MIDDLE AMERICA

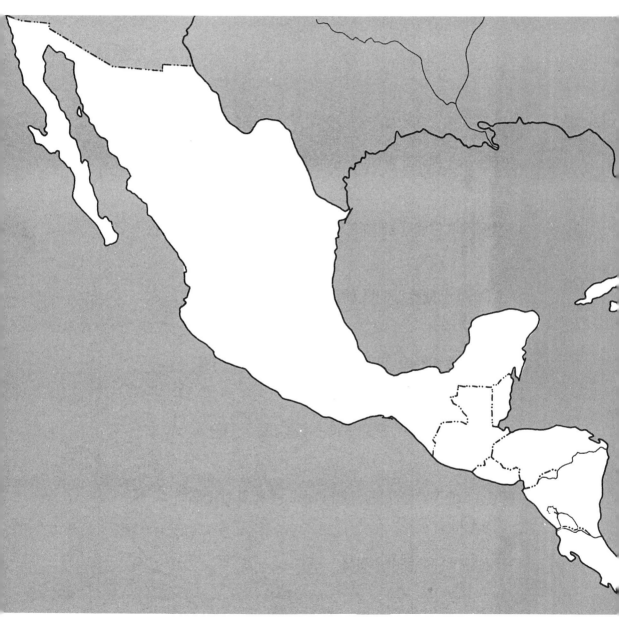

MIDDLE

AMERICA

Its
Lands
and
Peoples

ROBERT C. WEST
Louisiana State University

JOHN P. AUGELLI
University of Kansas

PRENTICE-HALL, INC.
Englewood Cliffs, New Jersey

MIDDLE AMERICA: ITS LANDS AND PEOPLES
by Robert C. West and John P. Augelli

PRENTICE-HALL INTERNATIONAL, INC., *London*
PRENTICE-HALL OF AUSTRALIA, PTY. LTD., *Sydney*
PRENTICE-HALL OF CANADA, LTD., *Toronto*
PRENTICE-HALL OF INDIA (PRIVATE) LTD., *New Delhi*
PRENTICE-HALL OF JAPAN, INC., *Tokyo*

Current printing (last digit):
19   18   17   16   15   14   13   12   11   10

Library of Congress Catalog Card No.: 66-14748

Preface

Middle America: Its Lands and Peoples presents the geography of an important and diverse segment of Latin America—the West Indies, Mexico, and Central America. This is the part of Latin America that is nearest to the United States; from its strategic and commercial importance alone, this is the part of Latin America that should be best known (but unfortunately is little understood) by North Americans. We hope that this volume may aid North American readers toward a better understanding of their nearest neighbors to the south.

The approach used in this book is strongly cultural and historical. We believe that such an approach is necessary to comprehend the complex medley of peoples and cultures that characterize Middle America today. The comprehension of the contemporary cultural scene of any long-inhabited land is rooted in an understanding of its past. Consequently, chapters on the pre-European aboriginal, European colonial, and nineteenth- and twentieth-century human geography of the West Indies, Mexico, and Central America comprise much of the book.

While we share joint responsibility for the entire book, we did not feel bound to maintain complete uniformity of style or in the content emphasis of the various chapters. The division of labor was such that the sections dealing with Mexico and Central America fell to West, while the first and last chapters and those focusing on the West Indies fell to Augelli.

Several people contributed to the art work for this volume. Joseph W. Wiedel, assistant professor of geography at the University of Maryland, drafted most of the maps. Judy Josserand and Morris Morgan executed the line drawings.

We thank the Association of American Geographers for permission to include Figures 1.3, 1.4, 1.5, and 7.5, first published in the *Annals* of that organization. We are indebted to the editors of the *Geographical Review* and *Focus* for borrowing freely from their published maps in constructing Figures 6.3, 6.4, 7.44, and 7.45. We are also indebted to Otis P. Starkey, Arilin D. Fentem, and Robert C. Kingsbury for using many data from their Technical Reports (numbers 1 through 11) on the commercial geography of the eastern Caribbean, prepared under Office of Naval Research Contract 908 (13).

R.C.W.

J.P.A.

Table of Contents

List of Illustrations

1

Cultural Diversity of Middle America

Middle America is an arbitrary geographic expression which refers to a mosaic of peoples, places, and cultures. Mexico, Central America, and the West Indies, the area which the term usually defines, share a general focus on the Gulf of Mexico and the Caribbean Sea and an intermediate location between North and South America. Each of the units formed part of the first locus of European settlement in the New World and, in each, post-Columbian domination and exploitation by outside powers has more or less deeply affected the patterns of land and people, the institutions, and other aspects of the culture. Partly because of this historical experience, there is some similarity in the current makeup of the component units. The three units have emerged into the twentieth century with economies which, for the most part, are still colonial. Their populations, which are stratified socioeconomically into the privileged few and the underprivileged many, comprise multiple racial elements. Their resources have been exploited to the point of abuse in some instances and inefficiently developed in others.

Despite such similarities, however, Middle America is characterized by diversity rather than uniformity. Each island and each mainland nucleus of settlement is a distinctive composite of people, habitat, historical tradition, and cultural orientation. The climate ranges from the aridity of Baja California and northern Mexico to the tropical rain forest of some of the Antilles and the Caribbean lowlands of Central America. Soil, vegetation, and landforms run almost the entire gamut of possibility (see Chapter 2). Mexico boasts useful mineral resources, but most of the territories have little exploitable mineral wealth.

Populations differ in number, density, and racial composition. The population of Mexico, more than 34,500,000 in 1960, contrasts sharply with that of the West Indian islands of Montserrat and the British Virgin Islands which, combined, is less than 24,000. Population density is as variable. Many of the West Indies, for example, have more than 500 people per square mile, while Central American areas such as the Petén of Guatemala and parts of Panama are almost empty (Figure 1.1). Racial and ethnic heterogeneity are everywhere apparent. The people of Costa Rica, Puerto Rico, and the Cayman Islands are largely Caucasian, those of Guatemala are predominantly Indian, the populations of Haiti and Jamaica are largely Negro, and many natives of Trinidad are of East Indian origin. In Mexico there are marked regional differences in racial composition, especially between the north and the south (Figure 1.2).

Poverty and limited opportunity characterize all of Middle America, but there is a considerable distance between the Haitian peasant's constant flirtation with famine and the improving conditions of the Puerto Rican. And the differences in living standards become glaring when we compare the conspicuous consumption of the privileged few with the lot of the masses, or the cities of each territory with its rural areas. Economies may be purely commercial, as in Cura-

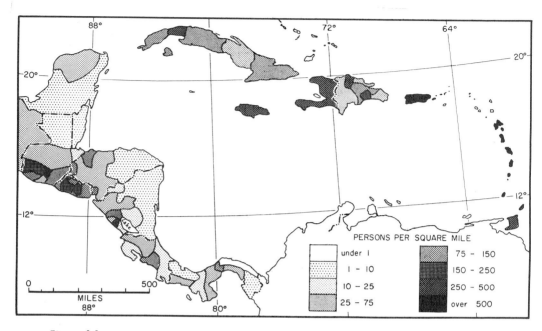

Figure 1.1
Central America and the West Indies : Population Density, 1960.

Figure 1.2
Middle America : Aspects of Racial and Cultural Diversity.

a. East Indian Hindus, Trinidad.

b. Negro boys, Haiti. (*Alcoa Steamship* Company, *Inc.*)

2

c. Guatemalan Indians watching a religious drama which combines Roman Catholic and pre-Columbian pagan symbols. (*Delta Air Lines*)

d. Muslim Mosque, Trinidad. (*Alcoa Steamship Company, Inc.*)

e. Roman Catholic Monastery, Mexico. (*Eastern Air Lines*)

f. Dutch house types, Curaçao. (*Alcoa Steamship Company, Inc.*)

çao, or almost completely subsistence, as in some of the Indian communities of Guatemala.

Middle America includes some territories which continue some political association with outside powers such as Britain, France, the Netherlands, and the United States, but the form of government is different in each such dependency. Most of Middle America is politically organized into so-called democratic republics, but while Costa Rica and Puerto Rico are models of democracy and stability, other countries often suffer one-man rule and recurrent revolution. There are equally broad differences in language, religion, and education, as well as in settlement, house types, land tenure, agricultural tools and practices, transportation, commerce, and other aspects of material culture.

These are only some of the more important aspects of the diversity of Middle America, but they are sufficient to invalidate any claim that the area meets the usual criteria of homogeneity which distinguish a *region*. Because of the area's general focus on the Gulf and the Caribbean Sea, a weak case may be made for the existence of a *nodal region,* but such nodality would have to embrace the United States Gulf coast as well as the Guianas, Colombia, and Venezuela, which are excluded from the present work.[1]

PRINCIPAL ROOTS OF DIVERSITY

The causes of cultural diversity in Middle America are legion, but in addition to the nature and variety of the physical environment and the consequent historical adjustments to it, the most important appear

to have been: (1) variety in the numbers, densities, and technological levels of the pre-Columbian Amerindian populations; (2) the cultural baggage, motives for conquest, and colonial methods and policies of the European groups who entered the area in the early period of settlement; (3) the origin and extent of subsequent immigration; and (4) the varying play of isolation and localism.

Pre-Columbian Indian Populations

Middle America was an Indian world before the arrival of the European and the African and, to a considerable extent, it still is. The degree of Amerindian influence on the racial composition and cultural patterns of any part of the area roughly correlates with the number, density, and level of civilization of the indigenous population before the conquest. This correlation is, however, not applicable to the West Indies, where the aborigines were unable to withstand the initial cultural shock of conquest and most were all but extinguished less than a century after the arrival of the first Europeans. A further exception is found in the few areas of the mainland which have retained an Indian flavor despite low population densities and standards of culture because such areas have been remote and unattractive to the European.

We have no count of the total Indian population of Middle America on the eve of Discovery, and estimates vary enormously. A conservative approximation is 15 million: more than 14 million in Mexico and Central America, and perhaps one million in the West Indies. This total, far larger than the combined pre-Columbian populations of all Anglo-America, was even greater than the Andean concentrations among the Indian populations of the New World.

The Europeans found conspicuous cultural and demographic differences among the aboriginal groups of Middle America. The high-culture areas of *Mesoamerica* (the southern Central Plateau of Mexico and

---

[1] Despite the widespread use of the term "Middle America," there is no general agreement about its definition. Some include only Mexico and Central America; others add the West Indies and, infrequently, even Colombia, Venezuela, and the Guianas. Occasionally, the term is used synonymously with "Central America," and some German geographers use *Mittelamerika* to refer to the isthmian territories from Panama to Guatemala.

Yucatan, and the highlands and the Pacific lowlands of Central America, e.g., of Guatemala, western Honduras, and western Nicaragua)[2] were the most populous and technologically most advanced. Here the inhabitants were densely settled, often in large communities and even cities. Their agriculture was intensive and stable enough to assure an adequate food supply, they had domesticated a large number of plants, and they often practiced terracing and irrigation. Their economy was regulated by highly sophisticated social organizations and theocratic states. In the West Indies, and in most of the Caribbean lowland areas on the mainland and in arid northern Mexico, the Indian populations were smaller, primarily because of their inferior food-producing methods—slash-and-burn agriculture, gathering, hunting, or fishing. Food was thus less certain, settlements were smaller and less permanent, and the entire economy was less stable. Except for the nomadic tribes of northern Mexico, which depended largely on the chase, the vast majority of the pre-Columbian people of Middle America depended upon agriculture. This difference between the aborigines of Middle America and the smaller and culturally less advanced Indian populations of what is now the United States accounts, in part, for the superiority of the Middle American Indians, both in number and in post-Columbian influence.

The cultural shock resulting from European conquest caused vast changes among the aboriginal populations of Middle America. In the West Indies the Indians died off virtually en masse, leaving a mere handful of survivors and a few vague traces of their former occupation of the islands. Elsewhere, and particularly in the large settlements of Mesoamerica, the initial European impact resulted in a drastic reduction of population. The Indians had no immunity to imported diseases, and they were ill-prepared for the brutality of the Spanish handling of labor. Perhaps more important, their food supply was sharply curtailed by the diversion of their lands to large tracts, or *latifundia,* which were conferred upon the white colonists and then allowed to lie almost idle.

The small number of Spanish colonists who entered Mexico and Central America in the early colonial period used every means to pacify the Indians, including military action, economic pressure, and intermarriage. Except where the number of Spaniards was more nearly equal to the Indian population, however, pacification did not always result in assimilation to the culture of the conqueror. Today, more than 450 years after Columbus, there still exists on the mainland of Middle America an unassimilated or partially assimilated indigenous population which accounts for at least three persons in five in Guatemala and one in ten in Mexico. Both countries are keenly conscious of what they refer to as their "Indian problem."

Even where assimilation with the European pattern has gone further, however, the biological and cultural mark of the Indian past is apparent. Except in Costa Rica and British Honduras, the racial composition of the mainland of Middle America is basically Euro-Indian or mestizo.[3] Indian languages remain locally important and the Indian motif permeates much of the artistic expression and thought of Mexico and Central America. Equally important to the student of

---

[2] The term "Mesoamerica" is attributed to the anthropologist Paul Kirchoff. It designates the high-culture areas occupied by the Aztec, Maya, Zapotec, etc., and their predecessors in Mexico and Central America (see Chapter 8).

---

[3] Mestizo (feminine, mestiza) means a person of mixed blood, usually the offspring of a European and an Amerindian. In Middle America, the term has also acquired a cultural connotation. Mestizo culture implies assimilation with the European pattern, as distinguished from the Indian. A person whose way of living is European may be racially a pure Indian but culturally a mestizo. Similarly, a white person who lives like an Indian may be classified as an Indian, culturally. In Guatemala and other parts of Central America, the term "Ladino" is used to describe anyone whose speech and way of life are Spanish.

geography are the crops, farming practices, diet, settlement patterns, house types, and other aspects of the material culture which, in varying degree, are a heritage of the Indian tradition.

The European Cultural Intrusion

Many nations have left their cultural stamp upon the people, landscapes, and institutions of Middle America. The list includes Spain, England, France, The Netherlands, Denmark, and the United States, as well as assorted African, oriental, and other elements. The role of Spain must be judged by far the most important, however, if only because the European tradition of the vast majority of the people and the territories of Middle America is Hispanic. Other ethnic groups have been significant primarily in the West Indies and in parts of the Caribbean coast of Central America, but even the West Indies—Cuba, Puerto Rico, the Dominican Republic and, to a much lesser degree, Trinidad and Jamaica—came under early Spanish influence. Therefore, in this section we shall deal exclusively with the role of Spain, leaving for elsewhere the assessment of the influence of the other nations.

The Spaniard brought to Middle America an entirely new fabric of life which was imposed amidst and upon the indigenous forms. The resulting human geography speaks loudly of the colonist's Iberian background, his motivations, and his institutions. At the time of the discovery of America, Spain was emerging from a 700-year struggle to evict the Moors, and the conquest of America was in many respects a parallel to and a prolongation of the conquest of the Moors. Many institutions and much of the national character developed during the fierce Moorish wars became part of the Spaniard's method and policy of colonization in the New World. Unlike England in North America, Spain never attempted to establish small, slow-growing colonies which could develop themselves. What Spain undertook

was an imperial expansion, aimed at imposing her language, religion, and customs upon millions of colonial subjects of a different race and culture. The symbolism of the cross and the sword, the fanatic missionary zeal, the strongly centralized control of every phase of colonial life from town planning to trade, the tolerance of racial fusion, the fierce intolerance of contrary ideas, religious and other, the contempt of the conquering soldier for manual labor, the attitudes of the aristocratic exploiter—all these and more formed the cultural baggage which the Spaniard carried to Middle America.

Spain's approach to colonization differed radically from that of every other western European power, with the exception of Portugal, partly because many of the forces which had transformed western Europe from a feudal to a modern condition had bypassed the Iberian Peninsula. The Reformation, the Enlightenment, the industrial and mechanical revolutions, laissez-faire capitalism, and other movements created little impression on Spain. Thus, during much of their formative colonial period, Spanish settlements received their principal cultural nourishment from a medieval and feudalistic fountainhead which was strikingly different from the rest of western Europe.

Spain faced two major disadvantages in the conquest and colonization of the New World: a lack of surplus wealth and a small population (the population of Spain in 1492 is estimated to have been only ten million). In order to overcome her need for money, Spain borrowed heavily from European bankers and paid back with gold and silver from her colonies. This necessitated a strict commercial monopoly of colonial trade, so that all the profits could go back into Spain's coffers. In essence, the colonies were viewed as instruments for the benefit of the mother country. Trade was restricted, and any colonial endeavor which might compete economically with the mother country was discouraged. To overcome the disadvantage of a small Spanish population, the Spaniards incorporated Indian populations into the feudalistic structure of colonial society. The small group of Spanish colonists formed the aristocracy, and the indigenous people supplied the labor force.

The primary motivation of the Spanish colonists was to obtain precious metals. But when stores of precious metals were not to be had or had been depleted, emphasis was given to the creation of large landed estates owned by Spaniards and worked by Indians. Large Indian concentrations were sought out, not only to satisfy the burning missionary zeal but also to supply cheap and abundant labor.

While the gold and missionary fevers burned, the Spaniards located their settlements very carefully. Not every piece of real estate would do—only such zones as contained large Indian populations and precious metals. This was the principal reason for the rapid exploration and envelopment of Middle America, which contrasts with the slow, systematic, westward movement of the Anglo-American frontier. It also partially explains the nucleated pattern of settlements separated by empty or lightly populated areas, a pattern of population distribution which often has persisted to the present.

Of the various tools used by Spain to mold the patterns of land and people in the New World—trade legislation, religion, racial fusion, and land tenure systems—the last was probably the most important. After the initial gold rush, land became the basis of most fortunes. Landed property became the chief institution of colonial production, and its ownership the hallmark of social prestige in a society which disdained trade and industrial pursuits. The large European-owned estate was early entrenched in Middle America. It has remained the principal form of land tenure and one of the major obstacles to progress in most of the area.

Landed property, without a labor force, would have been worthless, however, and the Spanish colonists had to be assured of an adequate supply of workers. Some Negro slaves were imported, particularly into the

West Indies and, to some degree, into Mexico, but on the whole this type of labor was not an important factor in the Hispanic exploitation of the land. The African slave was too expensive for the haphazard production of the Spaniard's *hacienda*; and the *plantation*, which was geared to the intensive production of commercial crops such as sugar and so created the heaviest demand for African slave labor, was only spottily developed by the Spaniards in Middle America. More important, the large Indian populations in the principal Spanish settlements in Mexico and Central America obviated the need for Negro slaves.

The Spaniards used various techniques to acquire and hold Indian workers. In the early days of the Conquest, the most important method of supplying a gold mine of human labor was the *encomienda* system, perhaps the most misunderstood institution established by the Spaniards in the Americas. Its origins go back to medieval Europe, where it was the practice of peasants living in a given locality to "commend" themselves to the lord of the neighborhood manor, rendering him specified personal services in return for protection. In the Americas, the *encomienda* was instituted by the Spanish Crown, with the support of the Catholic Church, to protect the Indians, establish a stable and working economy, and gradually incorporate the large indigenous population into Spanish colonial society. Under the terms of the encomienda the Crown "commended" Indians to the colonists "in order that you may employ them on your lands and in your mines, and it is your duty to instruct them in the Spanish language and our Holy Catholic Faith." The grant did not *ipso facto* include ownership of land itself. It gave the colonist, as trustee, the right to collect tribute and demand certain services from his Indian wards. Since even the rendering of services was abolished by law in 1549, the primary function of the encomienda became that of tribute payment by the Indians to the encomenderos. Thereafter,

Indian labor for agriculture was supplied mainly through the *repartimiento,* a work-levy system which the Spanish authorities imposed on Indian villages.

As conceived in Spain, the encomienda seemed a humane method of bringing about an economic and social transition of the lands and people of the New World, and certainly it was less brutal than the slave and tribute systems imposed by the Aztecs on their subject tribes. In practice, however, the system resulted in abuse for at least two reasons. First, it rested on the mistaken assumption that the encomenderos were God-fearing gentlemen. The truth is that many of the early colonists represented the very dregs of Spanish society. They made magnificent explorers, soldiers, and sires of the mestizo races, but most of them proved to be miserable economists and rulers of men. A second reason was the inability of the Spanish Crown to enforce the letter of the law in the far-off colonies. The law regulated the treatment of the Indians and the amount of services and tribute that could be required from them, but it was almost impossible to enforce these regulations in the colonies. Any effort the Crown and the clergy made to improve the lot of the Indians was fiercely resisted by the colonist who needed the labor.

The encomienda system never worked in the West Indies, where the natives, unaccustomed to hard labor, were rapidly decimated. In the major centers of Indian population of Mexico and Central America, however, where the natives were already organized into a well-disciplined labor force, the system largely accomplished its aims. It brought about an initial transition from pre-Columbian to Spanish colonial patterns and was an important instrument in cementing the feudal, master-serf relationship which to this day persists in many parts of Middle America.

According to law, the encomiendas were made for two generations—to the original encomendero and to his heir—after which they theoretically reverted to the Crown.

The system was gradually reduced by attrition and was abolished outright in 1720, by which date debt peonage was well enough established to assure the landholders of a continued labor supply.

The other two most important Spanish institutions which laid the groundwork for the land-and-people patterns of Hispanic Middle America were perhaps the town and the mission. Most Spanish landholders lived in the towns and went to their holdings only for tours of inspection. The estates (and the mines) were the sources of production of goods. The towns were the consumers, and the collecting, trading, and distributing of the goods took place there.

In contrast, the religious missions were often independent, self-contained economic units. The role of the mission in encouraging Spanish settlement, particularly of areas which lacked minerals or a large Indian population, was an important one. The Catholic mission, serving as the other arm of Spanish colonization, helped to bring about a less painful transition of land and people from the indigenous to the Spanish form. It placed religion above labor requirements and persuasion above force. Wherever the mission came into conflict with the encomienda, however, it was the encomienda which won out.

Origin and Extent
of Subsequent Immigration

The diverse human geography of Middle America was molded not only by the initial wave of Hispanic settlers, but by subsequent immigration as well. Following the first flush of conquest and colonization, which involved a relatively small number of settlers, the flow of Spanish colonists to Middle America dwindled down to a mere trickle. This reduced flow is explicable partly by Spain's small population and her numerous interests in other parts of the world and partly by a policy of restricting the immigration of non-Catholics and colonists from other nations, but perhaps its chief cause was the lack of opportunity in the Spanish colonies of Middle America. The early grants of large holdings to Crown favorites and others preempted the supply of vacant public lands which could serve as a magnet to immigrants, as it did in Anglo-America. Moreover, the restrictions imposed on commerce and manufacturing stunted the development of these activities and further limited opportunity. Thus, unless he possessed capital, and most potential immigrants did not, the new immigrant was doomed to competing with Indians and slaves in the labor market. No Spanish or other European peasant, no matter how harsh his lot at home, preferred the even harsher lot of the peon and slave of Middle America. Spanish immigration to the area did not become significant again until the nineteenth and early twentieth centuries; even then, it was primarily in response to the opportunities created by the commercial development of Cuba and Puerto Rico.

The establishment of northern European colonies (by England, France, Holland, and Denmark) in the West Indies and, to a far lesser degree, along the Caribbean coast of Central America brought new European immigrants to Middle America. But again, the number of arrivals was not large, and again the principal restriction was lack of opportunity. The West Indian territories occupied by the northern Europeans had little arable land, and this quickly became concentrated in a few hands. True, the development of plantation agriculture in these areas created a huge demand for labor, but early experiments proved that this demand could not be met by importing European workers, even when they were brought in as indentured servants.

The development of plantations by the northern Europeans was instrumental, however, in what is perhaps the largest migration of people into Middle America. This was the forced slave movement from Africa. An accurate count of the number of Negroes brought into Middle America during the slave period is difficult to determine, but it was sufficient to make Negro and part-Negro people the dominant population in virtually all the West Indies. On the Caribbean coast of Central America, the colonial slave population was later reinforced by the free migration of Jamaicans and other West Indian Negroes who were attracted by the growth of banana plantations, by work on the Panama Canal, and by other employment opportunities in the nineteenth and twentieth centuries. The total of this migration has been sufficient to give this sector a strong Negro component.

The vast bulk of the immigrants entering Middle America arrived from the sixteenth to the first half of the nineteenth centuries. The arrivals since 1850, such as the East Indians in Trinidad, have been relatively few and are only locally significant.

Isolation and Localism

Isolation has been a major factor in crystallizing and perpetuating the vast diversity of human geography in Middle America. The circulation of people, goods, and ideas within the area has always been limited. This was true when much of it formed part of Spain's colonial empire, and the individual colonies were forbidden to trade with each other, and it is almost equally true today. Most of the population move within an economic orbit which essentially provides only subsistence, and they have little need for commerce or contact outside their own communities. Exports, primarily plantation crops and minerals, directly involve only a small percentage of the total population, and these exports do not move within Middle America but are directed chiefly to middle latitude markets such as the United States and Europe. The nature of the economy, the nucleated pattern of settlements, the different cultural traditions, the difficulty of transportation and communication, the restriction of migration, and other isolating forces have engendered in the component units of Middle America a degree of localism which has virtually no equal in Anglo-America. This localism not only separates the territories from one another, but is found even within the same political unit.

RESULTING CULTURE AREAS

The interplay of physical environment and history, reinforced by isolation, has given to Middle America a myriad of culturally differentiated areas and landscapes. Only a vast, and perhaps impractical, number of detailed and narrowly focused studies could reveal the extent of this diversity. The culture-area classification of the outline which follows, and which is also depicted in Figures 1.3, 1.4, and 1.5, emphasizes gross pat-

Figure 1.3
The Rimland–Mainland Divisions of Middle America.

terns, rather than detailed distinctions. Consequently, it should be considered only an approximation of the truth.

Generalized Culture Areas of Middle America

I. The Euro-African (Caribbean) Rimland
  A. Central American Sector
    1. Plantation Zone
    2. Others
  B. West Indian Sector
    1. Hispanic Zone
      a. Dominican Republic
      b. Cuba
      c. Puerto Rico
    2. North European Zone
      a. The Netherlands Antilles
      b. British West Indies
      c. French Culture Complex

(1) Primary
  (a) Martinique and Guadeloupe
(2) Secondary
  (a) Haiti
  (b) Dominica, St. Lucia, Grenada[4]

II. The Euro-Indian Mainland
  A. Mesoamerican Sectors (*Marked* Indian Influence)
    1. Southern Plateau of Mexico and Yucatan
    2. Guatemala and Chiapas, western Honduras and western Nicaragua
  B. Mestizo Sector (*Moderate* Indian Influence)
    1. Honduras
    2. El Salvador
    3. Nicaragua
    4. Panama
    5. Central Mexico
  C. European Sectors (*Limited* Indian Influence)
    1. Costa Rica
    2. Northern Mexico

Racial Differentiation of the Culture Areas. The primary basis for the proposed culture-area classification of Middle America rests upon a twofold division of the area between what may be termed the "Euro-African Caribbean Rimland" (Figure 1.4) and the "Euro-Indian Mainland" (Figure 1.5). This delimitation is based in part, of course, upon the racial makeup of the population of the two segments. In general, the dominant strain of the Rimland is Negro or part-Negro, and even where Negroes do not form a majority (as in Cuba, Puerto Rico, and some segments of the Caribbean coast of Central America), they represent a significant minority (Figure 1.4). On the Mainland it is the Indian or, more commonly, the part-Indian (mestizo) who forms the racial

---

[4] Dominica, St. Lucia, and Grenada, although British territories, retain many French cultural characteristics because of their past association with France.

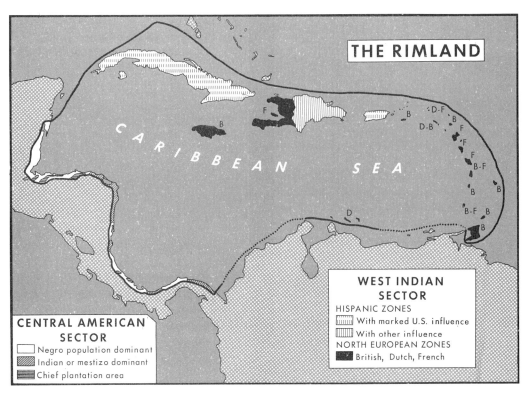

THE RIMLAND

CARIBBEAN SEA

WEST INDIAN SECTOR
HISPANIC ZONES
▦ With marked U.S. influence
▥ With other influence
NORTH EUROPEAN ZONES
■ British, Dutch, French

CENTRAL AMERICAN SECTOR
☐ Negro population dominant
▨ Indian or mestizo dominant
▤ Chief plantation area

Figure 1.4
The "Euro–African" Caribbean Rimland.

Figure 1.5
The "Euro–Indian" Mainland.

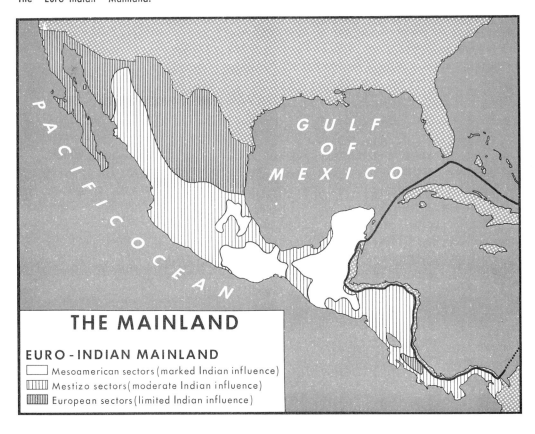

PACIFIC OCEAN

GULF OF MEXICO

THE MAINLAND

EURO–INDIAN MAINLAND
☐ Mesoamerican sectors (marked Indian influence)
▥ Mestizo sectors (moderate Indian influence)
▥ European sectors (limited Indian influence)

matrix of the population. The incidence of Indian blood may vary, but it is present to some extent everywhere, including the more European-like areas of Costa Rica and northern Mexico (Figure 1.5).

Cultural Differences. The racial differentiation is only a symptom, however, of the far more important contrasts which stem from cultural orientation, human habitat, and the economic organization of land. The Mainland retains strong pre-Columbian Indian cultural remnants and the post-Columbian culture brought to it has been almost exclusively Hispanic. The Rimland retains virtually no indigenous forms; it has some imported African traits; and in its post-Columbian history, it has been exposed to a variety of European (including Anglo-American) ethnic cultures. These contrasts are responsible in part, at least, for the differences between the two areas in landscape, material culture, and other facets of man-land relations.

The Culture Areas as Human Habitats. Viewed as a human habitat, the Rimland is essentially a tropical lowland, varying in humidity from rainforest conditions to savanna, with occasional patches of steppe. True, many of the West Indian islands are mountainous, but the vast bulk of the Rimland population lives on coastal plains and river valleys well below 1,000 feet in elevation. Because of its island and coastal character and sea location, the Rimland habitat has been more accessible to the play of outside forces than that of the Mainland. Its lowland tropical conditions are conspicuously expressed in the general landscape, the nature of the subsistence and commercial crops, the building materials, and the types of houses, as well as in other ways. The Mainland habitat is largely a tropical or subtropical highland, characterized by subhumid to arid conditions over much of its Mexican and Pacific slope components and by a wide range of humid conditions in the highlands

of Central America. With the exception of Panama, Nicaragua, and northern Yucatan, the major population concentrations of the Mainland are both more remote and at considerably higher elevations than in the Rimland. The climatic variation and the location of the habitats of the Mainland population help to account for their restricted contact with the outside world as well as for much of the distinctiveness of their crops, their use of the land, their diet, and other aspects of their adjustment.

The Plantation vs. the Hacienda. While it is impossible to focus on every cause and consequence of the contrasting human geography of Mainland and Rimland in Middle America, at least one more merits special attention. This is the difference in economic organization of the land.

The expansion of European enterprise into Middle America following the Discovery eventually gave rise to two outstanding modes of land organization: the hacienda and the plantation. The two are similar in a number of respects: (1) both are European techniques for the exploitation of land and labor; (2) both require large amounts of land and cheap labor (though labor costs have been characteristically cheaper on the hacienda); (3) both have been developed on the best land in their respective spheres, discouraging the emergence of a strong, independent class of small farmers and of a balanced economy; and (4) both have been historically characterized by agglomerated, village-type settlements of workers grouped near the big house of the landowner.

As institutions which have shaped manland relations, however, they differ fundamentally, mirroring the differences in the surrounding environment and in the availability of indigenous labor and, perhaps above all, reflecting the gulf which separated the economic values of the Spaniard from those of the northern European. The hacienda is an almost exclusively Hispanic institution, now confined largely to Mexico and Central America. The hacienda was characteristic of Cuba, Puerto Rico, Santo Domingo and perhaps even Trinidad during much of the colonial period, but the destruction of the indigenous population, the high cost of imported labor, and the development of the more efficient plantation largely doomed the hacienda organization in those territories.

Part of the land on the hacienda is devoted to cash crops which often supply the food for the populations of nearby towns and cities. The hacienda is fairly self-sufficient, in that the workers are provided with subsistence plots and meet most of their needs from this production and from home crafts. There is far less specialization than on the plantation, capital is scarce, and family ownership of land is characteristic. Land is used extensively rather than intensively, and production is notoriously inefficient. Traditional methods of cultivation are employed, little use is made of machinery, and the movement of products to any except nearby markets is often beset with difficulties. While there has been some desire for profit, it would appear that the hacienda owner's desire to live like a proper Spanish *caballero* has been more important to him than financial gain. The acquisition of hacienda property has had more to do with the prestige of land ownership than with any desire to expand production and increase profits. Under these circumstances, much hacienda land remains unused, a testimony to the inefficient Hispanic concept of aristocratic living.

Without a large and cheap supply of indigenous labor, the hacienda might never have developed. Its inefficiency made even slave labor prohibitively expensive. In the centers of large Indian population of Mexico and Central America, however, conditions were well suited to its development. The Spaniard developed his hacienda by obtaining grants of land that once belonged to Indian nobility and of unoccupied areas abandoned by Indian villages; then he ac-

quired a cheap labor force first through the encomienda and repartimiento, and later by debt peonage, custom, and political legislation.

The plantation, in contrast to the hacienda, became associated largely with the Rimland and was authored primarily by northern Europeans, and later the Anglo-Americans, who established themselves in the West Indies and the Caribbean lowlands of Central America. Hispanic groups engaged in some plantation development, particularly in Cuba and Puerto Rico during the nineteenth century, and at various times along the southern Gulf coast of Mexico. But the plantation was never a forte of Hispanic agricultural economics, and least so during the colonial period. Following the political break with Spain, the Hispanic territories of the Rimland—Cuba, Puerto Rico, and the Dominican Republic—developed important plantation economies. The so-called coffee plantations, developed chiefly by local entrepreneurs of Hispanic origin in the uplands of Central America and Mexico, are a special economic form which in many respects is more akin to the hacienda than to the typical sugar or banana plantation of the Caribbean rim.

The Rimland plantation has been more than an economic institution. With some modification, it has persisted as a way of life from the colonial period to the present. It has been an important, and often the chief, determinant of racial composition, population numbers, densities, and distributions, land tenure and land use, commerce, transportation, and other cultural aspects of the Caribbean.[5] Of course, the plantation has

---

[5] Sociologists and anthropologists stress that the plantation has functioned as a political and social force as well. It represented the political organization through which the authority of the whites was imposed on colored colonial peoples; it established the framework of a system of social relationships between the European masters and Negro laborers, including the tradition of white paternalism and the other guiding principles of race relationships. The over-riding impact of the plantation on

not remained unchanged by time and space. There is considerable difference between the family-owned West Indian sugar plantation of the eighteenth century, for instance, and the corporate organization of the present. Equally significant differences exist between a twentieth-century United Fruit Company banana plantation in Central America and a French sugar plantation in Martinique.

Nevertheless, certain aspects of the Middle American plantation are always the same:

1. Its *location* is generally on the coast, roughly coinciding with the humid tropical lowlands of Middle America.
2. *Production* is almost exclusively for export, usually of a single crop.
3. *Capital,* technology, and managerial skills are often imported, giving rise to absentee ownership and the export of profits.
4. *Labor* is seasonal and, historically, had to be imported because the indigenous Amerindian labor force was inadequate.
5. While the *utilization of land* is more efficient than on the hacienda, the plantation must hold considerable idle land in reserve for expansion of production, crop rotation, grazing of work animals, and other uses.

Both the plantation and the hacienda have undergone great changes in the twentieth century. The plantation has evolved from the family-owned enterprise of the colonial period to the corporate factory in the field of the present. In Mexico, the hacienda has been dealt a heavy blow by the concept of the *ejido* and by other land legislation stemming

from the Mexican Revolution. Elsewhere, improved transportation and social unrest are creating problems and opportunities which are forcing hacienda owners to produce more efficiently and for export. Despite these changes, however, the two institutions —the Rimland plantation and the Mainland hacienda—continue to differentiate the man-and-land relationships of the two culture areas.[6]

Secondary Division of the Culture Areas

In most instances, the bases for subdividing the Rimland and Mainland are self-evident. The Central American sector of the Rimland, for example, stands apart from the West Indies for several reasons. Among them are the facts that the plantation in Central America was a postcolonial development, that it was developed by Anglo-Americans rather than northern Europeans, that it specialized primarily in bananas rather than sugar and that, while drawing much of its labor from the Negro populations of Jamaica and the other West Indies, it also attracted some workers from the Indian and mestizo areas of the interior uplands. The distinctiveness of the Central American sector of the Rimland is further reinforced by the presence of numerous settlements of English-speaking, Protestant communities which tend to resist assimilation with the predominantly Catholic and Hispanic cultures of the adjacent Mainland.

The differentiation between the Hispanic and northern European islands in the West Indies is obviously based in part upon their cultural histories and in part upon the history of occupance, the racial composition, and other factors. In the Hispanic territories the plantation did not develop significantly

---

land, people, and society was not restricted to the Caribbean Rimland of Middle America. It is manifest in the United States South, northeastern Brazil, and wherever else the institution became important. Gilberto Freyre's brilliant study of the Brazilian plantation as a social institution would be applicable in large measure to the West Indies and to the American South. See G. Freyre, *The Masters and the Slaves,* 2nd ed. (New York: Alfred A. Knopf, Inc., 1956).

[6] Some differences also exist between the Rimland and Mainland in other forms of land organization and utilization, such as peasants' small holdings, Indian communal lands, sharecropping, etc., but these are less significant. They are discussed in appropriate sections of the book.

until the nineteenth and twentieth centuries, and it used slave labor only for a short period. As one result, Negroes are less numerous in Cuba and Puerto Rico than in the northern European territories.

Further differentiation within the Hispanic group stems in large measure from United States influence in Cuba and Puerto Rico following the Spanish American War, as opposed to Haitian influence in the Dominican Republic (see Chapters 5 and 6). Within the northern European group of islands, the "French cultural complex" extends beyond France's current possessions, Martinique and Guadeloupe, into Haiti, Dominica, St. Lucia, and even Grenada, because of France's former occupation of and cultural influence on these territories.

On the Mainland, the Mesoamerican centers of southern Mexico and Guatemala are distinguished by the far greater influence of indigenous forms and race in these two centers than is found elsewhere. Northern Mexico and Costa Rica, on the other hand, are loosely designated as "European," in part because of the racial composition and in part because of the more Europeanlike economy, settlement patterns, and other features of these areas. The remainder of the Mainland, where Indian influence is moderate, is designated as "mestizo."

THE IMPORTANCE
OF MIDDLE AMERICA

"Middle America," as we have seen, is an arbitrary geographic term for a complexity of land-and-people patterns. But, although it is not a region in the sense that geographers ordinarily define one, its study as a single geographic unit is not without justification. Its very diversity provides a fertile field for the comparative study of human adjustment under different physical and historical conditions.

Moreover, Middle America is one of the two richest repositories of Amerindian cultural remnants; it was the birthplace of the post-Columbian world in the Americas; it witnessed the arrival of the first Europeans, the first Africans, the first Jews and the first members of other religious minorities in the New World; it was the experimental area in which the tools, plants, animals, political and economic institutions, and other instruments used for the eventual conquest and settlement of the Americas were first used. The study of the variety of human habitats and cultural forms which have evolved in Middle America constitutes an intellectual challenge which can be found in few other areas in the world. While this challenge alone would justify our study of Middle America, the area is important, particularly to the United States, for many other reasons.

Strategic Significance

Middle America's Caribbean Sea, often called the "American Mediterranean," is one of the world's most important circulation routes. It is athwart the major trade routes between the Atlantic and the Pacific which go through the Panama Canal. And, together with its mainland and insular rims, it links the Americas. For good reason, control of the Caribbean has been imperative to the defense of the United States for more than a century, perhaps as far back as the proclamation of the Monroe Doctrine. A potential enemy with bases in the area could not only disrupt the vital trade lanes which flow through the Canal and those that bring strategic materials such as petroleum from South America; he could also mount an attack on the very heart of the United States. This accounts for the presence of American military establishments in Puerto Rico, the Canal Zone, Guantánamo Bay in Cuba, and for the lend-lease bases temporarily acquired elsewhere in the West Indies during World War II. Changes in military technology and in transportation have given and may again give different expression to the strategic value of Middle America, but its location and its arrangement of sea and land are, in Sauer's words "an elemental and permanent fact" whose strategic significance does not diminish.[7]

Economic and Social Significance

The economic importance of Middle America as a market for finished products,

fuel, and food, and as a source of raw materials such as tropical products and minerals has already been implied. The annual value of goods absorbed by the area's markets in the post-World War II period is in excess of two billion dollars, and the value of raw materials exported is even greater (Figure 1.6).

The economic importance of the area also rests, however, on its capacity to absorb foreign capital investment. The pattern of foreign investment originated in the early colonial era and has continued to this day.

[7] A. C. Wilgus, ed., *The Caribbean: Its Economy* (Gainesville, Fla.: University of Florida Press, 1954), p. 15.

Figure 1.6
Middle America : Generalized Flow Map of International Commerce.

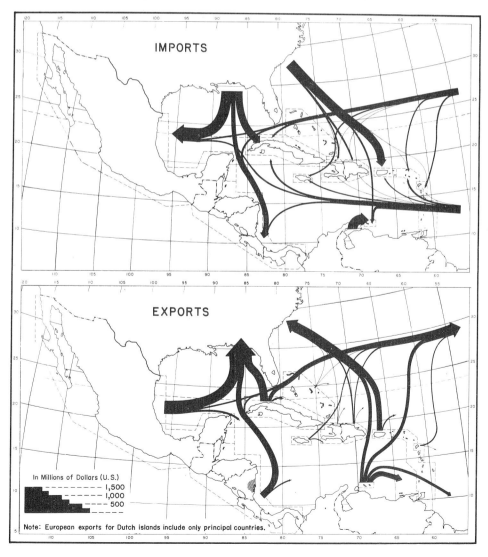

In the past, capital came primarily from England, France, and The Netherlands, and while investments from these countries are still important, the vast bulk of the money now comes from the United States. American capital permeates virtually every sphere of commercial activity. It is found in the plantations of Central America, the Dominican Republic, and Puerto Rico, in the oil refineries of Trinidad and the Dutch islands, in the bauxite mines of Jamaica, in the mines and ranches of Mexico, in the public utilities of Central America and elsewhere, in the industries of Puerto Rico, in the tourist hotels of the West Indies, and in countless other enterprises. Despite the unfavorable investment climate created by the expropriation of American interests in the Mexican oil industry, the confiscation of United States property in Cuba, and the numerous threats which American capital has faced in Central America and elsewhere, Middle America continues to rank along with Canada and Venezuela as one of the major areas of United States investment abroad.

The social importance of Middle America is complex, but perhaps its greatest value stems from its being a human laboratory sitting on the United States' doorstep, a potential pilot area in which to study many of the problems of the underdeveloped world. Such study is suggested not only by altruistic considerations; it is dictated by more pragmatic reasons, for many segments of Middle America are, in Hussey's vivid summary, "boiling cauldrons of human miseries and resentments likely to blow their lids at any careless stoking of the heat."[8] In the event of a blowup, such as has already occurred in Cuba, the United States and the West in general stand to lose. The conditions are such that Middle America could easily become a battlefield between democracy and communism.

Despite proximity and obvious importance, Middle America occupies only a small portion of the international consciousness of the United States. The American man in the street tends to think of most of the area as a vaguely defined backyard of banana republics, comic opera revolutions, exotic vacation spots, and attractive dance rhythms. The territories of Middle America, in the words of Sumner Welles, "...are among those of the American Republics with which the people of the United States are least familiar.... [To] most of us the national problems...the manner of being, the culture, and the economy [of Middle America] is a closed book."[9]

It is the purpose of this volume to view the lands and peoples of Middle America against the background of their geographic, historical, and cultural settings, placing particular emphasis on the relationships between the people and the land on which they live. We hope to make a small contribution to the better understanding of this fascinating area.

---

[8] A. C. Wilgus, ed., *The Caribbean: British, Dutch, French, United States* (Gainesville, Fla.: University of Florida Press, 1958), p. 248.

[9] D. Perkins, *The United States and the Caribbean* (Cambridge, Mass.: Harvard University Press, 1947), p. 7.

SELECTED REFERENCES

Adams, R. N., "Cultural Components of Central America," *American Anthropologist,* LVIII (1956), 881–907.

Augelli, J. P., "The Controversial Image of Latin America: A Geographer's View," *Journal of Geography,* LXII (1963), 103–12.

———, "The Rimland-Mainland Concept of Culture Areas in Middle America," *Annals of the Association of American Geographers,* LII (1962), 119–29.

Brannen, C. O., *Relations of Land Tenure to Plantation Organization,* U.S. Department of Agriculture, Bulletin No. 1269. Washington, D.C.: Government Printing Office, 1924.

Freyre, G., *The Masters and the Slaves: A Study in the Development of Brazilian Civilization,*

2nd ed. New York: Alfred A. Knopf, Inc., 1956.

Gillin, J., "Mestizo America," in R. Linton, ed., *Most of the World.* New York: Columbia University Press, 1949, pp. 156–211.

Herskovits, M. J., *The Myth of the Negro Past.* New York: Harper & Row, Publishers, 1941, pp. 54–85.

Klass, M., *East Indians in Trinidad: A Study of Cultural Persistence.* New York: Columbia University Press, 1961.

McBride, G. M., "Plantation," *Encyclopaedia of the Social Sciences* XI (1937), 148–53.

Ots Capdequi, J. M., *El Régimen de la Tierra en la América Española durante el Período Colonial.* Ciudad Trujillo, S.D.: Editora Montalvo, Universidad de Santo Domingo, 1946.

Perkins, D., *The United States and the Caribbean.* Cambridge, Mass.: Harvard University Press, 1947.

Price, A. G., *White Settlers in the Tropics.* New York: American Geographical Society, 1939.

Rubin, V., ed., *Caribbean Studies: A Symposium.* Kingston, Jamaica: Institute of Social and Economic Research, University College of the West Indies, 1957.

———, "Social Cultural Pluralism in the Caribbean," *Annals of the New York Academy of Sciences,* LXXXIII (1960), 796–815.

Simpson, L. B., *The Encomienda in New Spain* (rev. ed.). Berkeley, Calif.: University of California Press, 1950.

Wilgus, A. C., ed., *The Caribbean: Its Culture.* Gainesville, Fla.: University of Florida Press, 1955.

Wolf, E. R., and S. Mintz, "Haciendas and Plantations in Middle America and the Antilles," *Social and Economic Studies,* VI, No. 3 (1957), 380–412.

2

Physical Patterns

Diversity, as we have already noted, is the keynote of the physical landscape in Middle America. In few other areas of similar size are there, within short distances, such great variations of surface configuration, climate, soils, vegetation, and animal life as are found in Mexico, Central America, and the West Indies. With the exception of those features derived from continental glaciation and from frost action in high latitudes, almost the entire gamut of known landforms is represented in this area. Flattish alluvial and limestone plains are in close juxtaposition with high plateaus and rugged mountains that vary in type from fault blocks and folded ridges to volcanic cones. There is a magnificent variety of coastal forms, ranging from cliffed headlands through extensive barrier beaches and lagoons to coral reefs. This diversity of surface configuration in Middle America stems primarily from the complex geological history of the area and its position within one of the world's regions of contemporary active mountain building.

The mountainous character of Middle America is one of the important reasons for the complex pattern of climate types and associated vegetation cover. For example, on the eastern escarpment of the Mexican Plateau one may, in one or two hours, drive from a hot, jungle-covered coastal plain into the cool pine and fir forests of the Sierra Madre, passing on the way through rain-drenched windward slopes and dry protected valleys. Moreover, Middle America straddles the northern limit of the tropics. Thus, climates in Mexico vary from mid-latitude types

through most of the subtropical and tropical ones. The diversity of plant and animal life also derives from the fact that Middle America is the meeting zone between North American (Nearctic) and tropical American (Neotropical) flora and fauna.

SURFACE CONFIGURATION AND RELATED GEOLOGY

Because of their complexity, the landform patterns of Middle America might best be described on the basis of large physiographic regions, in each of which there is a general uniformity of surface characteristics. In the following section on surface configuration, Middle America is divided into 11 major physiographic provinces, beginning with those of Mexico (Figures 2.1 and 2.2).

The Mexican Plateau (I)[1]

One of the largest landform units of Middle America, and one of the most significant in terms of human settlement, is the Mexican Plateau. This upland is a tilted block of earth that stands a mile or more above the sea. Elevations are greatest in the southern portion, where some parts of the plateau surface rise over 8,000 feet above sea level. As one travels northward from Mexico City, near the plateau's southern edge, elevations gradu-

---

[1] The Roman numerals in parentheses refer to areas of Figure 2.1.

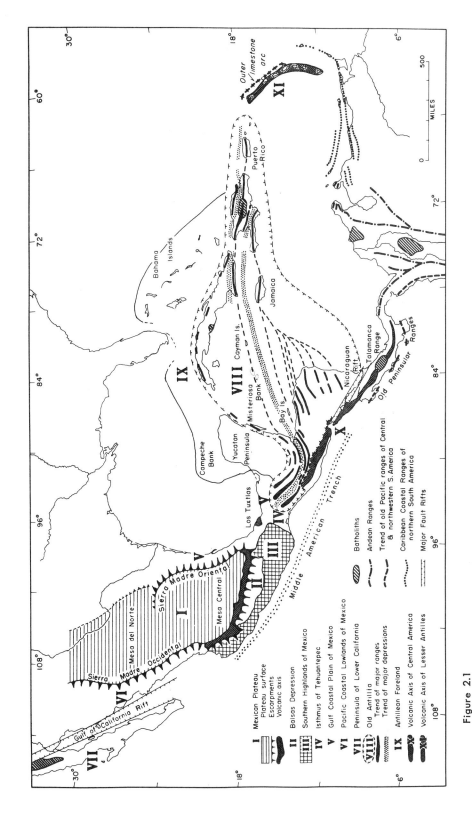

Figure 2.1

Physiographic-Tectonic Provinces.

21

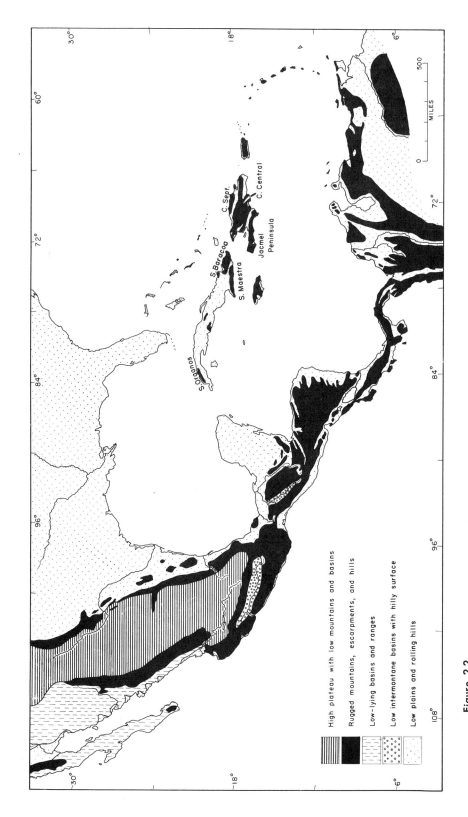

Figure 2.2
Landform Regions.

High plateau with low mountains and basins

Rugged mountains, escarpments, and hills

Low-lying basins and ranges

Low intermontane basins with hilly surface

Low plains and rolling hills

S. Organos

S. Baracoa

S. Maestra

C. Sept.

C. Central

Jacmel Peninsula

MILES

0   500

ally decrease to less than 4,000 feet at El Paso on the United States-Mexican frontier.

The Plateau Surface. The arid northern half of the plateau is sometimes called the *Mesa del Norte.* This part extends from the international border southward to about the latitude of San Luis Potosí (22°N.), where it blends indefinitely into the higher and more moist southern half of the plateau, often known as the *Mesa Central.* The surface of both parts of the plateau is characterized by low mountains separated by basins. Flattish basin floors occupy perhaps two-fifths of the total area. The ranges of the Mesa del Norte trend generally northwest-southeast and rise 500 to 2,500 feet above the adjacent basins. In the eastern section of the

plateau the ranges are of limestone and shale, while on the western side volcanic materials prevail. Northern Mexico is arid and there are few permanent streams. The desert basins (*bolsones*), flanked by sloping alluvial fans and rock pediments, form plains between the ranges. Usually lacking exterior drainage, the flat centers of these basins are often occupied by intermittent or playa lakes which contain water only after rare heavy showers. The two large areas of interior drainage that cover much of the Mesa del Norte are shown in Figure 2.3.

The southern half of the plateau, or Mesa Central, is a land of geologically recent volcanic activity. A row of high, widely spaced volcanoes lines the southern rim of the plateau. This range, called the Transverse Volcanic Axis or the Neovolcanic Range of Mexico, contains the snow-capped peaks of

Figure 2.3
Natural Drainage Types of Mexico and Adjacent Areas.

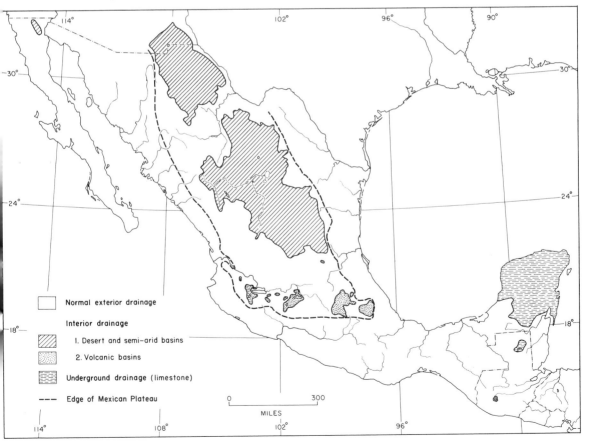

Figure 2.4

The Highland Basin of Amecameca (8,300 Feet Elevation), Immediately South of the Valley of Mexico. The snow-capped volcanoes Ixtaccihuatl (left) and Popocatepetl (right) border the basin on the east. Cinder cones and lava flows interrupt the flattish surface of this densely inhabited basin. (*Compañía Mexicana Aerofoto*)

Figure 2.5

Principal Basins of the Mesa Central. The basins are shown with stippled pattern; the edge of the Mesa Central is indicated by the broken line.

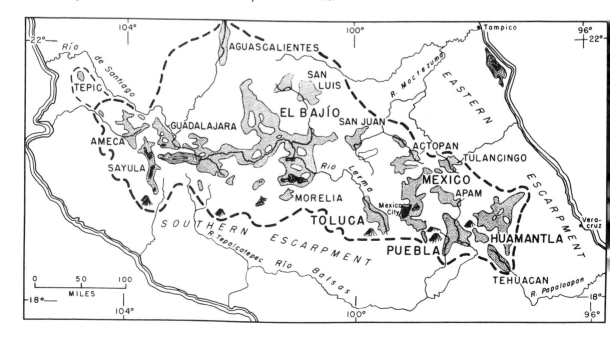

Popocatepetl (17,900 feet), Ixtaccihuatl (17,300 feet), Toluca (15,000 feet) and, near its western end, Colima (14,200 feet). Most of these large volcanoes were formed about ten million years ago in Late Tertiary time, but some, like Colima and Popocatepetl, are still active occasionally. Mexico's newest volcano, Parícutin, which erupted in 1943, lies within the volcanic axis. Low cinder cones, crater lakes, and lava flows add to the many volcanic forms within the mountainous area (Figure 2.4).

Immediately north of the volcanic range, the surface of the Mesa Central is composed of eroded remnants of old volcanoes, between which are flat-floored basins. During moist Pleistocene times most of these basins contained lakes, formed by the interruption of normal stream drainage through damming by ash fall and lava flows. Tapped by headward eroding tributaries of the main rivers and filled by sedimentation, the majority of the lakes have now disappeared, and their beds remain as the present level surfaces within the basins. Since prehistoric days, these basins have been the most culturally significant landforms of the plateau. An abundance of aquatic wildlife in and around the remaining lakes and the fertile soils on adjacent volcanic slopes and basin flats have attracted dense settlement. Today Mexico obtains the bulk of her food supply from the crops cultivated in the originally fertile lacustrine soils. Such basins vary greatly in size, from a few square miles to extensive areas 30 by 40 miles. The largest basins include the valleys of Mexico, Huamantla, Puebla, Toluca, Morelia, Guadalajara, and a series of connected basins called the Bajío of Guanajuato (Figure 2.5). Some of the basin lakes, such as Pátzcuaro, are still intact; others, such as the five original lakes of the Valley of Mexico, have been artificially drained within the last century; still others are in the process of disappearing through filling and natural dessication.

Three main river systems drain the greater part of the Mesa Central. The Santiago-Lerma system, the largest in Mexico, drains the western two-thirds of the plateau. Originating in the Basin of Toluca, the Lerma River passes through the Bajío, forms Lake Chapala within a long depression, and flows out as the Río Santiago to plunge over the western edge of the plateau in a deep canyon toward the Pacific Ocean. Much of the eastern third of the Mesa Central is drained by the Pánuco-Moctezuma river system, the tributaries of which have cut deep canyons into the edge of the plateau. Lastly, tributaries of the upper Balsas River serve as drainage for the southeastern section of the Mesa Central. Tributaries of all three drainage systems, as well as those of minor rivers, are continually eroding headward farther into the plateau surface. Within the last century, some streams have formed sizable canyons in once level farmland around the periphery of the highlands.

The Plateau Escarpments. The most spectacular features of the Mexican Plateau are the steep escarpments which flank it on the east, west, and south. Each of the escarpments is overlooked by a mountain range which forms the respective rims of the plateau. On its eastern flank the plateau is bordered by the *Sierra Madre Oriental*, a series of elongated limestone ranges. Trending generally north-south, the higher ranges of the Sierra rise from 7,000 to 8,000 feet elevation, with some peaks reaching as high as 13,000 feet. Viewed from the plateau, most of the Sierra Madre Oriental appears to be insignificant and seems to form only the eastern upturned lip of the highlands. But from the Gulf Coastal Plain, the Sierra rises in a series of parallel ridges and valleys to create a formidable escarpment. The ridges and valleys are the result of geological folding of the limestone bedrock. The upfolds, or anticlines, often form the elongated ridges, while the downfolds, or synclines, give rise to long, narrow valleys, similar to those of the folded Appalachians of the eastern United States. The southern portion of the eastern escarp-

Figure 2.6

At Their Northern End the Folded Ranges of the Sierra Madre Oriental Veering West-ward. This sector of the Sierra is called the Arteaga Anticlinorium. The city of Monterrrey (lower right) occupies a plain along the intermittent Santa Catarina River. (*Compañía Mexicana Aerofoto*)

ment bordering the Mesa Central is rimmed by the eastern end of the volcanic axis mentioned above. Here towers the great snow-capped volcanic peak of Orizaba, or Citlaltepetl (18,700 feet), the highest point in Middle America. Near Monterrey, northeastern Mexico, the Sierra Madre Oriental suddenly veers westward forming a spectacular series of folded ridges and valleys, called an anticlinorium (Figure 2.6). North of Monterrey the plateau escarpment, composed of low folded ranges, gradually decreases in elevation toward the Rio Grande.

On its western rim, the Mexican Plateau is flanked by the *Sierra Madre Occidental.* The elevation of this range is similar to that of the eastern sierra, but its geology and physiography are quite different. The Sierra Madre Occidental, as well as the western side of the plateau, has been built up of vast quantities of volcanic material that has issued from vents. The western side of the Sierra, which forms the plateau escarpment, has been frayed with deep canyons, or *barrancas,* by streams flowing westward from the plateau. Some of these barrancas such as that of El Cobre rival the Grand Canyon of the Colorado in depth and grandeur. The steepness of the escarpment and the presence of the deep barrancas make this section of Mexico most difficult of access. Not until 1945 was an auto road completed across the sierra from Durango on the plateau to Mazatlán on the Pacific coast; the first railway to cross it (from Chihuahua City to Topolobampo) was finished in 1962.

On the south the Mexican Plateau is bordered by the volcanic axis, already discussed. Overlooking the deep Balsas River depression, the volcanic range forms the southern escarpment of the plateau. Low passes between the large volcanoes, as well as the presence of occasional plateau remnants and basin fills on the escarpment slope, make the southern approaches to the Mexican Plateau much less difficult than those on its eastern or western sides. The valleys of Iguala and Cuernavaca, south of the Valley of Mexico, are examples of the steplike arrangement of basin fills on the escarpment that ease the climb from the Balsas depression to the central highlands.

The Balsas Depression (II)

This low, hot, and dry basin separates the Mexican Plateau from the southern highlands of Mexico. A jumble of low hills, through which the Balsas River and its tributaries twist and turn, characterizes the surface of the depression. In only a few places has the Balsas River formed sizable pockets of alluvium along its course. Near the Pacific Ocean the river breaks through the southern highlands to the sea. Geologically, the depression continues northwestward along the foot of the Mexican Plateau. In this section the lowland is occupied by the Tepalcatepec River, a tributary of the Balsas.

The Southern Highlands (III)

South of the Balsas depression lie the Southern Highlands of Mexico. The western part of this mountainous area within the state of Guerrero is often called the *Sierra Madre del Sur;* small discontinuous ranges continue northwestward along the Pacific coast as far as Cabo Corrientes. The wide eastern section of the highlands within the state of Oaxaca is known as the *Mesa del Sur.* The entire southern highlands form a mountain mass of ancient crystalline rock that represents some of the most rugged terrain in Mexico (Figure 2.7). Average elevations of mountain crests range from 7,000 to 8,000 feet above sea level, some 3,000 to 4,000 feet above adjacent stream valleys and basins. A few peaks rise to more than 10,000 feet above the sea.

Along the Pacific coast, the southern highlands descend abruptly to the sea in a steep escarpment, in places forming a rugged, cliffed coast. Only a few short stretches of narrow coastal plain occur from Cabo Corrientes to the Isthmus of Tehuantepec. There is little level land in his rugged mountain mass. The hundreds of small, swiftly flowing streams that drain the highlands have carved

Figure 2.7

Aerial View of the Mesa del Sur East of Oaxaca City. This view shows the rugged, stream-dissected surface and the scattered subsistence maize fields of the Indian inhabitants. In the center background is Cerro Zempoaltepec (11,000 feet elevation), the highest point in the southern highlands of Mexico.

deep V-shaped valleys into the surface, creating a land of precipitous slopes and knife-edged ridges. Only scattered remnants of a former plateau area and a few basins in the Mesa del Sur have extensive flattish surfaces. The Valley of Oaxaca is the largest basin— a down-faulted trench 60 miles long and some 15 wide that lies at an elevation of 5,000 feet above the sea.

The Isthmus of Tehuantepec (IV)

This lowland depression lies east of the Southern Highlands and is often taken as the physical divide between North and Central America. In this section, only 125 miles of land separate the Gulf of Mexico from the Pacific Ocean. Isthmian America truly begins here. Although the maximum elevation at the drainage divide of the isthmus is only 800 feet, streams have dissected the surface into a rough hill area. Plains occur only on the Gulf and Pacific sides.

The Coastal Lowlands of Mexico (V and VI)

The *Gulf Coastal Plain* (V), which fringes the eastern side of Mexico, is one of the most extensive lowlands of Middle America. A continuation of the Gulf Coastal Plain of the United States, this lowland belt extends from the Rio Grande for a distance of 850 miles to the Yucatan Peninsula. In width, the lowland varies from a maximum of 100 miles near its northern and southern extremities to a few miles in its center, where a spur of the eastern escarpment reaches the sea a short distance north of Veracruz. Swamps, lagoons, and barrier beaches occur along many parts of the immediate coast, such as the long stretch from the Rio Grande to below Tampico and along the shore of Tabasco. Inland from the coast are extensive plains and rolling surfaces underlain by young sediments of marl, shale, and sandstone. Toward the escarpment of the plateau,

the plains grade into elongated ridges and valleys that trend north-south. Occasionally the plain surface near the coast is interrupted by isolated hills and low mountains that have resulted from past volcanic eruptions, local folding, or the uplift of young coastal sediments by large masses of granite rock that have intruded from below. The Sierra de Tamaulipas between the Rio Grande and Tampico is an example of folding and intrusion, while the Tuxtla Mountains, which rise abruptly from the coast south of Veracruz, exemplify recent volcanic activity. In addition to the low mountains, a great number of volcanic plugs, or remnants of old volcanoes, form isolated steep-sided hills that stand like vertical shafts 100 to 900 feet high in the plains inland from Tampico.

A number of rivers originating on the eastern side of the plateau cross the coastal lowlands and have built alluvial flood plains in their lower courses. With adequate water for irrigation, the flood plain of the lower Rio Grande has, in recent years, become one of Mexico's major agricultural areas. Farther south, the Río Pánuco at Tampico, the Coatzacoalcos and Papaloapan rivers in southern Veracruz, and the large Grijalva river system in Tabasco discharge a large volume of water and sediment into the Gulf, and have formed extensive deltaic plains (Figure 2.8). Such areas afford future possibilities for agricultural development.

In contrast to the Gulf area, the *Pacific Coastal Lowlands* (VI) of Mexico are much less extensive and are characterized as much by hills and low mountains as by level plains. The Pacific lowlands are widest in the north near the United States frontier, where they form the Sonoran or Altar Desert, one of the driest sections of Mexico. There low, worn-down mountains, oriented north–south with desert basins between, characterize the surface. As one goes southward into the state of Sinaloa, the lowlands form a narrow coastal strip between the western plateau escarpment and the Pacific Ocean, continuing as far as the Santiago-Lerma delta in Nayarit.

Figure 2.8
The Flat Alluvial Plain of the Lower Usumacinta River in Tabasco, Southeastern Mexico. The town of Montecristo (upper center), now called Emiliano Zapata, occupies the natural levee of the river on its left bank, back of which lie marshes and lakes. (*Compañía Mexicana Aerofoto*)

Even in this narrow lowland, north-south trending hills of granite—remnants of formerly higher ranges—dominate the landscape. Some hills abut upon the sea, in places forming natural harbors, such as that of Guaymas, Topolobampo, and Mazatlán, with small islands off coast. Some of the larger streams, such as the Fuerte and Mayo rivers, which cross the lowlands, have formed large delta plains along the coast. These deltas afford extensive level areas of alluvium, and the rivers supply adequate water for the large-scale irrigated farming that has been developed along the northwest coast of Mexico in the last 25 years. Numerous lagoons fronted by sand bars extend along the southern part of the coast, and swamps abound immediately back from the sea in Nayarit state.

The Peninsula of Lower California (VII)

In the extreme northwest of Mexico, the Peninsula of Lower California extends southeastward from the international frontier for a distance of 800 miles. This long strip of mountainous land is separated from the Mexican mainland by the equally long Gulf of California. The latter is a rift, or down-faulted block of earth, that has been invaded by the sea; the northern part of the same rift extends into the United States in the form of the Imperial and Coachella valleys of southeastern California. Discharging its water and sediment into the northern part of the Gulf, the Colorado River has built a deltaic plain of fertile alluvium, now an area of intensive irrigated farming on both the Mexican and American sides of the frontier.

The greater part of the peninsula of Lower California is an elongated fault block mountain whose steep escarpment faces eastward toward the Gulf and whose backslope inclines gently toward the Pacific Ocean. Large areas of volcanic outpourings cover much of the backslope, forming rough, plateaulike features. In the north the high, rugged granitic ranges of Juárez and San Pedro Mártir are but southern extensions of similar mountains in southern California. Another mountainous mass of granite forms the Cape area, or southernmost tip of the peninsula.

Northern Central America
and the Greater Antilles (VIII): Old Antillia

The oldest and most complex physiographic and tectonic area of Middle America comprises both northern Central America (including the state of Chiapas in southeastern Mexico) and the islands of the Greater Antilles. The association of these two areas— one an isthmian portion of the continent, the other a group of large, mountainous islands, separated by the Caribbean Sea—becomes understandable in view of the similarity of present landforms, geologic structure, and tectonic history. Some investigators believe that at one time in the geologic past, probably 100 million years ago during the Cretaceous era, the two present areas formed one large land mass, to which the term "Old Antillia" is often applied.

The surface of both northern Central America and the Greater Antilles is characterized by a series of east-west trending mountain ranges and intervening depressions. Most of these ranges are extremely rugged. Some of the mountain surfaces are composed of limestone and sandstone into which streams have carved deep canyons, exposing ancient crystalline rocks that are sometimes rich in gold and other minerals. Erosion has stripped other mountain surfaces almost completely of their former limestone covering, and has exposed large masses of granite *(batholiths)* which have intruded upward from depths within the earth's crust.

Three ranges and one depression of northern Central America can be reasonably identified with those of the Antilles and can be traced across the floor of the Caribbean Sea in the form of submarine ridges and deeps. One range begins in the Mexican state of Chiapas as the plateaulike Sierra de San Cristóbal (9,000 feet elevation). Continuing into central Guatemala as the plateau of the Alto Cuchumatanes (10,000 feet elevation) and the highlands of Cobán, it joins with minor ranges in southern British Honduras to descend into the Caribbean as the Cayman Ridge. This range is expressed in the shallow Misteriosa Bank and the Cayman Islands with their adjacent shoals. Eastward it rises in southernmost Cuba as the high Sierra Maestra (5,000 to 6,500 feet elevation), continues into the island of Hispaniola where it forms the Cordillera Central, and finally ends in the central mountains of Puerto Rico (4,500 feet elevation) and the Virgin Islands. In the Dominican Republic, on the island of Hispaniola, the Cordillera Central has been intruded by a huge gold-bearing batholith, the summit of which is Mt. Duarte (Mt. Trujillo), 10,400 feet above the sea and the highest point of the Antilles. A lower mountain range, called the Cordillera Septentrional, borders the northern coast of the Dominican Republic. Between the northern and central mountain ranges lies a depression known as the Cibao, a wide alluvial-filled valley of prime agricultural importance.

A second large mountain structure of Old Antillia lies south of the one already described. It begins as the granitic Sierra de Chiapas along the Pacific coast of southernmost Mexico. Passing through Guatemala in a series of low crystalline ranges, it joins with the Sierra de Omoa in northwestern Honduras, forms the Bay Islands off Honduras and possibly Swan Island in the mid-Caribbean, and continues toward Jamaica. Farther south, a series of east-west ranges in Honduras and northern Nicaragua dip beneath the Caribbean to form the numerous shoals and banks off the coast (the Nicaraguan Swell). Most of Jamaica is covered with limestone that has been highly eroded and dissolved to form an extremely rugged surface (this topography is called "karst") averaging 2,500 feet above the sea. The island's highest elevations occur in its northeastern portion, where the Blue Mountains, a deeply dissected mass of crystalline rock, rise to 7,500 feet. The same structure continues eastward as the southern range of Haiti in the Jacmel Peninsula (elevation 8,000 to 9,000 feet).

Between the two Antillean mountain ranges described above, there occurs a depression that can be traced from the Valley of Chiapas in southern Mexico, eastward through the Motagua Valley of central Guatemala, and thence into the Caribbean as the Bartlett Deep, a submarine trench which in places attains depths of more than 22,000 feet below sea level. An eastward extension of this depression is seen in the lowland basins of Cul-de-Sac in Haiti and Enriquillo in southeastern Dominican Republic. The latter basin is one of the two spots of land in Middle America that are below sea level (− 154 feet), the other being the southern portion of the Salton Sink which extends across the Mexican border to Mexicali in Baja California.

The third and northernmost range that formerly connected the Antilles with Central America appears to be expressed in low hills that trend northeastward in British Honduras and along the east coast of Yucatan. The structure passes into Cuba to form the intensely eroded limestone mountains called the Sierra de los Organos along the island's northwestern coast. It appears again in the Baracoa Highlands in the southeastern part of the island. This northern axis of Old Antillia appears to have determined the long east-west extent of Cuba. Although most of the central part of this narrow island is generally low and has a rolling surface underlaid by limestone, a series of east-west hills arranged in *en echelon* pattern expose a backbone of crystalline rocks. Occasional granitic intrusions or batholiths, such as the Trinidad Mountains, give additional relief to the island surface. Broad marine terraces in many parts of Cuba indicate a long period of successive uplift, and coral reefs abound along the northern and southern shores.

The Antillean Foreland (IX)

On the northern side of the extensive belt of east-west ranges and depressions that has been called "Old Antillia" lie two separate areas of similar surface configuration and tectonic history. These are the Yucatan Peninsula and the Bahama Islands. Both are low-lying, almost level plains of recently emerged limestone resting on deep-seated platforms of stable crystalline material. Because of their peculiar tectonic nature, these two areas are often termed the *Antillean Foreland*.

Most of the Yucatan Peninsula is characterized by a karst, or limestone solution surface. In its northern half there are no surface streams, for rain water sinks quickly through the porous rock to form underground courses. Round, steep-sided hollows, called "sinkholes" (*cenotes*), the result of caving of surface rock above subterranean stream channels, are the most common landform, and are the main sources of water supply (Figure 2.9). The red *terra rossa* soils derived from limestone are thin over most of the northern part of the peninsula. Bare, fluted limestone is exposed over large areas, and the little soil available for cultivation has accumulated through rain wash in low, scattered pockets (*joyas*). Farther south into the Petén of northern Guatemala, low, elongated limestone hills frequently interrupt the extensive plains. There surface streams are more common than in the drier north, and round or oval lakes of all sizes indicate shallow sinkholes and solution channels.

North and west from the peninsular mainland lies a large submarine platform, the

Figure 2.9

Vertically-Walled Sink, or Cenote, in the Limestone Plain of Northern Yucatan, Mexico. The water level lies some 60 feet below the scrub-covered surface.

Campeche Banks, with depths of less than 600 feet and many shoals and reefs. The shallowness of these tropical waters has made them an ideal habitat for many kinds of fish and crustaceans, giving rise to a sizable fishing industry.

Immediately north of Cuba, the Bahama Islands—low, flat patches of porous limestone and coral—perch slightly above the sea on a vast shallow platform, or bank. Approximately 700 islands and over 2,000 reefs, cays, and rocks comprise this peculiar area. The Bahama Platform is separated from the crumpled Antillean area to the south by a submarine trench which eastward merges with the Brownson Deep (− 30,000 feet) off the north coast of Puerto Rico.

The Volcanic Axes of Central America and the Lesser Antilles (X and XI)

Both the western and eastern sides of the Antillean area of Central America and the West Indies are flanked by long zones of geologically recent volcanic activity. A continuous line of young volcanoes borders the Pacific edge of Central America for 800 miles, from the present Mexico-Guatemala frontier to Costa Rica. This volcanic axis forms the longest and most spectacular mountain range of Middle America. The Caribbean counterpart of the Central American chain is the volcanic arc of the lesser Antilles, a festoon of small islands 500 miles long, which forms the southeastern limits of Middle America.

The old Antillean east-west structure along the Pacific margin of northern Central America has been buried by recent volcanic materials. Thick deposits of older volcanic ash and lava cover much of the southern highlands of Honduras and north-central Nicaragua. The most recent volcanic activity lies near the Pacific coast, where more than 40 large volcanic peaks have ejected enormous quantities of ash, cinder, and lava. Among these volcanoes are the famous Fuego (12,600 feet) in Guatemala and Irazú (11,300 feet) in Costa Rica. Many volcanoes within the Central American axis are still active, especially in Guatemala and Nicaragua. As in the Mesa Central of Mexico, volcanic activity has formed lake-studded basins that range from 1,000 to 6,000 feet in elevation (Figure 2.10). Favored by fertile volcanic soils, these tropical highland basins and adjacent mountain slopes are the areas of densest settlement within Central America. The largest of these highland basins is the Meseta Central of Costa Rica with elevations between 3,000 and 5,000 feet. South of the Meseta Central the volcanic axis is interrupted by a huge batholith known as the Talamanca Range with elevations over 12,000 feet. In Panama, vulcanism resumes with the volcano of Chiriquí (11,410 feet) and continues in diminishing degree almost to the Canal Zone. Costa Rica and Panama have sometimes been called a volcanic bridge that connects Central and South America. Beyond the Canal Zone, the geology of Panama is closely related to a northwestern prong of the Andes, characterized by low mountain ranges along both the Caribbean and Pacific shores.

Between these coastal ranges is a low basin occupied by the Chucunaque River.

The middle of Central America is rent by a large crustal fracture, or rift, which forms the lowlands of Nicaragua. This long, narrow depression trends northwest-southeast between the Old Antillean structure and the volcanic axis of Central America. The central portion of the lowland is occupied by the largest fresh-water lakes of Middle America: lakes Managua and Nicaragua. Both drain to the Caribbean by way of the San Juan River, which flows through the southeastern part of the depression. Extending to the northwest of the lakes are plains covered with fertile soils derived from ash spewed from the volcanoes nearby. This rich lowland has been one of the most densely populated areas of Central America since pre-Conquest times. Near its northwestern end the depression helps to form the Gulf of Fonseca, the largest indentation along the Pacific shore of Middle America.

The *Lesser Antilles* are composed of a double arc of small islands. The inner arc

Figure 2.10
Lake Ilopango (El Salvador) with the Volcano of San Vicente in the Background. This view typifies much of the volcanic landscape of Central America.

consists of the high volcanic islands, which are volcanic cones or groups of cones. The tops of these cones rise out of the sea to elevations of 4,000 or 5,000 feet. Most of the surface of the volcanic isles, such as those from St. Kitts to Grenada, is composed of steep slopes, with narrow coastal plains and gently sloping piedmonts of deep, rich soil which ring the mountainous centers. The outer, and smaller, arc is made up of a few low flattish islands that are covered with limestone which overlays older volcanic or crystalline materials. This section of the Lesser Antilles includes the small isles of Barbuda, Antigua, the Grande Terre portion of Guadeloupe, and Marie Galante.

The Geological Hazards of Middle America

Situated in one of the world's most intensive zones of active mountain building, much of Middle America is subject to frequent earthquakes and volcanic eruptions. Often, in the past, these geological hazards have caused widespread damage to man and his works in Mexico, Central America, and the West Indies. In the future they will undoubtedly cause much more.

During historic times, several serious eruptions and explosions have occurred in all three of the main volcanic axes of Middle America. Probably the worst, in terms of loss of human life, was the 1902 explosion of Mt. Pelée on Martinique Island in the Lesser Antilles. A mass of fiery lava and superheated gas (*nuée ardente*) completely destroyed the town of St. Pierre and suffocated its 30,000 inhabitants within seconds. In 1835, Mt. Cosigüina, on the Gulf of Fonseca in northwestern Nicaragua, exploded. Many villages were half buried and farmland temporarily damaged by falling ash and dust within a radius of 100 miles. Much more serious destruction, accompanied by the loss of 6,000 lives, was wrought in 1902 by the eruption of Santa María volcano in Guatemala. Even the eruption of the relatively small Parícutin in Mexico in 1943 caused considerable damage

to forests and crops over a large area through ash fall; moreover, a flow of lava completely engulfed one Tarascan Indian town. Where ash fall was light, however, soils were improved by the addition of minerals. In 1963 Costa Rica's long dormant Irazú volcano suddenly erupted, spewing vast quantities of fine, grayish ash over the Meseta Central. Coffee groves, pasture lands, and forests were seriously damaged. In the long run, perhaps, the benefits of rich soils derived from the weathering of volcanic ejecta may outweigh the damage inflicted by occasional catastrophes.

As geological hazards, earthquakes have been far more destructive and widespread than volcanic eruptions in Middle America. Zones of seismic disturbance extend along most of the Pacific coast of Mexico and Central America and around much of the island rim in the Caribbean, as indicated in Figure 2.11. Severe quakes frequently occur in those coastal areas adjacent to deep submarine troughs, where slippage along faults sets up heavy shock waves within the earth's crust. Southwestern Mexico, near the Acapulco Deep off coast, and portions of the Dominican Republic and Puerto Rico, adjacent to the Puerto Rico Deep, are good examples. The Pacific coast of Central America is subject to frequent shocks that are associated with both volcanic activity and the deeply seated fault zones off coast.

The catastrophic effects of earthquakes are seen most frequently in the destruction of buildings and the causing of landslides. A less frequent, but equally destructive, effect is the creation by submarine earthquakes of tidal waves, called "tsunamis," which may inundate extensive sections of the coast, causing great destruction of property and life. There is hardly a town or city in western and southern Mexico, the Pacific side of Central America, or the West Indies that has not experienced earthquake disasters sometime in its history. The city of San Salvador, capital of El Salvador in Central America, has been completely or partially destroyed and rebuilt

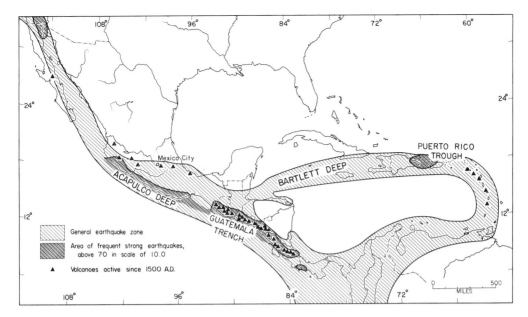

Figure 2.11
Geological Hazards.

nine times since its founding on the present site in 1528.

WEATHER AND CLIMATE

The physical diversity of Middle America is expressed, again, in its weather and climate. The distribution of air temperature and precipitation, the two principal elements of weather and climate, is highly complex in Middle America. Almost the entire range of subtropical and tropical climates, as well as some mid-latitude types, occur in this small segment of the earth's surface. Among the reasons for such diversity are: (1) latitudinal position; (2) complicated terrain and varied altitude; (3) influence of the adjacent seas and oceans; and (4) the various dominant pressure areas and accompanying wind systems.

General Temperature Characteristics and Controls

Latitude. Middle America's latitudinal position near the northern margin of the New World tropics is one of the basic controls of its weather and climate. The greater part of the area is within the tropics. Approximately two-thirds of the land and most of the adjacent seas lie south of the Tropic of Cancer (23½°N.). At least half of Mexico, however, lies north of the latitudinal limit of the tropics; in terms of weather and climate most of this area is subtropical or mid-latitude. The effect of latitude is reflected mainly in seasonal temperatures. As Figure 2.12 indicates, within the tropics there is a relatively small difference, usually less than 15°F, between the average temperatures of the coldest and warmest months (the annual temperature range). That is, in terms of temperature, there are no distinct summer and winter periods in the tropics. The difference between day and night temperatures (the diurnal range) is usually far greater than the annual range; hence, the well-known expression, "Night is the winter of the tropics." In much of northern Mexico, which is outside the tropics, the annual temperature range increases rapidly poleward, demarcating definite summer and winter seasons similar to those in the southern United States. Killing frosts occur every winter in the Mesa de Norte; but in the Pacific and Gulf coastal lowlands of northern Mexico they are rare.

Altitude. Within the Middle American tropics, altitude strongly influences air temperature. Since the temperature of the air decreases with altitude at the normal rate of approximately 1°F per 300 feet elevation, it follows that on high mountain slopes there occurs an altitudinal zonation of weather and climate. This fact is keenly recognized by the inhabitants of the Latin American tropics, who know the temperature belts by the terms given in Figures 2.13 and 2.14 and described below.

Within Middle America, altitudinal zonation of temperature is best seen in the escarpment areas of central and southern Mexico and in the mountainous sections of Central America. There, weather and climate, vegetation, soils, and man's use of the land vary according to altitude. In such areas, one may pass through three or four types of climate types·within a horizontal distance of only 25 miles. Variation in altitude within mountainous terrain is one of the most important reasons for the great complexity of weather and climate in tropical Middle America.

Following is a brief description of the extent and general temperature characteristics of the major altitudinal zones recognized in the Middle American tropics. Varying local conditions make it difficult to indicate the precise limits of these zones but, in general, the upper altitudinal limits of each zone tend to increase equatorward, and in Central America and Mexico they tend to occupy somewhat lower elevations on the Pacific slope than on the Gulf or Caribbean slopes.

1. The *tierra caliente* ("hot land") of Middle America lies generally between sea level and 2,500 feet elevation. Within these limits are included all of the tropical coastal lowlands, large plains areas (e.g., Yucatan Peninsula), low interior basins (e.g., the Balsas River Valley), and the foothills or low mountains of southern Mexico, Central America, and the West Indies. Thus, approximately one-half of the Middle American tropics is *tierra caliente*. In general, high but not excessive daytime temperatures (85 to 90°F)

Figure 2.12

Mean Annual Temperature Range.

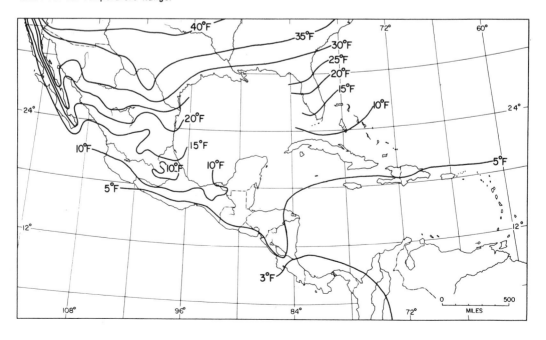

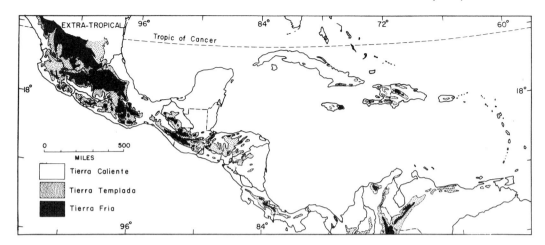

Figure 2.13
Altitudinal Temperature Zones.

contrast with cool nighttime conditions (70 to 75°F) most of the year, with small differences between summer and winter months. Frost is unknown, and rarely do night temperatures fall as low as 50°F. The *tierra caliente,* a land of tropical agriculture, is of growing importance throughout Middle America.

2. The *tierra templada* ("temperate land") is roughly between 2,500 and 5,500 to 6,000 feet in tropical Middle America. This zone, together with those that lie above it, constitutes the tropical highlands. The *tierra templada* includes the intermediate mountain slopes and much of the plateau surface of Central Mexico and Central America; only the higher interior mountains of the Caribbean Islands qualify as tropical highlands. Mild daytime temperatures (75 to 80°F) prevail, although hot afternoons with temperatures of 90 and 95°F sometimes occur in the warmer months of April or May, just prior to the start of the rainy season. Nights are delightfully cool (60 to 70°F). The difference between summer and winter temperatures increases poleward, so that in the Mesa Central of Mexico, on the northern margin of the tropical highlands, periods of cold and occasional night

frosts are not uncommon in December and January. However, the escarpment areas of Mexico and Central America are usually frost-free. Most Latin Americans and visitors from the mid-latitudes consider the *tierra templada* to have the most desirable temperatures for human comfort in Middle America. In Mexico and Central America, much of the population and the agricultural production is found in the *tierra templada.*

3. The *tierra fría* ("cold land") generally lies above 5,500 to 6,000 feet elevation. Only a small part of the Middle American tropics—possibly 10 per cent of the land surface—is considered to be *tierra fría.* Most of the cold land lies in the high

Figure 2.14

A Schematic Representation of the Altitudinal Temperature Zones of Middle America, at Approximately 15°N. Latitude.

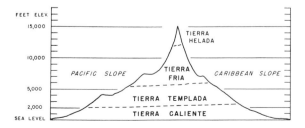

basins and mountain slopes of the Mesa Central of Mexico and in the highlands of Chiapas and Guatemala. These are areas of warm, pleasant days (75 to 80°F) and cold nights (50 to 55°F). Frosts are common during the cooler months of December through February; even in mid-summer, killing frosts have occurred in the higher basins of central Mexico, though rarely. Only hardy highland or mid-latitude crops thrive at these altitudes; however, many of the cold but fertile highland basins, such as the Valley of Mexico and those of western Guatemala, are among the most densely populated spots of Middle America.

4. The *tierra helada* ("frozen land"), generally lying above 12,000 feet elevation, occupies only the highest mountain peaks of Mexico and Central America. Temperatures below 50°F prevail almost all year. Freezes occur nightly in the cooler months and frequently in midsummer, and permanent ice and snow occupy the upper portions of the highest peaks.

Water Masses and Ocean Currents. Although their effect on temperature is less spectacular than altitude, the influence of adjacent water bodies must be considered. Air that overlies large water areas tends to take on the same temperature as the water surface. Thus, the air temperature of the coasts and the smaller islands of Middle America is profoundly influenced by the adjacent seas and oceans. Warm water borders the shores of most of Middle America. Of prime importance to the weather and climate of adjacent land areas are the Caribbean Sea and the Gulf of Mexico, both practically inland seas fed by warm offshoots of the Atlantic North Equatorial Current (Figure 2.15). As the temperature of their surface water ranges between 73 and 84°F, these two water bodies are veritable caldrons, over which forms a tropical marine air mass. This air mass extends warm conditions somewhat northward of their normal latitudes and carries tropical air into the southeastern and central United States during the summer period.

Warm surface waters fed by the northern

Figure 2.15
Ocean Currents and Sea Surface Temperatures.

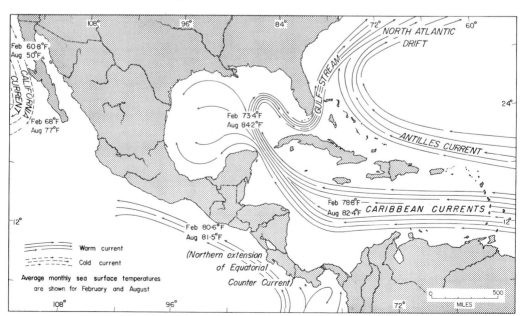

extension of the Pacific Equatorial Counter Current occur on the western side of Central America and southern Mexico. The Pacific maritime tropical air mass forms over these warm waters and transfers high year-round temperature and low annual range along the adjacent coasts.

In contrast, the relatively cold water of the California Current, which borders the Pacific shore of Lower California, brings cool year-round temperatures along the coast, but lowers the annual range to almost tropical proportions.

Continentality. Relatively narrow land masses, isthmuses, and islands characterize the southern two-thirds of Middle America. Thus, few points within this area are far from the influence of the sea. But toward the United States frontier, northern Mexico widens to continental proportions, introducing another temperature control, termed "continentality." Distance from the ameliorating conditions of the oceans and increasing latitude combine to give north-central

Mexico the cold winters and hot summers common to the interior mid-latitudes.

Rainfall and Its Controls

The rainfall map of Middle America (Figure 2.16) shows a complex areal pattern of abundance and paucity of moisture. The aridity of northern Mexico contrasts with the humidity of the southeastern part of the country. In general, the east coasts receive more rain than the west coasts, and small spots of dryness occur in the midst of areas with heavy precipitation throughout Middle America.

For the most part the rainfall is seasonal. The rainy period usually comes during the hotter months, May through October. The drier part of the year corresponds to the cooler period, December through April, and February and March are usually the months of least rain. Over most of the plateau and Pacific coast areas of Mexico and northern Central America, 75 to 80 per cent of the yearly rain falls between May and October.

Figure 2.16
Mean Annual Precipitation.

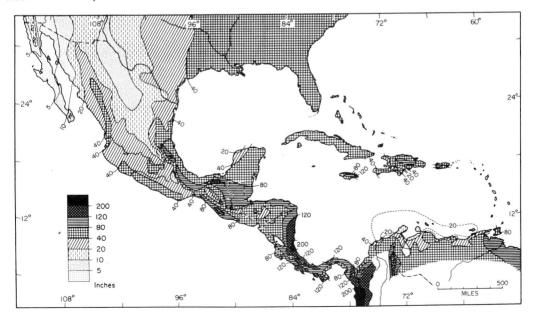

In the Spanish-speaking areas of the Middle American tropics, the wet season is called *invierno* ("winter") ; the dry season, *verano* ("summer").[2] In the tropics, seasons are determined by rainfall distribution and not, as in the higher latitudes, by temperature.

This simplified picture of seasonal rainfall distribution, however, is complicated by several significant exceptions. In particular, the eastern sides of the Caribbean Islands and Central America have short dry periods of less rain than usual, during January and February, rather than a true dry season with no or little moisture. Moreover, parts of the West Indies have double rainy and dry periods during the year, the longer dry season coming in January and February, the shorter one in June or July. Again, over most of Central America a ten- or fifteen-day period, called the *caniculas* or the *veranillo* (little summer), occurs in July or August, whereas the *verano,* or long dry season, lasts from November through March.

Both the areal and seasonal distribution of rainfall, as of temperature, are controlled by various natural factors. In Middle America the main controls of rainfall are: (1) pressure areas and associated winds; (2) air masses; and (3) configuration of the land surface. Usually all three controls operate together to effect the lifting and cooling that is necessary to produce precipitation.

The Northeast Trade Winds are the prime "weather machine" of eastern Middle America (Figure 2.17). These winds blow out of the Bermuda-Azores subtropical high-pressure cell, the center of which lies over the mid-Atlantic around 30°N. latitude. As they move toward the equatorial low pressure belt,

the earth's rotation deflects the Trades to the southwest. By the time they reach Middle America, they blow from the northeast and east, sweeping across the West Indian Islands and the warm Caribbean Sea to Central America and southern Mexico. As the air imported by the Trades sweeps over the warm waters of the South Atlantic and the Caribbean, it is heated and absorbs vast quantities of moisture, forming an unstable maritime tropical air mass. Along the windward slopes of highlands exposed to the Trades, the unstable, moisture-laden air is forced to rise and cool, forming great cloud banks and precipitating abundant rain on the mountain slopes. Thus the northeastern, or windward, sides of the West Indian Islands and the eastern side of Central America and southern Mexico are the wettest areas of Middle America, with an average yearly rainfall between 80 and 120 inches. In these areas, nearly every month is rainy, although there is a short, dry period during February and March when the tropical air mass is more stable. Interior valleys and the lee sides of mountains and mountainous islands receive comparatively little rain (20 to 40 inches), owing to the dryness of the descending air; such areas are said to be in the "rain shadow." Moreover, low-lying areas in the Trade Wind belt (northern Yucatan and the Bahamas for instance) receive little moisture, owing to the absence of high elevations to induce ascent and cooling of air.

During the warmer months, when the pressure areas have shifted slightly northward, the tropical air mass over the Caribbean and adjacent waters becomes quite unstable, and various kinds of tropical disturbances frequently interrupt the steady Trades. Afternoon thunderstorms over both land and sea are common during this period. Also, weak tropical disturbances with ill-defined fronts, called "easterly waves," move westward and northward through the Caribbean Islands and Central America, and bring prolonged rains (called *temporales* in Central America and southern Mexico) that last from three to four days. A more spectacular disturbance

---

2 These terms, as used in the Latin American tropics, are often confusing to mid-latitude dwellers, who think of winter and summer in terms of temperature. The inversion appears to have originated in the sixteenth century, when the newly arrived Spaniards applied their customary terms to the dry and wet seasons. In Spain and other parts of the Mediterranean area, the rainy season comes during the cool winter period (*invierno*) and the hot summer (*verano*) is the dry season.

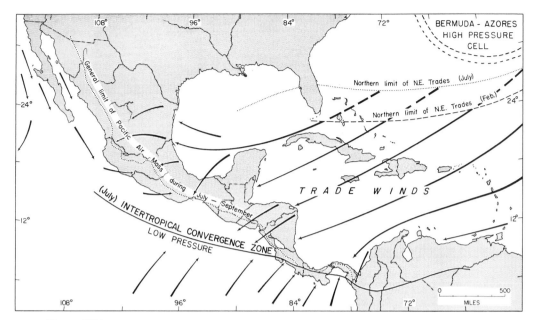

Figure 2.17
Pressure Areas and Prevailing Winds.

during the warmer period of the year is the tropical hurricane, discussed below under Weather Hazards.

Closely associated with the summer disturbances in the Trade Wind area is the northward movement of the equatorial low pressure belt (doldrums), or Intertropical Convergence Zone (ITC), into Central America and the Caribbean coast of South America. This zone is one of converging and rising warm, unstable air fed by the Trade Winds of the northern and southern hemispheres. Intense thunderstorms during the afternoon and night, and occasional weak tropical fronts, characterize the weather of this zone, which helps to usher in the summer rainy season on the Pacific coast of Central America and southern Mexico. The so-called monsoonal winds that blow from the Pacific into the Central American coast during this period are probably induced by the ITC as it moves periodically into the land. Destructive hurricanes also originate over the warm Pacific waters off the southern Mexican coast, as indicated below.

Because of its aridity and its position out-side the tropics, northern Mexico stands apart climatically from the rest of Middle America. Two large areas separated by the Sierra Madre Occidental comprise the arid section of the north: (1) the high, central desert of the Mesa del Norte; and (2) the low desert of Baja California and western Sonora. The low desert is the most arid section of Middle America, containing some points in Baja California which receive less than four inches of rain annually. Baja California and Sonora are often considered to be a southern extension of the Great Basin Desert of the United States, but their aridity is caused principally by the eastern end of the Pacific subtropical high-pressure cell which lies over northwestern Mexico most of the year. The dry, subsiding air of this high-pressure cell precludes much rainfall. The high, central desert of the northern Mexican plateau, on the other hand, owes its aridity mainly to its interior position, relatively far from oceanic sources of moisture. Furthermore, high escarpments effectively bar the entrance of much moist air from the Pacific or the Gulf of Mexico. In summer, occasional afternoon thundershowers bring isolated rains; in winter, the southern extension of mid-latitude cyclonic storms cause light rains and sometimes sleet and snow. In semi-arid northeastern Mexico, tropical disturbances, including the edges of hurricanes that form in the Gulf of Mexico, occasionally bring heavy rainfall during September and October.

Weather Hazards

Middle America is plagued as much by meteorological as by geological disasters. Its position at the poleward margin of the tropics makes this area vulnerable to atmospheric disturbances that originate in both low and middle latitudes. As we just mentioned, prolonged droughts are particularly prevalent in the central Mexican plateau, at the margin which lies between humid and arid zones. Excessive, flood-producing rains occur periodically in all parts of Middle America, even in the dry northwest, though at rare intervals. The killing frosts of northern Mexico and the tropical highlands have already been mentioned; in addition, summer hailstorms

sometimes destroy crops in the highlands of Mexico and Guatemala. The most spectacular and widespread of the weather hazards that affect Middle America, however, are storms of two types: (1) the tropical hurricane; and (2) mid-latitude cyclonic disturbances (Figure 2.18).

Tropical Hurricanes. These destructive storms occur on both the Carribbean and Pacific sides of Middle America. Those of the Caribbean are notorious; during the normal hurricane season—July through October— from five to a dozen occur. They are usually no more than 100 miles across, but the high winds within them whirl about a small, abnormally low-pressure center at velocities of over 75 miles per hour. They originate within the maritime tropical air mass over the warm waters of the Atlantic, the Caribbean Sea, and the Gulf of Mexico. Once generated, the storm centers move slowly westward or northwestward and eventually recurve to the north and northeast, to be dissipated in the mid-latitudes. The Atlantic hurricanes often pass through the West

Figure 2.18
Weather Hazards.

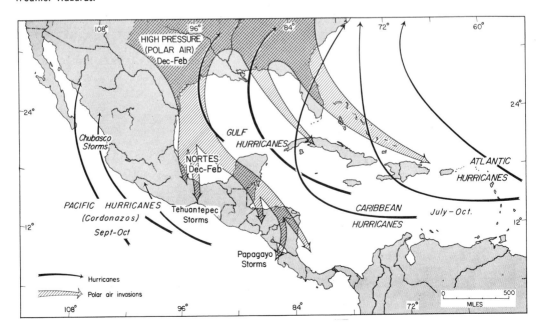

Indies and recurve to the northeast, striking the eastern coast of the United States or dying out in midocean. The storms that originate in the Caribbean Sea affect mainly the Greater Antilles, Yucatan, Florida and, occasionally, the east coast of Central America. Those of the Gulf of Mexico often hit the east coast of Mexico and the Gulf coast of the United States. The high winds of the hurricanes cause enormous destruction of human life and property, both directly and through the creation of large tidal waves along coasts, and the torrential downpours within the hurricane structure frequently flood large sections of land.

The hurricanes that originate over the warm Pacific waters off the southern Mexican coast during the months of June to October or November are little known, and are usually less dangerous than the Caribbean variety. These storms, locally called *chubascos,* frequently proceed northward from their point of origin and veer suddenly to the northeast, causing extensive damage along the west coast of Mexico as far north as Baja California and southern Sonora (27°N. latitude). In November, 1961, a large *chubasco* swept across the coast north of Acapulco in southwestern Mexico, causing many deaths and much destruction of property.

Mid-latitude Storms. The second type of destructive storm is the mid-latitude cyclonic disturbance, which often invades the Middle American tropics. Winter atmospheric conditions in the United States affect the weather and climate of Middle America to a greater extent than is normally supposed. Mention already has been made of the winter cyclonic rains of northern and central Mexico. From November through March, incursions of northern polar air into the Middle American tropics are frequent. Fronts (lines of contact between cool polar air and warm tropical air) often penetrate into central Mexico, Yucatan, and Cuba, and sometimes extend as far as Nicaragua in Central America and Puerto Rico in the West Indies. Along these weakened polar fronts heavy rains occur, principally along the eastern escarpments of Mexico and northern Central America where uplifting takes place. On the plateaus of central and southern Mexico and of Guatemala, the arrival of the front is accompanied by extensive overcast with light rains, variously called, *chipichipis, equipatas,* or *cabañuelas.* Such rains, as already mentioned, are highly beneficial to agriculture and grazing in the drier plateau areas. Following the passage of the weakened front, however, are stiff, cold winds which cause temperatures to drop suddenly as much as 10 or 15°F and which have caused killing frosts along the Gulf coast of Mexico as far south as northern Veracruz (as in January, 1962). These winds, which come from a northerly direction, are called *nortes* (northers) in Middle America. *Nortes* are most frequent along the Gulf coast of Mexico, where normally 15 to 20 occur each winter, prolonging the rainy season in places into December and January. Within this area and the Caribbean coast of Guatemala and Honduras, the north winds often destroy extensive sections of banana plantations and seriously damage coastal shipping. Northers also blow through the natural corridors across Central America, causing rough seas in the Pacific south of the Isthmus of Tehuantepec (where they are known as Tehuantepequer storms), the Gulf of Fonseca, and in the Nicaraguan Lowlands (where they are known as Papagayos storms). The stronger *nortes* pass over the highlands of northern Central America, causing occasional freezes and snow storms; they then descend to the Pacific coast as hot, dry winds, often dessicating coffee and banana plantings.

CLIMATE TYPES
AND ASSOCIATED VEGETATION
AND SOILS

Figure 2.19 indicates the distribution of climatic types according to the Koeppen

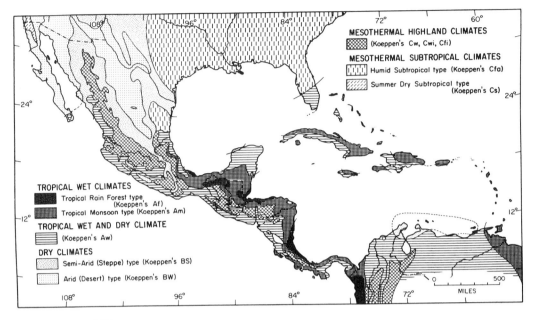

Figure 2.19
Climatic Areas.

classification. Mathematically, these types are based mainly on yearly and monthly averages of temperature and rainfall. However, vegetation is often used as a climatic indicator when temperature and rainfall data are lacking, since the area covered by each type of climate corresponds roughly to a given native type of vegetation. As we shall see, this correspondence of native vegetation and climatic type is often wanting.

The Tropical Wet Climates: Koeppen's Af and Am

These climates have high temperatures all year, the average for each month being above 64°F. Annual rainfall is heavy, usually over 80 inches, and there is no pronounced dry season. In Middle America these climates correspond mainly to the *tierra caliente,* or hot tropical lowlands, in exposed positions within the Trade Wind area; that is, the northeastern sides of the Caribbean Islands and the greater part of the eastern half of Central America and southern Mexico. A

narrow belt of tropical wet climate extends northward along the lower eastern escarpment of the Mexican Plateau where heavy orographic rains result both from the Trades in summer and the occasional northern cyclonic storms in winter. On the Pacific side of Central America, two small areas of high annual rainfall come within the tropical wet climates. One includes the coast and seaward-facing slopes of southwestern Panama and southeastern Costa Rica; the other is a narrow strip along the volcanic escarpment of Guatemala at an elevation 2,000 or 3,000 feet above the adjacent coastal plain.

Most of the areas of tropical wet climate in Middle America are characterized by a short dry period during the cooler months, but sufficient rain falls during the year to support heavy rain-forest vegetation. This is Koeppen's Am type, the tropical monsoon rain-forest climate. Only a few sections of the rainiest areas, such as the windward sides of the Lesser Antilles, a few parts of the Caribbean coast of Central America, and a portion of the Tabasco lowlands in southeastern Mexico can be classed as true tropical rain-forest climate (Koeppen's Af), with no dry season.

Vegetation. A heavy forest of tall tropical trees—properly called the "rain forest"—was probably the original vegetation that covered the greater part of the tropical, wet climatic area of Middle America (Figure 2.20). Just what may have been the natural vegetation of any area, however, is often hard to determine. Man, exploiting native plants, on the one hand, and clearing by cutting and burning, on the other, has greatly modified much of the natural cover of most of the world. This human process has been going on in Middle America since the coming of the first Indians, possibly more than ten millennia ago, and the rate of cultural modification of the vegetation has been greatly accelerated since the beginning of European settlement in the sixteenth century. In all of Middle America, there are probably few parts of the rain forest untouched by man.

The less modified tropical rain forests in eastern Central America and the West Indies are composed of a great number of distinct species of large, broad-leaved, evergreen trees, some of which are more than 150 feet tall (Figure 2.21). Most have straight, broad trunks, and many are heavily buttressed at their bases. Pure stands of single species are rare, and in Central America they exist naturally only in swampy areas. A dense canopy of overlapping tree crowns shuts out almost all sunlight from the forest floor, making it free of dense undergrowth except for occasional clumps of shade-tolerant palms and wide-leaved aroids. A myriad of large climbing vines (lianas) and clinging epiphytes often cover the trunks and larger branches of many trees. Dense undergrowth (jungle) occurs where sunlight can penetrate, as along stream banks and in scattered tree falls (Figure 2.22).

Many valuable hardwoods, such as mahogany, tropical cedar, and guayacan, were once abundantly scattered through the rain forests of Middle America, but large specimens of these trees are now found only in isolated spots. A peculiar feature of the forest near the Caribbean coast of Honduras and

Figure 2.20
Natural Vegetation.

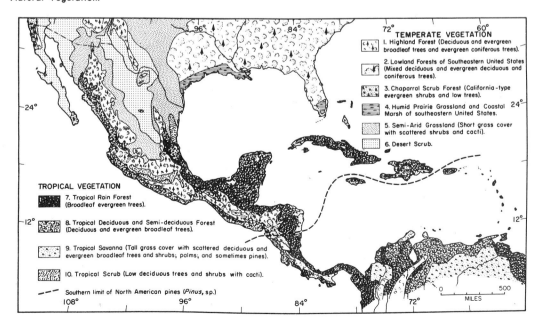

Figure 2.21
Tropical Rain Forest Along Edge of Clearing in the Tuxtlas Mountains, Southern Veracruz State, Mexico. The large trees, often buttressed and festooned with lianes and epiphytes, range from 60 to 80 feet in height. Palms and young trees form the understory vegetation.

Figure 2.22
Dense Tropical Jungle Growth Along a Stream Bank in the Lowlands of Northern Chiapas, Mexico.

on either side of the Yucatan Peninsula was the abundance of dye-yielding logwood, which was heavily exploited, particularly by English loggers, during colonial times. These stands are now badly depleted. In the dense rain forest of the Petén, or northern Guatemala, certain trees valuable for human food, such as the breadnut (Brosimum) and sapodilla, or chicle tree (Achras sapota), are often found in groves or solid stands, although their distribution is scattered. Such conditions seem to point to the probable influence of Indians, who planted these trees around settlements now abandoned or who protected them by cutting away competing vegetation.

Today, large areas of the once extensive rain forest of Central America and southeast Mexico have been destroyed to make way for plantations and pastures, and native farmers have reduced even greater areas to low growth by repeatedly cutting and burning in order to clear small plots for cultivation. In the West Indies, only isolated groves of rain forest remain on steep mountain slopes.

One of the most puzzling features of the natural vegetation in the tropical rainy areas of Middle America is the presence of large expanses of grassland, called "savannas," in areas that receive as much as 80 to 100 inches of rain annually, with no dry period or a quite short one. In terms of climate, such areas should be covered by a heavy rain forest. The largest of the humid savannas is found along the Caribbean margin of Nicaragua and northeastern Honduras (the Mosquito Coast). Open stands of tropical lowland pine (Pinus caribea) add to the curious aspect of this wet area (Figure 2.23). Such vegetational anomalies may be caused by edaphic (soil) or cultural factors, and the chief reason for the Nicaraguan pine-savanna is probably the porous, gravelly soil, which will support only drought-tolerant plants. Smaller areas of humid savanna associated with open stands of pine or palms within the rain-forest zone occur in British Honduras, the Petén of northern Guatemala, the Tabasco coast of southeastern Mexico, and in Cuba. Little is known about the origin of these grassy areas; most are probably edaphic, but some may have been culturally induced through burning.

Soils. Over a long period of time, and under given climatic conditions and kinds of vegetation cover, certain types of soils tend to develop. Such soils are considered mature, or *zonal,* types. In tropical rainy climates, where high temperatures and excessive moisture permit the weathering of rocks to depths of 30 to 50 feet below the surface, a thick layer of clayey red and yellow soil, or *latosol,* tends to develop as the general zonal type. In the tropical rainy areas of Middle America, however, there appears to be a great variety of zonal soils, most of which have received little study. In the Caribbean lowlands of Central America, red and yellow latosols are often encountered in the rain forest on well drained slopes. Latosols are usually leached

Figure 2.23
Open Pine Savanna, Mosquito Coast of Nicaragua, Near Bluefields. This area receives an annual average rainfall of nearly 100 inches with a short dry season during March and April. (James J. Parsons)

of plant nutrients and, when the forest is cleared, they prove to be quite infertile for agriculture. In Cuba, on the other hand, most of the red latosols derived from the weathering of hard limestone are among the most productive of mature tropical soils.

Large sections of the Middle American rain forest contain soils that develop under special drainage conditions or are derived from a given rock that imparts peculiar soil characteristics (*intrazonal* types). For example, the tropical weathering of soft limestone and marl in the Petén of northern Guatemala has produced a leached, heavy, black clay known to scientists as *rendzina*; in spite of the leaching, this soil still contains abundant calcium and thus is more fertile than the more normal reddish latosols. It is significant that the ancient Maya Indian civilization reached its apogee in precisely this area of tropical rendzina soils. Another intrazonal soil of the rain forest is the water-logged, blue and grey, mottled clay (gley) found in the swampy Tabasco lowlands of southeastern Mexico and in other wet areas along the east side of Central America.

Probably the most fertile soils in the wet tropics of Middle America are the *azonal* types derived from the weathering of recently deposited alluvium and young volcanic ejecta. Immature, these soils have not yet been leached of valuable plant nutrients and minerals; consequently, they have been considered premium farmland since aboriginal times. Primarily because of such fertile soils, the wide alluvial flood plains along the Caribbean coast of Central America were densely occupied by Indian farmers in pre-Conquest times, and today they are the sites of large tropical plantations. Likewise, the rain forest-covered volcanic slopes on the Pacific side of Guatemala, parts of the eastern escarpment of Mexico, and the Lesser Antillean islands contain fertile soils rich in minerals needed for the cultivation of coffee and sugar cane.

The Tropical Wet-and-Dry Climate : Koeppen's Aw

The temperature of this climate is similar to the tropical humid types, but it is distinguished by a definite dry season of four to six months during the cooler part of the year. It should be emphasized that this dry period may not be entirely without rain. However, the dryness is sufficient to induce a seasonal rhythm in vegetative growth.

In Middle America, the tropical wet-and-dry climate is characteristically developed in the lee of the Trade Winds, along the southern and western coasts and in interior basins of less than 3,000 feet elevation. It characterizes more than half of the *tierra caliente*. The largest continuous area of this climate is found on the Pacific side of Mexico and Central America. Smaller areas occur on the lee sides of the Caribbean Islands and in extensive low plains on the east side of Mexico. The latter include the northern half of the Yucatan Peninsula and much of the central Gulf coastal plain of Mexico.

Vegetation. The long dry season has a pronounced effect on the natural vegetation. Within Middle America, most of the tropical wet-and-dry areas are covered by a low forest of mainly deciduous trees that shed their leaves during the dry period. Occasional giant trees, such as the guanacaste (Enterolobium) and the silk-cotton tree (Ceiba pentandra) rise above the general forest level; frequently, clumps of palms grow in low wet spots. In Spanish-speaking areas, this type of forest is locally called *monte alto* ("high bush"). A less luxuriant association, called *monte bajo* ("low bush"), composed of thick growths of low, thorny scrub and cacti of many forms and species, often covers hill slopes having thin, rocky soils (Figure 2.24). A similar thorny scrub is also dominant in the drier interior basins, on the leeward coastal strips of the mainland, and on many of the Caribbean islands. The brilliant green foliage of both the low- and high-bush vegetation during the rainy season contrasts with the dull greys and browns of the bare trees relieved only by scattered clumps of green palms and an occasional evergreen broad-leaved tree, during the dry period. Possibly in response to the length of the dry period, there is an extraordinary concentration of gum and tannin-yielding plants and of dye-woods within the deciduous forest. Milky-sapped evergreens, such as the American fig (Ficus), are also abundant. In contrast to the low deciduous or semideciduous growth on hill slopes, the moist soil of the alluvial flood plains and stream banks supports a luxuriant cover of broad-leaved evergreens that is much like the rain forest.

One of the significant features of the vegetation associated with the tropical wet-and-dry climate in Middle America is the paucity of extensive areas of savanna grassland, which in South America and Africa forms the dominant plant cover in a similar climate. Only one large natural savanna, that of central Panama, occurs on the Pacific margin of Middle America. This and smaller spots of savanna elsewhere in Central America and the West Indies are more likely the result of soils and drainage conditions than of climate.

Man has altered the tropical deciduous

Figure 2.24

A Low Forest of Columnar Cactus and Deciduous Trees. The forest forms this tropical *monte bajo* vegetation characteristic of the rocky, rain-shadow mountain slopes in southern Oaxaca, Mexico.

and semideciduous forests of Middle America more than he has the rain forest. The tropical wet-and-dry lands have always been the part of the *tierra caliente* more favorable for human occupation, and they still today support a much denser population than the rain forest areas. Consequently, in many sections, particularly in alluvial flood plains and the more fertile hill sections, the original forest has been almost completely replaced by cultivated fields or pastures. Man-made grasslands, with scattered palms and broad-leaved trees, cover large areas of the tropical wet-and-dry climate of Middle America, giving a false impression of natural savannas. Landowners maintain such grasslands by annual burning during the dry season in order to improve forage for livestock and to destroy ticks. Once burning is stopped for a number of years, the low, woody growth begins to retake the land.

In many savannas of Middle America, scattered palms form a significant element of the vegetational landscape. When forests are cleared, the palms are usually saved, for they are highly regarded as sources of food and building material. Extensive groves of wild palms of a single species are often found in valleys and on hillsides on the Pacific coast of Mexico and Central America. It has been suggested that such groves owe their origin to long years of protection—practically semi-cultivation—by man.

As in many other tropical areas of the world, there occur, along the shores of quiet, muddy bays of the Middle American coasts, a special type of vegetation called a "tidal forest" or "mangrove swamp." This curious swamp vegetation may occur in all types of tropical lowland climates along muddy shores. Various species of salt-tolerant trees compose the mangrove swamp, the most typical being the red mangrove (Rhizophora) renowned for having a mass of stilt roots which grow up from the malodorous tidal mud flats (Figure 2.25). In bays and

Figure 2.25
Red Mangrove Forest Along the Honduras Shore of the
Gulf of Fonseca, Pacific Coast of Central America.

lagoons along the Central American coasts
the mangrove forest is tall, some trees reaching 100 feet or more. Northward, along the
Mexican coasts and in many sections of the
West Indies where the winters are cooler, the
mangrove becomes a scrubby growth. The
swamps, almost impenetrable except along
tidal channels, form an effective barrier between the coast and the interior. Much of
the taller swamp growth has been altered in
the past century as red mangrove has been
cut down for its tannin-rich bark and white
mangrove for wood to make charcoal.

Soils. The soils, like those of the tropical
rain-forest area, are various. Owing to the
dry season, soils that develop in the tropical
wet-and-dry climate are not as deeply
weathered or leached as those of the rain
forest.

The highly infertile red lateritic soils that
cover the surface of so much of the tropical

savannas of South America and Africa are
found only rarely in Middle America. However, such soils, with the characteristic hardpan layer of iron oxide nodules, may underlie
the natural savannas of western Panama, the
Mosquito coast of northeastern Nicaragua,
and the savannas of Tabasco in southeastern
Mexico, as well as parts of Cuba and Hispaniola. Young azonal soils, derived from
volcanic material, are found in most of the
Pacific coastal lowlands of Central America,
and they may be responsible for the luxuriant, semideciduous tropical forests that once
covered this area. In the wet-and-dry lowlands of Mexico there is a bewildering variety
of zonal, or mature soils, which seem to defy
attempts to associate them with climate.
According to recent surveys, many of the
soils of the Mexican Pacific lowlands and
some on the Gulf coast are *chernozemic,* a
general type that is usually associated with
semiarid regions of the mid-latitudes. Alkaline, little leached, and red-brown to black
in color, such soils are quite fertile and often
contain an abundance of lime. The northern
half of the Yucatan Peninsula is characterized by its thin, red, limey soil (*terra rossa*),
another chernozemic type more characteristic of arid regions than of the humid
tropics.

The Mesothermal Highland Climates: Koeppen's Cw, Cwi, Cfi

These climates correspond generally to the
tierra templada and *tierra fría,* or the tropical highlands. As indicated previously, the
tropical highlands of Middle America are
confined almost wholly to Mexico and Central America; only scattered patches occur in
the Caribbean Islands. Because of their elevation, the temperatures are lower than in
the tropical lowland climates, at least one
month of the year averaging less than 65°F.
Seasonal temperature differences are slight;
the highland climate in southern Mexico and
Central America is *isothermal,* that is, it has
an annual temperature range of not more

than 9°F. In Mexico, a wide strip of meso-thermal highland climate follows the Sierra Madre Occidental northwestward almost to the United States border. The northern half of this range has cold winters, often with snow, and warm summers.

In most of the tropical highlands of Mexico and Central America, precipitation is seasonal, the rains coming as thunderstorms during the hotter months (annual total precipitation, 30 to 80 inches). Occasional light winter rains of cyclonic origin are common in the Mesa Central of Mexico. On high slopes exposed to the Trade Winds, particularly along the eastern escarpment of southern Mexico and the Caribbean side of Central America, heavy rains fall every month. The annual total is 80 to 120 inches (Koeppen's Cfi).

Vegetation. The mountainous relief and the consequent variety of slopes exposed to wind and sun makes for a multiplicity of types of vegetation in the highlands. The most widespread highland plant association is an oak and coniferous forest, which extends from northern Mexico southward into Central America. The coniferous trees, however, extend only as far as the highlands of northern Nicaragua, where the North American pine (Pinus) reaches its southern limit. Both evergreen and deciduous oaks continue along the volcanic axis of Central America into Costa Rica and Panama. In the West Indies highland, oak and pine forests are found in the higher mountains of Cuba and Hispaniola. The Cordillera Central in the Dominican Republic and the Jacmel Peninsula of Haiti form another equatorward limit of the genus Pinus.

An altitudinal sequence of plant associations usually occurs in the forested highlands of Mexico and Central America. Within the Mesa Central of Mexico, for example, grass and scattered oaks probably formed the original vegetation of the basin floors. On the slopes of adjacent volcanic mountains (e.g., Popocatepetl) this association grades into for-ests of evergreen and deciduous oak. At approximately 7,000 feet, pines begin to appear in these forests, and at 10,000 feet solid pine predominates. Above the pine zone, fir (Abies) is found. It appears at 11,500 feet and continues as solid stands almost to the tree line, between 12,500 and 13,000 feet. A similar vegetational sequence occurs as far south as northern Central America, where the pine zone usually begins at a lower elevation than in central Mexico. Throughout the pine-covered mountain areas of Mexico and northern Central America, the solid forest is interrupted by grassy meadows in small flat-floored basins which afford pleasant sites for settlements and pastures.

In Central America and southern Mexico, on windward slopes, a highly interesting vegetation association, called the *cloud forest,* occurs above the pine zone. Beginning at elevations of 6,500 or 7,000 feet, these are almost continually enveloped in cloud even during the drier part of the year, and they drip with moisture. Giant evergreen oaks, laurels, deciduous sweet gums (Liquidambar), and thickets of tree ferns make up the greater part of this eerie forest (Figure 2.26). Owing to the abundance of moisture, the trunks and lower branches of the larger trees are covered with epiphytes such as bromelias, orchids, and mosses, which enhance the fairyland aspect of the vegetation. Somewhat similar cloud forests occur on the higher windward sides of the volcanic mountains in the Lesser Antilles and along the upper edge of the eastern escarpment of central Mexico.

Of all the vegetation types of Middle America, probably the oak-pine highland forests of central and southern Mexico have been the most seriously altered by human action. The process of destruction by man, principally by clearing for cultivation, has been in progress for at least 3,000 years. Large areas of the Mesa Central of Mexico, once oak and pine forest, now appear to be semiarid grass and bushland. Since the Mesa Central has for so long been an area of dense

Figure 2.26
A Remnant of the Cloud Forest, Much of Which Is Now Practically Destroyed by Man, in the Talamanca Range, Costa Rica. Giant buttressed oaks comprise the bulk of the formerly magnificent vegetation.

rural population, the amount of forest destruction is not surprising, especially when one realizes that since the Spanish occupation in the sixteenth century, cutting for lumber and fuel has increasingly diminished the extent of the pine and fir forests. Today, the only extensive reserve of pine in Mexico is in the Sierra Madre Occidental. On the other hand, in Honduras and northern Nicaragua, man may have accidentally extended pine growth by destruction of an original tropical forest; the latter appears to have been replaced by pine on eroded mineral soils.

Soils. The soils of the tropical highlands and the adjacent mountains of Mexico and Central America are extremely complex in type and distribution, as would be expected in an area of rugged relief and varied geology. The most important, in terms of human occupance, are the azonal soils derived from volcanic material found in the Mesa Central of Mexico and in the highlands of Central America. Two kinds of volcanic soils prevail.

Those weathered from recent basic volcanic ejecta (basalt, andesite) are the most fertile and widespread. The second type, derived from older acidic material (rhyolite), as in the southern highlands of Honduras, are thin and infertile. In the Mesa Central, many of the old volcanic basins contain mature, dark-colored chernozemlike soils derived from ancient lake-deposited alluvium. High in calcium and organic material, these soils are renowned for their fertility. Unfortunately, overcropping and overgrazing on the lower slopes of the basins has caused serious gullying and sheet erosion. The erosion so caused has often exposed an underlying hardpan of lime (caliche, or *tepetate*), rendering sizable amounts of land useless for cultivation.

The Mesothermal Subtropical Climates: Koeppen's Cfa, Cs

In Middle America, these climates occur in only two small areas of northern Mexico. The southernmost *humid subtropical climate* (Koeppen's Cfa, typical of southeastern

United States) is found in the extreme north-east of Mexico on the Gulf coastal plain and adjacent hill lands. In this area, winter temperatures are lower than normal for the latitude because of the frequent incursions of cool polar air from Texas; hot, muggy summers are induced by the presence of the tropical maritime air mass from the Gulf of Mexico. Rain, although relatively meager (20 to 40 inches), falls every month, reaching its maximum during the hot summer; frequent cyclonic storms bring most of the winter rainfall. The low annual precipitation and the porous, limestone-surface rock encourage a thorny semideciduous bush vegetation which covers most of northeastern Mexico. True forest occurs only in the higher elevations (such as the Sierra de Tamaulipas) and along streams, where cottonwoods and bald cypress are common. The soft limestone and marl of the lower coastal plain is responsible for the development of a belt of rendzina soils, a southern extension of the black soils of Texas.

The extreme northwestern part of Baja California is the southernmost limit of the summer-dry mesothermal climate (Koeppen's Cs), which characterizes the coastal valleys and ranges of upper California. Marked by severe summer drought and light winter rains (15 to 20 inches), this subtropical climate embraces the pine-covered mountains of the northern part of the peninsula and extends to the chaparral-covered plain around the town of Ensenada.

The Dry Climates:
Koeppen's BS and BW

The dry climates of Middle America, including the *semiarid*, or *steppe* (Koeppen's BS), and the *desert* (Koeppen's BW) types, are confined mainly to the northern interior and the northwest of Mexico. Small areas of dry climate, principally of the semiarid type, occupy rain shadow positions in deep valleys and in the lee of high mountains in many parts of the Middle American tropics. For example, a narrow corridor of semiarid climate extends southward from the dry, northern plateau of Mexico into the central and southern parts of the country that lie directly behind the eastern sierra. The Tepalcatepec Valley south of the Mesa Central in Mexico, the middle Motagua Valley of Guatemala, and the Enriquillo depression of Hispaniola in the West Indies are rain-shadow basins. Another area of dry climate that borders Middle America includes a portion of the Venezuelan coast of South America and islands offshore.

Moisture deficiency is, of course, the outstanding characteristic of the dry climates. Generally, the semiarid type receives twice the rainfall of the desert, but this is still insufficient for the growth of forest vegetation. In north Mexico, most of the scant precipitation comes during the summer months in the form of scattered thundershowers, but occasional winter cyclonic rain and drizzles are of exceptional importance where dry farming is practiced. In the northern part of Baja California, however, winter cyclonic rains and summer drought prevail.

In terms of temperature, the Middle American dry climates are mainly subtropical (Koeppen's BSh and BWh), with hot summers and mild winters. On high mountain slopes within the northern plateau, there are probably many spots of cold steppe and desert (Koeppen's BSk and BWk) with severe winter temperatures. Owing to the unusually clear, dry atmosphere and rapid radiation, the difference between day and night temperatures is extreme. In winter, nightly freezes are not uncommon in north central Mexico, whereas midday temperatures may be uncomfortably hot.

The Steppe Lands. In terms of human occupation, the semiarid steppes of Middle America are the more significant of the dry climatic areas. Generally, the steppe is a transition zone between the true desert and the more humid climates. In north central Mexico, the steppe occupies the higher

Figure 2.27
Steppe, or Short-Grass Pasture Lands in the Semiarid Portion of the Mexican Plateau, Near Durango City. Scattered huisache trees and mesquite shrubs form the sparse woody growth.

plateau surface that flanks the sierras on the west and east and the Mesa Central on the south. In northwestern Mexico, a wide belt of semiarid climate covers the ridge and basin lands between the Sierra Madre and the Altar Desert, narrowing southward along the Sinaloa coast. In northeastern Mexico, a semiarid climate extends almost to the Gulf coast south of the Rio Grande. The annual rainfall on these steppes averages between 15 and 20 inches.

The relatively small amount of rainfall in the semiarid regions is sufficient for the growth of a short grass, the most distinctive landscape feature of the steppe (Figure 2.27). Low, spiny shrubs, such as mesquite and cat's-claw, and various cacti grow in scattered fashion as associates of the low grasses. In low swales and along intermittent stream courses where the water table is high, mesquite bushes grow in dense thickets, and on the higher mountain slopes open stands of scrub oak and juniper prevail. The nutritious grasses and the protein-rich mesquite

pods afford a natural basis for the development of the Mexican livestock industry. In contrast to the north Mexican grasslands, the small spots of semiarid climate within the dry basins of tropical Middle America mainly support thorny scrub, vegetation similar to that of the drier sections of tropical wet-and-dry climates.

Soils of the steppe areas of north Mexico are typical of those that develop in semiarid climates; they are principally chernozemic, with a layer of lime accumulation that lies a few inches below a humus-rich, black-to-brown, upper soil layer. Except in irrigated areas, however, the deficiency of moisture unfortunately precludes intensive cultivation of these rich soils.

The Deserts. The true deserts of Middle America are limited to northern Mexico. That of Baja California and Sonora in the northwest is the most arid, a large area receiving less than four inches of rain annually. Along the Pacific coast of Baja California, the cold California current reduces air temperature; warm air from the Pacific, drifting over the cold water, produces extensive fog banks. Thus the coastal areas present the anomaly of a cool, foggy desert with atmospheric conditions similar to those of the Peruvian coastal desert in South America. The temperature range of the desert that borders on the Gulf of California, however, is quite distinct, with extremely hot summers and mild winters. Some of the highest summer temperatures in Middle America have been recorded along the arid coastal plain of Sonora and northern Sinaloa, where extremes of 115 to 120°F are not uncommon.

Less extreme temperatures and somewhat more rainfall (5 to 15 inches) prevail in the interior plateau desert of northern Mexico. Some of the higher mountain slopes may receive more than 20 inches of precipitation yearly. As in most deserts, the amount of annual rain is highly variable. Prolonged droughts of several years duration may be followed by periods of plentiful moisture and even floods.

Climatically and botanically, the deserts of northern Mexico are southward extensions of arid zones in the southwestern United States. Compared to the barren deserts of the Sahara and Arabia, the Mexican areas support a relatively lush plant cover. Plants are low xerophytes having special adaptations to long periods of drought. On the rocky hillsides and alluvial fans, the spindly ocotillo, the creosote bush, and the palm-like yucca form the dominant woody vegetation; between these plants grow succulent-leaved agaves, a bewildering variety of cacti, and a few widely spaced clumps of bunch grass (Figure 2.28). The alkaline surfaces of the *barreales,* or dry lakes, support only scattered growths of a wiry, unpalatable Hilaria grass; but along intermittent watercourses, low mesquite and acacia bushes and clumps of prickly pear cactus form narrow strips of more luxuriant desert vegetation. Areas

Figure 2.28
Desert Scrub in Coahuila State, North Central Mexico. The spiny plant at the right is ocotillo; the dark-toned ones are creosote bush. Lechuguilla forms low clumps between rocky outcrops.

completely devoid of vegetation are found in the few small shifting dune fields, such as those of Salamayuca in Chihuahua, 100 miles south of El Paso, Texas. In contrast, the mountain crests above 10,000 feet elevation often support scrub oak and occasional pine forest, forming spots of semiarid or even humid climate within the desert.

The desert vegetation of north central Mexico appears to be invading the margins of eroded or overgrazed steppe lands. That even the desert plants have not been free of destructive exploitation by man is evidenced by the depletion, in many areas, of various wild agaves and spurges collected for fiber and wax during the past few decades.

A definite zonal soil type is associated with the desert climate of Mexico in those areas where there has been sufficient accumulation of weathered material, as in basin fills and old alluvial fans. These desert soils are generally called *sierozems*. Because of the deficient rainfall and the slowness of plant decay, they are low in organic matter, high in lime and other soluble salts, and usually gray-brown in color. The soil is often so alkaline as to be useless for cultivation, but with proper treatment large sections of basin floor in the north Mexico deserts have been brought under irrigated agriculture. On the rocky hill slopes of the desert, however, little soil forms.

NATIVE ANIMAL LIFE IN MIDDLE AMERICA

Native animals, like plants and soils, form a significant part of the natural landscape of any area, and have been important to man in various ways. Broadly speaking, a correlation exists between climate, vegetation, and certain forms of animal life; however, various animals are mobile enough to extend their range into several climatic and vegetational zones, and the correlation often becomes blurred.

As are the other aspects of the physical environment, native animal life in Middle America is rich and highly varied, and faunal types have developed a complex distributional pattern. Again, the fundamental basis for such diversity is Middle America's highly complex surface configuration and its position astride the transition zone between the equatorial tropics and the midlatitudes.

Zoologists place the animal types of the Americas into two major faunal regions: the *Nearctic region* of the midlatitudes, in which native animals are of North American affinity, and the *Neotropical region* of the low latitudes, in which the fauna is mainly South American. The narrow zone separating these two large regions passes through central Mexico and the Florida Strait, leaving the West Indies within Neotropica (Figure 2.29). Specifically, the Transverse Volcanic Axis of Mexico has served as a partial barrier to north-south animal movements and, in general, marks the dividing zone between the two faunal regions. Neotropical animals, such as monkeys, various water rats, parrots, and the leaf-cutter ant, are characteristic of the fauna south of this barrier, but they also extend northward along the tropical Gulf Coast as far as Tampico and along the Pacific coastal lowland to Sinaloa. Nearctic animals, such as pronghorn, deer, various small rodents, and North American birds, inhabit the Mexican plateau, the northern parts of the coastal lowlands, and most of Baja California. The dividing zone, however, is not an absolute barrier; many South American forms, such as the armadillo and opposum, have migrated far into the United States; and some North American fauna, such as the white-tailed deer, have penetrated as far south as central Panama.

A significant feature of general animal distribution in Middle America is the relative paucity of West Indian fauna. At the time of the Discovery, aside from a large variety of bats, two genera of a small, curious shrew and three kinds of rodents were the only land mammals in the Greater Antilles. One of the rodents, the *hutía*, was an important game animal for the Taino Indians on Cuba and

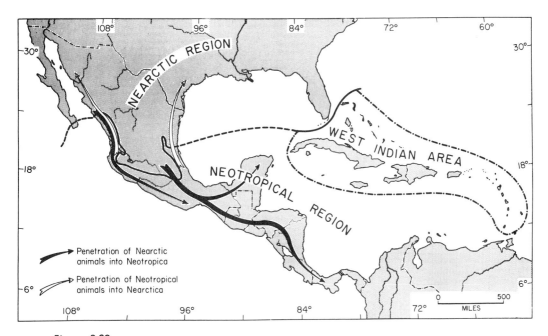

Figure 2.29
Faunal Regions of Middle America.

Jamaica. In the Lesser Antilles only two mammals were present—the *agouti*, a large South American water rat highly prized for its tasty flesh, and an insignificant spiny tree rat. The larger mammals, such as the deer and peccary, so important on the mainland as game, and the predators, such as foxes, coyotes, and jaguars, were completely absent. Birds and reptiles, however, are fairly abundant. The latter include the iguana, a large edible lizard, caymans and nonpoisonous snakes. Undoubtedly, the paucity of types of mammals in the West Indian islands reflects their insularity and long geographical separation from the adjacent continents.

In Mexico and Central America, a general interrelationship exists between vegetation associations and animal life. Faunal types in the tropical rain forest and highland cloud forest area exhibit certain peculiar characteristics. Mammals, for instance, are relatively few; many are arboreal, such as the monkeys, the opossums, tropical squirrels, and the racoon-like coati, cacomistle, and kinkajou. Because of paucity of grass in the shaded forest floor, the ground mammals are represented by only a few ungulates, the largest of which is the tapir. Others are two kinds of peccaries, which wander about the forest in large droves, feeding on roots and palm nuts, and the small brocket deer. Along streams, large edible rodents like the agouti and the spotted cavy live in abundance. All such ground mammals, and some of the arboreal ones, are hunted by the jaguar and his relatives and by man. The monkeys have been driven into isolated sections of the humid tropical forests, and the tapir has become a rarity. But a large number of reptiles, including many types of noisy frogs, the iguana lizard, and a great variety of snakes abound in the rain forest. Of the poisonous snakes of the Central American forests the fer-de-lance, the bushmaster, and the small coral are the most feared by man.

The greatest faunal variety of the forest is found in the birds and insects. More than 500 species of tropical birds are known to exist in the rain and cloud forests of southern Mexico and Central America alone. Among these are the showy macaws, parrots and parakeets; the big-billed toucans; the big game birds, such as the curassow, crested guan, and ocellated turkey; and, especially, the brilliantly colored trogons. The most renowned trogon is the beautiful quetzal which once inhabited the cloud forests from Chiapas in southern Mexico to Costa Rica. Hunted since ancient times, when the Mayas and their neighbors valued the bird's long, showy feathers for priestly headdresses, the quetzal is now found only in remote spots within the Honduran and Costa Rican highlands. Since the parrots and their close relatives like to feed on cultivated grains, these birds are the scourge of the tropical farmer. For this reason and for their demand as pets, these birds have been greatly depleted in number. In some areas, as in Cuba and Puerto Rico, they have been almost exterminated.

In spite of their great variety and numbers, insects in the tropical forests of Middle America are not readily apparent to the observer, except in clearings, around tree falls, and along stream banks, where sunlight can penetrate. In such places and at the top of the forest canopy clouds of colorful butterflies, gnats, and locusts swarm in abundance. Within the forest, long columns of leafcutter ants crisscross the ground, and on tree trunks are large, brown termite nests. If the abundance of insects is not immediately visible to the wanderer through the forest, the presence of these animals is soon evidenced by painful bites of flies and mosquitos and festering sores caused by burrowing chiggers that soon cover the entire body.

With some exceptions, the assemblage of animals characteristic of the dense rain forests in Central America and southern Mexico also inhabits the drier tropical deciduous forests of northern Yucatan, the Pacific coastal lowlands, and the interior basins. In the drier forest, however, the variety of mammals is almost double that in the rain forest. The increase of sunlight on the forest floor produces a varied ground cover of shrubs and grasses that supply food for small rodents, and especially for the North American white-tailed deer, which has penetrated far into the dry tropical forests and savannas of Central America. Complementary to the rodents and ungulates is the large number of predators, particularly the cats (jaguar, ocelot, maragay, jaguarundi, and bobcat), the Nearctic coyote, and carnivorous birds (owls, hawks, and the ubiquitous carrion-eating black vulture). During pre-Columbian times in the Yucatan Peninsula and the Pacific coastal lowlands, the deer and the peccary furnished the bulk of the meat diet for the Indian population, while the jaguar and his relatives have, for millennia, been important to man for their skins and as representations in religious symbolism.

Apart from the inland areas, the coastal margins of the Middle American tropics are distinguished by a rich amphibian and aquatic fauna. The numerous kitchen middens composed of clam and oyster shells found along the shores of the Greater Antilles and Caribbean Central America attest to the wealth of shellfish available for human consumption. Reptiles, including the iguana and the crocodile, and his close relative, the cayman, abound along the lower river courses, in estuaries and in lagoons. Though greatly reduced in numbers, the giant green sea turtle still supplies food in the form of eggs and flesh along some of the Caribbean beaches of Central America and the West Indian islands. Aquatic birds—ducks, herons, and grebes—some of them winter visitors from the north, inhabit the coastal lagoons. In colonial times the sea cow, or manatee, a huge aquatic mammal prized for its meat and fat, abounded in the estuaries of Caribbean shores. The West Indian seal was also once numerous around the islands. Today, few of these mammals are left, and the seal may be extinct.

The Nearctic faunal region of Middle America corresponds, in general, to: (1) the steppe and desert areas; and (2) the high land oak and pine forests of northern and central Mexico. Relatively few large mammals inhabit the highland forests. Probably the most important for human food is the white-tailed deer. Overhunted, this animal was already scarce in the densely populated Mesa Central when the first Europeans arrived early in the sixteenth century, however. The northern part of the Sierra Madre Occidental marks the southernmost extent of some typically North American mammals, such as the mountain sheep and the black and grizzly bears. A large array of small rodents and their natural predators, the coyote and the kit fox, are widespread throughout the highland forests. For birds, the pine and oak forests of Mexico seem to be a transition area between Nearctica and Neotropica; consequently, the highlands contain almost as many species of fowl as the tropical forests. The numerous lakes and marshes of the plateau attract millions of aquatic birds from North America in their seasonal migrations southward. These same lakes abound in many small fishes that for centuries have supplied surrounding human populations with protein-rich food.

The steppes and deserts of northern Mexico, including both the coastal lowlands and the plateau, contain a surprisingly large faunal assemblage. Most of the animals belong to the Nearctic region, but many in the lowlands are of Neotropical affinity. The extensive grasslands of the plateau once attracted large numbers of deer and pronghorn antelope; even herds of bison from the Great Plains of the United States grazed as far as northern Durango. Of these animals, only the white-tailed deer is left in any number. In the desert scrub of the coastal lands, peccary is still widely hunted. As in the highland forests, the rodents are the most numerous of the mammals, and the coyotes, kit foxes, bobcats, and ocelots are their main predators. The northern desert is also the dispersal center of the rattlesnake; at least one species and several varieties of this animal extends into southern Mexico and Central America, where it early became significant in religious symbolism among the Maya and Aztec civilizations.

SELECTED REFERENCES

Baker, R. H., "The Geographical Distribution of Terrestrial Mammals in Middle America," *American Midland Naturalist,* LXX, No. 1 (1963), 208–49.

Denevan, W. M., "The Upland Pine Forests of Nicaragua: A Study in Cultural Plant Geography," *University of California Publications in Geography,* XII, No. 4 (1961), 251–320.

Jaeger, E. C., *The North American Deserts.* Stanford Calif.: Stanford University Press, 1957.

Johannessen, C. L., *Savannas of Interior Honduras,* Ibero-Americana, No. 46. Berkeley, Calif.: University of California Press, 1963.

Lauer, W., "Klimatische and pflanzengeographische Grundzüge Zentralamerikas," *Erdkunde,* XIII, Heft 4 (1959), 344–54.

Leopold, A. S., "Vegetation Zones of Mexico," *Ecology,* XXXI, No. 4 (1950), 507–18.

——, *Wildlife of Mexico: The Game Birds and Mammals.* Berkeley, Calif.: University of California Press, 1959.

Ordóñez, E., "Principal Physiographic Provinces of Mexico," *Bulletin of the America Association of Petroleum Geologists,* XX, No. 10 (1936), 1277–307.

Parsons, J. J., "The Miskito Pine Savanna of Nicaragua and Honduras," *Annals of the Association of American Geographers,* XLV, No. 1 (1955), 36–63.

Portig, W. H., "Central American Rainfall," *Geographical Review,* LV, No. 1 (1965), 68–90.

Sapper, K., "Über Gebirgsbau und Boden des südlichen Mittelamerika," *Petermanns Mitteilungen,* Ergänzungsheft 151, 1905.

——, "Über Gebirgsbau und Boden des nördlichen Mittelamerika," *Petermanns Mitteilungen,* Ergänzungsheft 127, 1899.

Schuchert, C., *Historical Geology of the Antillean-Caribbean Region.* New York: John Wiley & Sons, Inc., 1935.

Termer, F., "Zur Geographie der Republic

Guatemala: I Teil, Beiträge zur physischen Geographie von Mittel- und Süd-Guatemala," *Mitteilungen der Geographischen Gesellschaft in Hamburg,* XLIV (1936), 89–275.

Tamayo, J. L., *Geografía General de México* (2nd ed.). Mexico, D.F.: Instituto Mexicano de Investigaciones Económicas, 1962.

Vivó, J. A., and J. C. Gómez, *Climatología de México,* Instituto Panamericano de Geografía e Historia, Publication No. 19. Mexico, D.F., 1946.

Wallén, C. C., "Some Characteristics of Precipitation in Mexico," *Geografiska Annaler,* XXXVII, Nos. 1–2 (1955), 51–85.

West, R. C., ed., *Natural Environment and Early Cultures. (Handbook of Middle American Indians,* Vol. I.) Austin, Tex.: University of Texas Press, 1964.

3

The West Indies: Early Setting

It is impossible to disassociate geography and history; the landscape is made up of their synthesis. Nature gives us the frame, but men, even in their most humble manifestations, are caught up in the currents of history. Almost always the present can be explained only by the past. It is by the integration of history into geography that one attains the very soul of a country.—Jean Sermet.

The important changes which have taken place in the human occupance of Middle America from pre-Columbian times to the present may be grouped historically into a series of formative periods during which major forces reshaped the area's land-and-people relations into new and distinctive forms. Since historical continuity makes overlap inevitable, it is seldom possible to cite the specific beginnings of such periods and even less possible to fix endings. At best, historical divisions are approximate and often arbitrary guides for surveying the evolution of spatial patterns and relationships.

That the critical formative periods of Middle America's various segments do not coincide is a further complication. On the Mainland, for example, the Amerindian past and the sixteenth-century Spanish Conquest have had far more important long-range effects on human geography than the same periods in the Caribbean Rimland. Plantation agriculture, the vital agent of post-Columbian change in the Rimland, did not reach its peak in most of the West Indies until the eighteenth century, while in Cuba, Puerto Rico, the Dominican Republic, and the Central American coast, the plantation was of only limited importance until the nine-

teenth and twentieth centuries. The human geography of Middle America is so deeply rooted in the past, however, that it is mandatory to try to classify and evaluate the play of time despite the complications.

For the West Indies, four major periods of occupance are suggested: (1) the pre-Columbian, Amerindian prologue; (2) the European Conquest and spread of settlement, which may be dated from 1492 to the latter seventeenth century; (3) the sugar revolution and the colonial plantation, encompassing roughly the two hundred years from the latter seventeenth to the latter nineteenth centuries; and (4) the modern plantation and current occupance, from the late nineteenth century to the present.

THE PRE-COLUMBIAN, AMERINDIAN PROLOGUE

The patterns of the Amerindians in the Antilles on the eve of Discovery defy detailed reconstruction. None of the Indian groups possessed a written language, and most of the indigenous cultures were so quickly wiped out by the shock of the European Conquest that our knowledge of them is derived primarily from the limited writings of early explorers and settlers and from later archeological study of burial caves, middens, and village sites.

Evidence indicates that the West Indian islands were swept by at least three Amerindian cultural waves before the arrival of the Europeans. The first of these was the primitive hunting and gathering Ciboney culture, whose origin is unknown. This was followed by the Arawak and the Carib cultures, both of which originated in South America and island-hopped their way into the Antilles. By the time of the Conquest, the Arawaks were centered on the Greater Antilles but also occupied the Bahamas and southern Trinidad. They had eliminated Ciboney holdings everywhere except for pockets on the coast of western Cuba and southwestern Haiti (Figure 3.1). The Caribs who arrived later had displaced the Arawaks in the Lesser Antilles and northeastern Trinidad and were raiding eastern Puerto Rico when the arrival of the Spaniards checked their expansion.

The Ciboneys subsisted primarily on fish, turtles, the sea cow, and other sea animals, on the iguana, and on the wild fruits of the forest. Their villages were small, semipermanent settlements made up of rock shelters and caves; they practiced no cultivation and, aside from the crudest tools and weapons, their chief possession was the dugout canoe.

The Arawaks and, to a lesser degree, the Caribs had more advanced material cultures than the Ciboneys. Both groups practiced agriculture, although the economy was far better developed among the Arawaks. Starchy tubers, such as bitter manioc (or cassava), yautia, sweet potatoes, and arrowroot; pineapples; peanuts; and some maize were products of Indian farming on the islands. In addition to food crops, the Arawaks also raised tree cotton for netting, and tobacco, which was used as a drug and as a means of exchange. Both groups relied heavily upon fishing and hunting.

In their languages and other cultural traits, the Arawaks were divided into various subgroups, such as the *Igneri* of Trinidad, the *Tainos* of Puerto Rico, Hispaniola, and eastern Cuba, the *Sub-Tainos* of Jamaica and

Figure 3.1
Pre-Columbian Indian Cultures of the Antilles.

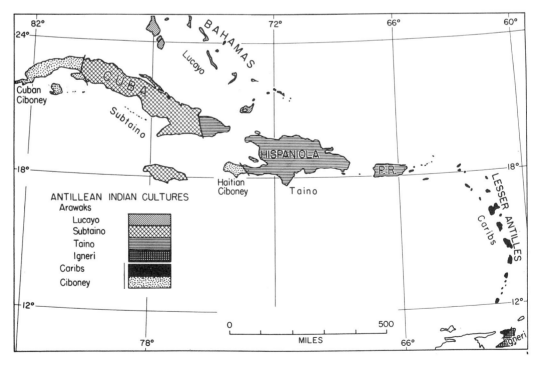

central Cuba, and the *Lucayos* of the Bahamas. While the technology of these sub-groups was by no means uniform, Arawak material culture generally included service-able pottery, good baskets, and polished stone tools such as knives, adzes, scrapers, and axes. Fishing equipment included nets, weirs, hooks, harpoons, and canoes. The existence of true weaving is uncertain, but the Arawaks are known to have made hammocks, aprons, and bags, probably from netted cotton. The Taino of Hispaniola also washed gold from stream gravels and, by beating the larger nuggets with stone, they formed ornaments worn by chiefs and others of high social rank. These golden objects immediately attracted the attention of the first Spanish invaders and led to their early exploitation of the island's gold deposits.

The Arawak settlements, generally located some distance inland as protection against Carib raids, ranged in size from single-family units to villages of up to 3,000 people. Their houses were of two types: the *bohio,* a rectangular, gabled structure used by the *caciques* or chiefs; and the *caneye,* which was circular with a conical roof, used by com-moners. The houses were generally built of palm thatch, sometimes plastered with mud.

The Caribs were far fewer than the Arawaks, culturally less advanced, and much more warlike. They depended more heavily on fishing, hunting, and gathering than on agriculture. In addition, the practice of eat-ing the flesh of their captured male enemies, whether for ritual purposes or merely for food, was sufficiently widespread so that the very name "Carib" came to mean cannibal. According to their own legends, the Caribs came into the West Indies about a century before the Discovery. They established their small villages either on the windward side of the islands or on low hills adjacent to the coast, where they were safest from surprise attacks. Their houses were either oval or rectangular structures of poles thatched with palm leaf. Outstanding among their material

possessions were canoes. Some canoes could carry 40 or 50 Carib warriors and these played an important part in their northward push along the Lesser Antilles.

Estimates of the total Indian population of the West Indies vary enormously. Las Casas, who observed the initial European impact on the Indians, sets the figure at six million, at least three million of whom were in Hispaniola. Later, the German naturalist, Alexander von Humboldt, esti-mated the indigenous population of Cuba alone at one million. While these numbers appear exaggerated in the light of the limited food-producing capacity of the Indian eco-nomies, the archipelago appears to have been heavily populated. A total of about one mil-lion, with the greatest concentrations in His-paniola, Cuba, and Puerto Rico, seems reasonable.

It is noteworthy that none of the Antillean Indians had developed the concept of private ownership of land. Land existed only to satisfy the necessities of life; it was never bought or sold or used for commercial profit. Since Rimland cultures included no wheeled vehicles or other sophisticated tools, and no beasts of burden or sources of energy other than human muscle, this attitude toward the land made for a relatively low standard of living, but it also usually meant security. Sub-sistence was never a problem, and famine occurred only if war and the forces of nature destroyed the productive effort of man.

EUROPEAN CONQUEST
AND SPREAD OF SETTLEMENT

The conquest and settlement of the West Indies by the Europeans between 1492 and the latter seventeenth century may be divided into a number of phases. First came the Spaniards, who discovered the area and who immediately proclaimed an exclusivist policy of trade and colonization. For almost a century the Spanish claims to lands discovered by Columbus went largely unchallenged, and Spain attempted to legitimize her possessions by occupance. Eventually, however, northern Europeans, lured by the possibility of trade, loot, and new lands invaded the Spanish monopoly and ushered in a period of intense political, economic, and cultural competition. French, English, Dutch and other north European powers not only attacked Spanish settlements and trade monopolies; they also established their own colonies, bringing into the Caribbean a multiplicity of national interests and cultures.

Less spectacular but equally important is the fact that, during this period of conquest and settlement, the Antilles served as a testing ground and dispersal base for the plants, the animals, and the new techniques which European man was to use in his conquest and colonization of the rest of the Americas.

Discovery and Spanish Colonization

Spanish discovery of the Caribbean borderlands at the close of the fifteenth century was followed by rapid envelopment of those areas which were deemed economically desirable. Within 50 years of the arrival of Columbus, the conquistadors had established themselves on the larger islands of the Antilles and had pushed on to Panama, Mexico, and other segments of the Main. Occupation of these territories was never total, however. The preferred settlement sites possessed advantages such as proximity to gold deposits, facility of external communications, abundant land for agriculture and grazing, and an ample Indian population to supply labor. If gold was the only consideration (and it generally was), the settlement was often either abandoned or died out when the metal gave out.

The first locus of Spanish colonization was Hispaniola, in the West Indies, and the initial objective was to found a mining and farming colony which could produce its own food, send gold back to Spain, and serve as a base for further exploration. To this end the Spaniards imported a whole society in miniature—tools, seeds, plants, livestock, and colonists who included not only priests and soldiers, but also farmers, artisans, and miners. The earliest settlement was established at Isabela on the north coast of the island (Figure 3.2). Moving southward through the Paso de los Hidalgos across the Cordillera Septentrional, the Spaniards discovered the great lowland of the Cibao which Columbus himself named the *Vega Real* ("Royal Vale"). From here, they moved rapidly through the Cordillera Central towards the south coast, founding the city of Santo Domingo in 1496.

Within a few years, the Spaniards had founded numerous small settlements on Hispaniola (Figure 3.2). These original settlements, formed by miners and encomenderos, and by such merchants and craftsmen as served their needs, relied on gold and Indian labor, and most of them (including the original settlement of Isabela) proved to be almost as ephemeral as the gold deposits and the Indians. Only the city of Santo Domingo, which was founded near the Jaina gold mines and which had the advantage of a good harbor at the mouth of the Ozama River, achieved and retained even modest importance during the colonial period. In fact, this city was so dominant that its name was used to designate the entire island.

The Spaniards' quest for gold became a determinant of both the initial economy and the location of many of the early settlements on Hispaniola. Gold was found in a variety of locales, including the south coast, but the richest finds were along the streams flowing from the Central Mountains northward to the Cibao depression. As indicated in Chapter 2, this central mountain mass is a granitic batholith, the eastern part of which is riddled with gold-bearing quartz veins. Oviedo indicates that the major mining activity of the early years focused on two areas: (1) along the Río "Cotuy," in the vicinity of the present town of Cotui; and (2) along the

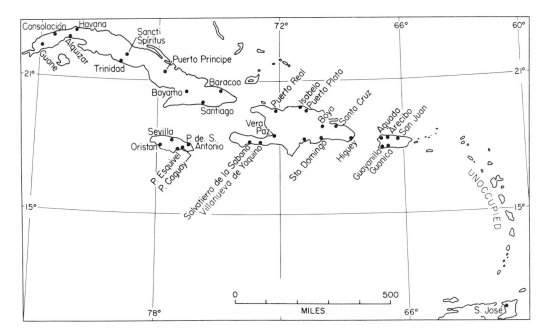

Figure 3.2
Early Spanish Settlements in the West Indies.

Río "Cibao," by which he probably meant the upper drainage of the present Río Camú. Placer mining along the streams reached a peak annual output of roughly 450,000 pesos between 1515 and 1520, after which production declined rapidly.

The decline of mining created some impetus for the production of commercial crops, especially sugar. Sugar cane had been brought to the island by Columbus in 1493, but production for export did not begin until after 1520. Records indicate that by 1535 there were more than 30 sugar mills or *trapiches* in the rich Cibao valley and along the south coastal plain near the capital, and that by the end of the sixteenth century most of the influential citizens of the colony were sugar planters. Despite the advantage of this early start, however, the Spanish colonists were too preoccupied with gold to develop sugar production on a significant scale.

Hispaniola, an object of colonization in itself, also served as a base for the conquest and settlement of the adjacent Antillean islands and the continent. From Santo Domingo, Ponce de León settled Puerto Rico, del Campo and Velásquez went to explore Cuba, Esquivel colonized Jamaica, Balboa set out to discover the Pacific, Pizarro conquered Peru, Heredia founded Cartagena on the Caribbean coast of Colombia, and Díaz Solís discovered the Plata estuary on the southeast coast of South America.

The settlement of the other West Indian islands from the Hispaniola base was also determined largely by the lure of gold. The Spaniards tended to occupy permanently only those islands where this precious metal was available. Where there was no gold, as in the Lesser Antilles, Jamaica, the Bahamas, and even western Hispaniola (Haiti), Spanish settlement was either limited or nonexistent. These vacuums were later filled by north European colonists.

In Puerto Rico, gold was panned in the beds of various streams, such as the Guanajibo River which flows out of the western mountains near the town of San Germán, and in the sands of the Gurabo and other rivers flowing from the Cordillera Central towards the north coast. The gold fever on the island lasted for about 30 years (1508–1538), but the total value of the metal found probably did not exceed 300,000 pesos and no permanent settlement in Puerto Rico was founded as a consequence of gold mining. The first colony was founded by Ponce de León at Caparra, a few miles inland from the Bahía de San Juan on the north coast, but the site proved so unhealthy that in 1521 the settlement was transferred to San Juan, which had the advantage of external communications. Other early settlements, such as Arecibo, Aguada, and Guánica (Figure 3.2), also tended to hug the coastline, and significant colonization of the interior of the island did not get under way until well into the eighteenth century.

The gold deposits of Cuba proved to be richer than those of Puerto Rico. Alluvial gold was found in rivers such as the Arimao, the Escambray, and the Holguín, and at several other sites such as La Mina near Havana and at Bayamo. The exploration for gold and the settlement of Cuba began at the eastern end of the island adjacent to Hispaniola and proceeded westward to Havana. The first settlements were established at Baracoa, Santiago, Trinidad, Puerto Principe, Bayamo, and Sancti Spíritus (Figure 3.2). Havana was founded in 1519, but it remained second to Santiago in importance until the center of Spanish interest shifted from Hispaniola and the other Antilles to Mexico and the continent. The sixteenth-century Spanish population of Cuba initially numbered 300 and probably reached a maximum of 3,000 between 1518 and 1520, after which it dropped sharply as the colonists followed Cortes and others to the greener pastures of the mainland.

Jamaica, which had little gold, was the least attractive of the Greater Antilles to the Spaniards. Colonization, begun in 1512, was based largely on the grazing of cattle and other livestock and upon limited agriculture. So few colonists were attracted that

when the English conquered the island in 1655, there were no more than 1,500 Spaniards. Most of the tiny Spanish settlements were little more than cattle ranches located along the coast. They included (Figure 3.2) Port Caguay (Port Royal), Port Esquivel (Old Harbour), Sevilla la Nueva (St. Ann's Bay), Santiago de la Vega (Spanish Town), Puerto de San Antonio (Port Antonio), and Oristan (Bluefields).

The Spaniards discovered and named virtually all the Lesser Antilles but, except for a token settlement in Trinidad, they found these islands unattractive for colonization. The small islands afforded no gold, and the Caribs who inhabited them were fiercer than the Arawaks of the larger islands. The dense forests which covered most of the archipelago discouraged grazing, and whatever logwood resources the islands possessed could be more easily obtained elsewhere. Moreover, while the approach to the Lesser Antilles by ships coming from Spain was made easy by the northeast trades, sailing back to them from the Spanish centers in the Greater Antilles was difficult. Some of the tiny islands off the coast of Venezuela, such as Margarita and Cubagua, attracted the early Spaniards because of their pearl fisheries, but no significant settlements were established there.

The West Indies remained at the center of Spanish interest for only a few decades after Discovery. Once Mexico, Peru, and other more desirable areas of the mainland were found, the islands quickly fell into decay. With their gold and Indian labor force largely exhausted by 1530, the insular economies were reduced to virtual subsistence. The flow of colonists from Spain ceased; worse, most of the original settlers joined the bands bound for the continent, taking with them much of the wealth of the islands in the form of horses, arms, tools, and other supplies. *"Qué Dios me lleve a Perú"* ("May God take me to Peru") became the prayer of the colonists who remained, and total depopulation of the islands was avoided only by invoking the sternest penalties—including cutting off a leg of any settler who tried to leave the islands. Nevertheless, many escaped in small boats to join their fellows in Mexico and Peru.

Spanish Policy and the Colonial Economy of the Antilles. The guiding principle of Spanish colonial policy in the Antilles (as elsewhere) was that the colony existed for the benefit of the mother country. Spain implemented this policy by establishing a highly centralized monopolistic control under the supervision of the Council of the Indies. While the restrictions imposed by the Council varied from time to time, the general controls included:

1. Only Spaniards could trade with the colonies, all goods had to be carried in Spanish ships and, for protection, all ships had to move in convoy from designated ports at specified times.
2. Colonies were prohibited from producing any product which would compete with the merchants and manufacturers of the home country.
3. Colonies were forbidden to trade directly with each other, and for many years goods from one colony to another had to be transshipped through Spain.
4. Only proven Spanish Catholics could migrate to the colonies (though this rule was not always enforced, and the early colonists in the Spanish Antilles included small groups of Italians, Germans, Flemings, French, and Portuguese).

To make matters worse, a large number of taxes were levied on colonial goods, so that by 1600, many products cost from three to ten times as much in the colonies as they did in Spain. And the Antilles, in particular, were beset by two additional disadvantages which had negative economic ramifications: They had to bear the brunt of attacks by pirates and by Spain's north European enemies in the Caribbean; and Spain considered them of little commercial importance in comparison to other colonies.

Following the expansion of Spanish colonization to the mainland, the Antilles ceased to be an economic end in themselves and became only a means to an end. Spain came to view them as possible supply bases and strong points guarding her imperial lines of communication with Mexico, Peru, Panama, and even the Philippines. To this end, all of the major Antillean ports—Havana and Santiago in Cuba, San Juan in Puerto Rico, Santo Domingo—and others (such as St. Augustine, Florida) were heavily fortified and garrisoned. The defenses of San Juan illustrate the extent and costliness of these fortifications. The entire town was enclosed in a wall 50 feet high, into which was set the fortress of San Felipe del Morro, which rises 140 feet above the sea. The fortifications mounted 400 guns and spread over 200 acres of land, although the town itself occupied only 62 acres. Its construction continued intermittently from 1525 to 1785, and its ultimate cost was six million pesos. These colonial fortifications are still very much a part of the picturesque landscape of San Juan and other Caribbean cities (Figure 3.3).

Not all the fortified harbors proved to be equally important, however. Ultimately, Havana rose to be the chief fortress city of the Indies, not only because of its superior harbor but because of its prime location with respect to the Spanish fleet movements under the convoy system.

Under the convoy system which operated from 1561 to 1748, two fleets were supposed to leave Spain every year for the Caribbean. The ships would depart from Cadiz or Seville and proceed to the Canaries in order to enter the belt of the northeast trades for the westward journey. The first landfall in the Caribbean was usually near Dominica or on an island to the north. Here the fleet divided, one segment going to Cartagena and Puerto Bello, the other going to San Juan, Santo Domingo, and Veracruz (Figure 3.4). Then

Figure 3.3
Fortress of San Felipe del Morro at the West End of San Juan Island, Puerto Rico. (*Delta Air Lines*)

Figure 3.4
Route of the Spanish Convoy System.

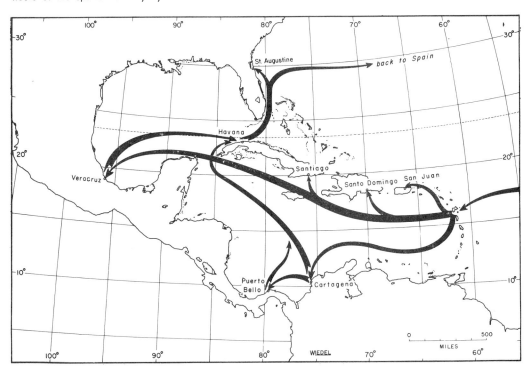

the entire fleet would reassemble in Havana for the journey back to Spain. From Havana, adjacent to the Florida Passage along the line of shortest distance between Veracruz and Spain, the ships entered the northeast-flowing Gulf Stream which carried them into the westerlies and thence into European 'waters.'

It was never certain that the Spanish fleet, which was the only legal link between the Antilles and the outside world, would always call, however. War, a shortage of ships, or other obstacles would prevent sailings, and Caribbean ports might go for two or more years without seeing a single Spanish ship. These and other conditions of the Spanish monopoly blighted commercial developments on the islands, discouraged free immigration, and caused finished products to become so scarce and costly that contraband trade with the English, Dutch, and French became necessary to survival.

With the exhaustion of gold and the shift of Spanish interest to the continent, the chief obstacle to economic development in the Spanish West Indies became shortage of labor. By 1530, immigration had come to a virtual standstill, many of the colonists had moved out, and the Indian population had been all but destroyed. African slaves began to be imported early in the sixteenth century to fill the labor gap, but this proved unprofitable in the Spanish islands until the nineteenth century, when plantation agriculture took significant hold. The labor shortage, coupled with other restrictions imposed by Spanish colonial policy, left open only two avenues of production—a largely subsistence agriculture and grazing.

The production of food crops (most of which had been inherited from the Arawaks) to feed the local population and to supply passing ships became a major feature of the economy of the Spanish Indies, and remained so for centuries. Manioc, which was made into *casabi* bread, was the most important subsistence crop—largely because

it kept in the ground until needed. Other crops included maize, plantains, pineapples, yams, and several European fruits and vegetables. Tobacco, which was produced in small quantities, had achieved some importance by the seventeenth century, especially in Cuba. Sugar cane, brought to the islands from the Canaries, became established early, but there was no significant production until the nineteenth century. Other crops of a commercial nature which were sporadically produced included ginger, *cañafístula* (a purgative), and tree cotton. Except for the growing of sugar, only the most primitive farm tools and equipment were employed—normally, the ax, knives and other cutting tools, and the hoe.

The shortage of labor and the abundance of land made grazing even more important than agriculture. The cattle and pigs brought over by the early colonists thrived and multiplied in the tropical forests and grasslands of the Antilles, where the flora provided adequate food and there were few natural predators. By 1620, there were 100,-000 cattle in Puerto Rico, and the numbers in Santo Domingo, Cuba, and Jamaica were probably even greater. The animals were allowed to run wild, for fencing was virtually unknown. Periodic roundups for branding netted only a small percentage of the animals. As a result, the *montería,* or the hunting of wild cattle and pigs, became an established right held in common by all the settlers. The beasts were valued chiefly for their hides and tallow, although some meat was eaten and some smoked or salted for sale to ships.

Such limited exploitation of the land did not lead to its being highly regarded as property. In keeping with Spanish tradition, all the land on the islands was originally considered *tierra realenga* ("royal land") which the Crown used to encourage colonization. In practice, land was granted by the *cabildos,* the local governing bodies in the islands. Early Crown grants included *caballe-*

rías and *peonías,* in accordance with the rank and service of the recipient, but when the colonists migrated to the continent, much of the granted land in the Indies was left *baldía* (without owners) for centuries.

Such landed properties as came into existence were loosely defined, usually in terms of a radius from a fixed feature, and little attempt was made to survey the boundaries. Land was popularly designated by its function: (1) *hatos* were lands used primarily for grazing cattle, horses, and burros; (2) *corrales* were used for pigs; (3) *estancia, sitio de labranza,* or *conuco* were lands used for crop production; and (4) *solares* were lands to be used for the establishment of towns. The *hatos* and the *corrales* were large, typically circular holdings, measured by the diameter of a circle passing through a fixed point. Where land was abundant, as in Cuba, the diameter ranged from two to four leagues. The *corrales* averaged about 22 square miles in size and the *hatos* embraced 80 square miles or more. These circular holdings are still apparent in the arcuate roads and fences of some areas. The grazing units were owned by the wealthier colonists, the *conucos* were held by small holders, who worked them for subsistence.

In addition to agriculture and grazing, there was some lumbering in the Spanish Antilles during the early colonial period. Exports included logwood, mahogany, and tropical cedar. A byproduct of lumbering was shipbuilding, particularly in Havana. Slave raiding among the Indians of the unoccupied islands (the Bahamas and the Lesser Antilles) was a noteworthy economic activity, as was the production of salt which was used to cure hides and meat.

The North European Intrusion

In answer to Spanish claims of monopoly in the Caribbean and elsewhere in the New World, Francis I of France is reputed to have said, "The sun shines for me as for others. I should very much like to see the clause in Adam's will that excludes me from a share of the world." A comparable attitude was adopted by other ambitious maritime nations of Europe, such as England and Holland: their challenge to Spain and to each other converted the Caribbean and its Rimland into a focus of intense international rivalry from the latter sixteenth century to the end of the eighteenth century.

The north European challenge to Spanish monopoly did not at first involve colonization. Searching for new routes to the great markets of Asia, privateering and pirating for booty, trading in contraband with Spanish colonists, cutting logwood, and making salt were the principal activities of the intruders, and these they carried out without establishing bases. Privateering expeditions were often business ventures financed by the merchants of Dieppe, London, Amsterdam, and other north European cities. In theory, privateers were supposed to operate against Spanish commerce only in wartime, but since "no peace beyond the line" (i.e., west of the longitude of the Azores and south of the Tropic of Cancer) was recognized even when there was peace in Europe, privateering continued as long as it was profitable.

As hopes for finding the straits to the Orient vanished and the profits from privateering began to decrease, however, the unemployed adventurers and their financial supporters turned their attention to the possibility of establishing colonies which might produce commodities such as tobacco and indigo, that commanded good prices in European markets. The result was a rapid colonization of the unoccupied Lesser Antilles, western Hispaniola, and other parts of the Rimland, beginning in about the first quarter of the seventeenth century.

The methods of the north European colonizers differed from those of the Spanish in almost every instance. Spain employed direct conquest, and her settlements were under the strict, centralized control of the home country; her aim was to create a monolithic empire which would faithfully mirror the language, religion, political institutions, and other cultural facets of the Castilian fountainhead. The north European nations used the trade and plantation company as the principal instrument of colonization. These companies were generally composed of merchants who subscribed capital for settlement and trade and received profits on a share basis from the enterprise. While the relationship between the company and the national government which granted the charter was a close one, there was far less political control and far less cultural integration with the mother country was required. Trade and profits were, from the very beginning, recognized as sufficient reasons for colonization.

English Colonization. The English mother colony in the Rimland was St. Christopher (St. Kitts), founded in 1623–1624. St. Christopher was also the first French colony in the Rimland, and it was jointly occupied by England and France until 1713. From this base, English colonization spread to other islands in the Leewards—Nevis, Barbuda, Antigua, Montserrat—and to the British Virgin Islands. Barbados, the Bahamas, as well as St. Andrews, Old Providence, and scattered points along the coast of Central America were also colonized during the seventeenth century; like the Leewards, they are considered colonies of original English settlement. Trinidad, acquired from Spain in 1797, and the Windwards, taken from France at various times in the eighteenth and early nineteenth centuries, fall into the category of conquered or ceded islands. Jamaica, although taken from Spain in 1655–1660, is to all intents and purposes considered an island of original settlement (Table 3.1).

Population in the newly founded English colonies, especially Barbados and the Leewards, increased rapidly for the first few decades. By 1640, there were nearly 30,000 white settlers on Barbados and 20,000 on St. Christopher and Nevis, making these the most densely populated territories in the Caribbean at the time. The early settlers relied upon agriculture, with privateering and the cutting of logwood as supplementary economies. Landholdings were small, and tobacco, followed by indigo, cotton, and ginger were the leading export crops. The white populace in most of the English West Indian colonies continued to increase until the advent of the sugar revolution and plantation agriculture, after which they were rapidly superseded by Negro slaves.

In the Bahamas and along the Central American coast of the Caribbean, the conditions for English colonization were less favorable than in the Lesser Antilles. Englishmen from Bermuda established colonies on the Bahamian islands of Eleutheria (1646) and on New Providence (1666), but the shallow limestone soils were unsuited to agriculture, and the numerous keys and islets came to serve primarily as the haunts of freebooters preying on the commerce moving through the Florida Passage. The pirates were eventually replaced by a scarcely less infamous group—the wreckers, who lured ships to destruction on the numerous reefs. Significant economic development did not take place in the Bahamas until well into the eighteenth century.

French Colonization. Following their joint occupation of St. Christopher with the English, French colonization was directed first to Martinique and Guadeloupe and later to western Hispaniola and the Windwards. Richelieu, one of the original directors of the French design in the West Indies, envisioned the establishment of strong peasant colonies which would protect the interests of France in the Caribbean; and, for a short time, Martinique and Guadeloupe developed in this image. From their founding in 1635 until the latter part of the century, the two colonies received thousands of Norman and Breton peasants who worked small plots for food crops, with tobacco as a cash commodity. As in the English colonies, this

Table 3.1

NORTH EUROPEAN COLONIZATION IN THE CARIBBEAN RIMLAND
IN THE SEVENTEENTH AND EIGHTEENTH CENTURIES

Colony	Date and Nationality of Original Settlement	Comments
English		
St. Christopher	1623 (English and French)	Jointly occupied by England and France until 1713
Barbados	1625 (English)	Uninterrupted English rule since original settlement*
Nevis-Anguilla	1628 (English)	Colonized from St. Christopher; British rule continuous since 1793
Antigua and Montserrat	1632 (English)	British rule unbroken since 1793
Barbuda	1661 (English)	Colonized from Antigua
British Virgin Islands**	1648 (Dutch)	English settlement began in 1680
Dominica	1635 (French)	Original settlements generally not permanent; became a bone of contention between England and France in 18th century; have remained English since 1804
St. Lucia	1650 (French)	
Grenada	1625 (French)	
St. Vincent	1762 (English)	
British Honduras	1638–1640 (English)	Logwood settlement; disputed by Spain; still disputed by Guatemala
Bahamas	1646–1666 (English)	Original settlements were temporary
Old Providence and St. Andrew's (Providencia and San Andrés)	1630 (English)	Taken by Spain 1641; English returned but no effective occupation resulted until 19th century
Tobago	1632 (Dutch)	Changed hands many times; English since 1814
Trinidad	1500's (Spanish)	Taken by England in 1797
Jamaica	1509 (Spanish)	Occupied by English in 1655
French		
Martinique	1635 (French)	Small, adjacent islands of Marie Galante, La De-
Guadeloupe	1635 (French)	

* Every other colony has changed hands at least once.
** St. Thomas, St. John, and St. Croix (American Virgin Islands) were occupied at different periods by the Dutch, English, and French during the seventeenth century. The Danish West India Co. occupied St. Thomas and St. John in 1671. St. Croix, which was administered for France by the Knights of Malta, came into Danish possession later. The three islands were purchased by the United States from Denmark in 1917.

Table 3.1 (continued)

NORTH EUROPEAN COLONIZATION IN THE CARIBBEAN RIMLAND
IN THE SEVENTEENTH AND EIGHTEENTH CENTURIES

Colony	Date and Nationality of Original Settlement	Comments
		sirade, Les Saints and others also colonized from Martinique and Guadeloupe
St. Domingue (Western Hispaniola)	1492–1493 (Spanish)	*De facto* occupation by French during 17th century; remained French until slave uprisings at the end of the 18th century
Dutch		
St. Eustatius	1632 (Dutch)	Dutch colonies were primarily trading centers
Saba	1640 (Dutch)	
St. Martin	1630's (Dutch)	
Curacao, Bonaire, Aruba	1634 (Dutch)	

pattern of dominantly white small landholders lasted only until the advent of sugar. After this, the whites were replaced by Negro slaves and the large estate became the characteristic form of land tenure.

The acquisition of western Hispaniola (St. Domingue, and later, Haiti) by France resulted from a combination of Spanish improvidence and Gallic *savoir faire*. Owing to the absence of gold, Spanish occupation of this area had never been heavy, and it became even sparser when Spain's interests shifted to the continent. Lightly settled and remote from the major Spanish strongholds in Santo Domingo and Havana, western Hispaniola became a refuge for outcasts and outlaws of many nationalities, including, in the latter sixteenth and the seventeenth centuries, French Huguenots. At first these made their living by buccaneering[1]—hunting wild cattle and hogs which had escaped from

Spanish settlements, smoking the meat, and selling it to passing ships. Eventually they branched out into contraband trade with Spanish settlements, pirating, and other profitable activities. Spanish efforts to dislodge the buccaneers proved unsuccessful, and France eventually won their allegiance and laid the foundation for what was to become the most prosperous plantation colony of the eighteenth century. In an effort to stop contraband and destroy the buccaneers, Spanish authorities ordered virtually all Spanish settlements in northern and western Hispaniola abandoned (1605), but this extreme move only gave the outlaws more elbowroom. When Spanish pressure occasionally became strong, the buccaneers would take refuge in coastal strongholds, the most famous of which was the island of Tortuga (Tortue) off Port Margot.

Except for minor settlements in Grenada, French colonization in the Windwards was unimportant through the seventeenth century. In fact, these territories were referred to as the "Neutral Islands" and were left largely to the Caribs until they became a bone of contention between France and England in the eighteenth century.

---

[1] The Arawak word "boucan" was applied indiscriminately to both the meat and the thatched sheds in which it was cured. From this usage came the term *boucaniers* and the English "buccaneers" to describe the practitioners of the trade. When the buccaneers turned to piracy, their name became synonymous with "pirates."

Dutch Colonization. Unlike the English and the French, the Dutch did not concern themselves with the establishment of agricultural colonies. Their interests lay primarily in trade, and the tiny islands which they occupied, particularly St. Eustatius and Curaçao, were developed essentially as trading centers. Salt for the herring industry of Holland was among the few products which the Dutch attempted to produce on their islands. Insofar as agriculture was attempted, tobacco was the chief cash crop. As will be shown later, however, the role of the Dutch in the development of the north European sectors of the Rimland was far more important than their territorial acquisitions. Their shipping, financing, and encouragement became important factors in the sugar revolution which developed in the English and French colonies.

In summary, the initial north European colonization in the Caribbean was (by comparison to the Spanish plan) haphazard and devoid of strict control from home. The major economic incentives were piracy, trade, the cutting of logwood, the production of salt, and the raising of cash crops such as tobacco. Piracy was spurred both by the rich shipments of Spanish bullion and by the hatred of Catholic Spain which stemmed from the Reformation and from European national rivalries. Much of the trade was a contraband trade with the Spanish colonies, a direct consequence of Spain's restrictive colonial policy. The production of salt from sea water along the dry leeward sides of the Antilles was encouraged by the important fishing economies of North Sea countries such as Holland and England. Tobacco, the first important cash crop of the north European colonies in the Caribbean, was best suited to small landholdings and the initial pattern of land tenure was, accordingly, one of small farms owned and worked by a white labor force. This early emphasis on commercial agriculture, coupled with the limited amount of available land on the small and mountainous islands of the Lesser Antilles, created higher land values in the north European colonies than in the Spanish.

EUROPEAN IMPACT AND EXPERIMENTAL ADAPTATIONS IN THE CARIBBEAN

The Europeans who colonized the Caribbean had to function in a milieu very different from anything they had previously encountered. The physical environment, the cultures of the indigenous people and of the later African imports, and the potentials of a new world presented the European with new situations to which he had to adjust and new problems to which he had to find solutions. In the process of adjustment and experimentation, he caused a radical alteration in the natural and cultural scheme of things which he found in the area: at the same time, his own cultural baggage was conspicuously modified. New features appeared on the land, new social and political forms evolved, and new values replaced old ones as European man adapted himself and his institutions to the new surroundings.

Impact on the Indian. Perhaps the most immediate consequence of European colonization in the Caribbean was the virtual annihilation of native peoples and cultures, especially in the West Indies. With the exceptions of some of the forest dwellers of the Central American coast, the Amerindian past in the Caribbean is now hardly a memory. In the Greater Antilles the destruction of the once numerous Arawaks at the hands of the Spaniards was so rapid and complete that, 75 years after Discovery, there were essentially no survivals. The Caribs of the Lesser Antilles survived a little longer, but only because the European came to these islands later. Within a half century of the start of north European colonization in 1623, the Caribs had been destroyed or had been driven off all their islands except Dominica and St. Vincent. Today, the only noteworthy remnant of the Caribs is a group of approximately 500 on a reservation in Dominica, and even most of these have a large admixture of Negro blood. There are also the Black Caribs, who live along the Central American coast, from Stann Creek in British Honduras to the Black River in the Republic of Honduras. The Black Caribs are, for the most part, descendants of the Carib Indians of St. Vincent and a cargo of Negro slaves which was shipwrecked off the island in 1675, a mixture which proved so hostile to the Europeans that the English exiled them from St. Vincent to Central America in 1797.

Many reasons have been advanced to account for the decimation of the Antillean Indians. The most basic appears to be that their technologically weak native culture was unable to compete for survival in the face of ruthless European methods. The Indian was at a disadvantage in military organization and weapons; he had no immunity to diseases such as smallpox brought in by the Europeans; he lacked the disciplined capacity for sustained hard work; and in the Antilles, the islands were too small to afford him refuge from the European onslaught. Perhaps equally important, the Indian lost his food supply when his European competitor took the land which produced it. A few survivors fled to the forested mountain interiors of the larger islands and became known as *Cimarrones* ("dwellers of the summits"). There they retained their way of life and continued to war against the European settlements on the lowlands. Eventually they were joined by runaway slaves, and Negro blood became dominant. Maroon bands persisted for a considerable time in a few of the islands, and in Jamaica the Maroons are still a distinct element of the population.

Even leaving aside the exaggeration of the Black Legend,[2] the history of the Antillean

Indian is a tragic one. The Europeans deprived him of his land, exposed him to smallpox, and permitted him to live only as a virtual slave laborer. The Indian either chose death over slavery, as did the Caribs, or he died because he lacked immunity to new diseases or was unable to adjust to the rigors of hard labor, as did the Arawaks. And about all that remains to prove his former occupancy of the Antilles is the tradition of raising tuber crops for subsistence, the *bohio* as a rural house type, the hammock, place names such as "Cuba" and "Haiti," and other Indian terms such as "hurricane."

The destruction of the Indian created both a labor and a cultural vacuum in the Caribbean, and history has filled the vacuum with a predominantly African labor force and a modified Euro-African culture.

The Plant and Animal Factors. Colonization of the Caribbean lands also had a disturbing impact upon the plant and animal associations of the region, particularly in the more densely populated zones such as the Antilles. Today, all the domestic animals and many of the useful plants of the Caribbean are Old World imports. Even some of the wild plants and animals were originally introduced from without and have since displaced some of the native species.

Descriptions of early travelers indicate that the Central American coast was almost entirely forested. In the Antilles, also, the vegetation was dominated by trees, the more

---

2 The Black Legend originated with the publication, by Bartolomé de las Casas in 1552, of the *Brevisima Relación de la Destrucción de las Indias,* in which it was charged that 15 million Indians had perished on account of the cruelty of the Spaniards. The book was eventually translated into virtually all the principal languages of Western Europe (including 18 Dutch editions, 8 German, 6 French, 4 English, 3 Italian, and 3 Latin). The report was welcomed as an exact picture of conditions in the Spanish colonies and of the inherent qualities of the Spaniards, who were hated by the Protestant people of that day as the leading Catholic power and by other people as the strongest nation in Europe. Despite the apparent exaggerations, this propaganda piece formulated an attitude toward Spain which survives to this day.

humid islands being forested right down to the water's edge. The forest of the Caribbean Rimland was not everywhere the same, however. The Antilles, for instance, had far fewer species[3] than the mainland coast. Moreover, it may be assumed that on the drier leeward sides and on the islands of low elevation, the true forest gave way to scrub woodland, savanna, and even steppe. Much of the area currently under grass or scrub vegetation in the Indies, however, was probably once forest which was altered by burning for agriculture, or by logging, charcoal making, and other post-Columbian disturbances. At present, small remnants of virgin forest in the Indies may be found only in remote mountain terrain such as in Dominica. In the Greater Antilles, even the mountain forests have generally had to give way to the need for farmland.

The native animal life of the insular sectors of the Rimland also consisted of a limited number of species, except in Trinidad, where proximity to South America resulted in a much richer fauna. Even these few, however, have been largely destroyed by post-Columbian man or by his animal imports, such as the mongoose and the rat. The iguana, a herbivorous lizard, the agouti, the hawksbill turtle, the green turtle, the manatee, and other animals have been nearly destroyed or sharply reduced on the islands.

In an effort to become self-sufficient in food, the Europeans, particularly the Spaniards, introduced a wide variety of domestic plants and animals to supplement the indigenous food supply. The vine and olive brought from Iberia proved unsuited to the climate, as did stoned fruits and wheat and

other European cereals. Oranges, lemons, and limes throve, however, and before long had passed from cultivated groves to a wild state in the forests. Bananas and plantains imported from the Canaries were an immediate success, as were sugar, rice, and numerous vegetables—lettuce, onions, cucumbers, cabbage, and others. Indian maize was used as a substitute for European cereals. Later plant imports included coffee, breadfruit, and the ubiquitous mango.

As we have already noted, grazing soon exceeded agriculture in the Spanish Antilles. The cattle, pigs, and horses imported from Spain and (more often) from the Canaries multiplied so rapidly that, by 1503, no further imports were necessary. Livestock was released on newly discovered islands so that permanent colonists who came later would have meat, and the Spanish Crown established farms and ranches to supply colonies on the mainland. A grant to the city of Panama (1521) from a Crown farm in Jamaica, for instance, included 500 cows, 500 yearlings, 1,000 pigs, and 200 loads of maize. In this way, the islands became suppliers to the conquerors of Mexico, Peru, and New Granada, and functioned as dispersal points from which animals, as well as plants, spread to the continent.

Because of the limited size of their territories and their greater emphasis on commercial agriculture, food was a more acute problem for the north Europeans than for the Spaniards, and initially they had to rely more heavily on indigenous food supplies. The diet of the early English and French colonist was built around sea food (turtles, sea cows, and fish), lizards, cassava, and maize. Later, the introduction of sugar and the consequent rapid increases in slave populations made land so valuable and food so scarce that large-scale importation became necessary. Sugar cane changed the drinking habits of the less well-to-do European colonists, from wine and ale to rum and *aguardiente*.

---

3 Gordon Merrill indicates that three species— gumlin trees (Dacryode excelsa), mountain cabbage (Enterpa globosa), and guava sweetwood (Aniba bracteata)—make up more than three-fourths of the forest in the upper slopes of several of the Lesser Antilles. In the Greater Antilles and on all the lowlands, the flora is richer.

Settlements and Houses. The evolution of settlements and house types in the Caribbean was dictated in part by European tradition and in part by local exigencies. In the Hispanic territories, the town was always the anchor point of European culture. Grazing and mining were somewhat seasonal and could be left to overseers. The leading settlers preferred to live in the towns, and the corporate town, rather than the country house, became the stronghold of the ruling class. The pattern of dispersed rural settlement characterized by the *bohio*—now in evidence in Cuba, Puerto Rico, and the Dominican Republic—developed later, authored primarily by the poorer whites and by Negroes.

The Spanish had a simple, standard plan of town construction. The central point was invariably a square plaza, around which were built the church, the *casa de ayuntamiento* ("town hall"), the prison, and other public buildings. If the town had a garrison, the barracks, facing a *plaza de armas* ("parade ground"), was located nearby. The streets were laid out in a chessboard pattern, intersecting at right angles where possible.

The settlement tended either to be square or to develop on two sides until it acquired an oblong shape. Public buildings and the homes of the wealthier colonists were generally of stone; the others were frame, of local wood with palm thatch roofing. Except for major centers like Havana, most Spanish settlements in the Caribbean during the first three centuries of the colonial period were very small, consisting of from 10 to 30 *vecinos* ("families").

The *bohio*, which became the most widespread house type in the rural areas of the Hispanic Antilles, was (as it is now, see Figure 3.5) a simple structure, often containing one all-purpose room, and closely resembling its Arawak namesake. It was generally rectangular, and was constructed of thin poles or boards with a thatched palm roof. In the wetter zones, the entire structure was set on four short poles above the ground and a floor of boards was added. There were virtually no furnishings. The family slept in hammocks which were folded and put away during the day, and cooking was done in the *batey*, or yard.

The town houses of the wealthier colonists

Figure 3.5
Cuban *Bohio*, or Typical Rural Dwelling, with Separate Kitchen in Rear, in Pinar del Rio Province.

had a strong Andalusian flavor. They were built flush with the street, with walls of thick masonry to keep out the heat and to give protection against hurricanes. Enclosed patios with an outside kitchen were characteristic, and the central bedrooms were often windowless. Major churches, such as the cathedral of Santo Domingo, were often designed by Italian architects and had a markedly Romanesque style.

Dutch settlements, like the Spanish, were also urban-oriented. The emphasis on commerce made the warehouses, port facilities, and the counting house the characteristic landmarks of the Dutch pattern. The merchants often lived in the rear or in an upper story of their business establishments, much as they did in Amsterdam.

In contrast, the English and the French tended more to rural living. Even before the profitability of sugar made expensive manor houses and estates possible, these two groups preferred to reside directly on the land. As a result, while the Spanish towns developed into well-planned settlements with imposing churches and public buildings, those in the English and French colonies were often haphazard collections of buildings. By the same token, however, there was nothing in the countryside of the Hispanic territories to equal the Georgian "great houses" of Jamaica and Barbados or the lavish estate residences that once dotted French St. Domingue.

Eventually, each European group left its cultural stamp upon the architecture of its colonies. The visitor to Havana, Curaçao, or once Danish St. Thomas has no difficulty in determining architectural origins. Where more than one culture has been at work (as

Figure 3.6

King Street in Kingston, Jamaica, About 1830. The towns on the English plantation islands were not famous for their distinguished architecture or cleanliness. *(Jamaican Government)*

Figure 3.7

"Chebictoo," an Eighteenth Century Jamaican Estate Mansion or "Great House" at Cave, Westmoreland. (*Jamaica Gleaner*)

Figure 3.8

Market Day at Falmouth, Jamaica, About 1850. (*Jamaican Government*)

in Trinidad), a variety of architectural forms are in evidence (see Chapter 7).

Other Adaptations. Our primary concern with land-and-people patterns precludes an analysis of other European adaptations in the Caribbean Rimland during the colonization phase, but they were many. Political instrumentalities, such as the Spanish *cabildo, regidores,* and *audiencias,* or the English representative assembly; methods of financing and credit; the encomienda and *repartimiento* technique; the socioeconomic relations between white and Negro, between master and slave or indentured servant—all these and more were originated or modified in the colonial period of the Rimland. The Caribbean was European man's initial area for experimentation in the New World, and much of what was developed here by trial and error came to affect not only the people of the Rimland but those of the rest of the Americas as well.

THE RIMLAND ON THE EVE OF THE SUGAR REVOLUTION

The end of the first phase of European occupance of the Caribbean may be set roughly at mid-seventeenth century, the eve of the sugar revolution. At this moment in time, the spread of European colonization in the Rimland was approximately as follows: in the West Indies the northern Europeans held the Leewards, the Windwards were largely unoccupied, and the Spaniards controlled Trinidad and the Greater Antilles (except for Jamaica, which they had lost to the English, and western Hispaniola, which was under the *de facto* occupation of France). Off the coast of South America, the Dutch held Aruba, Bonaire, and Curaçao, but the Spanish claims to other islands, such as Margarita, were unchallenged. Along the Central American coast the situation was fluid. Scattered settlements of English log cutters dotted the Gulf of Honduras; the

coast between Cape Gracias a Dios and the San Juan River was a no-man's-land often frequented by pirates; the islands of Old Providence and St. Andrew's had been taken by Spain in 1641 but were not held, so that the English returned for short stays on various occasions. Settlements everywhere were small and tended to hug the coast, and the principal centers of commerce and power were the port towns.

The economy of the area ranged from piracy and privateering to logwood cutting, trade, and agriculture. In the north European colonies of the West Indies, the initial economic phase, based upon the production of tobacco by small white landholders, was coming to a disastrous end as the tobaccos of Virginia and Maryland won preference in the European markets. The Spanish islands had lapsed into a pattern of sleepy colonialism awakened only by the raids of north Europeans. Grazing and subsistence agriculture was the economy of the countryside, and their function as fortresses dominated the port cities of Cuba, Puerto Rico, and Hispaniola.

The total population of the Rimland was probably around 100,000. Except on the Central American coast and in the Windwards, the Indians had been decimated. Negro slavery was established, but the Negro did not become numerically dominant until sugar became a major product. In most colonies, but especially in the north European territories, the white settler, functioning as small landholder, logwood cutter, or privateer still formed the matrix of the population. But all this was soon to change.

SELECTED REFERENCES

Deffontaines, P., "L'introduction du bétail en Amérique Latine," *Les Cahiers d'Outre-Mer,* X (1957), 5–22.

Las Casas, B., *Apologética historia de las Indias.* Madrid: Biblioteca de Autores Españoles, 1909.

López de Velasco, J., *Geografía y descripción universal de las Indias desde el año 1571 al de 1574.* Madrid: Establ. tip. de Fortanet, 1894.

Merrill, G., "The Historical Record of Man as an Ecological Dominant in the Lesser Antilles,"

Canadian Geographer, No. 11 (1958), 17–22.

Newton, A. P., *The European Nations in the West Indies: 1493–1688.* London: A. and C. Black, 1933.

Oviedo y Valdés, Gonzalo Fernández de, *Historia General y Natural de las Indias, Islas y Tierra-Firme del Mar Océano,* 4 vols. Madrid: Real Academia de la Historia, 1851–55.

Parry, J. H. and P. M. Sherlock, *A Short History of the West Indies.* London: Macmillan and Co., Ltd., 1956.

Parsons, J. J., "San Andrés and Providencia: English-speaking Islands in the Western Caribbean," *University of California Publications in Geography,* XII, No. 1 (1956), 1–84.

Parsons, J. J., *The Green Turtle and Man.* Gainesville, Fla.: University of Florida Press, 1962.

Roberts, W. A., *The French in the West Indies.* Indianapolis: Bobbs-Merrill Company, Inc., 1942.

Sauer, C., *Agricultural Origins and Dispersals.* New York: American Geographical Society, 1952.

Steward, J. H., ed., "The Circum-Caribbean Tribes," *Handbook of South American Indians,* Vol. IV. Washington, D.C.: The Smithsonian Institution, 1948.

Stroudemire, S. A., tr. and ed., *Natural History of the West Indies, by Gonzalo Fernández de Oviedo.* University of North Carolina Studies in the Romance Languages and Literature, No. 32. Chapel Hill, N. C.: The University of North Carolina Press, 1959.

Waibel, L., "Place Names as an Aid to the Reconstruction of the Original Vegetation of Cuba," *Geographical Review,* XXXIII, No. 3 (1943), 376–96.

4

Nature and Impact of the West Indian Colonial Plantation

What is there in these themes that the geographer ought to take notice of?...it is the sense of time, the attention to change, the focus upon the processes of peoples dealing with land, expanding and organizing space, and finally, the bold attempt to grasp the meaning of regionalism...—D. W. Meinig.

The present patterns of land and people in the Antilles are in a state of change, but they still mirror the effect not only of the varied tropical environment, but also of a history marked by colonialism, Negro slavery, mercantilism, monoculture, and absentee ownership. The initial author of much of this history was the classical device used by Europeans for the agricultural exploitation of newly acquired tropical areas—the colonial plantation. This early form of the plantation was developed to supply European markets with cane sugar and other tropical products. It became well established during the latter seventeenth century, reached its maximum development in the eighteenth century, and declined in the nineteenth century, to be replaced by today's modern plantation.

Initially conceived as an instrument for organizing the commercial possibilities of tropical land and labor, the colonial plantation in the Antilles had wide repercussions. It served as the vehicle for importing large numbers of Negro slaves and became a major determinant of racial composition and population patterns; it mined the soil and created a temporary but spectacular wealth over which European nations fought numerous wars; it made impossible the development of a European population composed of independent farmers and tradesmen, and gave rise to a two-class society divided by racial and economic gulfs. No institution is so vital to the understanding of past and present in the West Indies as the colonial plantation, for none has so deeply affected the patterns of land and people.

The colonial plantation based on sugar did not develop uniformly throughout the Rimland; in fact, it was confined almost exclusively to the West Indies. Along the Caribbean coast of Central America, sugar and the early plantation failed to take root, and when plantations began to emerge in the 1880's, they were the modern type, based on bananas and free labor rather than on sugar and slavery. But there were differences in development even within the West Indies. In the Spanish colonies (including Trinidad, until 1797), the sugar plantation worked by Negro slaves tended to be an exceptional feature of the economy until the nineteenth century. Its late development, as well as other circumstances, suggest that the nineteenth century Spanish plantation was a transitional type between the colonial and the modern forms.

On the basis of equipment, land tenure, labor force, time of occurrence, and other characteristics, the evolution of the colonial sugar plantation in the Caribbean may be classified into two phases and forms—the *trapiche* and the *ingenio*. The two Spanish terms described types of mills used for grinding sugar cane, but they may also be applied to the distinctive forms of the colonial plantation with which the mill types were generally associated.

The *trapiche* was a small primitive mill worked by animal power, although wind and even water were sometimes employed (Figures 4.1, 4.2, 4.3). Its grinding capacity was so limited that each farm had to have one or more depending on the amount of land under cane. The *trapiche*, family-owned land worked by Negro slaves, was the first plantation type everywhere. It had its beginnings in Santo Domingo, Cuba, and other Hispanic areas in the sixteenth century, but it reached its peak in the north European islands during the eighteenth century.

Figure 4.1
Surviving Example of a Primitive, *Trapiche*-Type Cattle Mill Common to the Colonial Plantation, Plaine du Nord, Haiti.

Figure 4.2
Ruins of a Wind-Powered Sugar Mill in Barbados. (*Barbados Tourist Board*)

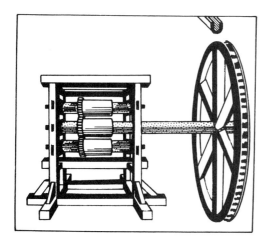

Figure 4.3

Sketch of a Water-Powered Mill Used on a West Indian Sugar Estate During the Eighteenth Century.

The *ingenio,* a larger and better-equipped mill which characterized the nineteenth century sugar plantation in much of the Caribbean, was run by water power, and later by steam. Most *ingenio* plantations were large family-owned estates, but corporate ownership was not absent, especially in Cuba during the latter nineteenth century. Depending on time and place, the labor force was either slave or free. In many respects, the *ingenio* was transitional between the earlier *trapiche* and the modern *central,* or factory in the field, which is discussed elsewhere in this volume.

Regardless of specific form, the characteristic colonial plantation, with its slave labor force and its emphasis on sugar production, was primarily a phenomenon of the English and French colonies, and it is to these colonies that we must turn for an analysis of the nature and impact of the institution on the Caribbean.

THE COLONIAL PLANTATION IN THE ENGLISH AND FRENCH WEST INDIES

Several conditions paved the way for the rise of sugar and the plantation which

began in the English and French Antillean colonies about the middle of the seventeenth century. As already noted, tobacco production, which had initially been the commercial mainstay of many of these territories, was being undermined by competition, in the European markets, from the higher-quality Virginia and Maryland product. Other possible cash crops, such as ginger and indigo, had only limited markets, and extensive cotton cultivation required more land than was available on the small islands. Coffee growing had modest possibilities and eventually achieved some importance, particularly in the mountain lands of St. Domingue and Jamaica. It was sugar, however, which offered the most promising alternative, not only because the islands were climatically suitable for the crop but also because an expanding European market promised the planters rich rewards.[1]

Once established, sugar caused a virtual revolution in the land-and-people complex of the Indies. Beginning in Barbados in 1640, the revolution swept through the Leewards a generation later and reached its climax in Jamaica and St. Domingue in the eighteenth century. Land values rocketed and the pattern of land tenure rapidly changed from small holdings to large estates. Successful sugar planters squeezed out the failing tobacco farmers, who left the islands in droves, and this, together with increased demands for labor, resulted in the importation of large numbers of Negro slaves. The population composition changed from dominantly European to dominantly African. The very appearance of the land was altered: as sugar planting expanded, the lowland forests were rapidly cut down and cane fields became the chief feature of the agricultural

---

[1] The technical know-how, as well as the credit and the shipping often needed by the early English and French planters, was supplied by the Dutch, who had learned the sugar business in Brazil. Expelled by the Portuguese from Bahia in the seventeenth century, the Dutch (including many Jews) moved to the Caribbean and supplied the necessary catalyst for sugar production.

landscape. The big house of the planter, with its village-like slave quarters, replaced the dispersed homestead of the small tobacco farmer. The sugar mill and its boiling house became an integral part of the West Indies scene.

Characteristics of Land Organization and Production

Physical Factors. Ideally, cane requires a frost-free, humid climate, and a relatively dry season immediately before and during harvest time. The perishable crop must be milled into raw sugar almost as soon as it is cut and, if the sugar is intended for overseas export, it must have easy access to shipping points. Planting should be on level to undulating land, to obtain the best yields and keep transportation costs low. Such requirements make it virtually mandatory to cultivate cane on tropical coastal plains and connecting interior valleys.

The colonial plantation territories were both advantageous and disadvantageous for sugar cane growing. Temperatures were nearly everywhere adequate. The mean monthly temperature on all the islands is above 64°F (see Chapter 2), frosts are unknown, and a year-round growing season is available particularly in the lowlands where the crop tended to be concentrated.

Precipitation is less than ideal, however. While on virtually every island there is a dry, or less wet, period during the cane-cutting season from roughly February to July, the total precipitation is often marginal, particularly on the leeward sides of the mountains and on the islands of limited elevation. Where the northeast trades are forced to rise over topographic barriers, the north or windward sides of the islands generally receive at least the 60-inch minimum required for efficient cane production in the West Indies. But on the south or leeward sides, where air is descending, and on the low-lying islands where there is too little surface relief to wring much moisture from the trades, total

precipitation may drop as low as 30 to 40 inches. In consequence, the colonial planters of the low-lying Lesser Antilles, as well as those of Jamaica's southern plain and the Cul-de-Sac of St. Domingue, often were beset with water problems. Irrigation was the answer, but irrigation was expensive and its practice was limited, especially in the English colonies.

The extent of level land adjacent to ocean transportation was also an important factor. In the smaller islands, such as the Leeward-Windward groups, proximity to ocean transport was never a major problem, but the paucity of level land often was. Especially on the high-lying volcanic islands, land suitable for cane was restricted to the narrow ribbons of coastal plains and to the even narrower, alluvium-floored valleys leading to the interior mountains. The smallness of the extent of suitable land had several effects: it limited the size of sugar estates, reduced the acreage which could be devoted to food crops, made for more intensive land use, and affected a variety of other conditions on the small islands. The most extensive planting areas were in Jamaica and St. Domingue, and in these larger territories sugar production and the colonial plantation attained their greatest development.

Land Tenure. The cultivation of sugar even under the colonial system could best be carried out by large-scale production. A plantation, to run economically, had to be big enough to keep the mill supplied with cane throughout the harvesting season. Small properties could not do this, nor could they pay the high costs of purchasing and maintaining slaves and equipment.

The size of sugar plantations varied, however, in the larger territories and the smaller ones, and between the English and the French colonies. In Jamaica, for instance, by mid-eighteenth century the average estate measured 1,000 acres, and a few were as large as 5,000; in the Leewards, they averaged about 100 acres and could be described as little more than family-sized farms with delusions of grandeur. French estates remained small until the 1700's, after which they tended to increase in size but, in general, they were smaller than their English counterparts.

The colonial plantation squeezed out most of the original small holders from the older colonies such as St. Kitts (Figures 4.4 and 4.5), Barbados, and Martinique, but they never completely disappeared anywhere. In the French territories, particularly Guadeloupe, there were always considerable numbers of *petits blancs* (small holders) as opposed to the *grands blancs* (large holders); in the Windwards, which were settled later and in which sugar seldom became dominant, small farmers remained an important segment of the total population. English small holders (such as the Red Legs of Barbados) were more numerous on the small islands than in Jamaica and eked out their living by cultivating food crops, minor commercial crops such as nutmeg and ginger, and by working as craftsmen on the estates.

Land Use and Occupancy. The patterns of land utilization in the English and French plantation territories were determined by sugar. Yet, on a typical plantation, sugar occupied only a fraction of the total land. Most of the estate land was pasture, provision grounds for food crops, woods, or waste, and much was used for buildings, roads, fences and other purposes. (See Figure 4.6 and Table 4.1.)

It was estimated that an efficient estate should have one-third of its land in cane, one-third in food crops such as yams, corn, and plantains, and keep the remainder partly in woodland for buildings and fuel and partly for miscellaneous uses. Few estates achieved such a balance, however. On the smaller and more intensively cultivated islands, such as Barbados, a higher percentage was devoted to cane; in the larger territories, such as Jamaica, the land in cane was well below one-third because the estates were large and often included slope land.

A characteristic land use, particularly in the larger territories of Jamaica and St.

Figure 4.4

St. Kitts: Agricultural Settlement in the Mid-Seventeenth Century Before the Rise of the Colonial Sugar Plantation. *(Based on map by Gordon Merrill)*

Figure 4.5

St. Kitts: Agricultural Settlement in the Mid-Eighteenth Century. Compare this with Figure 4.4 and note the differences caused by the advent of sugar. *(Based on map by Gordon Merrill)*

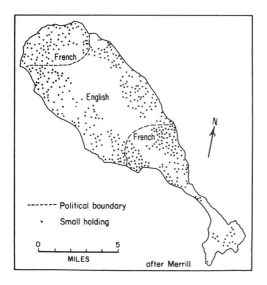

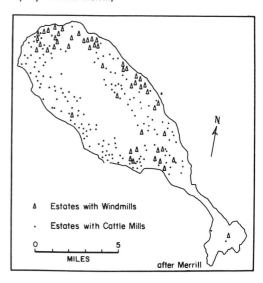

Table 4.1

LAND USE ON SIX SUGAR PLANTATIONS, PARISH OF ST. ANDREW, JAMAICA (1753)

Total Acreage	Cane	Coffee or Other Cash Crops	Food Crops	Animal Pens and Pasture	Woodland and Other
2,000	190	0	200	500	1,100
1,500	60	60	130	1,000	250
368	84	0	50	234	0
500	85	0	50	250	115
508	100	0	120	10	250
600	100	0	10	240	250

Source: Adopted from F. W. Pitman, "The Settlement and Financing of British West Indian Plantations in the 18th Century," *Essays in Colonial History* (New Haven: Yale University Press, 1931), p. 264.

Domingue, was the slaves' provision grounds (Figure 4.6). To meet their needs for food without involving the master in the expense of importing it, slaves were permitted to cultivate small gardens, sometimes in the immediate vicinity of their cabins but more often on marginal land in the foothills. In general, the slave was permitted one day every two weeks (except at harvest time), in addition to Sundays and holidays, to cultivate his plot and take the surplus to market. He might also be permitted to keep chickens, pigs, and even cattle. The products of the provision grounds were consumed on the estate and the surplus was taken to market and sold for the benefit of the slave. Sunday was market day; in Jamaica, as many as 10,000 Negroes might assemble in the market place of Kingston alone. The slave's rights to the products of his provision grounds became so deeply entrenched that they were sanctioned by custom. A Negro could designate an heir to his plot and could dispose of other possessions in any way he saw fit.

The institution of the slave's provision grounds was never firmly established in the smaller islands, where land was scarce. In Jamaica and St. Domingue, however, it became an integral part of the slave plantation economy. It also became a school whose teachings played a vital role in shaping the postemancipation landscape. Marketing the produce of the provision grounds taught

many Negroes entrepreneurial skills; it enabled the more industrious slaves to acquire

Figure 4.6

Sketch of a Mid-Eighteenth Century French Sugar Plantation on the Plain of Léogane, Haiti. In addition to the garden and orchard (G), the area designated as "estate headquarters" includes: (1) the estate house and related buildings, such as a separate kitchen and storehouse; (2) the sugar mill and rum distillery; (3) the manager's residence; (4) the slave quarters; (5) the coach house and blacksmith shop. (Based on map by G. Debien)

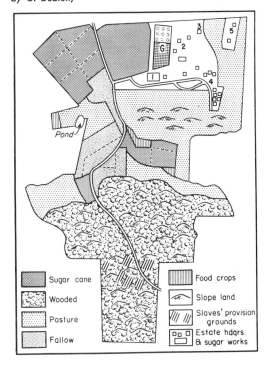

a modest capital which could be used later for the purchase of land; and it paved the way for the emergence of an independent peasantry which could abandon the sugar estates and take to the empty lands in the hills after emancipation.

The estates of Jamaica and St. Domingue also stood in contrast to those on the smaller islands in terms of the variety of functions. Their size, their more varied environment, and the restriction of sugar to accessible lowlands made possible additional commercial uses of land. In 1791, Jamaica had 767 sugar plantations, 607 coffee estates, and 1,047 grazing farms or pens on which were raised cattle and other animals needed by the sugar planters. In St. Domingue, coffee cultivation eventually ranked second only to sugar and probably involved more white planters, though fewer slaves. Diversification was, also apparent in the smaller French territories of Martinique, Guadeloupe, and in those of the Windward islands which France occupied before the English conquests. While sugar was of chief importance, the crop never reached the dominance in these islands that it did in the English colonies, or even in St. Domingue. The rapid spread of cane was actually checked by government policy; small holdings were encouraged and other cash crops were introduced. Coffee, for example, was introduced by order of the French government in Martinique and Guadeloupe, and it became a major export of these islands almost a decade before it was planted in St. Domingue and Jamaica.

Except on some of the small islands, such as Barbados, the plantation colonies never achieved total occupancy of their territories during the colonial period. The dictates of sugar gave emphasis to lowland occupancy, and the mountains were often left under forest.

In Jamaica, many of the mountain and plateau lands of the interior remained unoccupied until after emancipation. Through most of the colonial plantation period, the mass of the Blue Mountains, with their complex systems of ridges in the east, as well as the limestone hills pocketed with numerous valleys having no surface drainage in the rest of the island, were left unexploited and inaccessible. There were no roads to the backlands, and the only inhabitants were nomadic bands of Maroons (*Cimarrones*, see Chapter 3) who relied upon inaccessibility to retain their independence. Sugar cultivation was concentrated on the coastal fringes and in a few accessible interior basins such as the Rio Minho Valley and St. Thomas in the Vale. The most productive estate lands were on the broader southern coastal plain, especially in the parishes of Westmoreland and Vere. On the narrower north coastal lowlands and in the interior basins, the estates were only partially cultivated because they included considerable slope land. Some of the slope land which could not be used for cane was grazed and, during the eighteenth century, coffee growing penetrated a few choice spots in the Blue Mountains. Thus, through most of the colonial plantation era Jamaica was a sugar-oriented island with major development on the coast and an empty interior (Figure 4.7). This empty interior became a land frontier for Negro settlers after emancipation, a development which was to play a critical role in the redistribution of population, the emergence of new settlement forms, and in other changes of the landscape.

The other large colony—French St. Domingue—achieved a somewhat greater occupancy of its territory. As in Jamaica, the sugar planters sought out the lowlands. The first area to be developed was the Plaine du Nord, focusing on Cap-Français (now Cap-Haïtien). This fertile, well-watered plain was divided into large estates separated by hedges. Large mansions with typically imposing gates were built, a rectangular road network leading to the port city of Cap-Français was established, and a planter aristocracy lived in conspicuous opulence.

From the Plaine du Nord, sugar planting spread to two other lowlands—the Artibonite

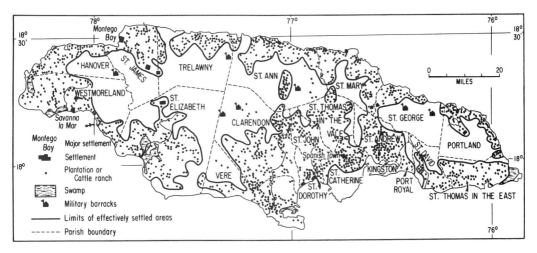

Figure 4.7
Jamaica : Land Use and Limits of Settlement About 1790.

Valley and the Cul-de-Sac–Plain of Léogane running east and west of Port-au-Prince. Eventually the Cul-de-Sac became the leading sugar area (and Port-au-Prince became the colonial capital) despite the inadequate precipitation. The French built a widespread irrigation system which changed the semiarid plain into the richest single sugar region in the eighteenth-century Antilles. In addition, the French tendency to diversify agriculture also made the production of cacao, cotton, and food crops important in all their lowland settlements. Coffee was introduced late but quickly became important. Coffee cultivation made possible the occupation of some of the mountain lands, particularly the slopes of the highlands south of the Plaine du Nord, but most of the mountain areas, such as the Massifs du Nord and de la Hotte, were not occupied until emancipation.

In summary, land utilization differed in intensity, diversity of production, and in other ways. Utilization was generally more intensive in the smaller islands but there was greater diversity of production in the larger territories. The French colonies consciously strived for greater diversification and a more balanced economy, while the English colonies were more prone to monoculture.

Agricultural Practices. Agricultural practices varied widely on the French and English sugar estates of the colonial plantation period, but some generalizations are possible. French methods of cultivation and sugar production tended to be superior. The French planters were more receptive to technical innovations, they practiced irrigation and fertilization more widely, and they were less guilty of absentee ownership than the English. As a result, the French obtained higher yields and greater profits, and the economies of the French colonies were more stable than those of their rivals.

These differences between the French and English were only in degree, however. Viewed *in toto,* efficient and effective farming practices were not the mark of the colonial plantation anywhere.

Soil differences were commonly ignored. Cane was planted wherever it would grow, with the result that production varied according to soil even on the same estate. In the English colonies irrigation was sparingly developed and, even in the French, the cost of construction imposed limitations. Constant use of the land quickly created a need for fertilization but, except for a limited supply of dung from work animals and the refuse of the sugar mills, no fertilizers were available. In the larger territories (particularly Jamaica), land was mined until it was exhausted and the planting was then shifted to virgin fields. On the smaller islands, where better care was given to the land, the estates were often too small to permit proper fallowing and crop rotation. Improvements which involved heavy capital expenditure and a consequent reduction in profits were avoided, and only such conservation as could be achieved through heavy slave labor input was practiced.

The most obvious kind of efficiency practiced on the sugar plantations was the utilization of large gangs of slaves equipped with simple tools for practically every task. The size of the slave force was generally determined on the basis of peak labor needs at crop or harvest time. Following the harvest, the slaves could not be discharged to cut down labor costs, as became the practice after emancipation. They had to be kept busy at tasks which could have been accomplished by a much smaller labor detail, with the result that there was little incentive to install labor-saving devices or to conduct operations more efficiently.

The biggest single chore on the estate was harvesting the cane and milling it before it spoiled. All other work ceased, the mill ground through a 24-hour day, and "there was no rest for man or beast." Other important plantation work included holing and forking the land, planting the cane, weeding, and trashing (removing outer leaves from the stalks). At planting time, holes about four feet square and nine inches deep were dug, and manure was forked into them before the cane cuttings were laid out. Weeding was particularly important when the young plants emerged. Trashing took place shortly before harvest.

All these tasks were accomplished with the simplest tools. Holing was done with heavy hoes, manure was carried in baskets by the slave women, weeding was done by hand, trashing with billhooks, and cutting with the ever-present cutlass or machete. The plow was virtually unknown until the end of the eighteenth century, and even then its use was by no means widespread. The argument against the plow was that in tropical soils, where a heavy, sun-baked hard pan offers resistance, a hoe was preferable. The abundance of slave labor is probably a more logical explanation; after emancipation, the plow was far more widely used.

The colonial plantation required many work animals. These were employed for transporting the cane to the mills and often for grinding it, as well as for other purposes. On a typical Barbados estate which had 200 acres in sugar, for instance, the livestock included 45 oxen, a dozen horses and mares, 11 asses and 8 milk cows; one in St. Domingue with 214 acres in cane used 45 mules and 16 oxen for transport, and an additional 60 mules at the mill. The stock was usually kept in permanent pens on estate yards, although some planters moved the pens onto fields being made ready for planting, to manure the land. Providing fodder for the livestock was a major problem, particularly on the smaller islands. A large part of the estate land was pasture, but the animals were often poorly fed and capable only of limited work.

Sugar yields varied from island to island and in accordance with labor input, fertilization, the number of ratoon crops and other factors. Yields were higher in the French islands and on the small English islands where estates were treated more like gardens than farms. Four tons an acre was an exceptional yield; 1.5 tons was a good average for the French territories and the smaller English islands; and in Jamaica, yields of .8 ton were common. The higher yields on the small islands and in the French territories were partly due to better care and partly to more frequent replanting.

Manufacturing Processes. The colonial sugar planter had to be a manufacturer as well as a farmer. Virtually every estate was

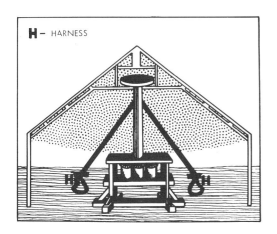

Figure 4.8
Sketch of Animal-Powered Sugar Mill.

equipped to grind its own cane to produce sugar (Figure 4.6).

Grinding techniques varied little until the nineteenth century. The typical *trapiche* operated on the principle of the clothes wringer, the press consisting of two upright rollers chocked closely inside a frame and meshed together by a row of pegs (Figure 4.8). The mills were of three types: cattle, wind, and water. Cattle mills, turned by oxen, mules, or horses, were the first type to be introduced and remained the most common through most of the colonial plantation period. These were small; they ground about 40 tons per year and could be easily dismantled and moved from place to place on the estate. Windmills (whose ruins are still present on many islands) also achieved considerable use, particularly in the English territories. These were generally larger than cattle mills, and were constructed of stone in the same manner as windmills in England and northwest Europe (Figure 4.2). Their chief disadvantage was that they could be effectively used only on the windward side of the island. Water-powered mills had the largest grinding capacity, but they were the least common because of the paucity of adequate sites on the level lands of the sugar estates. Regardless of the type of mill, the

apparatus was clumsy and developed too much friction, with the result that canes were not squeezed dry.

After the cane was ground, the juice was channeled from the mill into an adjacent boiling house, where it was boiled in a series of five or six graduated copper cauldrons heated over open fires. Certain agents, such as limewater and bone ash, were added to the boiling juice to bring oily impurities to the surface, where they were skimmed off. As the density of the molasses increased, its temperature was raised until, from the last of the cauldrons, the fire-hot, partially crystallized mass was scooped into small, clay molds to cool. The uncrystallized molasses was drained off and the crude brown sugar, *moscovado,* was packed in hogsheads for shipment. On some estates, particularly in the French territories, the *moscovado* was covered with a mass of wet clay. The water draining from the clay removed other impurities, and the resulting product was called "clayed sugar" or "plantation white." The ultimate refining of West Indian sugar was carried out in England and France.

Modern production methods give 8 to 11 parts of sugar for every part of molasses, but the crude colonial methods gave as little as 4 parts of sugar for every 3 parts of molasses. Molasses was thus an important byproduct of sugar processing on the colonial estate, and its sale, for table use or rum manufacturing, was crucially important to the estate economy.

Settlement and Houses. Settlement forms and houses on the colonial plantation were fairly uniform throughout the English and French West Indies. The most widespread type of settlement was the plantation village (Figure 4.6), consisting of the owner's mansion and the slave quarters. Close by were sheds for tools and equipment and for the work animals. A storehouse for food and other supplies was also a common feature. Completing the settlement were the mill, the boiling house, cisterns, stillhouse, curing

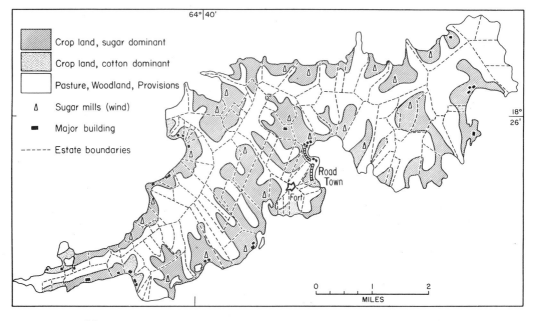

Figure 4.9

Land Use on Tortola, British Virgin Islands About 1810. Estate agriculture did not survive the sugar crisis of the nineteenth century on Tortola (see Chapter 7).

shed, and other buildings needed for sugar processing and shipping, as well as shops where the smiths, carpenters, and coopers worked. The total populations of such settlements varied but, in general, each had about 200 inhabitants.

Virtually every plantation had access to a town which often combined port and service functions. Whenever possible, the principal ports were on the leeward (west or southwest) sides of the uplands in order to afford better protection from the northeast trade winds. The most important port town in the territory, such as Port-au-Prince in St. Domingue, Port Royal (Kingston) in Jamaica, and Fort-de-France in Martinique, ultimately became the chief urban center and capital. Most of the coastal towns were dominated by a fort which overlooked the harbor and guarded against the numerous attacks to which the endless colonial wars of the West Indies gave rise (Figure 4.9).

Whether ports or simply service centers,

the colonial towns had little to recommend them as residential areas. Their streets were narrow and unpaved, most of the buildings were of wood and subject to periodic disastrous fires, and sanitation was so poor that virulent epidemics were frequent. Most planters preferred to live on their own estates and visit the towns only on business. As a result, the town population was generally made up of a few government officials, merchants, churchmen, soldiers and sailors, and servants. The architecture tended to reflect the national origin of the colonizing group— a differentiation which has continued in the West Indies to the present (Figure 1.2f).

Until almost the middle of the eighteenth century, most buildings in the West Indies, even the homes of the planters, tended to be simple frame structures often roofed with palm thatch. As the wealth from sugar increased, however, many planters built great houses, some of which still grace the West Indian landscape (Figure 3.7). These houses were constructed with an eye to their situation, their external appearance, and the spaciousness of their rooms. Whenever possible, the house was situated on a high spot facing the sea, in order to obtain a breeze, and was set back from the road. One approached it via an avenue of cedars, palmettos, or coconut trees. It was made of wood, preferably hardwood such as mahogany if available. In the wetter areas, the mansion stood on stone supports and had a single story; elsewhere, it might have two floors, the first of which was used for storage or workshops. Invariably, the planter's home had a wide hall which ran the length of the entire house and was flanked by bedrooms and the family's living quarters. (The kitchen was detached.) The roof was tall and pitched on all four sides, and the outside walls were partially made of jalousies, Venetian blinds which could be closed in bad weather and kept open at other times, to catch the trade winds and keep out the glare of sunlight. The interiors were plain, and the furniture consisted only of the most essential pieces.

The slave's hut was far simpler, generally 15 to 20 feet in length and consisting of two rooms. Hard posts were driven into the ground and interlaced with wattle and daub, a technique of African origin which is still used in the Haitian countryside. The floor was hard earth, the roof was of thatched palm and the furnishings generally included two or three stools, a platform of boards which served as a bed, a small table, a few jars, and an iron pot for cooking. The slaves normally built their own huts, using materials available on the estate.

African Slavery and Its West Indian Impact

The keystone of the colonial sugar economy was an abundance of cheap labor; economically speaking, it mattered little whether this labor was African, European, Asian or Amerindian; the emphasis was on cost. Approximately one field hand was needed for every acre of land in cane, and workers were needed for domestic service and other tasks, besides. Where was this labor to be obtained?

The dwindling Amerindian population was unused to hard labor. Records indicate that some Indians worked on plantations on a few of the islands such as Barbados, but from the beginning the Indian was never a major source of labor. Every effort was bent to the importation of European indentured workers, and the conditions of the European peasantry in the seventeenth and eighteenth centuries were so wretched that many poor people voluntarily indentured themselves for five years in the hope of getting a fresh start in the West Indies. Their treatment at the hands of the planters was so brutal, however, that the voluntary movement ceased quickly, and other methods of recruitment had to be resorted to. Prisoners, prostitutes, religious nonconformists (including many Irish Roman Catholics) and other undesirables were shipped to the islands. When all else failed, kidnapping, even of children, was used. "To be barbadoed" (sent to Barbados) became an infamous verb in the English language.

Ultimately, however, white labor proved too expensive, as well as too difficult to obtain. If the indentured European managed to survive his term of service, he had to be given some kind of compensation in money or land. More often he succumbed to the arduous plantation labor and to malaria, yellow fever, and other tropical diseases, against which the poor diet and poorer sanitation provided little protection.

There is evidence that the Spaniards experimented in importing Filipinos and Malayans, but the large pool of Asian labor was too far removed to be tapped. This left Africa as the only large and available source of labor.

Many reasons have been advanced for the heavy importation of Negro slaves to the West Indies. Western Africa, particularly around the Gulf of Guinea, had a large population located at a comparatively short distance across the Middle Passage from the Caribbean. The Negroes were felt to be inherently strong, they possessed some agricultural know-how, and many were already accustomed to slavery in their African habitat. Remote from his own cultural hearth and thrown in with fellow slaves who did not even speak the same language, the Negro could be easily controlled. Finally, the Africans seemed to possess some immunity both to tropical diseases and to the European varieties which had been the scourge of the Indian populations.

Slavery's Impact on Population. Everywhere that plantation sugar and slavery took hold in the West Indies the population changed: (1) the total population, as well as the ratio of Negroes to whites, increased rapidly; (2) miscegenation gave rise to a mixed-blood group which stood apart both from their maternal Negro and paternal white racial heritage; (3) population became concentrated on the coastal plains and other lowlands where sugar was cultivated; and (4) settlements took the form of Negro slave villages grouped around the great houses.

The impact of slavery on population is perhaps best illustrated by Barbados, the first territory to experience the sugar revolution. In 1640, the island had 43,000 people, of whom 37,000 were white and 6,000 Negro; by 1678, the white population had dropped to 20,000 and the Negro had risen to 40,000. By 1809, the island had 84,685 inhabitants, and the Negroes outnumbered the whites about five to one. The actual drop in the European population resulted from the departure of the small farmers, who could not compete with the large cane planters for land or with slaves in the labor market.

Elsewhere, the population trends illustrated by Barbados differed only in degree, mirroring differences in the size of the territory, the date of the sugar revolution, the history of settlement prior to sugar, and other local conditions (Table 4.2). Not unexpectedly, the largest population totals were ultimately achieved in Jamaica and St. Domingue, and the highest densities occurred in Barbados and the smaller islands, particularly the Leewards. An actual decrease in the size of the European population tended to take place only in the early-settled islands which already had a sizable number of small tobacco farmers.

Table 4.2

CONTRASTS BETWEEN SEVENTEENTH AND EIGHTEENTH CENTURY TOTAL POPULATION AND RACIAL COMPOSITION OF COLONIAL PLANTATION TERRITORIES

Territory	End of 17th Century			End of 18th Century		
	Total	White	Negro	Total	White	Negro
St. Domingue	10,000	7,091	2,909	640,000	40,000	600,000(?)
Guadeloupe	11,000	6,009	4,981	99,970	13,261	86,709
Martinique	16,500	5,000	11,500	91,815	11,619	80,196
Jamaica	48,500	8,500	40,000	280,000	30,000	250,000
Barbados	60,000	20,000	40,000	78,282	16,167	62,115
Grenada		Windwards		24,926	1,000	23,926
St. Vincent		largely		13,309	1,450	11,853
Dominica		unoccupied		16,203	1,236	14,967
Antigua	?	5,000	?	40,398	2,590	37,808
Montserrat	3,775	2,783	992	11,300	1,300	10,000
Virgin Islands	?	?	?	10,200	1,200	9,000
St. Kitts	7,381	3,521	3,860	22,335	1,900	20,435

Note: Data gathered from several sources; figures should be considered only approximate.

The rapid importation of large numbers of Negro slaves gave rise to very high population densities, particularly in the smaller islands. Barbados, for example, had densities of 400 people per square mile by 1684. In the other territories densities were lower, but everywhere the pressure of people on land was vastly greater than in the British North American colonies or the adjacent Spanish areas. The high densities of population in the West Indies today owe their origin in large measure to the influx of slaves authored by the colonial sugar plantation. But, as we have already observed, the mountain lands were relatively lightly occupied, a contrast which survives to this day on many of the islands.

Miscegenation occurred in all the slave-holding territories, but was probably most widespread in the French. The white planter, manager, or bookkeeper often chose an overlapping succession of concubines from among the slaves, and the mixed-blood group which developed ranged from 3 to 10 per cent of the total population. The importance of the mulatto group rested less in its size, however, as in the intermediate socio-economic position that it occupied. The possession of a lighter skin in a society obsessed with a Negro slave tradition gave the mulattoes a higher status. Even when they were not freed by their white fathers, as was customary, they were often considered too light to work in the fields and were used as domestic servants. Degrees of rank, depending on the exact admixture of race, developed, and society took careful note of the individual's composition. Light skin became the badge of the European, of racial superiority and high status, and dark skin was associated with slavery, field work, and low status. This prejudice has tainted the attitude of the West Indian towards agriculture and manual labor ever since.

Other Consequences of Slavery. Contrary to much opinion, the Negro slave did not arrive in the Caribbean a culturally naked savage. The region of West Africa which furnished most of the slaves to the sugar plantations was an area of well-developed cultures, including those of the Fula and Mandingo empires, the Hausa Kingdom of northern Nigeria, the Fanti and Ashanti states of the Gold Coast, and the eastern kingdoms of Dahomey, the Yoruba, and the Benin. In most of these places, the people lived in villages and even cities. They subsisted by means of complex systems of agriculture and animal husbandry; they possessed sophisticated social and political organizations; and, in some instances, they had developed handicrafts such as wood carving and working with metals.

The African culture brought by the slaves was not uniform, however, and crossing the Atlantic usually meant a radical break with African cultural tradition. The slave often assimilated, in varying degree, the European culture of his master. But there was some African cultural carryover, and it left its mark upon the social forms and the man-land patterns of the West Indies.

The Negroes seemed to have retained at least part of the African view of land tenure. Private ownership of usefully occupied or cultivated land was widely recognized in West Africa, but vacant land was considered the property of the tribe (or its king) and could be worked by any individual willing to invest the effort. After emancipation, the Negroes stubbornly asserted that unoccupied or unused land was open to settlement. They rejected the idea that perfectly good land could be left unoccupied at the mere whim of its owner.

Other African carryovers are discernible in agricultural tools and practices. In much of West Africa, farming resembled Amerindian cassava culture, which emphasized root crops and used fire for clearing the land. The chief tool was the hoe (often short-handled). Cultivation was done in gangs, with the laborers swinging their hoes in parallel rows to the beat of a drum. Friends and neighbors often worked together in cooperative, mutual-help groups. The slaves used these familiar tools and practices in plantation work or on their provision grounds, and the West Indian peasantry continued to use them after emancipation. Cooperative work, for example, variously called *combite,* "jollification," and other names is still practiced.

With the Negro slaves came new food plants. Among the more important were the ackee fruit, okra, the congo bean or black-eyed pea, the yam, millet, sorghum, and the mango, an Asian fruit which had been introduced into West Africa by Arab slavers. Breadfruit was introduced from the Pacific primarily to satisfy the need for cheap slave food, but the slaves refused to eat it and it did not become an important food crop until after emancipation. African influence has left its mark on the material culture of the West Indies in a host of other ways— including the wooden mortar for grinding grains, ways of preparing certain foods and even palm wine, and materials and modes for constructing huts such as the already-mentioned wattle and daub.

Economics of the Colonial Plantation

The colonial plantation became synonymous with spectacular wealth in its eighteenth-century heyday but, in retrospect, this wealth seemed to have had little rational basis. It was an artificial creation stamped with inefficiency, high prices, and exorbitant profits, and it can be understood only in the light of the protected market which West Indian planters enjoyed in England and France. The prevailing economic philosophy through most of the plantation period was mercantilism. Under this system, the mother country exercised a monopoly over colonial trade and, in turn, gave the planter a monopoly of the market in the home country. Assured of this protection, the planters, especially in the English colonies, often restricted production in order to keep prices up, and they felt no pressure to improve production methods in order to cut down costs. The planter class grew wealthy despite their inefficiency.

Capital and Credit. The sugar planter was of necessity a man of some wealth. The cost of land, slaves, and equipment was considerable, and sugar production was restricted to a comparatively few individuals. Once the initial investment was made, however, the plantation operated on virtually a barter economy. The estate generally had a close credit connection with a merchant in the home country who acted as agent for the sale of sugar and the purchase of needed supplies. In return for a monopoly of the estate's business which enabled him to charge noncompetitive commissions, the merchant extended easy credit to the planter and even lent him money to carry him through bad years. The ease with which advances could be secured resulted in gross extravagance. Caution was brushed aside in financial matters, and speculation and conspicuous consumption placed most planters in heavy debt to their merchant agents. For a planter to owe £150,000 was not unusual; in fact, a certain pride was taken in indebtedness. "Rich as a West Indian planter" became synonymous with opulence in eighteenth-century London and Paris, but this opulence was too often an illusion which covered a multitude of debts.

The credit system worked as long as a monopoly of the home market and high prices continued. When these disappeared, however, the planter could no longer meet his obligations, and the plantation economy collapsed like a house of cards.

Management. Nothing revealed the gross inefficiency of the colonial plantation economy as clearly as estate management. In contrast to the settler who went to the North American colonies and who usually intended to make his home there, the European immigrant to the West Indies generally hoped to make a fortune and return home to Europe. The planter's life in the West Indies was not a pleasant one. The climate was considered unhealthy and the death rate from tropical diseases was high; there was a lack of entertainment and of facilities for educating the children; above all, there was the isolation and the insecurity of living at close quarters with a numerically dominant slave population controlled by coercion. As a result, the successful planter returned to Europe, visiting his plantation only periodically.

Management of the estates was left to resident planters or to a handful of lawyers and merchants who acted as attorneys for the absentees and were paid 5 to 6 per cent of the gross product. A single attorney might be entrusted with as many as 20 estates; at best, he could exercise only cursory supervision. The real supervision of the estate generally fell to a resident overseer or bookkeeper whose primary qualification was often his white skin.

Absenteeism, while high everywhere, varied from place to place. It tended to be greater in the larger territories, such as Jamaica and St. Domingue, and it was definitely higher in the English possessions than in the French. In a few islands, as many as two-thirds of the planters were absent; in the English colonies 50 per cent was a common rate.

Absentee landlordship thus became a major characteristic of the colonial plantation, and its negative consequences were many. No attention was paid to economies, and the attorneys were often corrupt in discharging their duties. Long-range returns were sacrificed to immediate gains. The land was mined until exhausted, new land was brought into production reluctantly because of the large initial cost of clearing, and expensive improvements were seldom made. The plantation became a way of making money rather than a way of life, and the future impoverishment of the West Indies was guaranteed. The one advantage of absenteeism was that it created an influential group in the home country which lobbied tirelessly for the protection of the West Indian sugar monopoly.

Markets and Trade. Despite its gross inefficiency, the colonial plantation gave rise to far-reaching economic development in the mother countries. Within a half century of the sugar revolution, trade with the British West Indian islands employed 300 ships and 6,000 seamen, and was paying import duties of £100,000 in London alone. In 1798, Pitt estimated that four-fifths of British overseas investments were in the West Indies; in 1804, Admiral Nelson stated that 10,000 French troops could do more harm to British imperial interests in the Caribbean than in any other part of the world. Strange as it may appear today, the West Indian colonies of the eighteenth century were considered far more important than the North American settlements. Barbados, with its 166 square miles of territory, was worth more to British capitalism than Pennsylvania, New York, and New England combined. At the Treaty of Paris in 1763, France willingly gave up Canada in order to keep Martinique.

The West Indian colonies not only supplied England and France with tropical products whose sale in Europe established a favorable balance of trade; they also helped to stimulate shipbuilding and the growth of seaports at home; they gave impetus to the fishing economy of New England and Newfoundland; they gave rise to new industries such as rum distilling and sugar refining; and their needs in terms of clothing, food, and equipment benefited every aspect of the metropolitan economies. Is it any wonder that France and England fought so many wars for the control of these possessions?

The widespread economic development and the huge trade to which the colonial plantation gave rise can be understood only in the light of the institution's basic needs. Unlike its counterpart in the southern United States, the West Indian plantation never achieved any degree of self-sufficiency, and the planter was forced to import virtually all of his necessities. Chief among these were: (1) a large supply of slave labor, which had to be constantly replenished; (2) food, which could not be raised in sufficient quantities on the estate; (3) lumber for construction;

and (4) manufactured goods of all types, including clothing, tools, equipment, and luxury items.

During much of the colonial period, the slave trade was itself second only to sugar in its profit-making potential. The demand for slaves always exceeded supply. This was due to the rapid expansion of sugar planting, but also to the short life span of the slave and the inability of the Negro population to reproduce itself under slave conditions. Jamaica, for example, is supposed to have imported 800,000 slaves between 1690 and 1820, yet in 1820 the total Negro population was only 340,000. For this reason, the slave trade became a lucrative necessity in which virtually every country of Western Europe, as well as North America, participated actively. While the trade was abolished as early as the latter eighteenth century by some countries, slaves were imported into the Caribbean as late as 1888.

Feeding this large slave population posed a serious problem. Despite efforts to raise provisions on the estates and to keep the slave diet to a minimum, large quantities of food had to be imported, especially by the land-short smaller colonies. The imports generally consisted of the cheapest items, such as dried fish from New England and Newfoundland, a practice which continues; corn and beans from the Middle Atlantic colonies; and other necessities. So dependent were the colonies on food imports that when war or other calamities interrupted commerce, it was not uncommon for slaves to eat rats and clay and ultimately to starve in large numbers.

The trade which the movement of these and other goods created has been described as "triangular," although the sides of the triangle were not always the same. This trade involved the West Indies with three primary areas—England and France in Europe, the British North American colonies, and West Africa. The European countries supplied most of the shipping and manufactured goods; Africa supplied the human merchandise; and North America contributed most of the food and lumber.

The trade with North America was of special significance to both the English and the French West Indies. This area not only supplied the bulk of the food and lumber needs; it was also one of the most lucrative markets for molasses. The French colonies were prohibited by law from exporting molasses to France, where it might be manufactured into rum and compete with the brandy industry, but French molasses found a ready market in North America where it was used for cooking (Boston baked beans and brown bread, shoo-fly pie, molasses jack and corn pone) as well as for the production of rum. The continentals often gave preference to the French product, which was cheaper and of higher quality.

For the English colonies, a plantation economy would have been impossible without the food produced by the mixed husbandry of the North American colonies. In 1770, the North American settlements sent almost three-fourths of their food and animal surpluses to the West Indies, as well as half their lumber production in the form of barrel staves of oak for shipping sugar, wood planks, and other wood products.

In summary, the colonial plantation in the English and French West Indies was characterized by relatively large estates, monoculture, family ownership and absenteeism, primitive methods of production, slave labor, indebtedness, and the monopolistic protection of mercantilism. It began in the latter seventeenth century and remained dominant until the latter nineteenth, and it represented a European method for producing high-valued dessert crops which hitherto had been obtained in small quantities and at high cost over the long trade routes from Asia and Africa. Its principal commodity was sugar, although coffee, cotton, and other tropical products were also produced. As a technique for exploiting land

and labor, the colonial plantation was inefficient and destructive, and it bequeathed a legacy of poverty wherever it took root.

On the whole, the plantation functioned more effectively in the French colonies than in the English. This was due largely to French efforts to discourage absenteeism, to promote greater diversification of production, and to adopt improved methods of agriculture and sugar processing. Within the French group, St. Domingue came to represent the culmination of plantation development. Before it was destroyed by slave uprisings at the end of the eighteenth century, St. Domingue had become the richest European colony in the New World, and its production exceeded the combined total of all the English territories.

DECLINE OF THE WEST INDIAN COLONIAL PLANTATION

After reaching its height in the eighteenth century, the West Indian colonial plantation underwent a general decline in the nineteenth century and was ultimately replaced, in most instances, by the modern plantation. This decline and transition rocked the land-people complex of the West Indies into new forms, particularly in the English and French territories where the colonial system had been most completely established. On the Hispanic islands, where the colonial institution had not sent down deep roots, the transition from the colonial to the modern plantation was smoother. In fact, the Spanish possessions experienced an upsurge in plantation production precisely while production in the English and French territories was declining. Therefore, the following analysis of the decline of the colonial plantation will be focused primarily on the English and French territories.

General Causes and Consequences of Decline

There was no one major cause which led to the decline of the colonial plantation, nor were all causes equally important in all territories. For the Caribbean as a whole, the list includes: (1) slave uprisings and unrest; (2) the exhaustion of the soil; (3) the abolition of the slave trade and the emancipation of slaves; (4) the growing competition from other sugar producers, especially Cuba, as well as from beet sugar, which became established in Europe after the Napoleonic period; (5) the loss of monopoly of the home country market, especially by the English territories after 1846; (6) the independence of the American colonies, which obstructed the once-free commerce and increased the cost of food and lumber for the British sugar colonies; (7) absentee landlordism and heavy indebtedness; (8) new industrial and marketing arrangements and techniques; and (9) the destruction caused by the numerous wars in the Caribbean.

The collapse of the colonial plantation brought about revolutionary changes. The mainspring for most of these changes was the necessity to readjust land-people relations in the face of a sharp reduction in the production of sugar, the financial bankruptcy of the planter class, and an emancipation which freed a race but did not create a society.

Populations were profoundly affected. Their numbers, densities, distributions, movements, racial composition, and mode of settlement were changed. Land use and land tenure were altered; and the organization of commercial production was revolutionized. In virtually all of the islands, there was a decrease in the white population. Many planters were killed in slave uprisings, and many left for England, France, Louisiana, and elsewhere. The numerical loss was more than compensated for, however, by an increase in the Negro population. Once emancipated, the Negro population which had generally been unable to reproduce itself under slave conditions began to increase, a trend which has continued unabated to the present. In turn, the rise in Negro population increased population densities and pressure of people on land, and thereby set the stage for the current discrepancy between the population and the land resources of the West Indies.

Wherever possible, the ex-slave abandoned the coastal estates and occupied land in the hilly interior. This movement created in the larger territories a labor shortage which could be met only by the importation of cheap labor from the Orient and elsewhere; it tended, by transferring people from the crowded coastal plains to the interior, to more nearly equalize the population distribution; it emphasized the economic and social differences between the commercially utilized plains with their estates and their planter group, and the subsistence peasant groups in the uplands; it modified the settlement patterns, which had mainly been coastal cities and the slave villages of the estates by creating dispersed settlement and free villages.

Ultimately, the tendency of the freed Negroes to abandon the estates and establish themselves on small plots created a class of small farmers which came to be called "peasant." But the peasant class in the West Indies differed then, as it differs now, from its counterpart in Europe and Asia. There was little love for the land, little association with place, and little respect for manual toil. The association of field labor with slavery left a stigma on agricultural labor which continues to this day. And, since there was never enough land to go around, many of the Negroes came to form a landless peasantry whose unemployment or underemployment adds to the poverty of the present.

Readjustment also gave rise to change in the patterns of land use and land tenure. With the drop in the production and the price of sugar and the bankruptcy of a large number of planters, many estates were placed in receivership. Some of the estates were divided into small plots and sold or sharecropped to the ex-slaves. This caused a sharp increase in the number of small holdings and, as in the post-Civil War American South, it created the practice of sharecropping. The general reduction in the amount of land in cane condemned marginal lands to other uses. Land values tumbled. Those estates which remained sugar producers had to be made more efficient to stay solvent, and this set the stage for the modern corporate plantation.

The above changes occurred, in some measure, throughout the British and French West Indies, but there were numerous differences from island to island. The most important of these differences became apparent between the French territories on the one hand and the English on the other; between the large islands, such as Jamaica and Trinidad, which had unoccupied land and the smaller islands, such as Barbados, which were densely populated; and between the older colonies, such as the Leewards, where the plantation was strongly entrenched and the Windwards and Trinidad, whose history of plantation was briefer.

Decline and Adjustment in the French Territories

The colonial plantation suffered its most drastic blow in French St. Domingue, which had become the most prosperous of the plantation territories. The immediate instrument of downfall was slave revolt. The causes and the success of the slave revolt were, in turn, due to several conditions.

The rapid development of St. Domingue in the eighteenth century resulted in the importation of huge numbers of African slaves over a short period of time. In 1789, on the eve of revolt, the ratio of Negroes to Europeans was about 20 to 1, the most unbalanced slave-master ratio in the Caribbean. Equally significant, the importation had been so rapid that most of the colony's population had been born in Africa and had not been "civilized." Other contributing factors were the impact of the French Revolution, and of its preaching of liberty and equality, particularly on the educated mulatto element; the heavily mountainous nature of the island, which facilitated the defense of Negro bands; and the relative isolation from each other of three major nuclei of settlement—the Plaine du Nord, the Cul-de-Sac, and the Artibonite Valley.

The first uprisings occurred on the northern plain, where the ratio of slaves to whites was greatest. Within a few weeks the plain was a smouldering ruin scarred by savage bloodletting and destruction. Two thousand Europeans were killed, and 180 sugar plantations, and 900 coffee and indigo establishments were destroyed. All that remained of the prosperous plantations were the blackened foundation walls and the great gates of the mansions, which still distinguish the landscape of the Plaine du Nord (Figure 4.10).

From the north, the holocaust spread.

Years of French effort and large expenditures of men and money failed to quell the revolts and the ensuing independence movement. The mountainous terrain and tropical diseases helped the Negro and the fear of a return to slavery motivated him, and St. Domingue ceased to exist in name[2] and the colonial plantation system there came to an end.

But the triumphant Negroes who replaced the French planters as masters of Haiti inherited little save the devastated land, some coffee groves, and a legacy of internal strife and instability. All else—the mansions, the sugar works, the irrigation systems, the outbuildings, and the equipment—had gone up in flames or had fallen into decay during the turmoil of revolts and wars.

Moreover, the departure of the French did not bring peace. Sectional strife continued in the country, and this, coupled with

---

[2] The name was changed to Haiti, an old Indian name meaning "mountainous land."

Figure 4.10

Remnants of an Eighteenth Century French Plantation Mansion Which Was Burned During the Slave Uprisings, Plaine du Nord, Haiti.

the threat that the French might return, made necessary the maintenance of large armies for years. Since the money economy of Haiti had virtually disappeared, the numerous soldiery had to be paid with land from the confiscated French estates and the public domain. Large amounts of land were parceled into small plots and alloted to the troops according to rank. Other public lands were placed on sale at such low prices (in order to raise revenue) that thousands of Haitian peasants were able to acquire small holdings. These practices resulted in the disappearance of virtually the entire public domain of Haiti into small family plots, a pattern which continues to the present. The only exceptions to family-sized plots were the holdings of the highest echelons of military officers and the *Afranchis*. The latter were generally mulatto offspring of white planters who had inherited estates from their fathers and had managed to retain possession through the turbulent revolts and wars. Even these larger holdings could seldom be worked as estates, however. The owners, lacking the capital to hire laborers or to restore irrigation works and other equipment, often rented their land on a share basis.

The expulsion of the French also gave rise to the emphasis of many African cultural traits. Since 50 to 60 per cent of the slave population of St. Domingue in 1789 had actually been born in Africa, African culture was more fully retained in Haiti than elsewhere. The language of the Haitian peasant became a patois which blends both French and African forms. Roman Catholicism remained, in theory; in practice, African religious rites obtained a stronger hold on the Haitian masses. Of particular importance to the geographer, African culture manifested itself in the methods of house construction, in a growing emphasis on tree and garden crops, and in other agricultural practices (see Chapter 6).

The transition from the colonial plantation in Martinique and Guadeloupe, the

only important sugar colonies left to France after the Napoleonic period, was less painful than it had been in Haiti or in the English colonies. There were a number of reasons for this. On the smaller French islands, absentee owners were less common. Smaller holdings were more general, especially on Guadeloupe, and the basic economy was more diversified. Moreover, the planters were less debt-ridden, efficiency was greater, and the entire plantation system was on a much stronger footing, giving them a competitive advantage in the world markets over the English islands. Equally important, France, unlike England, never completely abandoned her colonies to the mercies of free trade.

However, the transition was not without difficulties. Many planters left the islands, especially Martinique, and returned to France. A temporary labor shortage made necessary the importation of some Oriental labor (Table 4.3). The biggest problem was the virtual explosion of the Negro population following emancipation. The peasantry found it difficult to obtain land, and small holdings, which had tripled by 1900, did not solve the problem. Poverty became widespread, and Martinique and Guadeloupe continued to turn to France for a solution.

Decline and Adjustment in the English Territories

The plantation economy of the English territories was temporarily benefited by the fall of St. Domingue, but not for long. Conditions both abroad and within the islands themselves were ripe for the decline of and changes in the plantation structure.

The independence of the North American colonies destroyed the mercantile system and discredited the old colonial scheme on which the sugar territories of the West Indies depended. With independence, North America became a foreign area, and thus subject to all the restrictive provisions of the British Navigation Laws. As a result, the West

Indian plantation islands were impeded from free intercourse with what had previously been both a market for some of their products and a source of cheap food and other provisions.

Roughly coinciding with American independence were several adverse trends. These included the growing tempo of industrialization in England, the shift of British imperial interests from the Caribbean to the Indian Ocean, and the increasing clamor for abolishment of the slave trade and for the emancipation of slaves. Industrialization increased the political influence of British manufacturers and gave them visions of worldwide markets for their products, but such markets could be obtained only by encouraging free trade. Moreover, an industrialized society demanded cheap food, and West Indian sugar was not cheap. In their fight against the West Indian lobby in Parliament, the industrialists finally won the day, and of all the dates marking the decline of the West

Table 4.3

CRITICAL DATES MARKING THE DECLINE OF THE COLONIAL PLANTATION IN THE BRITISH WEST INDIES

1783—Independence of North American colonies imposes restriction of British Navigation Laws to West Indian commerce with the United States.

1807—England abolished the slave trade.*

1825—Mauritius given access to British sugar markets.

1834—Slaves emancipated in English territories.

1836—*Moscovado* sugar from India admitted to British market at par with West Indian product.

1845—Sugar duties reduced by Britain, enabling foreign sugar to enter British market at par with the colonial product.

* The slave trade was also abolished by Denmark in 1804, the United States in 1808, Sweden in 1813, Holland in 1814, France in 1818, and Spain in 1820. This did not put an end to the trade, however. The huge demand for slaves in the expanding plantation economies of Cuba, the United States, and Brazil gave rise to a contraband commerce in slaves which continued until almost the end of the nineteenth century.

Indian colonial plantation (Table 4.3), none was more critical than 1845, when foreign sugar was admitted to the British market on a par with colonial sugar.

While the industrialists were attacking the West Indian sugar monopoly, abolitionists were attacking the other great prop of the colonial plantation—slavery. The planters were compensated for the loss of their emancipated slaves at a rate of about ten shillings to the pound, but the bulk of the planters' capital was tied up in slaves and emancipation proved a devastating economic blow. The inevitable collapse of the colonial sugar plantation in the British West Indies which followed abolition and free trade was made more complete by soil exhaustion, absenteeism, indebtedness, and other deficiencies inherent in the system.

Jamaica. Within the English colonies, the impact of readjusting land-labor relations after the fall of the colonial plantation was felt most severely in Jamaica. In no other territory was the attrition rate among the estates as high. By 1847, one-third of the Jamaican sugar estates which had existed at the beginning of the century were gone and, by 1865, fully one-half had disappeared. During the same period three-fourths of the coffee estates had also become ruinate. The rapid fall of estate agriculture in Jamaica was due in part to the high absenteeism, the widespread indebtedness, the inefficient utilization of marginal land, and other inherent weaknesses. It is significant that the survival rate among the absentee estates was lower than those of resident proprietors, that marginal estates virtually disappeared, and that the larger plantations weathered the storm with less difficulty than the smaller ones. But perhaps the chief factor in the decline of Jamaican estates was the labor shortage created by emancipation.

One of the freedoms which emancipation gave to the Negro was the right *not* to work for the planter, a right which the ex-slave exercised so freely in Jamaica that many estates lost two-thirds of their labor force. The principal cause of abandonment was the availability of land for subsistence agriculture, both in the mountainous interior and on the abandoned estates. Many resident planters opposed the sale of land to Negroes, but the economic condition of the absentees was so desperate that they made cheap land available. Good provision plots were sold for £5 to £10 per acre, mountain land was rented for 20 to 30 shillings per year, and, when money was lacking for either purchase or rental, the Negro did not hesitate to squat.

Where land was readily available, as in the interior, the Negro tended to sever his connection with the estate altogether. Elsewhere, a system had to be developed whereby the Negro laborer rendered estate service, partly for money and partly for the use of provision grounds and a house provided by the planter. The task of finding the correct balance between the estate's labor requirements and the self-subsisting economy favored by the Negro was a difficult one. The ideal solution was to retain Negro settlements on the estate, each family possessing

provision grounds and working for the planter when its labor was required, but the parties seldom agreed on terms. It seemed that the planter always asked too high a price for the provision grounds, and the Negro always asked too much for his services.

In consequence of the shortage of Jamaican estate labor, its cost continued to increase until it reached two-thirds of the cost of the entire operation. Coming precisely when the white planters were most hard-pressed, this increase in wage rates increased the bitterness between the white planter and the Negro peasant and paved the way for new importations of labor (Table 4.4).

Not all of the consequences of the Jamaican Negro's movement away from the estates were negative, however. The spread of Negro small holders in the interior brought new prosperity to the mountains. Agriculture on the peasant plots was not completely subsistent; there was often a surplus of food crops for local sale, and even some ginger, allspice, and coffee for the export market. By mid-nineteenth century, a lively trade had developed between the mountains and the plains where estates remained. The

Figure 4.11
Relic of a Slave Plantation Past. Slaves returning from the fields at dusk entered one at a time through the slit in the great gate to be searched and manacled.

Table 4.4

IMPORTATION OF ORIENTAL LABOR INTO THE WEST INDIES AFTER EMANCIPATION

Colony	Indians Imported	Period
Trinidad	134,183	1845–1917
Jamaica	33,533	1845–1917
Grenada	3,033	1856–1878
St. Kitts	337	1861
St. Lucia	4,427	1858–1893
Guadeloupe and Martinique	78,453	1862(?)–1885
St. Croix	351	1862

Source: N. Deerr, *The History of Sugar* (London: Chapman and Hall, Ltd., 1949), p. 398.

Note: In addition, 4,845 Chinese were imported into Jamaica (1860–1893) and 2,645 into Trinidad (1852–1872). Jamaica also experimented with the importation of Germans, Scots, Irish, and Maltese.

Jamaican peasant farm woman (called "the higgler") who took the produce to market became an institution. New towns sprang up in the interior of Jamaica. In St. Thomas-in-the-Vale, for example, Linstead became an important center where middlemen bought produce for shipment through the Rio Cobre Gorge to Spanish Town, Kingston, and the sugar lands of Vere. By 1865, there were 50,000 small properties and, while most were not self-supporting, they made a significant contribution to the island's economy. At crop time many of the small holders migrated to the plains to supplement their income, and this seasonal migration continues to this day.

Trinidad and the Smaller Islands. The problems of transition from the colonial to the modern plantation were of a somewhat different nature in Trinidad than they were in Jamaica. As we have already indicated, the Trinidad colonial plantation had existed for only a few decades when emancipation and other factors set the stage for change. The number of slaves imported between the end of the eighteenth century and abolition, in 1834, was small. Settlement had been largely restricted to the western valleys of the Northern Range and the plain south of Port of Spain. As a result, when emancipation occurred, Trinidad had the lowest people-land ratio and faced the severest labor shortage in the West Indies. Lack of workers posed a problem, not only to the existing plantations but for the expansion of commercial agriculture as well.

Along with other West Indian colonies, Trinidad made a desperate effort to find new sources of cheap labor (Table 4.4). Small groups of Chinese, Portuguese peasants from the Madeiras, free Negroes from Africa, and other people were imported. The final solution to Trinidad's labor problem, however, rested on large-scale imports of indentured workers from India and on the voluntary influx of immigrants from the crowded smaller islands such as Barbados and the Leewards. The East Indians were brought in for five years, after which they could either return home or remain and receive a grant of about five acres of land. Most returned to India, but in Trinidad enough of them chose to stay so that they now represent a significant minority (see Chapter 6).

In Barbados, the Leewards, and the Windwards, the problems stemming from the decline of the colonial plantation were less severe than in Jamaica or Trinidad. On some of the smallest islands, such as the British Virgins, plantation agriculture disappeared and was replaced by a peasant economy. In Barbados and the more densely settled Leewards, the shock of emancipation did not create a labor shortage. There was little unoccupied land available, and the freed Negro had to stay on the plantation, unless he chose to migrate. In the Windwards, where the history of the plantation was shorter and the dependence on sugar less, the changes which were ushered in by emancipation and the decline of the colonial system were similarly less difficult.

SELECTED REFERENCES

Bennett, J. H., Jr., "The Problem of Slave Labor Supply at the Codrington Plantations," *The Journal of Negro History,* XXXVI, No. 4 (1951), 406–41; XXXVII, No. 2 (1952), 115–41.

Cumper, G. E., "A Modern Jamaican Sugar Estate," *Social and Economic Studies,* III, No. 2 (1954), 119–60.

Debien, G., *Une Plantation de Saint-Domingue: La Sucrerie Galbaud du Fort: 1690–1802.* Cairo: Les Presses de l'Institut Français d'Archéologie Orientale du Caire, 1941.

Deerr, N., *The History of Sugar.* London: Chapman and Hall, Ltd., 1949.

Díaz Soler, L. M., *Historia de la Esclavitud Negra en Puerto Rico: 1493–1890.* Madrid: Revista de Occidente, 1953.

Edwards, B., *History, Civil and Commercial, of the British Colonies in the West Indies.* Dublin: Luke White, 1793.

Harlow, V. T., *A History of Barbados: 1625–1685.* Oxford: The Clarendon Press, 1926.

International Labour Organisation, *Definition of the Term "Plantation."* Geneva: International Labour Office, 1953.

Lowenthal, D., "Caribbean Views of Caribbean Land," *Canadian Geographer,* V, No. 2 (1961), 1–9.

McWilliams, C., *Factories in the Field.* Boston: Little, Brown & Co., 1939.

Merrill, G. C., *The Historical Geography of St. Kitts and Nevis, The West Indies.* Mexico, D.F.: Pan-American Institute of Geography and History (Pub. No. 232), 1958.

Pan-American Union, *Plantation Systems of the New World.* Social Science Monograph No. 7. Washington, D.C.: Pan-American Union, 1959.

Pares, R., *Merchants and Planters.* London: Cambridge University Press, 1960.

Pitman, F. W., "The Settlement and Financing of British West India Plantations in the Eighteenth Century," in *Essays in Colonial History Presented to Charles McLean Andrews by His Students.* New Haven, Conn.: Yale University Press, 1931, pp. 252–83.

Reid, M., *The Maroon: Or Planter Life in Jamaica.* New York: R. M. DeWitt, 1864.

Sires, R. V., "Negro Labor in Jamaica in the Years Following Emancipation," *Journal of Negro History,* XXV, No. 4 (1940), 484–97.

Thompson, E. T., "The Climatic Theory of the Plantation," *Agricultural History,* XV, No. 1 (1941), 49–60.

Waibel, L., "The Tropical Plantation System," *Scientific Monthly,* LII (1941), 156–60.

Westergaard, W. C., *The Danish West Indies under Company Rule: 1671–1754* (with a supplement chapter, *1755–1917*). New York: The Macmillan Company, 1917.

Williams, Eric, *Capitalism and Slavery.* Chapel Hill, N. C.: The University of North Carolina Press, 1944.

Zelinsky, W., "The Historical Geography of the Negro Population of Latin America," *Journal of Negro History,* XXXIV, No. 2 (1949), 153–221.

5

The Greater Antilles: Cuba and Puerto Rico

TRANSITION IN THE ANTILLES

The period from the latter nineteenth century to the present in the Antilles (both Greater and Lesser) has been characterized by at least two important land-and-people themes: (1) the emergence of the modern plantation; (2) a strong upsurge in population which has overtaxed the few resources of most territories. The past century has also been colored by an intense social dissatisfaction with the legacy of the plantation, slavery, and colonialism; and by a painful search for adjustment both to this legacy and to the discrepancy between an increasing population and a limited economic potential. The search for adjustment has not ended; on the contrary, it is a basic cause of the current instability and desire for change in the West Indies.

Emergence of the Modern Plantation

The economic crisis which followed emancipation and the decline of the colonial plantation gradually brought about a drastic reorganization in commercial production, particularly of sugar. The principal instrument of reorganization was the modern plantation. It emerged in the late nineteenth and early twentieth centuries, and with the rare exception, it continues as a dominant institution in the region (see Chapter 1).

Unlike its small, family-owned colonial predecessor, the modern version of the plantation is a large-scale corporate enterprise. In order to assure an adequate supply of cane and to provide for future expansion of production, the corporations have acquired huge landholdings. Cane is processed in a few *centrales* ("large mills") equipped with expensive machinery. Since the *centrales* have to be accessible both to vast areas of cane land and to ports, narrow gauge railroads and highways were built, and trucks, trailers and other types of rapid transport came into use. Efficiency and low production costs are stressed in every operation from farming to marketing. The enterprise has been aptly described as a modern factory in the field.

In retrospect, credit is due to the modern plantation for many positive achievements. It has placed sugar and other plantation crops on a sounder economic footing; its scientific agriculture has often improved worn-out land; it built new transportation; and through increased yields and lower production costs, it has made sugar available to a much larger market. But the modern plantation is also responsible for a variety of problems in the Antilles. It is a more efficient instrument for land and labor organization than the colonial *trapiche* and *ingenio*, but has done little to bring about a more equitable distribution of resources and income. The best land has continued to be concentrated in the hands of the few and the relationship between the rural proletariat which has replaced the slaves and the landowners has been marred by conflict. With only rare exceptions, the economy of the islands is more painfully dependent upon monoculture. A large share of the considerable profits go to foreign stockholders, leaving the local population with only incidental benefits. Large amounts of idle land, which might be used by the peasantry, are tied up in corporate holdings as a hedge against future needs. Work is at best seasonal, and the management is not obliged to give its workers year-round care, as were the colonial slave-owning planters.

These conditions, in a region of rapidly increasing population and limited resources, often make for a social environment of abject poverty and dangerous restiveness. The modern plantation in the Caribbean can be defended on many grounds, but there is little doubt that the bulk of the local people resent it as an instrument of exploitation, often a foreign-owned instrument, at that. The Cuban Revolution under Castro indicates that this resentment can sometimes become explosive.

Population Pressure

Some of the negative conditions created by the emergence of the modern plantation were gradually intensified by the growing pressure of people upon land. Beginning approximately in the latter nineteenth century, the West Indies witnessed a rapid growth of population. In most islands, this was a natural increase, made possible by the abolition of slavery, by rising health standards, and by other factors. In others, notably Cuba, Trinidad and, to a lesser degree, Puerto Rico, there were also a significant number of immigrants who were attracted by an expanding economy. In the British possessions, for example, the total population rose from roughly 760,000, in the middle of the nineteenth century, to more than 3.5 million in 1960. Trinidad, which had the greatest amount of unoccupied land, witnessed a tenfold expansion of population during this period, but even crowded Barbados and the Leewards experienced something of a population explosion.

For many years emigration alleviated the growing population pressure. Significant numbers of people moved from areas which had a surplus of labor (such as Haiti, Barbados, Jamaica, and the Leewards) to labor-deficient areas such as Cuba, Trinidad, the Dominican Republic, the Caribbean coast of Central America, and even to the United States and Europe. Emigration has continued to be important in some islands, especially since World War II, but the outflow has not counterbalanced the marked increase of births over deaths. As a result, the pressure of population upon land and other resources has continued to rise.

Agriculture remained the economic mainstay throughout the archipelago, and the rise in population soon pushed the ratio of people to cultivable land to critical levels on many islands. Despite the dispersion of the former slave population following emancipation, the arable acreage in most of the Antilles became saturated in the first decades of the present century. On many islands, rural densities approaching the order usually associated with urban concentrations were reached by the 1920's. As a result, the percentage of the total labor force employed in agriculture began to decline. Surplus labor became a permanent feature of the archipelago, especially in the more crowded territories such as Barbados, Haiti, Jamaica, Puerto Rico, and the Leewards.

Unemployment has been further intensified during the past half century by other socioeconomic conditions. Since much of the agricultural employment is in sugar cane production and other highly seasonal occupations, even the employed may work only a few months a year. On most of the islands, of course, there are large numbers of peasant farmers who work their own land or rent subsistence plots. The average peasant plot, however, is seldom more than two or three acres of marginal land, the yield from which is not enough even for bare subsistence. No independent peasantry has emerged, because even those who own land must depend on outside employment to supplement their incomes. The needs of the landless workers, and there are many of these everywhere, are even greater.

Consequences of Land-People Discrepancies. The most obvious consequence of the growing discrepancy between population and resources has been abject poverty. While figures on real, per-capita income are difficult to compute, the regional average in the Antilles is less than $300 a year. Income has been increasing since World War II, especially in Puerto Rico, but the cost of living has also risen. The peasant's income is spent on necessities, and he has little opportunity to save and get ahead. Food is surprisingly expensive. Most of the better land is held by large holders and corporations who emphasize commercial export crops, so virtually every island has to import food, just as it did during the slave period. As a result, many West Indian families spend as much as three-fourths of their total income for food alone.

Among West Indians, particularly those of the lower classes, which are made up of Negroes and colored elements, there is a growing tendency to blame the largely white upper classes and the governing powers for the plight of their communities. This feeling has intensified class and racial frictions, and has given rise to a growing demand for greater political autonomy and a stronger voice for the Negro masses. Nationalism and popular unrest have characterized the West Indies for many years, particularly since World War II. Universal suffrage has become accepted at least in theory everywhere, and the government, which in many territories was the privilege of the upper class, has fallen increasingly under popular control.

Popular unrest has brought about other political changes in the archipelago. The French islands have become overseas departments of metropolitan France, with full representation in the French Parliament; the Netherlands Antilles have achieved equality in a joint partnership with Holland and Surinam; the British territories (minus the Virgin Islands and the Bahamas) experimented unsuccessfully with federation; and Puerto Rico has become a commonwealth, freely associated with the United States. In the independent territories, political change since World War II has been of a different order, but the rise of Castro in Cuba, the overthrow of Trujillo in the Dominican Republic, and the various upheavals in Haiti are symptoms of the same unrest which characterize the rest of the archipelago.

The roots of unrest and political change in the West Indies are deeply imbedded in the problems of land and economics. Political moves, whether revolutionary, as in Cuba, or voluntary associations, as in the British territories, or other, are dominated primarily by a desire to improve economic conditions. Regardless of the strength of the desire for independence in Puerto Rico, economic necessity dictated a compromise solution. The French and Dutch territories chose to continue their associations with the mother countries because their economies would not otherwise be viable. The British territories federated largely in the hope of obtaining economic advantages, and both Jamaica and Trinidad chose to withdraw and go it alone because they foresaw little economic gain from the association.

Local Variations. The foregoing discussion has touched on transition for the Antillean archipelago as a whole, but its generalizations are seldom totally applicable to any individual territory. At local levels, there have been many variations on the central themes and on the search for new adjustment during the last century. Differences from island to island in population growth and density, political connections, availability of foreign capital, the history of commercial crop production, location, size and resources of the territories, industrial development, opportunities for emigration, and in other factors have resulted in the occurrence of a wide range of local patterns and problems.

This variety of local patterns, however, can

be more effectively appreciated from the analysis of individual territories.

Cuba and Puerto Rico

Cuba and Puerto Rico have run surprisingly parallel courses through much of their post-Columbian history, even though the role of the larger island has been more important. Both were among the first colonies established by Spain in the Caribbean. Through the early colonial history both served as springboards for the exploration of the mainland and as island fortresses guarding the sea lanes between the mother country and the richer settlements on the mainland. Except for these functions, however, neither island was given much importance by Spain following the conquest of Mexico and Peru; and the growth of population and economy was consequently retarded in the two colonies.

While sugar and slaves were introduced in Cuba and Puerto Rico in the sixteenth century, neither island experienced an early plantation development comparable to the English and French West Indies colonies. Until the nineteenth century, the limited economy of both islands remained essentially subsistent. Grazing, food crops, and small quantities of tobacco, sugar, and other cash crops were the mainstays of the largely white population.

In the first quarter of the nineteenth century, when Spain's mainland colonies achieved independence, Cuba and Puerto Rico were left behind. Agitation for freedom swept both colonies, but their small size and insularity enabled Spain to retain control until the Spanish-American War (1898). Nevertheless, the long-delayed economic and population growth finally overtook the two colonies during the 1800's. The plantation became firmly established and Negroes came in large numbers, first as slaves and then as free workers. The economy became increasingly commercial—sugar and tobacco in Cuba; coffee, sugar, and tobacco in Puerto Rico.

Both islands became pawns in the Spanish-American War. Following the war, Cuba was granted a questionable independence and Puerto Rico became a territory of the United States. This difference not withstanding, however, the economic and political destinies of both islands became intimately inmeshed with those of the United States.

On paper at least, the commercial economies of the two islands forged strongly ahead during the first part of the twentieth century. With preferential treatment in the rich United States market, the production of sugar, tobacco, and other cash crops expanded at a prodigious rate. This spelled wealth for a number of Cubans, Puerto Ricans, and foreign investors, but it left the growing masses of people on both islands far from satisfied with their lot.

Following World War II, the restive populations called for change. Both islands achieved change of a sort: Puerto Rico chose the road of political and economic evolution to improve the lot of its people; Cuba followed the path of revolution. The destinies of the two islands seemed to have parted company.

CUBA

Cuba has become an enigma with a beard. Castro's revolution and the swing to communism has placed the island behind an iron curtain. Current information is skimpy and unreliable. But from the Spanish-American War until Castro's takeover, Cuba's economy functioned as a tropical adjunct to that of the United States. Commerce, agriculture, industry, tourism, mining—all bore the deep stamp of the American connection. Now this relation has come to an abrupt end. Trade with the United States has dwindled to virtually nothing, and the island looks to the U.S.S.R. and other communist countries. One can only assume that this disruption, coupled with the radical political, social, and land reforms going on in Cuba will, if continued, bring about major modifications in the island's land-people patterns and relations. Details are lacking, however, and long-range forecasts are risky. The following analysis does not wholly disregard the beginnings of change in Cuba's land-man relations set in motion by the revolution, but the backbone of the presentation is supported largely by data of the pre-Castro period.

Physical Setting

Location.   The historical and strategic values of Cuba's location have already been cited. The island sits astride three important narrows: the Straits of Florida; the Windward Passage; and the Yucatan Channel (see Figure 3.4). For much of the colonial period, Spain looked on Cuba (and especially Havana) as the "bulwark of the Indies" and "the key to the New World." The acquisition of Guantánamo Bay by the United States following the Spanish-American War was further recognition of the island's strategic position at the principal gates to the Gulf of Mexico and the Caribbean Sea.

Cuba's location has also paid rich economic dividends. Within a radius of 1,500 miles from Havana lies the vast market of east-central United States, much of it accessible by cheap water transportation. Before Castro, this market absorbed virtually all of Cuba's tropical products and minerals. Proximity to a large group of well-heeled Americans also meant a tourist income of almost $100 million a year.

The island's ocean-borne commerce is aided by a highly articulated coastline. Because of its narrow width, no part of the island is far from one of the 200 harbors that dot the coast. Except for Matanzas and Cárdenas, all of the principal harbors are pouch-shaped and, as a result, Cuba has an extraordinarily large number of well-protected anchorages.

Relief and Rainfall.   With an area of 44,218 square miles, Cuba is easily the largest of the Antilles. The long, narrow island stretches southeastward for almost 800 miles, from Cape San Antonio on the Yucatan Channel to Punta Maisí on the Windward Passage, and its width ranges between 25 and 120 miles. Cuba is the least mountainous of the Greater Antilles, and her soils are well adapted to large-scale, machine agriculture. Most of the terrain consists of the gentle slopes and lowlands which form the Peneplain of Cuba. This "almost plain" runs the length of the island and represents the final stages of great erosional cycles that have reduced large limestone accumulations to gentle relief. In zones of more resistant rock, the plain is marked by erosional remnants of bolder relief; elsewhere, a series of terraces have been formed, now somewhat dissected by short streams, so that the land is moderately hilly.

There are three distinct mountain systems (Figure 5.1), all roughly oriented east-west and generally known in Cuba as the *oriental,* the *central,* and the *occidental.* In extent, altitude, mass, and complexity, the eastern system is the most striking. It covers most of Oriente province and parts of adjacent Camagüey, and consists of two main ranges: the Sierra Maestra, which parallels the south shore; and a line formed by a number of mountain groups, such as the Sierra de Nipe and the Cuchillas de Toar, which runs along the north shore. Between the two ranges is the lowland of the Central Valley and the Cauto River. The Sierra Maestra, which reaches elevations of over 6,500 feet, is indented here and there by embayments such as those of Santiago and Guantánamo but for the most part the range is bold, continuous, and difficult to penetrate.

The central mountain system of Cuba is much lower than the eastern, and covers less area. It consists of several low ranges, of which the most important is the Trinidad-Sancti Spíritus in southern Las Villas province. The western system is in Pinar del Río and is made up largely by the Sierras de los Órganos and del Rosario. The mountains

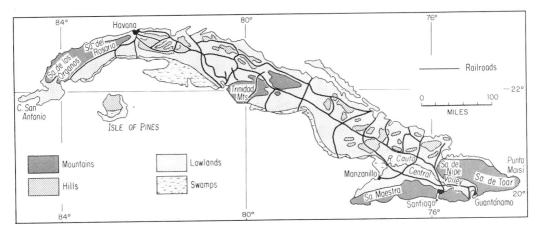

Figure 5.1
Cuba : Surface Configuration and Railroads.

rise in the marshy lands near Cape San Antonio and run eastward for more than 100 miles. The rocks of this system are primarily limestone, and the erosive action of water on the limestone has resulted in thousands of caves. Knobs of more resistant rocks, called *mogotes,* resemble gigantic organ pipes, and it is from this characteristic feature of the western landscape that the Sierra de los Organos derives its name.

The interaction of this generally moderate relief and the Trades results in less contrast in precipitation than is found between the windward and leeward sides of the more mountainous Antilles. Rainfall ranges from over 65 inches annually, in the Sierra de los Organos and the Trinidad Mountains, to less than 40 around Guantánamo, in the rain shadow of the Sierra Maestra (Figure 5.2). No part of Cuba is truly deficient in moisture.

Land and the Cuban Economy

Land Use. The present use of land in Cuba's economy reflects a variety of influences, but especially the interplay of physical conditions, market possibilities, and the impact of institutions which have controlled agricultural organization and tenure. A favorable combination of climate, relief, and soils gives Cuba one of the highest ratios of cultivated to cultivable land in Middle America. Roughly

Figure 5.2
Cuba : Soil Groups and Rainfall.

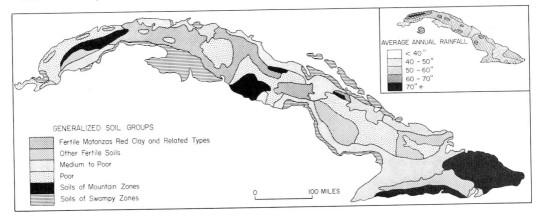

one-fifth of the island is under crop and two-fifths are in pasture. If permissive physical conditions were the sole criterion, almost two-thirds of Cuba's total surface (28 million acres) could be classified as arable.

Not unexpectedly, sugar cane normally occupies over half the cultivated land. No other single crop takes up as much as 10 per cent, although food crops, including corn, yucca, plantains, beans, yams, and others, account for about one-third of the land in crops. No significant percentage of the land is planted either in tobacco or coffee. The amount of land in pasture indicates the importance of livestock, the practice of rotating pasture and cropland, and the conditions which have kept land use extensive rather than intensive in Cuba.

Of the nonarable land, over 10 per cent is classed as woods, but much of this woodland consists of scrub growth from cutover forests and is of little economic value. Nonarable land also includes large areas of *marabú*, a leguminous shrub which was brought to Cuba from its native South Africa as an ornamental plant. It has since spread so rapidly that it now covers hundreds of square miles with an impenetrable tangle which is encroaching on crop and pasture land.

Like every other facet of the Cuban economy, these land-use patterns have developed largely in response to market possibilities, particularly those offered by the United States since 1900. As the nearest and most accessible of the low-latitude lands, the island became a convenient source of tropical farm products and other raw materials for the American market and a reciprocal buyer of American finished goods. In the decade preceding the communist takeover, the United States supplied an average of three-fourths of Cuba's imports and absorbed almost four-fifths of her exports. This relation gave the island favorable access to the world's richest marketplace and to a large supply of development capital, but it also entailed some serious disadvantages. Cuba's dependence on its northern neighbor came to verge on the

slavish. Everything from food, machinery, and lipstick to airplanes and roller skates came neatly wrapped from the United States and was expensive. The exploitation of Cuba's land resources, which was determined by the needs of the American market, became grossly uneven, and the unbalanced economic posture which resulted was a classic illustration of monoculture. Heavy emphasis on the production of a few profitable commercial crops, such as sugar, retarded agricultural diversification; the pressure to buy American finished goods tended to discourage industrialization; and above all, the United States tie helped to intensify the spread of the plantation and the *latifundium,* with all their inherent drawbacks.

Land Tenure. Although neither the *latifundium* nor the plantation was a twentieth century innovation introduced by American investors in Cuba, both institutions were strengthened by such investment. The trend to large landholdings can be traced back to the *hatos* and *corrales* of the colonial grazing era (see Chapter 3), and the plantation had undergone considerable development in the nineteenth century.

Nevertheless, before 1900, Cuba still had a large number of small independent farms and family-size *ingenio* plantations. With the passage of time, many of the large land grants made in the colonial period had been replaced by *comuneras* (collective holdings). As a result of the multiplication and scattering of heirs, as well as other difficulties of inheritance, the large properties came to be roughly divided into *pesos de posesión* (shares of possession), whose title was held in common by the descendants of the original owners. Up to 1900, other land-people conditions were also less intense. Thus, land values (while higher than they had been before the rise of the nineteenth century plantation) were moderate, particularly in the thinly settled eastern provinces. Squatting was widespread, and squatters were seldom evicted from private property. Landless peasants did not have a significant cash income, but under the easygoing paternalistic system of the times, money was not essential to survival.

Then came the Americans with their profitable market potential, their genius for corporate enterprise, and more than a billion dollars to invest in Cuba's sugar industry. The effects of this invasion on the island's land tenure structure and economy were revolutionary. Land values shot upward; the collective holdings of the *comunera* gave way to direct private ownership; the small owner was squeezed out; and the corporation, whether foreign or national, became the chief instrument of agricultural organization and land ownership. Many of the small farmers who lost or sold their holdings became *agregados* (hired hands). With the emergence of a highly specialized sugar plantation agriculture based on *latifundium* and efficient corporate management, Cuba was transformed into an industrial wage economy. This helped to destroy the traditional paternalistic relation between landowner and worker; it made squatting more difficult for the increasing number of landless peasants; and it pegged the well-being of the *guajiros* (peasants) to a money wage.

The rapid concentration of land in Cuba took place over the first two decades of this century, and then began to reverse itself. Overproduction had saturated the market for sugar by the 1920's, and it was no longer profitable to continue acquiring more land. In addition, the growing resentment of Cubans against a virtual monopoly of the industry by a handful of companies, often foreign-owned, resulted in restricting legislation. The most important of the measures taken were contained in the Sugar Coordination Law of 1937 and in certain provisions of the 1940 Constitution. The legislation was aimed at protecting the *colonos* (small sugar cane farmers who either own their own land or rent it from the *central*, and are dependent on the *central* for milling their cane), limiting the maximum amount of land which a

corporation or individual might own, improving the wages of cane workers, and encouraging the transfer of ownership from foreigners to Cuban nationals. These measures brought about some relief from the burden of the *latifundium,* and resulted in the transfer of a number of mills and other property from foreign to Cuban ownership. Apparently the relief was not sufficient, however, for Castro's major rationalizations for his swing to the left became "agrarian reform" and the abolishment of "foreign monopoly."

Castro's Agrarian Reform Law (May 17, 1959) is an emotional testament against the *latifundium* and foreign monopoly. It prohibits large landholdings and sharecropping and it prevents sugar manufacturers from operating their own plantations. The law also provides that only Cubans can buy or inherit land and that each family (of five persons) is entitled to receive a "vital minimum" of 67 acres, "provided that the...land is available and the economic and social conditions of the region so permit." The instrument for implementing these and other measures is the INRA (*Instituto Nacional de Reforma Agraria*) but, like other instruments of the revolution, INRA has fallen into the hands of inexperienced men who appear more dedicated to a policy of totalitarian politics than to reform.

The kindest observation that can be made about Castro's agrarian reforms is that it is too early to evaluate their impact. The initial period of reform has been characterized by political instability and international pressures, by social disruption which has made refugees of a large segment of Cuba's technicians and professionals, by a radically new market orientation for the island's exports, and by the inability to replace American-made equipment as it breaks down or becomes obsolescent.

These handicaps not withstanding, it was apparent by the 1960's that Castro's agrarian reform had failed to achieve its more important goals. The *latifundium* and monopoly are not dead—they remain in the form of large government-owned farms worked by a landless peasantry under a state monopoly. Slavish dependence on foreign markets, equipment, and capital has not been abolished—it has merely been transferred from the United States to the U.S.S.R. and other communist countries. Monoculture has not disappeared—it has only become less efficient. True, there is less importation of food; but this may be due more to a tightening of belts than to greater production.

Sugar

Spread and Transport Impact. Sugar cane has been called "the grass of Cuba," and for good reason. The island possesses an almost ideal environment for growing the crop (see Chapter 4). It has large areas of level-to-gently-rolling land which facilitate harvesting and the rapid transportation of the cane; its tropical climate generally provides sufficient rainfall and the necessary dry season for the *zafra* (harvest) ; and the sugar lands are within easy distance of the coast with its numerous pouch-shaped harbors.

Despite these natural advantages, a combination of inadequate land transport, political instability, and other obstacles restricted sugar to a few select zones until 1900. The bulk of production was concentrated in the western part of the island, particularly in the provinces of Habana, Matanzas, and Las Villas. The larger, eastern end of the island was devoid of sugar, except for spotty development such as along the coast southwest of Manzanillo and the Central Valley—Guantánamo Basin area of Oriente.

With the influx of American capital after 1900, Cuba's sugar frontier started to move out in all directions. Ultimately, however, its major direction became eastward, toward the unoccupied or thinly settled lands of Camagüey and Oriente provinces. There was some penetration into Pinar del Río, but there the Sierra de los Órganos, poor soils, and a high population density of small tobacco farmers posed obstacles. Cane also was blocked from

most of Cuba's south coast by widespread swamps or by the rugged relief of the Trinidad and Sierra Maestra ranges (Figure 5.1).

Sugar's initial thrust outward from its western center after 1900 generally followed the line of the productive Matanzas red clay soils to eastern Camagüey. These soils are deep (in places exceeding 25 feet), and are composed of residues from dissolved limestone. They are so fine-grained and permeable that, despite a clay content of 75 to 90 per cent, they may be cultivated even after heavy rains. The Matanzas soils, which extend from Artemisa in Pinar del Río to Ciego de Ávila in Camagüey (Figure 5.2) provided the first avenue for cane's expansion and still account for fully one-third of Cuba's sugar production.

In its rapid eastward march across the rest of Camagüey province and the virgin lands of Oriente, the sugar frontier had to adjust to less desirable soil types (Figures 5.2 and 5.3). Whenever possible, however, cane producers continued to seek out clay soils, and ultimately all of Cuba's leading sugar areas were in zones of soil with a high clay content.

Relief and precipitation also played a significant part in the spread of sugar across Cuba. As already indicated, cane was ruled out of mountain zones. Practically no cane took hold on elevations higher than 1,000 feet above sea level. Currently, over three-fourths of production is concentrated in areas below 300 feet, and gentle slopes, which assure good drainage without serious erosion, are preferred. As to rainfall, most cane areas on the island receive between 50 and 60 inches per year. When other conditions are positive, cane may be grown where totals drop to as low as 40 inches.

The eastward push of the sugar frontier in Cuba not only authored the occupation of new lands and the intensification of *latifundium* and plantation; it also carried with it waves of population and brought about the development of modern transportation facilities, mills, and other major features of the landscape. Of these, perhaps the most obvious are transportation and the *centrales* (Figures 5.1 and 5.3).

Under Spanish rule, Cuba's land transport system had grown little, and most of this growth coincided with the zones of denser settlement in the western provinces focusing on Havana. The spread of cane, which must be moved rapidly from field to mill, gave rise to a widespread rail network after 1900. At present, roughly two-thirds of Cuba's more than 9,000 miles of railroads consist of narrow-gauge tracks built directly by sugar corporations. The remainder were constructed by English and American capital attracted by the sugar boom. The much-maligned sugar interests gave Cuba the densest rail network in Latin America. Over 90 per cent of the island's population are within hearing distance of a train whistle (Figure 5.1). If fewer highways than railways have been built, one important explanation is that the sugar industry took less interest in automotive transport.

Centrales and Regions. The new large sugar mills (*centrales*) are more than factories for grinding the crop. They have functioned as mechanisms for owning land and controlling the *colonos,* as reference points for the transportation network, and as nerve centers for administering the total operations of the large sugar plantations. The amount of sugar land needed to feed the *centrales* varied but, before Castro, the average mill owned (or controlled through *colonos*) about 40,000 acres, and the largest serviced 165,000 acres.

The *centrales* came into their own in Cuba after 1900. Prior to that, the island's cane was milled for the most part in moderate-size, closely spaced *ingenios*. In 1860, for example, Cuba had about 2,000 such mills, but by 1900, the destruction ensuing from the wars of independence had reduced their number to 207. Only about 100 of the larger *ingenios* were subsequently retained, and most of these are in the old sugar areas of the western provinces (Figure 5.3).

The need for larger modern mills to facilitate the development of sugar production resulted in the construction of over 60 *centrales* between 1902 and 1927. Most were constructed by American companies on their newly acquired cane lands in Camagüey and Oriente in eastern Cuba. In contrast to the older, smaller, and largely Cuban-owned mills which controlled relatively small plantations, the modern *centrales* built by foreign capital came to control huge blocks of land.

Thus, the location and spacing of sugar

Figure 5.3
Cuba : Sugar Lands and Centrales.

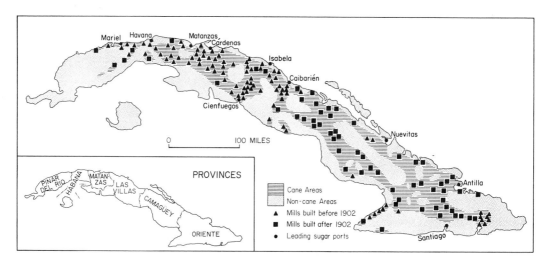

mills in Cuba (Figure 5.3) are revealing not only of the industry's history, the size of land-holdings, and the degree of foreign ownership, but also serve as important criteria for regionalization. Using these as criteria, Dyer delineated 13 sugar districts in Cuba but, to avoid detail, we are combining them into three major units: (1) the eastern, consisting primarily of Camagüey and Oriente provinces; (2) the central, which focuses on Las Villas; and (3) the western, which includes the provinces of Matanzas, Habana, and Pinar del Río.[1]

Briefly, the eastern region is the most recently developed and the most distinctive of the three. Prior to 1900, this region was devoid of sugar except for spotty development on the coast, such as around Manzanillo and Guantánamo, in Oriente, and the hinterland of Nuevitas, in Camagüey. The mills of these older areas tend to be smaller and more closely spaced and a high percentage of them were owned by Cubans. Elsewhere, particularly in northwestern Oriente, the mills are more modern, larger, and were primarily American-owned. It was here that the *latifundium* and foreign ownership reached their extreme. Cane in the eastern region has had to adjust to generally poorer soils and to a greater variety of environmental conditions than is the case farther west. The adjustment was made primarily in the form of more extensive plantings, fewer ratoon crops, and more rapid rotation with pasture. For shipping, the eastern cane lands rely on 11 ports, of which the most important, in terms of tonnage, are Nuevitas in Camagüey and Santiago and Antilla in Oriente.

The central region in Las Villas is the least important. The mills are generally smaller, older, and have been owned by Cubans. The holdings are smaller, there are more *colonos* and land use is more diversified. The principal sugar port of this region is Cienfuegos, on

the south coast, but the ports of Isabela la Sagua and Caibarién, on the north coast, are of some importance.

Cuba's western region (Pinar del Río, Habana, and Matanzas) is set off by a number of characteristics. It includes most of the highly productive Matanzas clay soils and the old pre-1900 nucleus of sugar production; within it is refined most of the sugar used on the island, as well as a limited amount which is exported; and it includes some of the most intensively utilized sugar land in the country. The mills are less densely spaced than in Las Villas, but they are denser than in the eastern region. Many are small, older carryovers from the nineteenth century and are associated with Cuban ownership, but the region also includes several larger *centrales* constructed after the establishment of the United States connection. Not unexpectedly, the chief outlet is the port of Havana, which has been second only to Nuevitas in the export of sugar from Cuba. Other important sugar ports serving the region are Matanzas, Cárdenas, and Mariel (Figure 5.3).

Problems. Cuba's sugar economy was beset with a multiplicity of problems well before Castro added further to its woes. It has been technologically stagnant ever since the middle 1920's. Neither the government nor the producers devoted significant sums to research following the sugar depression in the third decade of this century. The most widely planted cane on the island, for example, was developed by the Dutch in Java after World War I and is not necessarily the best suited to Cuba's soil and climatic conditions. No new *central* was constructed in Cuba after 1927 and, while the existing mills were kept in repair before Castro, the equipment and the technique for grinding cane have undergone only slight improvements in the last half century. Machinery for the agricultural phase of production has been kept more up-to-date, but the fierce opposition to labor-saving innovation by farm workers who feared for

[1] D. R. Dyer, "Sugar Regions of Cuba," *Economic Geography,* vol. 32, 1956, pp. 177–184.

their jobs has kept mechanization well below that of Hawaii and other advanced sugar producers. Planting, weeding, and cutting are still largely done by hand, and the ox is indispensable both for plowing the fields and hauling the cane to railroad sidings. Yields can be substantially increased by fertilizing and irrigation, but during the 1950's only about one-tenth of the crop was fertilized and slightly over 1 per cent was irrigated. Cuba's cane yields have been above the average of most other producing areas, but this reflects the large blocks of land held in reserve and the rapid rotation, rather than efficiency in production.

The industry has also been plagued by a market fluctuation which has affected both production and national income. Sugar output rose rapidly during the first decades of this century, increasing from less than a half million tons in 1900 to four million tons in 1919; it continued to be high until market saturation and the effects of the Great Depression caused a drop (from five million tons in 1930 to two million in 1933); and thereafter, output rose irregularly to all-time highs after World War II, only to tumble to less than four million tons when Castro took over. Price as well as production reflected varying market demands. For example, in 1920, the average price of a pound of sugar was 11.95 cents bringing about what Cubans call the "dance of the millions"; in contrast, the 1932 crop sold for only 0.71 cents per pound, bringing hard times to the door. Some price stabilization was achieved after 1933, when Cuban sugar was included in the United States quota system, but considering that sugar and its byproducts continued to make up more than 80 per cent of the value of its exports, the island's economy remained and remains vulnerable to the vagaries of sugar prices. Probably no other national economy in the world is so completely dependent on the sale of a single product.

In other respects, Cuba's sugar problems parallel those of other sugar areas. There is the usual seasonality in the use of both labor and equipment. After the *zafra,* which lasts

for about four months, the mills stop grinding, most of the labor force is laid off, and a vast array of equipment, including railroads, highways, ports, and other facilities, is underutilized. The large amount of uncultivated land which the sugar plantations have held in reserve not only created a landless peasantry but made necessary a heavy and expensive importation of food. In recent years, the island has had to import over 40 per cent of its food calories. Food importation under Castro is less, but so is the caloric intake of the population. Many argue that, nevertheless, the sugar industry gave pre-Castro Cuba one of the highest standards of living and per-capita incomes in Latin America. Such arguments are academic, however, if the *guajiro* was ill-fed and dissatisfied.

Other Cash Crops and Grazing

Crops other than sugar in Cuba are many, but of limited importance. Cane has so completely dominated land use during this century that other products, even when commercial in nature, have been relegated to lands considered unsuited for sugar plantation requirements. Similarly, since "big money" was interested solely in sugar, production of other cash crops has been left largely to the small landholders and the sharecroppers. Land use for subsistence food crops has been at an even greater competitive disadvantage. We have observed that the amount of land devoted to subsistence is large, but of poor quality. With some exceptions, grazing also has been associated with the small holder and poor land.

Tobacco. Despite its worldwide fame, tobacco normally occupies less than 3 per cent of the land under cultivation and provides slightly more than 5 per cent of the exports by value. But Cuban tobacco has been important in other ways. It was the island's first significant export crop, and during the colonial period it was the economic backbone of the white, small landholder.

Tobacco cultivation began in Cuba during

the late seventeenth century and, by 1717, its export had become so profitable that the Spanish Crown imposed a monopoly on sales. Despite an armed uprising by the *vegueros* ("tobacco farmers"), the monopoly was retained for a century, helping to discourage any major expansion of tobacco growing. The abolishment of the tobacco monopoly and the liberalization of trade in 1817 were followed by a sharp increase in the number of *vegas* ("tobacco farms") and by the first factories for producing cigars and other tobacco products. At the start of the wars of independence (1868), there were over 1,000 small factories, primarily in Havana, and over 10,000 *vegas,* mostly in Pinar del Río and Las Villas provinces. The wars destroyed a major segment of the industry and sent tobacco workers as refugees to Florida, where they established cigar manufacturing in Tampa and Key West. By the end of hostilities there were fewer than 500 factories left on the island.

Unlike sugar growing, tobacco production received little impetus from the establishment of the United States connection in 1900. Neither American nor Cuban investors showed interest in producing the crop. Tobacco farming was too risky, required far too much care and labor and, compared with sugar, promised too few profits to attract the investment dollar. As a result, Cuba's tobacco

production experienced only a modest increase between 1900 and 1960, and the export of quality cigars actually decreased. On the eve of Castro, there was little *latifundium* associated with tobacco, although sharecropping was widespread. In Pinar del Río, for example, the average *vega* measured less than two *caballerías* (66 acres). Even such small plantings required 20 to 30 hired hands or sharecroppers.

While tobacco is grown practically everywhere on the islands, Cubans traditionally recognize five major regions (Figure 5.4). The most important of these is the famous Vuelta Abajo, which is concentrated for the most part along the lowlands and foothills south of the Sierra de los Órganos in Pinar del Río. There, a combination of undulating terrain with excellent drainage, red to greybrown soils with a high sand content, and tobacco farming know-how which goes back more than two centuries, produces the island's finest crop. This leaf is bright brown, aromatic, and mild, and is used for better grade cigars. The region consists of several districts (Llano, Lomas, Remates, Guane, Costa Norte, and Costa Sur) and the tobacco of each district is recognizably different, the very finest wrapper leaf being grown under cheesecloth in the Llano. A smaller region, called the Semi-Vuelta, adjoins the Vuelta Abajo to the southeast. In the Semi-Vuelta,

Figure 5.4
Cuba: Tobacco, Coffee, and Rice.

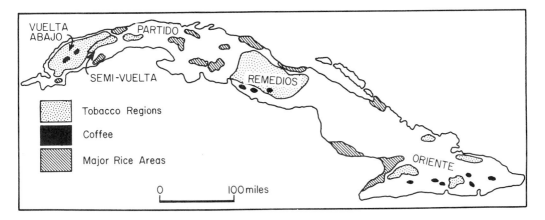

Figure 5.5
Cuba : Vuelta Abajo District Near Viñales. Note the typical Cuban bohios ; malanga, a common food crop in the foreground ; and a sector of the Sierra de los Órganos in the background.

the leaf has a heavier body and a stronger aroma, and is blended with other tobaccos as cigar filler. The soils of the tobacco lands in Pinar del Río are too poor for sugar, and there has been little competition for their use.

In contrast, the rich red soils of the Partido region to the southeast of Havana have been increasingly taken over by winter vegetables and sugar. Production has dropped from over 7 million pounds, before World War I, to less than 1.5 million pounds at present. Much of the Partido tobacco is grown under shade to produce a large, light-colored leaf of fine texture which is used as wrapper on clear Havana cigars manufactured for the English export market.

In terms of area and production, Cuba's leading tobacco region is the Remedios (also called Vuelta Arriba), most of which is in Las Villas province. A combination of swampy coasts and generally mountainous terrain in this province has functioned to keep much of the area the domain of the small farmer. The tobacco leaf grown on the slope land of the Remedios is of poorer quality and is characterized by a heavy, gummy texture. However, it blends well with lighter leaf for cigar fillers and, before Castro, it was largely exported to the United States for use in machine-made cigars. The tobacco grown in the four widely separated districts of the Oriente region is of even lower quality. Most of the production is too poor for export and is sold in the Cuban market.

The bulk of Cuba's tobacco is exported in leaf form, but a reduced number of small cigar and cigarette factories continue to operate on the island. At present there are about 1,000 such factories, employing an average of eight workers. These are found in all parts of the island but, as in the colonial period, the major concentration is in Havana.

Coffee and Rice. Coffee is a cash crop, primarily sold in the Cuban market. Introduced into Oriente province by French refugees from St. Domingue in the late 1700's, the plant flourished during much of Spanish colonial period. At mid-nineteenth century, for instance, Cuba counted over 2,000 coffee *fincas,* producing over 50 million pounds per year. This was sufficient not only for the island's needs, but for considerable export as well. With the advent of sugar, coffee was neglected, particularly at the turn of the century. Recent attempts by the Cuban government to aid the industry have resulted in an occasional export surplus.

As in Puerto Rico, coffee grows in the highlands. The chief producing region continues to be in the mountains of southern and eastern Oriente province, where the French introduced it. A second region is in the mountains between Cienfuegos and Trinidad in southern Las Villas province, and the third is in the uplands of Pinar del Río (Figure 5.4). Most of the crop is grown under shade trees by small farmers or sharecroppers.

Government encouragement has also stimulated rice production since World War II. Rice with beans makes up a substantial part of the Cuban's food intake. Prior to the War, Cuba imported over 90 per cent of her rice, mostly from the Orient. The small amount of rice produced locally was of the dry or upland type, because Cubans feared the mosquito and malaria-breeding potentialities of wet rice fields. When the War cut off imports from the Orient and forced the importation of much more expensive rice from the United States, wet rice production in Cuba became potentially profitable as long as the needs of the wet rice industry for level land did not displace any sugar. Most production is clustered on poorer soils around Manzanillo in Oriente, La Florida in Camagüey, Consolación del Sur in Pinar del Río, and elsewhere (Figure 5.4).

Grazing. Grazing was Cuba's first industry (see Chapter 3), and it remained in the lead until surpassed by sugar in the late 1700's. It was unable to compete with plantation agriculture, however, and was pushed off the best lands during the nineteenth century. Grazing was dealt a further blow during the wars of independence, when more than three-fourths of the island's cattle were wiped out. After 1900, the herds were slowly built up again, aided by imports from Venezuela and the introduction of special breeding stock from the United States and India, but there are reports that the food shortage under Castro is again causing depletion of the herds.

Cuba's climate permits almost year-round pasturing, providing cheap feed, particularly for the cattle, which are the most important livestock. Cattle are fed exclusively on grass (principally Guinea and Pará). Lack of supplementary fodder becomes a problem during the dry season when much of the grass becomes dry and unpalatable.

Since almost 40 per cent of Cuba's total area is classified as pasture, stock raising is of some significance throughout the island. However, the major concentration occurs in the poorer lands in the east-central part of the island (Camagüey-Oriente) where, before Castro, there were large ranches. Elsewhere, grazing was either carried on by the small-scale operator, who owned an average of less than 100 head, or functioned as a supplementary economy on the sugar plantations. The widespread use of oxen for plantation work and the large blocks of land rotated with pasture by the cane growers made cattle raising an important adjunct to sugar production. Much of Cuba's cattle is of poor quality *criollo,* or native, stock, but there has been constant upgrading by crossing local cattle with imported brahma from India and Santa Gertrudis cattle from Texas.

Population

Historical Growth. The growth and the composition of Cuba's population may be closely correlated with the island's commercial economy, especially plantation agriculture based on sugar (Figure 5.6). Other important influences include the impact of political disturbances, and the elimination of tropical diseases such as malaria and yellow fever.

The history of Cuban population growth lends itself to a fourfold division: (1) the preplantation period, from the early sixteenth century to the British capture of Havana in 1762; (2) the *ingenio* plantation period, from 1762 to the outbreak of the wars of independence in 1868; (3) the war period, from 1868 to 1900; and (4) the *central,* or modern plantation period, from 1900 to Castro's revolution.

The growth of Cuba's population in the preplantation years (1512–1762) was slow and erratic. Such colonists as arrived during the first decade or two of colonization were largely siphoned off by Cortes' venture to Mexico and other expeditions. In 1537, the estimated population of the island was 5,800, of which 300 were Spaniards, 500 were

Figure 5.6

Cuba : Sugar and Population.

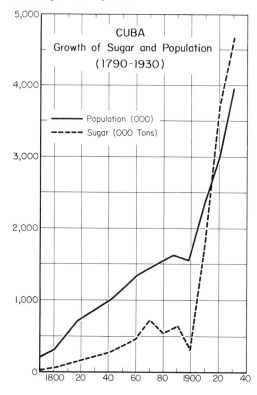

Negro slaves, and 5,000 were Indians. Thereafter, the Indians were largely wiped out and European immigration dwindled to a trickle except for a block of 8,000 Spaniards that arrived from Jamaica following the English capture of the island in 1665. The total number of African slaves imported during the preplantation period is estimated at 60,000. A few of these were employed in the tiny *trapiche*-type sugar industry, but most of them were absorbed by the more important occupations of grazing and tobacco-food crop agriculture. Except in and around Havana, Cuba remained thinly occupied through most of this period. In 1762, the population was probably less than 150,000.

The brief English occupation of Cuba (1762–1763) set the stage for the expansion of sugar production based on the plantation and slavery. The first census, 1774, counted a total population of 171,620, composed 56 per cent of whites and 44 per cent of Negroes. Despite some political unrest before 1868, population expanded rapidly, along with sugar production (Figure 5.6). A small part of this was due to natural increase, but most of it was due to new arrivals, including French refugees from the slave uprising in Haiti, a steady flow of Spanish immigrants, the arrival of Chinese indentured servants and, above all, the importation of roughly one million Negro slaves.

During the period of instability resulting from the wars of independence, 1868–1899, the population of Cuba tended to decrease. The insular economy was badly disrupted; immigration was drastically reduced; slavery was abolished (1886–1887); and large numbers of people died. In an effort to deprive Cuban rebels of popular support, the Spaniards herded much of the rural population into concentration camps. There are no precise figures as to the number of people who lost their lives from famine and disease in these camps, but estimates place the number of dead at almost 200,000 under the regime of the infamous Valeriano Weyler alone.

With the coming of independence, integration with the huge United States economy, and an unprecedented expansion of sugar and other industries, Cuba's population again rose dramatically, increasing more than fourfold between 1899 and 1959. Large-scale immigration again played an important role, although natural increase, prompted by general political stability and the elimination of dreaded diseases such as malaria and yellow fever, was also responsible. The major growth (ranging from 3.1 to 3.4 per cent annually) occurred from 1899 to the eve of the Depression of the early 1930's. Thereafter, the rate of increase dropped as immigration was substantially reduced.

The correlation between population growth and sugar production has been all but absolute in the history of Cuba. Not only has the total number of inhabitants risen in almost direct proportion to sugar output, but the greatest population increases have taken place precisely in the provinces of rising cane production. For example, in 1911, the eastern provinces of Oriente, Camagüey, and Las Villas contained 52 per cent of the total population and accounted for 60 per cent of the island's sugar output; in recent years the percentage of population and sugar production in these same provinces has risen to roughly 60 and 75, respectively. The correlation is even more striking when one considers the fact that the three western provinces (Pinar del Río, La Habana, and Matanzas) include the huge urban concentration of metropolitan Havana.

Migrations and Racial Composition. Migrations in Cuba have been the chief determinants not only of population growth but also of racial composition. With the destruction of the Indians, the leading elements in the racial matrix became Spaniards, Negroes, and a wide range of mixtures between the two. As noted above, Spanish immigration to the island was limited during the first two and one-half centuries of colonization.

The first major wave of Spaniards was attracted to Cuba by the growth of sugar plantations between the latter eighteenth and the end of the nineteenth centuries. This influx was small, however, compared to the Spanish migration in the first half of the twentieth century. In the three decades from 1903 to 1933, 723,381 Spaniards entered Cuba and, while the number of later entrants was much smaller, Cuba has remained a favorite of Spanish immigrants. Spaniards on the island tend to be identified with the regions of Spain from which they came (chiefly Galicia, Asturias, and Santander). Before Castro, numerous regional clubs called *Centros Asturianos, Gallegos,* and so forth, were foci of cultural and social activity.

Immigration of other European groups to Cuba has been far less than the Spanish, and has varied according to economic and political conditions. The arrival of 30,000 French refugees from Haiti at the end of the eighteenth century has already been mentioned. At various times before 1900, Cuba also received small groups of Italians, Germans, and other Europeans, but the major influx of non-Spanish whites occurred after 1900. Among the more than one and one-quarter millions of immigrants between 1900 and 1950, there were more than 25,000 Americans and, after 1919, considerable numbers of European Jews.

The Negroes, who constitute the other important racial ingredient in Cuba's population, fall into two groups. The first, and by far the most numerous, arrived as slaves between the 1520's and the abolition of slavery in 1887. The bulk of the slaves were brought in after 1790, and the influx was so great that, by 1817, the colored population outnumbered the white. The colored continued to form the majority until past the middle of the nineteenth century. Then their number decreased partly because of the heavy toll taken by the wars of independence. Negroes made up a large percentage of the rebel armies, and lived in the rural areas most devastated by the wars. Also, because they lived more poorly than the whites, they were felled in larger numbers by the epidemics of cholera, yellow fever, and other diseases. After independence, the percentage of Negroes decreased, in part because of the heavy Spanish immigration and in part because of widespread miscegenation.

The second Negro group arrived in Cuba as free laborers, primarily from Haiti and Jamaica after 1900. In the 30-year period from 1902 to 1932, approximately 190,000 Haitians and 121,000 Jamaicans entered the island, the peak years of this immigration coinciding with the sugar boom of World War I and its aftermath. The collapse of the sugar market in 1921–1922, coupled with the growing desire to "keep Cuba white," sharply reduced the importation of West Indian Negroes.

Other nonwhites brought to Cuba include Chinese and small numbers of Yucatan Indians. Labor shortages during the nineteenth century resulted in contracts for 132,-435 Chinese indentured laborers (13 per cent of whom died in passage) between 1853 and 1873. Small numbers of Chinese came in later as free migrants, but the total of pure Chinese in Cuba now is less than 20,000 and the shortage of women is causing the gradual extinction of this Oriental group. The number of Yucatan Indians brought in probably did not exceed a few thousand, and no trace of these is left.

Emigration has been of minor importance in Cuba except in times of political stress. The largest single block of emigrants (over 250,000) has been composed of refugees from Fidel Castro's regime. Most went to the United States, but also to other Caribbean areas, such as Puerto Rico, Costa Rica, and Venezuela.

Density and Distribution. With a present population of 7.3 million, the ratio of people to arable land in Cuba is the lowest in the West Indies. Despite the rapid population increase following independence, the island has not experienced land hunger except when it has been man-made. If arable land were the sole criterion, it would take almost 150 million people to saturate Cuba to the present densities of Puerto Rico.

The spread of settlement in response to economic growth since the colonial period has periodically altered the relative distribution of population on the island. Until the end of the eighteenth century, Havana and its immediate hinterland contained the only significant population nucleus in Cuba. With the beginnings of large-scale sugar production, population movement tended to be to the western lands lying closest to the capital city and chief port. By the middle of the nineteenth century, the western provinces of Pinar del Río, La Habana, and Matanzas, only one-fourth of the island's area, had almost two-thirds of the total population. Transportation to the rich lands of the eastern interior remained so poor during the wars of independence that Cuba's population center remained well to the west until the twentieth century. After 1900, the growing pressure for new sugar lands and the construction of railways and roads pushed settlement eastward. By 1943, the center of population coincided with the east-west geographic center of the island, and the shift to east continues slowly, counterbalanced by the rapid growth of Havana.

The spread of settlement was by no means uniform, however. It varied according to soil fertility, accessibility, transportation, and the growth of industry. As a result, the density and distribution of population is still quite irregular. The lowest densities occur on the poor and often swampy soils of the Isle of Pines and on the peninsulas of Guanacabibes in Pinar del Río and Zapata in Las Villas. Poor soils or poor drainage are also responsible for the scarce population of the coastal regions of Camagüey and the north coast of Las Villas. Other areas of low densities are the result of low precipitation, as exemplified by Oriente's leeward coastal strip from Guantánamo to Cape

Maisí, or are associated with the more rugged mountain zones, such as parts of the Sierras Maestra and de los Órganos. It is significant, however, that despite the abundance of land, many of the mountain areas in Cuba have considerable populations. Small farmers squeezed off the more desirable lowlands by the plantation have found refuge in the highlands, as they have elsewhere in the West Indies.

At the opposite end of the density scale are the immediate vicinities of the larger cities such as Metropolitan Havana, and the *municipios* of Santiago, Camagüey, and Holguín. These, of course, include many of the major commercial, industrial, and political centers. Following these urban zones are the Vuelta Abajo tobacco region of Pinar del Río and the sugar lands of northwestern Matanzas, central Las Villas, western La Habana, and the Central Valley focusing on Holguín. The high density pattern of the Vuelta Abajo stems from the large numbers of small tobacco farmers. The densities of the sugar lands reflect chiefly soils of high fertility, such as the famous red clay Matanzas varieties and the alluvial deposits of the Central Valley.

Urbanization has proceeded with striking rapidity in recent decades. All the island's urban centers of over 25,000 inhabitants have experienced unusual growth, especially Greater Havana, whose 1.2 million population is more than five times that of Holguín, the second largest city. (Other large cities in the order of their size are Camagüey, Santiago, Santa Clara, Guantánamo, and Cienfuegos.) Another type of population shift has resulted from the movement of the *guajiros* (peasants) from their dispersed *bohíos* to small agricultural villages, usually of less than 1,000 inhabitants. During the last 30 years, hundreds of such villages have sprung up in the Cuban countryside, especially in Oriente. Cuba's communist geographer, Núñez Jiménez, claims that more than two-thirds of the island's population may now be classified as urban, but this figure probably

disregards the largely agricultural function of many of the new villages. There is little doubt, however, that well over half the population is legitimately urban and that the movement to town continues unabated.

The trend to urbanization is due in part to the expansion of urban functions such as industry, commerce, and government, but much of it reflects simply the desire of the *guajiro* to escape the often drab and wretched existence of rural life. The concentration of political largess, social services, and entertainment in the cities serves as a magnet. The dispersed *bohío* pattern remains characteristic of rural settlement, however, especially in the mountain districts.

The Balance Sheet :
Cuban Man-Land Relations

A disturbing continuity of inadequate institutional equipment and external forces has plagued man-land relations in Cuba. The *latifundium* of Spanish grants and the monopoly of colonial trade created the beginnings of a landless peasantry and limited the utilization of land to a few products. The connection with the United States after independence intensified both the *latifundium* and monoculture and added the burden of large foreign ownership of land and resources. Castro's brand of communism eliminated foreign ownership, but actually intensified the *latifundium*. The fact that the *latifundium* is now based on state rather than private ownership has not altered its negative effect on the *guajiro*. Thus, despite a favorable location, a well-articulated coastline, good climate and topography, a plentitude of arable land, and other resources, most Cubans have experienced, and continue to experience, want in the midst of plenty.

A major cause of this unfortunate discrepancy has been international interference, attracted by Cuba's favorable location and economic potential. From its earliest post-Columbian history, the island has been buffeted by international stress which placed the strategic, political, and economic interests of outsiders above the welfare of the Cubans. Under Spain, the island had neither economic nor political independence. Cuba rid herself of Spanish colonialism only to fall victim to the economic colonialism imposed by sugar and the American market, and now her break with the United States has plunged her into an even more brutal colonialism as a satellite of the U.S.S.R.

Cuba has become an enigma with a beard. Her future is uncertain, but there are grounds to believe that this future, like the past, is not likely to be wholly in the hands of the Cubans themselves.

PUERTO RICO

There seem to be too many Puerto Ricans for Puerto Rico, and for many years the discrepancy between its limited resources and growing population appeared hopeless. But there has been a new optimism abroad on the island since the end of World War II. The birth rate has been leveling off and even dropping. Puerto Rico, with its "Bootstrap" program, has become a showcase for what a determined people can achieve even with puny natural resources. Equally important, their economic development is taking place within a democratic framework, without Castro-type revolution and dictatorship.

Physical Setting

In contrast to Cuba, Puerto Rico is a mere 3,500 square miles of eroded mountain land and tired alluvial soils. The island is slightly over 100 miles long, with an average north-south width of 35 miles (Figure 5.7). More than three-fourths of its surface consists of mountains and hills. The main mountain chain, called the Cordillera Central in the west and the Sierra de Cayey in the east, forms the island's backbone. Its average elevations are roughly 3,000 feet, and it

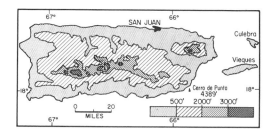

Figure 5.7
Puerto Rico : Relief.

reaches a maximum of 4,388 feet at Cerro de Punta south of the town of Jayuya. Other mountain masses are those of Luquillo in the northeast and the Atalaya range in the northwest. The remainder of the island consists of interior valleys, such as that of Caguas and a narrow ribbon of coastal plain which reaches a maximum width of 13 miles at Lares on the north side of the island.

Puerto Rico's dominantly mountainous terrain gives rise to sharp windward-leeward contrasts. Precipitation varies dramatically, from over 200 inches in the northeast-facing Luquillo mountains to less than 30 inches at Cabo Rojo in the southwest corner of the island. Most of the land to the south or leeward side of the central mountains is too dry to be cultivated without irrigation.

Compared to Cuba, Puerto Rico is more removed from the rich American market and her coastline is less well articulated. San Juan, the capital, is 1,600 miles from New York and 1,700 miles from New Orleans. The island has several harbors, such as San Juan, Mayagüez, and Playa de Ponce, but the number of anchorages with sufficient depth and protection are few and they are often located on the less developed south coast.

Agricultural Economy

Puerto Rico's industrialization has been so rapid that the island already lists manufactures as its leading export. But this can be misleading. The insular economy remains firmly rooted in agriculture. The number of people directly employed in farming is more than twice the number in manufacturing, and if to this is added the workers engaged in the processing of agricultural products, the ratio is much larger. The importance of agriculture is also apparent from its role in generating private income other than wages, and its high percentage contribution to the gross national product.

Land Use and Production Structure. The diversity of terrain, climate, and soils permits a wide range of agricultural activity in Puerto Rico. This, coupled with the high density of rural population, has resulted in the utilization of even the marginal lands on the island, so that almost four-fifths of the total area is under crops and pasture (Figure 5.8). Much of this is mountainous terrain which was once covered with tropical rain forest, and it is generally cultivated by the poorer, backward, small farmers. The more productive coastal plains and valley bottoms have been absorbed by the plantations and larger landowners.

Sugar cane still reigns supreme in the farming domain of Puerto Rico, and as long as the island remains within the United States quota system, there is little likelihood of its dethronement. The crop occupies almost half (the better half) of all the cultivated land; all other agricultural exports are relatively insignificant. Cane has traditionally dominated land use on the coastal plains and in the interior valleys, such as the Caguas lowland. In order to take advantage of the large sugar quota assigned to Puerto Rico by the United States, however, farmers are now planting cane on the lower mountain slopes and on other marginal land. The amount of land in cane has almost quadrupled since 1898, and, despite attempts to diversify agriculture, the island's farming is a typical example of plantation monoculture.

Tobacco, used largely as cigar filler in the United States, is an extremely poor second to sugar as an export product and it occupies less land than other major crops, such as coffee, bananas, corn, and starchy vegetables. Production is confined primarily to the humid eastern half of the Central Cordillera, where

Figure 5.8
Puerto Rico: Land Use.

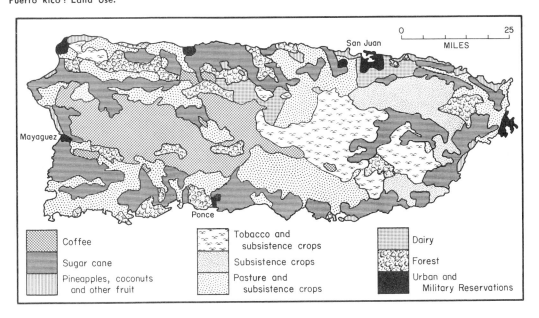

Coffee

Sugar cane

Pineapples, coconuts and other fruit

Tobacco and subsistence crops

Subsistence crops

Pasture and subsistence crops

Dairy

Forest

Urban and Military Reservations

it generally provides the cash income of small farms of less than 20 acres. Approximately one-fourth of each farm is planted in tobacco, the remaining land being devoted to food crops and pasture. Because of a fluctuating market and a tendency to overproduce, a tobacco quota restriction is imposed by the Insular Department of Agriculture.

Coffee occupies an amount of land second only to sugar, but it is no longer an important export. It is raised by small farmers in the western highlands, along with other tree crops such as oranges and avocados. In the last days of the Spanish regime, coffee was Puerto Rico's chief export, but current production is so limited that often it is insufficient to meet local needs. Unlike sugar, the robust Puerto Rican coffee found little favor in the United States.

About one-fifth of the cultivated land is in food crops, especially starchy root vegetables and plantains. In fact, food products often occupy more land than cash crops, everywhere except on sugar land. Fruits are raised in small quantities in all crop regions. Except for pineapples, which are exported, there is no outstanding fruit area, and most fruit is consumed locally. Dairying has expanded continuously since World War II, and the current value of production exceeds the combined income from tobacco and coffee. About half the island's fresh milk is produced on the north coast, within a short distance of San Juan. Despite this growth, Puerto Rico continues to be deficient in both dairy products and meat.

Farm Practices. While some improvements have been made in agricultural techniques in recent years, farming is still primitive by American or European standards. Hand labor continues to be dominant, but machinery is being introduced at a significant pace, particularly in dairying and in sugar production. Machines cannot be used on much of the land because of the steep slopes, the smallness of the holdings, and other obstacles. But even on large sugar farms which might profitably employ machinery, its introduction is often hampered by workers' unions, which fear displacement.

Tools are few and simple. The most ubiquitous is the long knife, or machete, which is used for cutting, digging, and a variety of other purposes. The ox-drawn plow is common except on the small farms and the steepest mountain lands. The typical peasant uses little more than machete and hoe.

The most widely used work animal is the ox, but many small farmers cannot even afford this animal. Small, wiry horses are used both for farm work and transportation, especially in the mountains. Virtually every small farmer keeps a few animals for food, chiefly scavengers such as pigs, chickens, and goats. Trucks for transporting cane to the mills and food crops to market are generally owned by the large farmers or merchants.

The farmland has been worked for so long that little will grow without heavy fertilization. The small number of animals does not provide sufficient natural fertilizer, and most has to be imported at a high cost from the United States. As a result, fertilizers are sparingly used, and crop yields tend to be low except in the better sugar lands. Large farms practice crop rotation and leave a substantial part of their land fallow. The small farmer also practices rotation, but his limited holdings prevent him from leaving sufficient land fallow. In fact, the peasant has to practice interplanting of beans, corn, and other food crops to obtain the maximum yield.

Since much of the planted acreage is on slope land, erosion is a major problem. Terracing is almost unknown, although contour plowing is making headway (Figure 5.9). The most widespread guard against erosion is the crisscrossed, diamond-shaped pattern of furrows that is dug on the mountain sides to reduce the velocity of runoff.

Land Tenure and Land Reform. The advent of plantation agriculture created a

Figure 5.9
Contour Farming on Puerto Rico's Heavily Populated Mountain Lands. (*Government of Puerto Rico*)

landless peasantry in Puerto Rico, as it did everywhere else in the West Indies. The attack on this problem is one of the major features of the postwar "Bootstrap" program on the island. Significant results have been achieved, but what remains to be done is even more significant.

Viewed historically, large-scale sugar monoculture, with its typical patterns of large plantations, developed only to modest extent in Puerto Rico during the last century of the Spanish regime. Before the United States occupation, about three-fourths of the cultivated land on the island was in small holdings averaging about 12 acres. The United States military reported in its Census of 1899 that "this general ownership of farms has unquestionably had a great influence in producing the contented conditions of the people on this island, as contrasted to the restlessness of Cuba, where a large proportion of the cultivated area is in the hands of comparatively few landlords."

Between the time of United States occupation and World War II, however, profound changes occurred in the island's pattern of land tenure. Small growers were swallowed up by great plantations, which were owned by a handful of wealthy local families and absentee Americans. Sugar farming spread to areas previously used for food production, and the cost of living behind the protection of United States tariff walls proved very expensive. The patrimony of the small farmers was bought by the sugar companies, and people often found themselves working as *agregados* (hired hands) on land that their fathers had owned for centuries. By 1940, only 16 per cent of the cultivated land was in small farms of less than 20 acres. Most of these were in the mountains or on marginal lands unsuitable for sugar, and few were sufficiently productive to provide a living for their owners. More important, the bulk of Puerto Rico's farm workers had no land at all. The plight of Puerto Rico's landless population grew steadily worse, especially during the Great Depression (1929–1940).

In an effort to avoid land monopoly by large corporations, the United States Congress had added the Five-Hundred-Acre Law as part of the original Organic Act for the newly acquired territory. This law was conveniently disregarded and, 40 years after its passage, 51 corporations controlled 249,000 acres of Puerto Rico's best land. One of these actually had over 50,000 acres. This was the situation and the problem on the eve of Puerto Rico's famous *jalda arriba,* the "uphill push" under Governor Muñoz which is transforming Puerto Rico into a showcase for progress.

In brief, Muñoz's reform program began with the enforcement of the Five-Hundred-Acre Law. About half the land illegally held by the corporations was purchased by the government for various uses. Some of it is incorporated into proportional profit farms owned by the government, with profit-sharing by workers, and some has been sold to small farmers in plots not exceeding 25 acres; more, while owned by the government, was given in usufruct to communities of landless farm workers. Land that was not suitable for farming was turned over to the forestry service. In addition, the Insular Land Authority was empowered to acquire barren and swampy lands for purposes of reclamation.

Not all the corporate land in excess of 500 acres was forced into sale, but enough was acquired to drastically weaken the stranglehold of large land owners on the farming economy. Today the sugar corporations of Puerto Rico are primarily industrial enterprises which run the *centrales.* Government farms and *colonos* supply most of the cane.

Puerto Rico's land reform is part of an over-all development program which includes industrialization, expanding the tourist trade, and improving transportation, housing, education, medical, and other social services. As such, it is difficult to isolate the specific benefits derived from land reform. It is

obvious, however, that: (1) thousands of landless peasants have acquired land or otherwise improved their lot; (2) there has been some crop diversification, leading to a slightly more balanced agricultural economy; (3) new lands are being reclaimed and the standard of land use has been made more efficient; and (4) the government is in a position to stimulate more scientific agricultural practices. These have not eliminated the problem of insufficient land for a growing population, but in the words of the *jíbaro* (peasant), *"Algo es algo"* (It's better than nothing).

Manufacturing

Since 1940, figures on the total number of new manufacturing plants established in Puerto Rico have had a way of being always obsolete. By mid-1962 the number was approaching 700 but, considering the growth trends of the past decade, this figure may increase by the score with each passing year. Puerto Rico has become the example to emulate, not only for the rest of the Caribbean but for all of the Free World's underdeveloped areas. How is an overcrowded tiny piece of tropical real estate lacking in minerals, energy fuels, capital, and many technical skills achieving industrialization?

Factors in Industrial Growth. There is no single answer to this question. Industrialization is part of an over-all developmental program which was started in 1941, initially aided by money coming into the island during World War II. The program fostered improvement in health, education, and housing to raise living standards and increase labor productivity. It built modern roads, airports, fast communication, and supplied abundant electrical power to facilitate manufacturing and commerce. Government agencies were created to aid the development of private enterprise and, when necessary, to invest directly in industrial and agricultural ventures.

The government's role in aiding new industry has numerous facets—direct and indirect subsidies, free plant sites and factory buildings, training of workers and supervisors, and an endless number of services ranging from the entertaining of potential investors to conducting advertising campaigns in the United States. Under Puerto Rico's Industrial Incentives Act, new manufacturers are exempt from corporate taxes, personal income taxes, and property taxes for periods of from five to ten years. An additional incentive was provided by the establishment of a Foreign Trade Zone, an enclosed area near the western city of Mayagüez where foreign and domestic merchandise may be entered without being subject to customs law.

Finally, there are the all-important advantages stemming from the connection with the United States. Puerto Rico is characterized by political stability and the democratic process in government. It offers the American investor cheap labor and other incentives, without the dangers common to investments outside the United States. There are no tariff walls separating the island from the continental market, and there is complete freedom of movement for both goods and people. American rule has helped to develop a well-trained officialdom and an efficient corps of civil servants.

Nature and Distribution of Manufacturing. Lest we be blinded by figures, the most important manufacturing industry in Puerto Rico remains the processing of the island's chief cash crop—sugar cane, although there are other old industries, such as the manufacture of beer and rum, which existed before the new industrial surge. Except for some of the sugar mills, most of the older industries are owned by Puerto Ricans and either process agricultural products or produce goods for the local market. Factories owned by local capitalists tend to be family enterprises rather than corporations.

The new industries which are coming to the island are characterized by a large number of small factories employing an average of 70 workers each; they are often branch plants of United States corporations and are largely owned by American stockholders (Figure 5.10). (Puerto Rican capitalists are still shy about investing in industry.) Manufactures cover a wide range of products, from handkerchiefs to electronic equipment, and

Figure 5.10
New Industry for Puerto Rico. Many of the island's new factories are branch plants of United States corporations.

most industries can be classified as light, labor-oriented enterprises. The United States provides the bulk of the raw materials as well as the markets for the new manufactures.

The new industries are generally located in large urban centers which have port facilities and other services. The San Juan metropolitan area, which contains about a third of the island's population, has received almost half the new jobs created by incoming industries. Next in line of preference are the port cities of Mayagüez, on the west coast, and Ponce, on the south coast, two cities which follow San Juan in total population. Large port cities are preferred because they afford cheap external transportation for both the raw materials and the finished products which move by sea between Puerto Rico and the United States. In addition, the major cities have larger labor pools and the necessary legal, banking, and recreational facilities.

The smaller interior towns, especially those in the highlands, have received only a small share of the new industry. Most of these interior centers have adequate electric power and are easily accessible by all-weather roads, but the added cost of transportation and the paucity of essential services have worked against them. In an effort to foster location of industry in towns outside the major urban clusters, the government offers special incentives. The island has been divided into incentive zones, and subsidies are paid in indirect proportion to the desirability of the location.

Tourism

Hundreds of thousands of free-spending visitors are annually providing still another substantial income for Puerto Rico. In the 1959–1960 season, the gross income from tourism was estimated to be over 50 million dollars, and is still rising. Tourism, like other segments of the insular economy, has been expanding constantly since 1941. During the

1950's it increased more than sixfold, and it now ranks third in economic importance, agriculture and manufacturing being the first two. Tourism is part of the over-all developmental program.

Because of its climate and natural beauty, Puerto Ricans call their island *La Isla del Encanto* (The Isle of Enchantment). But this beauty yielded only poetry and songs until the Puerto Rican government and a series of gratuitous circumstances conspired to attract the Yankee dollar. In the absence of private capital, the government built the now-famous Caribe-Hilton hotel in 1948 and leased it to the Hilton chain, a venture which was so successful that the government has recouped its investment and is now netting a profit of over one million dollars a year from it. The success of this and other hotels (such as La Concha) built at public expense stimulated private investment, and numerous hotels, including Laurence Rockefeller's sumptuous nine-million-dollar Dorado Beach, have been built or are on the drawing boards (Figure 5.11).

Other factors have combined to stimulate tourism: the continuous postwar prosperity of the United States; the capture of much of the Cuban tourist trade following Castro's Revolution; and, perhaps above all, "the biggest airline bargain in the world." The cheap air fare between the island and major United States cities originally aimed at migrating Puerto Ricans; now it also provides transportation for tourists at less cost per mile than a New York subway.

Like the new manufacturing industries, tourism tends to be concentrated in the large coastal cities, especially San Juan. That the shortage of facilities in the interior is only a partial explanation for this was demonstrated when a beautiful hotel built in the highlands at Barranquitas failed soon after it opened its doors. Tourists have not discovered the interior, and it may be that most of them prefer the sea and the night clubs of San Juan to the fresh air of the mountains.

Figure 5.11
New Hotels for the Booming Tourist Trade, San Juan, Puerto Rico. (Government of
Puerto Rico)

Population

Growth and Racial Composition. For almost three centuries following its initial colonization in 1508, Puerto Rico's population grew very slowly and remained essentially European. The first official census (1765) counted fewer than 45,000 inhabitants, of whom about 5,000 were Negro slaves. Most of this population was thinly distributed along the humid north coastal plain, the island's interior being largely unsettled. The dominantly subsistent economy and the small importance which Spain attached to the island effectively controlled population growth.

Beginning in the latter eighteenth century, the tempo of population growth began to increase, and the frontier was rapidly pushed to the mountainous interior. During the nineteenth century, 35 new towns were founded, mostly in the highlands—almost the number of settlements which had been established in the previous three centuries. By 1830, the island had 315,000 inhabitants and, by 1899, the population had almost trebled to 953,000.

The growth in population was stimulated largely by the expansion of the island's commercial economy, coupled with some immigration. Land under cultivation increased from 117,000 acres, in 1830, to 183,000 acres, in 1862, and reached a total of 274,000 acres by the end of the century.

This increase in land under cultivation was prompted primarily by the expansion of commercial crops such as sugar and coffee (Table 5.1). With the Schedule of Grace in 1815, Spain opened the island to world commerce. Significant plantation development occurred, aided by the immigration of French and Spanish planters from Louisiana, by royalist refugees from the revolutions in Venezuela and Colombia, and by immigrants from France and Corsica after the fall of Napoleon. These newcomers bought Crown lands on liberal terms, and engaged in the production of commercial crops.

The growth of plantations created the usual shortage of labor. Large numbers of Negro slaves were imported, and the plantation altered the racial composition in Puerto Rico as it had done elsewhere in the Antilles. In 1845, the island had over 50,000 slaves and about 175,000 free Negroes;; by 1898, there were 570,187 whites, 239,808 people of mixed blood, and 75,824 Negroes. The plantations and their Negro laborers were concentrated on the coastal plains, the highland interior remaining the domain of a large number of small white farmers who raised coffee and food crops.

Following the American occupation, there was a gradual decline in the death rate which, coupled with further expansion of commercial agriculture, kept the rate of growth of Puerto Rico's population high (Figure 5.12). By 1940, the total had reached

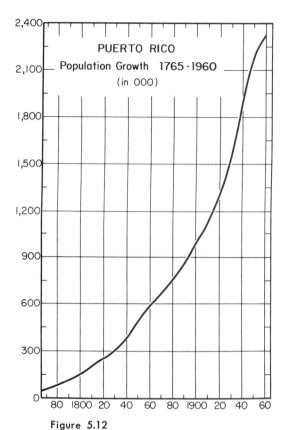

Figure 5.12

Puerto Rico: Population Growth, 1765-1960.

2 million, and a decade later it had surged to above 2.2 million despite considerable postwar emigration. Gradually, birth control, a rising standard of living, and emigration have begun to take effect. The birth rate has begun to drop, and future population increases are expected to be more modest.

Puerto Rico has the lowest percentage (20.3) of nonwhites in the West Indies. The ratio of Negroes to whites had decreased with each census taken during this century, and the colored element is being slowly absorbed into the basically white matrix of the population. Interestingly, the Negro population is still concentrated largely on the sugar lands of the coast. The population of the highlands continues largely white, and it is not uncommon to see blond Gallego youngsters running barefoot in the streets of the mountain villages.

Table 5.1

INCREASE OF LAND UNDER CULTIVATION IN PUERTO RICO: 1830–1896

Crop	Cuerdas* in 1830	Cuerdas in 1896
Sugar	15,242	62,000
Coffee	17,247	122,000
Food Crops	83,177	91,000
Other	5,334	7,000
Total	121,000	282,000

* One cuerda equals .97 acre.

Densities and Distribution. Population densities in Puerto Rico are close to the highest in the world. The simple ratio of people to land is almost 700 per square mile, but the number of persons per square mile of arable land is about 1,700, and many rural areas of the islands have densities as high as comfortably-spaced American suburbs.

Not unexpectedly, the zone of highest population density is the humid north coastal plain which runs from Luquillo in the east to Aguadilla in the west. Sugar, pineapples, dairying, and other farm enterprises make this the richest agricultural area on the island. Its cities are also the leading industrial and commercial centers. The major regional focus is the San Juan metropolitan area, with a population of over 400,000. There are other cities, however, with the result that the northern plain has the largest number of urban dwellers in Puerto Rico.

The eastern interior valleys and highlands focusing on the city of Caguas are the second most densely settled areas. Here agriculture is the dominant economy—sugar cane in the valleys, and tobacco and food crops in the mountains. During the recent industrial surge, some small factories have been established in the towns of this region.

Other zones of high density are the east coast, with its sugar and pasture lands; the western mountains, with its coffee; and the irrigated sugar lands of the south coastal plain. In fact, there are only a very few areas of low density. Chief among these are the Sierra de Luquillo in the northeast and the dry leeward margins of the southern uplands and unirrigated plain.

With well over 40 per cent of its 2.5 million people living in towns and cities, Puerto Rico ranks as one of the most urbanized islands in the West Indies. The movement from country to town has been especially strong since World War II. The flow, especially to greater San Juan, including the cities of Santurce and Río Piedras (but also to other urban centers, which have been growing rapidly), has been prompted by various forces, including industrialization and expanding education. For many people, the move to the city is the first leg of their emigration to the United States.

Cultural Characteristics of the People. Puerto Rico remains a Caribbean island of Hispanic culture. More than 60 years of involvement with the United States have failed to alter the basically Spanish cultural values of the people; in fact, it has often strengthened them. While English is widely taught, only about one-fourth of the people are truly bilingual, and most of these are urban middle-and upper-class people. The once-obligatory teaching of American history evoked little enthusiasm. The Anglo-Saxon, Protestant virtues illustrated by the tale of George Washington and the cherry tree he cut down were out of place in a tropical Catholic land without cherry trees. Despite the widespread efforts of American Protestant missionaries, the vast majority of the population remains Catholic.

There has been some selective borrowing from Americans. The democratic process in government is more firmly established in Puerto Rico than anywhere else in Latin America; Puerto Ricans have recognized the advantages of American managerial skills, planning, and technical know-how and are applying them with some modifications to their own environment, and they measure economic progress by United States rather than Caribbean standards. In most other respects, however, Puerto Rico is determined to retain its Spanish cultural heritage. Were it not for the economic advantages accruing from its relations with the United States, the island might well ask for total independence.

¿A Dónde Vas, Puerto Rico?

Puerto Rico, once the "poorhouse of the Caribbean," is now glowingly referred to as the "Laboratory for Democracy" and the

Figure 5.13
Feast of San Sebastián in San Juan, Puerto Rico. (Alcoa Steamship Co.)

"most rapidly developing territory in the Western Hemisphere." Glowing language aside, the island's economic and political achievements are indeed impressive. Since 1950, the total net income of the Puerto Rican economy has been growing at an average rate of 6 per cent yearly. Per capita income, $122 per year in 1939, is now the highest in Latin America. Incoming industry has created 100,000 new jobs, and wages paid to labor have gone from $125 million in 1940 to over $800 million in the early 1960's. During the same period, life expectancy climbed from 46 to 70.6 years. Measured by the yardstick of gadgetry such as tele-

phones and television sets, the growth is equally strong. Puerto Rico is by no means out of the economic woods, but the forest is thinning and the sunlight is shining through. By Latin American standards the island is well ahead of the pack, but Puerto Ricans insist on measuring economic progress by United States standards.

Puerto Rico has accepted a rational political compromise. There is little desire for statehood within the United States, but most Puerto Ricans have accepted the idea that total independence is a luxury that they cannot afford without disastrous economic consequences. The island enjoys a wide measure of local political and cultural autonomy, pays no federal income taxes, and has no direct representation in the United States Congress. Its people have full United States citizenship and are subject to United States law in matters of defense, international relations, tariffs, and currency. Except for a small minority of rabid nationalists and *independistas*, Puerto Ricans realize that this is as close as they can come to having their cake and eating it, too.

SELECTED REFERENCES

Baer, W., "Puerto Rico: An Evaluation of a Successful Development Program," *Quarterly Journal of Economics*, LXXIII, No. 4 (1959), 645–71.

Crist, R. E., "Some Notes on Recent Trends in Rice Production in Cuba," *Economic Geography*, XXXII, No. 2 (1956), 126–31.

Dambaugh, L. N., "Tobacco Production: Vuelta Abajo Region, Cuba," *Journal of Geography*, LV, No. 9 (1956), 442–46.

Doerr, A. H., and D. R. Hoy, "Karst Landscapes of Cuba, Puerto Rico, and Jamaica," *Scientific Monthly*, LXXXV, No. 4 (1957), 178–87.

Dyer, D. R., "Sugar Regions of Cuba," *Economic Geography*, XXXII, No. 2 (1956), 177–84.

Guerra y Sánchez, R., *Sugar and Society in the Caribbean: An Economic History of Cuban Agriculture*. New Haven, Conn.: Yale University Press, 1964.

Hanson, E. P., *Transformation: The Story of Modern Puerto Rico*. New York: Simon and Schuster, Inc., 1955.

Jones, C., and R. Picó, *Symposium on the Geography of Puerto Rico*. Río Piedras, P. R.: University of Puerto Rico Press, 1955.

MacPhail, D., "Puerto Rican Dairying: A Revolution in Tropical Agriculture," *Geographical Review*, LIII, No. 2 (1963), 224–46.

Marrero, L., *Geografía de Cuba*. Havana: Editorial Minerva, 1950.

Matthews, H. L., *Cuba*. New York: The Macmillan Company, 1964.

Mintz, S. W., "The Culture History of a Puerto Rican Sugar Plantation: 1876–1949," *The Hispanic American Historical Review*, XXXIII, No. 2 (1953), 224–51.

Nelson, L., *Rural Cuba*. Minneapolis: The University of Minnesota Press, 1950.

Noyola, J. F., "Aspectos Económicos de la Revolución Cubana," *Investigación Económica* (Mexico), XXVIII (1961), 403–25.

Núñez Jiménez, A., *Geografía de Cuba: Adaptado al Nuevo Programa Revolucionario del Bachillerato* (2nd ed.). Havana: Editorial Lex, 1959.

Ortiz Fernández, F., *Cuban Counterpoint: Tobacco and Sugar*. New York: Alfred A. Knopf, Inc., 1947.

Picó, R., *The Geographic Regions of Puerto Rico*. Río Piedras, P.R.: University of Puerto Rico Press, 1950.

Steward, J. H., *et al.*, *The People of Puerto Rico: A Study in Social Anthropology*. Urbana: University of Illinois Press, 1956.

Wilgus, A. C., *The Caribbean: Peoples, Problems, and Prospects*, Caribbean Conference Series One, No. 2. Gainesville, Fla.: University of Florida Press, 1952.

6

The Greater Antilles: Hispaniola and Jamaica

Hispaniola

The boundary line separating Haiti and the Dominican Republic on the island of Hispaniola is one of the sharpest cultural divides in the Americas. To the west of the line, the Haitian landscape is characterized by a predominantly rural occupance strongly reminiscent of West Africa. Irregularly oriented thatched houses are dispersed through the countryside or come together haphazardly to form tiny agricultural villages. Surrounding the rural settlements are patchy networks of fields owned largely by the peasantry and devoted primarily to subsistence crops. The hoe and machete are the chief farm tools and, in line with African custom, farm surpluses are sold by women who carry the products to periodic markets in the towns. There is little on the Haitian landscape which suggests either the twentieth century or a European colonial origin. Transportation is largely accomplished by human porters and overloaded donkeys who walk along narrow trails; industry is all but absent; facilities for social services are rare; and enterprise is on the penny-ante scale. The descendant of the prosperous eighteenth-century French colony of St. Domingue is racially essentially Negro and culturally more African than European. Only the ruins of European estate houses, sugar mills, and irrigation canals which dot the Haitian countryside speak of the prosperous past.

To the east of the international boundary on Hispaniola is the Dominican landscape, also dominantly rural, but with differences. Large estates, worked by landless tenants and devoted to commercial crops and cattle grazing, are more conspicuous than small peasant holdings. The plow, and even an occasional tractor, may be found side-by-side with the machete on the large farms. A sizable network of roads connects the major settlements and facilitates circulation; Dominican products move to market largely by trucks and rail. Industry is less conspicuously absent than in Haiti, and buildings, housing, hospitals, schools, and other services are not so rare as to evoke surprise from the passing observer. The Dominicans are primarily mulatto, but a history of bitter opposition to Negro Haiti has them fiercely Hispanic and European in their cultural attachment and orientation. It has been said that "the Dominican thinks white," regardless of his color.

The contrasts are due, in some measure, to differences in man-land ratios and relations. Haiti has few empty areas. Although its population is concentrated on the heavily mountainous western third of the island, it has well over 3 million people, and over-all densities exceed 300 persons per square mile. The intense search for land and living has often driven the Haitian *paysan* to the Dominican frontier, Cuba, and elsewhere. In the Dominican Republic, on the other hand, land hunger, and hunger in general, is far less acute than in Haiti. With a population only three-fourths as large as Haiti's, the Dominicans occupy a territory almost twice as large. There are still many thinly settled areas apt for colonization, particularly in the border provinces facing Haiti. In fact, one of the oldest themes in Dominican history has been the search for a means of safeguarding

Figure 6.1
The Haitian-Dominican Boundary on the International Bridge at Dajabón.

their borderlands against the burgeoning population pushing eastward from Haiti. This theme, and its inherent danger, is still very much present.

Physical Setting

Terrain. "Beyond the mountains are more mountains," runs an old Haitian saying, and it is an apt description of Hispaniola's rugged and complex terrain. Steep-sided highlands dominate the physical landscape virtually everywhere on the island. While the four major mountain systems and the parallel ribbons of lowlands which separate them are oriented roughly east-west, individual ranges and valleys within the system strike out in a variety of directions. The relief patterns of Hispaniola are the most complex in the West Indies, and generalization with reference to landforms is possible only at the sacrifice of important detail.

A simplified landform classification of the island points up several major regions (Figure 6.2). Beginning in the north, the first of these is the Cordillera Septentrional or Sierra de Montecristi, which lies wholly within the Dominican Republic. This region consists of several parallel ranges and isolated mountain blocks separated by intermontane valleys and patches of coastal plain. Elevations in the northern highlands seldom exceed 2,500 feet, but the steep, narrow-crested ranges form a distinctive landscape feature running southeast from near the Haitian border toward the Peninsula of Samaná.

To the south of these mountains are the extensive Cibao lowlands which continue westward into Haiti under the name of the Plaine du Nord. The Cibao varies in width from about 10 to 35 miles, and it includes within its limits a variety of drainage, relief, soil, and climatic patterns. Near the city of Santiago, the Cibao is divided into two parts by a low, hilly watershed. To the east of the divide, drainage follows the Yuna River to Samaná Bay, passing through one of the most impressively fertile districts in the world. This eastern portion of the Cibao, called the Vega Real, is easily the richest agricultural area of Hispaniola and contains one of the island's large population clusters. West of the

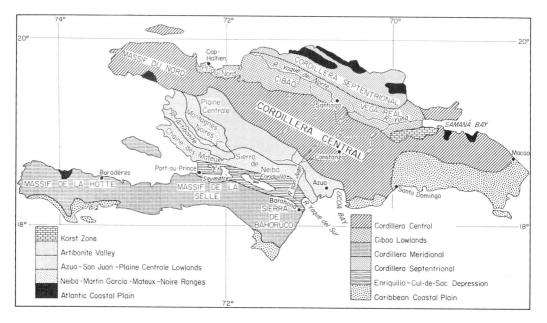

Figure 6.2
Hispaniola: Generalized Surface Configuration. *(Based on map by Schuchert)*

watershed, near Santiago, the Cibao region is less well-favored. In the valley of the Río Yaque del Norte, increasing aridity and less fertile soils limit both agricultural production and population concentrations.

Paralleling the southern edge of the Cibao is the Cordillera Central (called the Massif du Nord in Haiti), the main mountain backbone of Hispaniola. Formed from a checkered array of volcanic, metamorphic, and sedimentary rocks, the central mountains present a tangled maze of peaks and ridges with, here and there, a flat-bottomed intermontane valley. The system reaches both its maximum width (about 80 miles) and its highest elevations (over 10,000 feet) in the east central part of the island. Together with the geologically related highlands of the Samaná Peninsula, the Cordillera Central makes up more than one-third of Hispaniola. It is a significant divide between the northern population nuclei, such as those of the Cibao and Cap-Haïtien, and those to the south focusing on Santo Domingo and Port-au-Prince.

On the southwest flank of the Cordillera Central is a complex of alternating lowlands and ranges. Included in this complex are: (1) the Azua-San Juan Valley-Plaine Centrale lowlands; (2) the Sierra de Neiba range which continues into Haiti as the Chaîne de Mateux and Montagnes Noires; (3) Haiti's Artibonite Valley; and (4) the Enriquillo—Cul-de-Sac Depression. The sierras are for the most part rugged limestone mountains trending WNW–ESE; the adjacent lowland troughs are dry because of the rain shadow cast by the mountains. Geologically, the most arresting of the lowlands is the Enriquillo—Cul-de-Sac Depression. It resembles a rift valley which was once a marine strait. The depression was uplifted in such recent geologic times that it still remains largely unchanged by erosion. Parts of its dry surface are below sea level and are covered by large salt lakes such as those of Enriquillo and the Étang Saumâtre (Lac Azuey).

The only significant stretch of coastal plain in Hispaniola is on the Caribbean side of the island, between Ocoa Bay and Macao. In the Dominican Republic this coastal lowland is second only to the Vega Real in agricultural production and population concentration. It is the principal sugar plantation zone and forms the rich hinterland of Santo Domingo, the country's chief port and capital city. Smaller areas of coastal plains are also found on the peninsulas of Bahoruco and of southeast Haiti, but inadequate rainfall limits the value of these lowlands.

The last of Hispaniola's major landform regions is sometimes called the Cordillera Meridional. It consists of the Sierra de Bahoruco in the Dominican Republic and the Massifs de la Selle and de la Hotte in Haiti. This region includes several small interior lowlands, of which the most important is the Asile Valley south of Baradères in Haiti.

Climate. The complexity of terrain in Hispaniola is matched by a comparable complexity of climate and other physical elements. Tropical conditions stemming from the island's low-latitude location are modified by insularity, altitude, and the trade winds. Mean annual temperatures in the lowlands are about 78°F, except in a few walled-in spots such as Gonaïves, Port-au-Prince, and the Enriquillo Depression, where averages go above 80°F. In contrast, winter temperatures in the higher mountains, such as at Constanza, frequently drop below freezing. Thus,

temperature conditions on Hispaniola vary, with altitude, from those of the *tierra caliente* to those of the *tierra fría* (see Chapter 2). Temperatures also tend to increase from north to south and from windward to leeward as the trades sweep across the complex terrain.

Precipitation totals and distribution are equally varied, and humidity patterns on the island run the gamut from tropical rain forest to virtual deserts. As a general rule, rainfall decreases from northeast to southwest, from highlands to lowlands, and from windward to leeward exposures (Figure 6.3). For example, at Samaná, where the northeast trades sweep in off the ocean, precipitation is over 100 inches per year; at Barahona, in the southwest, totals drop to 25 inches; and in the San Juan Valley, which lies in the rain shadow of the central mountains, the total is 20 inches or less. This makes irrigation necessary or desirable for farming in much of western and southern Hispaniola, including the Artibonite Valley, the Plaine du Nord and the Western Cibao, the Culde-Sac, and other lowlands.

Vegetation. The patterns of vegetation of Hispaniola are as kaleidoscopic as the climate and terrain. There is considerable overlap,

Figure 6.3
Hispaniola: Mean Annual Rainfall.

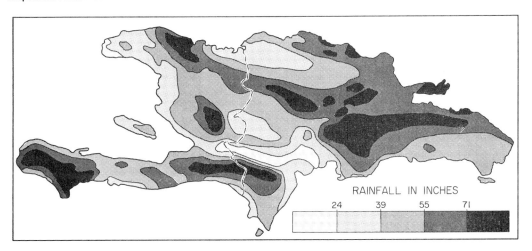

RAINFALL IN INCHES

24   39   55   71

but differences in elevation, precipitation, and other factors create a wide range of plant associations.

The driest zones, such as the Enriquillo-Cul-de-Sac Depression, the Azua lowlands, and sectors of the island's west coast, are characterized by xerophytic groupings of cactus, thorn brush, and dry scrub. In sub-humid areas such as the Artibonite Valley and the western Cibao, vegetation tends to savanna with scattered palms. Mangroves are the mark of coastal swamps, particularly at the head of Samaná Bay and the southeast coast. There is evidence that tropical rain forests once covered many of the humid lowlands in the north and northeast parts of the island, but most of this cover has been destroyed.

Hispaniola's remaining forests are confined largely to the mountains, particularly to the upper slopes facing the moisture-bearing northeast trades. The tree line on the leeward slopes is at a higher elevation than on the windward, and at the base of the mountains forests are everywhere thinner. Mountain trees vary with temperature. In the *tierra fría* of the Cordillera Central and parts of the Cordillera Meridional, pine forests cover considerable areas. Heavy cutting, particularly in Haiti, has removed virgin forests even in the mountain zones, however, and much of the cover currently classified as forest is secondary growth.

In summary, few areas of comparable size in the world offer the range and variation of ecological conditions present on Hispaniola. Elevations vary from over 10,000 feet above sea level in the Cordillera Central to 150 feet below sea level in the Enriquillo Depression. Abrupt changes from desert to jungle, from savanna to alpine forests, and from mangrove swamps to salt flats occur over comparatively short distances. The island offers a veritable laboratory for agricultural experimentation.

Haiti and the Dominican Republic have often made different adjustments to this medley of environments, largely because of the contrasting history, ethnic origin, cultural values, and institutional equipment of the two countries. Culture, rather than nature, has made Hispaniola's international boundary a sharp divide.

THE DOMINICAN REPUBLIC

A bountiful nature and an unstable history seem to have been at loggerheads with each other in the Dominican Republic. Where nature might have encouraged development, political instability has impeded it. Dominicans have seldom enjoyed the political equilibrium necessary to realize the potential of their environment and, today, after more than four and a half centuries of post-Conquest occupance, their land and resources are rarely well used.

The legacy of history was a bitter one almost from the start. Spain lost interest in her Santo Domingo colony soon after the discovery of Mexico (see Chapter 3). During the seventeenth and eighteenth centuries, while the French settlers in western Hispaniola imported large numbers of African slaves and developed the richest plantation economy in the Caribbean, Spanish Santo Domingo in the eastern part of the island remained small, economically stagnant, and largely white in racial makeup. Three hundred years of Spanish colonization had made only a dent on the landscape. By the end of the eighteenth century, Santo Domingo, with twice the territory of the neighboring French colony, had barely half the population. Its mountains and western border zones were uninhabited; its fertile savannas were divided into great haciendas, haphazardly used for cattle grazing and subsistence crops; and its Creole population, with a small number of slaves, led a slow-paced, isolated, and self-sufficient existence. This was the state of things in 1795, when Spain ceded all of Hispaniola to France and exposed Santo Domingo to the turmoil of slave uprisings that began against the French planters in the west (see Chapter 4).

From this period on the Dominican's history has been scarred with savage bloodletting engendered by the racial and cultural hatreds of the Haitians and with alternating periods of foreign domination and domestic dictatorships. To the Dominicans, the dark age of this history was the Haitian occupation (1822–1844), during which trade came to a virtual standstill, most of the white families of wealth left the country, and a planned policy of Haitianization bore heavily down on the Hispanic culture of the remaining population.

Independence, achieved with the expulsion of the Haitians, did little to bring peace and economic growth, however. Between 1844 and the United States occupation (1916–1924), the Dominican Republic was wracked by scores of revolutions, further armed invasions from Haiti, another period of Spanish domination (1861–1865), and a war to expel Spain. Fear of Haiti remained constant even after armed attacks ceased, kept alive by the peaceful penetration which occurred as the pressure of population mounted in Haiti, and its peasantry began to spill over the thinly settled Dominican border provinces.

Despite this instability, some progress was achieved in the late nineteenth century. A group of unreconstructed United States Southerners arrived in 1865, established a colony on Samaná Peninsula, and began to raise cacao. From there, cacao spread westward into the rich lands of the Vega Real, where it ultimately became a major cash crop of the rural population. Refugees from the Cuban wars of independence came during the decade 1868–1878, and created the impetus for sugar production. Later, American capital helped to make sugar plantations an important feature of the landscape, especially on the southern coastal plain.

Along with this limited economic development the population began to increase but, except for the Vega Real and the southern plains, much of the country's territory was

still sparsely occupied at the end of the nineteenth century. The mountains were uninhabited, and the western borderlands contained almost as many Haitians as Dominicans. Equally important, the chief population clusters of the Cibao and the south remained sharply separated by inadequate transportation and the barrier of the Cordillera Central.

The economic development of the Dominican Republic in the twentieth century was achieved largely during two periods of political stability. The first of these was the United States occupation (1916–1924), during which there were considerable advances in transportation. The second period of stability came with Trujillo's absolute dictatorship from 1930 to 1961.

At the cost of all personal freedom, the Era of Trujillo fomented vast changes on the landscape and in the general structure of the Dominican Republic. Population increased rapidly, new areas of settlement were opened up, and planned colonization bolstered the settlement of the borderlands on the frontier facing Haiti. Agriculture was strengthened by irrigation and the introduction of new crops. An impressive network of roads, linking all the major centers of population, was constructed. In addition, the foreign debt was paid off, new industries were created, and foreign investment capital received an encouraging welcome. Unfortunately, only a small measure of this progress filtered down to the bulk of the people, and the present patterns and problems of population, land, and resource use indicate that a continuing struggle for adjustment lies ahead.

Economic Patterns

Land is the fountainhead of the Dominican economy, but the economic structure erected on the land is far less sophisticated than that of Cuba or Puerto Rico. Most Dominican peasants are self-sufficient, to the extent that often their only cash needs are for *sal y candela* ("salt and candles"). Even the commercial phase of the national economy is distinctive in the Caribbean. The Dominican plantation is of very recent vintage. It has not achieved the intensity of production, the monopoly of land, nor the marked dependence on foreign markets that it has in most of the other Antilles. Under Trujillo, the Dominican economy resembled a feudal, patriarchal state of the past. The serflike peasants worked for and owed allegiance to the landowners, particularly to *El Benefactor,* the biggest landholder of them all; in turn, the lords of the land were supposed to take care of their peasants' minimum needs. With Trujillo's assassination in 1961, this antiquated socioeconomic structure began to change, but it is too early to determine the long-range nature of this change.

Land Tenure and Use.   One of the critical problems facing the Dominican Republic in the post-Trujillo period is the impossible legal tangle of land titles. Nowhere else in the Caribbean is the pattern of land ownership so thoroughly confused.

Originally, most land titles were derived from grants made by the Spanish Crown or by the government of the republic after independence. Many of the records of these titles are nonexistent, however, having been destroyed or lost during the turbulent period of Haitian occupation or in subsequent wars and revolutions, and much of the land now held was acquired through adverse possession, that is, through unchallenged claim or squatting over a period of years. Acquisition through adverse possession is seldom supported by clear-cut legal title.

Another factor contributing to confusion is the continued practice of *comuneras,* common holdings comparable to those existing in pre-twentieth-century Cuba. Dozens, even hundreds, of heirs of the original owner may hold *pesos de posesión,* or shares, in the *comuneras.* There may also be numerous fraudulent *peso* titles. It has often been the custom that any shareholder in the common property, though he own even one share, may enter and cultivate any part of the land not occupied by other co-owners. In the past, this haphazard way of exploiting communal holdings gave rise to a minimum of friction because there was plenty of land. With the rapid increase in population and with the growing importance of sugar and other commercial crops, however, conflict over the *comunera* system is bound to increase.

The land tenure problem has been further complicated by the expulsion of the Trujillo clan. Trujillo and his numerous relatives and favorites acquired vast holdings between 1930 and 1961. These acquisitions, including the finest sugar and grazing areas in the country, came in part from the public domain or from newly irrigated areas, but in most instances they were bought at arbitrary prices or confiscated from enemies of the state. The new government has consequently fallen heir to a large number of well-developed properties, but it has also inherited a myriad of unsatisfied claims against these holdings, and must work out a rational plan for their redistribution.

While large landholdings are more common in the Dominican Republic than in Haiti, there are exceptions to the general pattern, depending on location, accessibility, land use, values, and other conditions. Larger holdings characterize the sugar lands of the Caribbean coastal plain, the grazing areas in the uplands and savannas of El Seibo, the arid zones of the Bahoruco Peninsula, and the new, irrigated paddy rice areas in the western Cibao. Elsewhere, properties are often smaller. This is particularly true in the Vega Real, where there is a long-standing tradition among the farmers never to sell their fertile land. As a result, inheritance has fragmented holdings until they are little more than garden plots of a few tareas (1 tarea = 628.8 square meters). Thus, the *latifundium* is typically associated with cattle grazing, sugar, and paddy rice and the *minifundium* is more commonly associated with cacao, coffee, tobacco, and food crops.

For a variety of reasons, including a favorable land-people ratio and the limited importance of commercial agriculture until recent years, land use in the Dominican Republic tends to be extensive rather than intensive. Current estimates indicate that less than a fourth of the country's total area is under crop, and that an additional 12 to 15 per cent is in pasture. Much of the pastureland, however, has traditionally consisted of *sabanas,* the local designation for unimproved grasslands; *potreros* ("planted pastures") are of recent origin and less widespread.

Cropland has been substantially increased since 1930 through irrigation, reclamation, and the colonization of the western frontier. Over 100 irrigation projects costing about $125 million had been completed by 1960, and the amount of irrigated land jumped from a few thousand acres, in 1930, to almost 400,000 acres, in 1960. Except for a few projects established in leeward basins of the Cordillera Central, most of the irrigation was of semi-arid lowlands such as the western Cibao, the San Juan Valley, the Enriquillo Depression, and the coastal fringes from Azua to Santo Domingo. Significantly, about one-fourth of the newly irrigated land is located within 20 miles of the Haitian border, where frontier colonization has been emphasized.

The intensity of land use is closely correlated with population density. The most intensively utilized region in the country is the Vega Real, where small farms are characteristic. Land use is least intensive in the higher mountain zones and in the arid areas of the south and west. The current tendency of the peasants to invade the higher mountains (where they cut down the forests to establish their *conucos* or slash-and-burn plots) poses one of the most serious land use problems in the republic.

Agriculture. The commercial phase of Dominican agriculture rests upon the trinity of sugar, cacao, and coffee, reinforced by rice, tobacco, and bananas. Crops for local consumption include peanuts, which supply the national needs for vegetable oil, corn, beans, peas, and the usual wide range of tropical vegetables and fruits. Stock raising is sufficient to supply both local demands and to make this one of the very few countries in the West Indies which has an exportable meat surplus. Food has been relatively cheap, and the peasants, who continue to be largely self-sufficient, are among the best fed in the Caribbean.

The cornerstone of cash farming is sugar, which normally makes up more than half the country's exports. Small quantities of sugar are raised in many places, but the major production comes from the southeast coastal plain and adjacent interior lowlands (Figure 6.4). Secondary sugar regions are found in the Cibao, on the north coast near Santiago and Puerto Plata, and in the lower valley of the Río Yaque del Sur. As we noted earlier, cane was brought to Santo Domingo in the sixteenth century, and small quantities of sugar were produced throughout the colonial period. Significant production based on the modern plantation, however, did not begin until the arrival of Cuban refugees in the latter nineteenth century. Since then, production has increased steadily, rising from less than 5,000 tons, in 1870, to roughly 1 million tons, in 1960. Most of the Dominican sugar was exported to the United Kingdom and other European countries, but with the abolishment of the Cuban quota, an increasing amount is being sold to the United States. Trujillo, who owned much of the country's sugar industry, introduced the most modern machinery for both the farming and processing, and approved the importation of cheap, seasonal labor from Haiti to keep wage costs low.

In contrast to cane, cacao and coffee are raised by small farmers using primitive tools and simple agricultural techniques. The machete, the hoe, and, where terrain permits, the ox-drawn plow are the chief instruments of cultivation. Cacao is largely grown on the rich soils of the Cibao between Moca and San Francisco de Macorís. In this region, the typical cacao farm consists of a small property set off by a live fence of a spiney

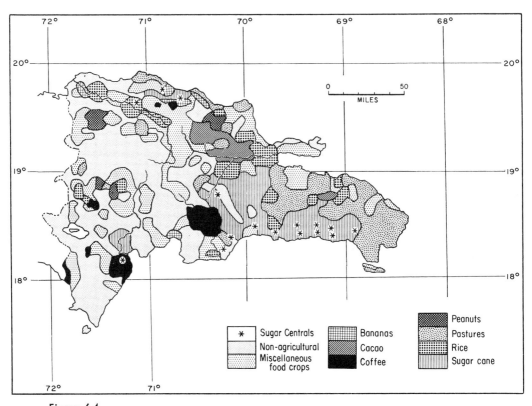

Figure 6.4
Dominican Republic : Land Use.

plant called the *malla*. The cacao trees are generally invisible because they are shaded by amapola trees whose falling flowers and leaves help conserve the humidity around the sensitive cacao roots. The soil on these small farms is coal-black, and produces a variety of food crops. A characteristic feature of the landscape is the small, drying platform for cacao beans (Figure 6.5).

Coffee and rice growing are less localized than cacao farming (Figure 6.4). Coffee is raised on the lower slopes of many mountain areas, including the Cordillera Central. Upland or dry rice is also widely scattered, but paddy rice is produced primarily in the irrigated districts of the western Cibao and the reclaimed marshlands near the mouth of the Yuna River in Samaná. With the expansion of irrigation since 1930, the production of paddy rice has increased sufficiently to

change the Dominican Republic from a large-scale importer to a modest exporter of the crop. Bananas are widely raised for local use, but those for export are concentrated in the irrigated lands of the western Cibao. A substantial part of the country's banana trade is in the hands of the American-owned Grenada Company, which raises the crop on its own plantations and also buys from small farmers.

Other Economies. Compared to agriculture, the other components of the Dominican economy are of only modest proportions. The principal mineral production is of salt and gypsum in the southern province of Barahona, and of iron ore in the Hatillo-Maimón area in the central highlands. Two small oil wells were operating near Azua in 1959, and exploration for bauxite in the extreme southwest was promising. Except for salt and gypsum, production is insufficient even for local needs.

Industry is still largely confined to the processing of agricultural products, although in recent decades plants producing cement, glass, textiles, and comparable products have been established. Most of these are in the capital city of Santo Domingo. Lumbering of pine in the Cordillera Central is threatened by the encroaching *conucos* of small farmers, but it is still sufficient to provide many of the country's wood needs. Mahogany and tropical woods have long been a minor export. Trujillo built several luxury hotels in an effort to stimulate the tourist trade, but the Dominican Republic has captured only a tiny fraction of the Caribbean tourist dollar.

Transportation. Prior to the United States occupation (1916–1924) and the Trujillo dictatorship (1930–1961), inadequate transportation was a major obstacle to both economic development and political stability in the Dominican Republic. Much of the land

in the interior was condemned to bare subsistence production or no production at all. The population nucleus around the capital was so poorly integrated with that of the Cibao that each region functioned almost independently of the other. The two population clusters communicated more easily by sea than along the tortuous trails across the intervening Cordillera Central. Indeed, were it not for the Haitian threat, the Cibao and the *capitaleños* might have formed separate political states. Poor transportation also made it difficult for the central government in the capital to enforce the law in the more remote parts of the country and, as a result, local caciquism, or bossism, and revolution flourished in defiance of national authorities. Moreover, the remote frontier zone which could not be integrated with the rest of the state was left exposed to the encroachment of Haitian influence and settlers.

The expansion of the road network has partially corrected these shortcomings. There are now roughly 3,000 miles of highways, of which about half are paved, all-weather

Figure 6.5
Drying Cacao Beans West of San Francisco de Macorís, Dominican Republic. The shelter can be rolled forward to cover the platform in case of rain.

roads. Three major arteries fan out from Santo Domingo to the north, east, and west, connecting the capital with the major urban centers. Secondary roads feed into the main highways, creating an effective grid over much of the country, including the sensitive frontier. Only in the more rugged mountains and in the arid southwest is a road network still largely absent. Cargo hauling on a government-owned narrow-gauge railroad which connects the Cibao with the port of Sánchez on Samaná Bay is being eclipsed by the increasing use of trucks.

Population and Settlement

If Dominican statistics are trustworthy, the population of the country increased from roughly one million in 1930 to over three million in 1960. This exceptionally rapid rate of growth, even for Latin America, took place during the only significant period of stability which Dominicans have enjoyed since the end of the eighteenth century. Except for the clandestine infiltration of Haitian settlers and workers, immigration has played only a slight role in the rise. Most of the population growth has been due to higher rates of natural increase stemming from improved health and economic conditions during the Trujillo dictatorship.

Sharp increases in population are exceptional in Dominican history. Santo Domingo was the first European colony in the New World, but its post-Columbian population growth was probably the lowest in Middle America before 1930. The total destruction of the colony's Amerindian groups, its lack of attraction for Spanish and other European immigrants, the absence of the plantations and their need for slaves, political instability, and economic stagnation—all these served as barriers to population growth until recent times.

There are no accurate data, and only a few estimates, about Dominican population trends before this century. The early sixteenth-century concentration in Santo Do-

mingo was rapidly decreased as adventurers left to conquer the other Antilles and the mainland (see Chapter 3). Thereafter, virtually abandoned by Spain, the population of the colony increased at a snail's pace. By the latter eighteenth century, it is estimated, the total number of inhabitants in the territory came to about 150,000, of whom 20 per cent were Negro slaves. The Haitian invasions reduced this figure by almost two-thirds, partly through slaughter and starvation, and partly by prompting the wholesale emigration of the better-to-do white families. Estimates of population at the beginnings of independence in 1844 vary from 80,000 to 125,000. There were modest increases during the rest of the nineteenth century, but as we have noted, the total did not reach one million until 1930.

With a current population in excess of three million and a national territory of 18,817 square miles, over-all densities in the Dominican Republic approximate 160 people per square mile. This ratio is low compared to other West Indian islands, but high in comparison to most Latin American countries. The distribution of people on the land is very irregular, however, and mathematical densities are only a crude index of actual densities.

The country's major population clusters continue to coincide with the historical nuclei of the Cibao and the southern coastal plains. The Cibao, together with adjoining parts of the north coast such as Puerto Plata and Montecristi, contain over half the Dominican population. Densities are especially high (600 per square mile) in the black-soil belt of the Vega Real between Santiago and San Francisco de Macorís. Concentrations in the semiarid Cibao lowlands west of Santiago are small, except in the irrigated zones, and, east of San Francisco de Macorís to Samaná Bay, densities are lower than in the heart of the Vega Real because of less favorable soils and poorer drainage. The metropolitan zone of Santo Domingo and the sugar lands of the Caribbean coastal plain between San Cristóbal and La Romana account for roughly one-third more of the population. The remainder is distributed along the approaches to the Haitian frontier, on the grazing lands of El Seibo, and in the various mountain regions.

Among these nuclei, the largest proportional increase in recent decades has taken place on the southeast Caribbean coastal plain. This has been caused by the rapid growth of the capital city of Santo Domingo and its environs and by the increasing importance of sugar cane, which is the agricultural mainstay of the area. Proportional increases have also been high along the frontier and its lowland approaches, such as the Enriquillo Depression, the San Juan Valley, and the westernmost Cibao. Population growth in the traditionally empty borderlands was due primarily to a policy of planned colonization under Trujillo. Since much of the frontier is subhumid, the expansion of irrigation played a leading role in this colonization. Finally, it is noteworthy that the rapid over-all increase in population, the expansion of plantation agriculture through large land-holdings, and the tendency to import cheaper Haitian labor for seasonal work on the estates is forcing population into the higher mountain zones, including the Cordillera Central. Unlike Puerto Rico and Cuba, the Dominican peasant did not have to occupy mountain areas in the past, because limited plantation development on the lowlands left ample room for settlement. Currently, however, there is a marked push into the mountains, and many of the forested mountain zones, even in the *tierra fría*, are being cleared for occupation.

Population movements such as those to the mountains, the frontier, and the city are all of comparatively recent origin. Historically, Dominicans have exhibited a strong tendency to stay put. Unlike the Haitians, Puerto Ricans, and other West Indians, the Dominican peasantry has never been forced to migrate because of land hunger at home. On the contrary, the Dominican Republic has experienced immigration rather than emigration in

this century. Similarly, while there has been a movement from country to town in recent decades, it never reached the intensity that it did in other Latin American countries. In fact, under Trujillo's frontier colonization policy, an effort was actually made to send urban slum dwellers back to the land.

In addition to comparative lack of mobility, the Dominican population is also distinctive in the Caribbean in terms of racial composition. Cuba and Puerto Rico, the other Hispanic islands of the region, are primarily white. The territories of north European colonial association are largely Negro. Only in the Dominican Republic is the bulk of the population mulatto. As we noted earlier, Spanish Santo Domingo continued to be primarily white during the colonial period. A small number of slaves were imported, but the low profits from cattle grazing did not warrant the importation of any large number of slaves. As usual, some miscegenation took place between white masters and slave women but, still, at the end of the eighteenth century, the population of Santo Domingo was basically European. The change to mulatto composition must be largely attributed to the Haitian invasions and occupation. Many white families fled, as we have said, and the death rate among the remaining white Dominican males rose sharply. It was not uncommon for invading Haitian troops to slaughter the men and boys in a captured town and mate with the women. The Hispanic family names have been retained, but much of the mulatto population of the Dominican Republic issues from nineteenth century Haitian soldiery and captured white women.

In round numbers, the racial distribution is as follows: about 25 per cent are more or less white, 12 per cent are Negroes, and the remainder of the population falls into a wide range of mixture between the two. In addition, there are a few thousand Chinese, concentrated in the cities where they all but monopolize the restaurant trade, and a few hundred Japanese living in agricultural colonies. The Japanese were brought in after World War II, when Trujillo's open-door policy failed to attract many Europeans. It is unlikely that the Japanese immigration will continue; in fact, some Japanese are already returning to Japan. Negroes are heavily concentrated along the Haitian border, particularly in the Montecristi area, and above-average concentrations of Negroes are also characteristic of the sugar lands of the southeast.

Settlement. Types and patterns of settlement in the Dominican Republic attest to the importance of farming and to the rural orientation of most of the people. The percentage of the population classified as urban rose from 16.6, in 1920, to over 26, in 1960, and the trend to urbanization continues; but most Dominicans are attached to the land and dwell in agricultural settlements, both dispersed and nucleated.

The average Dominican peasant lives in a *bohío* constructed of split royal palm siding and thatched with palm leaves. The unit usually consists of two rooms with a dirt floor, plus an occasional secondary shelter which serves as a kitchen or a storage shed. *Bohíos* are often built by a *junta* of neighbors, in a cooperative effort which resembles the old house-raising bees in the United States. Furnishings are few—a table, a few chairs, a bed for the parents, and hammocks for the children.

Traditionally, the *bohíos* were dispersed through the countryside, and some dispersed settlement is still apparent, particularly in the Cibao and in the mountain areas of *conuco* or slash-burn agriculture. More recently, however, the general trend has been to village groupings which often develop stringlike along the roads. This trend has been encouraged by the growth of a highway network in the last 30 years, and also by the government, which has found it easier to provide social services for village nuclei than for scattered homesteads.

Under Trujillo, the government-sponsored agricultural colony emerged as a distinctive rural settlement on the Dominican landscape. There are now dozens of such colonies scattered over the country, particularly along the Haitian borders (Figure 6.6). Their functions include bolstering the frontier against the growing pressure of Haitian population, developing previously unexploited areas, resettling surplus population both from urban slums and overcrowded farm zones, and attracting foreign immigrants. In 1960, a few of these colonies were classified as "foreign" and were made up of recently arrived immigrants, such as Japanese, Spaniards, Hungarians, and Jews. But since the Dominican bid for immigrants went largely unanswered, the bulk of the colonies were "national" or "mixed," that is, composed of Dominicans or a mixture of Dominicans and foreigners.

Except for Santo Domingo and, to a lesser extent, Santiago, most of the country's urban settlements have few specialized functions. Centers along the western frontier, such as Dajabón, Elías Piña, and Jimaní, include so many soldiers that they are almost garrison towns. By and large, however, the towns and cities of the Dominican Republic are either ports or service centers for surrounding agricultural areas.

Most of the larger towns and cities are in the Cibao or along the southern coastal plain.

Figure 6.6

Dominican Republic: Agricultural Colonies, 1960.

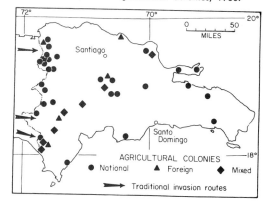

Figure 6.7
Town House: Moca, Dominican Republic.

The road running eastward through the Vega Real from Santiago passes in rapid succession through important centers such as Moca, Salcedo, San Francisco de Macorís, and Sánchez. Similarly, on the south coast, La Romana, San Pedro de Macorís, Santo Domingo, San Cristóbal, and Baní follow each other in close order. Outside the two major population regions, towns such as San Juan, Barahona, and Azua are more widely spaced, reflecting lower economic production and smaller population concentrations.

All the country's urban centers have been experiencing rapid growth, but none comparable to that of Santo Domingo (formerly Ciudad Trujillo). The population of the capital increased more than tenfold in recent decades, jumping from about 30,000, in 1920, to over 360,000, in 1960. Santiago, the second largest city, has yet to reach 100,000, and no other Dominican urban center had reached 30,000 by 1960. Santo Domingo was largely destroyed by a hurricane in 1930, and its subsequent growth mirrors a rapid expansion of its government and port functions,

as well as of its role as the country's chief center of industry, transportation, and banking. Trujillo lavished huge sums of money on this city which bore his name until 1961. At its center, Santo Domingo is one of the cleanest and most attractive cities in Middle America, but even Trujillo was unable to wipe out the odoriferous slum fringes which characterize Caribbean urban centers.

The Outlook. At an incredible cost in terms of liberty and other human values, Trujillo brought about major economic improvements which left an impressive mark on the Dominican landscape. That the dictator was largely motivated by self-interest is now unimportant; what is important is that with Trujillo's death and the expulsion of his clan, the country's new rulers inherited a legacy of amassed wealth, improved transportation, and other instruments for bettering the lot of Dominicans. No revolutionary government of modern times has come into power with such a legacy. If the new democratic government fails, it will strengthen the argument that the Dominican Republic (together with much of Latin America) is not yet ready for the responsibilities of democracy.

The task of maintaining and improving upon the material achievements of Trujillo will not be easy. The rapid and continuing growth of Dominican population is wiping out the traditionally favorable land-people ratio; the problems of land titles and redistribution are more complex and acute than ever; the pressure from the Haitian west may grow greater. Above all, there is the great difficulty of changing the relation of a quasi-feudal society to the land, so that the peasant will give up the security and shackles to which Trujillo accustomed him and match his new freedom with economic initiative and political responsibility. The revolution following Trujillo's death was easy; it is the unfinished business of the revolution which is hard.

HAITI

There is no more arresting theme on the Haitian landscape than the hopeless disequilibrium of its people, land, and resources, and the grinding human poverty which ensues from this. All of Haiti's potentials appear submarginal, save the child-bearing capacity of its women. The mountain lands which make up almost 80 per cent of the national territory's 10,240 square miles are eroded; the lowlands often suffer from inadequate rainfall; minerals are virtually nonexistent; the forests have largely been cut down; and fishing makes only a puny contribution to the food supply of the nation.

On this weak resource base live 3.5 million people—or is it 4 million? No truly accurate count has ever been made. Population densities are high almost everywhere, for people

Figure 6.8
Haitian Peasants in the Drought-Stricken Department du Nord-Ouest, 1959.

have had to spread over mountains and plains, wet areas and dry ones, regardless of conditions. And still the population increases!

Under these conditions, poverty is etched on the landscape in bold relief. In Port-au-Prince it can be seen in the distended bellies of children begging for tourist nickels, in the eyes of the men and women scavenging alongside the pigs in the city dump, and in the swampy slums of La Salene. The countryside is equally bad. People "forage on the hillsides like nature's lesser creatures. As soon as something green grows...they chop it down, to eat or burn as fuel."[1]

Haiti's change, in less than two centuries, from the richest plantation colony in the Caribbean to the poorest independent nation in the Americas, is due to a multiplicity of causes. First of all, much of the equipment and organization for production developed by the French went up in the flames of slave revolts (see Chapter 4). Estate houses and sugar mills were symbols of slavery and of the hated *blancs*, and they were destroyed outright; other features, such as roads, aqueducts, irrigation works, and coffee groves, were not maintained and often reverted to nature. The turmoil and instability which began with the slave uprisings at the end of the eighteenth century did not end with independence. They have continued in varying degree of intensity to this day. When the Haitians stopped fighting Europeans, they fought the Dominicans, and they fought each other—north against south, republic versus kingdom, mulatto against black. Added to this instability were the burdens of inexperience, lack of know-how, political corruption, and perpetual distrust of the white world.

Through this turbulent history the pressure of people on the poverty-stricken land has gradually increased to saturation and beyond. As in other slave societies, freedom from bondage was often interpreted as freedom from work—at least freedom from supervised work (see Chapter 4). The Negroes took to the hills to scratch out a bare but independent living, and the peasant plot replaced the large plantation. In this way the national economy became dominantly subsistent, estate agriculture became an anomaly, erosion of mountain lands became rampant, and poverty became the way of life for the constantly increasing population.

Figure 6.9
Haitian Fisherman from Gonaïves. Note the ravages of disease and malnutrition.

---

[1] T. Wolfe, "Haiti Crumbling Back into its Primitive Past," *The Washington Post,* December 4, 1960, p. E-1.

While many Haitians deny it, the most constructive period in recent times seems to have been the United States occupation (1915–1934). As in the Dominican Republic, the Americans were not popular, but they built roads, improved sanitation, stabilized the budget, and left the national treasury with a surplus. The surplus had disappeared by 1937, and it now requires a strong back and a sturdy jeep to traverse some of the roads built by the Americans.

Agricultural Patterns

The mark of economic activities other than agriculture is barely legible on the Haitian landscape. Mining, forestry, grazing, and transportation are of minor consequence; tourism is of modest significance, and only in a few centers such as Port-au-Prince and Cap-Haïtien; and manufacturing installations are few in number and largely associated with the processing of farm products.

The chief molder of the landscape and the backbone of Haiti's economy is the *petite culture* of peasant farmers. Plantation agriculture (*grande culture*), so important in most West Indian territories, is insignificant except for a few minor cash crops such as sisal. The dominance of peasant farming throughout the production structure is reflected in land ownership and use, local marketing and foreign trade, agricultural practices and tools, and a variety of other characteristics.

Land Tenure. The current patterns of land ownership in Haiti may be grouped into three major categories: (1) peasant plots; (2) bourgeois holdings; and (3) the public domain. Of these, peasant ownership is the most important, both in terms of cultivated acreage and over-all crop production. Peasant plots vary from a fraction of an acre to upwards of 100 acres. Estimates are that average holdings are less than 1.5 *carreaus* or 5 acres (1 *carreau* = 3.33 acres or 1.2 hectares). Peasant properties of over 10 *carreaus*

are exceptional, and their owners form a rural middle class called *gros habitants.*

Bourgeois holdings include both the estates of Haitian nationals and the lands owned by foreign corporations and individuals. There are probably about 1,000 estates (of 300 acres or more) owned by the local town-dwelling elite. Only a few of these holdings are intensively cultivated under the direct supervision of owners. Most are haphazardly exploited through rental and sharecropping under a peasant *gérant* ("manager"). The owners who prefer to live in town are interested only in the income from their land. They seldom visit the properties, and as a result, the estates are undercultivated and mismanaged. Prior to the United States occupation (1915–1934) there were considerably more of such holdings. The elimination of many town jobs by the efficiency-minded military government forced many of the unemployed elite to sell their lands in order to live.

The United States occupation also resulted in the repeal of laws against foreign ownership of land in Haiti. At present, there are several large holdings which are owned and operated in typical plantation fashion, using agricultural wage labor for the production of cash crops.

The extent of Haiti's public domain has never been accurately established, but most of it consists of marginal lands in the mountains and in arid areas. In order to produce revenue and relieve the pressure on private lands, the government rents parts of the public domain for annual fees. The rental theoretically varies according to environment and productivity, being highest in well-watered mountains and favored locales. In practice, however, local politics are more important than environmental considerations in determining rent.

Renting land from the government and estate owners goes hand-in-hand with widespread sharecropping, or *métayage,* in Haiti. Both practices reflect the growing pressure of population on the limited supply of land.

Fragmentation of small holdings through inheritance has forced many families to sharecrop additional land to eke out a living. Even when a peasant's total inheritance is large enough, it is often scattered in patches over a wide area, and, unable to farm the scattered properties, the small owner is forced to relinquish some of the land to *métayage*. References to the preponderance of small properties in Haiti tend to obscure the fact that many of these holdings no longer provide an independent living to the peasant owners. Moreover, the small holders are constantly haunted by insecurity of tenure. With no adequate cadastral survey, a long tradition of squatting, widespread illiteracy, and increasing land hunger, many property titles are subject to legal challenge.

Land Use. Data concerning agricultural land use in Haiti are, at best, guesses which tend to vary with the source of information. Estimates of cultivated land, for example, range from one-half to over two million acres. Considering the physical limitations and the pressure of population, it is possible that a seventh of the country's total of roughly seven million acres is either cultivated or under tree crops. Of this, about 60 per cent is in the lowlands such as the Cul-de-Sac, the Plaine du Nord, and Les Cayes, and the remainder is scattered through the several mountain chains.

Except for the few plantation nodes, detailed tracing of land use and crop regions is equally unreliable, especially in the highlands. Mixed farming is the rule on peasant plots, and seldom is any one crop outstanding. The chequered pattern of cultivated plots may change from one year to the next, as advanced erosion causes the abandonment of some mountain areas; and even on the plains, farming is stable only in the irrigated or well-watered sectors. Elsewhere, the unreliability of rainfall, flooding by the debris-loaded streams, and other conditions result in a discontinuous and shifting patchwork of cultivation. Since the great majority of Haitians

are farmers, a general notion of at least the intensity of land use from place to place may be inferred from population distribution (Figure 6.13). A crude classification of regional crop areas is that coffee is cultivated on the humid windward slopes, sugar and rice on irrigated lowlands, cotton on the semi-arid plateaus and plains, and food crops for local use anywhere that they will grow.

Coffee and Other Export Crops. Haitian exports are almost exclusively agricultural. In recent years, coffee has accounted for almost three-fourths of the total trade, and sisal and sugar together make up 15 per cent more. Other noteworthy commercial products are essential oils, cacao, cotton, and bananas.

The position of Haitian coffee (see Chapter 4) has undergone a number of modifications since the end of the eighteenth century: it has surpassed sugar as the leading export; it has changed from a plantation product to a peasant cash crop; and its chief center of production has shifted from the hinterland of Cap-Haïtien to the southern massifs. Coffee production was able to survive the destruction of the colonial plantation. Its exportation surpassed that of sugar and it became the leading cash crop of the peasants—largely because the plantings were self-perpetuating. In the chaos which followed the ousting of the French, little care was given to the coffee estates, and the crop would have died out, except that berries which fell to the ground were decorticated by rats, and thus provided seed for the new trees which began to grow wild on the mountain sides. The postrevolutionary population which occupied the former estates seldom attempted to restore the groves, and coffee came to be gathered as a wild fruit from the forest. Even today, there is little actual cultivation of the crop. Most thickets from which the peasantry gathers berries are natural growth, *café rat,* derived from the French colonial plantations.

The southward shift of major coffee production from its old eighteenth century locus around Cap-Haïtien is due in part to the nineteenth century struggles which separated the Haitian north from the south, making the Artibonite a no-man's land. The north, under radical Negro militarists such as Christophe, experienced greater destruction and instability than the south, which was ruled by moderate mulattos such as Pétion and Boyer. The shift of the coffee-growing areas may also be explained in terms of land distribution policies, climate, and other factors.

Currently, Haiti's chief coffee area is the mountainous Southwest Peninsula between Tiote and Jérémie (Figure 6.10). Production in the Massifs de la Hotte and de la Selle amounts to over three-fifths of the national total, making the south's production well above that of the north and the Artibonite. Since the south experienced less destruction from slave revolts and has had greater stability in the postindependence period, the investment of the region's highlands by peasant farmers was more orderly. Under the enlightened land distribution policies of Pétion and Boyer, the property rights of small holders were more firmly established and respected and, as a result, the peasantry seems to have taken better care of the land. Deforestation and erosion, which are major threats to the coffee economy in mountain zones, have occurred less in the southern massifs

than elsewhere. Equally important, the rainfall of the windward slopes of the southern highlands is almost ideal for coffee, especially the dry fall period when the crop is reaching maturity. These favorable historical and climatic conditions for the crop were also reinforced by the region's proximity to Port-au-Prince, Haiti's chief port and coffee mart.

The coffee areas of the north and the Artibonite rank a poor second and third, respectively, to those of the south. The heart of the coffee country in the Massif du Nord is on the windward slopes, extending from the vicinity of Port Margot eastward through Limbé, Marmelade, and Pilate. The crop is also found on the lowlands, such as those near Port-de-Paix, Milot, and Cap-Haïtien, where it is often raised in association with cacao and bananas. Production in the Artibonite centers on a number of upland fringes, including the Chaîne de Matheux and the Montagnes Noires.

Despite the vital importance of coffee as Haiti's chief cash crop, production is beset by numerous difficulties. The peasant farmers who produce the bulk of the crop seldom prune or top the trees, with the result that plantings have become dense thickets of stems and leaves which yield only about 100 pounds of berries per acre. There are very few large plantations, and most peasants own only a few hundred trees. Equipment for processing the crop is very primitive; the berries are dried in the sun and then pounded in mortars to remove the dry pulp. Pounding breaks many of the beans and improperly cleans others, and the over-all quality of the product is greatly reduced.

There are indications that recent destruction by hurricanes and other factors may reduce production even more in the future. Since coffee raised between sea level and 4,000 feet in Haiti requires shading, the amount of land available for the crop depends in large measure on the availability of forest cover, and the necessary cover is being constantly depleted. Government efforts at reforestation failed because the peas-

Figure 6.10

Haiti: Commercial Crops.

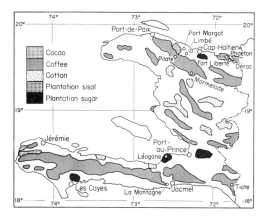

ants quickly pulled up the young trees in the desperate search for fuel. Moreover, the increasing cost of food has forced many small farmers to clear coffee land in favor of subsistent food crops.

Sugar and sisal, the other two significant exports, are primarily associated with the *grande culture* of the plantations. Both crops are of comparatively recent commercial development and both are largely tied to United States corporate ownership. While some sugar continued to be produced in Haiti after the downfall of the colonial estates, the modern sugar plantation of the *central* type had to await the United States occupation (1915–1934). The Americans not only abolished the laws against ownership of land by foreigners, but they also improved the transportation and provided the capital necessary to stimulate plantation development. A prime illustration of the effect of this United States influence is the Haitian American Sugar Company, which owns some 27,000 acres of productive cane lands. The chief regions of commercial sugar production are the irrigated lowlands of the Cul-de-Sac, the plain of Léogane near Port-au-Prince, the Plaine du Nord south of Cap-Haïtien, and the coastal zone of Les Cayes (Figure 6.10). An unknown quantity of cane is also raised on peasant plots for local use. This goes into making *rapadou* (a solid sweetner) and *tafia* and *clairin*, the favorite alcoholic beverages of Haiti.

Sisal production received a major boost during World War II. Currently, a few large plantations, located mainly on the north coast between Cap-Haïtien and Fort Liberté (Figure 6.10), raise the crop. Mills for processing sisal in this area have been built at Phaéton and Dérac. Chief among the plantations is the American-owned Daphne holding of over 10,000 acres, in northeast Haiti.

Peasant Farming. As already implied, the *petite culture* of Haitian peasant farming rests upon the intensive cultivation of small plots. Labor input is large, capital investment is limited and is largely restricted to the own-

ership of the land itself, tools are few and simple, the use of animal power is restricted primarily to marketing, and farming practices are primitive. While generally described as subsistent, *petite culture* shows considerable market orientation at the local level.

Peasant production emphasizes numerous food crops, of which the more important are cassava (*manioc*), yams (*igname*), sweet potatoes (*patate*), and other root varieties. In the drier areas the African grains, sorghum and millet (*petit mil*), are widely cultivated. Other food crops brought from Africa and grown by the Haitian peasant include the vegetables, okra (*gombo*) and pigeon bean (*pois congo*); the cooking banana, or plantain (*banane*); and the all-important yam. Virtually all the fruit, vegetables, and grains (especially maize) of Middle America's *tierra caliente* and *templada* zones are raised, and in addition there are some cooler latitude plants (such as peaches, strawberries, and figs) which are grown at higher elevations. Fibers such as cotton, native sisal, and others (used in making rope, cloth, and so forth) are second to food crops in importance.

Peasant farming practices and tools may appear primitive to outsiders, but they are often convenient adaptations to local physical and economic conditions. The principal tools include the hoe, machete, the billhook (*digo*), an iron bar or dibble (*louchette*), and various types of knives, such as the curved *serpette* and the *collins*. The machete is used for clearing, and the hoe, billhook, and dibble are variously used for cultivation, depending on slope and type of crop. In some especially steep mountain lands where the peasant can only work with a rope to hold him up, even the hoe is ruled out. No use is made of the wheel; crops are carried by man or animals in baskets; and the mortar serves as decorticator. The plow has never won acceptance, in part because of the small size of holdings and in part because of the broken surface of the ground. Actually, plows and other less primitive tools would have loosened the mountain soils more deeply and thus increased erosion.

Farming practices are roughly comparable to those of *conuco* agriculture elsewhere in the West Indies, but with some suggestion of African influence. In planting, for example, the peasant drops seeds from a calabash and covers them with his feet, as is done in parts of West Africa. Plural-storeyed, mixed planting is common, with maize and beans above and root crops below. In the absence of fertilizers, crop rotation and fallowing are necessary for even the barest yields, but they are not always practiced. Burning weeds and brush before cultivation is common, even though forbidden by law. Burning impoverishes the soil by consuming some of the humus content, but it does add some needed potassium to the land.

The heavy work of clearing and hoeing is done by the men who often invite their neighbors to form a working *combite*. Although comparable in spirit to the American husking bee, the *combite* is supposed to be a West African carryover. The workers line up and hoe in unison to the beat of a drum or the cadence of a chant. Payment by the farmer to the members of the *combite* may be made in a variety of ways, including return services, cash, or a large meal and a measure of white rum (*tafia*). Once the heavy work has been accomplished, women and children take over the weeding and other light tasks.

Women play a vital role in Haitian peasant agriculture, not only in light farm work but in management and marketing as well. As we have already noted, peasant holdings are often fragmented and scattered, making it impossible for the farmer to work all his plots. Under the circumstances, he may either give part of his land to others for sharecropping or he may take a second wife (*placé*) and put her in charge of his plot. Thus, if a peasant increases his holdings or inherits a second plot on the other side of the mountain, it is only common sense for him to take a second woman, raise a family

by her, and assure himself of an overseer, a labor supply, and a marketing agent on each of his properties. Practical needs determine the number of women to each man.

Marketing in Haiti, except wholesale and export, is also largely in the hands of women. The surplus of peasant farming is walked to market in loads of anywhere from 20 to 50 pounds on the heads of women, or on donkeys (Figure 6.11). Every town and hamlet has a market, and there are others in the countryside, at crossroads or other convenient locations. Groups of walking women may spend half the week on the road and in the market place. They sleep wherever nightfall catches them, and many walk as much as 30 miles to a more distant market to get a slightly better price. If all the produce carried by the woman or burro is sold at a fair price, she may return home richer by a few *gourdes* (20 or 30 cents). If, as often happens, the market is glutted, she has to sell for less or carry the stuff back home. Markets serve a social as well as economic function. The market women are the rural gossip columns of Haiti, and often they won't sell until they have had a chance to socialize and gather the news.

Figure 6.11
Haitian Peasant Women Walking to Market.

Figure 6.12
Rural Market on Roadside Northwest of Kenscoff, Haiti.

Marketing by women began in revolutionary times with the breakdown of the French communication system. During the troubled periods, men had to hide to escape death or the army, and women had to take over the disposal of farm surplus. Once established, marketing by walking women was reinforced by custom and economic conditions. Inadequate transportation and lack of refrigeration and other facilities make any other form of collecting and marketing too difficult and costly.

While most of the production of Haitian peasant agriculture is for subsistence, the widespread local marketing suggests a significant commercial emphasis. The peasant depends not only upon the disposal of such obviously cash crops as coffee, but upon the small surpluses of virtually everything his plot produces. Part of the peasant surplus goes to feed the country's urban population and to supply export, but much of it is sold within the rural peasant population itself. The walking women often buy from each other the different produce grown under different climatic conditions only a short distance away. There is an obvious exchange between lowlands and highlands, between the *tierra caliente* (*té cho*) farmers and those of the *tierra templada* and *fría* (*té fret*) zones, and between the coast and the interior.

Population

Densities and Movements. The growth of Haiti's population was comparatively slow until this century. The territory contained over 500,000 people, the largest block in the West Indies, in the eighteenth century, but the subsequent proportional increases have been well below those of Puerto Rico, Cuba, and even the Dominican Republic. Historical turmoil served as a Malthusian barrier to rapid population growth, but this is of little comfort in the light of current population pressures and patterns.

Estimates in 1960 indicated an over-all density of roughly 320 persons per square mile, but the figure is close to 1,000 per square mile when population is related to arable land. The rural population concentration tends to be high over much of the country, but densities vary considerably with climate, terrain, soil productivity, and other factors. The heaviest concentrations are generally on well-watered or irrigated lowlands, and on the lower and middle slopes of windward facing uplands; the lowest densities are associated with dry, leeward areas on the upper slopes of the high mountains.

Rural population reaches its highest density in two widely separated zones. The first of these consists of parts of the Plaine du

Nord, behind Cap-Haïtien and the humid slopes of the Massif du Nord between Port-de-Paix and Saint-Raphael. The coastal lowlands centering on Cap-Haïtien were a major locus of plantation development and slave population in the colonial period (see Chapter 4), and they remain heavily populated. Fertile alluvial soils, in combination with a relatively humid climate and accessibility to ocean transportation, make the Cap lowlands one of the most valuable farming areas in the country. Much of the population now living on the northern slopes of the Massif Central stems from postslavery migrants from the Cap lowlands.

A second zone of maximum rural concentration is in the south, extending from the western Cul-de-Sac through Port-au-Prince into the Southwest Peninsula. Densities in this zone, as well as in the hinterlands of Port-au-Prince, Jacmel, and Jérémie, are especially high on the coastal plains of Les Cayes and the Asile Valley (Figure 6.13). More localized zones of high rural population are found in the lower Artibonite Valley and in small coastal concentrations elsewhere.

These environmentally favored zones make up only 17 per cent of Haiti's area, but they contain over half the country's population. At the other extreme of the density scale are lands which comprise 24 per cent of the total area but house only 8 per cent of the population. These include the eastern Cul-de-Sac, the semiarid Plaine Central, the alkaline

Figure 6.13
Haiti: Rural Population Densities.

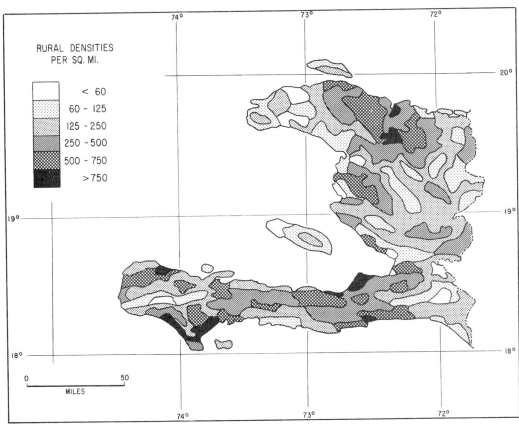

lands of the Artibonite, and the rain-shadow zones of the Northwest Peninsula and the west coast.

The pressure of increasing population has led many Haitian peasants to emigrate during this century. Whenever possible, the workers have preferred permanent to seasonal moves. For this reason, official figures on Haitian emigration seldom reveal the true extent of movement. The migrants avoided being counted and identified, to reduce the chance that they would be returned to Haiti. As noted elsewhere, the major directions of Haitian migration have been toward the labor-short Cuban sugar economy and the Dominican Republic. Official records indicate that 75,000 immigrants entered Cuba from Haiti during the period of maximum flow, from 1913 to 1921; after 1921, the sugar depression and Cuba's fear of Africanization reduced the flow. By 1931, 80,000 Haitians were listed as living on the island, but more than a third were later repatriated. Those who remained, including many who escaped official notice, have largely blended into the local Negro population. Cuban doors are now totally shut to Haitians.

The flow to the Dominican Republic may be divided into two streams. The first, and older, was the unsanctioned infiltration of Haitians into the thinly settled Dominican border provinces. This movement goes back a century or more and, while no statistics exist, it undoubtedly involved a considerable number of migrants. Despite the wholesale slaughter and expulsions of Haitians in the latter 1930's, the Haitian mark is still evident on the Dominican border landscape, in the more Negroid composition of the population, the occasional distinctively Haitian peasant house, and the ability of the border people to speak the Haitian patois as well as Spanish. Before Trujillo's campaign to Dominicanize the frontier, the Haitian gourde circulated as freely as the peso, voodoo rites were common, and much of the population consisted of *rayanos,* a Dominican term for frontier people of dubious nationality.

The second type of movement to the Dominican Republic was the seasonal migration associated with the growth of the sugar economy. Haitian workers were contracted for specified periods, quartered under guard on the plantations, and repatriated after the harvest. The fall of Trujillo may largely shut off the seasonal migration, but it may spur the infiltration movement across the border.

Composition, Caste, and Culture. With the exception of a tiny colony of white business families in Port-au-Prince, Haiti's population is about 95 per cent Negro (*brun*) and 5 per cent mulatto (*jaune*), the latter descendants of eighteenth-century French fathers and African mothers.

The slight difference in eighteenth-century ancestry has burgeoned into a wide gulf between the minority of *jaunes* and the masses of *bruns*. There are few Caribbean areas where color and classes are so closely related as in Haiti. The mulattoes constitute the elite and are separated from the Negro majority by class barriers which have the rigidity of caste. The elite do not work with their hands; they live in the urban centers and are engaged primarily in business, the professions, industry, and government. In contrast, the Negro majority constitutes a rural peasantry whose life is bound to the cultivation of the land. The two groups are also sharply differentiated by language, religion, dress, education, cultural orientation, and other ways of life.

Haiti is actually a bilingual country. French, the official language, is spoken only by the elite. The peasantry speaks a Creole patois which is a mixture of French, Spanish, and English, with some African and Indian vocables. The two groups can communicate only because the elite learn the Creole dialect, as children, from the servants. The masses dress in cotton and go barefoot, but the mulatto aristocracy copies the latest European fashions. The elite adheres to Catholicism as a badge of their part-European ancestry and wholly European cultural values and orientation; the Negroes may be nominally Catholic, but they also practice *voudon* ("vodoo"), an African carryover. In short, while the *jaunes* represent the veneer of sophisticated twentieth-century French culture in Haiti, the *bruns* symbolize the more primitive African cultural forms stemming from the colonial slave period. Money breaches the barriers however: "a poor *jaune* is a *brun,* and a rich *brun* is a *jaune.*"

Settlement

Rural Patterns. Nine out of ten Haitians live in a rural setting, either in dispersed homesteads or in tiny villages consisting of from four to ten dwellings. In general, the peasant hut (*caille-paille*) is a one- or two-room thatched cottage whose walls are loosely made of twilled bamboo or other flexible creepers and coated with mud and lime (Figure 6.14). The shelter tends to be small,

averaging 10 by 12 feet; it has a beaten-earth floor but no ceiling; and its roof thatching is of straw, palm leaves, or similar materials. Cooking is done outside, or over a charcoal fire in a metal brazier. Furnishings are few. Perhaps one *caille-paille* in four contains a bed. The others have hammocks or straw mats for sleeping. A few crude chairs, occasionally a table, cooking utensils, and the family chest complete the list of household goods. The more fortunate village groupings may have a community privy nearby. In the colder mountain zones, families shiver around small braziers, or simply shiver. About three-fourths of Haiti's rural housing consists of vermin-infested hovels which are wet during the rainy season and suffocating at night when the doors and windows are shut tightly against ghosts and the night air.

Despite general uniformity, some variations exist in the *caille-paille,* reflecting both the owner's economic status and the region in

Figure 6.14
Haiti : Peasant's *Caille-Paille* on the Plaine du Nord.

Figure 6.15
Haiti : Tiny Peasant Village in the Highlands. (*Delta Airlines*)

which he lives. The house described above is characteristic of the small landholder who typifies the Haitian peasantry. Landless families, locally called *sans maman* ("disinherited ones"), may dwell in even poorer circumstances. In contrast, the *gros habitant,* whose land holdings are above average, may live in a frame house with a corrugated iron roof, a veranda, and other marks of status. Many parts of Haiti have been so denuded of trees and other vegetation that construction materials are very expensive even for

the better-to-do. An ordinary *caille* often costs 400 or more *gourdes* ($80), which is well above the annual cash income of a Haitian peasant family.

Regional variations in the peasant house are reflected in the nature and durability of the construction material. In some areas, such as the higher parts of the Plaine Centrale adjacent to the Dominican Republic, for example, houses are often built of unfinished palm boards, and resemble the Dominican *bohio*. On the Plaine du Nord, the filling is commonly a mixture of clay and brick fragments gathered from the numerous small kilns that dot the plain. Fillings made from the sandy materials and alluvium of the coastal areas, the Cul-de-Sac, and other valleys are less resistant than those made from the denser red soil of the mountains. Hence, lowland houses are often pock-marked, as if by smallpox. Roofing material shows even greater diversity. The most widely used thatch consists of palm branches or Guinea grass, but the leaves of banana trees, bamboo, and other plants are also used. Climatic conditions also exert their influence. The *caille* of the colder mountain zones is broader, more sturdily built, and capped by a heavier thatch than its lowland counterpart.

The presence of rural dwellings on the Haitian landscape is generally denoted by clumps of fruit trees. These trees are most commonly bananas, plantains, breadfruit, avocado, and mango, but there is some variation with climate and region. At higher elevations, such as in the mountains around Kenscoff, there are peach and other middle-latitude trees. Beyond the fruit groves which screen the houses are cultivated patches of field crops and occasional thickets of coffee trees. Not infrequently, the family tomb, built of masonry and much sturdier than the *cailles,* is also hidden by foliage.

Dispersed rural settlement is much more frequent in Haiti than elsewhere in the Antilles. In part this is due to the necessity to seek out the small patches of cultivable land, but in part it seems to stem from historical insecurity. In the turbulent past, agglomerated settlements were frequently pillaged by roving bands of marauders and soldiery. The peasant learned that there was less danger in dispersed settlements hidden by a screen of thick foliage. Even today, the unwary observer may walk for miles through densely settled rural zones without seeing a *caille.*

The village grouping of four to ten houses, less common than the dispersed homestead, in some parts of the country seems to be dis-

appearing altogether. Neither highways nor social services are sufficiently developed to play any important role in stimulating the growth of agglomerated rural settlements in Haiti, as they have in the Dominican Republic. Most of the tiny villages of Haiti are inheritance groupings which develop on family lands, and the *habitants* are usually blood kin, with common parents or grandparents.

Rural Patterns. Despite the practice of census officials of designating even hamlets of a few hundred inhabitants as *villes,* cities and urban settlements in general have made only a slight dent on the Haitian landscape. This is due in part to the limited importance of commerce, industry, and other city-building functions. Perhaps equally important, however, is the strong psychological attachment of the Haitian *habitant* to the land. From the time that the emancipated slaves escaped from the French plantation villages and the colonial towns, the Haitian masses have avoided the urban centers except for marketing. Currently, Haiti is one of the few countries in Latin America without a burgeoning (and often artificial) country-to-town movement.

Estimates in the early 1960's indicated that less than 7 per cent of Haiti's population (250,000 out of over 3.5 million) lived in centers of 5,000 or more inhabitants. Of these 250,000, almost 150,000 were concentrated in Port-au-Prince. Cap-Haïtien, the second largest city, had slightly under 25,000 inhabitants, and the rest of the "cities" had between 5 and 13,000 people. With the exception of Pétionville, which is really a satellite of Port-au-Prince, all other cities are located on the coast (Figure 6.16). Typically, the chief functions of the Haitian city are to serve as port, administrative headquarters, and regional marketplace for the more favored and densely populated agricultural zones. Its residents always include the mulatto elite of the region.

The Haitian town (*bourg* or *bouc*) is

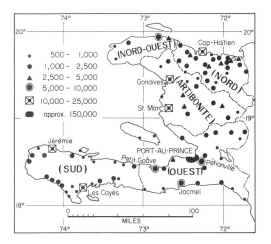

Figure 6.16
Haiti: Urban Centers and Departments.

smaller than the city, is located inland, and its major function is to serve as a marketplace for Haiti's "walking women." The size of the *bourg* appears to be proportional to its market. In turn, the size of the market depends on the population density and the productivity of the immediate hinterland, plus the nature of the terrain over which the peasant woman must walk. The internal structure of the average town includes a *place* ("square") around which are grouped the church and public buildings. The houses of the better-to-do residents are on the principal streets leading to the *place*. These residences are small, rectangular constructions which are built of wood plastered over with clay, painted in bright colors, and roofed with sheet iron. Most houses near the center of the town have a veranda and an interior courtyard which has a cookhouse and a storage shed. The huts of the poorer elements on the edge of town are no different than the *caille-paille* of the rural *habitant*.

The Balance Sheet. Probably nowhere else in Middle America is man so closely tied to nature as he is in Haiti, but it would be difficult to find another place where man's struggle to wrest a living from the land is so bitterly unrewarding. History and environment

seem to have conspired to foster hopelessness in Haiti.

Economically, the country appears to be worse off today than under French rule. In 1789, fewer than 10,000 French planters, aided by about 0.5 million slaves, cultivated almost as much land as do over 3 million Haitian peasants today; and the value of the plantation exports in 1789 were over $75 million, roughly double the amount of Haiti's current annual exports. The contrasts are almost equally sharp in terms of transportation, irrigation, the processing of plants for crops, and other features of the economic landscape. After more than a century and a half of independence, Haiti has not only failed to recover from the destruction of the French colonial plantation, but has actually retrogressed.

This retrogression may be attributed in part to the lack of order in man's relation to land. A growing pressure of population on a limited resource base has been compounded by deforestation and erosion, by fragmentation of holdings to a point where they are no longer viable, and by disregard of the most elementary rules of conservation. But Haiti's current plight can also be attributed to lack of order in man's relation to man. Until recently, a Western world, obsessed with the notion of European racial and cultural superiority, looked upon the Negro republic as a hopeless throwback to Africa and made no effort to lend a hand. The negative attitude of the outside world has been more than matched by that of the Haitian elite itself. In a society almost wholly dependent on agriculture, the governing aristocracy has shunned the countryside for the towns and poured its talents into professions largely unrelated to farming. Legislation which might have aided the peasant in making better use of the land has been inept because the legislators themselves have known little about the problems. Burdened with this legacy of disorder, the Haitian peasantry has had to forego progress in an elemental struggle simply to survive. In many respects, the future of Haiti appears even more desolate than the past.

Jamaica

It is not surprising that Jamaica was the first to withdraw from the West Indies Federation.[1] With over 1.6 million inhabitants and a territory of 4,411 square miles, the island had more than half the land area and people of the ill-starred union. Many Jamaicans reasoned that separate independence within the British Commonwealth was preferable to political association with the other small, widely scattered, and poorly endowed British colonies. Jamaica's resource base is limited, however, and its viability as an independent nation is subject to some doubt.

---

[1] The federation was formed in 1958, when all the British West Indian territories except the Bahamas and the Virgin Islands "agreed to dwell together in unity." The withdrawal of Jamaica in 1961 and, later, of Trinidad brought about its collapse.

The Resource Base

Jamaica is handicapped by numerous disadvantages—some natural, and others resulting from man's misuse of the land. Level areas suitable for farming are scarce. Well over half the island's surface consists of rugged slopeland lying 1,000 feet or more above sea level (Figure 6.17). In the east, an uplifted core of igneous and metamorphic rocks has been heavily dissected by rivers into a topography of twisting valleys and sharp-crested ridges dominated by the Blue Mountains. Elevations in this sector average well above 3,000 feet and reach a maximum of 7,402 feet at Blue Mountain Peak. Except for a fringe of coastal plain, the rest of the island consists of a limestone plateau which has been considerably broken up by faulting, and on which the erosive action of water has etched a typically karst landscape.

The widespread karst terrain is both an asset and a liability. In some areas, such as the Cockpit Country (Figure 6.17), the honeycombed limestone, with its network of

Figure 6.17
Jamaica: Gross Surface Features.

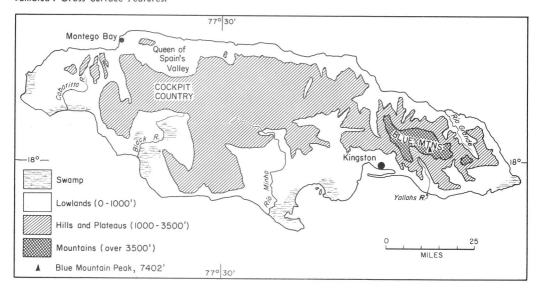

collapsed caverns and sinkholes, diverts drainage underground and makes for inadequate surface water supply despite heavy rainfall. Here, farming is largely ruled out, transportation is difficult, and population is sparse. Elsewhere, erosion of the limestone has produced a rolling upland of rounded hills which provided a living for a larger number of people. The heaviest rural settlement in the limestone areas, however, is to be found in the great solution basins with their deposits of rich, red soils. The largest and most productive of these are St. Thomas in the Vale, the valleys of the Black, Minho, and Cabaritta rivers; and the Queen of Spain Valley near Montego Bay. A number of solution hollows also contain a byproduct of limestone weathering which is rich in alumina. This is bauxite ore, now Jamaica's leading mineral export.

As a mountainous trade wind island, Jamaica receives its heaviest precipitation in its northeast highlands (Figure 6.18). The higher slopes of the Blue Mountains, for example, are drenched by 200 or more inches of rain per year. In contrast, the southern lowlands (such as those west of Kingston), which lie in the rain shadow of the mountains, are often too dry for agriculture without irrigation. The island's humid zones once had a dense forest cover, but most of this has been cut down, and many of the woodland areas shown on Figure 6.19 represent secondary growth of limited value for lumbering.

Deforestation has deprived Jamaica of useful timber resources and has also intensified soil erosion and leaching. Without a protective cover, a combination of steep slopes, high temperatures, and (in the humid areas) torrential rains has washed away much of the topsoil. Often the entire upper horizon has been removed; where it has not, the rate at which nutrients have been leached from the soil has increased.

Natural disasters have added to the problem. Crustal instability periodically gives rise to severe earthquakes, such as the tremor

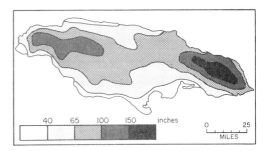

Figure 6.18
Jamaica: Mean Annual Rainfall.

which largely destroyed Kingston in 1907. Hurricanes are even more of a problem. At least once in every decade of this century, the island has suffered from varying degrees of destruction from the "dread wind of the Caribees." Loss from these storms was particularly heavy in the 1940's.

Economic Patterns

The meagerness of Jamaica's resource base is strikingly revealed by Table 6.1. Despite the vital importance of agriculture, only about 15 per cent of the island's area is considered cultivable, and even much of this is marginal or is under tree crops. Unbridled exploitation of the lowlands by the plantations and of the uplands by the peasantry has rendered ruinate much of Jamaica's soil resource. Perhaps as much as three-fourths of the area now classified as unused and un-

Table 6.1

JAMAICA: GROSS LAND USE RATIO

Category	Percentage of Total Area
Cultivable land and orchards	15
Pasture	21
Forest	17
Urban, roads, etc.	5
Unused, but potentially productive for agriculture or forestry	30
Permanently useless	12
Total	100

productive can be restored to productivity for farming and forestry. As the Yallahs Valley project[2] illustrates, however, restoration requires the expenditure of considerable effort and capital.

Land Tenure. The usual contrast, between the plantations (called "estates" in the British-connected territories) in the lowlands and the peasant holdings in the uplands, characterizes Jamaica, also. In 1960, 300 estates of 500 or more acres comprised almost two-fifths of all the land, and most of this acreage was in the fertile solution valleys and coastal plains. The largest of these (called "Frome") is located in the Cabaritta Valley of Westmoreland (Figure 6.19) and encompasses 30,000 acres. At the other extreme, holdings of less than 25 acres, over 70 per cent of the farms, comprised only 15 per cent of the land. The vast majority of these peasant holdings are on the less fertile interior

----

[2] The Yallahs Valley (see Figure 6.17) is a badly eroded area of 70 square miles which is being improved at government cost through reforestation and the introduction of new crops and farming techniques.

slopeland, with some spillover into the least desirable lowland zones.

As elsewhere in the Antilles, the contrast between peasant farming and estate agriculture in Jamaica goes far beyond the differences in size, location, and fertility of holdings. Except for a limited number of large holdings in drier areas which emphasize cattle production for local consumption, most Jamaican estates have the typical organization and production structure of the modern plantation (see Chapters 1 and 4). They emphasize the production of a few cash crops for export, using machinery and hired labor under an efficient corporate management. In contrast, the peasant farmer uses hand tools and family labor to raise a large number of crops. A small part of his production may be for export, but the vast bulk is for subsistence, or for sale (by his "higgler" spouse) in local markets. His holding, reduced in size and fragmented into small, scattered plots by successive inheritance, seldom provides an independent living; he must either sharecrop additional land or seek wage labor on the estates and elsewhere. Without reserve capital, the peasant is vulnerable to drought, hurricanes,

Figure 6.19
Jamaica : Land Use.

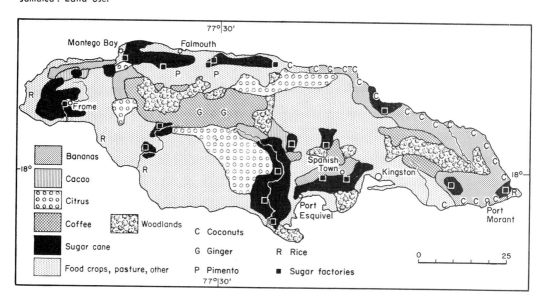

Figure 6.20
Jamaica : Peasant Farmer and His Wife en Route to Market. (Jamaica Tourist Board)

cold spells, and to his neighbors' bad habit of stealing crops.

Despite these handicaps, Jamaican peasant farming has come a long way from its eighteenth-century predecessor, the slave's provision grounds (see Chapter 4). The growth of urban centers, especially Kingston, coupled with an expanding network of roads, has encouraged peasants throughout the island to earn cash income from the sale of vegetables and fruit. The value of the food crops produced on peasant plots is now considerably greater than that of all the export crops combined. Moreover, an increasing number of small holders are planting crops such as sugar cane, which were once grown exclusively on the estates.

Sugar Cane. It took the Jamaican sugar economy more than a century to recover from the collapse of the colonial plantation (see Chapter 4). The island's record output of 100,000 tons in the early nineteenth century remained unsurpassed until the latter 1930's. Since then, however, production has soared. In 1961, it reached 440,000 tons, of which more than 85 per cent was exported. The key factor in this expansion has undoubtedly been the guaranteed market quota which Jamaica enjoys under the Commonwealth Sugar Agreement with Great Britain.

With the expansion of sugar production in recent decades, cane has come to occupy more than a third of the cultivated land on the island. Interestingly, independent farmers, many of whom are small holders, now cultivate three-fifths of the total land under cane in Jamaica. The estates continue to produce well over half the sugar, on the remaining two-fifths, however, largely because they control the more fertile lowland areas.

A comparison of Figures 6.17 and 6.19 suggests that the leading cane areas are located primarily on the plains along the coast and in the interior solution basins, while subsistence crops are more characteristic of the uplands. In many instances, however, the division of land use between the plains and the adjacent hills is not always clear-cut. For example, at Frome, the largest of the sugar estates, food plots planted by company workers are found throughout the lowland sugar areas, and the hills nearby are dotted with numerous plots of cane cultivated by peasant holders. Since the small producers often have to rely on estate-owned transport facilities and grinding mills, independent cane farming tends to decrease as one moves away from the periphery of the estate. According to G. E. Cumper, "the quantity of cane grown at distances greater than five miles from the estate railheads at Frome is insignificant."[3] The location of the 20 *centrales* (Figure 6.19) imposes comparable restrictions.

Bananas. In the spring of 1870, one Lorenzo Dow Baker sailed his sloop "Telegraph" from Morant Bay, Jamaica, with a risk cargo of 160 stems of bananas. Two weeks later he disposed of the fruit in Jersey City, New Jersey, at a profit of $2 per stem, and both the enterprising Yankee skipper and Jamaica were in the banana business.

Captain Baker eventually returned to the island to preach the benefits of commercial banana cultivation to a very willing audience.[4] Jamaicans were still in the grip of the depression stemming from the decline of sugar which followed the fall of the colonial plantation (see Chapter 4), and they were desperate for a new export crop. Under these conditions, the banana (primarily of the Gros Michel type) quickly took root, particularly in the more humid northeastern parishes of Portland and St. Mary (Figure 6.19).

The new cash crop gave an economic lift to large and small landholders alike, but perhaps more to the small holder. For the peasant farmer, the banana has a number of advantages: it provides income the year round; it can be interplanted with other crops, and is especially useful in providing shade for coffee and cacao plants. Moreover, while better suited to level land, it yields relatively well on the slopeland on which most of the small farms of the island are located.

Beginning in the 1880's, the export value of bananas increased so rapidly that by 1900 it had surpassed that of sugar. Thereafter, until the eve of World War II, the fruit represented the most important commodity in Jamaica's external trade (Table 6.2). Cultivation spread from the northeast to other sectors of the island, including the drier southern parishes where the crop was raised by irrigation. Bananas, often intermixed with other crops, came to occupy over one-third of the island's cultivated land.

[3] G. E. Cumper, "A Modern Jamaican Sugar Estate," in H. D. Huggins, ed., *Social and Economic Studies,* Vol. III, No. 2 (1954). Mona, Jamaica.

[4] In the process, Baker established a business which was to develop into the mighty United Fruit Company.

Table 6.2

JAMAICA: BANANA EXPORTS BY SELECTED YEARS: 1910–1960

Year	Millions of Stems	Per Cent of Export by Value
1910–14 (average)	14.35	49.4
1922	12.71	44.2
1927	21.15	49.8
1937	26.95	51.2
1943	0.28	1.1
1947	5.51	20.6
1953	10.21	18.4
1960	10.27	8.0

Even in its heyday, however, the Jamaican banana economy was not without its problems. The banana trees, with their weak, pulpy trunks and heavy stems of fruit, were pushovers for the hurricanes which lashed the island periodically. And in between the two World Wars, the Panama disease, to which the Gros Michel is especially susceptible, took its toll. This fungus killed the trees and so infected the soil as to rule out further banana cultivation for years in the affected areas. Several estates went out of production, and the local manager of the United Fruit Company is said to have advised Jamaica to give up bananas and "go in for coconuts." In 1936, a second disease, called "Sigatoka" or "leaf spot," added further to the burden of banana cultivators. Finally, the wartime shortage of shipping during the 1940's so drastically curtailed exports (see Table 6.2) that the banana economy would have been wiped out, had it not been for the subsidy paid to growers by the British Food Ministry.

The postwar period has witnessed both recovery and new trends in Jamaica's banana economy. The Lacatan, a variety immune to Panama disease, has largely displaced the Gros Michel banana. Production continues to center in the humid hills and valleys adjacent to the north and east coasts, but there is also some on the irrigated estates in the drier areas. Currently, about 20 per cent of the island's cultivated land is in bananas, as compared to 35 per cent before the war. But perhaps the most disturbing trend is the decrease in the number of peasant cultivators. The Lacatan banana, which now makes up over 80 per cent of the exports, is easily damaged. It must be packed in plastic bags or boxes and requires regular spraying against Sigatoka. Unable to meet these and other rigorous requirements as easily as the estates, many small farmers, especially those in the hills, are giving up banana cultivation.

Other Land Use Patterns and Crops. The land use patterns shown in Figure 6.19 are, at best, a highly generalized version of reality. With only 15 per cent of the island under cultivation or in orchards, much of the area shown in crops includes considerable acreage which is not farmed at all or is used only for grazing. This is particularly true in the eroded uplands and on the drier leeward coast. Similarly, the cultivation of food crops is so widespread that items such as corn and yams often make up the bulk of the farmed land even in the zones shown to be under bananas, coffee, and other largely commercial products. As we have already indicated, food crops (for subsistence and local sale) constitute the most valuable output of the island's farming.

In addition to sugar and bananas, Jamaica produces a variety of secondary agricultural exports. The most important of these has been coffee but, in recent years, citrus fruit, pimento (allspice), and even cacao have commanded a higher value in the island's overseas trade. Most of the secondary exports are raised on small upland farms, and their chief importance is that they provide a cash income for the peasantry.

Jamaican coffee, and especially the famous Blue Mountain product, acquired a very favorable reputation during the colonial plantation period. As in French St. Domingue, the crop was raised on estates and, while it ranked well below sugar, it was one of the island's significant exports during the eighteenth and early nineteenth centuries. But the combined effects of labor shortages, the bankruptcy of the planter class, and the occupation of many coffee estates by the peasantry following emancipation, as well as the recurrent havoc of hurricanes, dealt the industry a blow from which it has never recovered. Recent government efforts to increase output have met with only modest success. The island exported but two million pounds in 1960—a figure well below the estimated market potential.

Mining and Manufacturing. Thanks to the recent growth of the bauxite industry, minerals now surpass agricultural products in Jamaica's foreign trade. Bauxite was discovered in the course of wartime explorations in 1942, but the first shipment of the ore was not made until 1952. Since then, however, bauxite and the alumina processed from it have become the island's leading earners of foreign exchange.

A number of factors have favored the rapid rise of Jamaican bauxite production. Chief among these are the huge ore reserves which the island possesses, and the ease and low cost of mining operations, including the shipment of the ore to market. Most of the bauxite is found in limestone solution hollows averaging 20 to 30 feet deep, with only a thin overburden of soil covering the ore. This makes it possible to carry on inexpensive open-pit mining with power shovels and scrapers. And the mines are located a short distance inland, on the north and south flanks of the limestone plateau, so that the bauxite can be hauled cheaply to port or to local processing plants by truck, rail, and even aerial tramway for eventual shipment to nearby markets in North America. The relatively low alumina content of the ores (46 to 50 per cent) is more than compensated for by the huge reserves, which are estimated to be the world's largest. At the present production rate of about seven million tons per year, they are expected to last for a century.

Capital and know-how for the development of bauxite has come primarily from the United States and Canada. Of the three companies operating in 1964, two—Kaiser and Reynolds—were American; the third, Alcan of Jamaica, is a subsidiary of Canada's Aluminium Limited. (Another United States firm, the Aluminum Company of America, is expected to begin mining in the near future). The Canadians process much of their ore into alumina at plants near Mandeville and Edwarton before shipping it through Port Esquivel; the American companies send their kiln-dried bauxite directly to aluminum refineries in the United States. Reynolds ships through Ocho Rios on the north coast to Corpus Christi, Texas, and Kaiser through its own port on the south coast to Baton Rouge, Louisiana.

The impact of bauxite production on the Jamaican economy and landscape is reflected in a variety of ways. By 1960, this comparatively new industry comprised roughly half the value of the island's exports, employed about 5,000 workers, and accounted for almost a fifth of all government tax receipts. Mining interests have improved existing transportation and shipping facilities, and, as in the case of Port Kaiser, have actually built new ones. Equally significant are the consequences of the laws which oblige bauxite companies to restore mined lands to at least previous fertility and to maintain agricultural production on land being held in reserve for future mining. Before bauxite can be dug in a given area, six or more inches of topsoil must be stripped and stockpiled for restoration to the same location later. In most cases, the companies fertilize the restored soil. In addition, the bauxite firms have undertaken reforestation, planted food crops, improved water supplies and pastures, and developed considerable herds of beef and dairy cattle on their properties. Of the 80,000 acres owned by Reynolds, for example, 60,000 are under some form of cultivation, including a large area planted to Pangola and Guinea grasses. The companies have also imported Santa Gertrudis, Charolais, and Brahman stock to improve the island's cattle strains.

In addition to bauxite, Jamaica also mines gypsum, a nonmetallic mineral widely used in cement, plaster of Paris, and other building materials. Rich, 85-per cent-pure, massive deposits of gypsum are located near Bull Bay about ten miles east of Kingston. Most of the 246,000 tons produced in 1960 was sent to New Orleans and Jacksonville, but some was retained for use in local cement and plaster board factories.

Tourism and Trade. Except in the war years, tourism has grown constantly ever since the flow of visitors first assumed significant proportions in the mid-1920's. Prior to the war, most tourists came by sea, on cruise ships and even banana boats. Port Antonio, for example, once ranked along with Montego Bay and Kingston as a tourist center, largely because it served as a port of call for vessels in the banana trade. Since the war, the rapidly increasing movement of vacationers to the island has been largely by air. Like Puerto Rico, Jamaica's tourism has been benefited in recent years by the rising prosperity of the United States, which supplies most of the visitors, and by the United States proscription of travel to Cuba since Castro came to power. In 1960, the island was host to almost a quarter of a million people, and tourism is now ranked (after minerals and sugar) as the third most important industry. Only bauxite surpasses it as a dollar earner. In addition to the expansion of facilities in the old tourist centers of Montego Bay and Kingston, the large postwar influx has given rise to new developments on the north coast beach zones between Falmouth and Port Maria, and more recently, in the Negril district at the western end of the island. Interestingly, some of the old manor houses of the colonial plantation period are, along with the new hotels and guest houses, serving the tourist trade.

The pattern of foreign trade has been undergoing very great changes. In 1950, for example, sugar and bananas accounted for 65 per cent of the exports; the bulk of the trade was with Britain and the sterling block; and the value of all goods shipped was £14.8 million. By 1960, the value of exports had leaped to £55.7 million; sugar and bananas comprised 35 per cent of the trade, as compared to 49 per cent accounted for by bauxite and alumina; and most of the trade was with the dollar countries (United States and Canada) rather than with Britain. The major cause of these changes has been the dominant role assumed by bauxite mining and processing in the island's economy. Britain continues to take most of the agricultural products.

Population and Settlement

As already suggested in Chapter 4, the

historical occupance of Jamaica may be broadly divided into two stages: (1) the colonial plantation-slave period, during which there was selective settlement of lowland areas suited for sugar production; and (2) postemancipation, roughly to 1910, during which a population of peasant farmers invested the unoccupied limestone uplands to the limits of cultivation. With the disappearance of the settlement frontier in 1910, the gross patterns of population distribution were complete. Thereafter, there was no significant extension of the settled area; instead, land use became more intense, densities continued to rise and, above all, there began a marked trend to urbanization which has continued at an ever-accelerating tempo. Over-all population densities, 86 in 1844, reached 365 persons per square mile in 1960.

The current distribution of population tends to be correlated closely with terrain, the history of settlement and urbanization, and the productive capacity of agricultural land. The heaviest concentration is the urban sprawl of Kingston–St. Andrew which continues westward along the irrigated southern lowlands, through Spanish Town, to Port Esquivel. Densities are also high in St. Thomas in the Vale and other well-watered solution valleys such as those of the Black and Minho Rivers; in the Montego Bay area and south through the lowlands of the Great River; and along the humid north and east coasts from Falmouth to about Morant Bay. Elsewhere, population densities are less, and ratios are especially low along the driest sectors of the southwest coast, the Cockpit Country, and in the highest mountain zones of the central and eastern parts of the island.

Emigration. Population pressure has made Jamaicans prone to emigration for almost a century. The first large-scale flow from the island was to Panama between 1881 and 1886, when the French were working on the Panama Canal. This was followed by a significant movement to Costa Rica, where railway construction was in progress. Resumption of work on the Canal by the United States, in 1904, again directed the major flow to Panama. The expansion of sugar cultivation in Cuba, the development of banana plantations along the Caribbean coast of Central America, and the growing commercial ties between Jamaica and the United States in the latter nineteenth century provided other foci for emigration (see Table 6.3). Prior to the post-World War II movement to Britain, the major period of Jamaican emigration was 1881 to 1921. After 1921, immigration restrictions imposed by most countries which had received the islanders reduced the outflow to a mere trickle.

In the post-World War II period Jamaicans have been the most numerous group of West Indians moving to the United Kingdom. Annual net migration to Britain rose from 1,700, in 1950, to about 30,000 in 1960, but this flow is now largely cut off by restrictions imposed by the British Parliament. Unlike former emigrants who were largely unskilled, many of those who have been leaving Jamaica in recent years come from the small reservoir of skilled labor. Remittances from the emigrants are important to the island's economy.

Settlement Types and Patterns. The bulk of Jamaica's population lives in dispersed homesteads or in small clusters which, depending on size and function, may be classified as neighborhoods or villages (Figure 6.21). In most parishes, the chief town is on the sea coast and serves as a port. Except for Kingston, the term "city" is difficult to apply to the urban centers.

Some differences exist, however, between the interior uplands, with their large number of small holders and subsistence agriculture, and the lowlands, with their estates, commercial farming, ports, and fishing villages. In the hilly interior, dispersed settlement is the rule, although discontinuous ribbon clusters of households often form neighborhoods along the motor roads. At more important road junctions, the ribbonlike clusters of buildings are more closely spaced and form the typical village. In addition to residences, the village also includes shops, a primary school, a post office, and facilities for a weekly market. While the lowlands also have some dispersed settlement, one sees more village clusters here than in the uplands. This is especially true of the sugar estates and the fishing settlements. Often the estate villages consist of barracks and other housing built by the landowners for the workers. The lowland village tends to be more nucleated and less ribbonlike than its upland counterpart.

Kingston, which, together with its suburbs, had a population of 380,000 in 1960, is far and away Jamaica's chief city. Founded in 1693 after the destruction of Port Royal, the city has been aided by a sheltered and once easily defended harbor and a rich agricultural hinterland. Kingston suffered heavy damage by earthquakes in 1907, but was rebuilt and now functions as the island's chief port, as well as its major administrative, fi-

Table 6.3

ESTIMATED NET EMIGRATION FROM JAMAICA: 1881–1921

Period	To the U.S.	To Panama	To Cuba	To Other Areas	To All Areas
1881–1891	16,000	17,000		10,000	69,000
1891–1911		26,000			
1911–1921	30,000	2,000	22,000	23,000	77,000

Source: G. W. Roberts, *The Population of Jamaica,* London: Cambridge University Press, 1957, p. 139.

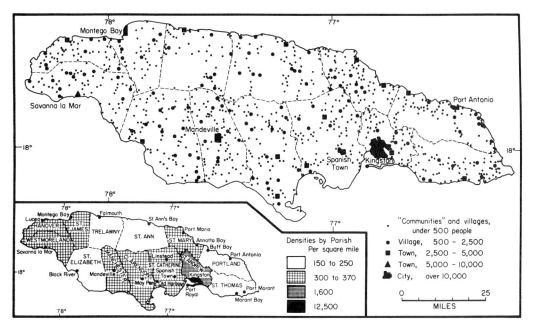

Figure 6.21
Jamaica : Settlement Types and Patterns.

nancial, and transportation center. In recent decades, its suburbs have spread rapidly into the parish of St. Andrew across the Liguanea Plain and up into the encircling foothills. Kingston has been, by far, the leading terminus of Jamaica's country-to-town movement since 1911. Other significant urban centers are Montego Bay (population, 24,500 in 1960) which functions both as a port and the leading tourist mecca; Port Antonio, a banana outlet on the northeast coast; and Spanish Town, the former insular capital, located on the southern lowlands.

THE CAYMAN ISLANDS

Some 200 miles northwest of Jamaica are the three Cayman Islands: Gran Cayman, Little Cayman, and Cayman Brac. Low, flat, and covered with limestone, these islands lie atop the Cayman Ridge, a submarine extension of the Sierra Maestra of Cuba and one of the mountain systems of Old Antillia (see Chapter 2). Formerly the Caymans were a dependency of Jamaica, but in 1959 they became a separate British colony with internal self-government.

In sharp contrast to Jamaica's predominately agricultural population, the Cayman Islanders are a seafaring people—fishermen, turtlers, and shiphands, who find their way to many parts of the Caribbean. About 9,000 live on the three islands, most of them on the larger Gran Cayman. Some 30 per cent are white, 50 per cent mulatto or "coloured," the rest Negro; nearly all are descendants from English colonists and African slaves who settled from Jamaica in the eighteenth century.

Since the late seventeenth century, the economy of the Cayman Islands has revolved around the exploitation of the large, green sea turtle. The wide, sandy beaches of Gran Cayman were once the nesting grounds of countless green turtles. During the eighteenth and early nineteenth centuries, the turtle population of the Caymans was virtually destroyed by Caymanians and English seamen who sold the salted flesh as slave food to the sugar estates on Jamaica and the Lesser Antilles. Still today, a large portion of the male inhabitants of Gran Cayman are turtlers, but the turtle fleet now operates in

the Miskito Cays off the Nicaraguan coast or off the Tortuguero Coast of northeastern Costa Rica. For their main market, the Caymanian turtlers look to the New York area and to London, where both live turtles and quick-frozen meat are used to make the gourmets' green turtle soup served in plush restaurants.

SELECTED REFERENCES

Augelli, J. P., "Agricultural Colonization in the Dominican Republic," *Economic Geography,* XXXVIII, No. 1 (1962), 15–27.

Blaut, J. M., *et al.,* "A Study of Cultural Determinants of Soil Erosion and Conservation in the Blue Mountains of Jamaica," *Social and Economic Studies,* VIII, No. 4 (1959), 403–20.

Crist, R. E., "Cultural Dichotomy in the Island of Hispaniola," *Economic Geography,* XXVIII, No. 2 (1952), 105–21.

Cumper, G. E., "Population Movements in Jamaica: 1830–1950," *Social and Economic Studies,* V, No. 3 (1956), 261–80.

de Young M., *Man and Land in the Haitian Economy,* Latin American Monographs, No. 3 Gainesville, Fla.: University of Florida Press, 1958.

Dyer, D. R., "Distribution of Population on Hispaniola," *Economic Geography,* XXX, No. 4 (1954), 337–46.

Edwards, D., *Report on an Economic Study of Small Farming in Jamaica.* Mona, Jamaica: University College of the West Indies, Institute of Social and Economic Research, 1961.

Holly, M. A., *Agriculture in Haiti.* New York: Vantage Press, 1955.

"La Historia Azucarera y su Evolución en la República Dominicana," *Revista Secretaria Estado Industria Comercio Banca,* XLII (1955), 59–86.

Logan, R. W., *Haiti and the Dominican Republic.*

London: Royal Institute of International Affairs, 1963.

Moral, P., "La Culture du Café en Haïti," *Les Cahiers d'Outre-Mer,* VIII (1955), 233–56.

———, "La Maison Rurale en Haïti," *Les Cahiers d'Outre-Mer,* X (1957), 117–30.

———, *L'Économie Haïtienne.* Port-au-Prince: Imprimerie de l'État, 1959.

———, *Le Paysan Haïtien: Étude sur la Vie Rurale en Haïti.* Paris: G. P. Maisonnueve et Larose, 1961.

Moscoso Puello, F. E., *Cañas y Bueyes.* Santo Domingo, Dominican Republic: Editorial La Nación, 1935.

Pearson, R., "The Jamaica Bauxite Industry," *Journal of Geography,* LVI, No. 8 (1957), 377–85.

Roberts, G. W., *The Population of Jamaica: An Analysis of its Structure and Growth.* London: Cambridge University Press, 1957.

Street, J. M., *Historical and Economic Geography of the Southwest Peninsula of Haiti,* University of California, Department of Geography, Office of Naval Research Technical Report. Berkeley, Calif., 1960.

Thomas, C. Y., "Coffee Production in Jamaica," *Social and Economic Studies,* XIII, No. 1 (1964), 188–217.

Wood, H. A., *Northern Haiti: Land, Land Use and Settlement.* Toronto, Canada: University of Toronto Press, 1963.

7

The Lesser Antilles and the Bahamas

The Lesser Antilles

The geographic variety which characterizes the larger West Indian islands is no
less pronounced in the Lesser Antilles.[1] Behind the seemingly uniform facade of tropical
insularity, a widespread dependence on farming, and a largely Negroid population, lie
significant physical and cultural differences.
Some of the islands belong to the high-lying,
humid volcanic arc of the Antilles; others
fall into the less humid, low-lying limestone
arc; and still others, such as Trinidad, are
fragments separated from the South American continent (see Chapter 2).

Agriculture is the cornerstone of most of
the insular economies, but land use and
tenure, commercial crops, and other aspects
of farming vary. Estate-grown sugar is still
the chief cash crop on Barbados, Trinidad,
St. Kitts, and Antigua. Elsewhere, cane cultivation declined sharply or disappeared after
emancipation, and peasant-grown cash crops,
such as sea island cotton, arrowroot, nut-
megs, and bananas, are now the mainstay of
the economy.

Patterns of population, political orientation, language, and religion are equally
diverse. Many of the islets and reefs are too
small or inhospitable for human occupance;
others, such as Barbados, are among the
world's most densely populated territories.
The official languages are English, French,
and Dutch, depending on current political
connections, but the language of the people
may have older origins. Thus, a French
patois is spoken in British-connected Dominica and St. Lucia; Hindi is heard in the
East Indian villages of Trinidad; and the
Barbadian peasant's English is unique. As
for religion, Trinidad alone probably has as
great a variety as most of mainland America.

TRINIDAD

Although each of the Lesser Antilles
has its own geographic flavor, none approaches the distinctiveness of Trinidad. The
island is the largest and most populous in
the archipelago, the richest in natural resources, and the most heterogeneous in ethnic
composition. It is also the only Lesser Antillean territory with sufficient economic viability to be politically independent.[2] These
advantages stem partly from its physical
geography and partly from its unique history
of settlement and exploitation.

---

[1] We include, among the Lesser Antilles, Trinidad, Barbados, all the territories from the Virgin
Islands in the north to Grenada in the south, and
Aruba, Bonaire, and Curaçao, which lie well to the
west of the Antillean chain. There is no absolute
agreement about the inclusiveness of the designation. For many students, especially geologists, the
Lesser Antilles begin with the islands east of the
Anegada Passage, such as Sombrero and Anguilla,
and end with Grenada or Tobago in the south
(Figure 7.1).

---

[2] Trinidad followed Jamaica's example both in
withdrawing from the West Indies Federation and
in electing for independence within the British
Commonwealth.

Physical and Historical Setting

A detatched fragment of South America, Trinidad shows the imprint of close connection with the continent in both its physical and historical geography. The island's geology, including the oil-bearing Tertiary formations, its surface configuration, and its plant and animal life, is more akin to the adjacent Orinoco region of Venezuela than to the more distant volcanic and limestone arcs of the Lesser Antilles (see Chapter 2 and Figure 7.1).

Figure 7.1

The Lesser Antilles.

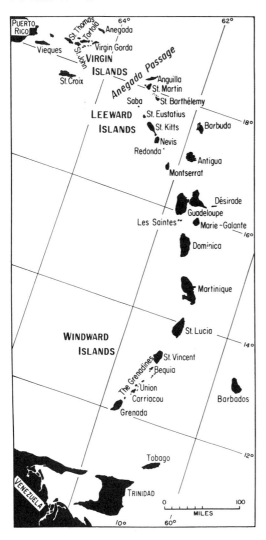

In contrast to the rugged Windwards, for example, Trinidad's relief is generally subdued. The major exception is the Northern Range, a line of steep-sided mountains which rises abruptly from the sea to elevations of 3,000 feet (Figure 7.2). Even this range is punctuated on its southern flank by several large, pouch-shaped valleys. The only other uplands are two low, narrow ridges of hills, with elevations of 1,000 feet or less, which extend across the center and south of Trinidad. The rest of the island is lowland whose chief handicap is poor drainage. Because of its comparatively large size (1,864 square miles) and its gentle relief, the island has more level, cultivatable lowland than any of the other Lesser Antilles.

Trinidad also possesses a major climatic advantage. It lies south of the main path of hurricanes and seldom experiences them. Because of its lower latitude and other influences, the climate is distinctly hot for the West Indies. The high temperatures and generally high precipitation (Figure 7.3) often create hot-house weather, uncomfortable for people but ideal for tropical crops such as cacao. Soils vary widely but, on the whole, the most fertile are along the west coast and in the southern valleys and foothills of the Northern Range.

Trinidad's unarticulated coastline is a drawback, however. A combination of steep barrier mountains in the north, widespread coastal swamps, and winds and currents make sea communications difficult, except in a few spots along the western margins of the island.

Its soil, its adequate rainfall, its year-round growing season, and its relative protection from hurricane provide Trinidad with an agricultural potential far exceeding that of the other Lesser Antilles. Yet, Spain, which controlled the island from its discovery until the British annexation in 1797, sent only a few colonists, and these developed little agriculture. There was a little cultivation, particularly of cacao, during the seventeenth and eighteenth centuries, but by 1783

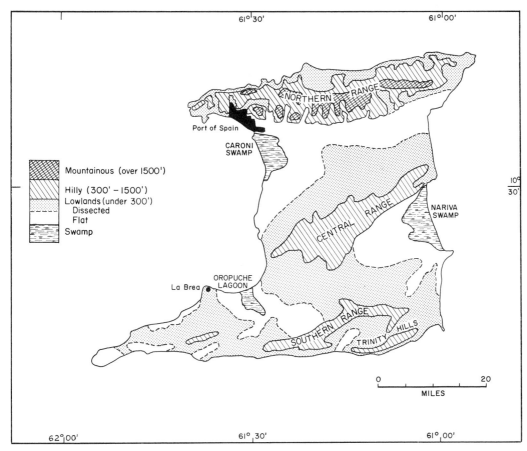

Figure 7.2

Trinidad : Generalized Surface Configuration.

the total population of Trinidad was only 2,763.

In 1783, Spain liberalized its colonization policies, permitting all Roman Catholics to enter, remitting taxes, and conceding land to new settlers. As a result, the island began to receive a moderate flow of immigrants, largely planters from revolt-torn St. Domingue and other French West Indian colonies. On the eve of the British occupation, there was some production of sugar, the population had risen to about 20,000, and settlement had expanded from a tiny nucleus around Port of Spain to adjacent areas on the Caroni Plain and in the valleys of the Northern Range.

The tempo of economic development and the spread of settlement picked up dramatically after 1797. The plantation-minded British settlers expanded commercial agri-culture, and cash crops such as sugar and cacao provided a firm economic foundation throughout the nineteenth century. The economy was further strengthened by petroleum

Figure 7.3

Trinidad : Mean Annual Rainfall.

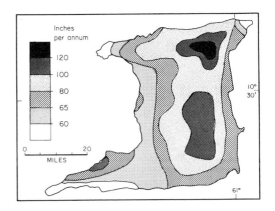

after 1910 and, more recently, by manufacturing, tourism, and other sources of income.

The steady demand for workers attracted immigrants not only from nearby islands but also from India, China, and other distant places (see Chapter 4). As the population increased, the frontier was gradually thrust southward from Port of Spain. By the 1870's, much of the western part of the island had been occupied. The settlement of lands in the east came later, with the development of cacao plantations.

Economic Patterns

In most respects, Trinidad's economy is typically West Indian. Agriculture employs most of the people; export crops occupy so much of the best land that much food must be imported. For its food, as well as for a wide range of other imports, including most finished goods, the island is slavishly dependent on the export value of a limited number of products. Unlike most of the other Antilles, however, Trinidad exports more petroleum and related products than agricultural commodities.

Petroleum and Asphalt. Leases for oil exploration have been granted for more than 90 per cent of Trinidad's surface, including its offshore areas. Most of the oil, however, comes from a small zone adjacent to the Pitch Lake (Figure 7.4) and from the offshore Soldado field in the Gulf of Paria. Proven deposits are associated primarily with the Tertiary formations located in the southern part of the island, opposite the delta of the Orinoco, and may be considered a geological extension of Venezuela's Orinoco oil province.

Trinidad's oil industry was developed after 1910, primarily by British capital. In 1956, however, Texaco, an American firm, bought the English-owned Trinidad Oil Company and became the largest owner. Texaco together with British Petroleum and Shell now account for 90 per cent of the production; the remainder is pumped by more than a half-dozen small companies.

Because of complex subsurface conditions, low yields, and other handicaps, the cost of petroleum exploration and production is exceptionally high. Most wells have to be drilled to 4,000 feet; a few have gone down to 16,000 feet. Even so, they produce less than one-fifth the average of Venezuelan wells. The industry is bolstered, however, by the refining of both its own and imported crudes.

Trinidad now refines over twice as much oil as it pumps. Crude is imported chiefly from nearby Venezuela and Colombia, but smaller quantities come from as far as Saudi Arabia. The refineries are at Pointe-à-Pierre, Brighton, and Point Fortin—all at tidewater locations on the west coast near San Fernando. By the early 1960's, an average of over 100 million barrels was being refined annually.

Despite foreign ownership, oil is the nerve center of Trinidad's economy. In the early 1960's, taxes, custom duties, and royalties from petroleum accounted for over one-third of the island's general revenue and over one-fifth of the income of the government-operated railway, telegraph, and port services. Oil, and associated products such as asphalt, accounted for more than 80 per cent of the value of Trinidad's exports and contributed twice as much to the gross domestic product as agriculture, forestry, and fisheries combined.

Geologically associated with oil are considerable reserves of natural gas and asphalt. Although most of the asphalt is a by-product of oil refining, the island is famous for the natural deposits at Pitch Lake, near La Brea (Figure 7.4). The lake's natural asphalt is a semisolid bituminous material which results from the mixing of gas and oil with clay. In a few spots the material is soft and sticky but, over most of the surface, it is hard enough to cut into blocks. It is then loaded on light railway cars and carried up the steep lip of the lake to a factory where asphalt cement and other by-products are made, and the finished product is hauled by overhead cable to a nearby pier.

Pitch Lake is the world's chief deposit of natural asphalt. Annual output is over 150,-000 tons, cumulative production since mining began in 1867 is about ten million tons, and the reserves are estimated at several million tons. Removal of the asphalt causes the lake to drop a few inches every year, and the surface is now over 30 feet below the rim.

Agriculture

Land Use and Tenure. Nearly half of Trinidad's total area is in forest, but the wood-land cover appears even more extensive because tree crops occupy more than half the cultivated land. The remaining farmland is mostly in sugar cane and food crops (Figure 7.4).

The land is held both in estates and in small peasant plots. The estates, which comprise less than 1 per cent of the farms but control over 40 per cent of the farm land, dominate sugar and coconut production; the smaller holdings produce all the food and half the cacao and coffee. The peasant plots are of more commercial importance in Trinidad than in most of the other Antilles.

Sugar. For several decades following the

Figure 7.4
Trinidad : Land Use.

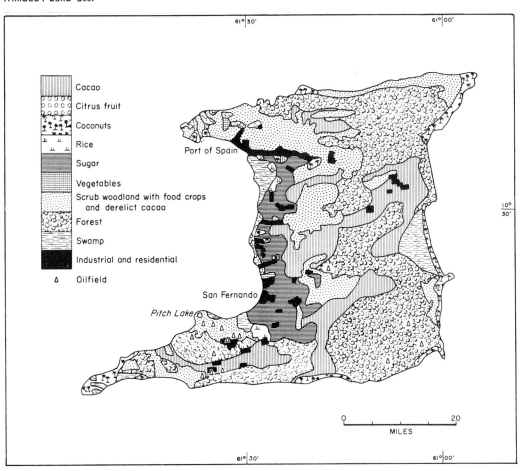

British occupation, Trinidad's sugar production was based on a modification of the colonial plantation (see Chapter 4). Estates were generally family-size farms, widely dispersed in the valleys of the Northern Range and along the west coast; virtually every estate was equipped with a *trapiche*; and transportation and milling costs were high.

Despite these inefficiencies and the "labour problem," an abundance of virgin land enabled Trinidad to weather the postemancipation sugar crisis of the West Indies until the 1870's. By that time, however, the island's competitive position in the world sugar market had become weak and there ensued a rapid changeover to the modern plantation. The family estates gave way to corporate ownership and the *central*. The more remote cane lands were planted to cacao and other crops, and sugar production was increasingly concentrated in a belt running south of Port of Spain to the Oropuche Lagoon. Here were the best conditions—level terrain, better soils, a more favorable climate, and easy access to ports. Little cane is now grown elsewhere on the island.

Currently, cane occupies about a quarter of the cropland, the ownership being about equally divided between the estates and some 11,000 small holders. The capital resources, mechanization, and efficiency of the estates, however, enable them to produce twice as much sugar as the small holdings and to process the entire crop. Many of the small sugar farms are owned by East Indians who also work as wage laborers on the estates. Great Britain is the chief buyer, and Canada and the United States also purchase significant amounts.

Cacao and Other Agricultural Exports. As we noted earlier, cacao was grown very early in the colonial period, but it became a significant crop only in the late nineteenth century. When sugar declined, the cultivation of cacao increased rapidly and, by 1900, it had become the island's leading export. Eventually, cacao occupied much of the former cane land in the west and spread over the unsettled virgin lands in the eastern part of the island.

Cacao prospered until the 1930's. Then, the witch's broom disease, combined with competition from the African Gold Coast and the Great Depression, brought about a decline. Many cacao farms were abandoned, others became coffee or citrus groves, and still others became cane fields or were put to other use. In the valleys of the Northern Range, for example, the cacao lands closest to Port of Spain became urban areas; those more removed from the capital became citrus groves.

At present, more of Trinidad's land is classed as "cacao" than "sugar" (Figure 7.4), but this is misleading because many of the cacao plantings are derelict. Moreover, cacao is generally intercropped with other plants and seldom occupies more than half the land. Currently, cacao production centers in the Central Range, northeast of San Fernando. The crop is produced both on estates and on small holdings, but the estates use superior methods so that, with substantially less acreage, they produce more.

Other Trinidad export crops of some importance include citrus fruit and coconuts. Citrus fruit has replaced cacao, especially in the valleys of the northern range. Coconuts grow on the sandy soils of virtually all of the island's coasts (Figure 7.4), and almost three-fourths of the output comes from large estates. The bulk of the harvest is dried to make copra for the manufacture of edible oils, soap, and cosmetics. Most of these products are consumed locally, but some are exported to other West Indian territories.

Food Crops. Food crops are grown largely in an area of small holdings which skirts the sugar belt and runs to the south of San Fernando. Rice, the most distinctive food crop, is raised mainly in the low, wet areas of the Caroni Swamp. It is grown during the wet season between June and

December; the rest of the year the fields are often planted to vegetables. Rice is produced almost entirely by East Indians who plow the land with the water buffalo and use other Asiatic techniques. Most of the harvest is consumed by its growers and a large part of the island's rice, as well as other food, has to be imported.

Secondary Industries. In the postwar period there has been a marked increase in manufacturing in Trinidad, much of it developed with government financing and other support. Its growth has also been aided by a modest local market, cheap power, and comparatively low labor costs. Manufacturing began with the processing of oil, asphalt, and agricultural products, but now includes cement, textiles and clothing, pharmaceuticals, plastic goods, and numerous other products.

The government of Trinidad is also subsidizing an effort to increase tourism. The new Trinidad-Hilton Hotel, which opened in 1962, is the largest of some 30 hotels and guest houses. In addition to its natural beauty, Trinidad's attractions include its fascinating variety of cultures and races and its importance as a hub for air transportation. Much of the tourist trade is from stopover visitors. The majority of these (over 125,000 in 1961) come from nearby Venezuela, from other Antillean territories, and from North America.

Population

As we noted elsewhere, the economic development of Trinidad following the British occupation was accompanied by the rapid growth and ethnic diversification of the population. From a mere 20,000 in 1797, the population climbed to 75,000 by 1851, to 300,000 by 1911, and reached over 800,000 in the early 1960's. Besides the East Indians who came between 1845 and 1917 (see Chapter 4), there arrived, at various periods, smaller numbers of Chinese, Madeiran peasants, Syrians, European Jews, Venezuelans, and others. The largest group came, after emancipation, from overcrowded territories elsewhere in the British Caribbean, especially from Barbados and the Windward Islands. Even today, about one Trinidadian in ten was born in one of the other British territories in the Lesser Antilles.

Distribution. The current distribution of the population reflects Trinidad's settlement history, terrain, land use, and a variety of other conditions. The lowest population densities coincide with the rugged terrain of the Northern Range and the zones of poorer soils, inadequate drainage, and inarticulate coastlines in the east and south (Figures 7.2 and 7.5). The heaviest concentrations are in the west, which was settled earlier, has a more articulate coastline, and whose fertile soil is more intensively and commercially cultivated. The western counties also include most of the oil fields and refineries, the Pitch Lake, and the urban complexes of Port of Spain and San Fernando (Figure 7.4).

Trinidad's people have been moving to the towns, particularly since 1940, and it is now one of the most urbanized territories in the West Indies. By the 1960's, the population of metropolitan Port of Spain was well over 200,000, and the entire area between the capital and Tuna Puna, ten miles east, was gradually fusing into one urban sprawl. The urban thrust of the metropolitan zone was being felt even in the island's third largest city, Arima, 24 miles to the east (Figure 7.5). San Fernando, the second largest city, has also grown vigorously.

In the rural areas, population densities tend to vary with the labor requirements of the dominant crop. Thus, sugar cane, which requires a large labor force, is associated with high concentrations, and many parts of the sugar belt, which extends south of Port of Spain (Figures 7.4 and 7.5), contain over 200 persons per square mile. Rice and vegetable gardening are associated with comparable, and even higher, densities. Cacao,

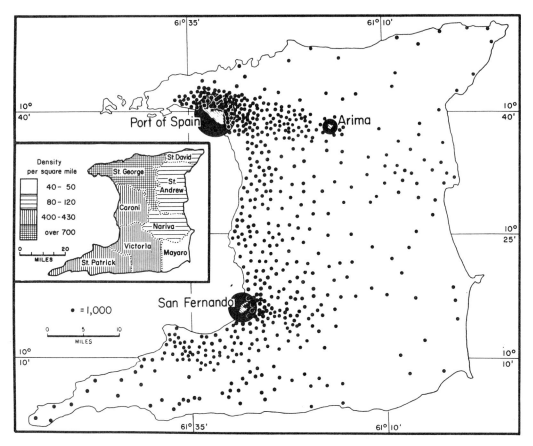

Figure 7.5
Trinidad : Population Distribution and Density.

which requires about one-half the labor force needed for sugar cane, is associated with less dense populations. Coconuts, the chief cash crop along much of the southern and eastern coastal margin, require a small labor force and hence are associated with low population densities.

Racial and Cultural Diversity. While there has been some mixing among Trinidad's diverse racial and ethnic groups, the island has not been a melting pot. The various segments have retained their distinctiveness and, as a result, Trinidad's landscape is marked by a variety of cultural features and flavors. The diversity of the population is expressed in distribution, as well as its settle-

ment, its land use, its agricultural systems, its place names, and in other areal phenomena; it is also mirrored in differences in religion, architecture, language, diet, class association, dress, and even politics. There is virtually no aspect of the island's culture which does not somehow express the diversity of its people.

Distributional contrasts between the Negroes and East Indians are especially sharp. The Negroes (or Creoles) markedly prefer the urban areas. They comprise about 57 per cent of the total population, but account for a far greater percentage of people in the cities and towns, in the oil fields, and in the Pitch Lake district; they comprise much less than 57 per cent of the population, in the intensively cultivated countryside. The distribution of the East Indians is almost the reverse. They make up about 40 per cent of the population, but contribute far less than this ratio to the urban areas and the oil fields; they form a much higher percentage of the population in the more intensively cultivated areas, especially the sugar belt.

Place names are truly diverse. Town names are French (Blanchisseuse), Spanish (Sangre Grande), Indian (Fyzabad), English (St. Mary's), as well as Irish and Scotch (Flanagin Town and McBean). In Port of Spain, O'Connor, De Vertueil, and Petra are adjacent streets and Fraser and Carlton run alongside others named Madras, Calcutta, and Bengal.

Religious architecture is equally heterogeneous (Figures 7.6, 7.7, and 7.8). There are stately English Gothic churches, Moslem mosques, and Hindu temples. There are many sects, but the major religious division

Figure 7.6
Hindu Temple: Port of Spain, Trinidad.

Figure 7.7
Episcopalian Church: Trinidad.

Figure 7.8
Cemetery: Port of Spain, Trinidad.

is between the Christian population, which includes practically all the European and Negro groups and the non-Christians, which include the East Indian Hindus and Moslems, the Jews and others.

The Christians are mostly Roman Catholics, but Presbyterians, Methodists, and Baptists are well represented. About 70 per cent of the East Indians are classified as Hindus, and the remainder are, in almost equal numbers, Moslems and Christians. In addition to the established religions, there are sects with a strong African flavor, such as the Shango, the Rada, and the Shouters.

Language is less varied. English is the official tongue and Creole English the ordinary language, but remnants of Spanish, French patois, and Urdu and Hindi survive.

Tobago

Tobago, which has an area of 116 square miles and a population of over 30,000, is politically bracketed with Trinidad. But its history, economy, and landscape are noticeably different.

In size and general character, Tobago bears a closer resemblance to the Windward Islands than to Trinidad, which is only 20 miles away. The uplands of the Main Ridge, which dominates the northeast, consist of igneous materials; the lower, southwest portion of the island is made up largely of coral terraces. Tobago was settled early, unlike Trinidad, and during the seventeenth and eighteenth centuries, its sugar, cotton, and indigo made it a bone of contention among France, England and Holland. Before British rule was established in 1814, the island had changed hands more often than any other West Indian territory.

At that time, Tobago was an intensively cultivated plantation island with a prosperous, slave-supported sugar economy. The economy began to collapse, however, after 1838, when over 10,000 slaves were emancipated and by 1886, exports had fallen 90 per cent. Economic distress forced Tobago to unite with its more prosperous neighbor, Trinidad, in 1888.

Tobago has since experimented with several other cash crops, of which the most important are now cacao, which is raised on the humid windward side and coconuts, which are more characteristic of the leeward side. About 40 per cent of the total area is under cultivation (Figure 7.9), but the economy is a weak one. A long history of exploitation has depleted the soil, and yields are low. Erosion is a major problem on the

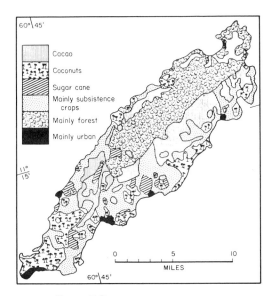

Figure 7.9

Tobago : Land Use.

tion densities had reached 700 people per square mile by 1834–1838, the period of emancipation. And, since nearly all the land was in the hands of the planters, the freed Negroes were unable to obtain holdings of their own and either had to continue to work for their former masters or migrate. The abundant supply of cheap labor enabled the economy to survive the sugar crisis of the nineteenth century. Barbadian planters were under less pressure to incorporate or to invest in new machinery and mills than were planters in Jamaica and Trinidad. Nor did they have to diversify; Barbados' land and labor force could still produce sugar more profitably than any other crop.

The Land

Barbados is the most easterly of the West Indies, located at least 100 miles further out in the Atlantic than its nearest neighbor, St. Vincent. From the west, the island looks flat and uniform. Closer observation, however, reveals considerable variation in relief. Rainfall, soils, and other physical characteristics are also varied.

Most of the island consists of a limestone layer over a core of strongly folded sedimentary rocks such as clays, sandstones, and shales. In the northeastern, or Scotland, district, the limestone cap has been eroded and the underlying rock has been weathered into rugged ridges and ravines. Elsewhere, the island is mostly a series of terraces, each with a retaining wall of coral rock, which ascend from west to east and culminate in Mt. Hillaby (1,115 feet) in the Central Uplands (Figure 7.10). East of the upland mass, the land often drops abruptly, forming cliffs which plunge hundreds of feet to the windward coast. South of the uplands, the land descends to St. George's Valley and rises again to about 400 feet at the Christ Church ridge.

Soils in the limestone areas, while shallow, are very fertile. In zones of higher elevation and rainfall, they are red or brown and, like

interior slope land, where most of the peasant plots are located, and even the coastal estates have suffered.

Tobago's dominantly Negro population has a high birth rate, but large-scale emigration to Trinidad has kept the net population increase relatively low in recent years.

BARBADOS

Barbados has been appropriately described as "a city with sugar cane growing in the suburbs." Over 230,000 persons are crowded into an area of 166.3 square miles, producing urbanlike population concentrations; yet, the island depends primarily on farming, and on one crop at that. For the past three centuries, almost all the cultivated land has been in sugar.

Barbados was the first of the West Indies to experience the sugar revolution in the seventeenth century, and the first to experiment successfully with the slave plantation (see Chapter 4). But emancipation caused relatively little disruption in Barbados. So many slaves had been imported that popula-

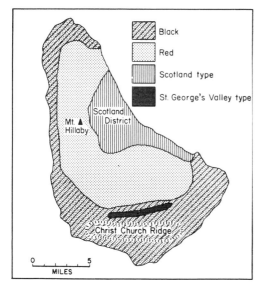

Figure 7.10

Barbados : Major Soil Types. *(Based on map by Starkey)*

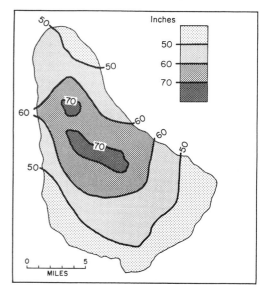

Figure 7.11

Barbados : Mean Annual Rainfall.

the Matanzas clays of Cuba, especially suited for cane. On the less wet limestone lowlands, the soil is black and less fertile. In the Scotland district, the soils vary in fertility, but are often so eroded as to be untillable. The black soils of St. George's Valley are highly productive when properly plowed and drained. All the soil is admixed with volcanic materials, which presumably were carried to the island from the Windwards, especially from Mt. Soufrière on St. Vincent.

The productive capacity of the land also depends on the water supply and drainage. Rainfall is irregular, both from year to year and from place to place. The annual average rainfall is about 63 inches, most of which falls during the rainy season (June to November), but it may be less than 40 inches or soar to almost 90. And 25-inch differences between the wettest zones in the Central Uplands and the driest zones on the leeward coast are common (Figure 7.11).

Immediately after a heavy rain, drainage becomes a problem. Soils become water-logged, and farmers have to bore holes, or "sucks," through the underlying coral rock to get rid of the excess water. There are no permanent streams on Barbados; the water seeps into underground, basinlike catchment areas which have been dissolved in the limestone. These reservoirs are tapped by wells, largely for domestic use, but some water is also used for irrigation.

Economic Patterns

Except for a very modest tourist industry, a scattering of manufacturing enterprises, and some entrepôt trade, the Barbadian economy rests almost exclusively on farming. The enormous pressure of population has resulted in much more intensive farming here than elsewhere in the Caribbean. Every bit of productive land is used. The forests

Table 7.1

BARBADOS : LAND USE

Use	Acres
Suger cane	59,350
Other crops	7,650
Pastures and "rab" land	25,000
Urban uses, roads, and waste	14,000
Total acreage	106,000

and thickets which once covered the island have vanished; over 55 per cent of the total area is tilled; and what land cannot be worked is put to other uses (Table 7.1). On the steep flanks of the terraces is grown grass for fodder and for cane mulch, while "rab" land, unfit even for pasture, is being planted with hardy trees or supports peasant dwellings. Farming practices are similarly intensive.

Sugar. Agriculture and cane cultivation have been virtually synonomous on Barbados for three centuries. The crop occupies almost 90 per cent of the cultivatable land; sugar and its by-products, rum and molasses, constitute up to 95 per cent of the exports. The well-being of every person, be he merchant, peasant or politician, is tied to cane. Nowhere else in the Caribbean has sugar reigned so long and absolutely, and nowhere else is its reign more secure.

The sugar plantation or estate is the dominant holding. Four-fifths of all the land is held in about 240 estates which range from 10 to 1,000 acres, and average between 150 and 200 acres. The remainder of the land is held in small peasant plots averaging less than 10 acres. Cane is produced both on estates and on peasant plots, but the estates with more and better land and more efficient management, produce almost six times as much sugar as the small holders.

Farming practices, as well as yields, reflect the pressure of population. Labor-saving machinery is little used (Figure 7.12). Holes for planting, for example, are still dug by hand. Production has been increased largely

Figure 7.12
Harvesting Sugar Cane with a Machete or Cutlass in Barbados. (*Barbados Tourist Board*)

through the use of fertilizer and better plant varieties and by the elimination of pests and plant diseases. By such measures, the island's annual output of raw sugar was increased from 55,000 tons, in the 1920's, to almost 200,000 tons in the 1960's. Efforts have also been made to cut production costs by reducing the large number of antiquated mills or factories, especially those which were powered by wind. The island's cane is now processed in 21 factories, roughly the same number used to process Jamaica's much larger crop. Obviously, the sugar factories are not very efficient but, with so many people in need of work, mechanization has its limits.

While cane is grown throughout the island, the center of production is in the parishes of the central uplands. The heavier and more reliable rainfall, together with the fertile red and black soils, result in best yields (see Figures 7.10 and 7.11). In this area, cane occupies virtually all the cultivated land and the large landholders control over 90 per cent of the acreage.

The sugar industry of Barbados has little prospect of further growth. There is no unused land; the unreliable rainfall is a major problem; irrigation is costly and subsurface water supplies are limited; yields are already almost maximum; mechanization is of dubious advantage when labor is overabundant. Moreover, the sugar market is glutted; prices are low and, could the island produce more, there would be few buyers. Under International and Commonwealth Sugar agreements, Barbados can dispose of less than 200,000 tons per year, with the bulk of the exports going to the United Kingdom and Canada. The continuing growth of the island's population in the face of its limited economic future is Barbados' greatest problem.

Food Products. On the estates, at least, food crops are grown, largely by force of law. In order to keep down the huge cost of importing food, the government obliges estate owners to devote at least 12 per cent of their cultivatable land to such provisions as corn, yams, pulses, sweet potatoes, eddoes, and cassava. But since there is a price ceiling on food crops, no planter grows more than he has to. When the food is not planted on the poorest land on the estates, it is raised in the cane fields after the last ratoon crop is harvested and before the new cane is planted. The peasants also prefer to raise cane instead of provisions, but often their land is too poor for sugar.

Barbados is fortunate in having an abundance of tropical fish, notably flying fish, in surrounding waters. Its fishing industry is one of the most important in the West Indies, but the annual catch of over ten million pounds is insufficient for its own people. Fish still must be imported.

Other Economies. The Barbadian economy derives some income from tourism, from a small but growing number of manufactures, from remittances from workers who have left the island, and from warehousing. Tourism increased when Pan American Airways was induced to serve the territory, and tourists, mostly Americans and Canadians, spent over $10 million a year in the early 1960's.

Barbados is the first port of call for many ships sailing from Europe to the southern Caribbean and an important stopping point for schooners engaged in interisland trading. The income derived from the sale of supplies and from harbor fees is significant. Bridgetown's harbor, once little more than an open roadstead, has been improved and now accommodates larger ships.

Population and Settlement

Barbados is extremely populous. By the early 1960's, there were 1,400 persons per square mile and, despite emigration and one of the lowest birth rates in the West Indies, the ratio continues to climb. Lowenthal estimates that the densities are equal to those of suburban London and exceed those of suburban Philadelphia and most United States cities.[3] Along with a few spots in the Nile Valley and the Orient, Barbados heads the world list of densely occupied agricultural areas. The island now has about four persons per cultivated acre. As we noted earlier, Barbados was densely populated before emancipation. Periodic waves of emigration to Trinidad, the Guianas, Central America, the United States, and the United Kingdom, have served only to slow the rate of growth. Current emigration is a mere trickle, primarily to the United Kingdom.

The distribution of population on Barbados is somewhat irregular. Over one-third of the people are in metropolitan Bridgetown, which extends well beyond the municipal limits of the city proper (Figure 7.13).

_____

[3] D. Lowenthal, "The Population of Barbados," *Social and Economic Studies,* VI (Jamaica: University College, 1957).

Figure 7.13

Barbados: Population Distribution. *(Based on maps by Lowenthal and Starkey)*

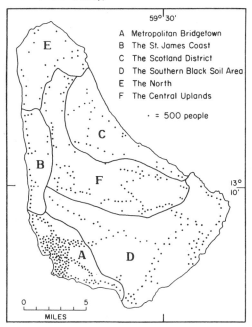

Here, densities range from ten to twenty thousand per square mile. The least crowded areas, the rugged and eroded Scotland district and the semiarid southeast coast, have densities of about one person per acre.

Compared to Trinidad, and even to Jamaica, the population is relatively homogeneous. About four-fifths are descendants of African slaves; slightly over 5 per cent are whites; and the remainder are Euro-African mixbloods, locally called "coloured." Since the island had a surplus of labor after emancipation, there was no need for immigrants from India, China, or elsewhere.

The correlation between race and class is more obvious on Barbados than on the other West Indies. In general, the whites occupy the top of the social hierarachy and the mixbloods and Negroes rank below them, but there is considerable stratification within each group. The poorest whites, the Red Legs, have a standard of living lower than that of most Negroes, and are looked down on by everyone. But the island's "colour bar" excludes even the highest officials of Negro blood from membership in elite white social clubs. Despite such distinctions, however, racial relations have been comparatively peaceful. The average Barbadian has an English respect for tradition and the law, born of over three centuries of uninterrupted British rule. This helps to explain why the island is sometimes described as "a little bit of England, and Victorian England, at that."

Clustering is the predominant settlement pattern. Outside of the urban nuclei such as Bridgetown and Speightstown, most Barbadians live in village clusters located on estates or on "rab" land along the highways or at the crossroads. On the estates, the workers' villages stand apart from the factories and the residences of the managers and owners, as they did in the slave era. The other villages are extremely compact, and generally have a few shops, a church, and a school. Only in the less fertile and less populous eastern areas, where peasant plots are common, does one find dispersed houses.

Barbados has one of the densest road networks (four miles of roads to each square mile) in the world. As a result, no community is more than a half-hour bus ride from Bridgetown, and the entire island is heavily influenced by its capital.

THE BRITISH LEEWARD AND WINDWARD ISLANDS[4]

The Leewards and Windwards underwent the full, stormy history of conquest and counterconquest by France and England before finally becoming British (see Chapters 3 and 4). Both groups experienced the growth of the colonial sugar plantation in the eighteenth and early nineteenth centuries, and both felt the impact of its downfall.

Most of the islands have suffered almost continuous economic depression since emancipation, and their prospects seem as bleak as their past. Small, limited in resources, and with expanding populations, they cannot maintain themselves without outside help. It was this lack of viability which made the Leewards and Windwards the most enthusiastic supporters of the now-defunct West Indies Federation and which obliges them to cling to Britain.

Antigua

Land and Economy. Although classified as a low-lying, semiarid, limestone island, Antigua's geology, relief, and rainfall are sufficiently varied to permit a threefold regional division (Figure 7.14). The south-

---

4 There is no rational basis for the trade wind nomenclature applied to these islands. The Leewards are not to the west, or leeward, of the Windwards but to the north. To complicate matters, Saba and other Netherlands territories, which lie in the midst of the British Leewards, are called *"Bovenwindse"* ("windwards") by the Dutch. The nomenclature is used here only as a device for distinguishing two British administrative units.

Table 7.2

THE LEEWARD AND WINDWARD ISLANDS

Territory	Area (In square miles)	Population (1960)
Leewards		
Antigua and Barbuda	170.5	54,000
St. Kitts, Nevis, and Anguilla	152.0	56,600
Montserrat	32.5	12,000
Windwards		
Dominica	305	60,000
St. Lucia	233	86,000
St. Vincent	150	80,000
Grenada	133	89,000

west consists of eroded volcanic remnants, where steep-sided hills rise to an average of 1,000 feet, reaching 1,330 feet at Boggy Peak. Paralleling these volcanic uplands is the central plain, a lowland some ten miles long and three miles wide which runs northwest-southeast through the heart of the island. This zone of lagoon-deposited clays is flat to undulating, with elevations which seldom rise above 50 feet. The third region is a belt of low limestone hills which extends from the northeast to the southwest coasts.

The average rainfall varies from less than 40 inches over much of the coastal lowland

Figure 7.14

Antigua : Regional Divisions.

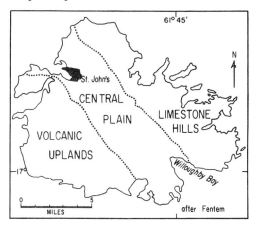

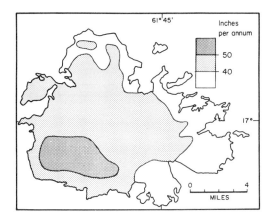

Figure 7.15
Antigua : Mean Annual Rainfall.

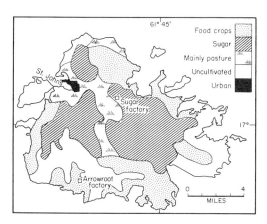

Figure 7.16
Antigua : Land Use.

to slightly over 50 inches in the volcanic uplands (Figure 7.15), but may fluctuate sharply from year to year. Drainage is a problem; it is poor in the clay soils of the central plain and is too rapid through the porous limestones of the northern hills. Surface streams are rare, yet floods are not unknown, especially after the heavy downpours associated with hurricanes.

The scarcity of water, as well as other physical limitations, is sharply mirrored in Antigua's agriculture. The uncultivated areas are generally those with less than 40 inches of rain on the steep, eroded slopes of the volcanic uplands; pastures are located primarily in the most poorly drained sections of the central plain; and subsistence farming is practiced only where commercial crops are ruled out (Figures 7.14, 7.15, and 7.16). Sugar cane, the leading cash product, occupies the best lands in the central plains and valley bottoms, and cotton, which is second in commercial importance, dominates the limestone hills. Yields are comparatively low and drop dangerously in the dry years. During the 1953–1954 drought, for example, the cash crops dropped by more than half. Water is in such critical supply that much of the farm work on the island consists of repairing catchments, making ponds, and drilling wells.

Sugar, which comprises about four-fifths of Antigua's exports, is raised both on estates and on peasant plots. As elsewhere, the estates own the best lands, use more scientific methods, and obtain the higher yields. The estates control the single sugar factory which mills all of the island's cane.

Cotton is also raised on both large and small holdings, but the greater part of the cotton crop is produced by peasants. Antigua now has the largest cotton acreage in the Antilles; unfortunately, this is no panacea. Production fluctuates with rainfall and price, both of which are highly unreliable, and the crop is often ravaged by insects. To protect the peasantry, the government buys the entire crop, gins it at a local factory, and sells it at the best price available in England. There is increasing emphasis on the production of cottonseed oil and cake for local consumption and for export.

The rest of Antigua's farm production consists largely of food raised on peasant plots, mostly roots, such as yams and sweet potatoes; tree crops, such as bananas; and pigeon peas. The government is encouraging the production of arrowroot as a peasant cash crop and has established a factory for processing it.

Population and Settlement. Antigua's population fell from over 40,000, in the heyday of the eighteenth-century sugar boom, to less than 30,000 in 1921. This decline was largely the result of emigration (to Cuba, Panama, Central America, and the United States), which reached its peak in the early twentieth century. Emigration was largely cut off after 1921, and the population increased to over 50,000 by 1960. The average density of population per square mile is about 500, but there are 2,000 people per square mile of cultivated land. Almost three-fourths of the population is concentrated in the more productive northeast half of this island.

Except for the capital, St. John's (13,000 people), settlement is rural and is typified by clusters of tiny wooden houses. Most of the more than 60 rural settlements which now dot the island began as plantation villages.

Barbuda

The wealthy Codrington family, which owned Barbuda from 1691 to the latter nineteenth century, used it as a hunting preserve and as a stud farm to provide livestock and slaves for their sugar plantations on other islands. Today, making a living on this administrative outlier of Antigua poses a challenge.

Barbuda's 62 square miles are a flat, low-lying plain which rises to a height of 200 feet at its eastern edge, in a series of steep-sided limestone terraces. An alternation of droughts and occasional torrential rains discourages all but hardy bushes and grass. The population of about 1,200 maintains itself by fishing, keeping cattle, making charcoal, and catering to a few tourists. Such farming as exists is of food crops and cotton.

St. Kitts, Nevis, and Anguilla

St. Kitts, the largest territory in this administrative unit, is a sugar plantation island par excellence. It rivals Barbados as a striking example of a one-crop economy and a

landholding system dominated by estates. Equally striking, it has maintained cane production for almost three centuries without serious deterioration of its soil. The island is the most agriculturally efficient and prosperous of the Leewards and Windwards.

Land and Economy. Except for the tail-like southern peninsula, most of St. Kitts has a backbone of rugged volcanic mountains which rise steeply to average elevations of almost 3,000 feet and reach a maximum of 4,314 feet at Mt. Misery, in the northwest. Surrounding the base of this highland core is a gently sloping apron of volcanic ash cut by deep ravines, known as "gats" or "guts." The southern peninsula consists of a cluster of volcanic hills and the large Salt Pond.

Precipitation, more than 90 inches in the mountain zones at about 1,200 feet, decreases downslope to as little as 50 inches in parts of the ash apron and is even less in the southern peninsula (Figure 7.17). Virtually all of the troughlike "guts" are dry, but heavy rains often result in disastrous floods. The island is also subject to hurricanes.

These physical conditions impose definite limitations on land use. The semiarid southern peninsula, with its scrub trees, low

Figure 7.17
St. Kitts : Mean Annual Rainfall.

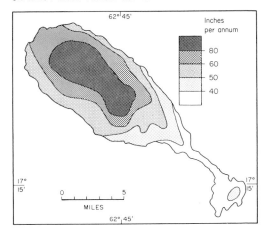

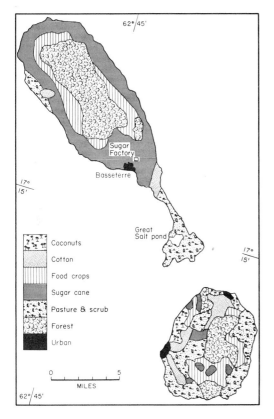

Figure 7.18
St. Kitts and Nevis : Land Use.

mills were replaced by a single *central* served by a narrow-gauge railroad; and other improvements were made in cultivating and manufacturing sugar. The amount of land in cane was doubled in the twentieth century, but the reforms were so effective that sugar production has increased fivefold.

Of the 16,000 acres currently under cane in St. Kitts, all but a few hundred are estate-owned. And, since the estates often extend from the sea to the mountain crests, they control much of the other land as well. The marginal slope land at the edge of the forests is usually rented to peasants.

All other economic activity is puny compared with sugar production. Sea island cotton, which occupied over 4,000 acres in the early 1900's, now occupies less than 200, and experiments with other cash crops, such as citrus fruit and tobacco, have failed. Food crops, grown on peasant plots and in rotation with cane on estate lands, are insufficient for local needs.

Population and Settlement. Population densities on St. Kitts are the highest in the Leewards, despite considerable emigration of

bushes, and cacti, is used primarily for grazing. The wet upper slopes of the highland core above 1,000 feet remain under a dense cover of rain forest and palm brakes, except for scattered patches of peasant cultivation. Only the ash apron and lower mountain slopes lend themselves to intensive agricultural use (Figure 7.18).

While the nineteenth-century sugar crisis necessitated some adjustment on St. Kitts, it did not seriously impair the sugar plantations. Their ability to survive was due in part to superior growing conditions and in part to efficient management. With careful cultivation, the fine volcanic soils of the island's ash apron continued to be highly productive despite long exploitation. The many small estates were consolidated into approximately 50 large holdings (Figures 7.19 and 7.20); the numerous, inefficient

Figure 7.19
St. Kitts : Agricultural Settlement in the Mid-Nineteenth Century.

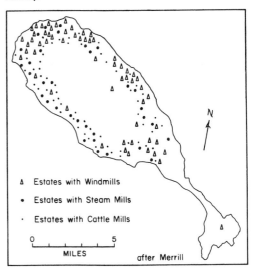

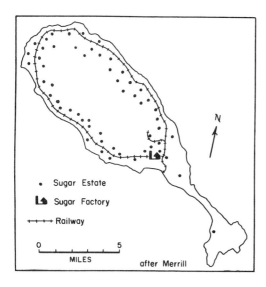

Figure 7.20

St. Kitts: Sugar Estates. Note that Figures 4.4, 4.5, 7.19, and 7.20 depict the evolution of agriculture and settlement on St. Kitts from the mid-seventeenth century to the present.

Legend in figure:
- • Sugar Estate
- Sugar Factory
- +--+--+ Railway
- 0 ————— 5 MILES
- after Merrill

Land use and tenure has changed greatly since the eighteenth century. Much of the cane land has reverted to scrub, and the approximately 7,000 acres still under crop are largely in cotton, coconuts, and provisions (Figure 7.18). Coconuts are estate-grown; the rest are produced by peasants who cultivate their own plots or sharecrop estate land. The coconuts are raised primarily along the north and west coasts, and provide the copra for the margarine produced in a small local plant.

The peasants grow enough food for the island and some, especially fresh fruits and vegetables, for export to St. Kitts. They also raise small quantities of sugar cane which is sent by lighter to St. Kitts for milling.

Anguilla. In contrast to volcanic St. Kitts and Nevis, Anguilla, which lies 60 miles north, is a dry, low-lying limestone island. With a maximum elevation of about 200 feet and an annual precipitation of 40 inches, most of the island is too dry or has soil too thin to support agriculture. Except for a few of the more favored spots, where peasants cultivate cotton and food, the land is used only for grazing or is not used at all.

Anguilla's second most important export is salt, which is produced by evaporating sea water. Her most important export is her young men, many of whom become sailors or migrate to the Dutch oil islands and elsewhere in search of work. The island's population in the 1960's numbered approximately 5,000.

Negro workers to Trinidad, the Dutch oil islands, Britain, and the Dominican Republic. The outflow of younger men in search of employment is so great that there is a large surplus of women.

Much of the population is concentrated along the lower courses of the "guts." The estate mansions are of stone; the houses in the peasant villages are built of imported lumber or, more recently, of cement blocks. The only town of any size is Basseterre, the capital. It is the chief port, though its harbor is little more than a sheltered roadstead.

Nevis. Like St. Kitts, Nevis is a relatively humid, high-lying volcanic island. At its center is the steeply rising cone of Nevis Peak (3,232 feet), whose base is surrounded by a volcanic ash apron. Like its larger neighbor, Nevis experienced a sugar boom in the eighteenth century, but only the ruins of estate houses and sugar works are left. The soils on Nevis are stonier and less fertile than those on St. Kitts, and most of the sugar estates were unable to weather the crisis in the nineteenth century.

Montserrat

The "little world" of Montserrat is a troubled one. Only 32.5 square miles large, its only resource is its land, which was depleted by the early sugar plantations and which has been heavily eroded by poor farming practices. It is burdened by a slavish dependence on cotton, the most unstable of West Indian cash crops. Yet the territory has a population density of almost 450 people per square mile.

Montserrat is a mountainous island consisting of three main volcanic groups. In the north is the heavily eroded volcano, Silver Hill, 1,285 feet high; southward are the Centre Hills, 2,450 feet high; and southernmost are the Soufrière Hills, whose maximum elevation is slightly over 3,000 feet. As on Nevis, the volcanic summits are steep and their bases flanked by stony ash aprons, deeply cut by "guts." Annual precipitation, which varies sharply, averages over 70 inches on the wet, cool uplands and well below 50 on most of the coast (Figure 7.21). Heavy rains ravage the soil on the deforested slopes and create destructive floods in the "guts."

About one-third of Montserrat is cultivated. The remainder is under scrub and grass, but there is still some forest in the more humid areas above 1,500 feet (Figure 7.22). Sea island cotton, the chief cash crop, is grown on the ash aprons and up to about 500 feet on the slopes. Most of the cotton

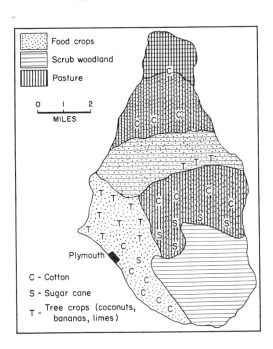

Figure 7.22
Montserrat : Land Use.

Figure 7.21
Montserrat : Mean Annual Rainfall.

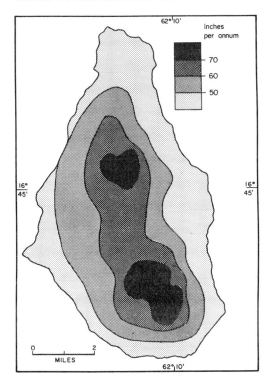

is raised on peasant-owned plots, although there is still some sharecropping on the larger landholdings. The value of the fruit and vegetables produced probably matches that of cotton, but they are used locally, and only about one-tenth of the harvest is exported. Tomatoes are the most important food export, but poor shipping facilities limit their production. Cold storage facilities and a tomato paste factory have been of some help. Most of the tomatoes are sent to nearby islands, such as St. Kitts, but they have also been shipped to Bermuda and even Canada. Sugar is now produced only in small quantities, for making rum. The production of limes, also once important, has been drastically reduced. As in the Windwards (see below), the cultivation of bananas has been expanding and may become the cash crop of the future, provided that shipping facilities are improved.

The scrub and grass support several thousand head of cattle, enough for the island's meat and milk and an occasional exportable surplus. Montserrat's economy is rounded out by income from minor occupations such as charcoal burning and boat building and, more important, by remittances from islanders who have migrated. The gap between exports and imports is so wide that, without these remittances and British Colonial Development and Welfare funds, the island would face disaster.

Emigration has become a way of life for the men of Montserrat. The island has the dubious distinction of being the only one of the Antilles whose population has seriously declined in the last century. Originally settled by Irish Roman Catholics from St. Kitts, Montserrat lost all but a handful of its white planter families after emancipation. These remnants, plus a few Syrian merchants, are now the only non-Negro elements on the "Emerald Isle of the Caribbean."

The Windwards

All the larger islands in the Windwards fall into the humid, high-lying, volcanic arc of the Antilles. The Windwards were settled later than the Leewards (see Chapter 3), but experienced an even more frequent alternation of French and English ownership than their northern neighbors. Their French heritage is still apparent in the language and customs of most of the islands. All the territories, except Dominica, experienced the rise and fall of the colonial sugar plantation. Bananas are now the chief cash crop of the group as a whole, but each territory also has at least one other important agricultural specialty.

Dominica

Land and Economy. A mountainous terrain, easily the most rugged in the Lesser Antilles, dominates Dominica's landscape. Patches of isolated alluvial flats, which comprise less than 3 per cent of the total area, are the only level land. The remainder is a tangled backbone of steep, volcanic ranges with peaks, such as Morne Diablotins and

Morne Trois Pitons, which rise to almost 5,000 feet. A maze of spurs, separated by steep-walled ravines, extends coastward from the axial ranges to form sheer sea cliffs hundreds of feet high. Geologically, the island is completely volcanic, and the presence of fumaroles and hot springs attests to continuing, albeit subdued, vulcanism.

Rainfall and vegetation vary with elevation and exposure to the trades, but both are heavy. On the highest windward-facing peaks, precipitation is between 250 and 400 inches (Figure 7.23). Even the driest leeward zone in the southwest receives 70 to 80 inches. A dense mantle of vegetation, much of it unaltered by man, blankets all but small portions of the island. Deciduous forests extend to about 1,000 feet, where they give way to the rain forest that climbs to 3,000 feet. Above this level, the characteristic cover

Figure 7.23
Dominica : Mean Annual Rainfall.

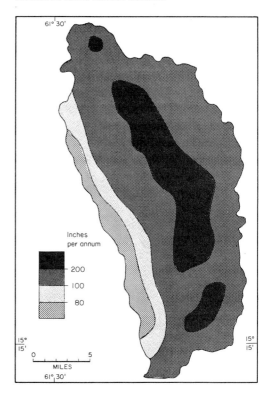

Inches
per annum

200
100
80

MILES

is an elfin forest of stunted, moss-coated trees and lichens.

This forbidding environment has stamped every important phase and facet of post-Columbian occupance in Dominica. The fierce Caribs, fighting from the forested mountain fastness, delayed European conquest until well into the eighteenth century (see Chapter 3). After the conquest, the scarcity of level land and other impediments limited the growth of the sugar plantations. Except for a few decades after the 1830's, when an effort was made to develop cane, the island's chief exports have been coffee, limes, cacao, vanilla, and bananas—all tree crops vulnerable to hurricanes. The environment has intensified the island's isolation, and the difficulty of the terrain still discourages effective settlement of the interior.

Probably less than 15 per cent of Dominica's total area is under crop, and most of that area is a narrow coastal strip within 2,000 yards of the sea. Even this strip includes sea cliffs and other impediments, and is not uniformly developed. Only the vicinity of Roseau and sections of the windward coast in the northeast and southeast are intensively farmed. Most of the interior is either not used or is haphazardly exploited by shifting cultivators (Figure 7.24). Shifting cultivation is more widespread on this island than anywhere else in the Antilles.

The most productive coastal land is owned by approximately 85 estates. Compared to St. Kitts, Barbados, and other sugar islands, however, the estate system is but weakly entrenched on Dominica. Only a few of the tree crops which have been the mainstay of the island's exports lend themselves to large-scale production. As a result, much of the land now cultivated is peasant-owned or unalienated public lands which the peasantry feels free to use.

Bananas, which became the chief cash crop after World War II, occupy more than a fifth of the cultivated acreage and are raised wherever transportation permits. About a fourth of the crop is produced on the

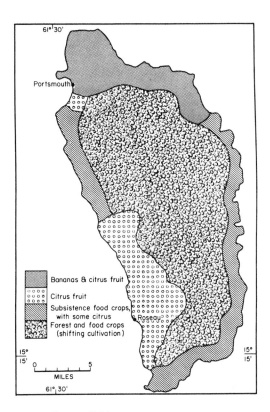

Figure 7.24
Dominica : Land Use.

estates, the largest of which are on the humid northeast coast. Citrus fruits, which are second only to bananas in commercial importance, are largely grown on estates on the southwest coast near Roseau. Grapefruit and oranges are shipped fresh to Britain, and most of the limes are first processed into preserves, juice, and oil. Other tree crops, such as cacao and vanilla, are raised mostly by the peasantry.

Dominica has the most extensive forest resources in the Lesser Antilles, but lack of transportation has so far prevented their exploitation.

Population and Settlement. Because it was colonized late and the growing of sugar was limited, Dominica had a comparatively small slave population at the time of emancipation (1834–1838). The island's population is still less than that of the other Windwards, and its population density is far below the average. In Dominica, however, average densities are meaningless, because about 90 per cent of its people are concentrated in the narrow coastal band of cultivated land within a mile from the sea. Here, the pressure of population and the lack of economic opportunity are such that permanent emigration to the United Kingdom and seasonal migrations of farm workers to nearby Guadeloupe are common.

The paradox of emigration and overconcentration on the coast while the interior remains uninhabited stems in no small measure from the inadequacy of transportation. The steep terrain, and the heavy rains which cause landslides, make roads prohibitively costly. Even the seacoast is, in places, so rugged that no continuous coastal highway has been built. For example, there is no direct connection between Roseau, the capital, and Portsmouth, 20 miles away on the west coast. In 1956, a transinsular road which had been begun in 1899 was completed, and one can now reach Portsmouth from the capital by driving northeast and then west, a distance of 50 miles. External communications are not much better. Roseau, the chief port, has only a jetty to accommodate small ships; larger vessels must stand offshore and be loaded and unloaded by lighters. The best natural harbor is at Portsmouth, but it is little used because of the unproductive and unhealthy swamps which adjoin it.

St. Lucia

Physical and Historical Setting. Like Dominica, St. Lucia is a high-lying, humid, volcanic territory, but without the high relief and great rainfall of its neighbor. The island's major surface divisions include a heavily eroded northern upland with an average elevation of about 1,000 feet, central *pitons* with a maximum height of more than 3,000 feet (Figure 7.25), and a

southern zone of worn-down volcanic cones covered with thick deposits of ash and rocks. Level land is scarce and scattered, consisting mostly of alluvial bottoms in the lower courses of the valleys. Rainfall varies with terrain, ranging from over 150 inches on the center *pitons* to 50 to 60 inches on the lower elevations in the extreme north and south of the island (Figure 7.26). Remnants of rain forest remain on the summits of the central peaks, but the rest of the original cover has been removed.

As in Dominica, the Caribs stemmed colonization of St. Lucia until almost mid-eighteenth century. The French effected the first permanent settlement in 1744, and between that time and the establishment of a permanent British connection in 1803, the island changed hands 14 times. The influence of the French, reinforced by proximity to Martinique immediately to the north, is still evident in place and family names, the French patois and Roman Catholicism of much of the population, and in many customs, including the law governing property.

The economic history of St. Lucia has been almost as unstable as its political history. The earliest economy, based on cotton and tobacco, gave way to cane. Emancipation created the same problems it created elsewhere and, despite the importation of East Indians and the construction of modern mills, the sugar industry never fully recovered. With the decline of cane, St. Lucia's economy ran a chequered course. The planters experimented with other cash crops, such as limes, with varied success, but the labor shortages resulting from emigration and nonfarm employment forced many large holders to subdivide their estates.

For almost a half-century beginning in the 1880's, Castries, which has an excellent harbor, was a major coaling station in the West Indies, and provided a livelihood for hundreds of workers. When oil replaced coal as ships' fuel in the 1930's, however, the island experienced a severe economic depression

Figure 7.26
St. Lucia: Mean Annual Rainfall.

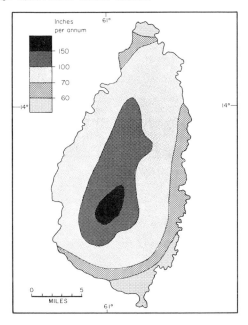

and many of the laborers returned to the land. Then came the unprecedented prosperity of World War II, when the United States used St. Lucia as a lend-lease base. Agricultural workers left the farms in droves to work for the free-spending Americans. But the closing of United States installations after the war created new economic distress, compounded by the reluctance of many of the workers to return to farming, the only economy of any importance on the island.

Agriculture. At best, less than one-third of St. Lucia's total area is devoted to agriculture. Bananas, sugar, coconuts, and cacao are grown for export, and the usual variety of vegetables and fruit is grown for local consumption (Figure 7.27). The exporting of bananas, which began in the 1920's, declined sharply when Panama disease struck in the 1930's and was halted by the lack of shipping during World War II. But bananas are now again the island's leading export. The fruit, although widely grown, is concentrated in the coastal valleys, and most growers take their harvest to collection points on the roads where it is weighed and graded before it is sent to Castries or Vieux Fort for overseas shipment. Bananas have been primarily a peasant crop, but are becoming increasingly important on the large land-holdings.

St. Lucia is still the chief sugar producer in the Windwards, but the crop is declining. By the early 1960's, the island was producing less than half the cane needed to satisfy both local demand and its assigned export quota. The sugar industry has suffered from labor problems, and also from the difficulty of achieving efficient concentration in view of the scattered location of patches of suitable level land. Cultivation is now restricted primarily to the Roseau and Cul de Sac valleys,

and total production is barely sufficient to keep a single *central* in operation.

Coconuts occupy more land than either sugar or bananas. They are raised on virtually half the farms, but the bulk of commercial production comes from large holdings. Most of the harvest is converted into oil at a factory in Soufrière, and the remainder is sent to Barbados for processing. The rapid growth of the crop since the 1950's has made St. Lucia the leading producer of coconut oil in the Lesser Antilles. Cacao, a very poor fourth among the cash crops, is raised over much of the island, especially the southwest, and small quantities of beans are exported to Britain via Port of Spain.

There are roughly 70 estates and more than 10,000 smaller holdings. The lack of clear titles, often stemming from the old French practice of vesting ownership in the family rather than in the individual, complicates the problem of land tenure, especially among the peasantry. Much of the land is worked by squatters who have no legal title.

Population and Settlement. Over 40 per cent of St. Lucia's population lives in towns, such as Castries, the capital, Soufrière, and Vieux Fort. Castries, which is built on a small alluvial flat, was largely destroyed by fire in 1948 and had to be rebuilt. Rural settlement tends to be dispersed; isolated huts are scattered along, or adjacent to, the roads. There are also clusterings around estate houses and hamletlike groups of huts (Figure 7.28) at the intersections of paths or tracks.

Population distribution is uneven. Almost four-fifths of the people live in two nuclei: the alluvial valleys and hills in the north, which include Castries; and the southern hills and lower mountain slopes. The remainder are scattered over the drier zones of the extreme north and south. The rugged mountain country in the center of the island is the most thinly populated.

Figure 7.27

St. Lucia : Land Use.

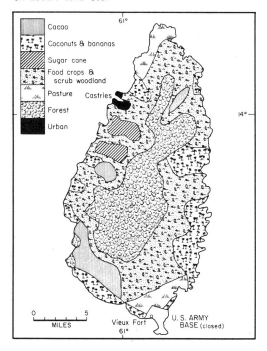

Figure 7.28
West Indian Hip-Roofed Cottage.

St. Vincent

Physical and Historical Setting. St. Vincent's natural landscape bears the deep brand of vulcanism. The island is composed almost entirely of ash and other porous volcanic materials, and of lava flows. In the north, Soufrière, one of the two most active volcanoes in the Antilles, rises abruptly from the coast to a height of over 4,000 feet. Its eruptions are sporadic, but violent; in 1902 they killed more than 2,000 people, devastated the entire northern part of the island, and choked the valleys with heavy deposits of ash.

South of Soufrière, St. Vincent is a maze of steep-sided ridges and deep gullies which the streams have cut through the soft volcanic materials. Mountain spurs from the central ridges often extend to the sea, giving much of the island an inarticulated, cliffed shoreline. The uplands are more steeply slanted on the leeward side of the island than on the windward. Patches of level land with less than five degrees of slope are few; most of these are on the south and east coasts where the sea has carved a number of natural terraces.

Arable land is limited not only by the rugged terrain, but also by rainfall and drainage. No part of the island receives less than 60 inches of precipitation (Figure 7.29), but seepage through the porous vol-

Figure 7.29
St. Vincent : Mean Annual Rainfall.

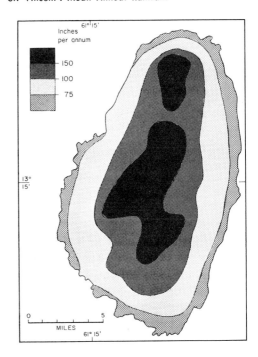

canic soils is so rapid that drought sometimes occurs on the leeward coast.

European settlement came late to St. Vincent, as to the other Windwards. The island was the chief stronghold of the Caribs, and resistance to white encroachment was especially fierce there. The French, who began to establish cotton plantations on the west coast in 1719, made little progress, but after the British seized the territory in 1763, large numbers of slaves were imported for the sugar plantations, and settlement was greatly expanded.

Plantation cane dominated St. Vincent until the latter nineteenth century. Then, a labor shortage and changing market conditions brought about a shift to arrowroot, and peasant-owned plots increased at the expense of the estates.

Economy. St. Vincent's economy differs from most of the Lesser Antilles in at least one important respect. There is a healthy balance between large plantations and commercial crops, on the one hand, and peasant food farming, on the other. The land ownership, as of 1960, was about equally divided between the small holders and the approximately 30 large estates of 500 or more acres, and peasant ownership is increasing as a result of government settlement projects which involve the acquisition of estate lands for distribution among the peasantry.

The relative importance of the small holder in the economy gives rise to better farming practices, such as mixed cropping, intensive cultivation, and careful attention to conservation. The volcanic soils of St. Vincent are very fertile, but their steep slopes expose them to erosion. To prevent rapid runoff, the farmers resort to extensive terracing, strip cropping, grass barriers, and other conservation techniques. Such farming is unusual in the haphazard West Indies.

Almost half the island's total area is cultivated. The ratio of cultivated acreage to woodland is more than two to one, despite the mountains. Only the steepest slopes of

Soufrière and the central mountain core are still forested.

St. Vincent's commercial crops are diversified. In addition to bananas, which rose to first place in the 1950's, the island exports arrowroot, sugar, cotton, coconuts, and even sweet potatoes. Bananas have proven so profitable a crop in the postwar years that their cultivation has become widespread. They are grown on the estates, and virtually every peasant raises at least a few stems even if he has to plant them at his doorstep. Since fruit is typically interplanted, its expanding production has not encroached seriously on the established crops.

St. Vincent's most distinctive crop is arrowroot. The island produces 98 per cent of world consumption of the starch derived from the roots of the plant. Arrowroot is raised on slope land and grows to a height of about five feet. The harvested roots are trucked to one of approximately 20 estate factories or to a large government-owned plant at Belle Vue where they are processed for starch.

In the postwar period, there has been a modest recovery of the island's cane industry. Enough is now grown for local needs, including rum making, and to permit limited export. Most of the crop is processed at a sugar factory in Georgetown.

The major share of the export products are raised in the coastal margins and up to 1,000 feet on the mountain slopes on the windward side of the island (Figure 7.30). Food crops are grown chiefly on the leeward coast, though provisions are also raised in a zone of shifting cultivation between the forest and the permanently cultivated fields everywhere on the island. Food production is sufficient for most of the local demand, and there is significant exporting of sweet potatoes and other vegetables to nearby islands, especially to Trinidad.

Population. Despite some recent emigration to Trinidad and elsewhere, St. Vincent's population rose to over 80,000 in the early

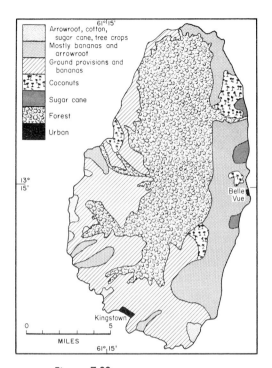

Figure 7.30
St. Vincent : Land Use.

1960's. The average population density is about 600 per square mile, and the ratio of people to cropland is almost 1,500 per square mile. In the British Leewards and Windwards, only Grenada has a higher pressure of people on its land.

The racial composition of the population almost rivals Trinidad in diversity. While the vast majority are Negro or "coloured," there are also British whites, Portuguese and East Indians who descend from laborers imported after emancipation, and a tiny remnant of Caribs. The whites include a small group of "Red Legs," who live in the hills overlooking Kingstown and trace their ancestry to Irish slaves originally sent to Barbados following Cromwell's conquest of Ireland. The total number of people classified as Caribs comes to slightly more than 1,000, but so many of the purebloods were wiped out in the Soufrière eruptions of 1812 and 1902 that only 200 remain. The others are Black Caribs, descendants of a Negro-Indian mixture which

resisted the Europeans so fiercely that most of them were deported to Central America at the end of the eighteenth century.

The bulk of St. Vincent's population hugs the coastal periphery of the island, especially the southwest coast near Kingstown. Kingstown, the capital and chief port, is a town of about 5,000. It has no deep-water pier, but it does boast an airstrip and a road which connects it with all the coastal settlements save those in the northwest.

Grenada

Physical and Historical Setting. Agriculturally, Grenada's terrain leaves much to be desired, but its soil and climate could be worse. The island is a high-lying volcanic mass consisting almost wholly of mountain slopes and ridges. Several peaks in the central ridges rise above 2,000 feet, and one, Mt. St. Catherine, reaches a maximum of 2,756 feet. The level land consists of scattered patches of alluvial flats in the small valleys and narrow ribbons of coastal plain compressed between the uplands and the sea. Grenada shows little evidence of recent vulcanism. Except for a few crater lakes, such as Grand Etang, its surface has been shaped primarily by the erosion of older volcanic deposits.

The island's best soils are associated with the alluvial flats. The next best are the red and red-brown types in the less humid lowlands. But even the poorest of the gray or yellow-brown soils of the wet uplands is arable.

The climate is generally adequate, except in the hurricane seasons, and other conditions are also generally favorable for farming. Temperatures are high enough to permit a year-round growing season even on high mountain slopes. Precipitation, though marked by the usual extreme differences between windward and leeward exposures (Figure 7.31), is sufficient everywhere but in the driest segments of the southwest coast.

Post-Columbian exploitation of Grenada

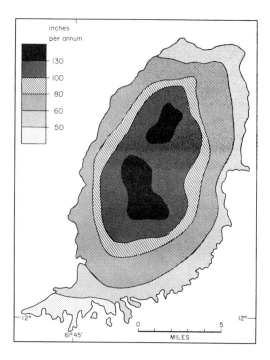

Inches
per annum

130
100
80
60
50

12°   12°

61°45'

0   5
MILES

Figure 7.31
Grenada : Mean Annual Rainfall.

began early. Carib resistance was weak, and the French were able to establish the first agricultural colony by 1650. Initially, tobacco and indigo were stressed, but by the mid-eighteenth century the chief cash crops were cotton, coffee, and sugar. The French, who held the island until its capture by the British in 1762, left a heritage which is still found in the language, religion, and place names.

As on St. Vincent, the arrival of the British resulted in a swift increase in the slave population, an expansion of cane, and the entrenchment of the plantation system. Also as on St. Vincent, Grenada's rapid development continued up to the mid-1800's, only to be followed by an equally rapid decline.

The postemancipation labor shortage was especially acute because more favorable working conditions in nearby Trinidad attracted many of the freed Negroes. Those who remained left the estates to occupy

mountain lands in the interior, just as did their counterparts on other West Indian islands (see Chapter 4). Efforts to attract indentured workers from India, the Madeiras, and elsewhere were largely unsuccessful.

Eventually, the labor shortage and other unfavorable circumstances brought about major changes on the land. Cane production dropped 75 per cent between 1840 and 1880; cacao replaced sugar as the chief export; and the hard-pressed planters sold small plots to the peasantry. The plantation did not disappear, but its grip was weakened.

Economy. Agriculture is Grenada's leading economic activity, but the growing pressure of population is a serious problem.

Cultivation has been pushed over two-thirds of the island's total area. Even the poorest slopes are now under crop, and there is no room for further expansion. Only the highest and most inaccessible mountain peaks have been left in forest. The patches of thorny scrub in the dry southwest are given over to grazing. Elsewhere, even the steepest slopes immediately below the forest hold nutmeg trees. Cacao follows nutmeg downslope and merges with bananas in the humid valleys. Food crops and sugar are raised in small quantities on the leeward coast, and coconuts occupy the sandy beaches of the sea margins (Figure 7.32).

The pattern of land tenure on Grenada has changed little in the twentieth century. About half the land is held in estates of 100 or more acres, and the remainder is in peasant plots of five acres or less. The smaller properties are owner-operated, but many of the estates are run by managers for absentee owners. The arrangement is unusual in that a large number of the peasant plots are at lower elevations along the coast, while the estates are frequently located in the interior hills. This pattern is probably due to the fact that the slope land is used for the commercially important tree crops.

The most distinctive tree crops are nut-

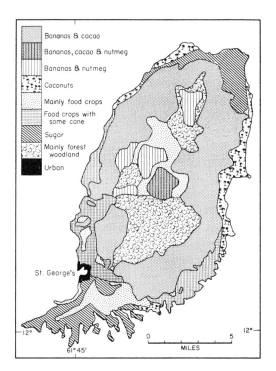

Figure 7.32
Grenada : Land Use.

escaped injury, and this was scant consolation since the island depends on its cash products to finance the buying of its food. Tree crops, especially bananas and cacao, are also more susceptible to disease than field crops. But with a dense population and a land which consists almost entirely of mountain slopes, what choice is there?

Population and Settlement. With 740 inhabitants per square mile in 1964, Grenada is the most densely populated island in both the Leewards and the Windwards. The increase in population was relatively moderate between the two world wars. Since 1946, however, a drop in emigration and in the death rate, coupled with a rise in the present birth rate, has resulted in a huge net increase.

Except for a small number of whites and an East Indian minority of about 5 per cent, the population is Negro or "coloured." English, well-laced with French and even African phrases, is the chief language, but a dominantly French patois continues to be spoken in many communities.

Settlement is largely rural. Farmsteads are scattered through the hills or strung out on roads leading to the coast, and hamlets consist of a dozen or so houses. These tiny villages often mark the site of former slave quarters on plantations. The only town of any size is St. George's, the capital, chief port, and major commercial and administrative center.

The Grenadines. Between Grenada in the south and St. Vincent in the north is a group of more than 100 small islands and countless reefs which together make up the Grenadines (see Figure 7.1). Those south of Carriacou are considered part of Grenada; the rest belong to St. Vincent. Only ten of the islands support a permanent population. Of these, the most important are Carriacou, some 13 miles square and with a population of 8,000, and Bequia, 7 miles

meg and mace. Small quantities are raised in other West Indian territories and in Indonesia, but Grenada is the chief source of these spices. The nutmeg tree is raised on the higher mountain slopes, where temperatures range from 70 to 75°F and precipitation exceeds 80 inches (Figures 7.31 and 7.32). The center of the fruit is a dark brown nut, covered with a fine web of mace, which splits when ripe. Most of the mace is sent to Britain, where it is used for baking and in the manufacture of cosmetics; the bulk of the nutmeg is sold to the United States.

Nutmeg production illustrates some of the peculiar problems of Grenada's agriculture. The slow-growing trees require 20 years to reach peak production, but they can be quickly destroyed by heavy winds. In 1955, for example, a hurricane reduced the crop over 90 per cent. The same storm also caused huge damage to cacao, bananas, and coconuts. Only ground provisions, such as yams, square and with 2,500 people. The population of the other inhabited islands is slightly more than 3,000.

The basic occupation in the Grenadines is subsistence farming, but the larger islands also export small quantities of cotton, limes, and coconuts. Cultivation is handicapped by the islets' mountainous terrain and their thin, worn-out volcanic soils. Other occupations include fishing and boat building. There is not enough work, however, and many of the young men emigrate or become seamen.

THE FRENCH WEST INDIES

Composite View

Martinique and Guadeloupe, together with the latter's dependencies, are all that remain of the once-considerable French holdings in the Caribbean. Even these remnants probably adhere to France as much from economic necessity as from sentiment. Small in size (1,112 square miles) and heavily populated, the islands suffer from many disadvantages. Arable land is their only significant resource, but the terrain is rugged and there is less than an acre per person. There are periodic hurricanes and very destructive volcanic eruptions and earthquakes, especially on Martinique. The agrarian economy is beset by monoculture, latifundia, and other liabilities characteristic of West Indian tropical plantation agriculture.

Thus handicapped, Martinique and Guadeloupe desperately need the protected market for exports, the government subsidies, and the outlet for surplus population which the French connection provides. This need was strongly manifested in 1946, when the islands overwhelmingly elected to end more than three centuries of political dependency and become overseas *départments* of metropolitan France. Their new status provides both the territories with direct representation in the French parliament and gives them all the advantages and disadvantages of being integral parts of France.

Transition to the Current Patterns

Economic. Emancipation in 1848 and the subsequent downfall of the colonial plantation created the problems with which the reader is by now familiar. A labor shortage developed as the freed Negroes abandoned the estates; much of the white planter class was bankrupted and returned to France; the amount of land under cultivation dropped, and so did the harvest; and the population increased.

In the readjustments, a class of small peasant holders emerged, sharecropping was introduced, and the sugar plantations were consolidated. The Negro peasantry acquired small plots either by squatting on unused land in the mountains or by buying it from hard-pressed estate owners, but their plots were not large enough to provide them with a living. Sharecropping was an attempt to meet the postemancipation labor shortage; once established, however, it remained, especially on the less desirable estate lands. The consolidation of family-size estates presaged the rise of the modern plantation (see Chapter 4). Corporate ownership, financed by French capital, became established in both territories, especially on Guadeloupe. With the emergence of the small peasant holders, however, agriculture became more diversified. The peasants grew food and, whenever possible, small quantities of coffee and cacao for sale.

Cane occupied the best land even at the height of the nineteenth-century sugar crisis. Sugar production was bolstered by an expanding demand for rum in Europe, and many planters, especially in the more isolated areas, began to convert their cane into alcohol. Later, the sugar economy received additional help through the establishment of a quota system which guaranteed the Antillean territories a share of the protected French market. French tariff protection, coupled with widespread hurricane damage of coffee and cacao crops in the 1920's, was also instrumental in effecting the last important change in land use. A 1928 law which gave preferential treatment to bananas from French possessions resulted in a gradual elimination of coffee, cacao, and even cane, in favor of commercial banana production in zones suitable for the fruit on both Martinique and Guadeloupe. At present, hardly enough coffee and cacao is produced for local needs, and the value of the banana exports surpasses that of sugar.

Despite these changes, the economy of the French Antilles differs only in degree from that of a century ago. It is still dominated by plantations controlled by local planters and absentee stockholders; its exports are few, with bananas, sugar, rum, and molasses accounting for over 90 per cent of the total; and its dependence upon the French market is almost absolute. While the plantations have undergone some modernization, they continue to use hand labor, animal power, and simple tools. The planters have felt little need to increase efficiency until recently, because French tariffs have shielded them from competition. Mechanization has recently been increasing, however, because of the French minimum wage law which became applicable on the islands after they became departments in 1946.

Subsistence farming is a very poor second in the agricultural structure. Export crops monopolize the best areas, and the consequent necessity of importing food from France is the principal drain on the insular economy. But virtually all of the arable acreage is already under crop, and expansion of subsistence farming is a dubious solution.

Industry is restricted to the processing of cane, the production of rum, and the manufacture of a few simple products such as textiles. Some fishing is carried on, but not enough to supply local demand. Tourists are attracted by the inexpensive French wines and perfumes, but hotel accommodations are sparse and poor. In a way, perhaps the second most important economy on the islands is the French government. Both departments receive much more from Paris, in the form of subsidies and public aid, than they pay in taxes.

Population. Except for the decade from 1895 to 1905, when the loss of life from the Mont Pelée disaster caused a slight drop (see below), the population of the French West Indies has grown steadily since 1635. Prior to 1848, the gain was due to immigration but, after 1848, the non-European population increased rapidly. More than 78,000 Orientals and 16,000 Africans were imported between 1852 and 1887, and the birth rate of the freed Negroes rose sharply. On the other hand, the white population decreased. Many emigrated, and those remaining suffered a disproportionately heavy loss of life in the destruction of St. Pierre. In addition, their birth rate was low, compared to that of the non-white groups.

The over-all growth of population has increased the pressure on the land. By the early 1960's, population totals were approaching 550,000, and average densities were over 480 persons per square mile. A mounting tide of migration to France, especially by the younger element, has been the only safety valve.

Except for the whites (who number less than 10,000) and the descendants of the imported Orientals, the racial composition of the French islands is Negro. Traditionally, the whites have possessed a disproportionate amount of economic and political power, but in recent decades, and especially on Martinique, they have been ousted from political power and their economic position is being weakened by the rise of an aggressive colored middle class.

The gross characteristics described above stem primarily from broad influences such as French colonial policy, the impact of the plantation, and the tropical environment—influences shared by all the French Antilles. The details of land-people patterns, however, tend to vary in accordance to the play of local factors.

Martinique

The Land and Its Use. Martinique, 385 miles square, is within the volcanic arc of the Lesser Antilles (see Chapter 2), and vulcanism has had an important influence on both the land and the people. A spectacular eruption of Mont Pelée wiped out the city of St. Pierre and laid waste over one-fifth of the island in 1902[5]; other eruptions of this volcano (in 1792, 1851–1852, and 1929) also have stamped Martinique's landscape. The huge base of the 4,583-foot volcano occupies almost the entire northern part of the island. Elsewhere, the land is characterized by steep volcanic ridges, deep ravines, and extensive massifs. Level land is restricted to the Lamentin Plain southeast of Fort-de-France (Figure 7.33) and to small patches between the ravines and along the coast. Rainfall (Figure 7.34) and vegetation vary with elevation and exposure to the trades. A fall of 200 inches supports a dense rain forest on the windward slopes, and the leeward coast, which receives less than 40 inches, contains a drought-resistant thorn forest.

These physical conditions are sharply reflected in the utilization of the land. About one-fifth of Martinique is under forest or other natural cover. In the deep ravines and on the windward mountain slopes, the tropical forest is too dense even for lumbering, so that most of the island's wood must be im-

---

5 On the morning of May 8, 1902, Mt. Pelée exploded, and in less than a minute had enveloped St. Pierre with burning lava and superheated gases (*nuée ardente*). All the ships in the harbor were burned, save one which broke from its moorings and reached St. Lucia with half its crew dead from burns and suffocation. A few sailors who had thrown themselves into the sea from other vessels were picked up by a French cruiser which arrived in the afternoon; the only other survivor was a Negro prisoner in a dungeon. The total loss of life was estimated at 40,000, with roughly 26,000 dead at St. Pierre and 4,600 at Prêcheur. Much of Martinique was totally devastated, its vegetation burned, its topography changed, and its drainage deranged.

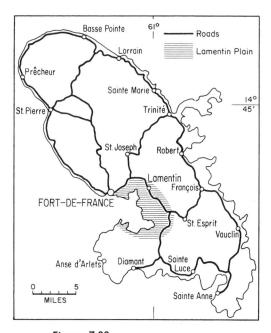

Figure 7.33

Martinique : Transportation and Settlement.

Figure 7.34

Martinique : Mean Annual Rainfall.

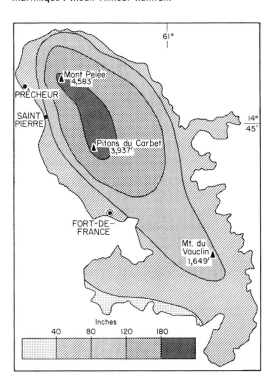

ported from the United States and France. An additional fifth of the island is in permanent meadows and pastures used for grazing; these are in the cool wet zones above 2,500 feet and on leeward exposure which receive limited rainfall.

It is officially claimed that about 45 per cent of Martinique is arable or under tree crops, but this figure includes a considerable amount of slope land which is farmed only intermittently. Perhaps less than one-third of the territory is cultivated in any one year. Sugar, the most important cash crop, occupies the level lands, especially the Lamentin Plain where cultivation is so intensive that no land is spared even for houses. Cane is also grown on smaller patches of level land along the north and east coast and in scattered mountain basins. Much of the cane, particularly from the less accessible areas, is used for distilling a rum which has an excellent reputation in France. Sugar and rum, together with less important commercial crops such as pineapples, coffee, and cacao, account for half of Martinique's exports; the remaining half is the bananas which are raised primarily on the humid lower mountain slopes.

Population and Settlement. Martinique's total population, 290,000 in the early 1960's, gives the island an over-all density of more than 700 persons per square mile and densities at least twice as high in relation to arable land. The population is concentrated in three major zones: (1) the west-central area, around the Bay of Lamentin and Fort-de-France; (2) the central massifs; and (3) the east coast. Most of the rural population within these nuclei lives in the transition areas between the lowlands and the mountains. Peasant dwellings are one- or two-room shacks measuring roughly 10 by 20 feet, usually located on rock outcrops or other sites unsuitable for farming. Fort-de-France, Martinique's capital, chief commercial center, and only city, contains over 20 per cent of its population. The city is situated on the leeward side of the island and has one of the largest and best protected harbors in the Antilles (Figure 7.35). Other agglomerated settlements function as fishing

Figure 7.35

Martinique: Fort-de-France. In the background the volcanic Pitons du Carbet rise over 4,000 feet above the sea. (*French Government Tourist Office*)

villages, coastal or interior sugar towns, and villages serving subsistence farmers.

Guadeloupe and the Dependencies

The Land and Its Use. Guadeloupe actually consists of two islands, Basse-Terre (364 square miles) and Grande-Terre (219 square miles), separated by a narrow channel (Figure 7.36). Basse-Terre, like Martinique, is high, rugged, and volcanic. Mt. Soufrière rises to 4,867 feet (Figure 7.37). In contrast, Grande-Terre is a low-lying limestone island, on which no point rises to more than 485 feet above sea level (Figure 7.38). The twin islands also differ in climate and vegetation; Basse-Terre resembles Martinique and Grande-Terre is more akin to the other low-lying limestone islands in the region (see Chapter 2).

As on Martinique, the chief farm exports are bananas and sugar, and they occupy the best land, virtually excluding other crops. Since the physical requirements of bananas and cane differ, there is little competition between the two. Cane requires level land and a precipitation of at least 45 inches (Figures 7.36 and 7.39), conditions which are best met on some of the flat limestone areas of eastern Grande-Terre and on the rolling volcanic soils of western Basse-Terre. Bananas grow on the well-watered lower

Figure 7.36

Guadeloupe and Dependencies : Mean Annual Rainfall.

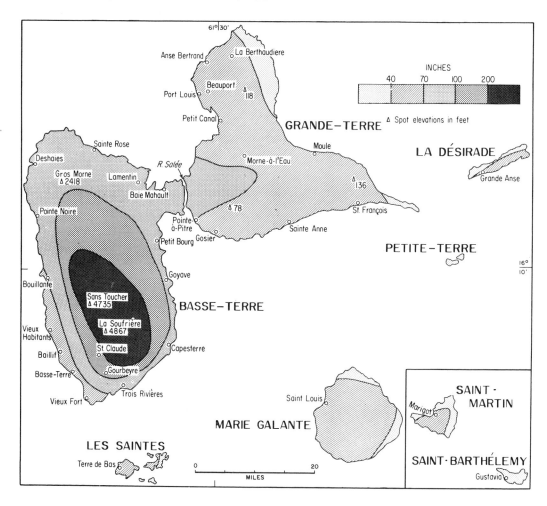

Figure 7.37

Guadeloupe : Basse-Terre. Volcanic mountains rise abruptly from the coast. *(French Government Tourist Office)*

Figure 7.38

Guadeloupe : Grande-Terre, Sainte **Anne.** *(French Government Tourist Office)*

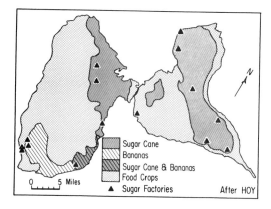

Figure 7.39
Guadeloupe : Land Use.

mountain slopes with deep soils, such as are found on southern Basse-Terre. The two leading exports compete and coexist only in the southeast of the island.

Sugar production on Guadeloupe is based on plantations, sharecrop holdings, and small peasant plots. The largest plantations, 2,800 to 20,000 acres each, own over half the sugar land and cultivate all but the less suitable parts. The less desirable plantation land is divided into small farms and worked on a sharecropping basis by *colons,* who often also raise some food and keep a few animals. With better land and more modern equipment, the plantation lands have a much higher yield than those of the *colons* and peasants.

Banana farms are smaller than cane fields, ranging in size from under 5 to 600 acres and averaging about 200. The smaller farms are owner-operated; the larger are worked by hired hands supervised by managers. On both types of holdings, food crops are often raised, as well as the coffee or cacao which provide insurance against droughts and other calamities which might affect bananas (Figure 7.39).

Population. The population of Guadeloupe increased until World War II, after which an increasing emigration to France, especially from Grande-Terre, caused a leveling off. By the early 1960's, the population was 220,-000, most of it concentrated on Grande-Terre and eastern Basse-Terre.

While Guadeloupe's racial composition resembles Martinique's, race and class lines are less rigidly drawn. Guadeloupe has a larger and more vigorous colored middle class, which appears more open to innovation than the conservative, aristocratic white families which hold sway on Martinique. This difference is probably based in part on land tenure patterns. On Guadeloupe, the peasant proprietor produces more of both the food and the export crops; sharecropping is more general; and there is less family ownership of estates and more ownership by foreign corporations. In part, the more democratic character of Guadeloupe's population also has its roots in the class origins of the early colonists. References to "les *gens* de la Guadeloupe et les *messieurs* de la Martinique" are frequent in French colonial literature.

Settlements on Guadeloupe resemble those on Martinique, except that each part of the island has its own city. The city of Basse-Terre has a population of 25,000 and is the capital of the whole island. But it is located on the less productive side of the island and has a poor harbor, and so is smaller and less important commercially than Pointe-à-Pitre, in Grande-Terre.

The Dependencies. Attached to Guadeloupe, for administrative purposes, are several small islands whose combined area is 105 square miles (Figure 7.36). The most important of these are Marie Galante, La Désirade, and the northern part of St. Martin, all limestone formations, and the volcanic islets of Les Saintes and St. Barthélemy.

Fishing and grazing are of some importance on all of the dependencies, but farming is the most common occupation. In addition to food, which is raised everywhere, the leading cash crops are cotton and sisal on La Désirade, sugar on Marie Galante, cotton on St. Martin, and a variety of products, including bananas, on St. Barthélemy.

The population of the dependencies was

25,666 in 1954 and 26,000 in 1960, and the slightness of the difference reflects the emigration of Negroes to France in the last decade, especially from St. Martin and St. Barthélemy. Densities vary, but are generally lower than on Guadeloupe proper. The exception to these patterns is Les Saintes, which has a higher population density than the main island and a predominantly white population which has been gaining in numbers.

THE NETHERLANDS ANTILLES

The Netherlands Antilles consist of two groups of widely separated islands. One, which the Dutch call the *Bovenwindse* ("windward") islands, is located almost at the head of the Lesser Antillean chain, and includes St. Eustatius, Saba, and the southern part of St. Martin; the other, named the *Benedenwindse* ("leeward") islands is in the southernmost Caribbean adjacent to Venezuela, and consists of Aruba, Bonaire, and Curaçao—the ABC islands. The islands differ in their landscape, their history, their economy, their demography, and in other ways. In fact, the six territories are so different that they seem to be held together by little more than the mechanics of Dutch administration.

Physical Landscape and Historical Setting

Of the three northern islands, St. Eustatius (sometimes referred to as Statia) and Saba belong geologically to the inner, or volcanic, arc of the Lesser Antilles, and St. Martin falls in the outer, or limestone, arc (see Chapter 2). St. Eustatius is dominated by two high-lying extinct volcanic peaks; Saba consists of a single cone which rises to 2,887 feet (Figure 7.40). Lower-lying St. Martin has a core of older igneous rocks beneath its calcareous cap, but is devoid of recent volcanic forms. In contrast, the southern, or ABC, islands are worn-down remnants of crystalline rocks from which most of an

overlying limestone layer has been removed (Figure 7.41). Their terrain is thus less striking, except for the distinctive, fan-shaped, bottle-necked embayments which were formed when a rise in sea level after the last ice age flooded the coastal valleys. The prime example of these is the Schottegat, St. Anna Bay, which forms the magnificent harbor of Willemstad on Curaçao (Figures 7.42 and 7.43).

Figure 7.40

The Netherlands Antilles.

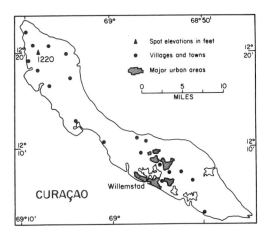

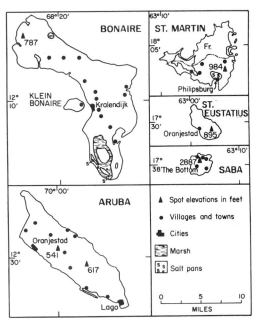

Figure 7.41

St. Martin: Air View of Philipsburg and Salt Pond. (*Netherlands West Indies Tourist Committee*)

Figure 7.42

Harbor Entrance at Willemstad. (*Foto Fischer*)

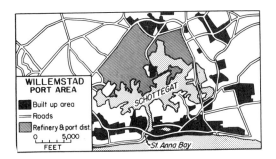

Figure 7.43
Curaçao : St. Anna Bay and the Schottegat.

The Netherlands Antilles receive scanty rainfall, but the northern trio which has a higher elevation and is closer to the hurricane paths, receives roughly twice as much as the southern. On Curaçao, for example, the annual total of 22 inches is so low in comparison with the mean annual temperature, 81°F, that the island's sparse vegetation is primarily xerophytic, or drought-resistant. Water for domestic use is obtained by catching rain in cisterns or is pumped from wells, often powered by windmills. On Curaçao and Aruba, the large population and the heavy demands of the oil refineries have made necessary the distillation of sea water. Equally discouraging, everywhere in the Dutch West Indies, is the scarcity of level land, the poorness of the soils and, except for small deposits of phosphate at Sta. Barbara on Curaçao, the absence of valuable minerals.

Obviously, it was not resources which first attracted the Dutch to their Antillean holdings. The southern islands, and especially Curaçao with its excellent and easily defended harbor, were occupied in the seventeenth century primarily as bases for preying on Spanish commerce. When privateering became less profitable, Curaçao was converted into an important slave-trade center. St. Martin, with its salt-rich lagoon (Figures 7.40 and 7.41), provided salt for Holland's herring industry. The Dutch made some effort to raise sugar and other cash crops, but the chief function of the Antillean islands during the seventeenth and eighteenth centuries was to serve as entrepôts and trading centers (see Chapters 3 and 4). Compared to the rich profits made from the trading marts at "Statia" and Curaçao, the return from farming was puny. With the destruction of "Statia" by Rodney, the English admiral, in the late eighteenth century and the subsequent abolition of the slave trade and the collapse of the West Indian colonial plantation system (see Chapter 4), all of the Netherlands Antilles entered a decline from which most have never recovered.

Economic Patterns

Oil Refining. In August, 1918, a tugboat called "Don Alberto" with the lighter "Wilemstad" in tow, sailed from Lake Maracaibo with the first shipment of oil for the newly built Curaçao refinery. For Curaçao, and later for Aruba, this was a revolutionary event. Immigrants began to pour in; banking and business assumed proportions unheard of in the Caribbean; and, almost overnight, the two islands were transformed from sleepy, subsistence areas to places of world-wide commercial importance. This revolutionary change started with the construction of large refineries by subsidiaries of Royal Dutch Shell on Curaçao, in 1916, and was given a tremendous boost when Standard Oil of New Jersey built its refineries on Aruba in 1929.

Curaçao and Aruba were selected as sites for the refineries for political and geographic reasons. Dutch oil interests were among the first to negotiate with Venezuela for the development of the Maracaibo fields. These interests wanted their refineries located on the Dutch islands because of Venezuela's political instability and because she lacked adequate ports near her oil fields. Curaçao, only 216 miles away and possessing the excellent natural harbor of Willemstad, was the logical location. Similar reasons probably prompted Standard Oil to fix on Aruba.

Currently, oil dominates the economy of the Dutch Antilles. It comprises over 85 per cent of the imports and 98 per cent of the exports; it enables Curaçao and Aruba to support a large population at one of the highest standards of living in the Caribbean; and it indirectly provides income and social services for the four agricultural islands in the federation.

Despite the prosperity of the last few decades, however, many a sober Dutchman views the economic future of the oil islands with apprehension. What will happen when the oil runs out or if it were refined elsewhere? Farming cannot be expected to support the large population now making its living from oil; minor occupations—fishing, phosphate mining, the manufacture of Panama hats—are not the answer; and mass emigration, particularly of the colored peasantry, seems out of the question.

Other Economies. Farming in the Netherlands Antilles has always been precarious. The southern islands have a rocky surface and a paucity of water; the northern islands have a rugged terrain and a paucity of arable land. Small quantities of cotton are grown on St. Martin and "Statia," and aloes are grown on Aruba and Bonaire; elsewhere, agriculture is generally confined to small-scale food growing on peasant plots. Local food supplies, including livestock and fish, are so inadequate that virtually all the food, especially on Curaçao and Aruba, must be imported. In an effort to alleviate the situation, the Dutch have established a hydroponics farm on Aruba and have also induced the oil companies to give workers who have gardens a few days of paid vacation at planting and harvest time.

But the islands' agricultural potential is so limited that the Dutch have pinned their major hopes for an economic future on tourism and on manufacturing. Luxurious new hotels have been built, duty-free zones have been established on Curaçao and Aruba, and widespread advertising has been undertaken. Success has been only modest, however, because the islands are off the beaten path, especially for Americans. The advancement of manufacturing enterprises not connected with oil refining and shipping has met with even less success.

Population and Settlement

The demography of the Netherlands Antilles is so closely linked with their economies that the contrast between the oil-refining islands and the others is enormous (Table 7.3). Between them, Curaçao and Aruba now account for 80 per cent of the total population and have densities of 765 and 828 persons per square mile, respectively; but the other four islands have had a quite different recent history. The outflow of persons, especially of men, from the agricultural islands to Curaçao and Aruba has been so marked that on Bonaire, for example, the

Table 7.3

THE NETHERLANDS ANTILLES—AREA, POPULATION, AND DENSITY: 1960

Territory	Area (In square miles)	Population (1960)	Density (Per square mile)
Curaçao	170	130,000	765
Aruba	70	58,000	828
Bonaire	108	5,700	53
St. Martin (Dutch section)	13	1,500	115
St. Eustatius	12	1,004	84
Saba	5	1,062	212

females outnumber the males more than three to one. The northern islands, also, are now populated by females and by males who are too old or too young to seek work elsewhere.

The people of the Netherlands Antilles are predominantly African, but there are some Europeans. The history of settlement and recent migrations, however, have given rise to somewhat different racial balances on each of the territories. On Saba, for example, Europeans have traditionally outnumbered Negroes, but the recent emigration of whites to the oil islands and elsewhere, coupled with the higher birth rate of the Negroes, is reversing the ratio. The same trend is apparent on St. Martin, whose population also included a high percentage of whites.

On Curaçao, the pre-oil population included descendants of Negro slaves, of seventeenth-century Jewish settlers from Brazil and Holland, and of Dutch, German, Danish, and Swiss colonists. On Aruba, the old peasant stock is of Amerindian ancestry. Oil has brought a variety of new groups to both islands, chiefly Negroes from the other West Indian islands and from Surinam. But there has also been significant immigration from the Netherlands, and the Madeiras, and smaller groups of Chinese, Syrians, and East Indians.

The islands' racial and ethnic pluralism is matched by their cultural pluralism. While the Dutch language has official recognition and is spoken by an increasing number of people, the most common tongue in the ABC group is *Papiamento,* a remarkable mixture based mostly on Iberian linguistic forms. *Papiamento* reflects the close contact with the Hispanic peoples of nearby Venezuela and the probable influence of Portuguese-speaking Jews. In addition, many of the immigrant minorities continue to use their own languages. The colored peasantry of the northern islands, for example, speak an English dialect.

Similarly, the vast majority, especially in the southern islands, are Roman Catholic, reflecting both Hispanic contact and the strong missionary effort of Dutch Roman Catholic priests. Various Protestant denominations, Jews, and others are also represented, however.

Settlement in the Netherlands Antilles tends to be agglomerated rather than dispersed, with villages predominating. The chief urban center is Willemstad, which has a population of over 50,000. With its distinctive harbor and drawbridges, the Amsterdam-like flavor of its architecture, and its cosmopolitan population, Willemstad is rated by many as the most colorful city in the Caribbean.

THE VIRGIN ISLANDS

Between the Anegada Passage in the east and Puerto Rico in the west are several dozen small islands and numerous reefs which, collectively, are called the Virgin Islands (see Figure 7.1).[6] Politically, the archipelago is unequally divided; two-thirds of its 200 square miles is governed by the United States and the remainder is British.[7] The bulk of the population and economic activity in the American islands is centered on St. Thomas, St. Croix, and St. John; the most important of the British holdings are Tortola, Virgin Gorda, Jost Van Dyke, and Anegada (Figures 7.44 and 7.45).

Physical and Historical Setting

Most of the Virgins are of volcanic origin and are characterized by rugged slopes which rises abruptly from the sea to elevations of

---

[6] Geologically, the Puerto Rican islands of Vieques and Culebra, sometimes called the "Spanish Virgins," are also part of the archipelago.

[7] The British Virgin Islands have often been administered as part of the Leewards. They are treated separately here, partly for convenience and partly because of their close ties with the American Virgin Islands.

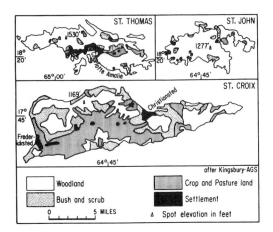

Figure 7.44
The American Virgin Islands.

1,000 to 1,780 feet. The remainder are low-lying limestone islets, such as Anegada, whose average height is barely 30 feet.

Except on St. Croix, level farmland is restricted to a few dry stream bottoms or "guts." Nor is the soil rich. On the limestone islands, it is either nonexistent or con-

sists of small pockets of an earthy substance composed of coral sand and humus. Elsewhere, the soil is a brown loam derived from volcanic material. Serious erosion, the result of deforestation, overgrazing, and the cultivation of slope land, is widespread. Even the best soils tend to be shallow and are exhausted from long use.

However, the Virgins' greatest physical drawback is the scarcity of water. The average annual precipitation in the archipelago is about 50 inches but, with year-round temperatures of 65 to 90°F, the rate of evaporation is high. Moreover, the seasonal distribution is highly variable; most of the rain falls in short, heavy showers during summer and fall. The runoff on the steep slopes is so rapid that the moisture is sufficient only for xerophytic vegetation.

"Water is our most precious resource, please conserve it," reads a sign found in many Virgin Island hotels. There are no rivers or lakes on the islands, and only a few perennial streams. Water comes from wells, a few springs, home cisterns, and, especially on

Figure 7.45
The British Virgin Islands.

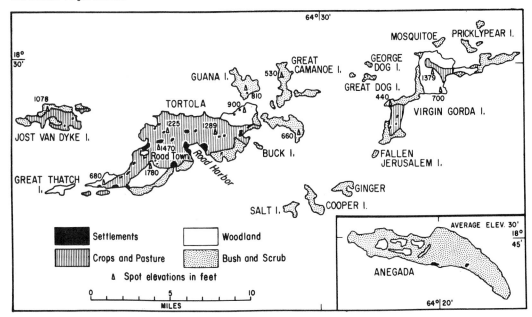

St. Thomas, from stone or cement catchment basins built on the hillsides. And it is imported in ever-greater quantities from Puerto Rico. With a record number of tourists in 1962, St. Thomas had to bring in more than 84 million gallons, in addition to distilling almost 26 million gallons of sea water at a local plant.

In the seventeenth and eighteenth centuries, this poor environment was contested far more than its economic potential warranted. The various islands have flown the flags of Holland, France, England, Spain, Denmark, the Knights of Malta and, intermittently, even the Jolly Roger of the buccaneers. Eventually, the Danes gained firm control of the western islands and the English of the eastern. The last political change occurred in 1917, when the United States purchased the Danish territories for $25 million.

The archipelago's economic history has been almost as chequered as its political history. Following early experiments with indigo and tobacco, the islands' economy was a slave-based estate sugar and cotton agriculture. While market and labor conditions remained favorable, the plantations enjoyed a small measure of prosperity. In 1787, for example, the sugar exports of Tortolan estates (see Figure 4.9) came to £164,000.

Handicapped by a mountainous terrain, poor soils, and a limited water supply, however, the marginal plantation agriculture of the Virgins was ill-equipped to withstand the problems created by emancipation and the drop in sugar prices during the nineteenth century. Its collapse on Tortola and other British islands was so complete that, by 1860, virtually all the white planter families had migrated, leaving the land to Negro subsistence farmers. The Danish islands were also severely affected. Only St. Croix, which is less mountainous, managed to retain a meager sugar economy. St. John was taken over by the Negro peasantry and its mansions became relics. St. Thomas suffered not only from the downfall of sugar, but also from a major reduction in shipping and warehouse revenues. In the days of slow-moving sailing ships, the island's excellent harbor at Charlotte Amalie (Figure 7.44) was an important transhipping and supply base. Its relative proximity to Africa and Europe made it the first port of call for vessels in need of stores. With the advent of the faster, wider-ranging steamship, Charlotte Amalie became an important coaling station, but it lost much of its former income.

Current Economy

The American Territories. Like Puerto Rico, the United States Virgin Islands have been reaping major economic benefits from being American-owned, especially since World War II. Federal subsidies and aid, the influx of tourists and small industries from the continent, an outlet for surplus labor— these, and other, advantages of the American connection are transforming the islands which Herbert Hoover once called a "poorhouse." There has been marked improvement in social services, including the establishment of the College of the Virgin Islands in 1963; per capita income rose from $412, in 1950, to $1,751 in 1964; and total annual income increased more than 500 per cent in the same 15-year period.

This progress has occurred despite agricultural stagnation and decline. On St. Thomas, farming has disappeared except in a small northern area where fruit and vegetables are planted on terraced plots (Figure 7.44). The peasant farming on St. John is largely subsistent, but production is sufficient to allow some exporting to the growing urban market of Charlotte Amalie. St. Croix continues to have a plantation economy based on sugar, but only by the grace of federal quotas and supports. The cane is produced on more than 150 small, uneconomical estates and it is milled in an obsolete and unprofitable factory run by the Virgin Islands Corporation, an agency heavily underwritten by the United States

Department of the Interior. Efforts are being made to induce a switchover to provision farming on St. Croix, and for good reason. Food, like water, is scarce, especially on St. Thomas. The cost of food imports rose from $2.37 million, in 1950, to $7.64 million in 1961, and will probably continue to rise.

While the new industries attracted to the islands have made some contribution, the major economic gains in the Virgins have resulted from tourism. Tourist expenditures, less than $5 million in 1952, were over $35 million in 1962. The vast majority of the 290,000 visitors in 1962 arrived by plane.

St. Thomas is less than 20 minutes by air from San Juan, and much of the heavy traffic bound for Puerto Rico (see Chapter 5) spills over into the Virgin Islands. A major attraction is the free-port status of the islands, which enables the visitor to purchase luxury goods for 20 to 50 per cent less than he would have to pay in New York.

The British Territories.   The British Virgin Islands have changed only slightly in the last century. Tourists have not yet discovered them, and a semisubsistent peasant farming is still their characteristic economy. If the people of these islands were permitted to do so, they would probably emigrate en masse to the American territories.

With crop cultivation largely ruled out by steep slopes, small rainfall, and poor soils, land in the British Virgins is mostly given over to scrub growth or pasture (Figure 7.45). Probably not more than one-tenth of the land is under crops, and the amount is constantly decreasing. Most of the cropland is in the bottoms and on the more fertile slopes; even so, the soil is so marginal that a modified shifting cultivation has to be practiced. Food crops are generally followed by pasture, croton thicket, and secondary woodland. Stock raising, particularly of cattle, is the principal farming activity.

Many of the islanders engage in secondary occupations such as fishing and boat building. Fish is the second most important ex-

port, cattle being the first, and is also an important part of the local diet. On islands such as Anegada, Salt, Peter, and Jost Van Dyke, where farming is even more difficult than on the main island of Tortola, fishing is often the principal economic enterprise.

Despite the poverty of their economy, the islanders have a higher standard of living than the people in most of the other British Lesser Antilles. The key to this paradox is hidden income, especially that derived from temporary employment of the British Virgin Islanders in St. Thomas and St. Croix. Such employment in the more prosperous American territories is a long-established practice and it has reached major proportions since the recent boom in tourism. It is estimated that, at any given date, as much as one-fourth of the labor force of the British islands is temporarily residing and working in the American Virgins. This, as well as other interaction between the two politically separated groups of islands, has led to a surprising degree of social and economic integration.

Integration in the Virgin Islands.   The relations which the British Virgins have with St. Thomas and the other American islands are based on a mutual interdependence. St. Thomas is largely urban and needs low-cost meat; the British islands are largely rural, and can export a limited number of livestock. The people on St. Thomas are reluctant to farm or do domestic service but they can and do migrate to better jobs in the United States, and the labor vacuum thus created is nicely filled by unemployed workers from the British territories. The money spent by St. Thomas for meat and wages is, in turn, spent by the British islanders on consumers' goods and services (e.g., banking and medical services) not available at home. St. Thomas serves as the port of call for the British Virgins. The economic bonds between the British islands and St. Thomas are as strong as those between any town and its rural hinterland.

Not all of the consequences of this integration have been positive, however. The work and wages available on the American island have created a strong movement, especially of young people, away from the land, and they seldom return to the farms. Since the older people are unable to do all the farm work, the current trend is to put less land in crops and more in grazing. Yet the shortage of labor affects even grazing, and greater dependence is being placed on unimproved natural pasture than on planted grasses. The net result is a less intensive use of land and a relative decline in its productivity.

Population. The population of the entire archipelago was approximately 42,000 in 1960. St. Thomas and St. Croix had approximately 16,000 people each, and St. John had about 800. The entire British Virgins supported 8,100, of whom more than 85 per cent lived on Tortola. Every other island had fewer than 300, except Virgin Gorda, which reported 564 inhabitants.

The vast majority of the islanders are Negro. There are not 20 whites in the British islands. The Caucasian population of the American Virgins, especially of St. Thomas, has increased with tourism, but the Negroid people still constitute more than three-fourths of the total.

Two minorities in the American islands are the Puerto Ricans of St. Croix, who are recent arrivals, and the French of St. Thomas, who came from St. Barthélemy in the eighteenth century. These French are one of the most interesting cultural groups in the Caribbean. They have retained their language, customs, and racial homogeneity despite two centuries of exposure to other cultures and races. They are concentrated in Charlotte Amalie, where the colors and the neatness of their tiny houses catch the eye. Even the straw hats worn by *Chachas,* as the French are called, are distinctive. Most of the group fish or make handicrafts; the rest are farmers who work the terraced plots on the north side of the island.

The Danes who once ruled the American Virgins have also left their mark, especially on the architecture of the older buildings and in place names (Figure 7.44). The Danish language, never widely used, is no longer heard at all.

The Bahamas

The people of the Bahamas have some justification for rejecting identity with the West Indies. In the last two centuries, their destinies have been more closely linked with continental United States than with the island world of the Antilles. Moreover, their way of life has never been typically West Indian. Plantation agriculture was an ephemeral development, and even today farming is of little importance. The Bahamians are a race of seamen, and it is the sea which provides the key to understanding their island habitat. In the words of one Bahamian, "We rely upon the sea for everything... through the centuries it has given us our food and our wealth...our products and our people move by boat."

Setting

The Bahamas are a sprawling archipelago of some 700 islands and more than 2,000 reefs and rocks which rise above shallow submarine banks to form the eastern rim of the Florida Passage (Figure 7.46). None of the islands rises as high as 400 feet above sea level and, on most of them, the highest point is well below 200 feet.

The archipelago is composed largely of calcareous materials derived from sea shells. At higher elevations on some of the islands, these materials were consolidated into rocks and have subsequently been weathered into a typical karst landscape of caves and other features; elsewhere, the calcareous sand has been piled into low ridges by the action of wind and water. Brackish water swamps cover large insular areas.

The soils of the Bahamas are therefore poorly developed and of low fertility. They

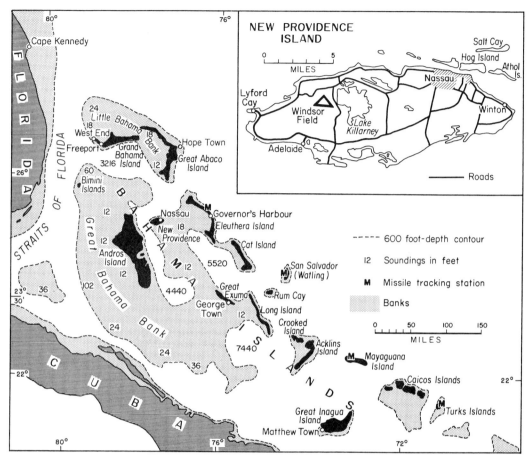

Figure 7.46
The Bahamas.

have little depth or humus content; they retain little water; and, once disturbed by cultivation, they are prone to erosion and depletion. Moreover, the islands are subject to hurricanes. Annual precipitation varies between 40 and 60 inches, and most of it falls in heavy showers between May and October and soaks quickly through the thin, sandy mantle, reducing its usefulness to the farmer. As on Barbados, well water is drawn for domestic use from subsurface reservoirs, but there is little for irrigation.

Nor is the land otherwise rich. A few of the islands have exploitable forests, but the vegetation elsewhere tends to be sparse. Except for bat phosphate found in the caves

and used for fertilizer, mineral wealth is insignificant. Resources are so limited that only about 22 of the several hundred islands have permanent populations.

Such prosperity as the Bahamas have experienced has stemmed largely from the advantages of their sea environment and their strategic location vis-à-vis the United States. These advantages have frequently made illegal activities profitable. During the seventeenth and eighteenth centuries, for example, the archipelago provided an ideal base from which pirates could prey on shipping sailing through the Florida Straits. The "wreckers," who lured unsuspecting ships to their destruction among the uncharted reefs, also prospered from stripping and selling the cargoes. The Bahamas experienced another brief prosperity during the American Civil War, when Confederate blockade runners came to the islands to exchange cotton for English munitions, medicines, and machinery. And the Bahamians also profited from the smuggling of liquor into the United States during Prohibition.

It was the location of the Bahamas and the difficulties of navigating among them which made possible these dubious but profitable activities. Channels deep enough for large ships are few, and they are difficult to follow in the shallow waters surrounding the maze of island and reefs (Figure 7.46), so that people familiar with them could easily elude pursuit. The present economic upsurge in the archipelago, while less spectacular and more legal, also stems in part from the advantages of location and a unique sea environment.

Economic Patterns

Agriculture. In addition to the drawbacks we have already enumerated, there is little arable land in the Bahamas. Moreover, transportation is poor and agricultural practices are primitive.

Less than 2 per cent of the archipelago's total area of roughly 4,000 square miles is considered suitable for crops. The arable pockets, widely scattered, are often so remote from Nassau, the chief market, that it takes a week for sailboats to transport produce and livestock. The peasantry clears the land by slashing and burning, a practice which destroys the humus, dries the soil, and subjects it to erosion. In general, yields are low and profits discouraging.

Nevertheless, the peasants produce enough fruit and vegetables for themselves and for the Nassau hotels (Figure 7.47). In addition, small quantities of tomatoes, onions, okra and pineapples are exported to the United States and Canada. Livestock production has been associated with this haphazard peasant farming, especially on Exuma and Long Island, but there are now some large and modern livestock farms, such as that established by a former president of the Chicago Stockyards on Eleuthera Island.

Figure 7.47
The Bahamas : Waterfront Market at Nassau. (*Bahamas News Bureau*)

Figure 7.48
The Bahamas : Fish Nets Drying at San Salvador. (*Bahamas News Bureau*)

Fishing and Forestry. Fish is the major staple of the Bahamian diet, partly because farming is so difficult and partly because the shallow waters of the archipelago provide rich catches. Fishing, from small boats and with primitive equipment, is practiced throughout the archipelago (Figure 7.48), but it is especially important on Grand Bahama, Abaco, and Harbour Island. Most of the catch is consumed locally, but there is some export, especially of crayfish, to the United States. The once-important trade in sponges was sharply curtailed by a disease which invaded the grounds of the Bahamas and of nearby Florida in the 1940's.

Forest products, especially pulpwood, account for over a third of the value of the exports. Most of these come from the extensive pine stands of Grand Bahama, Abaco, and Andros. In addition, there are mahogany and other hardwoods for constructing small boats, an industry of vital importance.

Tourism and Tax Refuge. The current economic boom in the Bahamas results largely from tourism and tax dodging. The islands are near the populous east coast of the United States, and they offer a subtropical climate without extremes of temperature, excellent fishing and bathing, and spectacular marine scenery. These natural advantages combined with the United States ban on travel to Cuba and an effective advertising campaign have resulted in a year-round tourist industry. The number of visitors, 200,000 in 1958, climbed to over a half-million in 1963, and the dollars spent by American and Canadian tourists have become the chief source of income. The center of tourism, and of everything else in the archipelago, is Nassau on New Providence but, as transportation improves, an increasing number of visitors are discovering the charms of the other islands.

The Bahamas have also acquired some well-heeled permanent guests from the United States and elsewhere. Some who came to the islands to retire have contributed know-how and capital for economic development. The former president of the Chicago Stockyards who established a modern livestock farm is only one illustration. The Ericksons, a Boston family who came to Great Inagua Island in 1934, provide an even more striking illustration. They found evidence of a once-important salt industry based on the solar evaporation of sea water, revived the industry, and now produce hundreds of thousands of tons of salt for annual export.

But the major attraction for most of the new settlers is an extremely liberal tax law. Except for import duties there are virtually no taxes. As a result, the Bahamas have become the legal residence of numerous American, Canadian, British, and other foreign firms, as well as of many wealthy individuals. One of the most promising consequences of the liberal tax laws was the establishment of a huge industrial reservation at Freeport, on the southern side of Grand Bahama, in 1955. Any new industry established on this site will pay no customs duties for 99 years, no taxes of any kind for 30 years, and will be free of the usual immigration restrictions against bringing in skilled labor.

The Bahamas have also benefited from United States military expenditures. During World War II, the archipelago was a lend-lease base. And more recently, the Americans have established missile tracking stations to spot rockets fired from Cape Kennedy, Florida (Figure 7.46).

Population and Settlement

After the destruction of the Indians by Spanish slave raiders in the early sixteenth century, the Bahamas remained virtually unsettled, except for pirates, until the "Eleutherian Adventurers" arrived in 1647. But these settlers and those who followed, including Palatinate Germans in 1721, were so few that by 1731 the archipelago had only 1,378 inhabitants. The major influx of settlers took place at the close of the American Revolution, when loyalists from the Carolinas arrived with their slaves to settle on Abaco and several other islands, then to raise sea island cotton. They prospered for the few decades during which the virgin soil lasted and slavery was permitted. But their plantations were wiped out in 1834, when slavery was ended and many moved to Nassau or left the archipelago altogether.

The present population of the Bahamas is small, but is growing rapidly. The 1963 census reported 130,721 people, a 54 per cent increase from the 1953 figure. This is due, in part at least, to the postwar influx mentioned above.

Among the 22 inhabited islands, there are enormous differences in the distribution and density of population. New Providence, with an area of 60 square miles, accounts for more than half the total and has a population density of more than 700 per square mile. The Bahamians apply the term "out islands" to all the Bahamas save New Providence, the site of Nassau "and therefore the capital of the world." Of the 21 inhabited "out islands," Andros, Grand Bahama, Abaco, and Eleuthera have a few thousand inhabitants each; the others have from less than a dozen to several hundred inhabitants.

TURKS AND CAICOS ISLANDS

Geographically, these 14 small isles are the southernmost of the Bahamas, but politically they form a separate British colony. Until 1960, they were a dependency of Jamaica. Like the rest of the Bahamas, the Turks and Caicos are low exposures of calcareous sand and coral deposits. Receiving an annual rainfall below 30 inches, they are among the driest of the Antilles. Mainly for that reason and the lack of good soil for farming, the production of salt by evaporation of sea water has been the chief enterprise of the islands since the late seventeenth century. Together with neighboring Great Inagua Island, the Caicos produce most of the salt exported from the Bahamas.

Like other Bahamians, most of the Caicos Islanders are fishermen. The commercial catch revolves around the collecting of a large shellfish called the conch (Strombus gigas) in clear, shallow water off coral reefs. The meat of the conch is dried for shipment mainly to nearby Haiti, where it brings good prices in that protein-starved land.

In 1960, some 5,700 people, mainly Negro descendants from slaves formerly used to rake salt, inhabited the island group.

SELECTED REFERENCES

Augelli, J. P., "The British Virgin Islands: A West Indian Anomaly," *Geographical Review,* XLVI, No. 1 (1956), 43–58.

————, and H. W. Taylor, "Race and Population Patterns in Trinidad," *Annals of the Association of American Geographers,* L, No. 2 (1960), 123–38.

Bureau of Foreign Commerce, U.S. Department of Commerce, "Basic Data on the Economy of the Bahama Islands." *Overseas Business Report* 64–38. Washington, D.C.: Government Printing Office, 1964.

Démographie des Antilles Françaises: Guadeloupe et Martinique. Paris: Institut National de la Statistique et des Études Économiques, 1955.

Fentem, A. D., *Commercial Geography of Antigua,* Indiana University, Department of Geography, Office of Naval Research Technical Report No. 11. Bloomington, Ind., 1961.

————, *Commercial Geography of Dominica,* Indiana University, Department of Geography, Office of Naval Research Technical Report No. 5. Bloomington, Ind., 1960.

Finkel, H. J., "Patterns of Land Tenure in the Leeward and Windward Islands and Their Relevance to Problems of Agricultural Development in the West Indies," *Economic Geography,* XL, No. 2 (1964), 163–72.

Harewood, J., "Population Growth in Trinidad and Tobago in the Twentieth Century," *Social and Economic Studies,* XII, No. 1 (1963), 1–26.

Hoy, D. R., *Agricultural Land Use of Guadeloupe,* National Research Council Publication No. 884. Washington, D.C.: National Academy of Sciences, 1961.

James, P. E., "Changes in the Geography of Trinidad," *Scottish Geographical Magazine,* LXXIII, No. 3 (1957), 158–66.

Kingsbury, R. C., *Commercial Geography of the British Virgin Islands,* Indiana University, Department of Geography, Office of Naval Research Technical Report No. 2. Bloomington, Ind., 1960.

————, *Commercial Geography of Trinidad and Tobago,* Indiana University, Department of Geography, Office of Naval Research Technical Report No. 4. Bloomington, Ind., 1960.

Lasserre, G., *La Guadeloupe: Étude Géographique.* Bordeaux: Union Française d'Impression, 1961.

Lowenthal, D., "Economic Tribulations in the Caribbean: A Case Study in the British West Indies," *Inter-American Economic Affairs,* IX, No. 3 (1955), 67–81.

————, "The Population of Barbados," *Social and Economic Studies,* VI, No. 4 (1957), 445–501.

————, "The Range and Variation of Caribbean Societies," *Annals of the New York Academy of Sciences,* LXXXIII, No. 5 (1960), 786–95.

Luke, S., *Development and Welfare in the West Indies.* London: Her Majesty's Stationery Office, 1955.

Macpherson, J., *Caribbean Lands: A Geography of the West Indies.* London: Longmans, Green & Co., Inc., 1963.

McFarlane, D., "The Future of the Banana Industry in the West Indies," *Social and Economic Studies,* XIII, No. 1 (1964), 38–93.

Netherlands Antilles Government Information Service, *The Netherlands Antilles: Their Geography, History and Political, Economic and Social Development* (3rd ed.). Willemstad, Curaçao, Netherlands West Indies, 1961.

Niddrie, D. L., *Land Use and Population in Tobago,* The World Land Use Survey, Regional Monograph No. 3. Bude, Cornwall, England: Geographical Publications, 1961.

O'Loughlin, C., "Economic Problems of the Smaller West Indies Islands," *Social and Economic Studies,* XI, No. 1 (1962), 44–56.

Paget, E., "Value, Valuation, and Use of Land in the West Indies," *Geographical Journal,* CXXVII, No. 4 (1961), 493–98.

Simmonds, N. W., "The Growth of Post-War West Indian Banana Trades," *Tropical Agriculture,* XXXVIII, No. 2 (1960), 79–85.

Starkey, O. P., *Commercial Geography of Montserrat,* Indiana University, Department of Geography, Office of Naval Research Technical Report No. 6. Bloomington, Ind., 1960.

8

Mexico and Central America: The Pre-Conquest Setting

To understand adequately the human geography of present-day Mexico and Central America, one must consider the aboriginal background as it existed in these areas before the European invasion in the early sixteenth century. Much of Mexico and parts of Central America are still considered to be largely Indian in character, although they have been variously modified by European culture. Probably one-third of Mexico's total population, and more than half of Guatemala's, is of pure Indian blood. In Mexico, more than 2.5 million people (8 per cent of the population) still speak Indian languages; in Guatemala, more than one million (40 per cent) speak native tongues. But more significant than race and language are the great number of Indian customs that are retained in the cultural heritage of Mexico and Central America. Among these are food crops and food habits, farming practices, and rural dwelling types, all of which give an aboriginal cast to the landscape of many areas. To be sure, most of the present dominantly Indian sections are found in isolated areas. On the other hand, many Indian customs, mainly food crops and diet, have become an integral part of rural life throughout much of Mexico and Central America. Moreover, certain aspects of ancient Indian systems of land tenure have been retained in many areas, and in Mexico the aboriginal custom of communal land use has been incorporated into the current agrarian program.

ABORIGINAL ECONOMIES IN ABOUT 1500 A.D.

Immediately prior to the Spanish invasion, two fundamentally different types of aboriginal economies were present in the Mexico-Central American area: (1) A *primitive hunting, gathering, and fishing economy,* which was practiced by the scant population that inhabited the steppes and deserts of northern Mexico; and (2) an *agricultural economy,* which prevailed over the rest of Mexico and Central America (Figure 8.1). The bulk of the Indians were farmers living in villages or in scattered dwellings and practicing a rudimentary slash-burn cultivation, although in various sections advanced farming techniques such as irrigation and terracing were utilized. The advanced methods were particularly important in parts of central and southern Mexico and of northern Central America. This was the area of highly developed aboriginal culture which the anthropologists call "Mesoamerica," the locale of the renowned Aztec, Maya, and other Indian civilizations.

The farming population of Mexico and Central America may be further classified into two groups on the basis of crop types. In the southeastern part of Central America, Indians of relatively low cultural status chiefly cultivated tubers of South American origin, such as manioc and arrowroot. In contrast, within northern Central America and Mexico,

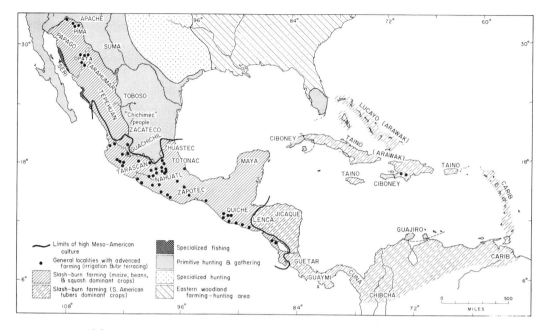

Figure 8.1
Pre-Conquest Economy and Culture Areas: 1500 A.D.

the Indian farmers relied principally on three seed plants of local origin: maize, beans, and squash. These three plants still comprise the major crop complex in the same area. The maize-beans-squash region may, in turn, be divided into two areas: (1) Mesoamerica, distinguished by its high native cultures, advanced farming techniques, and a great variety of domesticated plants; and (2) northwestern Mexico, characterized mainly by people of relatively low culture, but related culturally to both the Mesoamericans to the south and the well-developed farming cultures of southwestern United States.

Summary of Aboriginal Economies in Mexico and Central America

I. Primitive hunting, gathering, and fishing economy: desert nomads of northern Mexico

II. Agricultural economies
    A. Maize, beans, and squash farmers of Mexico and northern Central America

      1. Primitive and advanced farmers of Mesoamerica
      2. Primitive farmers of northwestern Mexico
    B. Primitive tuber farmers of southeastern Central America

PRIMITIVE HUNTING, GATHERING, AND FISHING

The desert nomads of northern Mexico held the lowest cultural status of any Indian group on the mainland of Middle America. They wandered in small bands from place to place, gathering seeds, roots, and fruits of desert plants; hunting with traps and bow and arrow for rodents, reptiles, and sometimes deer, and often fishing with nets in the streams and more permanent desert lakes. Along the eastern coast of the Gulf of California some nomads, such as the Seri and Guasave, became specialized fishermen.

The rudimentary shelters of these people

were crudely built lean-tos and domed huts of desert plant materials. Such dwellings could be quickly constructed where fruit and game were abundant and abandoned when the surrounding resources were depleted. Owing to the scantiness of the desert resources for people of such low culture, the number of the nomads was never large.

The Indians of Baja California, one of the least desirable areas of Middle America, were the least numerous and culturally lowest of the desert nomads. The Pericú in the southern Cape area, the Cochimí in the central Vizcaino Desert, and the Kiliwa in the north were some of the important language groups of the arid peninsula. Missionized by Spanish priests in the seventeenth century, these Indians were practically wiped out by introduced European diseases, and today only a handful remain scattered in isolated areas.

The nomads of the north central Mexican desert and steppes were more numerous and more culturally advanced than the lowly Baja Californians, particularly in social organization. Warlike and mobile, they were the scourge of the northern Aztec frontier, having more than once raided the settled farming areas near the Valley of Mexico. Quite likely, these people were the source of the periodic invasions that often overthrew the high cultures of central Mexico, the intruders finally being assimilated into the culture, much as were the Mongol invaders in central Chinese civilizations. The Aztecs themselves were probably descendants of desert nomads from the north.

Collectively, the northern hunters and gatherers were known as "Chichimecs," an Aztec term of derision. Linguistically, they comprised many groups, such as the Pame, Guachichil, and Zacateco in the south and the Toboso, Suma, and Coahuilteca in the north. Women gathered desert products and men hunted deer and smaller animals with their strong bows. One of the favorite foods of many bands was the pod of the mesquite bush. Stripped of their indigestible seeds,

the pods, rich in protein and sugar, were pounded into a meal and eaten as a gruel mixed with water. This is still a famine food for many people in isolated villages in northern Mexico.

We shall see later how the Chichimecs became a cultural barrier to northward expansion of Spanish settlement during the colonial period. Never numerous, these aborigines gradually died away or mixed with Spaniards or with settled Indians from central Mexico, so that today probably no Chichimecs are left. Quite in contrast to the civilized farmers of Mesoamerica, the desert nomads left no cultural heritage in northern Mexico. Today northern Mexico is largely non-Indian, providing a contrast to the central and southern parts of the country, which have a strongly aboriginal character.

THE MESOAMERICAN CIVILIZATIONS

Mesoamerica was the cultural hearth of ancient Mexico and much of Central America. It was one of the two areas of the Americas in which both high Indian civilizations and a major center of plant domestication developed, the other being the central Andes of South America. Thus we are dealing now with the most significant aboriginal area of Middle America. It is precisely within the bounds of ancient Mesoamerica that we find today the bulk of Indian population, the greatest number of spoken aboriginal languages, and most of the Indian ways of life that are retained in the culture of Mexico and Central America.

Significantly, the civilizations of Mesoamerica developed within the tropics of Mexico and Guatemala, in the high- and lowlands. On the northern periphery of aboriginal American civilization the Mesa Central of Mexico, the home of the Aztecs and their predecessors, was the largest and probably the richest of the tropical highlands (Chapter 2). The rugged uplands of

Oaxaca and the volcanic highlands of Guatemala were secondary foci of cultural development. In the tropical lowlands, the hot, damp Petén of northern Guatemala and the Yucatan Peninsula fostered the magnificent Maya civilization; almost equally advanced cultures, such as the Totonac, evolved on the Gulf coastal plain of Veracruz.

About 1500 A.D., on the eve of the Spanish invasion, the northern limit of Mesoamerican high cultures began on the Gulf of Mexico, at the latitude of present Tampico, and followed the Pánuco and Moctezuma rivers southwestward to the Río Lerma on the Mesa Central. Thence it extended northwestward, forming a narrow prong of high culture along the Pacific coast to the present town of Culiacán in central Sinaloa. This northern limit between high and low aboriginal cultures represents one of the most significant cultural boundaries in Middle America. It persisted through colonial times and though now blurred, it is still expressed as a transition zone between northern Mexico's predominately European-mestizo way of life and southern Mexico's prevailing Indian and mestizo cultures.

Prior to 1500 A.D., this cultural line had not been a stable one. On their arrival in Mexico, the Spaniards found the Chichimecs pressing southward into the area of high culture. Moreover, archeological evidence reveals that, probably during the ninth century A.D., Mesoamerican civilization extended northward into the steppe lands of Zacatecas and Durango along the eastern foothills of the Sierra Madre Occidental. By 1500 A.D., the Mesoamericans had abandoned their ceremonial sites and cultivated fields within this area, which was subsequently occupied by desert nomads and simple farmers.

The southern limit of Mesoamerica bordered on the simple farming culture of Central America. The boundary passed through western Honduras and thence southeastward, to include the Pacific coastal areas as far south as the Nicoya Peninsula of Costa Rica. This southern extension of high culture resulted from early (perhaps ninth century A.D.) migrations of Central Mexicans into the coastal lowlands of El Salvador (Pipil culture) and the lake shores in the Nicaraguan Depression (Nicarao and Mangue cultures).

Anthropologists have defined Mesoamerican culture on the basis of various attributes indicative of a civilization. Among these are advanced architectural knowledge, illustrated by the construction of large ceremonial centers with stonefaced or plastered, truncated, pyramidal temple bases; ball courts; and palaces. The ruins of these sites form part of the present cultural landscape throughout central and southern Mexico and northern Central America. Such centers imply the existence of a highly organized religion with an elaborate priesthood and ritual. A well-developed agriculture based on maize, beans, squash, and other plants; organized trade and markets; and knowledge of metallurgy are other significant characteristics of this culture level.

History of Mesoamerican Cultures

The Aztec, and other Indian civilizations that the Spaniards found in the Mesoamerican area, had been preceded by many highly evolved cultures entailing centuries of human development. Since remote times, man has favored the tropical highlands and lowlands of Mexico and northern Central America. One of the oldest human skeletal remains in the Americas, dated at approximately 7000 B.C., was found in the Valley of Mexico near the village of Tepexpan. Following a long period of slow cultural development, the immense ceremonial centers of Teotihuacán, Cholula, Xochicalco, and Monte Albán represented the culmination of native American art, architecture, and religion in the brilliant classical civilizations that developed between 200 B.C. and 900 A.D. in central Mexico (Figure 8.2). These cultures were followed by the Toltec period (900–1170 A.D.), when the great site of Tula was constructed north of the Valley of Mexico.

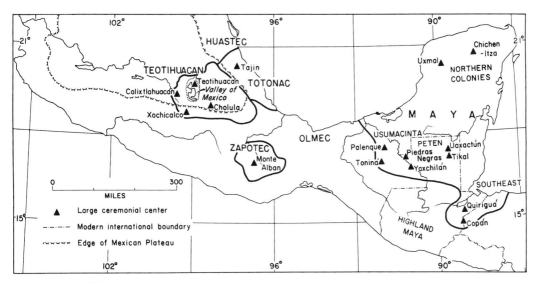

Figure 8.2
Mesoamerican Classical Cultures: 200 B.C. to 900 A.D.

From approximately 300 to 900 A.D., the renowned classical Mayan civilization flourished, paradoxically, in the tropical rain forests of northern Guatemala, Tabasco, and British Honduras. The ruins of hundreds of large Mayan ceremonial centers today lie hidden by dense forest within this region. After the sudden, and, as yet, unexplained abandonment of these centers in the last years of the ninth century, the Mayas continued their culture in the drier northern half of the Yucatan Peninsula. There the famous ceremonial centers and cities of Chichén-Itzá, Uxmal, Mayapán, and scores of others were occupied from around 850 to 1300 A.D. (Figure 8.3). Many of these sites had already been established during the classical period. In the north, practically every ceremonial center was located near a *cenote*, or sinkhole, which in many parts of the dry limestone peninsula is the sole water supply. When the Spaniards first penetrated Yucatan in the 1520's, the Mayan civilization, through a series of civil wars, had disintegrated into a group of 16 native states. Although most of the large ceremonial centers lay in ruins, an estimated population of 250,000 Mayans at that time were carrying on a thriving

agriculture and trading extensively with their Mexican and Central American neighbors. Approximately the same number of Maya-speaking Indians today inhabit the northern part of the peninsula.

To the south of Yucatan, in the highlands of Guatemala and Chiapas, lived close relatives of the Mayas. Although they lacked the pretentious ceremonial centers characteristic of the lowlands, they practiced advanced agriculture and were probably far more numerous than their lowland counterparts. Among the many linguistic groups related to Mayan speech were the Quiché and Mam of the volcanic highlands of Guatemala; the Kekchi or Pocomam of the limestone plateaus in the Alta Verapaz; and the Tzeltal and Tzotzil of the Chiapas highlands. The descendants of these groups who still speak the Indian languages number nearly 1.2 million souls.

By 1500 A.D., two powerful military states had evolved in the highlands of central Mexico. These were the Aztec domain in the east and the Tarascan state in the west (Figure 8.4). The Aztecs, who spoke Nahuatl, or Mexicano, had established the larger and more populous of the two states.

Figure 8.3

Central Part of the Great City and Ceremonial Center of Teotihuacán (200-600 A.D.), near Mexico City. This air view was taken before the recent reconstruction of smaller temples and plazas leading from the Pyramid of the Moon (lower left) past that of the Sun toward the Ciudadela (upper left). The entire archeological site covers about five square miles. (Compañía Mexicana Aerofoto)

According to legend, these people were migrants from the north who established themselves in the Valley of Mexico during the fourteenth century A.D. As all of the available land around the basin lakes was already occupied by sedentary farmers, the Aztecs were forced to settle on a small island near the western shore of Lake Texcoco. There, in 1325, they established a village and ceremonial center called Tenochtitlán, which later became a magnificent city and capital of the Aztec realm. The old central square (the Zócalo) and adjacent parts of the present metropolis of Mexico City lie over the ruins of Tenochtitlán, destroyed in 1521 by the Spanish conquerors. Through an alliance with the neighboring states of Texcoco and Tlacopán (Tacuba), the Aztecs gained political and military control over the Valley of

Mexico. In 1429, the rulers of the alliance began the spread of empire with well-disciplined armies. Within 75 years, the Aztecs had extended their political hegemony from the Pánuco River in the northeast to the modern frontier of Guatemala in the south. The Totonac and Huastec Indians of the eastern escarpment and Gulf coastal plain; the Otomí on the northern Chichimec frontier; the Mixtec and Zapotec of the southern highlands of Oaxaca—all became vassals of the Aztec. Only the Tlaxcalans east of the Valley of Mexico, the Tarascans to the west, and minor chiefdoms in the south were able to resist Aztec domination. When Cortes arrived on the Gulf coast of Mexico in 1519, the Aztecs were slowly pushing their realm southward into Central America.

The Aztec domain was not an empire in

the modern sense; rather, it was a tribute state. All conquered towns were subject to the payment of an annual or semiannual tribute in the form of grain, gold, textiles, cacao, or other economic products of the land. These were carried to the capital, Tenochtitlán, and there placed in the storehouses of the ruler or apportioned among the nobility. Although the Aztecs established military garrisons at strategic points within their realm to encourage the payment of tribute or to protect trade routes, they made no attempt to impose their language (Nahuatl), government, or religion upon the conquered.

Aztec conquests were motivated principally by the desire for economic gain through tributes. The hot lower escarpments bordering the plateau, the Balsas Basin, and the Pacific and Gulf coastal lowlands were particularly prized. These areas were the main sources of cotton and cotton cloth; of cacao, the beans of which were employed both as a

beverage for the nobility and as currency; and brilliant plumes of tropical birds and jaguar skins used in priestly and military garb. One of the last territories conquered before the landing of the Europeans was that of Soconusco (Xoconusco), along the Pacific coasts of Chiapas and Guatemala, famed for its extensive groves of cacao. For gold for ceremonial ornaments, the Aztecs depended mainly upon the stream placers of the upper Balsas Basin; however, professional merchants undertook long trading expeditions as far as the Caribbean coast of Honduras and Panama to obtain the precious metal, as well as other products. The Aztec state thus spread southward and eastward into the rich tropical lowlands; the dry northern plateau, inhabited by marauding nomads, was unattractive.

On the western part of the Mesa Central, the Tarascan Indians also established a native state, which, although not comparable in size and wealth to that of the Aztecs, was a

Figure 8.4
Ancient Political States: 1500 A.D.

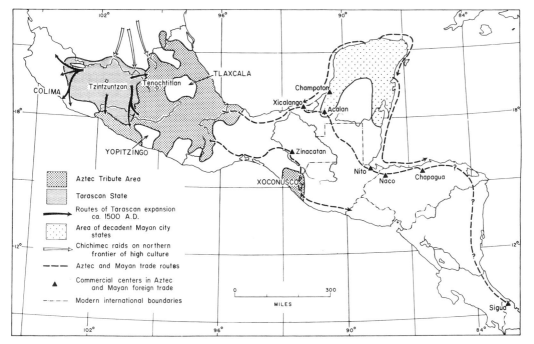

cohesive political unit. Pre-Conquest Tarascan territory corresponded roughly to the present Mexican state of Michoacán. The principal ceremonial center, Tzintzuntzan, like the Aztec capital, occupied a lake site— the eastern shore of beautiful Lake Pátzcuaro. Today the small remnant of Tarascan-speaking Indians live around the lake and the adjacent pine-covered volcanic highlands *(La Sierra)* in central Michoacán.

Like the Aztecs, the Tarascans expanded their frontiers outward from their highland core during the 75-year period preceding the Spanish conquest. To the east, approximately along the present Mexico-Michoacán state boundary, a stable military frontier, lined with forts of log and stone, was set up against the Aztecs. Tarascans made their military advances mainly to the south and west of the highland core. Southward they took over the hot, lower Balsas and Tepalcatepec basins, the sources not only of tropical products, but also of copper. Westward they conquered the highland areas occupied by culturally advanced Indians south of Lake Chapala, and penetrated into the rich lowlands of southeastern Colima near the Pacific shore. Another likely incentive for westward Tarascan expansion was the silver ore within the present state of Jalisco, south and west of Lake Chapala. The Tarascans and their subject peoples were the foremost metallurgists of Middle America; they were good goldsmiths and knew the art of refining silver and copper. Early Spanish assay records from Mexico are replete with references to plates and ingots of silver taken as booty from various Tarascan towns, and there have been many archeological finds of ceremonial copper axheads, bells or rattles, and other copper objects in Tarascan or pre-Tarascan graves.

The Tarascan state was probably more of a political empire than that of the Aztec. The Tarascans not only exacted tribute from conquered populations, but colonized their own people in frontier towns and, by this means, spread their language and culture by methods not used by the Aztecs.

Population and Settlement in Mesoamerica

During pre-Conquest times, the southern half of Mexico and northern Central America formed one of the most densely occupied areas of the New World. The actual numbers of people can never be known, but historians and anthropologists have made serious though highly discrepant estimates of the population of this area. Estimates for central Mexico alone vary from 3 to 25 million persons, and between 12 and 15 million might be considered a reasonable guess.[1] The inhabitants of the highlands of Chiapas and Guatemala may well have numbered over one million; of the Yucatan Peninsula, one-half million; and of southernmost Mesoamerica (El Salvador and western Nicaragua) perhaps another quarter million or more.

At the time of the Spanish Conquest, over 80 different languages belonging to more than 15 language families were spoken within Mesoamerica. The multiplicity of tongues and the fragmented areal distribution of many of the languages within this small densely settled area indicate that a great number of immigrations had occurred over a long period of time.

The dense aboriginal population was by no means evenly distributed. Undoubtedly, the highland basins of Central Mexico and Guatemala were the most favored spots for settlement, just as they are today. Nevertheless, the accounts of sixteenth-century Spanish chroniclers and the evidence of modern archeological surveys indicate that the tropical lowlands of Mesoamerica were far more densely occupied in the pre-Conquest period than at any time since.

The Valley of Mexico, 30 by 40 miles in size and the center of the Aztec realm, was the most densely inhabited spot of all Middle

[1] In recent studies on Indian population in Mexico, Woodrow Borah and S. F. Cook of the University of California, present convincing evidence that central and southern Mexico, alone, may have supported as many as 25 million people on the eve of the Spanish Conquest. See bibliography for references.

Figure 8.5

Dispersed " Ranchería " Type Settlement and Small Fields of Otomí Indians on the Western Slope of the Sierra de las Cruces Overlooking the Basin of Toluca, Central Mexico.

America. Recent studies indicate that between one and two million people probably lived in this basin during the early years of the sixteenth century. Since most of the basin floor was covered by five large lakes, settlement was heavily concentrated around the narrow lake plain and the adjacent slopes of the surrounding mountains. The most striking settlement feature of the Valley of Mexico was the large cities, almost unique in the aboriginal civilizations of the Americas. Estimates of the population of Tenochtitlán vary from 50,000 to 250,000. The cities of Texcoco and Chalco, on the eastern side of the basin, were less populous. Smaller compact towns and villages dotted the basin's periphery, probably much as they do today.

The most common type of aboriginal settlement throughout most of Mesoamerica and adjacent regions, however, was the small, semidispersed, rural village (*ranchería* or *caserío*), whose individual dwellings were scattered haphazardly over a large area and connected by footpaths (Figure 8.5). Such settlements are now typical of those in isolated mountain areas and are not uncommon in more accessible valleys and foothills. As we shall see (Chapter 9), the Spaniards eventually forced most of the Indians to live in the compact European-type rural village that is so common in Latin America today.

One of the most conspicuous features of human settlement of any area is the individual dwelling, the style of which may vary from place to place with the available construction materials and the cultural heritage of the inhabitants. In aboriginal Mesoamerica, there were a confusingly large number of house types, each characteristic of a given area. In many parts of rural Mexico and Central America, aboriginal types of house construction, little modified from those of pre-Conquest times, still prevail. Such houses are usually single-family units with but one room and a dirt floor—*chozas,* or huts.

In the highlands, houses were characteristically square or rectangular, and had walls of stone, adobe (sun-dried brick), or wattle and daub (mud-covered lattice of saplings) and roofs which were steep, highly pitched, and thatched with dried grass. In certain sections, however, such as the Valley of Mexico and adjacent areas, flat-roofed adobe houses, similar to those of the Pueblo Indians of the American Southwest, were common. In the tropical lowlands, there was a much greater variety of types. Floor plans were

Figure 8.7
A Typical Hearth in an Indian Kitchen, Valley of Mexico.

square, oval (apsidal), or round; walls were of loose wattle, sometimes covered with mud but more frequently left unplastered to permit the free entrance of air; roofs were of palm or grass thatch. The roofs of round houses were conical; the roofs of square or rectangular houses were either steep-hipped and four-sided or gabled and two-sided. Windows and chimneys were unknown (Figure 8.6).

Associated with the main dwelling were various outbuildings. These included the kitchen, a separate structure usually built in the rear of the main house. This was the place of the women, who prepared food and cooked over the hearth—three stones arranged in a triangle for placing clay pots over the fire (Figure 8.7). The granary, which had many forms, and often a semi-subterranean structure known as the *temazcal,* or sweatbath, completed the house assemblage (Figure 8.8).

Figure 8.6
Two Examples of Aboriginal House Types in Mexico. The round structure above is a Huastec house, northern Veracruz. Below, a Tzotzil house in Chiapas, Southern Mexico.

Food and Agriculture

The dense pre-Spanish population of many parts of Mesoamerica was supported by a well-developed agriculture. A large number of domesticated plants were cultivated, and by farming techniques sufficiently advanced to produce a food surplus. In Mexico and northern Central America, Indians cultivated nearly 90 different species of plants. Seventy of these were native to the area; the remainder, imports from South America (Table 8.1). We have already noted that the most important food crops of Mesoamerica were maize, beans, and squash, still the basis of life for millions of Mexicans and Central Americans. This plant trilogy affords a fairly well-balanced diet. Maize furnishes the starch or carbohydrate element and is also rich in oil and protein; beans provide the protein component, largely taking the place of meat; and squash offers a variety of essential vitamins in its oil-rich seeds, which are roasted, and in its flowers and flesh, cooked as vegetables. Indians cultivated all three crops together in the same plot, as they do today. Through centuries of cultivation, something of a symbiotic relationship has developed among these three plants: the tall maize stalks serve as supports for the climbing bean vines, which in turn enrich the soil with nitrogen; and the squash, being a creeper, covers the ground beneath the maize and beans with its wide leaves, protecting the loose soil from undue erosion by the heavy afternoon downpours characteristic of the summer rainy season.

The Indian farmers of Mexico and northern Central America made five important starch foods from maize, just as their pure- and mixed-blood descendants do today.

1. The *tortilla*—a thin, round pancake of maize dough baked on a large clay plate *(comal)*—was the most common food.

2. *Tamales* were made by filling maize dough with meat, beans, or chile peppers, wrapping in corn husks, and boiling.

3. *Pozole* was a thick soup of hominy (whole, cooked kernels of corn) with other vegetables, highly seasoned with chile pepper. In southern Mexico, *pozol* was a watery gruel of corn meal flavored with chocolate.

4. *Atole,* perhaps the most ancient of the maize foods, was a thick, starchy gruel of boiled maize dough, flavored with chile pepper, and drunk from a clay bowl.

5. *Pinole,* made by grinding toasted maize kernels to a coarse flour and often flavored with honey, could be carried on long trips without spoiling and a gruel could easily be prepared from it. Pinole was the road provision for travellers, merchants, and the military.

Figure 8.8

Aboriginal Granary Types of Central and Southern Mexico. All three types shown here are used for storing shelled maize. On the left is the *cuezcomatl,* a vasiform granary of clay and thatch.

Table 8.1

MAJOR DOMESTICATED PLANTS CULTIVATED IN MESOAMERICA:
1500 A.D.

Plants	Scientific Name	Place of Origin
Seed Plants		
Maize	Zea mais	S. Mexico; Guatemala (possibly)
Beans	Phaseolus (4 species)	S. Mexico; Guatemala
Amaranth	Amaranthus cruentus	S. Mexico; Guatemala
Sunflower	Helianthus annus	S.W. United States or western Mexico
Chía	Salvia hispanica	Mexico
	Chenopodium nuttalli	
Tuber Plants		
Sweet potato	Ipomea batatas	South America
Sweet manioc	Manihot esculentus	South America
Jicama	Pachyrrhizus erosus	Mexico
Vegetables		
Tomato	Lycopersicum esculetum	S. Mexico; Guatemala
Husk tomato	Physalis ixocarpo	S. Mexico; Guatemala
Chayote	Sechium edule	S. Mexico; Guatemala
Squash	Cucurbita (4 species)	S. Mexico; Guatemala
Fruits		
Cacao	Theobroma cacao	S. Mexico; Guatemala
Avocado	Persia americana	S. Mexico; Guatemala
Pineapple	Ananas comosus	South America
Papaya	Carica papaya	S. Mexico; Guatemala
Tuna cactus	Opuntia	Mexico
Cherimoya	Annona cherimolia	S. Mexico; Guatemala
Mamey	Calocarpum mammosum	S. Mexico; Guatemala
Chicosapote	Achras sapote	S. Mexico; Guatemala
Mexican cherry (capulín)	Prunus capuli	Mexico
Hog plum (jocote)	Spondias mombim	S. Mexico; Guatemala
Guayaba	Psidium guajava	S. Mexico; Guatemala
Vanilla	Vanilla planifolia	S. Mexico; Guatemala
Fiber Plants		
Agaves	Agave (5 species)	Mexico
Cotton	Gossypium hirsutum	South America
Condiments		
Chile pepper	Capsicum (various species)	S. Mexico; Guatemala
Dye Plants		
Achiote	Bixa orellana	South America
Indigo	Indigofera suffruticosa	Central America
Ceremonial Plants		
Tobacco	Nicotiana (2 species)	South America
Copal	Protium copal	S. Mexico; Guatemala
Ornamentals		
Dahlia	Dahlia coccinea	S. Mexico; Guatemala
Marigold	Tagetes patola	Mexico
Tigerflower	Tigridia pavonia	S. Mexico; Guatemala

Tortillas, tamales, and atole were prepared from a heavy dough *(masa,* or *nixtamal)* made by grinding boiled maize kernels on the metate, or stone quern (Figure 8.9).

In addition, fresh green corn was parched as roasting ears, and dried kernels of specific varieties were either parched or popped on the *comal.*

Besides maize, the Indians of southern Mexico domesticated another grain, amaranth, a weedlike plant that yields a colorful spike of tiny seeds rich in starch and oil. In pre-Conquest times in the Mesa Central of Mexico, this grain was almost as important a food as maize. Its significance as a ritual food presented to native gods in Aztec temples attests to its antiquity. Today only small plots of amaranth are cultivated in isolated localities in Mexico and Guatemala. Curiously, the small village of Tulyehualco, a few miles south of Mexico City, specializes in the cultivation of this tiny seed for making small cakes that are eaten only during Holy Week and Christmas.

Other food plants cultivated aboriginally included at least two starchy tubers—the sweet potato and the nonpoisonous variety of manioc (yuca), both of South American origin. Among the vegetables, besides several kinds of squash, were the tomato and the piquant condiment, chile pepper. High in vitamin C and an active stimulant of the salivary glands, chile enlivens the bland maize foods and adds to the human dietary requirements. Over 30 different species of fruits, most of them tropical plants of Mexican or Central American origin, were cultivated in Mesoamerica. Among the most important were pineapple; cacao, or the chocolate bean tree; avocado, or alligator pear; papaya, or melon tree; many kinds of soursops, such as the chirimoya; at least five different species of sapotes; the hog plum; and many others.

Most of the American food plants that we have mentioned have now spread to many parts of the world, particularly to the tropics and subtropics of Africa and Asia, where they have revolutionized native food habits

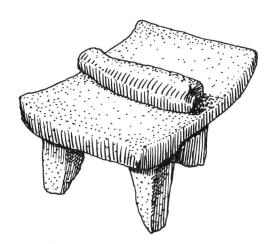

Figure 8.9

An Indian Metate, or Grinding Mill, Still Used in Most Parts of Mexico and Northern Central America.

and have increased the efficiency of human diet severalfold. Undoubtedly, their domesticated plants were the American Indians' greatest gift to the world.

The Mesoamerican Indians cultivated many plants for purposes other than food. Cotton and agave (the century plant) furnished fiber for weaving cloth. Several species of agave, called "maguey" in Mexico and Central America, were put to many uses; not only do these plants produce a stout fiber in their large, fleshy leaves, but they also yield a sweet sap, which, when fermented, becomes the famous pulque of central Mexico. Since this mild intoxicant contains ascorbic acid and many kinds of vitamins, it was, and still is, an essential part of the diet of the maize-beans-squash eaters in many parts of the highlands of Central Mexico. Tobacco for smoking and copal for incense were cultivated mainly for ceremonial use, while *achiote* was raised for its red dye, which was used to color food and to paint the body. Several flowers, such as the marigold and dahlia, were domesticated in central Mexico and used for decorating temples and graves.

In contrast to their wealth of agricultural plants, the Indians of Mexico and northern

Central America had only three truly domesticated animals. These were the dog, one variety of which was the short-legged, hairless, edible type; the turkey, domesticated probably in southern Mexico; and the small stingless bee, kept for its honey and wax. Two small scale insects were semidomesticated. One was the cochineal bug, which feeds on the nopal, or prickly-pear cactus, and was reared for a scarlet dye. Another scale bug, called *aje* or *ajín,* was raised on certain trees for its wax, which was used as a base for paint, lacquer, and for burnishing pottery.

The Mesoamerican Indian supplemented his predominantly vegetable diet by fishing, hunting, and gathering wild animal life within his environs. It was particularly around the environment of highland lakes within the volcanic areas of central Mexico and Central America that these activities became well developed among the farming population. Lakes usually afford a great variety of food for man, the edible animal life ranging from fish and aquatic birds to insects, including their eggs and larvae. At the time of the Spanish Conquest, the highland Indians of Mexico and Guatemala appear to have hunted little large game, which may have been a reflection of the depletion of wild life after centuries of human occupation. For these people, the lake fauna had become the main source of animal food.

Fishing was an important occupation around the lakes of the Mesa Central, especially in the Valley of Mexico and the lake-studded Tarascan country. Most of the lacustrine fish resource was composed of small, sardinelike varieties, formerly caught by the thousands in nets and dried for later consumption. So important was lake fishing among the Tarascans that the Aztec called their neighbors' area Michhuacan ("place of the fishers"), the origin of the present state name, Michoacán.

The hunting of aquatic fowl was probably as significant as lake fishing. Every year, myriads of migratory waterfowl (mainly ducks and coots) from North America nested in the reed-clogged lake shores in central Mexico. For fowling, the Indians employed long nets and forked spears thrown with the spear thrower, or the atlatl, one of man's most ancient weapons, still used today by a few Tarascans on Lake Pátzcuaro.

Probably the various insects, crustaceans, reptiles, and rodents hunted and gathered within the shallow, marshy sections of the lakes were equally important as food. Frogs, tadpoles, turtles, crayfish, and a larval salamander which the Aztecs called *axoxotl,* were netted and gigged in large numbers. Of especial esteem in the Valley of Mexico were the eggs of various waterbugs which the Indians gathered from reeds growing along the lake shores. These eggs formed the famous ahuauhtle ("Aztec caviar"). Until a few years ago, villagers in the southern part of the valley gathered and ate ahuauhtle. Moreover, the larvae of a salt fly as well as green algae were skimmed from the lake surface for food. Away from the lakes, Indians habitually gathered and ate as delicacies toasted grasshoppers; various ants and their larvae; the maguey grub, which feeds on the agave plant; and other insects. Although such animals are not considered proper food in Western society, they are rich in protein, niacin, riboflavin, and several minerals essential to the human diet. These seemingly weird foods helped to supply dietary deficiencies that might have occurred among a population dependent mainly on maize, beans, and squash, and, in times of drought (not infrequent on the central plateau), the lake resources served as famine food. During the past 200 years, the various activities that once centered around the lakes in central Mexico have greatly declined, owing to natural desiccation and artificial draining of the water bodies.

Systems of Tillage

To cultivate their many domesticated plants, the Indians of Mesoamerica developed various methods of farming consonant with natural conditions and their technical knowledge. At least two general systems of tillage prevailed in Mexico and Central America before the arrival of Europeans: (1) migratory slash-burn cultivation; and (2) advanced farming, which involved (a) systematic fallowing of permanent fields and, occasionally, (b) terracing and/or irrigation. Despite the availability of numerous European agricultural practices and tools during the past 450 years, Indian farming techniques persist in various parts of Mexico and Central America.

Several features were common to the two systems of cultivation. For instance, since farming was mainly for subsistence, fields were small, probably no larger than one-half to three acres in size. Moreover, the Indian farmer practiced horticulture, rather than the single-crop field agriculture characteristic of Western culture and now common in most of Latin America. The Indian gave special care to individual plants, cultivating a great variety within his small plot. Not only were maize, beans, and squash raised together; but a few tomato, chile, or amaranth plants, and perhaps one or two fruit trees, were also scattered about, until his holding took on an unordered, unkempt appearance. These practices are retained today in subsistence agriculture in many parts of Mexico and Central America, particularly on hillside plots, in kitchen gardens around the house, and even in permanent, plowed fields. Again, the same farming implements were employed in the two systems of cultivation. These were: (1) the simple planting stick, or dibble, with a sharpened, fire-hardened point; and (2) in some sections of central Mexico, the *coa*, a kind of spade with a triangular-shaped blade parallel with the handle (Figure 8.10). In the Tarascan area, *coas* with copper blades were used, but elsewhere they probably were wooden. Although today these aboriginal tools have been largely displaced by the European hoe and plow, they are still employed in some areas of Mexico. For instance, Indian farmers

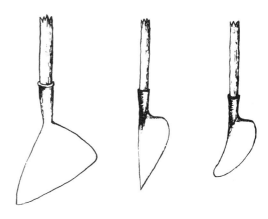

Figure 8.10
Types of Metal Coa Blades Used in Central Mexico.

living in the Xochimilco area, only 20 miles from the center of Mexico City, still use the triangular-bladed *coa* to cultivate flowers and vegetables.

Migratory Slash-Burn Cultivation. Probably man's most ancient tillage system, this was the simplest and most widespread type of farming in all the Americas. Fundamentally, it is a woodland type of agriculture. It was practiced on steep, wooded slopes in the highlands, and on both slopes and level land within the lowland tropical forests. Today this relatively primitive method of cultivation still prevails in subsistence farming throughout the tropical lowlands of Mexico and Central America; and its persistence in the West Indies has been mentioned frequently in previous chapters of this book. In the highlands, however, it is now practiced only on the higher or more isolated mountain slopes where forest still remains.

The system involves the clearing of small plots within the forest during the dry season and the burning of the dried branches and logs. The wood ash, rich in various minerals such as potassium and phosphorous, serves as a good fertilizer for crops. At the start of the rains, seeds and tubers are planted in holes punched into the ash-covered soil with the dibble. Yields are good the first year, but after two or three years of cultivation the soil is usually exhausted and weeds become such a problem that the plot is abandoned for perhaps 8 to 20 years, to permit the rejuvenation of the soil and the reestablishment of second-growth forest. After that time, when the decaying leaves and roots of the forest plants and microorganisms have renewed soil fertility, the same plot may be recleared and the cycle repeated. Meanwhile, in the surrounding forest, the farmer has cleared new plots which go through the same cycle of cropping and abandonment. Thus the farmer is continually shifting his small cultivated fields. In central Mexico today, subsistence farmers call such slash-burn plots by the Nahuatl terms *tlacolol* or *coamil;* the Spanish terms *roza* and *desmonte* are sometimes used[2] (Figure 8.11).

It is readily apparent that, owing to the

---

[2] Slash-burn cultivation is often mistermed "milpa" agriculture. In Mexico and Central America, the word "milpa" is applied to any cultivated field(but principally one in which maize is grown), regardless of the system of agriculture used.

Figure 8.11

A Slash-Burn Plot in the Coastal Lowlands of Veracruz State Mexico, Showing Charred Logs and Patches of Ash After Burning. Maize and bean seeds will be dibbled into the ash and thin soil after the first rains.

frequent shifting of cultivated plots, a large forested area is needed for the continued operation of the slash-burn system. Being an extensive type of cultivation, therefore, it can normally support only a low density of population. Yet with only this simple farming technique at their disposal, the lowland Mayas were able to produce sufficient food to support a highly advanced culture.

Another attribute of present-day slash-burn cultivation in Middle America is an associated settlement pattern of either small hamlets (rancherías) or completely dispersed dwellings scattered on the forested mountain slopes. Archeological findings and early Spanish accounts indicate that a similar settlement pattern existed in pre-Conquest times, in the Mayan area of Yucatan and in the Totonac and Huastec regions along the Gulf coastal plain and adjacent eastern escarpment of Mexico. Then, however, settlements were usually scattered around the vicinity of ceremonial centers.

One of the most serious effects of long, continued use of the slash-burn system in a given area has been the alteration and, often, the eventual destruction of the forest cover. This has been especially true when the need for food causes the period of abandonment of the plots to be unduly shortened, preventing the complete restoration of the forest and with it, the renewal of soil productivity. One of the hypotheses presented to explain the collapse of the classical Mayan culture in southern Yucatan and northern Guatemala involves possible overcropping by the slash-burn system, which led to forest destruction, soil exhaustion and even erosion, and encroachment of a heavy grass cover. Probably the destruction of much of the oak and pine forest that once covered portions of the Mexican Mesa Central has been partly due to the overuse of slash-burn cultivation in pre-Conquest and colonial times.

Advanced Farming: Fallow Land. Although somewhat akin to slash-burn cultivation, the fallowing of permanent fields in Mesoamerica was a more advanced agricultural technique and was more productive of foodstuffs. This method involved the initial clearing and burning of the vegetation cover, but two or three years of successive cropping was followed by an equal period of letting the land lie fallow. The farmer thus confined his attention to a few more or less permanent fields within a small radius, a system conducive to permanent village settlement and fairly dense population. Indians fallowed land generally in the cool highlands, particularly around the fertile volcanic basins on the Mesa Central of Mexico and in southwestern Guatemala and Chiapas, where the population was extremely dense. They kept mainly to the lower, gentle slopes surrounding the basins; it is doubtful that they would have been able to till the flattish basin floors, characterized by heavy soils and thick grass cover, with only the dibble and *coa*. The fertile lacustrine soils of most of the highland basins, now so important in the economy of Mexico and Guatemala, were probably little farmed until the Spaniards introduced the plow in the sixteenth century. Today the ancient fallow system is occasionally seen on slopes in the eastern part of the Mesa Central and in Oaxaca, Chiapas, and Guatemala.

Advanced Farming: Irrigation and Terracing. The most advanced and productive system of cultivation practiced in pre-Conquest Mesoamerica involved irrigation, sometimes accompanied by terracing on hill slopes. As far as we know, Mesoamerican irrigation was extremely spotty, but the technique was, of course, utilized in areas subject to a long dry season or to frequent drought. Early sixteenth-century Spaniards reported the use of irrigation at various points along the southern escarpment of the Mesa Central and the upper Balsas Basin, where river water was diverted onto fields through small canals. Moreover, most of the native cacao groves along the Pacific slope from Colima in Mexico to Nicaragua were cultivated by canal irrigation. But the Valley of Mexico and its

environs was the most significant center of irrigation and hydraulic engineering in Mesoamerica. The Aztecs and their neighbors commonly employed canal irrigation on the western and eastern sides of the Valley of Mexico, as well as in the basin of Puebla to the east. Aqueducts were also constructed to bring potable water from the springs of Chapultepec on the western side of the Valley of Mexico to the center of Tenochtitlán.

The most fascinating irrigation that the Indians developed in the Valley of Mexico was the *chinampa* system. This ingenious system is one of the most sophisticated and productive kinds of farming practiced by the American Indian. Chinampas were artificial plots constructed along the shallow margins of fresh-water lakes. They were made of long strips of aquatic vegetation cut from thick masses of flotant that had accumulated on the lake surface. These strips, sinking at first to the shallow lake bottom, were placed one above the other until the top one barely extended above the water surface. Then layers of rich mud scooped from the lake bottom were spread over the chinampa to form a planting surface. Thus, long artificial fields, 8 to 12 feet wide, more than 100 feet long, and separated one from another by narrow canals, resulted in the chinampa field pattern familiar today to most tourists who visit Xochimilco south of Mexico City. To anchor the plots securely, native willows were planted along the edges. Such trees give the present chinampa area its pleasant sylvan appearance (Figure 8.12).

From three to four harvests of maize, beans, chile, flowers, and other plants could be taken annually from one plot, for the crops were started in seed beds and transplanted to the chinampa surface. Continuous natural irrigation was effected by seepage from the canals through porous chinampa material, and young plants were protected from winter frosts with mats of grass. Fertilizer in the form of lake mud, rotted vegetable matter, and probably even human excrement was applied before each planting.

Figure 8.12

A Chinampa Plot Bordered by Willows and Canals Near Xochimilco, Valley of Mexico. The chinampa surface has been recently planted.

There is little doubt that the dense rural population and the large cities in the Valley of Mexico in pre-Conquest times were based mainly on the tremendous amount of food produced on these intensively cultivated plots. When Cortes and his party arrived in the Valley of Mexico in 1519, the chinampa area covered the shallow margins of the southern fresh-water lakes of Chalco and Xochimilco and extended northward along the western edge of Lake Texcoco beyond Tenochtitlán to Azcapotzalco (Figure 8.13). To prevent periodic incursion of the saline water of Lake Texcoco into the chinampa area and to regulate the lake levels, an elaborate system of dikes was constructed. Each of the causeways that connected the Aztec capital with the mainland served both as a road and a dike. Located east of the capital, the largest dike was that of Netzahual-coyotl, which effectively protected Tenochtitlán and the western margin of Lake Texcoco from salt water. Curiously, there is no evidence that the chinampa system was known outside the Valley of Mexico in pre-Conquest times, though other shallow fresh-water lakes abounded on the Mesa Central. The closest known parallel to the Mexican chinampas are the floating gardens of Kashmir, in northwestern India.

Chinampa agriculture still continues to be practiced in the Valley of Mexico, and as late as the middle of the last century new chinampas were being constructed around Xochimilco. But since the final desiccation of the lakes in 1900, the chinampa area has dwindled to a narrow strip along the south shore of former lakes Xochimilco and Chalco. Water for the canals is obtained from springs, and vegetables and flowers are still grown in the traditional manner for the Mexico City market.

Still another advanced agricultural technique occasionally practiced by the Meso-american farmers was directed toward soil conservation on permanently cultivated slopes. Stone retention walls, forming crude terraces (most of which are now abandoned), are found from the Valley of Mexico southward to British Honduras. A more common soil-retention device was to plant hedges of agave along the contour to hold the soil and reduce the gradient of the slope. This technique, called *bancal* or *pantli*, is still widely practiced in central Mexico (Figure 8.14).

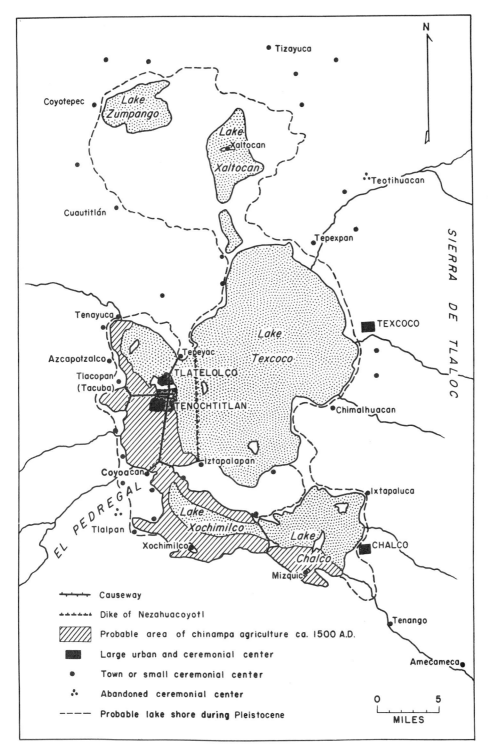

Figure 8.13
Central Portion of the Valley of Mexico at the Time of the Spanish Conquest.

Figure 8.14

The *Bancal,* or *Pantli,* a Semi-Terrace Technique Used Today on Both Steep and Gentle Slopes Near Apam, Central Mexico. Rows of maguey (agave) serve as low retention walls to prevent excessive erosion and to preserve moisture. (Compañía Mexicana Aerofoto)

Land Systems

Among most of the high cultures of Mesoamerica, agriculture was of such fundamental importance that rules of land tenure were carefully formulated. Especially in Mexico, some of these ancient Indian rules have persisted or have been reestablished despite 450 years of Spanish domination. Throughout most of Mesoamerica, the landholding village was at once the basic unit of settlement and the principal form of land tenure. Surrounding arable and wooded land belonged to the village. The village council assigned tillable land to each native family, and the family members held it as long as the land was farmed. Thus, individuals held

only use rights to the land; private individual ownership of land did not exist. This tradition of village land is retained in practically all Indian areas of Mexico and Guatemala today, and Mexico's recent agrarian program has incorporated many elements of the ancient landholding village into its program for redistributing the property of former large estates to the landless peasants.

The concept of the landholding village was best formulated in the Aztec area of the Mesa Central of Mexico, where much of the cultivated land was in permanent fields. There each village was organized into large kinship groups (*capullis*). Each *capulli* was given a tract of land in which tillable plots were assigned to each family of the group.

By the time of the Spanish Conquest, a second type of land tenure, somewhat like the European feudal estate, had been established among the Aztecs. Through various means, Aztec nobles and priests had been able to acquire large tracts of land from village holdings, and these estates were worked by serfs who were attached to the land. After the Conquest, these estates formed the first Spanish haciendas, the system of land holding that remained typical of Mexico's land tenure until the Agrarian Revolution of the present century.

Crafts, Trade, and Transport

Though the Mesoamericans were basically farmers, their society was sufficiently advanced to have developed some degree of craft specialization and an organized system of trade and transport. The ordinary farmers, like most pretechnical rural folk, were also craftsmen who fashioned household utensils during their spare time. But in the large urban centers, there were guilds of craft specialists—stonecutters, featherworkers, and goldsmiths—who made products for the nobility and the priesthood and sold their surplus wares in markets. Moreover, certain villages, favored by nearby supplies of raw materials, specialized in pottery, basketry, or weaving, much as many rural towns do today in Mexico and Central America. Thus, in certain strategically located villages, the periodic market (*tianguis*) where handicrafts and surplus agricultural products could be exchanged, became an integral part of Mesoamerican economic life. The largest markets were often held in or near large ceremonial centers. Within the Aztec realm, the great market of Tlatelolco, adjacent to Tenochtitlán, was one of the big centers of Mesoamerican commerce. In many respects, the present picturesque Indian village markets of Mexico and Guatemala are probably quite similar to those of pre-Hispanic times (Figure 8.15).

Both the Aztecs and the Mayas were great traders, engaging actively in foreign commerce. On their arrival in Yucatan, the Spaniards found the Mayas exporting large quantities of salt (from coastal lagoons), as well as cotton cloth, in large seagoing canoes to the Gulf Coast of Mexico and the Caribbean shore of Honduras. In those areas, the Mayas traded their products for cacao, which was cultivated in abundance in the alluvial river valleys and piedmont slopes of Tabasco and Honduras.

Among the Aztecs, foreign commerce was in the hands of a group of travelling merchants, called the *Pochteca*, an official trading

Figure 8.15

Native Market Scene, Village Square of Santiago Atitlán, Guatemalan Highlands. Women, wearing the village costume, squat before their wares as did their ancestors in pre-Conquest times.

Figure 8.16
Indians in Guatemala Hauling Pottery Attached to a Box-Like Carrying Frame, Called
the *Huacal*, or *Cacaxtli*. The load is steadied on the back by means of the tump line
placed over the forehead. (*Delta Air Lines*)

guild with special social status. With long trains of human carriers and protected from attack by armed guards, the *Pochteca* traveled southward to Tehuantepec, and into Central America as far as Nicaragua and Costa Rica, where they traded fine Mexican cloth, obsidian, and slaves for gold dust, jade, cacao, feathers, and jaguar skins. These merchants also served as spies in hostile territory, gaining information for Aztec rulers on rich areas ripe for conquest. Both their extensive trading activity and their tribute system helped to spread the Aztecs' Nahuatl speech. Nahuatl became the *lingua franca* of much of Mesoamerica, and it remained a trade language long after the Spanish Conquest.

Lacking large domesticated animals and utilitarian knowledge of the wheel, the Indian himself served as beast of burden on land. Professional carriers (*tamemes*), both freedmen and slaves, hauled on their backs loads weighing up to 200 pounds and supported with the tump line, or forehead strap. In isolated sections of Mexico and Central America today, it is not uncommon to see both Indians and mestizos using this ancient means of transport (Figure 8.16). For water transport, the Indians used dugout canoes of various designs and, at the time of the Spanish Conquest, thousands of canoes plied the lakes of the Valley of Mexico. Canoes remained the principal means of transport for the peasant farmers of the valley until the lakes were finally drained at the beginning of this century.

Since land travel was exclusively by foot, only paths served as roads. With the exception of the causeways of the Aztec capital, all well-made ancient roads that have been discovered archeologically in Mesoamerica were for ceremonial purposes. The Aztecs and their predecessors established several main pathways leading from the Valley of Mexico into the tropical lowlands. Some colonial and modern roads followed these same paths. But as Indians on foot usually employed the most direct routes, their trails were often too steep and arduous for the wheeled traffic later introduced by Europeans.

Eastward from the Valley of Mexico, the trail to the Totonac country in the coastal lowlands of Veracruz passed between the volcanoes of Ixtaccihuatl and Popocatepetl to Cholula; thence it continued through the basins of Puebla and Huamantla and, through a series of easy steplike valleys, descended the eastern escarpment probably near the present Mexico City-Veracruz highway via Jalapa. Another trail went northeastward into the Huasteca of northern Veracruz, following approximately the route of the present highway by way of Jacala and Tamazunchale. The most important trails, however, led southeastward to the Maya country and into Central America, which, by the beginning of the sixteenth century, had become the Aztecs' biggest market and source of imports. One of the southern roads passed through the Mixtec and Zapotec areas of Oaxaca, approximating the present Pan-American Highway; from Oaxaca the trail proceeded southeastward to Tehuantepec, the Soconusco cacao area, and Guatemala. An even more ancient and significant footpath ran south and east, along the coastal lowlands of Veracruz and Tabasco to the great Aztec-Mayan trading center of Xicalango on the Laguna de Términos; thence it followed rivers and paths through the rain forest of northern Guatemala to the Mayan trading posts of Nito and Naco near the Caribbean coast of Guatemala and Honduras. Probably this same trail continued along the Caribbean coast as far as the present Costa Rica-Panama frontier (Figure 8.4). Soon after the Spanish Conquest, trade areas and modes of transport changed, and this famous road was forgotten.

On the western side of the Mesa Central of Mexico, a trail which has been used possibly for thousands of years descended the escarpment following a series of step-basins via present Tepic, approximating the modern railroad and highway from Guadalajara to the coast. The northwestern extension of high Mesoamerican culture into the Pacific coastal plain probably followed this route.

PRIMITIVE FARMERS OF NORTHWESTERN MEXICO

On the northwestern periphery of Mesoamerica lived the primitive farmers of the Sierra Madre Occidental and the coastal plain of northwest Mexico. Since their farming was based on the maize-beans-squash complex, this area might be considered as a northern extension of simple agriculture from the cultural core, Mesoamerica. Within the northwestern area, however, there were small islands of advanced farming, such as the irrigated terraces of the Ópata in mountainous central Sonora and the irrigated fields of the Pima in southern Arizona and the Sonoran lowlands. Both Ópata and Pima may have derived their advanced farming knowledge from the Indian cultures of southwestern United States, particularly from the ancient Hohokam culture of southern Arizona. Most of northwestern Mexico, however, was inhabited by simple farmers practicing migratory slash-burn cultivation on hill slopes and along stream bottoms. Within the Sierra Madre Occidental, the Tarahumar and the Tepehuán were the largest groups of simple farmers, while on the coast, various tribes, such as the Cahita and Yaqui, planted along the river flood plains, utilizing the moist alluvial soils when the annual floods receded. Farther north, in the desert of western Sonora, the Papago Indians were known as cultivators of the drought-resistant tepary bean (still the commonest bean in the more Indian parts of Sonora), which they cultivated with maize and squash along intermittent water courses by flood irrigation. Most of the coastal farmers lived in small, permanent villages and supplemented their agricultural diet with seafood. The mountain people were more nomadic, living in scattered seasonal dwellings and relying on hunting and fishing for sustenance as much as on farming. Although greatly reduced in numbers, some Indian groups persist in the Mexican northwest. The Tarahumar, isolated in the rugged Sierra Madre in southwestern Chihuahua, are the most numerous; a few coastal people, mainly the Cahita, still cultivate their lands along the rivers as did their forefathers.

PRIMITIVE FARMERS
OF SOUTHERN CENTRAL AMERICA

The Central American Indians who lived south and east of Mesoamerica had a much lower culture status than the Mayas or Aztecs and their neighbors. Most of them were primitive forest farmers of South American origin, speaking languages related to Chibchan speech of Colombia. People speaking Cuna and Guaymí inhabited Panama. A large number of Chibchan languages were spoken in Costa Rica, but the Huetar of the central volcanic highlands were probably the most numerous group; in eastern Nicaragua, the Miskito and the Sumu lived on the coastal savannas and in the interior rain forest. Non-Chibchan groups, such as the Lenca, Jicaque, and Paya, occupied the rugged forested highlands of central Honduras along the contact zone with high Mesoamerican culture.

Like some of their more highly cultured neighbors to the north, the Central American Indians practiced only simple slash-burn farming. Hunting and fishing, however, was as important to their economy as agriculture. Moreover, the food crops of the Central Americans were much different from those of the Mesoamericans. Various tuber plants, all of South American origin, were raised from cuttings or part of the root, rather than from seeds. The tubers included sweet manioc, arrowroot, sweet potato, and the American

yam. Another significant food was the boiled and roasted fruits from the cultivated peach palm, called *pejibaye*, also a native of South America. Maize, beans, and squash, except in a few areas, were secondary as food crops. Maize was grown principally for preparing *chicha*, a South American beer made by fermenting grains of corn. The tortilla was unknown. After the Spanish Conquest, maize became a more important food crop in southern Central America, but still today, in most rural sections of eastern Nicaragua, Costa Rica, and Panama, the tubers predominate in the ordinary dishes. In addition to their food crops, the Central Americans, like the Mesoamericans, raised cotton (but not agave) for fiber, tobacco for ceremonials, and various dye plants. Their only animal domesticates were the dog, the stingless bee, and the small wax-producing scale insect.

Besides crops and food habits, other South American culture elements prevailed among the Indians of southern Central America. Among these were large, round communal houses of wattle and thatch, in which several families lived; the hammock for resting and sleeping; the blowgun as well as the bow and arrow for hunting and fishing; and weaving techniques similar to those used in the central Andes.

Although most of southern Central America was inhabited by forest farmers of low culture, there were at least two densely settled areas in which there existed a more advanced way of life. These were: (1) the area of Coclé culture and Cuna speech in south central Panama, including the Azuero Peninsula and the savanna lands along the Pacific coast eastward to the present Canal Zone; and (2) the area of Huetar culture, which centered on the volcanic highlands of Costa Rica and extended southward along the flanks of the Talamanca Range. Both areas contained various chiefdoms organized into social classes of nobles, commoners, and slaves, which lived in large villages around small religious centers. One of the most outstanding cultural achievements in both areas was skilled metallurgy in gold, a skill derived from northwestern South America, where the Quimbaya Indians of Colombia produced some of the best gold work known in indigenous America. Huetar and Coclé goldsmiths fashioned ear and nose pendants, breastplates, pins, figurines, bracelets, necklaces, and even fishhooks by casting, hammering, and soldering nearly pure gold but more often a gold-copper alloy (*guanín* or *tumbaga*). Since practically all the golden objects were ceremonial, they were usually placed in graves of chiefs and others of high social rank. Thus, after the Conquest, grave robbing became one of the main activities of the Spaniards, particularly in Panama and Costa Rica, as well as in Colombia. Other advanced skills of the Coclé and Huetar people included the manufacture of finely decorated polychrome pottery, well-woven cloth and, among the Huetar, elaborate ceremonial stonework. Moreover, the Coclé people developed a fairly extensive trade, involving the export of salt, hammocks and other cotton goods, gold dust and gold objects, and slaves in large sail-rigged canoes to various points along the Pacific cost of Central America and possibly even to Mexico.

Today nothing is left of these cultures. The Huetar are completely gone, and only a handful of Indian descendants of various Talamanca groups now live in isolated sections of the Costa Rican highlands. The present Indians of Cuna speech who now inhabit the San Blas coast of northeastern Panama are far removed in space and culture from their ancestors.

SELECTED REFERENCES

Armillas, P., "Land Use in Pre-Columbian America," *UNESCO Arid Zone Research,* No. 17 (1961), pp. 255–76.

Borah, W., and S. F. Cook, *The Aboriginal Population of Central Mexico on the Eve of the Spanish Conquest,* Ibero-Americana, No. 45. Berkeley, Calif.: University of California Press, 1963.

Barlow, R. H., *The Extent of the Empire of the Culhua Mexica,* Ibero-Americana, No. 28. Berkeley, Calif.: University of California Press, 1949.

Chapman, A., "Port of Trade Enclaves in Aztec and Maya Civilizations," in K. Polanyi, *et al.,* eds., *Trade and Market in the Early Empires.* New York: Free Press of Glencoe, Inc., 1957, pp. 114–53.

Coe, M. D., "The Chinampas of Mexico," *Scientific American,* CCXI, No. 1 (1964), 90–98.

Cook, S. F., "The Incidence and Significance of Disease among the Aztecs and Related Tribes," *Hispanic American Historical Review,* XXVI, No. 3 (1946), 320–35.

Deevy, E. S., Jr., "Limnologic Studies in Middle America with a Chapter on Aztec Limnology,"

Transactions of the Connecticut Academy of Arts and Sciences, XXXIX (1957), 213–328.

Dressler, R. L., "The Pre-Columbian Cultivated Plants of Mexico," *Botanical Museum Leaflets,* Harvard University, XVI, No. 6 (1953), 115–72.

MacNeish, R. S., "The Origins of New World Civilization," *Scientific American,* CCXI, No. 5 (1964), 29–37.

Morley, S. G., and G. W. Brainerd, *The Ancient Maya* (3rd ed.). Stanford, Calif.: Stanford University Press, 1956.

Sauer, C. O., *Agricultural Origins and Dispersals,* Bowman Memorial Lectures, No. 2. New York: American Geographical Society, 1952.

———, "The Personality of Mexico," *Geographical Review,* XXXI, No. 3 (1941), 353–64.

Stanislawski, D., "Tarascan Political Geography," *American Anthropologist,* XLIX, No. 1 (1947), 46–55.

Vaillant, G. C., *Aztecs of Mexico* (rev. ed.). Garden City, N.Y.: Doubleday & Company, Inc., 1962.

Wolf, E. R., *Sons of the Shaking Earth.* Chicago: University of Chicago Press, 1959.

9

Mexico and Central America: Conquest and Settlement

In many respects, the sixteenth century is the most significant period in the development of the cultural landscape in Mexico and Central America. Through their conquest and occupation of the land during that century, the Spaniards established a cultural pattern that prevailed during most of the colonial period. This pattern, which still exists in modified form over much of the area, stamped its impress on the land and in many places altered the relationships of the native inhabitants to their environment.

Fundamentally, the colonial cultural pattern and its manifestations in the landscape evolved from a fusion of native Indian and medieval Iberian peoples and customs. The degree of cultural and racial mixing, however, varied from place to place. In remote sections and in areas where the aborigines were especially resistant to change, as in the southwestern highlands of Guatemala, the Indian way of life prevailed and is even now little modified by Spanish culture. Where the Indians were of low cultural status and few in numbers, as in northern Mexico, or where they were quickly destroyed, as in Costa Rica, Hispanic culture took over almost wholly. The most complete mixing of Old and New World cultures seems to have occurred in central Mexico, particularly in the Mesa Central. In this tropical highland, the Spaniards found choice lands favorable for European settlement, but since the area was already occupied by a large Indian population with a civilization based on a well-developed agricultural economy, the Spaniards were forced to incorporate the Indian

and his culture into colonial society. Thus in central Mexico, as well as in other areas of Mesoamerica, there resulted a partial fusion of the two races and of the two sets of cultural patterns. The present kaleidoscopic cultural landscape of Mexico and Central America derives in large part from the uneven distribution of the Hispano-Indian cultural amalgam that developed in the sixteenth century.

In this and the next chapter, we shall trace the development of the cultural landscape in Mexico and Central America during colonial times—a period of some 300 years (1519–1821). Of prime significance in this development are: (1) the story of the spread of Spanish conquest and occupation of the land; (2) the impact of conquest on the physical aspects of the aboriginal population; and (3) the processes by which Spanish culture combined with the Indian to mold the landscape to its colonial form.

SPANISH CONQUEST AND SPREAD OF SETTLEMENT

As elsewhere within the Iberic sphere of the New World, the Spaniards' original motive for the discovery and settlement of Mexico and Central America was economic. Foremost in the minds of those who made up the conquering expeditions was the acquisition of quick wealth by exploiting the human and natural resources of the land. To the Spaniard, gold and silver, the standards of exchange in mercantilist Europe of the sixteenth century, were most desirable, but any other exploitable resources were acceptable, provided they could be sold for a huge profit. Thus, the Spaniards were first attracted to areas rich in mineral wealth and also to those with a dense native population which could supply large forces of labor and quantities of tribute. It was usually after the initial conquests had been effected that a more humanitarian motive of Spanish colonization—the spread of the Christian faith— came into play.

After the tragic decimation of the native population in the Greater Antilles and the consequent decline of gold production in Hispaniola, the Spaniards looked toward the Middle and South American mainlands to recoup their fortunes. By the second decade of the sixteenth century, various exploratory expeditions from the Antilles had touched many points along the eastern shores of

Mexico and Central America. From these reconnaissance voyages, the Spaniards obtained sufficient information to realize that the mainland probably contained great wealth.

The first successful points of Spanish conquest and occupation on the mainland occurred in two widely separated areas: (1) the isthmus of Panama; and (2) the highlands of central Mexico (Figure 9.1). Once these two areas were firmly occupied, they became dispersal centers for the conquest and settlement of the remainder of the Middle American mainland. The Spaniards were not slow to realize that both Panama and central Mexico were strategic spots. Panama, because of its isthmian character, was to serve as the transit zone between the Atlantic and Pacific oceans, a function it has performed ever since. Central Mexico, on the other hand, was the cultural focus of high

Figure 9.1
Spanish Conquest and Settlement of Mexico and Central America: Early Sixteenth Century.

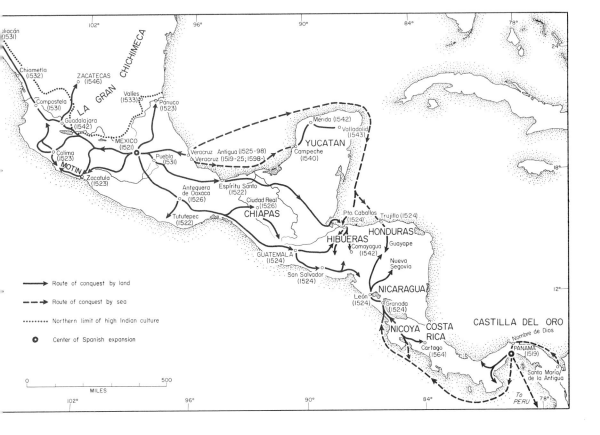

Mesoamerican Indian civilizations, the center of the Aztec and Tarascan tribute states—a land of dense population with a productive agriculture and great mineral wealth.

The Conquest of Panama

Panama was the first of the two dispersal centers to be occupied. Drawn by Balboa's discovery of the Pacific Ocean in 1513 and by the gold-rich Coclé Indian cultures within the southern coastal plain of the isthmus, Spanish officials established the town of Panama as the capital of Castilla del Oro (the isthmus area) in 1519. The Coclé area of south central Panama was quickly overrun; the golden artifacts looted from houses and graves were melted down into ingots; and the Indian population was either enslaved or dispersed into the surrounding hills. During the first half of the sixteenth century, a few small Spanish towns, such as Natá, were founded in the Coclé savannas. Small-scale stock raising was introduced, and various attempts were made to exploit the gold placers of Veraguas on the heavily forested Caribbean slopes of western Panama. But throughout the colonial period, the main function of the isthmian area remained that of a transit zone between the two oceans. Between Nombre de Dios and Puerto Bello, the Caribbean termini, and Panama City, on the Pacific side, mule trains and fleets of canoes hauled merchandise that came from Peru and Spain.

By 1524, expeditions exploring northwestward from the isthmus had brought most of the southern part of Central America into the jurisdiction of Panama. The most important *entrada* was that of Hernández de Córdoba, who conquered the culturally advanced Chorotega and Nicarao peoples of the densely settled Pacific lowlands of Nicaragua. In 1524, he founded the town of Granada on the northwestern shore of Lake Nicaragua and that of León on the northern edge of Lake Managua. Further exploration brought the Spaniards from the Nicara-

guan plain into the central highlands of Honduras, where they met the vanguard of exploring parties from Mexico. Thus a frontier of expansion between the Panamanian and Mexican expeditions was established approximately along the present Honduras-Nicaraguan boundary.

Within the densely settled Nicaraguan Pacific lowlands, the Spaniards engaged chiefly in taking Indian slaves during the first years of occupation. Before Indian slavery was abolished in 1542, thousands of these docile Nicaraguans were branded and taken in chains to Panama and later to Peru. Others, granted in encomiendas to various Spaniards, were forced to wash gold in the Nicaraguan highlands (Nueva Segovia) 100 miles east of the lakes. From 1527 to 1540, these gold fields became one of the main areas of Spanish activity in Nicaragua.

Later in the sixteenth century, following depletion of the gold placers and a drastic decrease in native population, the Spaniards turned to stock raising in the savannas around the lakes and in the scrub-covered Nicoya Peninsula. Minor colonial activities, all based on Indian labor, included cultivation of cacao and indigo in the fertile isthmus of Rivas which separates Lake Nicaragua from the sea; the gathering of naval stores in the interior pine forests; and the cutting of tropical timbers for ship construction along the Pacific coast. This pattern of resource and land use persisted in the Nicaraguan lowlands well into the nineteenth century. Still today, most of Nicaragua's population and economic activity centers within the lake lowlands and in the adjacent volcanic hills along the Pacific.

A southern appendage of the colonial province of Nicaragua included the Nicoya Peninsula and adjacent Guanacaste lowlands (today the northwestern extremity of Costa Rica). The conquerors of Nicaragua quickly occupied the Guanacaste plains, for they were densely settled by Indians of Chorotegan culture, similar to that of the lake area. Moreover, the Gulf of Nicoya, protected from the Papagayo storms that often plagued winter sea travel off the Nicoya coast, afforded an easy approach to Nicaragua via the Guanacaste lowlands. Throughout the colonial period, the Guanacaste was a part of Nicaragua province and became a land of cattle ranches and mixed Indian-Spanish blood, as it is today.

During the early period of northward expansion from Panama, the Spaniards bypassed the high mountainous area called Costa Rica. It was not until the 1560's that settlers from Nicaragua, drawn by rumors of rich gold deposits, finally penetrated the cool volcanic basins of the Meseta Central. In 1562, disappointed by the lack of abundant gold placers in this area of young volcanic rock, the settlers founded the town of Cartago in the damp eastern basin of the Meseta Central. By that time, disease had already decimated the warlike Huetar Indians of the highlands, and the low-cultured forest tribes of the Talamanca range to the south were few in number and little inclined to work for Spanish masters. Thus the small group of white settlers in the Cartago area remained free of Indian blood, a contrast to the mixed racial pattern in most of the Spanish provinces of Central America. They became small subsistence farmers who tilled the land themselves, without the aid of Indian laborers. These settlers formed the nucleus from which developed the present white highland-farming population of Costa Rica.

For almost a century, less than 100 Spanish peasant families living in the Cartago Basin comprised the only permanent European settlement in Costa Rica. Late in the sixteenth century, the Cartago farmers began to raise substantial amounts of wheat which were transported into the cacao-producing area of the Matina valley on the Caribbean lowlands of Costa Rica, into the Pacific lowlands of Nicaragua, and even to Panama and Cartagena by ship. Later, tobacco became an important crop exported from the highlands. By the end of the seventeenth cen-

tury, the Cartago basin was so crowded that farmers began to move to other parts of the Meseta Central. In 1706, the town of Alajuela was founded in the western part of the plateau and, by 1736, San José, the modern capital of Costa Rica, was laid out on its present site. At the end of the colonial period, the density of population in the Meseta Central exceeded 100 persons per square mile, and the expansion of white settlement into other parts of the forest-covered highlands and adjacent escarpments, which is still going on in Costa Rica, began.

Conquest from Central Mexico

The central highland of Mexico was by far the most significant area from which Spanish conquest and settlement spread over most of the Middle American mainland during the early sixteenth century. The true center of dispersal was the Valley of Mexico, the heart of the Aztec realm. In 1519, Cortes and his band entered the city of Tenochtitlán after their initial journey up the eastern escarpment from Veracruz, and finally conquered and sacked it in 1521. Upon the ruins of the Aztec capital, the Spaniards slowly built the city of Mexico, which became the administrative center of New Spain, the name given to much of the conquered territory of Mexico and Central America.

Spanish conquest and colonization outward from central Mexico occurred in two phases, each encompassing a definite geographical area. The first phase was characterized by a relatively easy and rapid overrunning of the areas of high Indian culture, or Mesoamerica, including central and southern Mexico and the northern third of Central America. The second and later phase dealt chiefly with the relatively slow conquest and settlement of northern Mexico, the arid lands of low Indian cultures described in the preceding chapter. It is significant that the two phases of Spanish conquest in Mexico, distinguished in time, area, and process, are also distinguishable on the basis of the differing Indian cultures they supplanted.

Conquest of Mesoamerica. Within 12 years after their landing at Veracruz, Cortes's men had taken over most of the area of high Mesoamerican culture, from Culiacán and Tampico in the north to Honduras in the south. Various factors contributed to the rapidity and ease of Spanish conquest. The docile nature of the Indian peasant farmers, accustomed to outside rule, may have played a part, but more important was the fact that the Spaniards who took the place of the defeated native overlords retained the Indian institutions that corresponded with those of feudal Europe, such as the tribute system and slavery. Other factors include the weakening of the native will to resist conquest through the accidental introduction of European diseases and the Spaniards' superior military tactics and weapons, including firearms, the awesome horse, and the large, fierce, hunting dog.

Two factors were especially significant in directing the course of the early conquests from Central Mexico. One was the location of areas of dense Indian population, the source of tributes and labor under the encomienda system. Immediately after their submission to Spanish authority, Indian villages were granted as encomiendas to members of the conquering force. Thus the densely populated basins of the Mesa Central and the adjacent escarpments, as well as the Valley of Oaxaca in the southern plateau, were areas highly prized by the Spanish encomenderos. During the early colonial period, the main income from the encomiendas was tribute in the form of gold, cacao, cotton cloth, and other products of the land that could be sold for profit. Until the mid-sixteenth century, the encomendero also forced his Indians to commute tribute to personal services, which could include labor of almost any sort. Thereafter, the use of encomienda Indians for personal services was prohibited by law, and the Spanish Crown began to

regulate Indian labor under a system called the *repartimiento,* a rationing of Indians to Spanish applicants of certain kinds of workers. The tribute system, however, continued for much of the colonial period.

The second factor that influenced the direction of conquest was the location of the major sources of Aztec and Tarascan gold. These were the placer deposits of stream beds that drain: (1) the areas of old crystalline rock in highlands of southern Mexico; and (2) the rugged Caribbean slope of northern Central America. The major gold belt extended westward from the Isthmus of Tehuantepec, through Oaxaca and the Balsas depression to Colima. The Spaniards' early routes of conquest thus led southward from the Mesa Central into the hot lowlands and the gold country, following the earlier pattern of Aztec and Tarascan expansion.

Even before the fall of the Aztec capital, the Spaniards, working out from the friendly independent chiefdom of Tlaxcala, had secured most of the densely settled highland basins and the adjacent escarpments east and south of the Valley of Mexico. Cortes had sent out small parties to reconnoiter the main sources of Aztec gold in the Balsas Basin as far as the Pacific and, in the upper Papaloapan River basin, to the southeast. A few months after the final conquest of the Valley of Mexico in 1521, most of the former Aztec state was securely in Spanish hands. Cortes acquired for himself many of the best areas of central and southern Mexico. One of these was the rich valley of Oaxaca, where, in 1526, the town of Antequera (now Oaxaca City) was founded in the center of the Zapotec Indian country (Figure 9.2).

In 1522, other expeditions overran the Tarascan state in the western part of the Mesa Central and continued down the southern escarpment of the plateau to the lower Balsas Basin and the mountainous Pacific coast. There the Spaniards found gold in abundance, especially in the isolated Motines area northwest of the Balsas River mouth. Still another expedition, in search of the

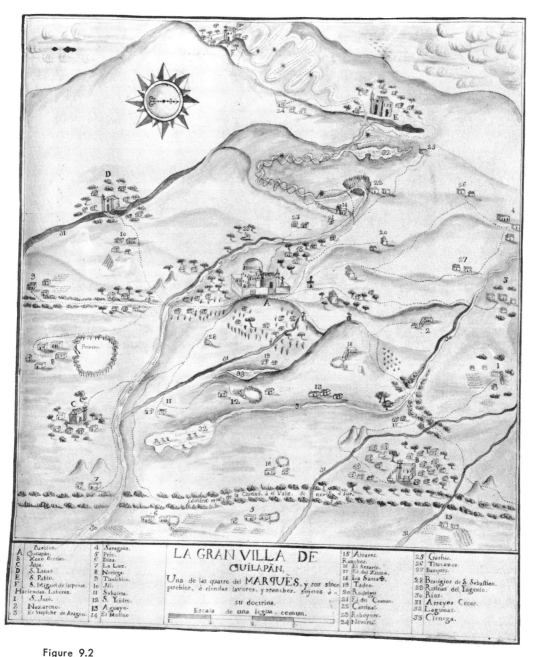

A	Pueblos.	4	Saragoza.	15	Alvares.	25	Gerhes.
B	Cuilapan.	5	Prio.		Ranchos.	26	Tirucozes.
C	Xoxo Ocotlan.	6	Diaz.	16	El Rosario.	27	Basques.
D	Jalpa.	7	La Luz.	17	El del Zauze.		
E	S. Lucas.	8	Noriega.	18	La Santa ✚.	28	Barrigios de S. Sebastian.
F	S. Pablo.	9	Tlanichico.	19	Tadeo.	29	Ruinas del Yngenio.
	S. Miguel de las peras.	10	Jili.	20	Rodrieu	30	Rios.
	Haciendas. Laberes.	11	Sabaleta.	21	El del Comun.	31	Arreyos Cecos.
1	S. José.	12	S. Ysidro.	22	Carrizal.	32	Lagunas.
2	Nazareno.	13	Aguayo.	23	Reboyero.	33	Cienega.
3	El trapiche de Aragon.	14	El Molino.	24	Neveria.		

LA GRAN VILLA DE
CUILAPÁN.

Una de las quatro del MARQUES, y sus sinco
pueblos, à ciendas lavores, y rranchos, sujeros à
su doctrina.

Escala de una legua, comun.

Figure 9.2

An Eighteenth-Century Map of Settlement Within the Jurisdiction of Cuilapan, Near Oaxaca City. Around 1775, Cuilapan was one of the four villas of the once vast holdings of Cortes that remained in the hands of his descendants. Besides the villa of Cuilapan (center, marked A) the map shows five Indian pueblos and various haciendas, ranchos, and smaller holdings. *(Biblioteca Nacional, Madrid)*

source of Tarascan silver and copper, descended the western escarpment to establish the town of Colima within an area of dense Indian population, gold placers, and cacao orchards. About the same time, punitive forays from the Valley of Mexico pushed southeastward into the cacao-rich chiefdom of Coatzacoalcos in the Isthmus of Tehuantepec and northeastward into the Huastec country as far as present Tampico, to quell rebelling Indians. Far from the central authority of Mexico City and lacking gold, the dense population of the Huastec area was ruthlessly exploited, and thousands of Indians were shipped as slaves to the island of Hispaniola in the Caribbean.

Until the 1540's, gold placering and collection of tributes from their encomiendas formed the main economic interests of the Spaniards in central and southern Mexico. By mid-century, new activities, and associated settlements, had been introduced. One was the mining of silver ore from small deposits found on the southern and western escarpments of the Mesa Central. Other activities included the farming of newly introduced Old World crops, such as wheat in the highland basins and sugar cane in the warmer escarpment valleys and, even more important, establishment of a livestock industry based on the herding of Old World animals on the highland pastures and the tropical lowland savannas.

Both the religious orders and lay Spaniards engaged in most of these new occupations. To administer their various activities and control the Indians, the Spaniards founded towns, or *villas*, at strategic points. By 1531, some 15 towns, including Veracruz, Mexico City, and Puebla, had been established within the former Aztec area. To control their economic interests and spread the Faith, the religious orders founded convents and churches in Spanish towns and Indian settlements throughout the area.

Subsequent conquests from the Valley of Mexico were directed southeastward beyond the Isthmus of Tehuantepec, into Chiapas, Guatemala, and other parts of northern Central America. As was indicated in Chapter 8, most of this territory was occupied by advanced Indian cultures of Mayan affinity, such as the Quiché and Cakchiquel. In 1524, accompanied by thousands of Aztec and Tlaxcalan warriors, the Pedro de Alvarado expedition penetrated the Guatemalan highlands and the hot Pacific coastal areas into what is now El Salvador. In contrast to the easy penetration of central and southern Mexico, the conquests of Guatemala and Chiapas were bloody affairs, owing to the stiff resistance of the natives, and Indian uprisings in those areas persisted into the mid-sixteenth century. Moreover, the Spaniards found little gold in the young volcanic materials and the limestone of the Guatemalan-Chiapas highlands.

Although the two important Spanish towns of Santiago de Guatemala and Ciudad Real de Chiapas (now San Cristóbal de las Casas) were founded by 1526, most of the highlands were lightly held and the native cultures were little disturbed for much of the colonial period. In these same areas today, Indian blood and culture predominate. In northern Central America, the Spaniards exploited chiefly the Pacific coastal areas and the low volcanic lands of El Salvador, where the cultivation of tropical products such as cacao, sugar cane, and indigo with Indian and Negro labor became the main colonial activities.

North of the Guatemalan and Chiapas highlands, the Mayan Indians of the Yucatan Peninsula offered even greater resistance to Spanish conquest. Not until the 1540's, when the towns of Mérida and Valladolid were founded, were the Yucatecan Mayas subdued and Spanish authority established. Again, the low, infertile limestone plain of Yucatan contained no precious metals and offered little promise to Spaniards bent on the acquisition of quick wealth. Like the Guatemalan-Chiapas highlands, Yucatan retains a predominantly Indian culture.

The sparsely occupied rain forests of the Petén between the Central American highlands and Yucatan, long abandoned by the Mayas, held no interest for the Spaniards and were untouched for the entire colonial period. Likewise, the equally unattractive coast of present British Honduras and the eastern shore of Yucatan were left for subsequent occupation by the English.

The farthermost southeastward thrust of Spanish conquest from Mexico was directed toward Honduras, a mountainous land of old, highly mineralized rocks that comprise the western side of Old Antillia. There the Spaniards found another center of gold production in the placer deposits of streams draining into the Caribbean. Spanish forces from Mexico, dispatched via sea by Cortes in 1524, took over points along the Caribbean shores of Honduras near fertile, densely populated alluvial valleys, such as the Aguán and Ulúa. Both valleys were rich in native golden artifacts and cacao orchards. Within the Ulúa Valley, the settlers established the town of San Pedro Sula and the port of Caballos (now Puerto Cortés); near the Aguán Valley, the port of Trujillo was founded. Later exploration revealed the fabulous gold placers of the Olancho Valley along the Guayape River and its tributaries in the eastern interior of Honduras, but political rivalry and Indian troubles delayed the effective colonization of Honduras for many years. By 1540, the Spaniards had partially subdued the recalcitrant Lenca and Jicaque Indians of the rugged interior, and had founded the towns of Gracias a Dios and Comayagua near gold and silver deposits. It was not until the 1570's, however, that the Spaniards discovered and developed the large silver mines of Tegucigalpa, which were to give the province of Honduras its colonial fame. Together with stock raising, mining continued to be the chief occupation of Honduras until the end of the nineteenth century. Owing chiefly to the early collapse of the native Indian population and the disinterest of the colonial government, the province of Honduras was never to approach the importance of Mexico as a producer of wealth for Spain.

Although nominally under the jurisdiction of the Viceroyalty of New Spain, Central America was so distant from Mexico City that, in 1543, the Spanish Crown established the Captaincy-General of Guatemala to administer the southern area. The captaincy comprised the Central American provinces from the Isthmus of Tehuantepec to Panama, including the present Mexican state of Chiapas. Colonial Panama, however, became part of New Granada (Colombia) and thus fell into the jurisdiction of the Viceroyalty of Peru. In 1548 Santiago de Guatemala (Antigua) was chosen the capital city of the captaincy-general and the seat of the *audiencia,* or circuit court, of Guatemala. It is significant that, with the exception of Chiapas, the major provinces of the captaincy later became the present nations of Central America.

The last important line of conquest within Mesoamerica was directed northward along the Pacific coastal lowlands of Mexico, following the northwestern extension of high Indian culture. This conquest was carried out in 1531 and 1532 under the leadership of the infamous Nuño de Guzmán who was in quest of gold and the fabled land of the Amazons. After desolating the northern part of the Tarascan area, Guzmán founded the towns of Guadalajara and Compostela on the western side of the plateau. Following a well-worn Indian trail down the western escarpment, the expedition continued into the hot, wet lowlands of Nayarit. Although some gold and silver deposits were uncovered within the western foothills of the Sierra Madre Occidental, the Guzmán party turned to slave raiding, ravaging the densely populated lowlands of Nayarit and Sinaloa. Near the limit of high aboriginal culture in northern Sinaloa, the Spaniards founded the town of Culiacán, which was to serve as a frontier base for slaving and subsequent expansion northward.

The Conquest of Northern Mexico. The second phase of Spanish conquest and settlement from central Mexico was concerned entirely with the occupation of the land north of the area of high Indian culture. The presence of the warlike Chichimec nomads who occupied most of the deserts and steppes in the north, as well as the apparent poverty of the land, at first dampened Spanish ardor for further conquest beyond the Indian agricultural frontier. The north looked so formidable to the Spaniards that they gave the regional terms *la Gran Chichimeca* and *Tierra de Guerra* ("Land of War") to the dry interior that stretched for nearly 800 miles from near the Lerma River in central Mexico to beyond the Rio Grande into Texas. Thus, during the 1530's, northward expansion halted momentarily at the zone of contact between the high Indian cultures of the south and those of low culture to the north.

Two events during the next decade finally breached this cultural barrier and permitted the start of Spanish conquest northward. One was the Mixton War (1541), in which the Spaniards defeated a large Indian force of allied Cazcán farmers and Guachichil nomads on the Chichimec frontier north of Guadalajara. The subsequent retreat of the Guachichil to the east opened an approach northward from Guadalajara into the grasslands of Zacatecas. The opening of this route led, in turn, to the chance discovery, in 1546, of the vast silver deposit of Zacatecas, which set off a veritable rush of Spaniards into the new area. The exploitation of silver deposits thus became the prime motive for further expansion into the Chichimec country, and eventually made New Spain the most lucrative of the Spanish colonies.

In contrast to the rapid overrunning of the areas of high culture to the south, effective occupation of northern Mexico took nearly 200 years. Although the chief silver-producing areas were rapidly blocked out, other sections, such as northeastern Mexico, portions of the central desert, and Baja California, were not settled until the mid-eighteenth century. Moreover, the Spaniards had to employ different methods of conquest and settlement than those used in the south. Among the intractible nomadic Chichimecs the encomienda system was impossible, and the few primitive farmers of the Sierra Madre Occidental who were subjected could offer little in way of tribute. For labor, the Spaniards were forced to rely on free Aztec,

Tarascan, and Otomí Indians from the south, and on sporadic importation of Negro slaves. Furthermore, the mining camps, rather than the villas, or the town corporations that operated so well in the south, became the chief centers of permanent Spanish settlement. Often, the richer mining camps (*reales de minas*) grew into large and opulent cities such as Zacatecas, Guanajuato, and Parral.

Because of repeated depredations made by the desert nomads, the Spanish administration in the north was chiefly military; the presidios, or forts, along the main trails became a common type of settlement and the origin of many present towns in the north. In addition, missionary endeavors were far greater among the lowly northern Indians than among the more cultured peoples in the south. Especially in those northern areas lacking in mineral wealth, the Church orders were often more important than the civil administration in advancing the frontier of settlement. Many present-day agricultural towns of northern Mexico and the southwestern United States can trace their origin to the colonial missions.

The discovery of the Zacatecas mines led to the settlement of the northern part of the Mesa Central, occupied since pre-Conquest times by the hostile Chichimecs. This area included the fertile Bajío, immediately north of the Lerma River, and the extensive grass-covered plains around Querétaro. Since the direct route of communication between Zacatecas and Mexico City traversed this territory, its occupation was imperative. By 1555, Spanish military forces had established fortified towns along the cart road over which silver bullion from Zacatecas was hauled to the capital. Gradually, Otomí and Tarascan Indian farmers from the south, followed by Spanish missionaries and ranchers, took over the Bajío and the Aguascalientes Valley, both of which soon became thriving livestock and agricultural centers supplying grain and animal products for Zacatecas. Most of the large towns, such as Celaya and León, that today serve as market centers in the Bajío, grew out of villages and ranch centers established in the mid-sixteenth century. In 1563, when the large Guanajuato silver mines were opened, the Bajío gained additional importance.

The importance of the Zacatecas mines also led to the establishment in 1548 of a new political province, called the "Kingdom of New Galicia." Initially, this province encompassed the entire northwestern part of New Spain, but it was later confined to an area that approximates the present states of Jalisco, Nayarit, and Zacatecas (Figure 9.3). Guadalajara was chosen as the administrative and religious center of New Galicia.

After the Zacatecas strike of 1546, the main line of Spanish advance northward followed a series of silver-bearing ores that outcrop along the eastern foothills of the Sierra Madre Occidental (Figure 9.4). Within 20 years, Spanish miners had opened many rich deposits, such as those in Fresnillo, Sombrerete, and around Durango, and had reached as far as the Santa Bárbara mines

in southern Chihuahua. From this frontier outpost, the famous Oñate expedition departed in 1599, to settle the upper Rio Grande Valley of New Mexico, 600 miles to the north within present United States territory. Later silver discoveries along the route of northward expansion included the famous Parral mines (1631) and those of Santa Eulalia (1703), the northernmost of the large silver lodes, near which Chihuahua City was founded.

This great Silver Belt of northern Mexico lay within a zone of semiarid grassland, or steppe, bordered on the west by the pine and oak-covered Sierra Madre and on the east by the lower central desert. This grassland served as the natural basis for the growth of a livestock industry that furnished the adjacent mines with meat, hides, and tallow. Moreover, streams flowing eastward from the Sierra afforded water for irrigating narrow stretches of fertile valley land to help supply wheat, maize, and other foodstuffs to the mining centers. Thus, along the main line of northward advance there evolved a mine,

Figure 9.3
Major Political Divisions: Viceroyalty of New Spain, ca. 1625.

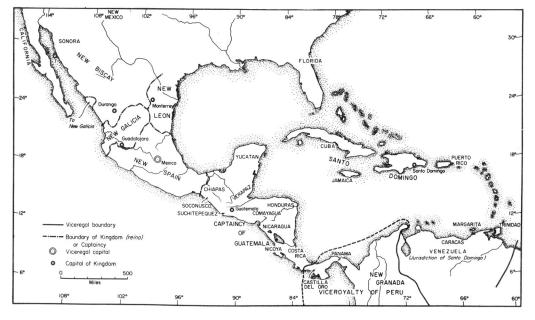

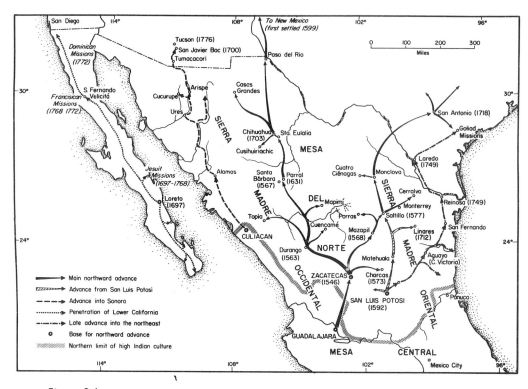

Figure 9.4
Spanish Settlement of Northern New Spain.

stockranch, and grain farm settlement complex that was to characterize much of the Spanish occupation of northern Mexico. This settlement complex, though modified, is still retained in many areas of the north. So significant was the northern silver area to the Spanish government that the northwestern quarter of colonial Mexico was made a separate province, Nueva Vizcaya ("New Biscay"), with Durango as its political and religious capital.

The spread of Spanish settlement outward from the Silver Belt of northern Mexico was slow, sporadic, and often accidental. The Sierra Madre Occidental discouraged settlement to the west. Gold and silver lodes within the sierra, covered by recent volcanic rock, were exposed only in the deep, almost inaccessible barrancas on the western slopes. Throughout the colonial period only one trail, via the mines of Topia, led across the sierra to the Pacific coast. To the east of the Silver Belt, aridity and the Chichimec men-

ace combined to discourage effective settlement. Nevertheless, during punitive forays into the desert to destroy or enslave marauding bands of Chichimecs, Spaniards accidentally discovered mines such as Charcas and Mazapil. They also found the grasslands on the eastern side of the plateau along the foothills of the Sierra Madre Oriental.

The final defeat of the combined Zacateco-Guachichil nomads in 1562 cleared the way for settlement across the desert to the eastern edge of the plateau, where Saltillo was founded in 1577. Shortly thereafter, the discovery of several small silver and lead mines drew Spanish settlement farther northward to Monclova and eastward across the Sierra Madre Oriental, to the sites of Monterrey and Cerralvo overlooking the Gulf coastal lowlands. Attracted by the grass-covered plateau basins along the western side of the sierra, stockmen from Zacatecas soon entered the Saltillo-Monclova area to establish large cattle ranches. By the beginning of the eighteenth century, ranchers and missionaries, pressing northward from Monclova, had crossed the Rio Grande into the grassy inner coastal plain of Texas, where San Antonio was established in 1718. This northward line of settlement from Saltillo and Monclova was eventually to reach the Sabine River bordering on French Louisiana.

Eastward from the Sierra Madre Oriental, the lowland basins and coastal plain of northeastern Mexico were, as early as 1579, formed into the province of New León, with the small village of Monterrey as the political capital. Sparsely settled and economically poor, with stock raising as the main activity, this isolated province remained a weakly held frontier area for most of the colonial period. Not until the mid-eighteenth century was the coastal area of northeastern Mexico finally settled under government supervision. A new province, New Santander (now the state of Tamaulipas and southernmost Texas), was formed to administer this forced colonization, which was carried out to subdue troublesome nomadic Indians and to discourage French designs for westward expansion from Louisiana.

Colonization directly northward from the Bajío of Guanajuato was blocked for a half century by the Chichimecs, especially by remnants of the Guachichil people who had taken refuge in the desert east of Zacatecas. With the final subjugation of these nomads in 1592, the town of San Luis Potosí was founded near a group of rich silver deposits. Spanish settlers soon entered to open mines on the mountain slopes and to establish cattle ranches in the surrounding grassy plains. Settlement northward, along a narrow belt of semiarid grassland, brought the Spaniards to the important silver deposits of Matehuala. Communications were established with Saltillo and Monterrey, forming an eastern trail continuous from Mexico City to New León. By the end of the sixteenth century, the settlers had overcome the Chichimecs in the southern part of the central desert. However, the Sumo, Apache, and

Toboso bands in the far north continued to plague ranches and mining settlements until well into the nineteenth century.

A third significant line of northward expansion proceeded up the western side of Mexico from the frontier base of Culiacán in Sinaloa. In the early 1530's, slaving parties under Nuño de Guzmán had reached the Fuerte River in northern Sinaloa, but no permanent settlements had been established above Culiacán. In 1540, enthused by Cabeza de Vaca's reports of large towns far to the north, Francisco de Coronado departed from Culiacán on his famed expedition in search of the legendary Seven Cities of Cíbola. Coronado followed an ancient Indian trail north through the Ópata Indian country in central Sonora to the Zuñi Pueblos on the Colorado Plateau. Throughout the colonial period and into the nineteenth century, this road was an important artery for trade and settlement. It connected Sonora and southern Arizona with Guadalajara and Mexico City on the central plateau.

Jesuit missionaries were the first to make permanent European settlements north of Culiacán, but not until the end of the sixteenth century. A few small missions were established along the main rivers in northern Sinaloa and southern Sonora among the Cahita and Yaqui tribes. However, the chief area of Jesuit mission settlement centered in northern Sonora among the Ópata, who practiced irrigation farming along the rivers within the low north-south trending basins west of the Sierra Madre Occidental. The principal mission towns of Ures, Arispe, and Cucurpe, founded in the mid-seventeenth century, occupied sites within the upper Sonora and the San Miguel river valleys, the most densely occupied areas of the Ópata and the heart of colonial Sonora. Within the fertile, grassy basins the Jesuits established large herds of cattle, using Indian neophytes as stock hands. Spanish stockmen and miners followed the missionaries, forming settlements and opening small gold and silver mines in the parallel ranges overlooking the valleys.

During the eighteenth century, the mining town of Álamos in southern Sonora grew into one of the largest silver producers of New Spain and became the center of white settlement in the northwest.

At the end of the seventeenth century, the Jesuits extended their missions into the Pima country of southeastern Arizona. There they founded the missions of Tumacacori (1687), north of present Nogales and of San Javier Bac (1700), near the site of Tucson. Again, Spanish stockmen followed, attracted by the lush pastures on the open oak- and grass-covered hills. Southeastern Arizona represents another northern terminus of a line of Spanish settlement into what is now United States territory.

The initial settlement of the arid peninsula of Baja California, like that of Sonora, was left to the Church. The Jesuits were the first to enter, founding Loreto mission on the barren gulf coast in 1697. Other missions, spreading north and south from the mother settlement, were established in the interior oases, where the Jesuits congregated the few nomadic Indians into agricultural villages. After the expulsion of the Jesuit order in 1767, the Franciscans and Dominicans completed the missionizing of the peninsula northward, as far as the present United States-Mexico border. But although colonists had followed the missionaries into Sonora, few followed them into the desolate peninsula. After the decimation of the Indian population by disease, the mission settlements declined, and only a few interior oases and one or two villages in the more humid Cape region at the southern tip of the peninsula survived into the postcolonial period.

A final northward thrust of Spanish settlement in North America took place during the last half of the eighteenth century, along the coast of Upper California. Alarmed by the gradual encroachment of Russian trading settlements from Alaska down the coast of northern California, the Spanish government in 1769 established San Diego, the first of the garrison-mission towns of the new province. Other garrison settlements, such as Los Angeles and Monterey, the capital, were founded soon after. By the close of the century, a line of 21 Franciscan missions extended from San Diego to Sonoma, north of San Francisco Bay. Moreover, Spanish stockmen established large ranches in the pleasant oak- and grass-covered coastal valleys and were soon profitably engaged in exporting hides and tallow. Upper California was the largest area that the Spaniards occupied within present United States territory. It also was the northward limit of Spanish colonial culture in the Americas.

North Americans often forget that the southern half of the present United States west of the Rocky Mountains was once part of New Spain and later of Mexico. But since this vast territory was ineffectively held and was settled by the Spaniards or Mexicans in only a few spots, it was easily acquired by the United States government as the aftermath of the war with Mexico in 1848. Nevertheless, Spanish cultural heritage is still strong in New Mexico and southern Arizona, and it is still cherished in California, if only in legend, mission remnants, and place names.

EVOLUTION OF
THE COLONIAL LANDSCAPE

The Spanish Conquest and occupation of Mexico and Central America during the sixteenth century brought many changes in the cultural and physical landscapes, and many of these modifications have persisted into modern times. One set of changes resulted from the impact of the Conquest on the physical characteristics of the Indian populations. Another kind of change came from the introduction of various aspects of Iberic culture, such as the Spanish language, Mediterranean settlement and architectural types, Old World plants and animals, Spanish agricultural methods, stock raising, and other economic enterprises. These innovations, often blended with the existing Indian culture, have given the greater part of the Middle American mainland its present geographical personality.

The Conquest and the Indian Population

The impact of conquest on the physical aspects of aboriginal population resulted in an early and drastic decrease in the number of Indians, and racial intermixtures. The latter process was to result in the mestizo racial element now so predominant in the area between the Rio Grande and the Panama Canal.

Decrease of Indian Population. On the mainland of Middle America the decline of native population was less severe than in the Greater Antilles, where the Indians were virtually exterminated. Nevertheless, it is estimated that the approximate pre-Conquest population of 12 to 15 million in Mesoamerica was reduced to about 2.5 million after the first century of Spanish occupation. Even by 1550, one of the most frequent complaints of the encomenderos of New Spain was the great decrease in tribute due to deaths among their Indians. The population of most highland villages had been more than halved and many lowland settlements had disappeared completely.

Various factors attributed to this appalling mortality. Warfare took a large toll of Indians in Mesoamerica during the first years of the Conquest and, for most of the colonial period, the Chichimecs of northern Mexico were hunted down until they were eventually absorbed or exterminated. Enslavement of many Indians during the first half of the sixteenth century also contributed to death and dislocation of population. Since the Spaniards followed the medieval custom of legally enslaving rebellious subjects, traffic in Indians early became a lucrative business, and remained so until it was outlawed in 1542. As we have already indicated, Spanish slaving parties based in Panama were particu-

larly active in southern Central America, where they desolated the Nicaraguan lowlands and the Pacific side of Costa Rica. In Mexico, the Huasteca of the Gulf Coast and the Indians of the Pacific lowlands of Nayarit and Sinaloa supplied large numbers of slaves to the mines and plantations of Central Mexico and in the Caribbean Islands. Harsh treatment, disruption of normal food production, and psychological despair may also have contributed to the death rates. The latter phenomenon is attested to by numerous contemporary reports of systematic abortion and infanticide, as well as mass suicide, among the Indians of Central America during the early sixteenth century.

The most important cause of Indian mortality, however, was Old World disease. As in the Caribbean Islands, the most virulent killers were smallpox, measles, and typhus, against which the natives had no immunity. The first smallpox epidemic swept central Mexico in 1520, even before the fall of the Valley of Mexico. The ability of the Aztecs and the Tarascans to resist the Spanish invaders was probably greatly weakened by this and subsequent epidemics of smallpox, measles, and other diseases which occurred throughout Mesoamerica at 10- to 15-year intervals for the rest of the sixteenth century. The worst were the measles epidemic of 1545 to 1546 and a scourge of typhus from 1576 to 1579. In the seventeenth century, the drastic decline of the Indian population of Mexico and Central America was to have significant economic and social repercussions.

Little is known of other Old World diseases that the Spaniards or their African slaves carried to the Middle American mainland. Quite probably, influenza, mumps, typhoid, and malaria took their toll. Still less is known about the diseases of the native Indians, who seem to have previously been surprisingly free from contagious ailments. Only syphilis has been definitely classified as an American disease, but various intestinal ailments were probably also endemic and may have become epidemic during periods of famine.

The Indian population in Mexico and Guatemala continued to decline slowly until the eighteenth century. Thereafter, a gradual increase in numbers followed, and this has continued at a growing rate until the present (Figure 9.5). The Indians gradually developed partial immunity to smallpox and measles, possibly through natural selection and the increasing miscegenation of white, Indian, and Negro.

The decrease of population brought about changes in the location of Indians in Mexico and Central America during the early colonial period. Many of the heavily settled lowland areas were almost depopulated within a century after the Conquest. With the exception of those living in the well-drained Yucatan Peninsula and the Nicaraguan depression, the lowland Indians seem to have suffered a far greater mortality from disease than did the people of the cooler highlands. The hot, damp, insect-infested coasts of the Gulf and Caribbean were particularly good breeding areas for the introduced diseases, especially for malaria, which was acquired and carried by the native anopheline mosquitoes. Later in the seventeenth century, yellow fever from

Africa, and its transmitter, the Aëdes mosquito, appeared on the east coast of Mexico and Central America.

As the lowlands were depopulated by disease and slave raids, the highlands acquired a relatively greater significance as the areas in which lived the remnant Indian populations. Throughout the colonial period and even into the present century, the fertile, nearly empty coastal lowlands of southern Mexico were feared by highlanders as places of sickness and hunger. Only in the last few decades has the reconquest of the lowlands, through health controls, gained real ground.

Racial Mixing. Probably the most lasting physical effect of the Spanish Conquest on much of the native population of Mexico and Central America has been the gradual dilution of Indian blood with that of the European Caucasian and the African Negro. The interbreeding of these three races has produced the present mestizo element which now predominates in all Middle American mainland countries except Guatemala (predominately Indian) and Costa Rica (predominately white).

Figure 9.5
Estimated Population Trends (Numbers and Racial Composition) of Central and Southern Mexico During the Colonial Period.

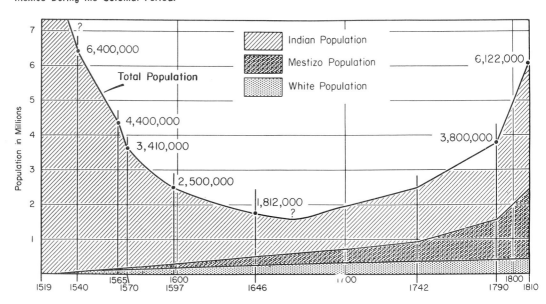

The mixing of Spanish and Indian blood began slowly. By 1570 there were perhaps 50,000 Spaniards in Mexico and far fewer in Central America, compared with an aboriginal population of possibly five million. As Figure 9.5 indicates, a sizable mestizo element was not created in Mexico until the beginning of the eighteenth century. Thereafter, the number of people of mixed blood increased rapidly, accounting at the close of the colonial period for nearly 40 per cent of the total population. In Mexico, interbreeding of whites and Indians occurred mainly in the Spanish towns in the central part of the country, where groups of native servants and laborers lived close at hand in the native quarter (barrio). Secondary centers of racial mixing were the mining camps, especially those in the north. Since Spaniards were legally forbidden to live in Indian villages, racial purity was maintained until rather late in most of the densely settled rural areas of central and southern Mexico and of Guatemala. In these areas, today, are most of the pure Indians remaining in Middle America.

Negro slaves were imported into colonial Mexico and Central America in sizable numbers. It is estimated that nearly 250,000 blacks were taken into Mexico, and an unknown but smaller number into Central America, during the colonial period. In any given year, however, the number of Negroes in New Spain was small, rarely exceeding 35,000. The Spaniards used their black slaves as personal servants, as laborers in the mines and in sugar and indigo processing, and as cowhands on stock ranches. Thus, Negroes were spread throughout most of the area of Spanish occupation, a few being employed even in the northernmost mines of Mexico. Most blacks, however, were concentrated along the hot coastal areas and in the port towns where the Indian population had been greatly reduced by disease. Negroes were particularly numerous in Panama, where they served as muleteers, canoemen, and carriers in trans-isthmian transport.

During the early colonial period, the Indi-ans interbred with Negroes probably as much as with whites, and whites with the Negroes, in spite of regulations to the contrary. Again, the mines and towns were centers of miscegenation. In addition, runaway Negro slaves often escaped to Indian villages; groups of runaways (cimarrones) often formed isolated settlements and took Indian wives from neighboring villages. Nearly 50 different racial castes were recognized in Mexico and Guatemala by the end of the eighteenth century.

Today, Negro blood in Mexico has been almost completely absorbed into the mestizo element. Occasionally one sees predominant Negroid physical characteristics such as short, kinky hair and broad, flat noses in some sections of the Veracruz coast and even in some of the mining areas. A single definitely Negroid group, stemming from colonial times, lives along the Costa Chica, eastward from Acapulco in Guerrero state. In Panama, the Negroid element is quite evident in the mixbloods living in the savanna areas west of the Canal Zone. In Honduras, people with Negroid features are often seen in the countryside surrounding the old mining centers near Tegucigalpa. As we shall see (Chapter 13), the predominance of Negroes along the Caribbean coast of Central America is a comparatively recent development, only 60 to 100 years old.

In 1810, despite racial mixing, probably more than half the total population of Mexico and Central America was still of pure Indian blood. The mestizos appear to have become predominant within the last century. After independence, the fine distinctions in racial types, according with skin color and facial features, tended to disappear, and the term "mestizo" now has a socioeconomic rather than a racial meaning.

The Introduction of Iberic Culture

The cultural changes that the Spaniards effected in Mexico and Central America during the colonial period were many and complex. Some Iberic importations, such as various domesticated plants and animals, were quickly adopted by the Indians; others, such as settlement forms and various economic enterprises were either forced upon the Indians or had little effect on their own way of life; still others, such as the Spanish language, filtered slowly into the Indian way of life.

Language Changes. Like the development of a racially mixed population, the supplanting of Indian speech by Spanish in Mexico and Central America appears to have been extremely gradual. Obviously, Spanish replaced the native tongues most rapidly in the lowland tropics, where the Indian populations were most reduced, and in northern Mexico, where the aboriginal population was quite sparse. In the densely peopled highlands and on the Yucatan Peninsula, however, native speech did not begin to give way to Spanish until the end of the colonial period. This persistence of native language was in part due to the Church, which usually taught the Faith in the local Indian tongue. Moreover, Nahuatl, one of the major languages, remained the language of trade in much of Mexico and Central America as late as the nineteenth century. Spanish tended to replace the Indian languages where European economic activity was greater and racial mixing more common, as around the Spanish towns, mining centers, stock ranches, and processing mills. Where European activity was weak or nonexistent, particularly in isolated areas, the Indian languages are still spoken. In scattered areas over east-central Mexico, nearly one-half million Indians and mestizos still speak Nahuatl, despite almost 450 years of contact with Hispanic culture. Still more striking is the persistence of the Maya-Quiché languages in the relatively isolated highlands of Guatemala, where one million speak them, and in the Yucatan Peninsula, where a quarter million speak Maya.

Changes in Settlement Forms. One of the Spanish activities that profoundly altered the

Indian cultural landscape during colonial days was the establishment of the compact European-type town and its associated architecture. The Spaniard was traditionally a town dweller, and it was only logical that he establish this type of settlement in Hispanic America. Today most people of Mexico and Central America, including many in the rural sections, live in compact towns or villages patterned after the sixteenth-century colonial settlements.

The first and one of the most important types of Spanish settlement was the Spanish town, or *villa,* to which we have already referred. An ancient Iberian institution, the villa was a municipal corporation, made up of a group of citizens (*vecinos*), governed by the town council (*cabildo*), and headed by an alcalde, or mayor. By custom, the town was given certain privileges enjoyed by its namesake in Spain and also a rank, according to its size or prestige. The more highly ranked towns carried the title of *ciudad* ("city"); the more lowly ranked ones were simply "villas." After a ceremony of formal establishment, streets were laid out, house lots and tracts of surrounding farmland were assigned to the citizens, and the town common (*ejido*) was delimited for pasturing animals near the exit of the settlement. By 1575, the Spaniards had founded nearly 35 towns in Mexico and more than 20 in Central America.

Since the prime function of the towns was administrative, their sites were selected with reference to trade routes or control of tributes and native labor. Hence, during the early years of occupation as many towns were established in the hot lowlands as in the cooler highlands. Following the decline of Indian population within the coastal areas, however, many of the lowland towns were abandoned or became insignificant, whereas in the highlands, where population declined less, most of the old Spanish towns grew to be large settlements, from which have developed many present-day cities, including national and provincial capitals.

Although the medieval towns of their

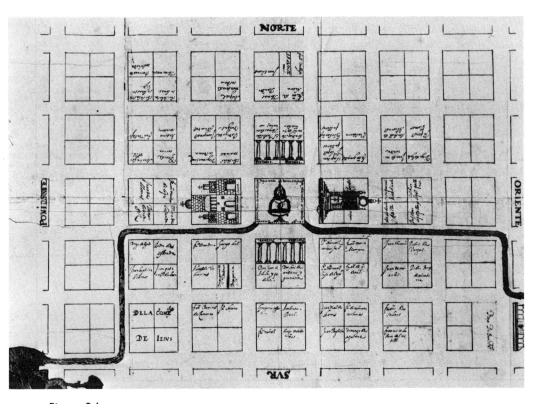

Figure 9.6

Original Town Plan of Nuestra Señora de la Concepción, a Villa Founded in 1603 Near the Mines of Sierra de Pinos, Northwest of San Luis Potosí. The plaza forms the center block of the grid plan and is surrounded by the church, the official buildings and portalled residences. Each block is divided into four lots, which were granted to the *vecinos,* or corporate members, of the town. *(Archivo General de Indias, Sevilla, Planos, Mexico)*

homeland had no regular pattern the villas that the Spaniards established in the American colonies were carefully laid out with a regular grid street pattern. A public square, or plaza, occupied the center of the town (Figure 9.6). Facing the square were the public buildings, often the church, the main business houses, and usually the dwellings of the richer and more socially prominent citizens. Commonly, the weekly or daily market was held in the square. Consequently, the central plaza became the economic and social center of the town. As is well known to every tourist who has traveled in Spanish America, most of the towns and cities have retained the grid street pattern and the central plaza (Figure 9.7).

A section of the town was invariably set aside for the Indians who served as house servants and laborers (*barrio de indios*), and who were usually more numerous than their white masters. In central Mexico, local Indians were brought in to settle the *barrio.* In northern Central America, the Spaniards often elected to import friendly Tlaxcalan or Aztecs rather than trust the local hostile Maya-Quiché people. Negroes and mulattos were housed in the native quarters of the towns in southern Central America, and many of Negroid blood penetrated the towns of Mexico. As we have already noted, the Indian and Negro *barrios* of the Spanish towns were centers of miscegenation. Often today, in the towns and cities of central

Figure 9.7

The City of Tepic in Western Mexico, Laid Out on a Grid Plan in the Sixteenth Century.
The main plaza lies near the center of the city. *(Compañía Mexicana Aerofoto)*

Mexico, the tradition of the old Indian quarter, now inhabited by the poorer class of mixbloods, is retained among the townspeople.

Other types of Spanish agglomerated settlements established during the colonial period included the mining towns and the habitation centers associated with various economic enterprises, such as the large estates, or haciendas, and the sugar processing plants. These settlement forms are discussed in relation to their respective economic activities (Chapter 10).

The Indian Congregations. The most numerous new settlements were the Indian villages established in Mexico and Guatemala during the colonial period by both the Church and the civil government. The main objective of resettlement was to congregate into compact, Spanish-type towns the Indians living in dispersed hillside hamlets, in order to better foster the Christian faith, collect tribute, and recruit labor gangs. The Indian congregation of the sixteenth century was the prototype of the present-day agricultural village, now the

prevailing rural settlement in Mexico and Guatemala.

Until 1565, the resettlement of the Indians in central and southern Mexico was in the hands of three missionary orders—the Franciscans, the Dominicans, and the Augustinians. These newly formed villages, each containing a church or at least a chapel, were actually missionary settlements. Between 1598 and 1625, however, the Spanish government took over Indian resettlement. Both the civil and the religious settlers attempted to choose sites near valley floors where plowland and water were available and, although some settlements were founded with little plan or foresight, most were laid out on the square grid arrangement with a plaza in the center.

The forced resettlement of much of the aboriginal population of central and southern Mexico sometimes had dire consequences. The environs were often unsuitable for Indian agriculture, with the result that food production decreased and famine ensued. Moreover, the compactness of the villages may well have encouraged the spread of contagious disease. Nevertheless, by the middle of the seventeenth century the compact agricultural village had become an essential part of the Mexican cultural landscape. Only in isolated Indian areas has the semidispersed hamlet, or *ranchería,* survived.

During the latter half of the sixteenth century another type of Indian congregation was begun in northern Mexico. Hoping to attract the desert nomads to sedentary life, the Spanish government established a number of colonies of Mexican (Nahuatl), Tarascan, and Tlaxcalan farmers from central Mexico at various points in the north. The first successful colony was Nombre de Dios, near Durango, founded in 1563 with Mexican and Tarascan Indians. In the 1590's, a large number of Tlaxcalans were induced to settle near Saltillo, San Luis Potosí, and other spots in the Chichimec country. From these centers the Tlaxcalans later established small agricultural villages in various parts of the desert, and many Chichimecs were induced to live with them. Indian blood is still much in evidence in the towns, such as Nombre de Dios, that have grown from these old colonies.

Architectural Introductions. Probably one of the most attractive aspects of the cultural scenery of Mexico and Central America is the Spanish colonial architecture—the old dwellings, public buildings, and religious structures that remain in the countryside and towns. These architectural forms are perhaps the most impressive reminder of the area's Spanish heritage.

Of all the types of buildings that the Spaniards introduced into America during the colonial period, the rural dwellings have been the least studied. Among the great variety of rural houses found in Mexico and Central America today, it is often difficult to determine which may be purely aboriginal and which are European; many are conglomerates of Indian and Spanish architecture.

It appears, however, that during the sixteenth century Spaniards introduced two main types of rural houses, both from south-

Figure 9.8

House Type of Southern Spanish Origin Introduced into Mexico and Central America. The roof of hollow red tile and ornately carved beams are characteristic.

ern Spain. One was the one-story, rectangular dwelling of whitewashed stone or adobe walls, with a gabled roof of hollow tile or straw thatch (Figure 9.8). This house is in widespread use in central and southern Mexico and in most parts of Central America, particularly in mestizo areas. It has also been adopted by many Indian groups, such as those of the Guatemalan highlands. The other general type, probably of Berber origin, was the squat, flat-roofed adobe house, often windowless, but frequently having a built-in hearth with a chimney (Figure 9.9). The adobe, somewhat similar in form to the flat-roofed Aztec dwelling, was spread with Spanish settlement into the dry mining areas of north-central Mexico, where it was adapted to the arid and semiarid climate.

The simpler Spanish dwellings were one- or two-room affairs; the larger and more pretentious ones, found mainly in the towns, were often of two stories and were con-

Figure 9.9

Flat-Roofed Adobe House, Common in Northern and Parts of Central Mexico.

structed around a courtyard, or patio, a feature of Moorish and Roman antecedents.
Invariably, the town houses abutted directly
on the street, just as they do today in most
Latin American towns.

Other types of rural and town houses introduced during the colonial period included
the charming one- or two-story Asturian
dwelling (of northern Spain), now found
chiefly in the state of Michoacán, Mexico.
Its gently pitched, gabled or hipped, tiled
roof, its wide, projecting eaves, its carved
rafters, and its wooden balconies distinguish
this house from all others in Mexico. Another
very interesting house, probably European
and possibly introduced in the eighteenth
century, is the notched-log or plank dwelling
(Figure 9.10), found today in many spots in
Mexico. It has been adopted by the Tarascan
Indians in Michoacán and by the Mije in
Oaxaca, and it also is found along the upper
eastern escarpment in Puebla, Hidalgo, and
Veracruz states. The notched-log house,
which is used in Scandinavia, in mountainous
areas of central and eastern Europe, and in
the Russian plains, may have been introduced
into Mexico by Catholic priests of German
or Austrian descent.

Some European architectural elements
have found their way into Indian architecture. The log or plank house of the Tarascans
and Mije and the Andalusian gabled house
of the Quiché of Guatemala have been men-

Figure 9.11

Granary of Notched Log Walls and Thatched Roof,
Commonly Used by Indians in Southern Mexico. The
technique of corner notching is probably of European
origin.

tioned. In central and southern Mexico there
is widespread use of notched-log construction
for outbuildings such as granaries and animal
pens (Figure 9.11). Moreover, many highland Indian groups have been gradually replacing the native palm and grass thatch
roofs with the Spanish, hollow red tile, which
has considerable prestige value. We do not
know how early the Indians began to adopt
these new building techniques, but the
Tarascans were constructing notched-log
houses by the end of the eighteenth century.
The adoption of other features of Spanish
architecture may not have occurred until
after the colonial period, for the process is
still going forward.

Most of the public buildings and many of
the private houses of the rich were more
pretentious and durable than the small rural
and town dwellings. The architecture of such
structures followed Roman antecedents long
established in southern Spain. Usually of
stone and mortar, each building was normally
constructed around a courtyard or patio, with
colonnaded porticoes or arcades facing outward on the plaza. Arcaded buildings of
colonial style still grace the plazas of many
old Mexican towns, such as Oaxaca, Morelia,
and Puebla. Other public structures of colo-

Figure 9.10

The Tarascan Plank House, Michoacán, Mexico. The
shake roof, wide eaves, and carved doors are typical
of this distinctive dwelling.

nial days included long, arched Roman aqueducts for bringing water into the towns. Although most of the colonial aqueducts are in ruins, some, such as those of Querétaro and Morelia in central Mexico, are still intact.

The various religious structures which were constructed in practically all types of settlements in Mexico and Central America during the colonial period were far more numerous than the civil buildings (Figure 9.12). The visitor to even the smaller villages of central Mexico is immediately attracted by the beautiful tiled domes and ornate belfry spires of the stone chapels and churches that tower high above the squat, whitewashed adobe houses. Most of the churches were constructed by Indians under the direction of the missionary orders during the first great period of church building in Mexico and Guatemala, 1530 to 1575. The disastrous typhus epidemic of the late 1570's so depleted the Indian labor force that religious construc-

Figure 9.12

The Cathedral at Campeche City, Completed Near the End of the Seventeenth Century. This cathedral is typical of the colonial religious structures of Middle America.

tion was not resumed until well into the seventeenth century. Some pilgrimage towns, such as Cholula in Mexico and Chiquimula in Guatemala, became noted for the great number of their religious structures. In the larger colonial towns that were chosen as diocesan centers, the sumptuous bishop's palace, as well as convents and monastaries, added to the wealth of religious buildings.

Although probably as many colonial churches were constructed in Central America as in Mexico, few have survived the frequent earthquakes within the volcanic axis along the Pacific. Even major cathedrals in the towns of El Salvador, Nicaragua, and Costa Rica are recent wooden frame buildings covered with decorated tin sheeting.

Colonial Urbanization and Vegetation. The large amounts of timber used in the Spanish villas and for the churches seriously depleted the oak, pine, and fir forests that had covered the mountain slopes and high basins of central Mexico and Guatemala. The beautiful forests around the Valley of Mexico were rapidly destroyed as the Spaniards rebuilt Mexico City on the ruins of Tenochtitlán. The abundance of pine and fir throughout the Mesa Central of Mexico actually encouraged waste of the tall trees which furnished the long beams for construction. Moreover, the customary heating and cooking fuel of the Spaniards was charcoal made from oak and pine wood, and the Indians quickly adopted this practice. Many became professional *carboneros,* or charcoal burners, who supplied the towns with fuel. Consequently, around Indian villages and Spanish towns alike, the forest began to disappear through overcutting. By the end of the sixteenth century, deforestation of the mountain slopes near the heavily populated areas of central Mexico had become so serious that erosion and lake filling had begun. Charcoal is still the main household fuel of Mexico and Central America, and the remaining stands of highland forest are in the process of disappearing.

SELECTED REFERENCES

Aschmann, H., *The Central Desert of Baja California: Demography and Ecology,* Ibero-Americana, No. 42. Berkeley, Calif.: University of California Press, 1959.

Aguirre Beltrán, G., *La población negra de México: 1519–1810.* Mexico, D.F.: Ediciones Fuente Cultural, 1946.

Cook, S. F., and W. Borah, *The Indian Population of Central Mexico: 1531–1610,* Ibero-Americana, No. 44. Berkeley, Calif.: University of California Press, 1960.

Cook, S. F., and L. B. Simpson, *The Population of Central Mexico in the Sixteenth Century,* Ibero-Americana, No. 31. Berkeley, Calif.: University of California Press, 1948.

Jiménez Moreno, W., *Estudios de Historia Colonial.* Mexico, D. F.: Instituto Nacional de Antropología e Historia, 1958.

Kubler, G., *Mexican Architecture of the 16th Century.* New Haven, Conn.: Yale University Press, 1948.

————, "Population Movements in Mexico: 1520–1600," *Hispanic American Historical Review,* XXII, No. 4 (1942), 606–43.

López de Velasco, J., *Geografía y descripción universal de las Indias desde el año 1571 al de 1574.* Madrid, 1894.

Marshall, C. E., "The Birth of the Mestizo in New Spain," *Hispanic American Historical Review,* XIX, No. 2 (1939), 161–84.

Morrisey, R. J., "The Northward Expansion of Cattle Ranching in New Spain: 1550–1600," *Agricultural History,* XXV, No. 3 (1951), 115–121.

Powell, P. W., *Soldiers, Indians and Silver: The Northward Advance of New Spain, 1550–1600.* Berkeley, Calif.: University of California Press, 1952.

Sauer, C. O., *The Road to Cíbola,* Ibero-Americana, No. 3. Berkeley, Calif.: University of California Press, 1932.

Simpson, L. B., *Studies in the Administration of the Indians in New Spain: The Civil Congregation,* Ibero-Americana, No. 7. Berkeley, Calif.: University of California Press, 1934.

Stanislawski, D., "Early Spanish Town Planning in the New World," *Geographical Review,* XXXVII, No. 1 (1947), 94–105.

Vásquez de Espinosa, A., *Compendium and Description of the West Indies,* Miscellaneous Collections, No. 102. Washington, D.C.: The Smithsonian Institution, 1942.

10

The Colonial Economy in Mexico and Central America

A study of the major colonial economic institutions of Mexico and Central America reveals processes by which a Spanish-Indian cultural landscape developed. Spanish settlement and economic activity in the New World, as we have seen, initially centered around precious metals and native populations which would pay tribute. Yet, though the bulk of the wealth came from the mines, the cultural complex of the area was even more affected by the cultivation of the land and the breeding of animals. Agriculture and stock raising, especially, functioned to produce a fusion of Indian and Iberic culture which formed a rural way of life that still prevails in most parts of the area.

The plow and the ranch entailed extensive use of the land. To be sure, the Spaniards opened up new areas previously unused by Indian farmers; but they also engulfed cropland which, under intensive tilling of the aborigines, had been producing far more food than it would henceforth. The introduction of European ways of using the land altered the relationship between man and nature in Middle America.

AGRICULTURE

Farming in colonial Mexico and Central America was based on a sometimes uneasy combination of native Indian and European crops, techniques, and systems of land tenure. The Spaniards brought with them most of their basic food plants, particularly the small grains, including wheat and barley. Wheat bread was the Spaniard's principal starch food, his staff of life, but the Indians had maize. His legumes—the horsebean, chickpea, and lentil—were introduced, but they never successfully competed with the Mexican and Central American Indian beans as protein food. Other Old World food plants included various vegetables: onions and garlic for flavoring; potherbs such as cabbage and collards; and a few roots, like the carrot, radish, and turnip. More significant were the tropical plants of Asiatic origin: sugar cane, banana, plantain, citrus fruits, and the mango, which spread throughout the *tierra caliente* and much of the *tierra templada* of Mexico and Central America. Mediterranean fruits such as the grapevine, fig, and pomegranate, as well as the more hardy apple, peach, and quince, were early introduced into the cool tropical highlands.

Spanish Farming and the Indians

The Indian farmers of the Middle American mainland, having already had a well-developed agriculture with an adequate plant and food complex, were slow to adopt most of these Old World plants. Some of the tropical plant introductions, however, such as the plantain (for starch) and sugar cane (for sweetening), spread rapidly among the lowland people of Mexico and Central America. Curiously, onions, garlic, and collards also soon became important adjunct foods among the highland Indians. On the other hand, wheat was rejected. Maize was an established staple, and the cultivation of wheat was limited to the highlands and entailed the use of an entirely new agricultural technique—the Old World plow pulled by a team of oxen. In many instances, the Indians learned to use the plow only when they were forced to work on Spanish farms or to give tribute in wheat to their encomenderos. To this day, wheat is a minor crop among most of the highland Indians of southern Mexico and Guatemala and is grown not for food, but as a cash crop.

The Church was probably the most important disseminator of Old World crops and agricultural techniques. Around every religious establishment in Mexico and Central America, the Spanish priests made fruit and vegetable gardens, a tradition of western European Catholic clergy. Their gardens served as colonial experiment stations and from them the priests spread European horticulture, especially among the highland Indian farmers. The cultivation of fruit trees, such as peach and apple, was admirably suited to the Indian way of farming. By the same process, Old World irrigation techniques and some agricultural instruments such as the hoe, spade, ax and, possibly, the plow were introduced into Indian culture.

For most of the colonial period, subsistence agriculture in Mexico and Central America remained largely in the hands of Indians and mixbloods. In the Mesoamerican area, the native maize, beans, and squash, plus a few Old World plants, were farmed by the ancient slash-burn system of tillage on hillsides, although some use was made of the plow on valley floors and gentle slopes. The small surplus that was raised either entered the local native markets, as of old, or was given in tribute to Spanish encomenderos. Commercial farming of both native and imported crops, on the other hand, was directed by Spaniards using Old World techniques. With some change in crops and techniques, this division between subsistence and commercial agriculture has persisted in Mexico and Central America to the present.

The Highland Crops

Wheat. Wheat was the chief commercial food crop in the Spanish colonies. In Middle America, it was cultivated chiefly in the highland basins of Mexico and Central America. Spaniards preferred their traditional wheat bread to the Indian maize foods, which they felt were detrimental to the health of Europeans.

However, there were difficulties in the way of large-scale production of wheat. The grain would mature well only in the cool highlands. Moreover, fungus diseases (*chahuixtle*) reduced yields when the grain was planted during the warm rainy season. Consequently, most Spanish farmers in the tropical highlands of New Spain and Guatemala cultivated wheat by irrigation during the cooler dry season. However, the better farming areas were often already occupied by Indians, and Spanish colonial law prohibited Europeans from usurping areas under native cultivation. The wheat farmers often acquired land titles by obtaining Crown grants of portions of former Aztec estates or of lands declared unoccupied (*baldíos*). Others, as *vecinos*, or members of a Spanish town, obtained rightful possession of agricultural plots surrounding the villa. Still others were able to amass large holdings by purchasing land from Indians or from other Spaniards.

The first large wheat-growing district in central Mexico was the Valley of Atlixco in the southwestern part of the Puebla basin (Figure 10.1). Favored by a flattish surface, light volcanic soil suitable for plowland, and plentiful water from streams fed by the melting snows from the adjacent slopes of Mt. Popocatepetl, the Atlixco Valley was by 1550 the foremost wheat-producing area of New Spain. There, and in other areas within the basin of Puebla, the Spaniards established the first large-scale commercial European farming in the New World (1532). Individual holdings, called *estancias de pan llevar* (wheat farms), averaged about 640 acres. Using

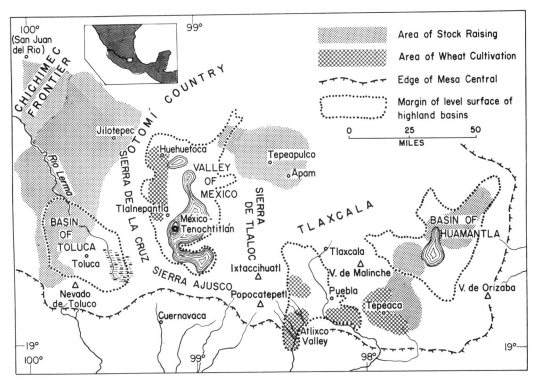

Figure 10.1
Spanish Land Use in the Eastern Portion of the Mesa Central: Mid-Sixteenth Century.

Indian labor from neighboring villages in encomienda, their owners often produced two crops of wheat and one of maize yearly. Not only was this fertile area the breadbasket for Mexico City and Puebla; it also early became a center of European fruit production, especially of pomegranates, citrus fruits, grapes and figs. The Atlixco Valley and its northward continuation around Cholula and Texmelucan is still noted for its irrigated farming, and supplies Puebla with wheat, fruits, and vegetables.

Other wheat-growing areas were developed around Spanish villas founded in the western part of the Mexican Mesa Central, particularly near Valladolid (modern Morelia) and within the volcanic basins around Guadalajara. After the opening of the northern mining districts in the last half of the sixteenth century, Spanish farmers and

Franciscan missionaries established wheat *estancias* in the Bajío and in the Valley of Aguascalientes, both on the northern edge of the Mesa Central. By the mid-seventeenth century the Bajío had surpassed Atlixco as the largest wheat-producing area of New Spain, and it is still considered to be the granary of Mexico. Farther north, Spanish wheat and maize farms were established near every large mining center, particularly in the valleys of Súchil and Poanas near Durango and the Valley of San Bartolomé (modern Allende) near Parral in southern Chihuahua. The Jesuit and Franciscan orders also cultivated wheat around the northern missions. In the northern mining and missionary frontier settlements, wheat became a more important food staple than maize among the mestizo and even in some Indian communities.

In colonial Central America, wheat cultivation was much less widespread than in Mexico. This might be explained by the relatively small Spanish population, the general poverty of the area, and the lack of extensive upland areas. The Cartago Basin of highland Costa Rica, with its purely Spanish population, was the most productive wheat area of the Central American provinces. Elsewhere, a few *estancias* for the cultivation of small grains were established around most of the Spanish highland towns, and a fair amount of wheat was cultivated within the highland basins of Honduras for the mines nearby.

Various agricultural tools and processes were associated with wheat tillage and the use of many of these was extended to the cultivation of other crops, both Indian and European. The most important, of course, was the plow. In sixteenth-century Spain, the chief farming implement was the ancient wooden ard, or Egyptian plow, of Neolithic origin. This instrument, drawn by a yoked team of oxen, merely scratches the soil; it does not turn it, as does our modern steel moldboard plow. The ard that the Spaniards brought to Middle America came from the provinces of Andalusia and Extremadura in southern Spain; essentially the same tool is used today in many rural areas of southern Mexico and Central America (Figure 10.2). With this simple instrument, the Spaniards were able to extend wheat and maize cultivation into the extensive grass-covered basin floors theretofore rarely cultivated by In-

dians, who had only dibbles and *coas*. The Spaniards also introduced rectangular field patterns, squares and strips, both of which are associated with plow cultivation. Such fields gave the rural landscape within the highland basins a European cast which contrasts with the irregular hillside fields of the Indians.

The plow, of course, could not be used on steep slopes, where native slash-burn cultivation persists to this day in Mexico and Central America. Nor could it be employed to advantage in flat areas with shallow, rocky soil, as in the Yucatan Peninsula, where still the Maya Indians till chiefly with the dibble. Even in areas suitable for the plow, as the coastal plains of the lowland Totonac Indians in Veracruz, strong native resistance to change has precluded its general use up to the present time.

The use of the plow greatly extended cultivation, but it resulted in the ruin and abandonment of much land in the most densely settled sections of the tropical highlands. In the late colonial period, when Indians and mestizos began to employ the plow on low slopes, sheet erosion and, finally, serious gullying of the soil ensued. The consequence is that extensive highland areas, from central Mexico into Central America, have been lost to agriculture.

Arabic irrigation techniques were also introduced, principally with wheat cultivation. These techniques consisted of the diversion of stream water through canals (*acequias*); the construction of dams across small, intermittent streams to form reservoirs (*jagüeyes* or *presas*); and the digging of wells and the use of water lifts, such as the noria. Spanish canal irrigation was similar to, but much more highly developed than, the ancient Indian methods. Reservoir irrigation became widely employed for both wheat and maize cultivation in the northern basins of the Mesa Central, where today the *presas* form a conspicuous part of the landscape, but the noria, so common in Spain and North Africa, apparently was little used in colonial Middle

Figure 10.2

The Wooden Plow, or Ard, Introduced by Spaniards into Their American Colonies.

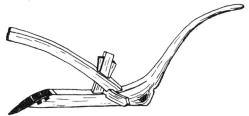

Figure 10.3
A Noria, or Wooden Water Lift, Operated by Donkey Hitched to the Long Sweep.
Few of these colonial-type wells remain in Mexico.

America. Today this ancient waterlift (Figure 10.3) is seen only in a few farming areas in the northern Mexican states of Aguascalientes, Zacatecas, and San Luis Potosí. It also survives in the Yucatan Peninsula, where it was introduced by Spanish priests and cattlemen.

The ancient threshing floor, the grist mill, and the bakeoven are three other imports that accompanied colonial wheat culture in the Middle American highlands. A round platform of tamped earth, the communal *era,* or threshing floor, was often located on the outskirts of the Spanish towns, while private ones became a feature of every wheat *estancia.* In many rural villages of central Mexico, wheat is still threshed by driving horses or mules over the sheaves placed on the *era* floor. Most of the flour mills were water-powered and were thus located along streams on the farms or within the Spanish towns. Today, only the ruins of such edifices in the highlands of Mexico and Central America testify to their importance in colonial times. On the other hand, the European outside oven for baking wheat bread spread far outside the area of wheat cultivation, and

is in widespread use in highland villages and isolated farm houses throughout Mexico and Central America.

Vineyards and Wine Making. Of the three plants of fundamental importance in the Mediterranean which were brought to Middle America—the small grains, the grapevine, and the olive tree—only the grains became firmly established. Climate and soils were favorable for the vine and the olive in most parts of the tropical highlands of America, but the Spanish government forbade their cultivation on a large scale except in the viceroyalty of Peru. This was done, apparently, to protect the colonial market for the wine and oil merchants in Spain. Nevertheless, in isolated spots of northern Mexico, far from central authority, both the missionaries and lay settlers succeeded in establishing small wine-producing areas. The largest vineyard district was Parras, a spring-fed oasis in the desert west of Saltillo, and during the latter half of the colonial period, the famous Parras wines and brandies were shipped to the northern mining centers. To this day, the wineries of Parras have retained their fame in Mexico. Smaller colonial vineyards were established in other northern localities, such as Aguascalientes, Saltillo, and along the Rio Grande downstream from El Paso del Río (modern Ciudad Juárez).

Commercial Farming in the Tropical Lowlands. Whereas commercial agriculture in the tropical highlands and the arid north of Middle America revolved chiefly around extensive cultivation of wheat, maize, and hardy European fruits, Spanish farming in the warm lowlands was based largely on tropical plants from both the Old and New World. Among these, the most significant were sugar cane, cacao, and the dyestuff, indigo. The commercial development of these three crops was particularly important to the colonial economy of Central America, which lacked Mexico's great mineral wealth.

Sugar Cane. Soon after their initial settlement in the 1520's the Spaniards brought sugar cane to Mexico and Central America from the island of Hispaniola, the distributing center for most of the tropical plants introduced from the Old World. In Mexico, the colonial cultivation of cane and the processing of sugar was limited to the southeastern and southern escarpments of the Mesa Central; in Central America the crop was concentrated in the Pacific piedmont along the base of the volcanic axis. Frostless, moist, and possessing the definite dry season necessary for the proper concentration of sugar in the plant, these areas were well suited for the cultivation of cane. The rich volcanic soils supported years of continuous cropping, and the swift streams flowing down the adjacent escarpments afforded water power for turning the wheels of the grinding mills.

In Mexico, during the 1530's, the earliest sugar estates and mills were founded around Cuernavaca in the *tierra templada* south of the Valley of Mexico and at the western base of the Los Tuxtlas volcanic mountains (southeast of Veracruz). Smaller enterprises

were later established along the eastern escarpment of the central plateau in Michoacán and Jalisco. By 1550, New Spain was the foremost sugar producer of the Spanish colonies, surpassing Hispaniola, in the Caribbean, in output. In Central America, the principal sugar areas lay along the Pacific piedmont of Guatemala, while less important districts developed in the coastal provinces of San Salvador and San Miguel (modern El Salvador) and in the lake lowlands of Nicaragua. Cane has been harvested from these areas for the last 400 years and they are still among the important sugar zones of the Middle American mainland.

The Spaniards needed large tracts of land, an abundant labor supply, and adequate capital for mill construction in order to develop the colonial sugar industry. Cortes, who acquired vast tracts of choice tropical lowlands in Mexico, was the first sugar baron of New Spain. Later, the missionary orders purchased or purloined sizable tracts for sugar estates from Indian villages. Since by mid-sixteenth century, disease had greatly reduced the native lowland population in Mexico and Central America, the abandoned lands (*terrenos baldíos*) were easily obtained through royal grants. Indians were at first employed to cultivate cane, but Negro slaves were used in milling and later as field hands.

The Spaniards introduced to the mainland sugar mills similar to those employed in the Antilles (see Chapter 3).

Cane brandy (*aguardiente de caña*), a hard liquor avidly sought by Indians, was a byproduct of sugar processing. Distillation, which the Spaniards introduced, may also have been applied to the juices of other plants, such as agave, from which the mezcal liquors (tequila) were made in the Mexican highlands.

Sugar cane cultivation also spread rapidly among the lowland Indian, who cultivated small plots for cane juice. The stalks of mature cane were cut into small lengths and chewed like a confection. In the markets of most Mexican and Central American villages, one sees neat piles of cut cane for sale; and, in the streets, the ubiquitous litter of chewed cuds that have been spat out by children and oldsters alike. Cane juice and panela cakes of brown sugar supplemented the native honey, which had been almost the Indians' sole sweetening.

Cacao. As we have already indicated (Chapter 8), cacao was one of the chief commercial products of tropical Mexico and Central America in pre-Conquest times. Soon after the Conquest, the Spaniards took over one of the most important of the native cacao areas—that of Soconusco along the Pacific piedmont of Chiapas and western Guatemala—and subsequently they extended cacao cultivation southeastward along the upper coastal plain of eastern Guatemala (Suchitepequez) into the Izalco area of western Salvador. The inner Pacific coastal region from the Isthmus of Tehuantepec to the Gulf of Fonseca thus became the cacao coast of colonial New Spain (Figure 10.4). The great pre-Conquest cacao area of the Tabasco lowlands in southeastern Mexico became a minor producing area during colonial times, as did other native districts such as Colima of western Mexico, the Sula valley of northern Honduras, the Rivas Isthmus of Nicara-

gua, and the Matina valley on the Caribbean coast of Costa Rica. In the Soconusco area, cacao production was left in the hands of the Indians, who paid most of the annual harvest as tribute to Spanish encomenderos. The new cacao areas of Suchitepequez and Izalco, however, were Spanish-owned plantations operated by skilled Indian laborers who were familiar with the starting of cacao seedlings in hot beds, with the irrigation needed during the long dry season, and with the planting of leguminous trees to shade the cacao plants.

For the first half of the colonial period, the chief market for cacao was the central highlands of Mexico, just as it had been in pre-Conquest times. In most of New Spain, cacao beans were made into a chocolate beverage drunk by Indians and Spaniards alike. They were also used as currency to pay Indian labor in many parts of the highlands.[1] Not until the mid-seventeenth century did Spain and other European countries become important markets for New World cacao. By that time, most of the groves of the Soconusco coast had declined and many had been abandoned as disease struck down their Indian cultivators. When cacao production shifted to Venezuela, beginning in the 1630's, the cacao industry in Guatemala and Salvador declined rapidly. Today only scattered groves along the Pacific coastal plain serve as a reminder of the former greatness of the cacao coast of Central America.

Indigo. The cultivation and exploitation of dyestuffs formed an important part of the colonial economy in Middle America. For nearly three centuries (1550–1850), American vegetable and animal dyes, including indigo, cochineal, and various dyewoods, were in great demand in the cloth manufacturing centers of northwestern Europe.

Figure 10.4

Cacao in Mexico and Central America: Sixteenth and Seventeenth Centuries.

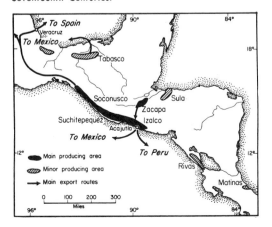

[1] During the sixteenth century in Mexico and Guatemala, 140 cacao beans were the equivalent of one Spanish real; 1,120 beans, the equivalent of one silver peso. During most of the colonial period, however, the purchasing power of the beans fluctuated widely.

Of these dyestuffs, indigo was the most important and widely grown in the Middle American tropics. The leaves of this low, weedy plant (Indigofera suffruticosa) yield a very fast dye of deep blue. About 1570, Spanish encomenderos along the Pacific lowlands of Guatemala and Honduras began to exploit the wild indigo, called *xiquilite,* and later they formed large plantations of the cultivated plant. By the middle of the seventeenth century, the chief indigo plantations of the Middle American mainland extended along the Pacific coastal plain from northwestern Guatemala to the shores of Lake Nicaragua. In effect, indigo replaced the failing cacao industry of Central America for the remainder of the colonial period. A second important indigo center was the low Yucatan Peninsula where, by 1600, more than 50 large processing plants were in operation.

The processing of indigo involved a large investment of capital in the construction of dye factories (*obrajes de añil*) along streams or irrigation canals. In the factory, the plants were soaked in stone vats to obtain a pasty residue which, filtered and dried, was cut into bars of blue dye ready for transport. Since the Spanish Crown forbade the employment of Indians in the indigo industry (it was thought to be an unhealthful occupation), Negro slaves were imported for labor. The Negro slave population was largest in the province of San Salvador, the center of indigo processing in Central America during the seventeenth and eighteenth centuries. By 1750, many tropical areas were competing with Central America for the indigo market, but the industry remained important in Guatemala and El Salvador until the introduction of analine dyes in the mid-nineteenth century (Figure 10.5). Even as late as 1921, El Salvador was exporting sizable amounts of indigo for dying special types of cloth. Today nothing remains of this once prosperous activity that upheld the colonial economy of many of the Central American provinces.

Cochineal. Cochineal, another notable native American dyestuff, also acquired special significance in the colonial economy of Mexico and Central America. As we mentioned earlier, the Aztecs used this scarlet dye which was extracted from tiny scale insects raised on leaves of the nopal or prickly-pear cactus. Unlike indigo, cochineal was a product of the cool tropical highlands, and in pre-Conquest times it was secured as tribute, chiefly from the Mixteca of northern Oaxaca. After the Conquest, the Spaniards also obtained the dye as tribute and forced the extension of its cultivation into the eastern part of the Mesa Central (Tlaxcala and the basin of Puebla). In Spain and northwestern Europe, this new dye commanded fabulous prices and cochineal gained an important place in the economy of New Spain. By 1600, it ranked in value next to the precious metals among Mexico's exports.

During the entire colonial period, the cultivation of cochineal remained in the hands of the Indians, who planted nopal cactus in small household plots and carefully tended the valuable insects. To protect the insects from wind and predators, each nopalry was enclosed by a high adobe wall (some of which remain today in isolated villages of southern Mexico). The red dye was ex-

Figure 10.5

Indigo in Central America : Eighteenth Century.

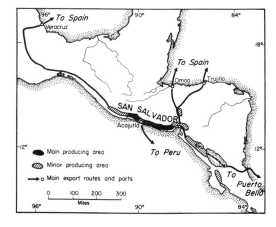

tracted from the dried insects by boiling them in water (Figure 10.6).

Toward the end of the seventeenth century, Spanish officials began to encourage the spread of cochineal culture into the Central American highlands as far as Nicaragua. In the 1770's, it was taken to the Canary Islands and eventually spread to other parts of the world. The production of cochineal remained important in Mexico until 1870, when the cheaper synthetic dyes destroyed the ancient industry.

Other Plant Resources

Dyewoods. Dyewoods were scarcely exploited by Spaniards along the tropical Caribbean coasts of Central America and Yucatan. This activity was left to the English, whose settlement and exploitation of the east coasts of Central America are discussed later.

Fiber Crops. Among the minor agricultural products that entered the colonial economy of the Middle American mainland were various fiber crops, the cultivation and processing of which were left in the hands of the Indians. Aboriginal cotton and cotton cloth came chiefly from the drier tropical lowlands, the Yucatan Peninsula and the lake area of Nicaragua being the largest producers. Rope and cordage made from fiber extracted from the native agave plant was produced by Indians in both tropical highland and lowland areas, but principally in the drier sections.

During the sixteenth century, Spanish officials introduced the Old World mulberry tree and the silkworm into the Oaxaca and Puebla areas of Mexico. Taught mainly by Catholic priests, the Indians of these areas rapidly took over the planting of mulberries, the raising of silkworms, and the spinning and weaving of high quality silk cloth. Unfortunately, the entrance of cheaper Asiatic silks into Spain after the establishment of the Manila trade in the latter part of the sixteenth century killed the Mexican silk

Figure 10.6
Early Eighteenth-Century Drawing of Cochineal Harvest in Oaxaca. (*Archivo General de Indias, Sevilla*)

industry. In various parts of the Mixteca of northern Oaxaca, one can still see remnants of old mulberry groves that the Indians retained after the decline of the industry.

Tobacco. Tobacco, native to Indian America, was another minor agricultural product grown commercially in various localities in Mexico and Central America during the late colonial period. Although production was hardly comparable to that of the famous colonial tobacco areas of Cuba and Venezuela, sizable crops were produced for local consumption and for export in the Costa Rican highlands, San Salvador, Chiapas, and especially the Copán area of western Honduras. In the Copán area's peculiar volcanic soils was grown high-quality tobacco for which the area is still known. In colonial Mexico, the largest tobacco-growing area was around Córdoba and Orizaba on the humid eastern escarpment above Veracruz.

STOCK RAISING

The introduction of Old World animals and of stock raising probably did as much as any other factor to change the cultural and physical landscape of Middle America during colonial times. The Indian, who lacked animal domesticates of his own in any number, was particularly affected by the incursion of this new economy. The peculiar vegetational and climatic factors of Mexico and Central America greatly favored the rapid reproduction of the new animals, and large areas of Mexico and Central America still attest to the occupance of the Spanish stockman and his herds.

In the sixteenth century, the Spanish stockman distinguished two general classes of Old World animals, all of which he introduced into the American colonies. One class he called *ganado mayor*. These were the larger domesticates, including range cattle, oxen, horses, mules, and donkeys. The other class—sheep, goats, and hogs—he termed *ganado menor* ("smaller animals"). To these we should add the barnyard fowls, particularly the chicken, the breeding of which spread so rapidly among the American Indians.

The first animals the Spaniards brought to Mexico and Central America were the horse and the hog. The horse, a symbol of rank and authority, was a most effective military weapon; later, the horse helped to herd other animals. Also accompanying every land expedition were droves of hogs, lean razorbacks. Easily driven and self-fed by scavenging, the hog formed a ready supply of pork and lard. Cattle, both the dun-colored, heavy-horned variety of western Europe and the black Iberian stock, were imported later, primarily for their hides and tallow, secondarily for meat; mules and donkeys were raised for

transport; and sheep and goats for their wool, meat, and milk.

The Indian farmers of Mexico and Central America were quick to acquire the smaller and more tractable of the Old World animals. In almost every Indian community, the hog and chicken became household animals, supplementing the native turkey and dog. Today the hog and chicken, both good scavengers (street cleaners, as it were), wander at will through village lanes and into doorways; they are rarely kept in pens except at night. Chicken eggs and, unfortunately, hog lard as well as the Spanish habit of frying foods, has been added to Indian cookery.

The small sheep (*rasa* variety), docile and easily handled, was readily adopted by the highland Indian farmers of Mexico and Guatemala, and wool soon replaced cotton as the chief cloth fiber in the highlands. The Indians also learned to breed sheep for certain natural colors of wool. Brown and black were the favorite hues for blankets and clothing, and the small flocks still tended by Indian children in the Middle American highlands include as many black and brown sheep as white ones. The Indians also adopted the Spaniards' hand-and-foot loom, reserving it for the weaving of woolens by men, while the women continued to weave cotton cloth on the native belt loom.

The Indians also accepted the slow, docile ox and the small donkey, or burro, which was used for transport, but feared and until late rejected the larger animals, such as the half-wild range cattle and the difficult mule. Only native nobles were permitted by the Spanish to keep or ride the horse.

Commercial stock raising remained in the hands of the Spaniards and mestizos during the colonial period. Cattle and, to a lesser degree, mules and horses were the principal range animals throughout Mexico and Central America. Raising of the merino sheep, introduced in the 1540's, was important chiefly in the cool, dry highlands and in northern Mexico.

On the Middle American mainland the

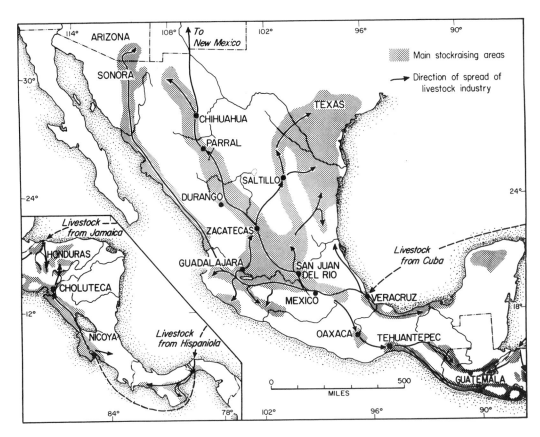

Figure 10.7
The Spread of Livestock Economy in Mexico and Central America During the Colonial Era.

Spaniards established the livestock industry in three types of natural situations:

1. The highland basins of Mesoamerica, already densely occupied by Indian farmers.
2. The tropical lowland savannas of the coastal plains and the interior valleys of Mexico and Central America.
3. The steppe lands of northern Mexico.

Each of these areas presented particular problems for animal husbandry, and in each there evolved a particular pattern of stock raising with particular consequences to the face of the land (Figure 10.7).

Stock Raising in the Highland Basins

In Mexico, stock raising developed first in the highland basins adjacent to the capital.

By 1535, sizable herds of cattle were roaming the grassy surface of Toluca and Puebla basins and the northern, drier part of the Valley of Mexico. In all three localities, despite regulations to the contrary, the Spaniards' herds overran the unfenced milpas of the Indians, causing the natives to abandon much of their farmland and flee to the surrounding mountains; other farmland was abandoned as the Indians died off. The Spaniards quickly took over this land for pasture, for the succulent pigweeds (amaranths and chenopods) that invaded the abandoned Indian milpas afforded even better pasture than the native grasses. Moreover, the paucity of serious predators, disease, and competing wild animals favored a rapid growth of herds in the central Mexican highlands. By 1550, there were an estimated 150,000 cattle and horses in the northern part of

Toluca Basin, where the abandoned Otomí town of Jilotepec had become one of the early centers of the Mexican livestock industry.

Checked by the Chichimec frontier from expansion into the semiarid grasslands farther north, the Spanish stockmen drove their herds westward into Michoacán and Jalisco in the 1540's, disrupting Indian agriculture as they advanced. The same phenomenon occurred farther south, in the Valley of Oaxaca, on the highlands of Chiapas and Guatemala and, to a lesser degree, in the basins of central Honduras. In all of these areas, Indian farmers were continually plagued by encroaching herds of cattle, horses, and mules. Cultivated land was abandoned, populations dislocated, and native food supplies depleted. Not until the mid-sixteenth century, when protective legislation was enforced and plow agriculture spread into the highland basins, were the herds controlled.

Within the cool highlands, commercial sheep raising became as important as cattle raising. Sheep were closely associated with agricultural areas, for they could be easily controlled by Indian shepherds and could feed on the wheat and maize stubble in harvested fields during part of the dry season. As in Spain, fields were unfenced and harvested areas were considered common pasture for livestock. Thus, the basins of Puebla, Tlaxcala, Toluca, and of northern Michoacán in central Mexico, the Valley of Oaxaca, and the highlands of Chiapas and Guatemala all became the early sheep-raising sections of Middle America. During the latter part of the colonial period in Mexico, the areas surrounding the Bajío of Guanajuato and the Saltillo basin, both major agricultural districts, also became important sheep-raising districts.

In some areas of central Mexico, the Spaniards and their Indian shepherds practiced transhumance, or the seasonal migration of flocks from summer to winter pastures. Around the end of the sixteenth century, during November and December, as many as

200,000 head would be driven from the summer (wet season) pastures of Toluca and Querétaro to winter at the eastern end of Lake Chapala in Jalisco, where green, succulent plants abound in the marshy areas through the dry season. Again, the flocks from the valley of Puebla wintered on the eastern escarpment of the Mesa Central in Veracruz, browsing and grazing on plants kept green by the frequent winter rains. By the mid-seventeenth century, as many as a half million sheep were being driven from central Mexico across the eastern sierra into the lush bluestem prairies of Nuevo León and Tamaulipas in far northeastern Mexico for winter pasture. Today, these former grasslands, destroyed by overgrazing, are covered by an acacia scrub.

By the end of the sixteenth century, overgrazing, which in some cases resulted in soil erosion, was already noticeable in a few areas of central Mexico. Deep gullies can now be seen, especially in the rolling grasslands west of Toluca in Mexico, near San Cristóbal in Chiapas, and in various parts of Guatemalan highlands where sheep have been grazing for nearly three centuries.

A colonial textile industry developed side-by-side with sheep raising. By the end of the sixteenth century, Spaniards had established small woolen mills (*obrajes*) in towns within the main sheep-raising areas: in Puebla, Tlaxcala, Querétaro, Texcoco, Mexico City, and even Saltillo in the far north. Such mills housed scores of small European hand-and-foot looms operated by cheap Indian labor and sometimes by Negro slaves. The colonial woolen mills were the first Mexican factories, and Puebla and Mexico City are still textile manufacturing centers.

Stock Raising in the Tropical Lowlands

In spite of high temperatures and an abundance of parasites, the tropical lowlands of Mexico and Central America early became important stock-raising areas. Cattle, horses, and mules were the main range animals;

sheep and goats did poorly in the hot and humid lowlands and the hogs that were introduced usually went wild, feeding on roots and fallen fruits and palm nuts in the forest.

The central savanna of Panama was the first lowland area of the mainland to be stocked with cattle and mules, imported from the Caribbean islands. From Panama, Spaniards introduced livestock into the Nicaraguan lake lowlands, the Guanacaste plain of Costa Rica, and the Choluteca Valley of southeastern Honduras. By the seventeenth century, Choluteca was famous for its mules, thousands of which were annually driven to Panama for use in the trans-isthmian traffic. In Honduras, the savanna areas on the Caribbean coast were populated with livestock brought in from Jamaica soon after the founding of Trujillo in 1524. By the middle of the sixteenth century, stockmen in Mexico began to take cattle from the highlands into the coastal lowlands in great numbers. The Gulf coastal plain, from Tampico south to Nautla and from Veracruz into Tabasco, as well as the Pacific coast, from the Isthmus of Tehuantepec into Guatemala, swarmed with cattle.

One of the chief reasons for the rapid growth of the cattle herds in the coastal lowlands was the availability of unoccupied land —farmland abandoned as smallpox and typhus decimated the Indians. Moreover, the fresh-water marshes near the coasts, especially those of Tabasco and Guatemala, afforded year-round pasture. Inland from the marshes, however, the natural grasses of the American tropics are poor in protein, and make poor feed. The succulent weeds of recently abandoned farmlands were far more nutritious. A variety of low leguminous trees and shrubs, whose young terminal buds and bean pods are rich in proteins, also afforded excellent forage for cattle. The young shoots of coarse tropical grasses are also fairly nutritious, and the Spanish stockmen annually burned the lowland pastures to clear away the dry stalks, thereby extending the grassy areas at the expense of the tropical woodland. The pres-

ent extensive coastal grasslands of Veracruz, Tabasco, and Tehuantepec are probably a product of such burning.

The underfed and ill-tended livestock in the lowland pastures were scrawny, half-wild beasts. The cattle were bred chiefly for tallow and for their hides, which were often riddled with holes by the larvae of parasitic ticks. Today, fires are set in the savannas as much to kill ticks as to clear the dry coarse grass for new growth.

Stock Raising in Northern Mexico

Stock raising in Middle America was most highly developed in the semiarid grasslands of the north Mexican plateau. These grasslands, stretching on either side of the central desert from the Bajío of Guanajuato northward to beyond the Rio Grande, afforded an extensive open range somewhat similar to the Great Plains of the United States.

Certain physical characteristics of this great range favored the growth of the Spanish herds. The original grass cover was black grama, a highly nutritious bunch grass which afforded year-round pasture. This valuable grass, green and tender during the summer rainy season, cures to a palatable natural hay in the dry winter period. Associated with it were other less palatable grasses—bluestem, tobosa, needlegrass, and many others. The shrubs that make up an important part of the semiarid vegetation in northern Mexico were as important as the grasses. The bean pods and young shoots of the thorny leguminous shrubs and low trees, such as mesquite and various acacias (huisache, screw bean), afforded excellent browse for cattle, sheep, and goats. Over most of the grassland area, an abundance of springs furnished water for livestock throughout the year, and these were supplemented both by intermittent and permanent streams flowing from the adjacent sierras.

Such conditions prevailed chiefly on the northern periphery of the Mesa Central and within the wide belt of semiarid grassland that lies between the Sierra Madre Occidental and the central desert. Within the latter area were the renowned pastures of western Zacatecas, central Durango, and Chihuahua, still the foremost stock-raising section of Mexico. As we pointed out earlier, the zone corresponded to the great Silver Belt and the main axis of Spanish northward advance in New Spain. On the eastern side of the plateau, the main grazing areas were around San Luis Potosí and from Saltillo northward into Texas.

Spanish stockmen first penetrated the semi-arid grasslands along the northern margin of the Mesa Central. This was the Chichimec frontier, which checked Spanish movement northward until the mid-sixteenth century. But by the 1550's, cattlemen had moved many of their herds into the grasslands of San Juan del Río and Querétaro, east of the Bajío of Guanajuato. Those areas, together with the previously occupied pastures to the south around Jilotepec, were the cradle of northern colonial stock raising (Figure 10.1). There Spanish herding techniques were adapted to the northern frontier; there the *vaquero* ("north Mexican cowboy") developed; and there some of the first big stock ranches, or *haciendas,* were established. From this center, the livestock industry and the mines spread northward as the Chichimecs slowly gave way. Beyond the mining districts, the Spanish stockmen and their herds joined with the Catholic missionaries to form the cutting edge of the frontier of settlement as it pressed northward into what is now United States territory. Although continually harassed by the Chichimecs, the northern cattlemen had advanced beyond the confining farmlands of the sedentary Indians to the south, and they were able to use Iberic herding techniques.

Stock-Raising Techniques

During the sixteenth century, the Spaniard introduced directly from his homeland most of the practices involved in colonial stock raising in Middle America. The rodeo, the annual or semiannual roundup to brand calves and to select stock for market; the use of the *desgarretadero,* a half-moon blade set on a long pole for hocking cattle, as well as the leather *lazo* for roping and the *garrocha,* or long lance, for controlling the herds; the emphasis on raising cattle for hides and tallow—all these practices appear to have come from southern Spain. The herder's use of leather clothing (jacket, chaps, even headgear) for protection from thorny shrubs may have been a New World development. In most parts of colonial Middle America, the earliest *vaqueros* were poor whites and Negros, slaves or freedmen, for Indians proved to be poor herders of the half-wild cattle. In Mexico, the interbreeding of Negro and Spanish cowboys with Indian women on the frontier produced the mestizo *vaquero,* who moved north with the cattle.

Stock Raising and Land Tenure

It was from the industry of stock raising as much as from commercial farming that the vast landed estates of Mexico and Central America evolved during the colonial period. Just as in the Greater Antilles, the Spanish stockmen of the Middle American mainland first obtained municipal or royal grants of certain pasture lands (*estancias, sitios,* or, as in Panama, *hatos*) for grazing. These grazing rights did not entail land ownership. The size of the grants varied according to the type of animal herded. Thus, the *estancia de ganado mayor,* a ranch for cattle, horses, or mules, usually measured around 5,000 acres; the *estancia de ganado menor,* for sheep and goats, about 2,300 acres. Through the accumulation of several contiguous grants through outright royal grant, or by purchase, or otherwise, rich and noble Spaniards came into possession of immense estates, particularly in arid north Mexico. The estate of the Marquis of Aguayo, which comprised almost the present state of Coahuila, was half as large as Texas. From the system of grazing rights, there gradually developed the recognition and confirmation of land titles by payment of nominal fees to government authorities. The resulting entailed properties based on stock raising, together with the agricultural holdings discussed above, developed into the large haciendas that still characterize the land tenure and dominate the economy of much of Central America and, until recently, of Mexico.

Most of the livestock haciendas of Middle America consisted not only of pasture, but also of small tracts of arable land, unusually along stream bottoms or alluvial terraces. Included on almost every grant of pastureland was at least one *caballería* (about 128 acres) of plowland. The wheat or maize harvested therefrom was used mainly for feeding the hacienda workers and overseers. On some *estancias* in central and northern Mexico, agricultural production became even more important than livestock.

The focal point of the hacienda was a compact cluster of buildings, sometimes called the *casco* (Figure 10.8). This included the often palatial house of the owner or overseer, the huts of the workers, the corrals, granaries, and usually an elaborate chapel tended by the hacienda priest. Invariably, the structures were of stone or adobe, and arranged around a central courtyard. The hacienda center was usually walled or strongly fortified against bandit attacks or, as in northern Mexico, against nomadic Indians. The New World hacienda center is highly reminiscent of the Andalusian *cortijo* of southern Spain, from which the architectural plan was probably taken. These hacienda centers, often abandoned and in ruins, dot the landscape of Mexico and parts of Central America.

LAND TENURE
AND THE LABOR SYSTEMS

The owners of the large colonial haciendas developed a labor system that pervaded New Spain. In the early colonial period, some haciendas, situated within the area of Mesoamerica, inhabited by sedentary Indians, were able to produce sufficient labor through the government-regulated *repartimiento* system, whereby a weekly levy of workers was made on nearby Indian villages.

Figure 10.8

The Casco, or Habitation Center, of Chimalpa Hacienda, Southern Hidalgo State, Mesa Central. Now an ejido center, this large casco was completely walled; atop the wall are parapets and turrets formerly used for defense against bandits. The hacienda church towers above all other structures.

Beginning in the sixteenth century, however, after the disastrous epidemics had reduced Indian population, most *hacendados* were forced to resort to extralegal means to get sufficient workers. Indians were induced to leave their old villages to settle on or near the estates by offers of relatively high wages paid in kind—such workers were called *gananes or peones*—and the owner or overseer advanced them goods on credit from the hacienda store (*tienda de raya*). In this way the workers fell into perpetual debt to be paid in labor. This was the origin of the pernicious system called "debt peonage," which bound the rural peasant to the landed estates. On the other hand, by freeing the Indian from the conservative customs of his native village and permitting him to satisfy his needs by exchanging his labor for food and clothing, the hacienda system became a powerful force for cultural change. On the haciendas, Indian workers became mestizo in culture, if not in blood. Debt peonage continued on the large haciendas of Mexico until the Agrarian Revolution of only 50 years ago, but the system, though greatly modified, is still in force in parts of Guatemala, El Salvador, Honduras, and Nicaragua.

A different labor system was practiced on the ranchos, or small holdings, which developed principally on the western and northern fringes of the Mesa Central of Mexico (in Jalisco and Guanajuato) and in the highland basins of eastern Guatemala and central Honduras. The ranchos required few workers. Occasionally the proprietor and his family composed the labor force; sometimes Indian workers were obtained through the *repartimiento* system; but, more commonly, natives and mixbloods were hired as free laborers to help cultivate crops and tend livestock. The modern, vigorous rancheros, freeholders in the Los Altos district in northern Jalisco and in the *valles* of central Honduras, are descendents of these colonial middle-class farmers who formed an anomaly within the general pattern of *latifundia* ("large estates")

in Mexico and Central America. Somewhat similar in size, land system, and labor force were the properties attached to the Spanish towns. The present system of *minifundia* ("small properties") of the Costa Rican highlands evolved from colonial town holdings.

In striking contrast to all of this, the Indian village lands of southern Mexico and Guatemala were set apart and, during most of the colonial period, were legally protected from encroachment by land-hungry Spaniards. In the Indian communities, the system of use rights and communal holdings of pre-Conquest days were retained, and they are practiced to this day in isolated areas. During the last years of the colonial period, and especially in the nineteenth century, the hacienda owners were permitted to acquire many of the Indian lands through illegal means, and the *latifundia* system was expanded at the expense of the Indian way of life. Such conditions were basic causes of Mexico's twentieth-century social revolution and land reforms.

COLONIAL MINING

We have observed that the acquisition of precious metals was the outstanding motive for initial Spanish settlement in Middle America, that the extraction of gold and silver became the leading business of New Spain, and that from these metals the mother country derived the greatest wealth from the Middle American colonies. On the other hand, mining engaged a relatively minor part of the population; most of the people, by far, lived by subsistence and commercial agriculture. Moreover, in only one part of Middle America—northern Mexico—did mining and its adjunct activities dominate the economic scene and leave a lasting impress upon the landscape. In the southern areas, heavily populated by sedentary Indians, agriculture was economically dominant and along with stock raising, the chief molder of the cultural scene.

Gold Placering

Gold placering was the earliest Spanish mining activity in Middle America. That carried on in the Carribean islands has been discussed (Chapter 3). On the Middle American mainland, the Spaniards engaged in washing gold from the streams that drained the old, highly mineralized rocks of southern Mexico and from the rivers on the Caribbean versant of Central America from Honduras into Panama. These early activities did little to change the aboriginal landscape. Indians who had worked the same streams before the Conquest served as miners for the Spaniards. With the exception of a few iron tools, such as crowbars, picks, and hoes, the Indian laborers used their own placering methods, including the batea, a round, shallow, wooden bowl for panning gold dust and nuggets. Moreover, the ephemeral nature of alluvial gold deposits resulted in continuous shifting of mining camps (called "ranchos") from one stream to the next, and few permanent colonial settlements resulted from gold placering in Mexico and Central America.

Although the period of active placer mining in these areas was short-lived (1525–1560), small family-sized operations continued, for most of the colonial period, in the tributaries of the Balsas River in Mexico and along several streams in Central America, particularly the Guayape River of northeastern Honduras. Such activity can still be seen in southern Mexico and Honduras, where a kind of folk mining with the ancient Indian placering techniques has persisted.

Vein Mining

With the abolition of cheap Indian slave labor and the depletion of the gold placers in the mid-sixteenth century, the Spaniards in Mexico and Honduras turned to the more difficult extraction of silver ores from vein deposits. This entailed permanent settlements. The exploitation of ore in veins required a large number of workers who lived in one place for long periods, and a large capital investment for the sinking of shafts and the construction of mills and refining plants. Most of the silver-mining centers of Middle America became sizable towns, and some grew to be large, opulent cities.

The first silver mines exploited by Europeans were relatively small deposits found within the area of high Indian culture. Although the Spaniards may have worked the Tarascan mine of Tamazula in western Michoacán as early as 1525, their first major silver-mining operation occurred in the 1530's at Taxco, an Indian tin-mining center on the southern escarpment of the Mesa Central, southwest of Mexico City. Soon a series of silver deposits were discovered to the northwest of Taxco, including those of Zacualpan, Sultepec, and Temascaltepec, and these were exploited. During the same period, the mines of Zumpango were opened farther south, in the Sierra Madre del Sur. In the early 1540's, a large number of small mines were exploited in the western escarpment of the Mesa Central in the vicinity of Guadalajara (Figure 10.9). The rich mines of Pachuca, discovered in 1556 just beyond the northern limit of the Valley of Mexico, and the lead-silver workings of Ixmiquilpan and Zimapán, in Otomí country to the north, were other deposits exploited within the area of high Indian culture of Mexico.

The largest and most productive colonial mining area of New Spain was northern Mexico, the locale of the great Silver Belt in the land of the Chichimecs. The opening of this area to Spanish settlement has been described (Chapter 9). Spain derived most of its colonial wealth from the mines within the Silver Belt, from Zacatecas and Guanajuato northward along the eastern foothills of the Sierra Madre Occidental to the mines of Santa Eulalia in Chihuahua. Outside of the main Silver Belt, other mines were opened in various sections of northern Mexico. An eastern line of deposits extended from San Luis Potosí to beyond Saltillo. In the far north-

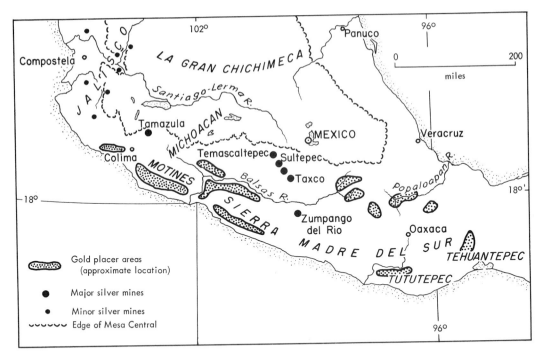

Figure 10.9
Spanish Mining Activities in New Spain : 1519–1545.

west, the mines of Sinaloa and Sonora formed a third area of silver production in northern colonial Mexico.

On the southern edge of the area of high Mesoamerican culture, within the highly mineralized highlands of central Honduras, the Spaniards developed another silver-mining area. A cluster of five mining settlements, centered around Tegucigalpa, was established soon after the initial discovery in 1569. But they were few in number, isolated from the main stream of colonial development, and neglected by the Spanish government, so the mines of Honduras, though rich in high-grade ores, could hardly compare with the opulent mining districts of northern New Spain.

The mining settlements of Mexico and Central America were physically not unlike modern ones, for both are closely associated with the peculiar nature of vein outcrops. Owing to various geological processes, mineralization of veins in underlying rock tends

to occur in clusters. These individual clusters, where mineralized veins outcrop, may cover many square miles. In colonial times, as to-day, such clusters usually make up a mining district in which the active mines might be scattered over a large area, each corresponding to the exploitation of one or several outcropping veins. In each colonial mining district, one large town was usually established as the administrative and refining center for the surrounding mines. Such a settlement was called a *real de minas* in northern New Spain and often termed *asiento de minas* in the central and southern parts of the viceroyalty. For example, the *real de minas* of Zacatecas was the administrative and refining center for the large number of mines within its district (Figure 10.10). Normally, the mining town was located along a stream where water was available for power and as an essential ingredient in the refining processes. Since most mineralized areas were mountainous, such streams flowed through deep narrow

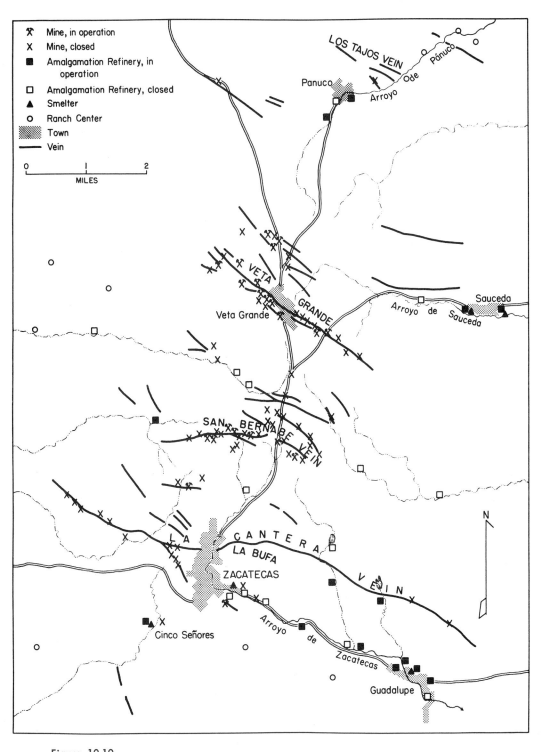

Figure 10.10

The Zacatecas Mining District at the Close of the Colonial Period. (*From Burkart, J.,
Aufenthalt und Reisen in Mexico in den Jahren 1825 bis 1834. Stuttgart*: *E. Schweizer-
bart, 1836*)

valleys which afforded little level ground for buildings. Consequently, most mining towns developed an elongated shape and an irregular street plan, in contrast to the regular grid pattern of the Spanish villas. The elaborate churches and other colonial structures; the steep, winding cobbled lanes; and the picturesque plazas tucked between intersecting streets—all give the old mining towns of Mexico a charming quality rarely found elsewhere in Spanish America (Figure 10.11). Another feature of most mining centers was the *barrio*, the residential quarter for Indian and Negro laborers, usually perched high on the valley sides above the main part of town. These sections are now the slum districts, still serving their old function as the living quarters for poorly paid laborers.

The extraction of silver from its ore in the colonial mining centers necessitated a large array of buildings, large numbers of workers, and the development of many subsidiary activities to furnish food, reagents, and fuel. Probably no other economy in colonial Middle America developed such an elaborate and interrelated system of activities as did the mining industry.

Few of the mining and refining techniques that the Spaniards used in their New World mines were brought from Spain. If the Spaniards knew little about gold placering, they knew even less about the refining of silver ores. During the formative years of silver mining in Mexico, the Spaniards relied upon Indian (mainly Tarascan) and German knowledge of vein mining and ore reduction.

Figure 10.11
The Mining City of Guanajuato, Founded in 1554, Crowded Within a Narrow Mountain Valley. Its winding, picturesque streets and alleys present an Old World, medieval atmosphere. Abandoned shafts of worked-out silver mines pock the surrounding hills. (*Compañía Mexicana Aerofoto*)

Many German miners were brought to New Spain from the Erzgebirge of Saxony, the chief mining area of fifteenth- and sixteenth-century Europe, to impart their knowledge of metals to the Spaniards. The stamp mill, powered either by animals or water wheels and employed throughout the colonial period for crushing ores, was introduced by the Germans in the early sixteenth century. Of a similar origin were improved smelting techniques and, quite probably, the famous amalgamation process for reduction of silver ores.

Until the mid-sixteenth century, smelting was the only known method of reducing silver ores. Large numbers of small rectangular furnaces of stone or adobe, operated with water-powered or hand-driven goatskin bellows, were constructed in every large mining center. In the smelting process, large amounts of lead and litharge were used as reagents; where there was no local supply, these materials had to be imported. The only fuel used in smelting was charcoal, made from the local wood supply, and around every mining center the woody vegetation was thus almost completely destroyed. The open stands of acacia and oak that once covered the hills around Zacatecas had completely disappeared by the end of the sixteenth century, giving rise to the present barren, wind-swept landscape around this once-prosperous *real*.

Around 1556, the amalgamation process of reducing silver ores was introduced into New Spain. This process involved the mixing of mercury with finely ground silver ores puddled in water to make a sludge. Salt and chalcopyrite were other ingredients mixed with the ore mud to aid chemical reaction. Mixing was accomplished by driving mules, and sometimes human workers, through the sludge. After a long period of curing, the sludge was washed, leaving behind an amalgam of mercury and silver. The mercury was volatilized by heating the amalgam in a retort, and the remaining metallic silver was then cast into bars.

With the amalgamation process, low-grade ores free of lead compounds could be cheaply refined. This process was employed in Mexico until the latter part of the nineteenth century, when the better, modern techniques of flotation and cyanidization were perfected. Extremely rich ores and those of high lead content continued to be reduced by smelting. Smelting and amalgamation were often carried on in the same mining center.

For these operations, the colonial miners constructed large plants of stone and adobe. Stamp mills, smelters, and amalgamation plants composed the *hacienda de beneficio,* several of which were located within a given mining town. The amalgamation plant consisted chiefly of large open courtyards, or patios, where the ore sludge was mixed with mercury and other ingredients for curing. Ruins of these buildings today abound in every colonial mining center of Mexico and Honduras.

The demand for reagents used in the refining processes, for animals used in mixing and hauling ore, and for food to feed the mine workers created a lively trade and a development of subsidiary activities within the mining zones. Lacking local deposits, the colonial miners imported mercury from Spain and Peru through a government monopoly. Lead and litharge were often brought in from afar. After the introduction of amalgamation, the salt industry in New Spain and Honduras became an adjunct of colonial economy. The close interrelationship of the mines and surrounding farms and stock ranches has already been mentioned; the ranches furnished tallow for the candles which illuminated the mine shafts, hides for ore sacks and ropes, mules and horses for mine work, and beef and mutton for food. The great demand for wheat and maize resulted in the development of small irrigated farms around the northern mines and in the expansion of commercial agriculture in the Mesa Central (Figure 10.12). Indeed, the economic survival of New Spain during most of the colonial period was based chiefly on the mining industry and the economic institutions related to it.

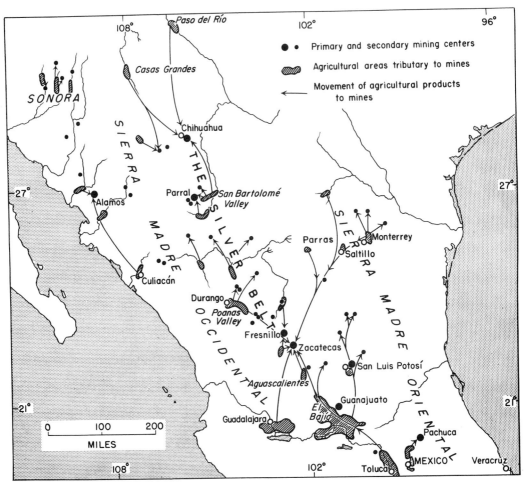

Figure 10.12
Mining and Agriculture in Northern New Spain: Seventeenth and Eighteenth Centuries.

Salt Gathering

Another significant economic activity related to mining was the gathering and making of salt for the amalgamation process. Fortunately for the mining centers of northern New Spain, the central desert nearby contained numerous salt-incrusted dry lakes formed in the lower parts of basins with interior drainage. The largest of these desert salines were those of Peñol Blanco, 45 miles east of Zacatecas. Partially covered by water after infrequent showers, the desert lakes dry up completely during the winter months, leaving a layer of salt on the surface. Yearly, during the dry season, Indian and Negro laborers raked the salt into piles and hauled it to the surrounding mines. Other desert salines farther north were exploited for the mines of Parral, Matehuala, and Mazapil. Salt for the interior mines was obtained from salines in lagoons and marshes along the Pacific coast of Mexico and the north coast of Yucatan. As in pre-Conquest times, the salines of Yucatan also produced table salt, which was transported to many parts of New Spain. So important were both the desert and coastal salines in colonial economy that they were placed under royal control; authority for exploitation was farmed out by contract. In southern Mexico, salt was obtained from springs and wells which had long been worked by the Indians.

TRANSPORT AND TRADE

The European modes of transport that the Spaniards introduced into America during the early sixteenth century were as instrumental as the Old World types of settlement and economic enterprises in molding the landscape to its colonial form. Two new factors revolutionized land transport in the New World: the pack animal and the wheel. Pack trains of mules and donkeys and the Mediterranean two-wheeled cart gradually replaced or supplemented the native Indian carrier.

Although the colonial trails and roads in the main followed those already used by the Indian, the Spaniards opened many new routes to exploit the wealth of the land. Sea transport necessitated the establishment of new ports on both shores of Mexico and Central America and also encouraged the growth of a rudimentary shipbuilding industry as well as the exploitation of naval stores, especially in Central America.

The Indians of Mexico and Central America were slow to use the new transportation. For most of the colonial period, they continued to transport goods on their own backs with the aid of the tumpline and the *cacaxtli* ("carrying frame"). Until the beginning of the seventeenth century and despite laws to the contrary, Spanish merchants and encomenderos retained the pre-Conquest system of professional Indian carriers (*tamemes*), although in reduced form. Moreover, the Spaniards first used Negro and mulatto slaves, rather than Indians, to drive mule trains. And, as indicated above, excepting the native nobility, Indians were forbidden to ride horses and mules.

The lowly, stubborn donkey, or burro, used as a pack animal, was probably the first European mode of transport that the Indian adopted. The two-wheeled cart, usually pulled by a team of oxen, was an expensive piece of equipment, and useful only in relatively level areas. Thus, although they proved to be excellent cart makers, most Indians within the areas of high culture did not adopt

wheeled vehicles for their own use until late in the colonial period. Today, the burro is a symbol of transport among the poorer rural Indians and mestizos of Middle America, and the ox-drawn cart is still employed in out-of-the-way places in Mexico and in many parts of Central America. Even so, in some aboriginal areas, particularly the Guatemalan highlands, the human still carries the burdens of the poorer families that cannot afford a burro or pay freight charges on trucks and buses.

The Colonial Road Pattern

The rugged terrain of the Middle American mainland did not lend itself to a widespread system of easily traveled land routes. Fortunately for the Spaniards, however, the lines of least resistance within the areas of high aboriginal culture had been established for centuries by Indian traders and warriors. Spanish exploration, exploitation, settlement, and transport followed most of the aboriginal routes of communication. In a similar manner, many of the auto roads and some of the railway lines of modern Mexico and Central America parallel old colonial thoroughfares. The colonial roads retained much of the character of the aboriginal pathways. Except in some places where the Indian trails were widened or bridges built, the famous *caminos reales* ("main roads") were often nothing more than narrow foot or mule trails.

In Mexico, the general pattern of the colonial road system was relatively simple. Most of the trails extended outward from the Valley of Mexico or other parts of the Mesa Central (Figure 10.13). One set of roads led northward into the mining country over the easy gradients of the plateau. Another set consisted of the more difficult trails that passed from the Mesa Central, down the steep escarpments, and into the adjacent tropical lowlands and the southern highlands beyond; these roads followed Indian routes. One led northeastward into the Huasteca and Tampico; in the eighteenth century it was extended northward, along the inner low-

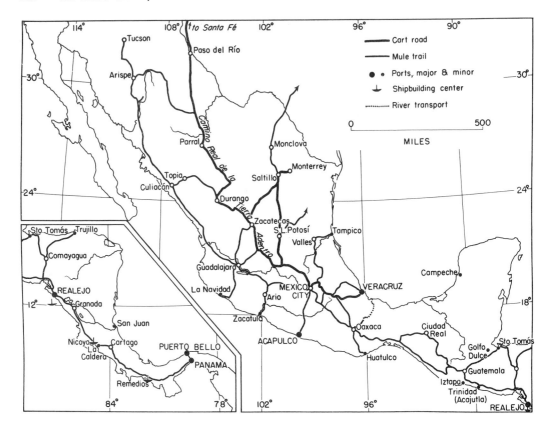

Figure 10.13
Colonial Transportation in Mexico and Central America.

lands basins, to Monterrey and Laredo. Eastward from the Valley of Mexico ran one of the most vital and heavily trafficked arteries of Mexico's colonial road system—the connecting link between Mexico City and the port of Veracruz. All of New Spain's legal trade with the mother country passed over this road.

In the colonial period, as now, there were two routes down the eastern escarpment. One skirted the northern slopes of the Volcán de Orizaba, following the old Aztec trail by way of Jalapa; the other passed south of the volcanic mass through Orizaba and Córdoba. So important was the latter route that, by the mid-seventeenth century, it was made suitable for cart travel despite the occasional steep grades on the escarpment.

Another significant road led southward from the Valley of Mexico into the upper Balsas Basin and continued to Oaxaca in the Mesa del Sur and thence to Chiapas and Guatemala. This was the main line of southward expansion of Aztec trade and conquest. It was the main route of trade and political contact between Mexico City, Oaxaca, and Guatemala during colonial days. And today it is the route of the Inter-American Highway.

Two other trails passed southward from the Mesa Central into the Balsas depression and thence to the Pacific coast. One of these joined Mexico City with the colonial port of Acapulco. In the latter part of the sixteenth century this road became the famous *El Camino Real*, along which oriental trade goods imported by the annual Manila galleon were packed into Mexico City and Veracruz for transshipment to Spain. The present Acapulco highway follows the same route. The other trail, called the "Ario Road," plunged over the escarpment south of Lake Pátzcuaro and continued to the old colonial port of Zacatula near the mouth of the Balsas River.

In addition, two roads descended the western escarpment of the plateau to the *tierra caliente*. From Guadalajara, one went southwest to Colima; the second descended the escarpment via the intermediate basins of Compostela and Tepic, and led thence to the coastal plain of Nayarit and northward, along the coastal lowlands, to Sonora. All of these escarpment trails were steep and rough. With the exception of the Mexico City-Veracruz road via Córdoba, they could be traveled only by mule train or by human carrier.

In contrast to the large number of escarpment trails, only two significant roads followed the easy gradients of the plateau surface from the Mesa Central into northern Mexico. One continued along the western edge of the plateau, through the great Silver Belt, from the Bajío of Guanajuato northward into Chihuahua and thence to the upper Rio Grande settlements in New Mexico. Over 1,500 miles long and heavily traveled, this road was one of the most significant of all Middle America. It was called the *Camino Real de la Tierra Adentro* ("the main road into the interior country") and, owing to its easy gradients, was the principal highway for cart traffic in New Spain. The other road into the north led through the dry basin and range country, along the western foothills of the Sierra Madre Oriental via San Luis Potosí, Saltillo, and Monclova, and into Texas as far as San Antonio. Again, modern railroads and paved highways pass near these old routes.

In colonial Central America, one main mule trail joined the various provinces of the Captaincy of Guatemala. This road, and its many alternates, led along the volcanic axis on the Pacific side of Central America, connecting the main towns and rural population centers from Chiapas in southern Mexico southeastward into Panama. Based on old Indian trade routes, this colonial road approximated the present Inter-American Highway.

A second set of trails in Central America formed the trans-isthmian routes connecting the Pacific and Caribbean shores. These also served as the main outlet for local products exported to Spain from the Caribbean ports. One led from Guatemala City, down the Motagua River depression, to the port of Santo Tomás, near present Puerto Barrios. Another crossed Honduras via the Comayagua Basin, from the Gulf of Fonseca on the Pacific side to the lower Ulúa River valley on the Caribbean. A third trail crossed through the Nicaragua lake depression and the San Juan River. The most important trans-isthmian highway was that between Panama City and Puerto Bello, near the site of the present canal, over which the products from Peru were packed by mule trains from the Pacific to the Atlantic side.

Transport Systems

With the rise of commercial agriculture and mining, freighting by pack train and carts became an important enterprise in colonial Mexico and Central America. The mule and donkey trains, called *recuas,* formed the most common type of commercial transport over the mountainous trails. Negroes and mixbloods were the original Middle American muleteers (*arrieros*), who packed the animals and drove them on their long and arduous journeys from production center to market or port.

The demand for animals for the transport business gave rise to the development of many mule-raising areas in various parts of Middle America. The pastures of Saltillo in northeastern Mexico supplied many of the northern freighters with mules; the highlands of Chiapas, especially the Comitán area, fur-

Figure 10.14

A Mule Train Entering the Old Mining Town of Sultepec, Southern Escarpment of the Mesa Central. In most parts of Mexico today *recuas* and *arrieros* such as these have been almost wholly supplanted by motor transport.

nished animals for the pack trains operating in southern Mexico and Guatemala; mention has already been made of the renowned savannas of Choluteca in southeastern Honduras, which supplied mules for the transisthmian transport of Panama. Today the pack train and the ancient institution of the muleteer persists in the back country of Mexico and Central America where modern auto roads and railways have not yet penetrated (Figure 10.14).

Until the middle of the sixteenth century, small two-wheeled carts (*carretas,* Figure 10.15) were the wheeled transportation in Middle America. These served for short local hauls in the basins of the Mesa Central. With the opening of the northern mining

Figure 10.15

The *Carreta,* or Two-Wheeled Spanish Cart.

districts of Mexico after 1550, the big two-wheeled cart (*carro*) was introduced. Pulled by 8 to 12 mules and equipped with iron-rimmed wooden wheels 5 to 6 feet in diameter, the *carro* hauled tons of heavy, bulky merchandise over the level surface of the northern plateau to and from the mines. Many miners became cart freighters, finding more profit in the exorbitant rates charged for hauling merchandise than in the extraction of silver. Moreover, the heavy, bulky *carro* was easily defended from the frequent attacks of Chichimec Indians along the northern roads. Caravans of 20 to 40 big carts, protected by royal cavalry, operated between the Mesa Central and the northern mines during the late sixteenth and seventeenth centuries. Many cart caravans were owned and operated by the Spanish Crown. In 1609, the Crown established a special caravan of big *carros* to supply the Franciscan missions in New Mexico. Six months were required to complete the 1,500-mile journey from Mexico City to Santa Fe over the *Camino Real de la Tierra Adentro*. During the last half of the eighteenth century, the pack train replaced the big carts in the northern mining areas mainly because Chichimec raids were no longer a severe problem. Today the *carro* has disappeared completely, and the small ox-drawn *carreta* is used only for short hauls and on isolated farms.

Sea Transport and Trade

On the Middle American mainland, colonial sea transport and trade consisted of local coastwise traffic and overseas commerce with Spain, the viceroyalty of Peru, and the Philippines. Spain prohibited her colonies from trading with foreign powers, but this law was often circumvented by smugglers.

The most extensive ocean transport and trade was, of course, with the mother country. French, English, and Dutch pirates operated in Atlantic and Caribbean waters, so that Spanish merchant vessels plying between Seville and the Middle American ports were required to sail in convoy escorted by men-of-war (see Chapter 3).

The greater part of the fleet for New Spain put in at Veracruz. Veracruz, protected by a group of coral and sandy reefs off her coast, was one of the largest and most strongly fortified ports of Spain's American colonies, and the official gateway into New Spain. The arrival of the annual fleet was the occasion for the big fair at Jalapa, on the cool eastern escarpment above the heat and filth of Veracruz.

Vessels occasionally broke from the convoy to call at the smaller Caribbean ports of Central America, such as Trujillo and Puerto Caballos in Honduras and Santo Tomás in Guatemala. Although insignificant in size and often occupied only when the ships arrived, these ports on the hot, sparsely inhabited Caribbean coast handled a large part of the trade of the Captaincy of Guatemala with Spain. The Central American sea transport has the same pattern today, since the large markets for its products lie on the Gulf of Mexico, the eastern seaboard of the United States, and in Europe.

The fleet destined for Panama was engaged chiefly in the Peruvian trade. Until the latter part of the sixteenth century, Nombre de Dios was the Caribbean port of the trans-isthmian route; thereafter, the terminus was transferred a few miles westward, to deeper water at Puerto Bello. Panama City,

the Pacific terminus, was changed to its present location after English pirates had destroyed the old town in 1671. On the annual arrival of the fleet from Spain, a large fair took place at Puerto Bello, and Peruvian merchants, who had come up with the Pacific fleet from Lima, purchased European goods. There, also, the silver bullion from the Peruvian mines, packed across the isthmus on mule train, was readied for transshipment to Spain.

During the latter half of the sixteenth century, a sizable trade was established between New Spain and Peru. Textiles, leather goods, woodwork, and luxury items of local manufacture were shipped to Peru from the colonial Mexican port of Huatulco, the Pacific terminus of the Oaxaca trail from Mexico City. Moreover, from the Central American Pacific ports of Trinidad (in the province of San Salvador) and Realejo (in Nicaragua), merchants shipped to Lima cacao for making chocolate and pine pitch for coating Peruvian wine jugs. In return, the merchants of Lima sent silver coins and bullion, mercury, and wine. Owing to the growing Manila trade and the increasing restrictions on inter-viceregal commerce, the Mexico-Peruvian trade finally ceased in the 1630's. Now nothing is left of the once-thriving port of Huatulco on the isolated Oaxaca coast of Mexico.

Local coastal trade along the Pacific coast of Central America, especially between Nicaragua and Panama, was important during much of the colonial period. In the early years of the sixteenth century, Indian slaves comprised the main cargo shipped from the Nicaraguan lowlands to Panama. Later, naval stores, cacao, and other foodstuffs left the ports of Realejo and Trinidad for Panama City, and wheat flour from Costa Rica was shipped from the small roadstead of La Caldera (near modern Puntarenas) to feed the Panamanian merchants.

The rise of the Philippine trade from Manila, during the final years of the sixteenth century, resulted in the development of the port of Acapulco on the southern coast of Mexico and in a flood of oriental goods into New Spain. The well-protected bay of Acapulco is the best natural harbor on the Pacific coast of Mexico. It is also the closest point on the Pacific coast to Mexico City. In colonial times, the chief disadvantage of the port was the extremely rugged terrain that separated it from the capital.

On the annual arrival of the galleons from Manila, a great fair was held in Acapulco, and merchants from all New Spain gathered to bargain for the rich oriental silks and brocades, jewelry, woodwork, and other luxuries from the Philippines and China. Many Chinese merchants came to Acapulco to live, and Chinese and Filipino slaves were imported into Mexico during the colonial period to work in mines and woolen factories. These immigrants probably added to the racial mixture of Mexico. It is thought that some elements of oriental culture, such as the palm rain cape so common in western Mexico, some types of stills for distilling hard liquors, methods of wet rice cultivation, and possibly the machete, may have been introduced into New Spain through the Manila trade. With the decline of Philippine commerce at the close of the colonial period, Acapulco degenerated into an isolated fishing village. It has never regained its former significance as a port, but has become one of the world's leading resorts.

Most of the colonial ports of Middle America had large fortifications, constructed to resist the pirate raids that were common on both coasts for nearly 200 years. The famous fortress of San Juan de Ulúa, constructed on one of the reefs off Veracruz, is typical of the military aspect of the colonial ports. Today such structures are poignant reminders of a turbulent past, adding to the colonial flavor of the old port towns.

Shipbuilding. Shipbuilding developed on the Middle American mainland as an industry subsidiary to sea transport. Most of the vessels used on the Atlantic voyages were made in northern Spain, but those that sailed on the Pacific side of Middle America were constructed locally. The principal shipyards were located on the Pacific coast of Central America, where tropical semideciduous forests supplied abundant timbers for construction. The fine-grained guayacan (Tabebuia) was the best of the tropical woods for ship construction. Durable, yet easily sawed and hewn, it was also resistant to the borings of the shipworm (Teredo) which infested the warm waters of Caribbean and Pacific shores of Middle America and often raised havoc with wooden ships.

The main shipyards were at Realejo, in Nicaragua, and Remedios, in the Veraguas area of southwestern Panama (Figure 10.13). From these two yards came most of the ships used in the Peruvian fleets and in local coastwise trade. Hundreds of Negro and mulatto sawyers were imported to cut timber in the Veraguas area. The strong Negroid element in the present-day mixbloods of western interior Panama may well stem from the African sawyers of colonial days.

Closely associated with shipbuilding in Central America was the gathering of naval stores in the highland pine forests of Honduras and Nicaragua. Pine pitch was needed in great quantities to caulk newly constructed ships and to repair old ones. Tons of pitch were shipped to Peru, not only for ship stores, but also, as mentioned earlier, for coating wine jugs to prevent leakage. Other ship stores supplied by Indians of Nicaragua and San Salvador included cordage of agave fiber for ropes and coarse cottons for sailcloth. In time, much of the colonial economic activity of the Central American Pacific coast centered around sea transport.

THE COLONIAL LANDSCAPE: CARIBBEAN COAST OF CENTRAL AMERICA

The hot, rainy Caribbean shore between northern Yucatan and eastern Panama held few attractions for Spanish settlers during the colonial period. As we have seen, in Central America the Spaniards kept to the highlands and the Pacific coast. On the Caribbean side the rocky northern shore of Honduras, adjacent to the mineral-rich interior; the small cacao-growing area of Matina in Costa Rica; and the Atlantic terminus of the Panamanian isthmus route at Puerto Bello were the only sections that the Spaniards more or less permanently occupied. The rest of the coast, low-lying and reef-strewn, was left to native forest Indians or to foreign interlopers such as the English pirates, smugglers, and woodcutters.

During the mid-seventeenth century, the English obtained a substantial footing in at least three sections of the Central American mainland and off-shore islands. One section included the various islands off coast, such as San Andrés, Providencia, the Bay Islands, Corn Islands, and others, which served initially as bases for pirates and smugglers operating in the western Caribbean. These islands also functioned as springboards for the English occupation of two coastal areas: (1) the portion of the east coast of the Yucatan Peninsula that lies within the Bay of Honduras; and (2) the Miskito (Mosquito) Shore of Nicaragua and Honduras, from the San Juan River to near Trujillo (Figure 10.16). The offshore waters of each of these coastal areas are shoal and strewn with coral reefs and cays. Moreover, the coastline is frayed with hundreds of small mangrove-bordered tidal inlets. Such conditions made for difficult navigation, but afforded ideal hideouts for pirates and smugglers. To this day, the influence of British occupation is seen within each of these areas —in the prevalence of English speech, in English place names, in the Anglican church, and in other Anglo-Saxon cultural carry-overs. The present colony of British Honduras traces its origin to seventeenth- and eighteenth-century English settlement along its coast. Such activity might be considered a western extension of England's political and economic interests from its holdings in the eastern Caribbean.

As early as the 1630's, English smugglers from Providence Island had established trade relations with the Miskito Indians and the sambos, or mixed Negro-Indians, on the Caribbean coast of Nicaragua. The sambos served as intermediaries in the profitable smuggling operations between the English and the Spanish colonials who were avid for cheap North European goods. Excellent fighters and superb boatmen, the Miskito Indians served on English raiding parties along the Spanish Main. About the same time, smuggling stations, called "stanns," were established along the western shore of the Bay of Honduras in an area called the "Cockscomb Coast," later to become British Honduras. The sites of the modern towns of Belize and Stann Creek were once occupied by such stations.

With the decline of piracy in the late seventeenth century, many of the English privateers and traders turned to the exploitation of logwood and mahogany which abounded near the coast and inland along the river courses of the Miskito and Cockscomb shores. The heartwood of the logwood tree was a source of fast red and brown dyes and the most valuable product of the English-held coast of Central America. The main stands of logwood occurred along the shores of eastern Yucatan, exploited as far north as Cape Catoche, the northeastern extremity of the peninsula. The English log cutters and smugglers of this area soon came to be known as the "Baymen." In the last quarter of the seventeenth century, the Baymen also established cutting areas in Campeche on the west coast of Yucatan. There the main areas exploited were the forests fringing the Laguna de Términos and the banks of the Champotón River, where Spaniards had previously cut logwood. Owing to Spanish hostility and depletion of the logwood stands, the English had quit Campeche by 1730 and returned to the Belize area.

Although periodically harassed by small

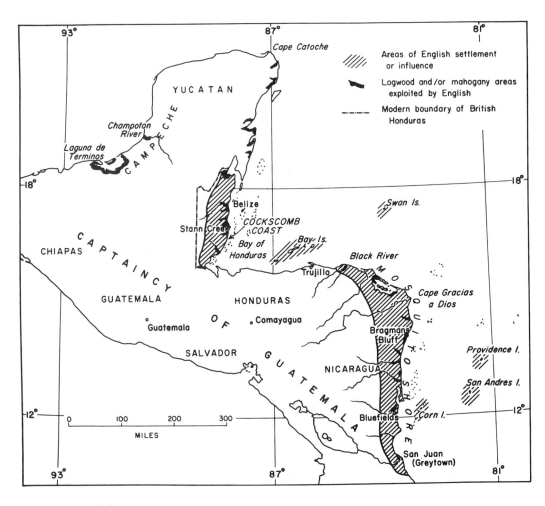

Figure 10.16

The English on the Caribbean Coast of Central America and Mexico: Seventeenth and Eighteenth Centuries.

Spanish forces bent on ousting the British from the Gulf of Honduras, the Baymen of Belize, aided by their Negro slaves and Miskito Indian friends from Nicaragua, were able to establish a permanent hold along the Cockscomb Coast. When the supply of logwood was depleted, mahogany, which was fashionable in eighteenth-century Europe, became the main export from the Belize area. Finally, in 1864, the settlements of British Honduras were officially made a crown colony of the Empire.

Along the Miskito Shore during the late seventeenth and early eighteenth centuries, English trading "stanns" had been made at Bluefields, Cape Gracias a Dios, Bragman's Bluff (modern Puerto Cabezas), and along

the Black River (Río Negro) in present Honduran territory. There was little logwood along this coast but, within the riverine forests that penetrate the interior savannas, mahogany was cut and sarsaparilla root gathered to be shipped to England. By mid-eighteenth century, a small agricultural colony had been started along Black River where, in 1761, nearly 200 Englishmen and 700 Negro slaves were cultivating sugar cane and tobacco. By treaty with Spain, the British government withdrew the white settlers from the Miskito Shore in 1778. But later the area was organized as the native Kingdom of Mosquitía, with its traditional capital at San Juan del Norte (Greytown). This kingdom was a virtual British protectorate until 1856, and was not abolished until 1894, when it finally came under Nicaraguan authority. The long and cordial contact with Englishmen is still evident among the remaining Miskito Indians and the sambos, most of who speak pidgin English and have a high regard for anyone of Anglo-Saxon descent.

The close of the eighteenth century saw another foreign cultural invasion on the Caribbean coast of Central America. In 1797, the British transferred some 5,000 troublesome Black Caribs (mixed Negro and Carib Indian) from the Lesser Antilles to the Bay Islands off Honduras. From there, these Carib-speaking mixbloods spread along the Honduran and Belize coasts from Trujillo to Stann Creek, where today their descendants live as subsistence farmers and fishers.

SELECTED REFERENCES

Bargalló, M., *La minería y la metalurgía en la América española durante la época colonial.* Mexico, D.F.: Fondo de Cultura Económica, 1955.

Bishko, C. J., "The Peninsular Background of Latin American Cattle Ranching," *Hispanic American Historical Review,* XXXII, No. 4 (1952), 491–515.

Borah, W., *Early Colonial Trade and Navigation between Mexico and Peru,* Ibero-Americana, No. 38. Berkeley, Calif.: University of California Press, 1954.

———, *Silk Raising in Colonial Mexico,* Ibero-Americana, No. 20. Berkeley, Calif.: University of California Press, 1943.

Brand, D. D., "The Early History of the Range Cattle Industry in Northern Mexico," *Agricultural History,* XXXV, No. 3 (1961), 132–39.

Chevalier, François, *Land and Society in Colonial Mexico: The Great Hacienda.* Berkeley, Calif.: University of California Press, 1963.

Dahlgren de Jordan, B., ed., *La Grana Cochinilla.* Mexico, D.F.: José Porrúa e Hijos, 1963.

Gibson, C., *The Aztecs Under Spanish Rule.* Stanford, Calif.: Stanford University Press, 1964.

Humboldt, A. de, *Essai Politique sur le Royaume de la Nouvelle Espagne.* Paris: F. Schoell, 1811. (Trans. by John Black, *Political Essay on the Kingdom of New Spain.* London: Longman, Hurst, Rees, Orme, and Brown, 1811–1822.)

Parsons, J. J., "San Andrés and Providencia; English-speaking Islands in the Western Caribbean," *University of California Publications in Geography,* XII, No. 1 (1956), 1–84.

Sandoval, F. B., *La industria del azúcar en Nueva España.* Mexico, D.F.: Instituto de la Historia, 1951.

Simpson, L. B., *The Encomienda in New Spain* (rev. ed.). Berkeley, Calif.: University of California Press, 1950.

———, *Exploitation of Land in Central Mexico in the Sixteenth Century,* Ibero-Americana, No. 36. Berkeley, Calif.: University of California Press, 1952.

Smith, R. S., "Indigo Production and Trade in Colonial Guatemala," *Hispanic American Historical Review,* XXXIX, No. 2 (1959), 181–211.

West, R. C., *The Mining Community in Northern New Spain: The Parral Mining District,* Ibero-Americana, No. 30. Berkeley, Calif.: University of California Press, 1949.

———, "The Mining Economy of Honduras during the Colonial Period," *Actas del XXXIII Congreso Internacional de Americanistas,* San José, Costa Rica, I (1959), 767–77.

11

The People and Economy of Modern Mexico

The foundations of Mexico's present geographical personality lie deep in its Indian and colonial past. True, the last 100 years, and especially the last 30, have brought great changes. Paved highways, diesel-powered trains, mechanized farms, modern cities, industrial suburbs, and rich oil fields impress the traveler. But never far away from such patches of modern Western life are the fields and villages that evoke the colonial period of which they are still a part. The varied cultural landscape of present-day Mexico is an Indian and colonial Spanish one on which has been superimposed an uneven veneer of modern European and North American materialism. Mexico, like so many other underdeveloped countries, is in a state of cultural transition which is reflected in the geographical scene.

Our purpose in this chapter is to describe and explain the more significant changes that have occurred in the Mexican landscape during the last 100 years. Many factors underlie these changes, but these are outstanding: (1) the Mexican Revolution of 1910 and the breakup of the large landed estates; (2) the postrevolutionary explosive increase in population which, in a country with a paucity of arable land, has resulted in serious food shortages; and (3) the geographical proximity of the United States and the concomitant ease of cultural borrowing and availability of technical knowledge and financial aid.

HISTORICAL SUMMARY OF THE POST-INDEPENDENCE PERIOD

Mexico's history since the close of the colonial era has been characterized by two periods of political turmoil, each followed by a phase of relative quiescence. In periods of political upheaval, the economy stagnated; with stability, it expanded, economic and social changes were effected, and the geographical landscape was transformed.

Beginning with the Wars of Independence (1810–1821), Mexico suffered nearly 70 years of intermittent political and military strife. Periodic civil wars, the Texan War (1836), war with the United States (1845–1847), and the French Intervention (1862–1867) made a shambles of economic and social progress. Although a scheme of land reform was devised by the patriot Benito Juárez in 1857, it could not be effected, and little change occurred in the colonial pattern which still dominated the economy and the landscape.

The dictatorship of Porfirio Díaz (1877–1910) gave Mexico a semblance of stability for the first time since the days of the Spanish viceroys. These 34 years of peace (often called the *Pax Porfiriana*) saw the beginning of the North American and European technological importations that have so greatly influenced present-day Mexico. The Díaz regime welcomed foreign investment and technology—

to build the country's railroad network; to revive the declining mines with modern techniques and management; to exploit the large petroleum reserves; and to begin modern manufacturing. At this time, Mexico established the close commercial ties with the United States with which it still maintains the bulk of its foreign trade. In addition, the government encouraged the cultivation of new commercial crops, such as coffee in Veracruz and Chiapas, and sisal (henequen) in Yucatan. In other respects, the colonial economic and social patterns of Mexico continued, and even expanded, during the *Pax Porfiriana*. The large estates became larger, although the influence of the Church declined. Most of the remaining Indian communal lands were usurped by the rich *hacendados*; Díaz gave away to foreigners and personal friends much of the public domain; and the poverty-ridden rural class became even more deeply enmeshed in the debt peonage system of colonial times.

The despotism of the Díaz regime and the problem of land distribution underlay the Revolution which erupted toward the close of 1910. Until the late 1920's rival armies and bandit groups, led by political aspirants from the Hispanic north and by rebelling native caciques in the Indian south, periodically ravaged the country. Mexican economy slowed to a halt and the population was reduced by warfare, starvation, and emigration. But out of this chaos came a social and economic revolution that is still in progress. The most fundamental change was the *ejido* system, the beginning of land reform—dissolution of the large estates and the reapportionment of the land in collectivized units or in small parcels among the poor rural population. The Revolutionary government also recognized the labor unions which were trying to better the wages, working conditions, and social security of the urban proletariat. A framework of public education was established. The concept of gradual nationalization

of the country's basic industries became a political tenet. The semisocialistic state that is present-day Mexico grew out of the Revolution of 1910.

From 1930 until the present, Mexico has enjoyed an unprecedented period of peace and stable national development, a period of rapid economic and social change as well as of fantastic population growth. The tempo —of land reform, urbanization, industrialization, highway development, and colonization of new lands—has steadily increased.

All of these factors have operated to change the face of many parts of the country. Perhaps the greatest change of landscape has taken place: (1) in the arid north, where agricultural production has been greatly expanded through large-scale government-constructed irrigation projects and through mechanization; (2) in various parts of the tropical lowlands, where the government has recently opened large areas to colonization through drainage, irrigation, and road-construction projects; and (3) in various urban centers throughout the country, where large industrial suburbs have mushroomed. Poverty is still the country's most pressing problem, however, especially in the heavily populated heartland of Mexico—the Mesa Central and the southern highlands. One-half of Mexico's 34.5 million people live on a bare subsistence level, ill-fed, ill-housed, and ill-clothed, and 40 per cent of the population is still illiterate, despite a vigorous educational program of 25 years standing.

The Mexican People

Since the close of the colonial period, changes of varying degree have occurred in the number, distribution, movements, and ethnic composition of the Mexican people. The population patterns of the eighteenth century continued little altered for almost one hundred years after Independence while Mexico awaited the twentieth century.

NUMBERS AND DENSITY
OF PEOPLE

One of the important developments in modern Mexico is the recent growth of population. Figure 11.1 shows that at the time of Independence (1821), Mexico's population was only 6.5 million, much less than before Conquest. When the Revolution began (1910), the population had increased to 15 million. Today, only a half-century later, the number has again more than doubled, to 34.5 million (1960 census). Like other countries of Middle America, Mexico's population is growing about 3 per cent annually. This is one of the fastest rates of human growth of any area on earth. It means an increase in the Mexican population of more than one million people in every year of the decade 1960–1970. At the present rate of increase, Mexico will have more than 60 million inhabitants by 1975 and 85 million by the year 2000.

This great increase began in the 1930's and reached its present rate just after World War II. This is the period during which the populations of practically all underdeveloped countries "exploded" to the point of serious shortages of food supply and living space. The reason for the rapid growth in Mexico

has not been increased fertility, for the Mexican birth rate has always been high, but rather a drastic decrease in the death rate, especially of infants, through the introduction of preventive medicine and sanitation. Moreover, the former killers in the tropics, yellow fever and malaria, can now be controlled with DDT sprays.

Despite the population boom of the last three decades, Mexico's over-all density is only 45 persons per square mile (the population density of the United States is 52). Over-all density figures are misleading, however. The ratio of people to arable land yields a more realistic picture of food supply. Mexico has a density of 450 persons per square mile of arable land; the United States, 250. Figure 11.2 indicates that almost one-half of the Mexican people are concentrated in the central part of the country, as they were during the colonial period.

In the Mesa Central and adjacent escarpments, densities of rural population, by states, range from 75 to well over 200 persons per square mile. In some sections of the plateau surface once favored by exceptionally fertile soils and plentiful water for irrigation, rural population densities exceed 500 and even 1,000 persons per square mile, equalling some of the maximum farming area densities

Figure 11.1
Population Growth in Mexico : 1790–1960.

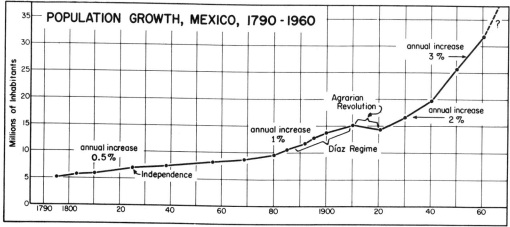

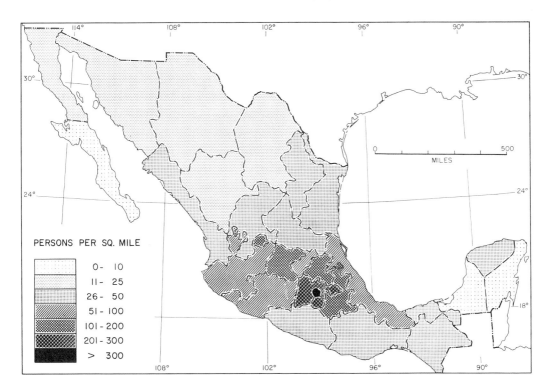

Figure 11.2
Population Density of Mexico : 1960.

in Southeast Asia. Such is the area in Tlax-cala state, around the northwestern base of Malinche Volcano and extending into the Cholula-Huejotzingo plain on the western edge of Puebla Basin. Similar densities occur in the southern part of the Valley of Mexico, within the ancient chinampa farming area around Xochimilco and in Toluca Basin near the headwaters of the Lerma River (Figure 11.3). The concentration of people around the basin rims within the Mesa Central is an expression of an old population pattern that goes back to colonial and even pre-Conquest times. Today, overpopulation and rural pov-erty in the Mesa Central, the traditional core of the country, are the roots of Mexico's greatest economic and social problems.

In contrast to the densely occupied Mesa Central, the rugged southern part of the country (states of Guerrero, Oaxaca, Chi-apas) have only moderate over-all popula-tion densities (about 45 persons per square mile). Within the mountainous terrain, peo-ple are unevenly distributed, many large areas being almost uninhabited, whereas in the highland valleys, such as that of Oaxaca, densities may be over 100 persons per square mile. Except for its well-settled northern part, the forest-covered Yucatan Peninsula and the adjacent Petén of northern Guate-mala form one of the empty areas (*despoblados*) of Middle America which have densities ranging from less than· three to only eight persons per square mile.

As in colonial and pre-Conquest times, dry northern Mexico is distinguished from the rest of the country by its sparse popula-tion. Average densities of less than 20 persons per square mile characterize most of the dry northwest, and there are only 2 per square mile in the arid territory of Baja California. In the last three decades, however, the

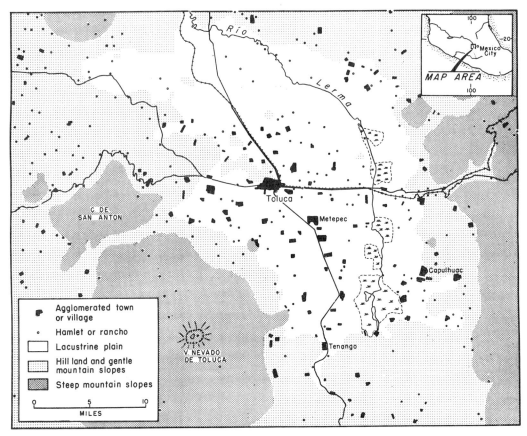

Figure 11.3

The Settlement Pattern of the Valley of Toluca, Mesa Central. Rural population densities between Toluca City and Tenango range from 500 to more than 1,000 persons per square mile.

opening of irrigation districts and increasing industrialization have drawn many people from the Mesa Central into the north. Overall population densities of over 40 persons per square mile now occur in the northeastern states of Nuevo León and Tamaulipas and densities as high as 100 are not uncommon in the recently established oases, such as the Laguna District in southern Coahuila and the irrigated river deltas of the Sonora and Sinaloa coastal lowlands.

Population Movements

Since the Revolution of 1910, there has been a great increase in the mobility of the Mexican people. The breakup of the hacienda system, which bound a larger part of the rural population to the estate as indentured laborers, enabled people to move about more freely. Growing industrialization and improved transport have also increased the mobility of the population. But more important, the great population pressure that has developed in the Mesa Central since the 1920's has induced movements of rural folk to: (1) the less densely settled farming areas and petroleum fields within the country; (2) the cities, especially to the capital; and (3) the United States, as either seasonal or permanent immigrants.

Although significant numbers of poor farmers from the Mesa Central have migrated to the northern irrigated districts and the tropical coastal areas, these movements have not appreciably decreased the population pressure within the core areas. Even many of the northern oases are now over-populated, and new irrigation districts are not being opened rapidly enough to absorb the growing local population. In the north-east, the opening of oil and gas fields in Tamaulipas, the exploitation of coal deposits in the Sabinas Basin (Coahuila), and the increasing industrialization of Nuevo León and Coahuila have attracted many migrants from central Mexico. Moreover, within the last decade, government-sponsored coloniza-tion of the tropical lowlands has drawn some highlanders to the Tepalcatepec Basin in southern Michoacán, the lowlands of Nayarit, and the Papaloapan Valley in south-ern Veracruz. Even in the Tabasco lowland, once a sparsely occupied, disease-ridden land, growing petroleum production and agricul-tural developments are now attracting popu-lation.

The most significant movement of Mexi-can population in recent years has been from the rural areas to the cities. Most of these migrants have poured into Mexico City and its extended metropolitan area. In 1900, the Federal District, which includes most of the capital's metropolitan area, contained but 4 per cent of the Mexican people; in 1960, with close to five million people, it had nearly 15 per cent. The next largest cities in Mexico (Guadalajara, 734,000 population; Monterrey, 600,000; Ciudad Juárez, 294,-000; and Puebla, 285,000) fall far below the size of the Mexico City megalopolis. This type of disproportionately large metro-politan area which is the political, economic, and social center of the country, is one of the most characteristic features of Latin Amer-ican urbanization.

The primacy of Mexico City goes back to the centralized government of colonial times and to the social prestige of its capital seat, but its position has since been strengthened by industrialization and by the recent influx

of poor rural folk. These people flock into the city in such numbers that they have created serious housing and sanitation prob-lems, as well as unemployment. The ram-shackle slums around the edges of Mexico City are adequate testimony of this growing urban problem that stems from the pressure of the rural population within the Mesa Central.

About 35 per cent of Mexico's people now live in cities and towns of over 5,000 population. This is approximately the urban population, for most localities of less than 5,000 people are agricultural villages with few commercial or other urban functions.[1] Mexico now has 40 cities of over 50,000 people and 17 with over 100,000 (Figure 11.4). Nearly half these urban centers are clustered in the Mesa Central, but large cities have grown up in the north within the past 30 years. These include industrial cen-ters such as Monterrey (600,000); the bor-der cities, fed by tourist traffic, such as Tijuana (150,000), Ciudad Juárez (294,-000), and Nuevo Laredo (93,000); and market and supply centers for the large irrigation districts, such as Torreón (180,-000), Mexicali (172,000), and Hermosillo (95,000).

Except in the Federal District, the popula-tion of the northern border states of Mexico is more urban than any other part of the country, for nearly half the people there live in towns of over 20,000. In contrast, outside Mexico City and its environs, the population of the Mesa Central is still mainly rural, despite the presence of many cities. The Indian south, with few cities, is even more rural.

The pressure of population in central Mexico has not only set up currents of mi-

---

[1] The Mexican census bureau (*Dirección Gen-eral de Estadística*), like that of the United States, considers places of over 2,500 people as urban. In Mexico, however, this is an unrealistic definition, because so many of the farming villages are large. Most students of Mexican demography use 5,000, or even 10,000, as the population which distin-guishes urban from rural settlements.

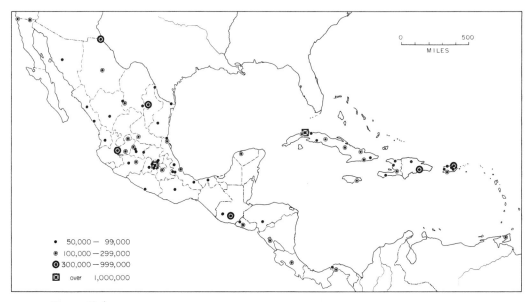

Figure 11.4
Urban Centers in Middle America : 1960.

gration within the country, but also has induced emigration to the United States. At present, nearly one million Mexican citizens reside across the border, and each year 250,000 more apply for resident visas, only a fraction of which are granted. The disturbed political conditions during the Revolutionary period and the present economic depression in many rural areas have been the main reasons for the outward flow of Mexicans. The permanent Mexican migrants to the United States have gone to the cities (especially to Los Angeles, where more than a half-million now live), and to many rural areas of the Southwest. Mexican nationals and United States citizens of Mexican descent now comprise the bulk of the permanent farming population of extreme southern Texas, between the international border and San Antonio.

Another type of Mexican migrant to the United States is the seasonal farm hand, or bracero, who is legally contracted as a worker on United States farms and plantations during the harvest period. Seasonal labor migrations from Mexico to the United States started on an unofficial basis after 1910, but this was followed by the controlled, contract labor, based on international agreement, which began on a large scale during World War II when the United States was short of farm workers. During the period 1951–1960, each spring between 200,000 and 450,000 braceros were legally contracted for, to work on the irrigated truck farms and orchards of the southwest and the Pacific coast, in the beet fields of Colorado and Michigan, in the cotton farms of Texas, and in other agricultural areas. Until recently, many thousands of Mexicans (called *wet-backs*) crossed the border illegally to find seasonal work. Most of the braceros and wetbacks came from the overpopulated Mesa Central, especially from the states of Michoacán, Jalisco, and Guanajuato, but many also came from the northern states of Chihuahua and Durango, the irrigated sections of which are now overpopulated. In many remote rural sections of central Mexico, there is hardly a village where one cannot find one or two men who have worked in the United States. Since 1960, the number of braceros coming to the United States has declined, and in 1964 the international agreement to continue the labor contracts was not renewed.

The dollars that the braceros sent home to their families were an important source of income and foreign exchange for Mexico. Equally significant was the knowledge of North American agricultural techniques and of modern Western ways that the Mexican worker took back to his country. The acculturating influence of the bracero is difficult to measure, but it has undoubtedly aided bits of North American culture to penetrate even the remotest villages of central Mexico.

RACE AND LANGUAGE

Since the close of the colonial period, the mixbloods, or mestizos, have gradually become the dominant racial element in Mexico. At present the population is estimated to be about 60 per cent mestizo, 30 per cent Indian, and 10 per cent white. More than half the Mexicans were pureblooded Indians in 1810, but the gradual breakdown of the aboriginal community by improved communication and interracial marriage, has been accelerating their decrease. By the end of this century the proportion may be greatly reduced from its present 30 per cent. For more than a century, the white element of Mexico has remained a nearly constant 10 per cent of the total population, whereas the Negro blood has been almost wholly absorbed into the mestizo majority.

Mexico's Indians

In Mexico, as in most parts of Latin America where advanced aboriginal culture prevailed before Conquest, the remnant Indian population presents a serious social and economic problem. Owing chiefly to the social stigma that the Spaniards and their descendents have attached to Indian life, but

also to the reticent nature of the aboriginals themselves, the Mexican Indians are usually at the bottom of the economic scale and have the lowest living standards in the country. Since the Revolution of 1910, however, the Mexican government has attempted to improve the lot of the Indian through land reform, special educational programs, and health measures.

It should be emphasized that, in most parts of Latin America, an Indian is defined much more in cultural terms than in racial terms. In Mexico, a person is considered to be Indian if he speaks an aboriginal language (though he may also speak Spanish), if he practices more aboriginal than European customs and uses more Indian than European tools, and if he thinks of himself as an Indian living within a recognized aboriginal community apart from his mestizo or white neighbors. Thus, a mixblood who conforms to these norms is considered an Indian, while pureblood aboriginals who no longer speak their language and have adopted predominately European ways are considered to be mestizos. Since many of the culture traits are hard to measure, government officials have usually taken language as the main criterion for determining the Indian population of Mexico.

In Mexico today, a total of 46 different native languages are spoken by nearly 2.5 million people (only 7 per cent of the entire population), and two-thirds of these also speak Spanish. From 1900 to 1940, Indian-language speakers comprised about 15 per cent of the population, but in the years following, this proportion decreased drastically, mainly because the non-Indians are increasing at a far greater rate than the aboriginals. Moreover, as the Indians come into closer contact with modern Mexican culture, they are slowly discarding their native tongues. The decrease in the number of monolinguals (Indians who speak no Spanish), from 1.2 million, in 1930, to less than 0.8 million, in 1950, has prompted some students of Mexican population to predict that the monolingual Indian will have disappeared by the year 2000.

Of the large number of aboriginal tongues still spoken in Mexico, only ten are used by groups of more than 50,000. Nahuatl, or Mexicano, the language of the Aztecs, is spoken by about 600,000 people scattered in fragmented groups in the east-central part of the country. Maya is spoken by 300,000 people in Yucatan. Zapotec (200,000) and Mixtec (185,000) are the main languages of the Indians of Oaxaca state. Otomí (185,000) is heard in the eastern section of the Mesa Central, north and northwest of Mexico City and Totonac (100,000) in northern Veracruz and Puebla states.

Figure 11.5, which shows areas of high concentration of aboriginal speech, also indicates the predominately Indian areas of Mexico and Central America. Almost the entire present Indian population is concentrated within the bounds of ancient Mesoamerica, the most populous part of Middle America before Conquest. In Mexico and Guatemala, the present distribution of predominantly Indian speech corresponds with the ancient Aztec and Mayan areas.

Today there are four outstanding Indian areas in Mexico: (1) the eastern Mesa Central and adjacent escarpments in which reside the fragmented aboriginal groups; (2) the rugged Sierra Madre and Mesa del Sur of Oaxaca and eastern Guerrero; (3) the Chiapas highlands of southeastern Mexico, which can be considered a western appendage of the Guatemalan highland Indian area; and (4) the northern Yucatan Peninsula, where Maya speech is concentrated. Within these areas live over 95 per cent of Mexico's Indians. The only significant groups outside these areas are the Tarascans of Michoacán, the small Cora and Huichol groups of Nayarit, and the Tarahumar Indians in the Sierra Madre Occidental of Chihuahua.

Except for the Maya of Yucatan, most of the Mexican Indians occupy isolated mountainous areas where modern transport is poorly developed or nonexistent and which

Figure 11.5
Areas of Indian Speech Concentration in Mexico and Northern Central America.

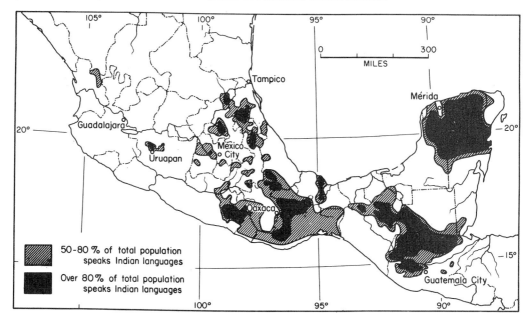

have an extremely limited agricultural potential. The Yucatan Peninsula, although a plains area, is covered by poor, thin soils, and until quite recently was an isolated cultural island only loosely attached politically to Mexican territory. In the more accessible and fertile areas of Mexico, the Spaniards and mestizos pushed out or assimilated the Indians. Thus, most of Mexico's aborigines now occupy refuge areas that are usually characterized by isolation, poverty, and high death rates. Difficulty of communication encourages the retention of old ways and discourages the entry of new ideas from outside.

The recent aim of the Mexican government has been to acculturate the remaining Indians sufficiently to incorporate them into the national life. The National Indian Institute (*Instituto Nacional Indigenista*), created in 1948, has established various educational centers in key Indian areas. Schools, roads, hospitals, and economic aid will in time destroy the remaining vestiges of ancient life. But, until that is accomplished, the Indian areas, with their steep, hillside fields, their scattered *ranchería* settlements, and their picturesque markets and wares, will remain an integral part of the Mexican landscape.

Mexico's White Population

The comparatively small white group, less than 10 per cent of the population, descends from Spanish colonial families and from European or North American immigrants who entered the country within the last century. As in colonial times, most of the whites live in the cities, forming the core of the remaining aristocracy and of the urban professional groups.

Mexico has received few white immigrants since the close of the colonial period, for political, economic, and social conditions within the country have not been favorable. During the nineteenth century, a few Europeans and North Americans came to cen-

tral Mexico to form agricultural colonies, but most of these were unsuccessful. More successful were various religious groups, such as the Mennonites, who formed farming colonies in sparsely settled areas of the North (see Chapter 12).

Besides these few agricultural colonists, there have been some individual Europeans, especially Germans and Spaniards, who have entered Mexican city life as merchants, professionals, and intellectuals, contributing a cultural influence out of proportion to their small numbers. Particularly significant to modern Mexican arts and letters was the influx of refugees from the Spanish Civil War (1936–1938), among whom were outstanding Castilian and Catalonian professors, artists, and writers. Most of the individual European immigrants have settled in Mexico City, but some found their way to the smaller towns, such as Puebla, Guadalajara, and Morelia.

Mexico's Economy in the Nineteenth and Twentieth Centuries

As we saw (in Chapter 10), the basic patterns of Mexico's present economy were formed in colonial days. Despite the recent industrialization and the surge of urbanization, Mexico is still a land of farmers (60 per cent of the population), most of whom eke out a bare subsistence by growing maize and beans on worn-out soils with tools not much improved over those of the eighteenth century.

Since the Díaz regime, commercial agriculture has developed at an increasing tempo. Irrigated cotton and tropical crops such as coffee and sugar are grown on some of the best lands. Stock raising is carried on in much the same way and in the same areas as in colonial times, but the livestock market has shifted from the mining centers to the United States. Mining, so important during the colonial period, is still basic to the economy. Mexico is still the world's lead-ing producer of silver, but the old mines are now yielding more lead and zinc than pre-cious metals. Moreover, interest in mineral exploitation has shifted to the vast petrole-um, natural gas, and sulphur reserves of the Gulf Coast lowlands.

Some of the greatest changes in Mexico's economy have come within the last 30 years, with the rise of large-scale industry and tourism. In the future, increasing industri-alization may reorient the entire economic structure of the country. The tourist trade, Mexico's newest addition to its economy, has been partly responsible for various land-scape changes, including a large network of paved highways and resort centers.

THE AGRICULTURAL ECONOMY

Although farming is its basic eco-nomic activity, Mexico is poorly endowed with arable land. Two-thirds of the country is mountainous, and one-half is too arid to produce crops without irrigation. Today a meager 10 per cent of Mexican territory is cropland. Moreover, in any given year only 5 per cent of the total land surface is cul-tivated, and only a bit more than 3 per cent actually yields crops. Optimists state that, by expanding irrigated areas in the north and

developing the tropical lowlands, 15 per cent of the total land surface can be made theo-retically arable. About three-fourths of the cultivated land is dry-farmed (*de temporal,* or dependent on seasonal rains); a twentieth is considered to be sufficiently moist (*de humedad*) to produce crops even in the dry season, and a fifth is irrigated (*de riego*).

As indicated in Figures 11.6 and 11.7, the larger part of the cultivated land is concen-trated in the country's heartland, or the Mesa Central, where the fertile soils of the volcanic basins and the usually sufficient summer rains afford an adequate physical basis for growing the traditional Mexican food crops. As one might expect, Figure 11.6 almost duplicates the patterns shown on the map of population densities (Figure 11.2). Within the states that comprise the Mesa Central, an average of 10 to 25 per cent of the total land surface is cultivated; in the small state of Tlaxcala, more than 40 per cent of the surface is tilled. In most parts of the densely peopled heart-land, almost all the arable land has been farmed for hundreds of years. However, since the colonial period, overcropping and the unwise use of the plow have caused depletion and erosion of the soil. Over wide areas of once fertile soils derived from the weathering of volcanic ash, sheet erosion has exposed underlying layers of limey hardpan, called *tepetate,* which renders the land useless for

Figure 11.6

Percentage of Total Area Planted, Cultivated, and Fallow: 1950.

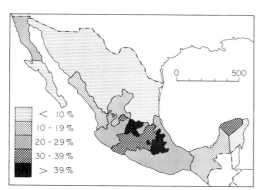

Figure 11.7

Percentage of Total Area Under Active Cultivation, Excluding Fallow Land: 1950

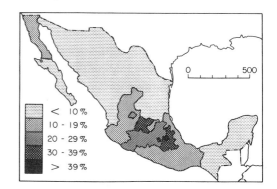

Figure 11.8

Serious Gulley Erosion Near Nochistan, Oaxaca Highlands. Plow cultivation on slopes has induced the destruction of most of the tillable surface shown in this scene; only small patches suitable for growing maize remain.

cultivation. The gutted lands of overpopulated Tlaxcala are probably the worst examples of this process. In other sections of the plateau and adjacent escarpments, as well as in many valleys of the Oaxaca highlands, disastrous gullying has transformed former corn fields and pastures into useless badlands (Figure 11.8).

The areas of Mexico having the least arable and cultivated land are the arid north and the forested, tropical lowlands of the southeast. In the plains of northern Yucatan and the mountainous southern highlands (Oaxaca, Guerrero, Chiapas), percentages of farmed land are much lower than in the Mesa Central. This is because of the broken terrain, the poor soils, and the predominance of slash-burn techniques, which utilize a relatively small amount of arable land in a given year.

Two fundamental changes in Mexican agriculture have been initiated during recent decades. One has been social and political in nature, involving changes in land tenure—

the fall of the hacienda system and the redistribution of land to peasant farmers. The other is a technical change that began about 1930, involving the introduction of modern European and North American farming techniques, such as large-scale irrigation, mechanization, the use of commercial fertilizers, and the planting of improved crop strains. Whereas changes in land tenure permeate all of Mexico, the technological changes have so far occurred only in a few places, chiefly in the north.

The Mexican Land Systems

The colonial hacienda reached its greatest development in Mexico during the last quarter of the nineteenth century. By 1910, 8,245 haciendas covered 40 per cent of the country's area. Ninety-six per cent of the rural families owned no land, and the majority of the landless worked as virtual serfs (*peones de campo*) on the big estates. As in colonial times, the haciendas were seldom smaller than 2,500 acres, and most were self-sufficient. Much arable land was left uncultivated because the hacienda system was based more on social prestige than on economic production. Through means both legal and illegal, the hacienda owners acquired the former church lands and usurped most of the Indian village properties that remained in the central part of the country. Many foreign individuals and land companies acquired vast tracts of territory, especially in the north. On the eve of the Revolution, the hacienda had become the most conspicuous feature of the rural scene in Mexico.

Other Mexican land systems of the nineteenth century included: (1) the rancho, or small private property of colonial origin; and (2) the few remaining Indian lands. The ranchos, 50 to 500 acres in size and operated by single mestizo or white families for subsistence, were scattered throughout the non-Indian areas of Mexico. These small holdings normally occupied the less productive hill lands bordering the large haciendas, which controlled the best farming areas. Though they held a relatively small part of the land, the nineteenth century *rancheros* formed, as they do today, the nucleus of a Mexican middle-class rural society.

The unalienated communal Indian holdings, before the Revolution, were chiefly in the isolated mountains of southern Mexico. Owing to misapplication of mid-nineteenth century land reforms, which had as their purpose the transfer of communal property to private ownership, most of the more accessible Indian villages lost their lands to speculators and neighboring haciendas. Nonetheless, the old Indian communal land organization served as a model for the present *ejido* system of Mexico.

Although the causes of the Revolution of 1910 are many and complex, the landless peasants' cry for land and food was fundamental. Thus, one of the principal aims of the Revolution was the expropriation of the large estates and the redistribution of the land among the rural proletariat. The redistribution program was promulgated by law in 1917, begun in 1922, and is still in progress. Under this program, expropriated land is turned over to a peasant community of at least 20 eligible heads of families (usually the workers on the former hacienda or those who live in villages within a radius of four miles of the expropriated property). Such newly acquired lands are called *ejidos*.

There are two types of *ejidos*. One is the *individual ejido*. An arable plot of 10 acres (of irrigated land) to 50 acres (of seasonal, or *de temporal* land) is distributed to each of the community members (*ejidatarios*). The *ejidatario* has only use rights to his plot; he cannot sell or mortgage it, and if he does not till it for two consecutive years, the plot reverts to the community and is reassigned. Pasture and woodland surrounding the community are used in common. These conditions are similar to those imposed under the ancient Aztec land system (*altepetlacalli*) and to the customs still observed in the Indian villages. The individual *ejido* has been established throughout the country, but it is most common in central and southern Mexico, where it is best understood by the peasantry of Indian and mestizo descent and where subsistence farming predominates.

The second type of *ejido* is called the *collective*. The community members do not receive individual plots for family use, but work the land collectively. Theoretically, the proceeds of the harvests are apportioned among the workers according to the type and amount of labor performed. The collective *ejido* is well-adapted to modern commercial agriculture, for mechanized cultivation of the large tracts, unencumbered by property lines, is possible. Only 5 per cent of *ejido* lands, however, are of the collective type. The more successful ones are in the northern oases, such as the Laguna area of southern Coahuila and the Yaqui Valley of Sonora (where cotton and wheat are raised commercially) and in the sugar-producing districts of Los Mochis (Sinaloa) and El Mante (Tamaulipas). Other collectives include the henequen-producing area of northern Yucatan (formerly in large plantations) and the coffee area of Soconusco in southwestern Chiapas.

Nearly half the cultivated land of Mexico has now been expropriated from the big estates and redistributed in *ejidos*. Most of the large haciendas have disappeared from the Mesa Central and the southern highlands, but smaller estates devoted to extensive cultivation of products such as maguey and pulque, have been left intact. Moreover, large holdings still prevail in the stock-raising areas of the north, for grazing in desert scrub and semiarid grasslands necessitates extensive tracts (Figure 11.9). When a hacienda is expropriated, the government permits the owner to retain as private property a portion of his land, the size depending on the use to which it is put.[2] Such land forms the residual estate, called the *pequeña propiedad*.

The breakup of the large estates did not significantly change the agglomerated rural settlement pattern that typifies most of Mexico. When not retained by the owner, the hacienda headquarters (*casco*) usually be-

[2] For example, a maximum of 250 acres of irrigated cropland may be retained or held privately; 500 acres of seasonal or unirrigated cropland; 370 acres for cotton; 750 acres for bananas, cacao, coffee, sugar cane, fruit trees, henequen, etc.; the amount of land required to maintain 500 head of cattle, depending on type of pasture, which rises to 125,000 acres of the most barren land.

Figure 11.9

Percentages of Total Land Area in Single Holdings of 12,500 Acres and Over: 1950.

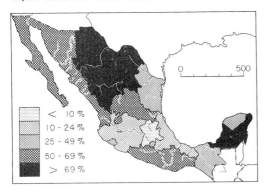

< 10 %
10 - 24 %
25 - 49 %
50 - 69 %
> 69 %

came an *ejido* village inhabited by the former hacienda workers, or *acasillados*. *Ejidatarios* also have established many new agricultural villages on expropriated land. And, to existing pueblos nearby, the government has returned the lands that the *hacendados* usurped during the last century.

The reapportionment of land through the *ejido* system has not resulted in the increased food production that the government envisioned. The *ejidos* that have successfully increased production of food crops are mainly those with irrigated land, such as the collectives in the northern oases and the individual *ejidos* of the Bajío of Guanajuato. Having little understanding of the profit motive, most of the individual *ejidatarios* of Indian origin in central and southern Mexico produce just enough food to feed their families, as did their ancestors in ancient times. Moreover, the plots of the individual *ejidos* are usually too small to raise surplus crops and are ill-suited to mechanized cultivation. Owing to decreased yields on overcropped soils, many peasants have abandoned their *ejidos*; such people, and those who were ineligible to receive *ejidos*, make up much of the recent influx of the rural element to the cities and to the United States. After expropriation of the estates was well under way in the 1930's, food production in Mexico fell, and only in the last few years has the country been able to feed itself through increased production from small, privately owned farms and the new irrigation districts in the north. The *ejido* system has, however, broken the power of the Mexican aristocracy and has lessened the evils of the stagnant economy inherent in the semifeudal hacienda system.

Besides the *ejidos* and the remaining haciendas, various types of small private holdings have acquired increasing importance in Mexico within the last few decades. Such holdings are composed mainly of: (1) old rancho properties of colonial origin; (2) the residual estates (*pequeñas propiedades*); (3) small tracts that individuals may purchase and hold in fee simple; and (4) small properties developed in government-sponsored agricultural colonies. These small private holdings may prove to be the solution to Mexico's land and food dilemma. Although most are quite small (less than 12 acres), those that range from 50 to over 500 acres are large enough for mechanized commercial farming.

The larger private holdings predominate in many of the irrigated districts of the north and in the agricultural colonies recently opened on national lands in the Gulf lowlands of Veracruz state. The current colonization program of the government has the purpose of resettling landless farmers from the overpopulated central highlands on the nearly empty tropical lowlands, and it sells the colonists 50- to 100-acre tracts at low prices and on easy terms. The government plans future colonies of private holdings on national lands in the Tabasco lowland and in the southern part of the Yucatan Peninsula (Campeche and Quintana Roo).

Subsistence Farming

Present-day farming in Mexico is characterized by great diversity in land tenure, cultivation methods, and crops. Patterns range from pre-Conquest Indian, through colonial, to modern forms. Subsistence tillage still occupies the bulk of the farming population, concentrated in the central and southern parts of the country, or within the bounds of ancient Mesoamerica.

The aboriginal crop trilogy of maize, beans, and squash, together with chile and pulque (the fermented sap of the maguey plant), is still the predominant subsistence food of most Mexicans. Maize is by far the most important single crop. In 1930, nearly three-fourths of the cultivated land of the country was planted in maize; today this proportion has dropped to about one-half, indicating a trend toward crop diversification. Although the bulk of the crop comes from the small subsistence farms of the Mesa Central and the southern highlands, where yields average

less than ten bushels per acre, maize production has doubled in the past 30 years, an increase due mainly to commercial, mechanized cultivation of high-yielding hybrid corn, which was recently introduced from the United States. The hybrid corn was developed as stock feed rather than human food, however, and most Mexicans despise its taste, and cling to the low-yielding native maize. The Mexican maize foods have changed little over the centuries (see Chapter 8, p. 239.) but, except in remote areas, the housewife has discarded the ancient metate, or grinding stone, and takes her lye-boiled corn to the modern motor-operated mill (*nixtamal*) now found in most Mexican villages. In the larger towns, tortilla-making machines are gaining ground against the ancient hand-patting method of fashioning the most important single item of Mexican diet. Most small farmers still grow beans and squash in the same fields with maize, and the maguey plants that form fences and property boundaries in the highland areas of subsistence farming furnish the sap, or *aguamiel,* for making pulque.

Throughout the steep escarpment areas bordering the Mesa Central, in the mountainous southern highlands, and in the forested tropical lowlands of the southeast, the ancient system of slash-burn cultivation is still a common technique of subsistence farmers. One of the most characteristic scenes on the steep slopes of the mountainous areas is the crazy-quilt pattern of small plots, some in crops, others temporarily abandoned to forest scrub (Figure 11.10). At the height of the dry season, in March and April, the atmosphere is filled with the blue smoke from burning plots being prepared for planting after the first rains of May or June. In these areas, slash-burn farming has changed little since pre-Conquest days. And, although the steel machete and iron hoe are now the main tools, many Indian farmers still use the wooden dibble and coa. Because of the pressure of population, the plots are now abandoned for only 3 to 4 years instead of from 10 to 15, with the result that yields are declining and the soil is becoming seriously eroded. The areas devoted to slash-burn cultivation are usually Indian village lands, though some are in *ejido* and others are national lands occupied by squatters. About 20 per cent of Mexico's cultivated land is still worked by the primitive slash-burn technique.

Within the more level areas of Mexico (Yucatan excepted), most subsistence farms are tilled with the ancient ard or wooden plow drawn by a yoke of oxen, much as in colonial times (Figure 11.11). Although many subsistence farmers of the Mesa Central and the North have adopted, via the United States, the more effective steel moldboard plow of North European origin, many, however, are either too conservative to use

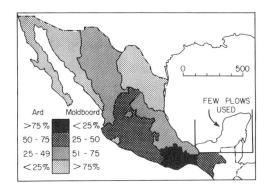

Figure 11.11

Ratio of Wooden Ard Plows to Steel Mold Board Plows in Mexico: 1950.

Figure 11.10

Slash-Burn Milpas (*Tlacololes*), or Maize Fields, on Steep Slopes, Southern Escarpment of the Mesa Central, Michoacán State. Old fields (*acahuales*), in various stages of secondary forest regrowth, and cultivated plots form irregular patches on the hillside.

it or do not have the price. In some sections where the steel plow is used, mules have recently replaced oxen for pulling it, chiefly because of the large destruction of oxen during the epidemic of hoof-and-mouth disease that plagued Mexico in the 1940's.

The few tractors and modern agricultural implements now used in subsistence farming are found largely in fertile irrigated basin flats, such as the Bajío of Guanajuato and sections of northern Michoacán and Jalisco in the western part of the Mesa Central. Little slash-burn cultivation is practiced today on the steep mountain slopes of the Mesa Central. However, on the slopes surrounding the Valley of Mexico and the basins of Toluca and Puebla, one still sees in use the aboriginal semiterrace (*bancal* or *pantli*) technique for permanent fields (see Chapter 8, p. 246).

Commercial Agriculture

Commercial agriculture, begun on a modest scale in colonial times, has greatly expanded during the nineteenth and twentieth centuries, so that today a crop such as cotton, cultivated by modern mechanized techniques, has become Mexico's leading export. Although some is scattered throughout the central highlands, most of today's commercial agriculture is in the irrigated oases of the arid north and in subtropical and tropical sections of the escarpments and coastal lowlands.

Mexico's commercial agriculture, unlike that of most Latin American countries, is well diversified, and many crops are cultivated both for home consumption and export. In terms of acreage, maize, beans, cotton, and wheat are the leading crops, followed by coffee, sugar cane, and sesame. Although the cultivation of some crops, for example, cotton and most wheat, is highly mechanized, others, such as maguey and sugar cane, are produced by techniques little changed since colonial times. Commercial production is carried on under practically all systems of land tenure present today in Mexico. Small amounts of wheat and sesame are grown for sale on Indian communal lands and individual *ejidos*; irrigated cotton, wheat, truck crops, and sugar cane are cultivated on collective *ejidos*, private holdings, and haciendas. Three large areas in Mexico produce important commercial crops: the Mesa Central; the northern oases; and the subtropical and tropical areas in the southern part of the country.

The Mesa Central. Albeit most of the arable land of the Mesa Central is devoted to subsistence agriculture, some of the more fertile basins are noted for commercial cultivation. One of these is the Bajío of Guanajuato and northern Michoacán, since colonial times considered the breadbasket of Mexico (Figure 11.12). Maize and beans are cultivated during the summer rainy season; in winter, wheat, truck crops, and alfalfa are grown by irrigation on the small private holdings and the *ejidos*. Farmers obtain water from the small reservoirs that dot the basin surface and surrounding hills, or pump it from deep wells with the diesel-powered engines which have replaced the colonial norias. A substantial part of Mexico's commercial maize and bean crop comes from the Bajío as well as from the *temporal* lands in the high basins of Zacatecas and Durango.

From colonial times until the 1940's, the Bajío produced the greater part of the country's wheat. Today, however, large-scale wheat production has shifted to the northern oases, where more than 80 per cent is now cultivated by irrigation on highly mechanized *ejidos* and private holdings. As in most Latin American countries, the consumption of wheat bread in Mexico is a status symbol. Bread was the food of the Spaniards, of their white descendants, and of other Europeans. Today, most urban folk in central and southern Mexico feel that wheat foods are prestige foods, and all eat them who can afford to do so. In the north, wheat bread, and even tortillas made from wheat flour, have been staple foods since colonial times. So important is the demand for white bread in urban areas and in the north that, in past years, the Mexican government was forced to import large quantities of grain and flour from the United States, expending valuable foreign exchange. With the shift of wheat production to the northern oases, Mexico now has grain even for export.

A more extensive type of commercial agriculture practiced in the Mesa Central is the large-scale cultivation of the agave plant, maguey, for the production of pulque, the ancient Indian intoxicant. During most of the colonial period, pulque making was chiefly a subsistence activity, the beverage being consumed in large quantities by the peasants. By the close of the eighteenth century, however, some landowners had established maguey haciendas in the dry northeastern part of the central plateau north of the Valley of Mexico, where the plant thrives under adverse natural conditions. The heyday of commercial pulque was the late nineteenth century; maguey plantings were greatly expanded and there was a large production for the increasing urban mestizo and Indian populations in the Valley of Mexico and in the mining establishments. Following the land reforms ushered in by the Revolution of 1910, the maguey-pulque producing area shrank to its present location in the dry,

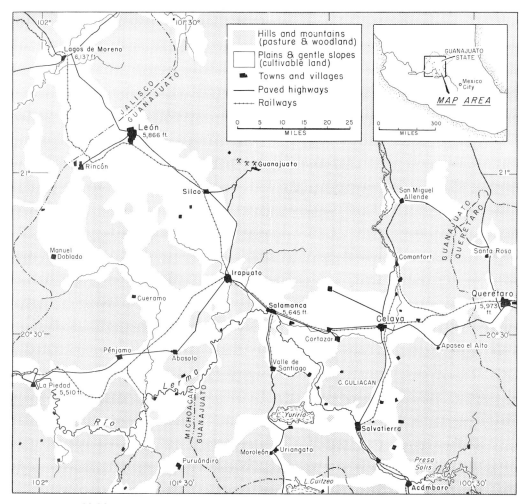

Figure 11.12

The Bajío of Guanajuato, a Series of Coalesced Volcanic Basins Which Forms One of the Major Agricultural Areas of Mexico.

rocky lands in southern Hidalgo and northern Tlaxcala states, north and northeast of Mexico City (Figure 11.13). Although nearly half the present area planted to maguey is now in *ejido*, 90 per cent of the pulque produced in Mexico comes from haciendas (200 to 500 acres in size) and smaller private holdings (Figure 11.14). Owing to the slow maturing of the maguey plant (8 to 15 years) and the decreasing market for commercial pulque, however, the maguey plantations are no longer the profitable enterprises of a century ago. To supplement income, barley for ani-

mal feed is often sown between the widely spaced rows of maguey. The sap collectors (*tlachiqueros*) still use ancient techniques, such as a large elongated gourd (*acocote*) to suck up the fresh juice that accumulates in a cavity made at the base of the plant. After fermentation in concrete vats, most of the pulque from the haciendas is still shipped into Mexico City, Pachuca, and Puebla, where it is consumed in the malodorous *pulquerías* in the poor sections of town. The less nutritious European-type beer, introduced into Mexico about 75 years ago, now

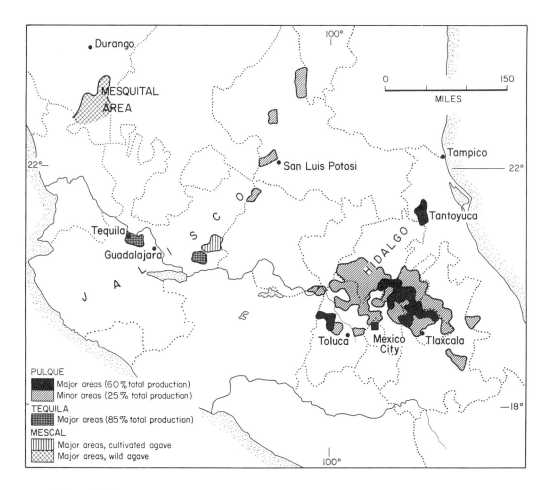

Figure 11.13
Areas Producing Alcoholic Beverages from the Agave Plant.

Figure 11.14
Maguey-Pulque Haciendas in Southern Hidalgo State, Northeast of the Valley of Mexico
Between the widely spaced maguey plants, barley and wheat are grown as cash crops
In the distance are several hacienda cascos, or processing centers for pulque.

offers stiff competition to pulque as a poor man's drink in the urban areas, however.

Closely related to maguey-pulque agriculture is the cultivation of other types of agave plants for the production of the distilled brandy called *mescal*. Small private holdings in Jalisco state, on the western side of the Mesa Central, produce most of this product, the center being the vicinity of Tequila (where the famous tequila, a type of mescal, is manufactured), northwest of Guadalajara. The juice used for distillation of tequila and other mescals is obtained by macerating the trunk of the agave plant.

The Northern Oases. Commercial farming in Mexico is best developed in the arid north, where, in the last 40 years, the government built dams and reservoirs on streams, thus creating large irrigated oases. Nearly 20 per cent of Mexico's arable land is now artificially watered, making it one of the world's leading countries in development of irrigation potential. The recent increase in food production and in the export of cotton has been due chiefly to the large-scale irrigation projects in the north.

Northern Mexico is not particularly well endowed for irrigated farming. Water is limited. Only two large rivers, the Colorado and the Rio Grande, affect north Mexican territory, and Mexico must share the water of both with the United States, which utilizes most of it. The greater portion of water for irrigation in the north derives from the modest rainfall and the melting snow of the Sierra Madre Occidental. The short streams that flow westward down the escarpment to the narrow Pacific lowland and those that run eastward into the Rio Grande or into areas of interior drainage carry most of the water used in cultivating the fertile alluvial soils of desert basins and delta plains. Moreover, the same streams maintain the ground water which is pumped from deep wells in the irrigated areas.

As we have already observed (Chapter 10), Spanish farmers maintained small patches of irrigated cropland in favored localities of northern Mexico throughout the colonial period. Much later, in the late nineteenth and early twentieth centuries, Mexican *hacendados* and North American land speculators developed sizable private irrigation projects, especially in the Laguna area of Coahuila and the Yaqui River delta in Sonora. It was not until the late 1920's, however, that the Mexican government began construction of large dams and reservoirs to develop the present irrigation systems that have revolutionized agriculture in the North (Figure 11.15).

The first irrigation district to be fully developed was the Laguna area of southern Coahuila, an immense desert basin once occupied by the now desiccated lakes of Mayrán and Viesca and fed by the Nazas and Aguanaval rivers. The western part of the basin was converted into a large, mechanized, irrigated farming area (400,000 acres) specializing in cotton, wheat, and alfalfa under the collective *ejido* system of land tenure. Deep wells that tap the once-abundant ground water supply of the basin furnish half the irrigation water, but excessive pumping has in recent years dangerously lowered the water table. During the 1930's, the Laguna area became Mexico's foremost cotton-producing region; the towns of Torreón, Gómez Palacio, and Lerdo, which cluster around the mouth of the Nazas River, grew into the large urban complex that today serves as an administrative, market, and supply center for the district.

Northwest of the Laguna area, in the state of Chihuahua, is the Delicias irrigation district on the Conchos River, the largest tributary of the Rio Grande in Mexican territory. Most of the surface water used for irrigation is supplied by the Boquilla Reservoir (Lago Toronto) constructed on the middle Conchos in 1916 for hydroelectric power. Other reservoirs built on the tributaries San Pedro and Florido, as well as deep wells, now supplement the Conchos water supply and help to irrigate 125,000 acres of fertile desert al-

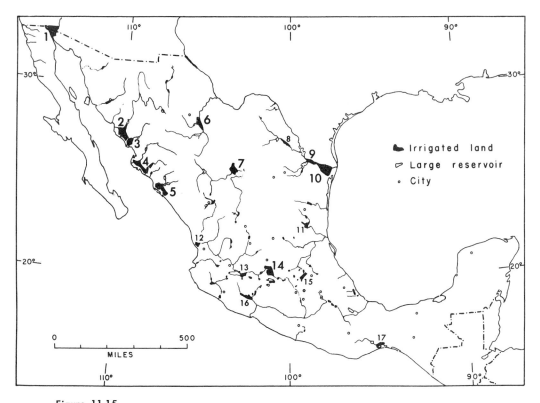

Figure 11.15

Major Irrigation Districts in Mexico. Numbers refer to the following districts:

1. Río Colorado (Mexicali)
2. Río Yaqui
3. Río Mayo
4. Río Fuerte-Sinaloa
5. Río Culiacán-San Lorenzo
6. Delicias
7. La Laguna
8. Río Salado
9. Río San Juan
10. Bajo Río Bravo (Matamoros)
11. El Mante
12. Bajo Río Santiago
13. Bajo Río Lerma ⎫
14. Alto Río Lerma ⎬ El Bajío
   ⎭
15. Río Tula
16. Río Tepalcatepec
17. Tehuantepec

luvium along the rivers. Cotton and wheat, grown by mechanized methods mainly on small private holdings, are the main crops of the area.

A third large region of recently developed irrigated farming lies within the lower Rio Grande drainage of northeastern Mexico. Within this area, nearly 700,000 acres of land are now cultivated with irrigation. Most of the farmland is within the Rio Grande delta, in the vicinity of Matamoros across the river from Brownsville; smaller irrigated areas occur along the Salado and San Juan rivers, tributaries of the Rio Grande. Developed

mainly since World War II, the Matamoros area has now overtaken the Laguna district as Mexico's leading cotton zone. The large international Falcon reservoir on the Rio Grande (completed in 1957) furnishes most of the water for the Matamoros area, while the Don Martín reservoir supplies the Salado section. As the lower Rio Grande carries little flow originating in the upper and middle courses of the river, the water for the reservoirs comes chiefly from erratic local rainfall, increased by the occasional passage of easterly waves and hurricanes. Slightly less than half of the Matamoros area is in *ejido,* the rest being private holdings, many of whose owners have managed to circumvent the land laws and consolidate their lands into virtual haciendas.

Within the past 20 years, arid northwestern Mexico has become the agricultural hot spot of the country and one of the most rapidly developing farming areas in the world. With the recent completion of a large network of canals, water from the lower Colorado River has been diverted onto the deltaic alluvium south of Mexicali in Baja California, to irrigate a half-million acres of cotton land. The irrigated Mexicali district now vies with that of Matamoros for the lead in Mexican cotton output. However, the Mexicali district receives only 10 per cent of the Colorado River water for irrigation, the rest being used by the United States. Unfortunately, much of the water utilized on the Mexican side is return flow that has already been applied on American fields and is thus often heavily impregnated with salts harmful to crops. The international dispute that has arisen over this question of water rights threatens to damage Mexican-United States relations.

The most spectacular development of irrigation in arid northwestern Mexico, however, has occurred within the lower courses and deltas of the streams that cross the dry coastal plain of Sonora and Sinaloa. Nearly two million acres are now under irrigation along the coast, from the small Caborca district on the Magadalena River in northern Sonora to the Río San Lorenzo in central Sinaloa. Beginning with the Angostura Dam on the Yaqui River (finished in 1937), the Mexican government has since completed reservoirs on most of the larger streams of the northwest and many more are under construction or planned. The largest irrigated areas comprise the flood plains and deltas of the Yaqui (550,000 acres) and Fuerte (600,000 acres) rivers (Figure 11.16). In some parts of the coastal plain, long canals bring water to the

Figure 11.16
The Alvaro Obregón Dam on the Yaqui River, Southern Sonora State. This dam impounds one of Mexico's largest reservoirs in the dry northwest. Water from this reservoir is used to irrigate the extensive cotton, wheat, and winter vegetable farms in the vicinity of Ciudad Obregón. *(Compañia Mexicana Aerofoto)*

interfluve areas, so that often there are continuous stretches of cultivation from one river valley to the next.

Wheat, cotton, and winter vegetables (principally tomatoes and melons) are the three main crops, and rice, sugar cane, and sesame are also important. Most of the acreage devoted to these crops is cultivated with modern machinery on both private holdings and *ejidos*. Wheat production has increased so much in the recent past that the river oases of Sonora and Sinaloa have replaced the Bajío of Guanajuato as the granary of Mexico. A large part of the winter tomato crop produced in the Fuerte and Culiacán areas has long been exported to the United States. The northwestern river oases now produce as much cotton as either the Matamoros or Mexicali districts, making Mexico the foremost cotton-producing country of Latin America. Associated with the cotton crop are the gins and the cottonseed-oil processing plants; associated with the winter vegetable crop are the packing sheds and loading stations. All of these form part of the modern landscape of the northern oases. Supply and market centers like Cuidad Obregón and Navajoa in the Yaqui and Mayo districts of southern Sonora and Culiacán in Sinaloa, are boom towns which exemplify the rapid urban growth that is accompanying the phenomenal farming development in the northwest.

The agricultural boom that is taking place in the irrigated lands of northern Mexico is closely related to the introduction of modern technology from the United States. Such technology includes the engineering involved in reservoir and canal construction, as well as the know-how required for the use of tractors, mechanical harvesters, and other modern agricultural machines. Other new techniques include the use of commercial fertilizers, insecticides, and improved plant strains. More fundamentally, the agricultural boom of the North is associated with Mexico's population and food problem and with direct government action in the development of water resources to increase food production. Free of the Indian conservatism and dense population that permeate central and southern Mexico, the newly developed farming districts of the North have witnessed the most spectacular and rapid changes in landscape in the country.

The Tropical Lowlands. Tropical commercial agriculture is still generally located in the areas developed by the Spaniards in the colonial period. The moist, nearly frost-free coastal lowlands and the adjacent eastern escarpments that border the Gulf are Mexico's outstanding regions of tropical farming. This area includes southeastern Tamaulipas, easternmost San Luis Potosí, practically all of Veracruz (Mexico's richest agricultural state), Tabasco, and parts of northeastern Oaxaca and northern Chiapas. It produces most of Mexico's coffee, sugar cane, bananas, copra, cacao, and pineapple, much of the citrus and minor tropical fruits, and quantities of maize, beans, and rice. Less significant areas of production of tropical crops are the valleys and slopes on the southern and southwestern escarpment of the Mesa Central, the semiarid lowlands of the Tepalcatepec Basin in Michoacán, and the narrow Pacific lowlands and escarpments from Nayarit to Chiapas. The hot, subhumid Balsas depression, with its hilly surface and infertile soils, still remains commercially undeveloped, as do most of the forested lands of the Yucatan Peninsula. The century-old henequen plantation area in the northern part of the peninsula is a special development in tropical agriculture in Middle America.

Diversity of commercial crops, rather than the monoculture found in other Middle American countries, characterizes tropical farming in Mexico. Of the dozen or more significant crops, however, coffee and sugar cane predominate in terms of acreage, production, and value. Mexico has been a self-sufficient grower of sugar since colonial times, and today competes with neighboring countries as an exporter, and, since 1950, Mexico

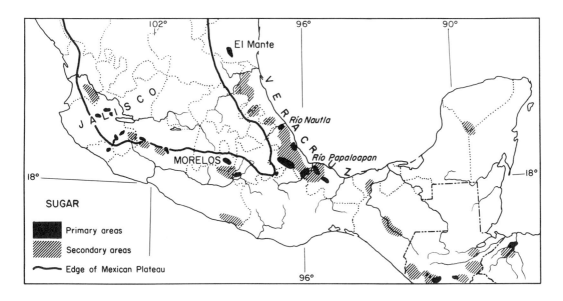

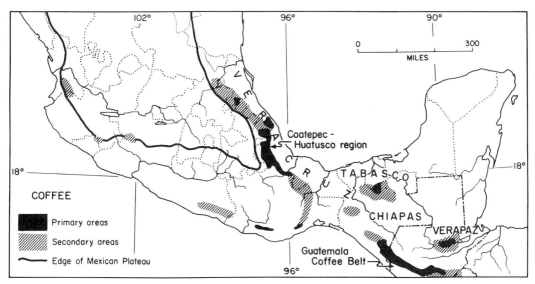

Figure 11.17
Sugar and Coffee Areas of Mexico.

has been the third largest coffee producer in Latin America.

The sugar-cane areas of Mexico have approximately the same distribution as in colonial days, with more than a third of today's production concentrated in the coastal lowlands and lower escarpment slopes of central Veracruz (Figure 11.17). At the close of the nineteenth century, some 30 large plantations and steam-operated processing plants (*ingenios*) plus hundreds of small animal-driven mills (*trapiches*) extended from the Nautla River to the Papaloapan lowlands. Today, the Veracruz sugar area has expanded southward, around the base of the Tuxtla volcanic mass, to the vicinity of Acayucan in the northern part of the Isthmus of Tehuantepec. The core of the sugar zone, however, still extends, as it did in the eighteenth century, southeastward from the Córdoba-Orizaba, or Las Villas area, along the lower flanks of the eastern escarpment to the Papaloapan River basin. Within the humid Gulf region, the northernmost sugar area centers around

Figure 11.18
The Sugar Hacienda "Villahermosa," in Morelos State. In the foreground the casco is composed of the "big house" of the former owner, the sugar mill, and remnants of abandoned warehouses. In the background are extensive sugar fields. Most of the land that formerly belonged to this hacienda is now operated as a collective *ejido*. (*Compañia Mexicana Aerofoto*)

the partly irrigated El Mante district in southernmost Tamaulipas, which was developed as a plantation just before the Revolution of 1910 and later made into large collective *ejidos*.

Although they were significant in colonial and pre-Revolutionary times, the sugar areas along the southern escarpment of the Mesa Central are now of relatively minor importance. Those of the *valles* of Morelos state (around Cuernavaca, Yautepec, Cuautla), of southeastern Puebla (Chiautla), and of the hot, narrow canyons and basins of southern Jalisco (such as Tamazula and Zapotiltic) were partially ruined during the Revolution, but have since been revived (Figure 11.18). The highly productive irrigated sugar area of Los Mochis in northern Sinaloa is the only one in Mexico that falls outside the humid tropical zone.

The pre-Revolutionary sugar haciendas were among the few large-scale Mexican agricultural enterprises that approximated the tropical plantation. Few, however, acquired the size and importance of the West Indian operations and, after the expropriation of the large estates, most of the sugar haciendas were converted into *ejidos* or broken down into smaller private holdings. In most of the sugar areas, cultivation has changed little since colonial times. The machete is still the main harvesting instrument since the rank, irregular growth of the tropical cane hardly permits the use of the harvester. Tractor-pulled cane racks are seen in the newer, more progressive holdings, but oxcarts still haul the cane to the mills in most areas. Large, mechanized processing mills and refineries, however, have replaced the old *ingenios*, though the mule or oxen-powered *trapiches* prevail throughout the sugar zone of Mexico for making the cheap

cakes of raw sugar (*panela* or *piloncillo*) consumed in large quantities by the poorer
classes. An important adjunct of sugar processing, begun in colonial times, is the manufacture of the rum and cane brandies for
which Mexico is famous.

Although the coffee plant was first brought
to Mexico in the late eighteenth century,
commercial production did not begin until
about 1860. Until recently it was a rather
minor crop in Mexico, most of the harvest
being consumed locally but, between 1950
and 1960, coffee acreage doubled. The crop
is now second only to cotton as an agricultural export and surpasses sugar in acreage
and value.

The first Mexican coffee-growing area to
be developed in the nineteenth century was
the humid eastern escarpment of Veracruz
state, in the vicinity of Córdoba and Orizaba.
From this center, coffee culture spread northward, beyond Jalapa, and southward, to the
Papaloapan Basin, along an altitudinal belt
of between 3,000 and 6,000 feet elevation,
which corresponds to the upper part of the
tierra templada. This belt is still Mexico's
leading coffee area, particularly that section
of rich volcanic soils that lies between Jalapa
and Orizaba. This area, known as the
Coatepec-Huatusco region, is one of Mexico's
lushest horticultural areas, where citrus orchards, banana plantings, coffee groves, and
scattered orchid-draped mango and avocado
trees blend into an almost continuous tropical garden.

Beginning in the 1880's, German planters
from Guatemala extended coffee cultivation
into the Pacific slope of the Sierra Madre de
Chiapas (the Soconusco), creating Mexico's
second producing area. Mexican colonists
have recently formed a third important
coffee district on the rain-drenched escarpment of northern Chiapas, overlooking the
Gulf lowlands of Tabasco; plantings are expanding rapidly in this virgin area, a product
of government-sponsored colonization of the
remaining tropical lowlands of the country.
There are other coffee zones along the east-

ern escarpment of Veracruz as far as the
San Luis Potosí border in the Huastec Indian
country; on the Pacific slope of Oaxaca and
Guerrero; and in small patches along the
southern and western escarpments of the
Mesa Central (Figure 11.17).

Before the Revolution, the Mexican coffee
farms (*fincas*) varied in size from 50 to over
5,000 acres and were chiefly owned by rich
Mexicans or foreigners. Many of the large
fincas, especially those in Chiapas, have been
converted into collective *ejidos*; in Veracruz,
many were apportioned in small individual
ejidos. Each former *finca* owner was permitted to retain a maximum of 750 acres in
coffee plantings, but many of these holdings
have been enlarged by combining contiguous
lands owned by relatives. As in most tropical
areas of America other than Brazil, coffee is
grown under shade trees, supposedly to improve quality of the beans. Since the prepara-
tion of the beans for market involves an
elaborate process of depulping, curing, and
drying, many smaller growers have established cooperative beneficiating plants; others
sell their crop directly to plant owners.

Rice, although hardly comparable to sugar
cane and coffee in acreage or value, is becoming an increasingly significant staple food
in the tropical lowlands of Mexico, as it is
elsewhere in the Latin American tropics. As
we mentioned in Chapter 10, the Spaniards
introduced rice into Mexico early in the
colonial period, but only in the past 50 years
has it become an important commercial crop.
In the lowland tropics, rice is a prestige food,
as wheat is in the highlands.

Traditionally, Mexico's main rice-produc-
ing area has been the irrigated valleys and
basins along the southern escarpment of the
Mesa Central, especially those of Morelos,
southern Puebla, and northern Guerrero. In
those areas today, farmers grow 30 per cent
of Mexico's rice crop in small holdings cultivated by techniques reminiscent of those employed in the Orient. Since the 1930's, much
of the Mexican rice growing has shifted to
the coastal oases of the northwest, where

nearly one-third of the country's crop is now produced by mechanized farming in the Río Yaqui irrigation district, southern Sonora.

The extent and location of many of the lesser tropical crops grown commercially in Mexico have undergone substantial changes within the past half-century. The traditional Mexican citrus district, for example, lies on the eastern escarpment between Córdoba and Jalapa, where oranges have been raised for the Mexico City market since colonial times. Minor citrus areas of less antiquity occur in sheltered basins in the western part of the Mesa Central, such as the Atotonilco el Alto orange district in eastern Jalisco and the lime-growing areas of Colima and the Tepalcatepec Basin of Michoacán. Since the 1930's, however, the center of citrus production has shifted to Nuevo León in the northeastern part of the country, where the Montemorelos district southeast of Monterrey, in 1950, produced more than half of the Mexican orange crop on small private holdings. Although favored by sufficient water for irrigation in abnormally dry years, the area is occasionally plagued by winter freezes caused by the incursion of cold air masses from Texas.

The banana industry has changed even more spectacularly. Small-scale commercial banana cultivation began in the late colonial period on the eastern escarpment around the Córdoba-Jalapa area of Veracruz, as did the cultivation of so many of the tropical crops. At the beginning of this century, local landowners established Mexico's first large banana plantations on the fertile river flood plains of the Tabasco lowlands. This development was part of the great banana boom that was taking place at the same time on the Caribbean coast of Central America. The Tabascan plantations reached peak harvests in 1936, when they produced half of the 14.5 million banana stems exported from Mexico that year. Thereafter, the expropriation of the large estates and the incursion of banana diseases caused a decline in production in the Tabasco area. Banana production has now

shifted to the Pacific (Soconusco) coast of Chiapas, especially to the vicinity of Tapachula, near the Guatemalan border. There, most of Mexico's banana crop is raised on small to moderate holdings (a maximum of 825 acres, by law). A secondary area, first planted in 1928, is in northern Veracruz, within the petroleum fields of Poza Rica and Papantla, where oil derricks, storage tanks, and gas flares are enveloped in the bright green of banana plants. Owing chiefly to disease, banana production in Mexico steadily declined after the 1930's; in 1956, the harvest yielded only 4.5 million stems. In recent years, however, production has increased following the planting of new banana acreage in the Pacific lowlands of Nayarit state.

Several native tropical plants, cultivated in pre-Conquest times, are now important commercial crops. The cultivation of practically all such plants, however, has also become far more significant in the Old World tropics and elsewhere. Among these are tobacco, first cultivated commercially in colonial days in Veracruz but now dominant on *ejidos* in the lowlands of Nayarit; pineapple, first cultivated on a large scale in 1906 around the area of Loma Bonita in southern Veracruz, which is still the foremost producing area in Mexico; cacao, the production of which has shifted from the Soconusco on the Pacific coast to the wet foothills of northern Chiapas and the river flood plains of Tabasco; and vanilla, of which Mexico still grows half of the world's production by ancient native methods in the Totonac Indian area of central Veracruz. The coconut, which grew along the Pacific coast of Central America before the Conquest, has become an important strand crop in this century, and is grown along both the Pacific and Gulf coasts of Mexico. The cultivation of the coconut on old beach ridges along the Gulf coast of Veracruz, Tabasco, and Campeche has recently reached boom proportions; these states now produce three-quarters of Mexico's copra.

An agave, or century plant called "henequen," is another commercially grown native tropical plant. The cultivation of this plant on a large scale in northern Yucatan during the nineteenth century gave rise to perhaps the best example of the tropical plantation in Mexico. Like its close relative, maguey, henequen thrives in thin, limey soil and in a hot semiarid climate. Its thick, fleshy leaves yield a stout fiber long used by the Indians for cordage and hammocks.

During the last century, the owners of cattle haciendas in northern Yucatan began to plant henequen to obtain fiber for manufacturing ship cables and other kinds of rope. The invention of the McCormick wheat binder in 1873, and the subsequent development of wheat lands in the central United States, created a large demand for binder twine. By the turn of the century, the flat, stony plains around Mérida in northwestern Yucatan had become a zone of large henequen plantations which employed cheap Maya Indian labor to cultivate and process the fiber exported to the United States for the wheat harvest. After the Mexican Revolution, several factors combined to effect a sharp reduction in Yucatan henequen production. Land tenure systems changed, demand for binder twine decreased with the invention of the wheat combine, and new sisal and henequen cultivators in other parts of the world began to offer strong competition. Today, the privately held Yucatan plantations are greatly reduced in size (maximum of 750 acres), and most of the henequen comes from collectively operated *ejidos* established on the former haciendas. Since the 1950's, small but rapidly growing areas of henequen production have been established in northeastern Mexico, especially around Ciudad Victoria in central Tamaulipas (Figure 11.19).

Tropical agriculture has been greatly furthered by the government's recent program for developing sparsely occupied lowland areas of the country in order to resettle landless farmers from the highlands and to in-

Figure 11.19

Sisal (Henequen) Near Ciudad Victoria, Tamaulipas State, Northeastern Mexico. About 10 per cent of the sisal grown in Mexico comes from this general area, whereas the remainder is produced in Yucatan.

crease food production. In 1938, the government undertook the development of the semi-arid Tepalcatepec Basin of southern Michoacán. The existing irrigation systems were enlarged, new ones established, and large areas within the plains of Apatzingan and Bellavista were opened for the cultivation of rice, maize, and tropical fruit.

A second scheme, far larger in scope, is the Papaloapan Project, ambitiously called "Mexico's T.V.A." This involves the agricultural and industrial development of the Papaloapan River Basin in southern Veracruz. The large Alemán Dam and reservoir on the Tonto River, a tributary of the Papaloapan, now controls floods, affords irrigation water in time of need, and generates electricity. In the lower part of the basin the government has constructed roads, straightened the sinuous river channel, instituted sanitary measures, and established several agricultural colonies in which small private holdings, rather than *ejidos,* are the rule. The best lands of the lower Papaloapan, however, are the fertile natural levees along the river. These are excluded to new colonization, for they are held by residual estates and *ejidos,* and have long been in sugar cane.

A third endeavor, the Grijalva Project, involves development of the Tabasco lowland, a tropical area of heavy rainfall, disastrous floods, and extensive swamps; most of the good farmland lies along the natural levees that border the active and abandoned river channels. The project involves flood control and sanitation in the lower part of Grijalva and Usumacinta river basins, to pave the way for large-scale colonization. The government has already constructed large artificial levees and drainage canals in the western part of the lowlands, particularly in the productive Chontalpa area west of Villahermosa, the capital city. In 1960, work began on the large dam and reservoir of Netzahualcoyotl at Mal Paso on the Grijalva River in northwestern Chiapas, which will control the flood waters of that river as it debouches from the mountains onto the coastal plain.

THE LIVESTOCK ECONOMY

Stock raising, in contrast to agriculture, has retained much of its colonial pattern. Neither the pasture areas nor the breeds of animals have changed appreciably since the eighteenth century.

Yet stock raising is still one of Mexico's most important economies. A third of the national territory is classified as pastureland; its landscape is characterized by widely spaced ranch centers, vast expanses of grassy or scrub-covered plains and hills, and scattered, ill-tended herds. According to the 1950 census, the monetary value of Mexican livestock actually exceeds that of cultivated crops.

As in colonial times, the Mexican livestock industry is divided into: (1) small-scale stock raising, including household animals associated with subsistence agriculture, which is found chiefly in the central and southern highlands; and (2) large-scale commercial ranching, which is found in some parts of the central highlands, in the arid north, and in the coastal lowlands. A third enterprise involving animals—dairying—has evolved only recently around the larger cities to supply fresh milk to a growing urban market.

Small-Scale Stock Raising

More than one-third of the country's livestock is kept by the subsistence farmers of the Mesa Central and the southern highlands. In addition to the work animals (oxen, mules, and burros) that he employs in cultivation and transport, many a farmer owns a few cattle, sheep, and goats which graze in the common pastures and woodland or on the stubble of cropped fields around his village. He also may have a hog or two which, like the oxen and burros, are kept near the house and are almost considered part of the family. Chickens and turkeys also comprise an important part of the household animals.

The occasional sale of a cow or hog, and the annual wool clip (one-half of the national production), bring the subsistence farmers some income. The little milk obtained from cows and goats is fed chiefly to the children or is processed into a soft, salty cheese common throughout the country. Many hogs are still raised commercially in the marshy sections of the Mesa Central, especially around Lake Chapala and the Cocula district in central Jalisco, which is as famous now as it was in colonial times for its hams and bacon.

As in colonial times, nearly half of Mexico's seven million sheep are concentrated within the high basins and mountain slopes in the eastern part of the Mesa Central, where Indian and mestizo villagers raise small herds. Owing to changes in land tenure and the increase in cultivated area, however, the great seasonal sheep drives between lowland Gulf pastures and the highlands no longer take place.

Large-Scale Ranching

The north, with 60 per cent of the nation's natural pasture, continues to be Mexico's outstanding commercial stock-raising area. During the Díaz regime, the cattle industry prospered, especially in the high, grassy plains of Zacatecas, Durango, and Chihuahua and in the low, scrub-covered hills of Sonora. Near the international border, North American land companies acquired large blocks of Mexican pasture, the Hearst estate alone comprising two million acres in western Chihuahua. United States ranchers introduced improved breeds of beef cattle, such as the Shorthorn, Hereford, and Aberdeen Angus, but most Mexican stockmen were content with the rangy *criollo* descendant of sixteenth-century Spanish stock. By the end of the nineteenth century, the market for Mexican cattle and mules had shifted from the local mining areas to the United States, and thousands of head were annually driven northward across the border.

The northern herds were devastated by guerrilla operations during the Revolution, but have again increased to about six million head, or one-third of the nation's cattle. The black grama pastures of the high plains and mountain meadows in northwestern Chihuahua, from Chihuahua City to the Casas Grandes area, form the present center of range cattle industry in Mexico. More than two million head now graze in this area (Figure 11.20). Other large northern cattle ranges are in the steppes of northwestern Zacatecas and central Durango and the lowland pastures in Sonora and northern Sinaloa. All of these were pasturelands in colonial times. Although 90 per cent of the range cattle are still *criollos,* the Hereford is slowly becoming the standard breed in northwestern Chihuahua, northern Sonora, and Coahuila.

As we have already mentioned, the land reforms following the Revolution of 1910 scarcely affected the size of the large cattle haciendas in northern Mexico. The carrying capacity of those pastures is so low (15 to 250 acres of land per animal) that a large holding is needed to graze a herd of profitable size. Foreign holdings near the United States border have been expropriated, however, and the land has been parceled out as *ejidos* for both farming and stock raising.

Goats and sheep are of minor importance on the northern stock ranches, although the hardy goat, able to survive the aridity and the sparseness of forage, is more numerous in the north than elsewhere in Mexico. The arid limestone hills and mountains of Coahuila, Nuevo León, and San Luis Potosí have the largest goat population in the country (over three million head, or about 40 per cent of the total). The goat belt of Mexico extends along the western flank of the Sierra Madre Oriental, from central San Luis Potosí through Saltillo to the Rio Grande. Most of the flocks are small, and owned and tended by villagers who live on the edge of the desert. In northeastern Mexico, *barbacoa* and *cabrito,* the delectable barbecued or roasted kid, are renowned regional dishes.

Of the two million sheep in northern Mexico, about one-half are in large flocks on haciendas; the remainder are in small flocks that belong to villagers. The large sheep ranches

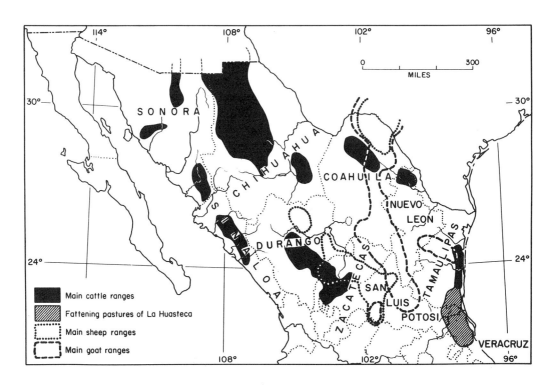

Figure 11.20
Main Livestock Ranges of Mexico.

Figure 11.21
Mixed Criollo-Brahman Cattle in the Tropical Lowland Pastures of Tabasco State, South-eastern Mexico. Improved animal breeds and planted pasture have greatly increased the value of the cattle industry in the lowland tropics of Middle America.

are concentrated in the steppes of northwestern Zacatecas, northern Durango, and in the semidesert scrub of northeastern Coahuila, south of Villa Acuña along the Rio Grande, which is a southern continuation of the great Edwards Plateau sheep and goat district in Texas.

The northern pastures have been overgrazed, particularly in this century. As a consequence, the vegetation has been modified and the carrying capacity of the pasture lands greatly reduced. The once extensive areas of nutritious black grama grasslands in the high basins of western Zacatecas, Durango, and Chihuahua are now severely depleted and have been invaded by noxious weeds, some of which are poisonous and annually cause the death of hundreds of animals. Other invaders include prickly-pear and cholla cacti, as well as mesquite and thorny acacia scrub. The invasion of desert scrub into the drier margins of the grasslands is especially noticeable in northeastern Mexico, where goats and sheep have drastically overgrazed and overbrowsed in formerly productive pastures.

Although stock raising in the tropical lowland savannas of Mexico dates from the colonial period, it is within the past 50 years that the industry has become especially significant in the Gulf coast area known as the Huasteca in southern Tamaulipas, in northern Veracruz, and in eastern San Luis Potosí. There, abundant rainfall affords year-round pasture. Most important, recent planting of nutritious African grasses, such as Guinea grass and Pará grass, has so increased the carrying capacity of the Huasteca pastures that they have become the foremost beef-fattening area of the country. Cattle from the steppes of Coahuila and Nuevo León, fattened in the lush lowlands, are shipped to Mexico City for slaughter. Like many stock-raising areas of the tropics, the pasturage in the savannas and marshes of southern Veracruz and Tabasco have been improved by the planting of African grasses. The permanent *criollo* herds in the Gulf lowlands have also

been improved by crossing with brahma stock from India and Brown Swiss from Europe (Figure 11.21). Today Veracruz is second only to Chihuahua as Mexico's leading cattle state.

The Dairy Industry

The newest development in Mexican stock raising is the dairy farm, scores of which have sprung up around the major urban centers within the past 50 years. Until recently the consumption of fresh milk was not significant in Mexico; it rarely has been in areas of Spanish culture. Its consumption, of course, was unknown to pre-Conquest Indians, and still today there are large numbers of people in Mexico who have never tasted milk. With the rise of urbanism and the influence of recent government propaganda, however, the use of milk and other dairy products has increased in Mexico.

The greatest concentration of dairy farms is near Mexico City, whose milkshed includes much of the northern and eastern portions of the Valley of Mexico where land reclaimed by lake drainage has been planted to alfalfa. In addition, alfalfa hay and other cattle feed are shipped in quantity from the Bajío of Guanajuato for the dairy herds, composed mainly of purebred Holsteins. Although most of the city's milk supply comes from United States-style dairies within the Valley, at least one-third is furnished by small, unsanitary establishments as far away as Querétaro, Puebla, and Tlaxcala. Guadalajara's daily milk supply is shipped in from small dairies scattered over a large part of central and eastern Jalisco, while Monterrey is supplied by farms close by. Modern pasteurizing plants and plants for processing condensed and powdered milk have made their appearance as dairying has grown.

The Poultry Industry

A still more recent innovation in animal husbandry in Mexico is the spectacular development of large-scale poultry raising around the large urban centers since World War II. Financed mainly by local capital, the large chicken farms on the outskirts of Mexico City, Guadalajara, and Monterrey are equipped with modern poultry-raising techniques and purebred stock imported from the United States. Such establishments have largely replaced the small peasant farmer as supplier of fowl and eggs for the growing urban population.

NONAGRICULTURAL RESOURCE EXPLOITATION

Apart from farming and stock raising, there are other activities based on the exploitation of the country's natural resources. These include lumbering, sea fisheries, and the extraction of mineral wealth. Mining, of course, has been of true economic and historic significance in Mexico; but all three together have never attained the fundamental position that agriculture holds in the Mexican economy.

Forest Exploitation

Man's use of the forest cover in Mexico has been highly destructive, as it has been in many parts of Latin America. At the beginning of the colonial period, possibly 60 per cent of Mexico was covered by tall forest; today, after nearly 450 years of indiscriminate cutting and burning, the forested area has decreased to less than 20 per cent of the country's surface.

The period of greatest forest exploitation began in the late nineteenth century with the coming of the railroads and the rise of the urban population. As we have already noted (Chapter 9), one of the chief reasons for the overcutting has been the demand for charcoal. Moreover, the gradual spread of slash-burn farming in both the mountainous highlands and the lowland tropics has reduced many forest stands to scrub growth. The con-

struction of the Mexican railroads at the close of the last century, which required millions of wooden ties, added to the problem. In the past 30 years, the phenomenal growth of the larger cities has required huge quantities of lumber; and recently, the synthetic fiber plants, which use paper pulp and cellulose, have caused further inroads to be made into the remaining forests. The recent large-scale exploitation of the Mexican forests was made possible by the introduction, from the United States, of steam- and diesel-powered sawmills, equipped with large rotary and band saws. Unfortunately, federal conservation measures have proved difficult to enforce after centuries of uncontrolled exploitation.

Today, Mexico's remaining forest reserves consist of: (1) the highland coniferous forests in the northern and central parts of the country; and (2) remnants of tropical rain forest in the southeastern lowlands. The Sierra Madre Occidental contains the largest stands of unexploited pine, the main source of construction lumber. In western Chihuahua, the municipality of Madero alone produces more than half the raw logs and railroad ties cut in Mexico. Smaller remnants of coniferous forests occur in the Sierra Madre Oriental, within the volcanic axis along the southern edge of the Mesa Central (where the cut-over pine forests now produce chiefly turpentine), and in scattered areas of the southern highlands of Oaxaca and Guerrero.

For more than 200 years, native and foreign loggers and collectors of vegetable products have exploited the tropical rain forest of the humid Gulf lowlands in southern Veracruz, Tabasco, and the Yucatan Peninsula. After the decline of the colonial dyewood industry along the coast in the mid-nineteenth century, (see Chapter 10, pp. 305–306), foreign interests started large-scale cutting of the mahogany and tropical cedar trees scattered throughout the Isthmus of Tehuantepec. Until the turn of the century, quantities of logs and beams were shipped to the United States and Europe through the small lumber port of Minatitlán on the Coatzacoalcos River and, by unsystematic and destructive cutting, the Tehuantepec and Tabasco forests were depleted of their valuable cabinet woods. Today, the exploitation of tropical woods has shifted to the rain forest of Campeche and Quintana Roo, in the Yucatan Peninsula. The sawmills and plywood factories of the towns of Campeche and Chetumal are busy processing mahogany and tropical cedar logs that are hauled in from the interior forests.

Sea Fisheries

Despite a long, 5,470-mile coastline and rich offshore fauna, Mexico's fisheries, like those of many Latin American countries, are underdeveloped. Throughout the colonial period and well into the nineteenth century, only a few subsistence fisherfolk lived along the coasts; commercial fishing was practically nonexistent. Mexicans have begun to develop their fishing resources only since the 1940's, after adopting modern North American fishing gear, freezing plants, and canning fac-

tories. Even so, only about one-third of the fish caught in Mexican waters is consumed within the country; the rest of the catch is exported, chiefly to the United States.

Although the reasons for the poor development of Mexico's fisheries may be partly cultural, natural conditions have also been responsible. Excepting on the Pacific shores of Baja California, the warm seas off the Mexican coasts contain a large fish population of many species, rather than the enormous schools of a single finfish found in cooler, mid-latitudes waters. The difficulties and expensiveness of catching a single marketable species of fish in warm tropical waters are somewhat analogous to those involved in lumbering a single species of tree scattered within the tropical rain forest.

The major commercial fishing grounds of Mexico lie off the Pacific coast of Baja California; within the long, narrow Gulf of California; and along the coasts of Sinaloa and Nayarit, to Cabo Corrientes (Figure 11.22). From these areas come 60 per cent of Mexico's annual catch. The nutrient-rich waters of the cold California current, along

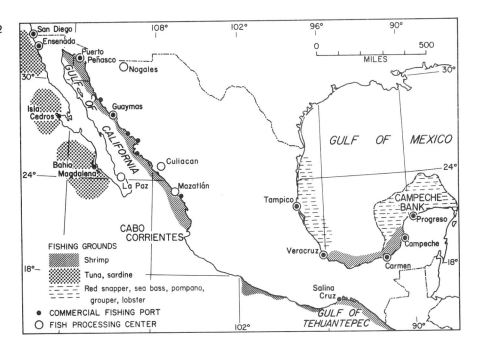

Figure 11.22
Mexican Fisheries.

FISHING GROUNDS
- Shrimp
- Tuna, sardine
- Red snapper, sea bass, pompano, grouper, lobster
- ● COMMERCIAL FISHING PORT
- ○ FISH PROCESSING CENTER

the Pacific side of Baja California, teems with large schools of sardines and tuna. These are taken mainly by United States boats operating out of San Diego and San Pedro, California, the Mexican government collecting a tax on the catch.

Extensive shrimp beds are found in the warm waters of the Gulf of California, particularly along the shallow, muddy shores of Sonora and Sinaloa and, since World War II, shrimping has been the mainstay of Mexican commercial fishing along the west coast. Most of the annual take is processed in freezing plants in Guaymas and Mazatlán and shipped to the United States. In recent years overexploitation of shrimp off Sonora and Sinaloa has drastically lowered production and has prompted many trawlers to migrate southward to the beds within the Gulf of Tehuantepec. At present about three-quarters of the total Mexican shrimp catch comes from the beds along the Pacific coast.

Mexico's second important fishing area lies within the tropical waters of the Gulf of Mexico. From the Rio Grande southward to Veracruz, the coastal waters afford an abundance of red snapper, sea bass, and pampano. The shallow, coral-strewn bottom of the Campeche bank, off Yucatan, is even more productive of these species, which are taken by boats from Tampico and Veracruz, where the catch is processed for national consumption.

The most spectacular fishing development of Mexico in recent years has been the rise of shrimping in the southern Gulf area. The main shrimp beds are off Tabasco and southern Campeche, where large rivers have deposited enormous quantities of silt and sand which make an ideal habitat for these crustaceans. The Gulf shrimping fleet, consisting of nearly 300 modern trawlers, is based mainly at Ciudad del Carmen, in southern Campeche. There, several freezing plants process the catch for export to the United States. Shrimp exports now constitute one of Mexico's most lucrative sources of foreign exchange.

Mineral Exploitation

As in colonial times, the exploitation and processing of mineral resources continues to be a significant part of the Mexican economy. The bulk of the metals extracted still comes from the old mining centers within the colonial Silver Belt (see Chapter 10, pp. 293 ff.). While Mexico remains the world's leading silver producer, the value of industrial metals, such as lead, zinc, copper, and iron, has risen to nearly 80 per cent of the country's metallic mineral production. Ferrous alloys, including cadmium, tungsten, molybdenum, and manganese, are also mined. In recent years, however, petroleum and sulphur have exceeded the metals in value and importance.

Metals. After the Wars of Independence (1810–1821), most of the old silver mines of northern and central Mexico lay in ruins. By mid-nineteenth century, with the introduction of British mining techniques and capital, silver production had gradually improved. Then, during the *Pax Porfiriana* (1877–1910), the output was greatly increased by the introduction of new ore-milling and refining processes, plus capital and management, from the United States. In 1880, gold and silver accounted for 90 per cent of the value of Mexico's mineral exports; at the turn of the century, lead, zinc, and copper production had surpassed that of the precious metals; and, on the eve of the Revolution (1910), large North American corporations held more than three-quarters of the producing mines and smelters.

Though many new mines were opened throughout highland Mexico, the greater part of the ores came from the old mining centers of colonial fame—Pachuca, Guanajuato, Zacatecas, Parral, and others (Figure 11.23). Below the worked-out silver veins of these mines there are ores abundant in zinc, lead, and sometimes copper. In the 1880's, an American company developed the rich copper deposits of Cananea in northern Sonora, and French interests opened the

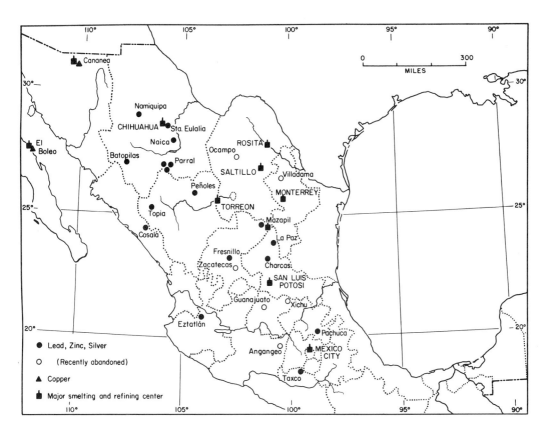

Figure 11.23
Mining and Refining Centers in Mexico : 1960.

Boleo copper mines at Santa Rosalía in Baja California. 1903 saw the opening of the large Cerro de Mercado, near Durango City, the chief source of iron ore for Mexico's growing iron and steel industry.

Although the mining industry faltered during the period of revolutionary turmoil, the production of silver and copper reached its peak in the late 1920's; that of lead and zinc, in the decades following. Since World War II, however, the extraction of these metals has declined, for the workable ores in the old mines are rapidly being depleted and foreign competition has depressed prices. Thus, many of the old mining centers of northern and central Mexico, such as Fresnillo, Pachuca, and several smaller towns, have become economic and social problem spots within the expanding economy of Mexico.

In 1961, the Mexican government established a law whereby the mining industry was to be "Mexicanized." Today only companies with majority Mexican ownership can obtain new mining concessions and such companies are entitled to half reduction of taxes on mineral production and exports. Designed to weaken the hold of foreigners on Mexico's mines and to spur mineral production with Mexican capital, the new law may help to revive the faltering industry.

Fuels. A profound change in Mexican mineral production occurred at the beginning of this century with the exploitation of the hydro-carbon fuel resources—coal, petroleum, and natural gas. In the 1880's, deposits of bituminous coal yielding an excellent grade of coke were discovered in the Sabinas Basin, northern Coahuila; by 1900, Sabinas coal had become an important fuel for railroad locomotives in Mexico, and later it fueled the iron and steel industry of Monterrey.

The exploitation of the large petroleum

and natural gas deposits along the Gulf coast began at the turn of the century. These fuel resources have been basic to Mexico's industrial growth for the past 30 years; gas and oil now furnish 80 per cent of the power used by Mexican industry and transport. First developed by North American and British corporations, the petroleum industry was nationalized in 1938; since that time the government agency PEMEX (*Petróleos Mexicanos*) has helped the industry to become the second largest Latin American oil producer.

In general, the petroleum zones of eastern Mexico are a southern extension of the Gulf coast fields in the United States. Similar oil-bearing structures, including ancient coral reefs, anticlinal folds, and salt domes, occur in both areas. By 1950, seven oil and gas provinces had been developed within the Mexican Gulf lowlands, extending from the Rio Grande to the Yucatan Peninsula (Fig-

ure 11.24). The most productive provinces lie in northern Veracruz and southern Tamaulipas, Tampico being the administrative and refining center and main oil port. In 1901, a North American company brought in the first well near Tampico. Later the famous Golden Lane (*Faja de Oro*) field, which once produced 400,000 barrels daily, was developed south of Tampico. Today, the Poza Rica province in northern Veracruz (discovered in 1931) is the most productive, yielding a fourth of Mexico's oil. Recently PEMEX has increased exploitation in the salt dome fields of southern Veracruz, on the Isthmus of Tehuantepec, and on the Tabasco coastal plain. This tropical lowland area, which also includes offshore deposits, may soon become the largest oil-and gas-producing region in Mexico. Although PEMEX has constructed several refineries in the Gulf area, much of the crude oil is transported to the Mesa Central, through

Figure 11.24
Petroleum Industry of Mexico.

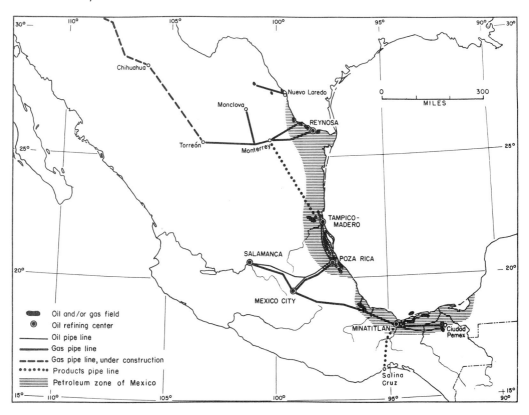

pipelines, for refining in the Valley of Mexico (at Azcapotzalco) and the Bajío (at Salamanca). Natural gas is piped from eastern Tabasco to Mexico City, and from the Reynosa fields in northeastern Mexico to the industrial centers of Monterrey and Torreón.

The exploitation of oil and gas has changed the landscape of the Gulf lowlands. Construction and operation of drilling rigs, storage tanks, depressurizing stations, pipelines, roads, and airstrips have transformed once isolated subsistence farming areas into semi-industrial regions. New settlements have been formed within the oil fields; some are permanent, well-planned modern towns, such as the administrative and refining center of Poza Rica in Veracruz and Ciudad Pemex in Tabasco; others are temporary camps for oil field hands and their families—agglomerations of wooden shacks that usually disappear with the completion of drilling operations. The network of all-weather roads within the petroleum provinces has given native farmers access to outside markets; and as laborers in the oil fields, many local inhabitants find a new source of income and are introduced to a new way of life. This acculturating influence of the petroleum industry is clearest among the lowland Totonac and Huastec Indians of northern Veracruz. The industry has also attracted from other parts of Mexico many workers and merchants who often remain in the lowlands as permanent settlers.

The exploitation of sulphur, which is associated with the petroleum deposits of southern Veracruz and Tabasco, has been the most recent development in the Mexican mineral industry. Large sulphur deposits occur near the top of salt domes that penetrate the coastal plain. First worked in 1956 by North American concerns, the deposits in the vicinity of Jaltipan, southern Veracruz, now produce 20 per cent of the Free World's native sulphur (by the Frasch process), most of which is exported to the United States via the nearby river port of Coatzacoalcos.

With the basic ingredients of oil, sulphur, and salt close at hand, a fledgling petro-chemical industry is now abuilding near the town of Minatitlán on the Coatzacoalcos River. Modern plants for the manufacture of commercial fertilizer, aromatics, synthetic rubber, plastics, and other products are in operation or are planned. Petro-chemical plants have also been established in various industrial centers on the Mesa Central, all of which are dependent on the petroleum of the Gulf coast.

MANUFACTURING INDUSTRIES

Manufacturing, partly as associated with the extractive industries discussed above, has become a significant factor in Mexico's economy and has created many changes in the landscape, particularly around urban centers. Industrialization began during the *Pax Porfiriana* of the late nineteenth century with the availability of foreign capital, the construction of railways, and the initial exploitation of power resources (petroleum, coal, and electrical energy).

Since 1940, manufacturing, like other elements of the economy, has undergone such phenomenal growth that Mexico is now one of the most industrialized countries of Latin America. It must be emphasized, however, that only 18 per cent of the Mexican labor force is engaged in industry; more than half the people are still farmers. Light industries, such as textiles, food processing, paper and wood products, and the like, predominate in Mexico's manufactures; heavy industries, including iron and steel, cement, and others, are secondary. Modern industry is restricted chiefly to the large cities, primarily within the densely peopled Mesa Central and, to a lesser extent, in those of the North.

Mexico has advantages over most Latin American countries—availability of raw materials, an adequate power base, and an abundant pool of cheap labor. On the other hand, the low purchasing power of the predominantly rural population, the inefficiency of production, the deficiency of local capital, and the lack of outside markets have tended to hinder an industrial growth comparable to that of West European nations.

Power for Industry

One of the most significant factors in the recent surge of Mexico's manufacturing industry is the availability of an adequate power resource. The hydrocarbon fuels (coal, petroleum, and natural gas) discussed in the last section are, of course, fundamental. These are used directly as industrial fuels or are converted into thermoelectrical power to operate machinery. Equally important is the development of hydroelectric power.

Figure 11.25 shows that the main hydroelectric systems, most of which have been developed in the last 20 years, are located on the eastern and southern escarpments of the Mesa Central. There, steep gradients and adequate streams afford the natural conditions necessary for hydroelectric power. The largest system is the Miguel Alemán complex, on the southern escarpment southwest of Mexico City. This complex of six hydroelectric plants, together with the Necaxa and newly constructed Mazatepec systems on the

Figure 11.25

Electrical Power in Mexico: 1964. Key to numbers and letters on map:

1. Cupatizio
2. Miguel Alemán complex
3. Necaxa
4. Mazatepec
5. Papaloapan system
6. Falcon system
7. Infiernillo (lower Balsas)
8. Malpaso (Grijalva River)
9. Novillo

  A. Mexico City (three large stations)
  B. Monterrey (two large stations)
  C. Minatitlán (one large station)

The dotted line indicates the edge of the Mesa Central.

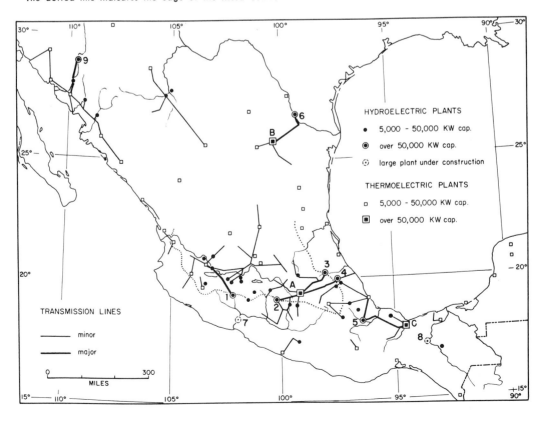

eastern escarpment, furnish the Valley of
Mexico with more than half its electrical
power. Other major hydroelectric systems include that of the Papaloapan Basin (serving
the industries of Veracruz City and Minatitlán) and the Falcon Dam Project on the
lower Rio Grande (an important power
source for the Monterrey industrial center).
The Mexican government considers electric
power so important that the industry is
almost totally nationalized.

The Textile Industry

Two of Mexico's outstanding industries—
textiles and steel—will serve as examples of
light and heavy manufacturing. Textile production is the country's oldest manufacturing
industry. The colonial, hand-operated woolen
mills (*obrajes*) established in the Mesa Central towns were discussed (Chapter 10). By
the mid-nineteenth century, European immigrants had built waterpowered woolen and
cotton mills on the eastern escarpment above
Orizaba in Veracruz state. With the development of hydroelectric power in the 1890's,
the textile industry was greatly expanded,
especially in the escarpment towns of Jalapa
and Orizaba and in the traditional cloth-
making centers of Puebla and Mexico City.
At the same time, the beginning of large-
scale cotton growing in the irrigated districts
of the north, plus the completion of trunk
railways connecting northern and central
Mexico, resulted in the rise of cotton cloth
manufacturing as the chief branch of the
Mexican textile industry.

Manta, heavy, coarse cloth used for clothing by low-income groups, is the main cotton
textile. Finer Mexican cottons found a ready
market in the United States and Latin
America during World War II, but today
little is exported.

The output of woolens has also declined.
Synthetic fibers, chiefly rayon and nylon, are
now made in Mexico. Today 20 per cent of
Mexico's industrial labor force works in textiles. As can be seen from Figure 11.26, the

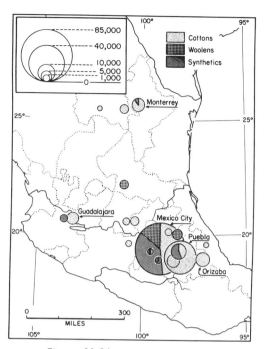

Figure 11.26
Mexican Textile Industry. Graduated circles refer to
number of workers.

main cloth centers are in Puebla and Mexico
City, where over 40 per cent of the textile
workers are concentrated.

The Steel Industry

Most underdeveloped countries, particularly those of Latin America, which have for
so long been dependent on the United States
and northwestern Europe for industrial
goods, consider iron and steel manufacturing
the basis of industrial growth. These countries
often try to force the development of this
heavy industry even if they lack the balance
of natural resources required for economic
production. Mexico, perhaps better endowed
with available raw materials for heavy industry than are most Latin American countries, was the first Latin American nation to
install a modern, integrated iron and steel
industry. This was begun in 1903, at Monterrey, in the northeastern part of the country.

Three essential raw materials are found

Figure 11.27
Aerial View of the Steel Mill at Monclova, Coahuila, Taken in 1952. Since that time the mill has been expanded to become one of Mexico's largest. (*Compañia Mexicana Aerofoto*)

in the north. There is high-grade iron ore at Cerro de Mercado, near Durango City; coking coal, in the Sabinas Basin of northern Coahuila; and limestone for flux, in the folded ranges of the Sierra Madre Oriental. But abundant water, needed in large quantities for making iron and steel, is lacking in the arid north. Monterrey, approximately halfway between the Durango iron ore deposits and the Sabinas coal field by rail, remains the chief center of the industry. In 1944, a Mexican company established a new steel mill and coking plant at Monclova, near the Sabinas coal basin northwest of Monterrey (Figure 11.27). The mills of Monterrey and Monclova now produce more than 65 per cent of the country's crude steel, the rest being made from imported scrap at the border town of Piedras Negras and in Mexico City. Mexico, whose iron and steel production has more than tripled since World War II, may become self-sufficient in the near future. Nevertheless, to exist, the industry must be protected by high tariffs; imported United States and European pig iron and crude steel is still cheaper than the local product. Although Mexicans point with justifiable pride to the rapid growth of iron and steel production in their country, the industry employs but 1 per cent of the industrial labor force and produces less than 5 per cent of the value of the total manufactures.

Distribution of Manufacturing

In Mexico, manufacturing is highly localized in a few industrial centers. Figure 11.28, based on numbers of industrial workers, shows that most of the centers are within the Mesa Central and that the Valley of Mexico, including Mexico City and surrounding towns, contains by far the greatest industrial concentration. Here, more than 60 per cent of the nation's industrial laborers work in 33 per cent of the total number of industrial establishments to produce 56 per cent of the value of Mexico's manufactures. And the concentration is still increasing. Almost the whole range of Mexican manufacturing is represented—from petroleum refining, iron and steel, and cement, through auto assembly, textiles, chemicals, electrical products, food processing, to jewelry, ceramics, and matches. The vast reservoir of cheap labor and the nearness of local markets in the densely populated Mesa Central are among the factors that may have caused this phenomenal concentration; the industrial concentration itself acts like a magnet, attracting into Mexico City more and more manufacturing plants and more and more job-seekers. Decentralization of industry is one of Mexico's pressing needs.

Other less significant manufacturing areas of the Mesa Central include the textile towns of the Puebla Basin and the eastern escarpment; Guadalajara and adjacent villages on the western side of the plateau; Toluca, west of the Valley of Mexico; and the larger towns in the Bajío of Guanajuato. The Bajío is a likely area for the construction of new industrial plants in order to relieve the overconcentration in the Valley of Mexico. In northern Mexico, the Monterrey-Saltillo zone forms the only significant industrial concentration, but around the city of Torreón in the Laguna district there is a growing manufacturing area.

The Cottage Industries

Traditional cottage industries of aboriginal or colonial origin still supplement the livelihood of many rural folk throughout Mexico. Most of these home occupations involve handicrafts, such as pottery making, woodworking, weaving, basketry, and others. They usually occupy the spare time of women and children in small agricultural villages.

As in times past, members of a given Indian or mestizo household may specialize in a particular handicraft, handing down the traditional techniques from one generation to the next. For example, the towns of Acatlán, Puebla, and Tlaquepaque, Jalisco, are renowned throughout central Mexico for their fine pottery; the towns of Olinalá, Guerrero, and Pátzcuaro, Michoacán for their lacquered woodwork; and Teocaltiche, Jalisco, for its woolen blankets. Probably the villages most highly specialized in many handicrafts are those of the Tarascan Indians in the state of Michoacán. And practically every Mixtec Indian village in the highlands of western Oaxaca specializes in making hats from palm leaf.

Commerce in cottage industrial products

Figure 11.28

Relative Importance of Manufacturing Centers in Mexico, Based on Number of Workers in Factories.

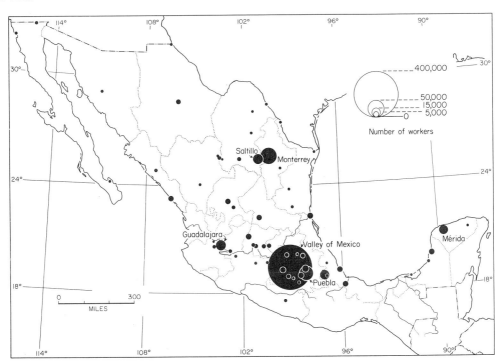

is usually confined to regional markets and fairs, although many local handicrafts are now sent to the cities for the tourist trade. The cottage industries play an insignificant role in the national economy, but they represent an integral part of traditional Mexican culture held over from the past.

THE TRANSPORT NETWORK

The development of modern transportation in Mexico is, of course, closely bound up with the growth of commercial agriculture and industry that began during the mid-nineteenth century. Most of the trunk railway lines in use today were built during the period of Porfirio Díaz, and with North American and British capital; only a few key lines have been added since 1910. The country's impressive network of surfaced highways, however, is recent; more than two-thirds of the present system was constructed after 1940, by Mexicans, and largely with Mexican capital.

The major pattern of both railroads and highways roughly follows the transport lines of colonial times. Most of the important routes converge on the Valley of Mexico, always the economic and political nerve center of the country. Main routes also connect the central plateau with the Pacific and Gulf coasts, with the north and the United States, and with southern Mexico and Central America (Figures 11.29 and 11.30).

Railways

Mexico's first rail line, finished in 1872 after 30 years of construction, connected the capital with the main port of Veracruz. The two main trunk lines, to El Paso and Laredo on the United States border, were easily constructed through the flattish desert basins and rapidly completed by 1885. The Pacific coast line to Nogales, however, was not finished until the 1920's. These routes not only served the big mining centers and irrigated farming districts of northern Mexico,

but also encouraged the growth of United States–Mexican trade. The two most recent additions to the railway network have been: (1) the line which joined the Yucatan Peninsula with Veracruz and Mexico City for the first time, completed in 1950; and (2) that between Chihuahua on the northern plateau and Topolobampo on the Pacific coast, the first railway to cross the Sierra Madre Occidental, completed in 1962. Owing to their importance to the country's economy, all Mexican railroads, except a few minor lines, are now nationalized.

Roads

The most spectacular change in Mexico's transport system in the last 30 years has been the development of highways. Full-scale automobile traffic may be said to have begun in 1936, with the completion of the Inter-American Highway link from Laredo to Mexico City. Today, with over 125,000 miles of auto roads (one-quarter of which are paved) and with well over a half-million automobiles, Mexican auto transportation is exceeded, in Latin America, only by Brazil and Argentina.

The highway pattern is much like that of the railroads. The densest net of paved roads is found in the Mesa Central, where even modern farm roads have been constructed. Four paved highways radiate northward from the Valley of Mexico to the United States border; several run from the Mesa Central to the southern and southeastern parts of the country (for example, the Inter-American Highway to Guatemala and the Gulf Circuit Highway to Yucatan); and many short transverse roads lead from plateau cities down the steep escarpments to ports along the Pacific and Gulf coasts. Unfortunately, poor maintenance often detracts from the usefulness of the Mexican highways.

Two factors have significantly promoted the rapid growth of the highway system: the tourist trade from the United States; and the development of truck freighting, which now competes successfully with the railroads.

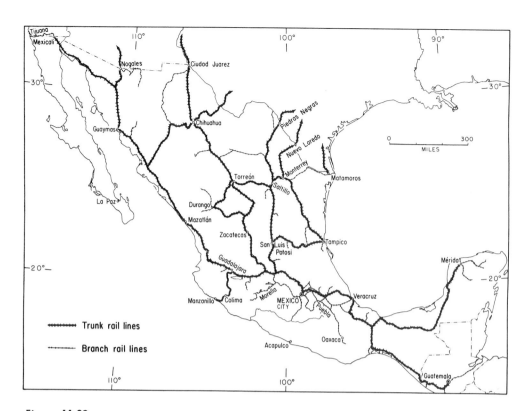

Figure 11.29
Railroad Network of Mexico.

Figure 11.30
Paved Highways in Mexico: 1960.

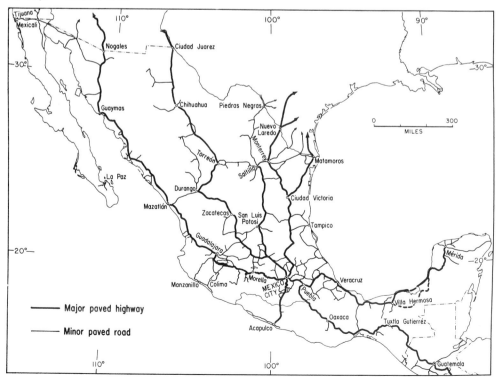

Between 1947 and 1960, the number of trucks in Mexico quadrupled; large, 12-wheeled, diesel-powered, truck-trailer combinations now carry farm and industrial products from one end of the country to the other.

Another aspect of modern transport in Mexico is the ubiquitous bus or passenger truck, heavily loaded with people and animals, bouncing along the most unlikely auto trails into remote areas of the mountainous countryside. On the paved highways, however, large Greyhound-type buses have become a major means of travel between the large cities of the country.

PORTS AND FOREIGN COMMERCE

Today, as in colonial times, Mexico's front door to overseas trade faces eastward on the Gulf coast. Since the early nineteenth century, the United States and northwestern Europe have replaced Spain as the main overseas market. At present, over 80 per cent of all foreign tonnage is cleared through the Gulf coast ports (Figure 11.31).

Veracruz remains Mexico's major port of entry, receiving half of the country's imports, but Tampico now handles more foreign commerce, including the bulk of oil exports (Figure 11.32). Tampico is the port for northeastern Mexico, which contains the industrial zone of Monterrey-Saltillo-Monclova, the oasis of La Laguna, and the oil fields of Tamaulipas and northern Veracruz. Tuxpan, a few miles south of Tampico, also ships out oil, and most of Mexico's sulphur and crude petroleum exports moves from the fields of southern Veracruz and Tabasco through Coatzacoalcos. A large part of the cotton exported from the Matamoros irrigation district of the lower Rio Grande is cleared through Brownsville, Texas, owing to the lack of port facilities on the Mexican side.

The west coast ports are much smaller and handle far less traffic than those on the Gulf.

Figure 11.31
Relative Size of Mexican Ports Based on Coastwise and Foreign Tonnage: Three-Year Average, 1959–1961.

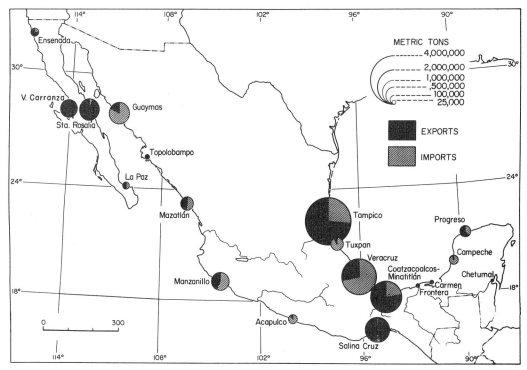

Figure 11.32

City and Port of Tampico on the Río Pánuco. Oil refineries line both banks of the river; the main wharves for commercial shipping lie just off the photograph, lower left. The main business district of the city occupies the area between the river and the Laguna Carpintero. (Compañía Mexicana Aerofoto)

With the increase of cotton production in the river oases of Sonora and Sinaloa, Guaymas, on the Gulf of California, has become the leading west coast port, shipping cotton chiefly to Japan. Cotton also leaves through the ports of Topolobampo and Mazatlán, but the exports of the Mexicali irrigation district pass through San Diego, California; approximately 50 per cent of Mexican cotton exports is cleared through United States ports. Other west coast ports engaged in foreign commerce include Santa Rosalía, in Baja California, from which copper concentrates are shipped; Venustiano Carranza, a new port on the west coast of Baja California, from which large quantities of industrial salt leave for the United States and Japan; and Manzanillo, the port for Guadalajara and the western part of the Mesa Central. Acapulco, one of the most renowned colonial ports on the Pacific coast of the Americas, no longer handles any significant cargo.

Prior to World War II, minerals, including crude petroleum, comprised three-quarters of the value of Mexico's exports, reflecting the continuation of the colonial overseas trade pattern. Since 1945, a drastic change in Mexican exports has occurred, and agricultural commodities—cotton, coffee, sugar, and cattle—now account for 60 per cent of the value of exports. Of these, cotton alone accounts for a quarter of the total. The change in the export pattern clearly reflects the revolution in Mexican commercial agriculture during the last 20 years, as well as the decline of minerals in the national economy. Mexican imports continue to consist chiefly of precision tools and machinery, automobiles and tractors, newsprint, and special foodstuffs.

Since the *Pax Porfiriana* of the late nineteenth century, the United States has been Mexico's best customer, followed by the north European nations. Recently, Japan, which imports a third of the Mexican cotton crop, has become second in Mexico's export list.

THE TOURIST TRADE

The significance of tourism to the Caribbean economy and landscape of Middle America in the past 30 years was described in previous chapters. Mexico shares with the rest of the area many of the physical factors that have attracted tourists, particularly North Americans: geographical proximity; a benign winter climate; tropical seascapes; varied mountain scenery; and the like. Mexico may be even more attractive because of its exotic folk culture of Indian origin (Guatemala also offers this); its abundance of prehistoric Indian monuments; and its many colonial vestiges, such as religious structures and quaint medieval-looking towns. The national capital, one of the world's great cities, is itself a special tourist attraction.

Tourism in Mexico began on a large scale about 1938, after the completion of the highway from Laredo to Mexico City. Thereafter, except for the war years (1941–1945), the number of foreign visitors has steadily increased. Now approximately 800,000 tourists annually spend well over a half-billion dollars within the country. As this sum accounts for more than a third of Mexico's foreign exchange income, tourism has indeed become a significant factor in the national economy.

To attract and accommodate the large influx of foreign visitors, the Mexican government has expanded its transport system. It has also encouraged the establishment of modern hotels in the larger towns, of United States-type motels along the main highways, and of resort areas in certain sections of the country. One of the most popular areas of Mexico is the formerly isolated southwest coast. This "Mexican Riviera," extending from Acapulco northward to Mazatlán, is rapidly becoming one of the world's foremost winter resort areas (Figure 11.33). A pleasant tropical climate, a scenic coast composed of rocky headlands that alternate with long stretches of sandy beaches, excellent fishing, and luxury accommodations now attract thousands of national and foreign vacationers to the main resort centers of Acapulco,

Figure 11.33
The Central Resort Section of Acapulco on the Mexican Riviera. (*Compañía Mexicana Aerofoto*)

Zihuatanejo, Puerto Vallarta, Manzanillo, Navidad, San Blas, and Mazatlán. Other rapidly developing resort centers include various sections of the warm southern escarpment of the Mesa Central, such as the Cuernavaca area immediately south of Mexico City and the hot-spring health resorts of San José Purúa in Michoacán and Ixtapan de la Sal in the state of Mexico. Easily accessible by air and highway, the large Mayan archaeological sites of Yucatan now attract a growing num-

ber of North American and European tourists. But the United States tourists spend more dollars in the Mexican border towns than in any other part of the country. With their expanding economies already firmly based on tourist trade, the usually drab border towns, from Tijuana near the Pacific to Matamoros near the Gulf of Mexico, are being beautified through the Mexican government's "Programa Fronterizo" to attract even more North Americans.

SELECTED REFERENCES

Bermúdez, A. J., *The Mexican National Petroleum Industry: A Case Study in Nationalization*. Stanford, Calif.: Institute of Hispanic America and Luso-Brazilian Studies, Stanford University, 1963.

Chardon, R., *Geographic Aspects of Plantation Agriculture in Yucatan,* National Research Council Publication No. 876. Washington, D.C., 1961.

Cline, H. F., *Mexico: Revolution to Evolution, 1940–1960.* New York: Oxford University Press, 1963.

Dozier, C. L., "Mexico's Transformed Northwest: The Yaqui, Mayo, and Fuerte Examples," *Geographical Review,* LIII, No. 4 (1963), 548–71.

Enjalbert, H., "L'essor économique du Mexique," *Les Cahiers d'Outre-Mer,* XI, No. 42 (1958), 173–96.

Gerstenhauer, A., "Die mexikanische Fischereiwirtschaft in geographicher Sicht," *Die Erde,* XCI, Heft 3 (1960), 178–90.

Kennelly, R. A., "The Location of the Mexican Steel Industry," *Revista Geográfica,* XIV, No. 40 (1954), 51–80; XV, No. 41 (1954), 105–29; XVI, No. 42 (1955), 199–213; XVII, No. 43 (1955), 60–82.

Lewis, O., *Life in a Mexican Village.* Urbana, Ill.: The University of Illinois Press, 1951.

McBride, G. M., *Land Systems of Mexico.* New York: American Geographical Society, 1923.

McDowell, H. G., "Cotton in Mexico," *Journal of Geography,* LXIII, No. 2 (1964), 67–72.

Maddox, J. G., "Economic Growth and Revolution in Mexico," *Land Economics,* XXXVI, No. 3 (1960), 266–78.

Mosk, S. A., *Industrial Revolution in Mexico.* Berkeley, Calif.: University of California Press, 1950.

Pedrero M., J. J., "Las obras de riego y el desarrollo económico de México," *Ingeniería Hidráulica de México,* XVIII, No. 3 (1964), 64–81.

Randall, L., "Labour Migration and Mexican Economic Development," *Social and Economic Studies,* XI, No. 1 (1962), 73–81.

Seawall, F., "Recent Developments in Mexican Sulphur Production," *Journal of Tropical Geography,* XV (1961), 39–45.

Simpson, L. B., *Many Mexicos* (3rd ed.). Berkeley, Calif.: University of California Press, 1963.

Tannenbaum, F., *The Mexican Agrarian Revolution.* Washington, D.C.: Brookings Institution, 1929.

Whetten, N. L., "Population Trends in Mexico," *Population Bulletin,* XIX, No. 7 (1963), 180–84.

————, *Rural Mexico.* Chicago: University of Chicago Press, 1948.

————, and R. G. Burnight, "Internal Migration in Mexico," *Rural Sociology,* XXI, No. 2 (1956), 140–51.

12

Culture Areas of Modern Mexico

In Chapter 11, we discussed the major features of Mexican culture which give expression to the geographical landscape, emphasizing the various changes in population and economy since the close of the colonial period. In this chapter, we shall suggest a possible division of Mexico into areas, basing the division principally on present-day ethnic and cultural characteristics, many of which derive from the pre-Conquest and colonial past. Such culture areas are geographical entities, within which particular cultural elements combine to pattern a landscape which is distinct from that of adjacent regions. These areas are often hard to define accurately and still more difficult to delimit precisely. In Mexico, culture areas sometimes coincide roughly with physical regions, for man's cultural manifestations within a given area are often closely associated with the nature of the land.

The largest and most fundamental cultural divisions of Mexico are the Indian-mestizo south and the European-mestizo north. The present boundary between these two divisions may be considered to be a wide zone, approximating the pre-Spanish borderland that separated the high Mesoamerican Indian farming cultures of southern and central Mexico from the nomadic hunting and gathering bands and primitive cultivators in the arid north. Figure 12.1 shows that the large regions are further divided into smaller culture areas, each with its particular cultural characteristics. Even these areas could be further divided, for the cultural scene of modern Mexico is almost as varied as its

physical character. For this reason, the term "many Mexicos" is often used to denote the multitude of regional differences within the country. Here, as in many other Latin American nations, the local inhabitants often refer to their *patria chica* ("little homeland"), the small culture area to which they and their families feel that they belong, and most Mexican rural folk feel a stronger political allegiance to their *patria chica* than to the nation. In predominately Indian areas, the inhabitant usually views his individual village and surrounding lands as a cultural and geographical entity to which he professes a strong social attachment.

THE INDIAN-MESTIZO SOUTH

This area is by far the more important of the two large cultural divisions of Mexico. It had a large population before the Conquest, and even today it contains nearly three-quarters of the Mexican people. It was the locale of the ancient Mesoamerican civilizations and the main center of Spanish colonial activity. Today its population is chiefly mestizo, but in many sections the people are pureblood Indians, in others, unmixed Caucasians. The over-all culture of the area is a mixture of Indian and Hispanic traits, but there are sizable sections, such as the Oaxaca Highlands and the Yucatan Peninsula, in which most of the people are of Indian blood and culture.

The northern border of the Indian-mestizo south coincides only partially with the pre-

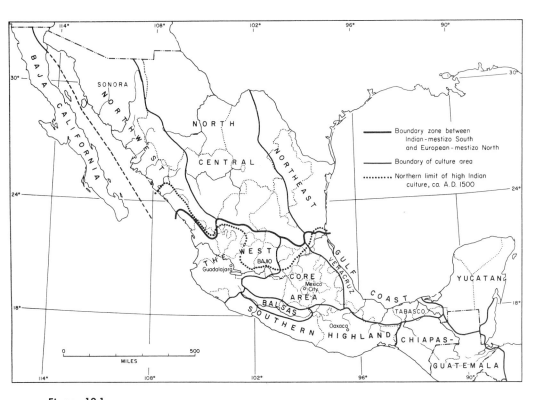

Figure 12.1
Culture Areas of Modern Mexico.

Conquest limit of high Indian culture. The middle portion of the border has been pushed northward, to the vicinity of San Luis Potosí and Zacatecas, through migrations of people from the central part of the country. A closer correlation perhaps exists between the northern border and the transition between the volcanic Mesa Central and the arid Mesa del Norte. The southern boundary of the Indian-mestizo south is little affected by modern international limits; it extends beyond Guatemala and includes parts of Honduras and El Salvador. For convenience of presentation, however, these areas will be considered in the chapter on Central America.

The Core Area

The outstanding culture area within the Indian-mestizo south occupies the eastern and middle portions of the Mesa Central, including the eastern and southern plateau escarpments. For lack of a better term, we shall call this "the core area." Since before the Conquest, it has been the cultural center of all Mexico. It contained the hearths of the Aztec and Tarascan states and is still an area of much Indian tradition. During the colonial period, it was the political and economic center of New Spain. Today it contains the national capital and the densest population of the country. An important agricultural zone, it is also the industrial and transportation hub of modern Mexico and contains many large cities which have a veneer of modern European-North American culture.

The well-watered volcanic basins on the plateau form one of the significant physical features of the core area. Probably for more than 3,500 years, the fertile soils of the basins and lower mountain slopes have attracted a dense farming population, and the food available in the numerous lakes that occupy many of the basin floors has been equally attractive. The most important volcanic basin is the Valley of Mexico, flanked by those of Toluca and Puebla. Located more than 1.5 miles above the sea, most of the basins enjoy a bracing, tropical highland climate (*tierra fría*).

The steep tropical escarpments bordering the plateau on the south and east form a part of the core area chiefly by reason of the close trade relations with the adjacent highland basins which have existed since pre-Conquest times. In the course of this active trade, many elements of highland culture have penetrated the upper escarpment valleys. The tropical basins of Morelos, south of the Valley of Mexico, not only furnish the highlands with sugar, tropical fruits, and rice in return for wheat flour and manufactures; but they also have become sites for winter homes of the Mexico City elite and recreational areas for highland urban vacationers, much as they were for Aztec nobility nearly 500 years ago.

Racially, the bulk of the population within the core area is mestizo. A sizable portion, however, is of pure Indian blood, and about 10 per cent, largely urban, is of Caucasian descent.

Enclaves of Indian speech and aboriginal mores dot the area. The total number of Indian-language speakers, however, is probably no more than one million, or about 7 per cent of the core area population. The Otomí, who number around 185,000 souls, occupy a large section north and northwest of the Valley of Mexico. One group, together with the closely related Mazahua (85,000), live in parts of Toluca Basin and adjacent mountain slopes, where semidispersed rancheria settlements and scattered hillside milpas have changed little since the Spanish Conquest. A still larger Otomí enclave covers the semiarid and highly eroded Mesquital Valley in Hidalgo state, one of the most forlorn of the *patrias chicas* in Mexico. Other important Indian groups within the core

area include the Highland Totonac in northern Puebla state, the highland Huastec of easternmost San Luis Potosí, and the Tarascans of central Michoacán. Scattered throughout the area are small groups of Nahuatl speakers, highly fragmented remnants of a once-solid distribution, who now number perhaps 600,000.

Although they have lost most of their aboriginal culture, including the Nahuatl language, the people of densely populated Tlaxcala state are mainly of Indian blood. Still cognizant of their pre-Conquest independence of Aztec domination, they occupy another *patria chica* within the main core area. The sharp contrast between the remaining Indian strongholds and the modern urban centers is one of the important cultural characteristics of the core area, and one that makes it perhaps the most interesting of all Mexico for the student of human geography.

Prior to the agrarian reforms of this century, two rural settlement forms prevailed in the core area: (1) the large colonial-type hacienda with its elaborate living center (*casco*); and (2) the agglomerated village, including the landholding Indian settlements and those of mestizos who had lost their land to the encroaching haciendas. The compact rural village still prevails but the hacienda has been almost completely destroyed, for the *ejido* program of land redistribution has gone farther in the core area than in any other section of Mexico. Some large holdings still exist north of the Valley of Mexico for the cultivation of maguey (for pulque), and a few stock ranches (some for the breeding of fighting bulls) remain. Most of the village and *ejido* farmers on the plateau raise maize, beans, and squash, as subsistence crops, and wheat and barley, as cash crops. Owners of small private holdings and some collective or individual *ejidatarios* in the escarpment areas cultivate commercial crops such as coffee and citrus.

Large urban centers form another component of the settlement pattern within the core area. Some of the cities, such as Puebla,

Orizaba, and the federal capital, have a long history of industrialization, especially textile, and are now leading manufacturing centers. Modern Western culture has influenced the cities so greatly that they provide an exceptional contrast to the surrounding rural scene, still largely colonial or even pre-Conquest in character.

Mexico City

Greater Mexico City and its satellite towns in the Valley of Mexico form a special cultural region within the core area. With nearly five million inhabitants, the Mexican capital is one of the world's great cities and the largest in Latin America. This vast urban sprawl is unique in Middle America, the much smaller metropolitan area of Havana, Cuba (1.2 million) being its closest rival in size.

Mexico City occupies one of the least favorable sites in the nation for the development of a large urban center. It was an historical accident that Cortes and his men chose to build the administrative center of New Spain upon the ruins of Tenochtitlán, which occupied a low, marshy island near the western shore of Lake Texcoco. The Spaniards soon learned that the waters of the lake would flood the site yearly. Consequently, attempts to drain the lakes of the Valley of Mexico by artificial means were started during the seventeenth century, but this engineering feat was not completed until 1900, when the tunnel of Tequixquiac was opened in the northern part of the valley. Through this breach, the lake waters now flow northward to the upper tributaries of the Río Moctezuma and thence to the Gulf of Mexico. The draining of the lakes has decreased the danger of flood within the older part of the city, but the partially dried bed of Lake Texcoco has become the source of saline dust clouds which are swept into the urban area by easterly winds during the dry winter season.

An even more serious problem arises from the peculiar character of the subsurface alluvium on which the city is built. The top 200 feet of basin fill consists of fine silt and clay saturated with water. In the past 40 years, overpumping from deep wells has caused the surface to sink at a rate which, in places, has increased to about one foot annually. A large portion of the city's business section has been affected by this sinking, which has damaged buildings, water lines, and sewage disposal systems. Lacking a firm foundation, some of the tall, modern buildings in the city are constructed on gigantic steel drums that float in the spongy alluvium.

Mexico City's most pressing physical problem is the lack of sufficient local water to meet its growing requirements. Only short, intermittent streams drain the surrounding mountain slopes into the closed basin; the numerous springs which issue from the porous lava flows bordering the Valley once supplied most of the city's water, but they now furnish only a small part. Since 1900, wells bored into the basin alluvium have supplied increasing amounts of water for the city; at present, one-third of the daily consumption is pumped from wells as deep as 1,000 feet below the surface. Even this supply has not kept pace with growing needs—and, as we have already noted, the rapidly lowering water table is causing the basin surface to sink. In the past few years, engineers have been forced to go outside the Valley for water. In 1951, the Lerma aqueduct, which carries water to Mexico City from the copious springs of the upper Lerma River in Toluca Basin, was finally completed with the blasting of a tunnel through the Las Cruces range. This abundant source now supplies the city with nearly 30 per cent of its needs, but the increasing demand will necessitate the further tapping of sources outside the Valley, and at enormous cost.

For 350 years after its founding, Mexico City's growth was inordinately slow. By mid-nineteenth century, the built-up section had reached beyond Alameda Park on the west; to the east, expansion was sharply

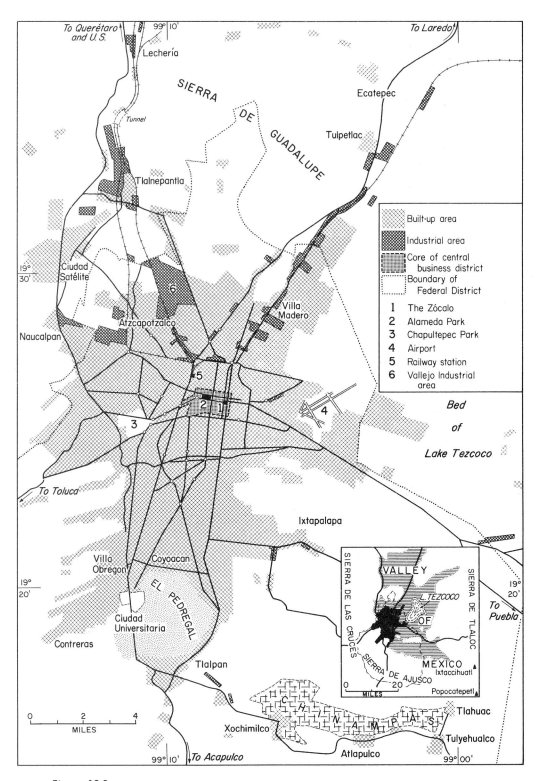

Figure 12.2

The Metropolitan Area of Mexico City. The heavy lines represent the main traffic arteries of the city. The floor of the Valley of Mexico is shown in the inset.

limited by Lake Texcoco. By 1920, the more elite residential sections had reached beyond Chapultepec Park to the lower foothills of the Las Cruces range. The city achieved its present phenomenal size in the past 30 years, during which it engulfed agricultural villages and market towns on the western side of the Valley. The solidly built-up areas now cover approximately 100 square miles and, in places where industrial suburbs are still expanding rapidly, extend far beyond the city limits (Figure 12.2).

The functional areas of Mexico City, as of many old European urban centers, form a highly complex pattern that has evolved with little planning. The traditional central business district lies between the Zócalo (the plaza that formed the center of the colonial city) and the Alameda to the west. Since 1940, the main hotel and office area has expanded southwestward along the famous Paseo de la Reforma, in lines of tall, ultra-modern buildings. As in most cities of the world, retail and service activities line the main traffic arteries (Figure 12.3).

Most of the older residential areas are composed of closely spaced apartment buildings or European-type chalets enclosed by stone walls. Even in the elite residential suburbs along the foothills west of Chapultepec Park, elaborate homes usually lack the spacious yards cherished by North American suburbanites. Slums are found throughout the city. The recent arrivals from the countryside have spawned the largest ones, especially around the industrial districts and along the edge of the dry Texcoco lake bed on the eastern edge of town. In certain sections of

Figure 12.3

Air View of the Central Part of Mexico City, Looking Eastward Over the Valley of Mexico Toward the Dry Bed of Lake Texcoco and the Sierra de Tlaloc. Snow-capped Ixtaccihuatl appears, upper right. In the foreground is the Alameda, a park formed in the seventeenth century; beyond is the old section of the city, including the Zócalo, or main plaza, built upon the ruins of Tenochtitlán, the Aztec capital. (*Compañía Mexicana Aerofoto*)

the city, however, the municipal government has destroyed many of the worst slums to make way for community apartment units, such as that of Nonoalco, housing 90,000 people.

Although Mexico City's industrial areas are scattered in many parts of the metropolis, the greatest concentration of plants clusters in the vicinity of Tlalnepantla, Naucalpan, and Azcapotzalco, former agricultural towns northwest of the old city. Another important manufacturing district lies northeast of town, along the Laredo Highway from Villa Madero to Ecatepec Morelos. The smoke and gaseous wastes from the industrial plants and from the exhausts of the thousands of automobiles that clog the city streets have created a serious air-pollution problem. The dull, grey haze and smog which envelop Mexico City most of the year obscure the beautiful views of surrounding mountains that one could enjoy only 20 years ago.

The West

The western part of the Mesa Central and adjacent Pacific slope form another culture area within the Indian-mestizo south. This culture area might be termed "the west" (*El Occidente*), as it includes the western part of Mexico's traditional heartland. Although in some respects similar to the core area, the west has sufficient cultural differences to set it apart as a separate region. Most of the area can be identified with the state of Jalisco, with Guadalajara as the regional capital. Peripheral sections include the states of Colima, Nayarit, Aguascalientes, and parts of Zacatecas and Guanajuato. Roughly, this area formed the core of the colonial province, New Galicia. Guadalajara was the administrative capital and seat of a circuit court (*audiencia*) that had jurisdiction over most of western and northwestern New Spain. The present-day cultural distinctiveness of west-central Mexico derives mainly from its colonial history. Characterized by a dense population, large agricultural produc-

tion, and growing industry, the significance of the west to Mexican economy and culture is second only to that of the core area.

The plateau surface of the west, like that of the core area, is composed of highland basins filled with fertile lacustrine soils bordered by volcanic hills and mountains. In the west, however, the basin floors are 1,000 to 1,500 feet lower and, consequently, enjoy a milder tropical highland climate (*tierra templada*). The productive Bajío of Guanajuato is the largest basin, followed in importance by those of Guadalajara, Ameca, and Sayula near the western edge of the plateau. Along the Pacific escarpment, at lower altitudes (2,000 to 3,000 feet), the attractive basins of Tepic, Autlán, and Colima form fertile spots of level agricultural land amidst a jumble of steep, rugged slopes. The Pacific coastal plain forms a narrow ribbon of *tierra caliente* in Colima and Jalisco states and widens considerably in Nayarit, where rich alluvial deltaic plains alternate with extensive tidal swamps.

The most distinctive cultural feature of the west is its lack of a strong Indian tradition, in contrast to the rest of central and southern Mexico. Although it was part of the ancient realm of high aboriginal culture, its pre-Conquest population was apparently never as dense as that to the east. Moreover, during the first years of Spanish Conquest, the mortality of the Indian population of this area was very great so that Indians were few in number throughout the colonial period. A handful of Hispanicized Nahuatl speakers near the town of Tuxpan, southern Jalisco, forms the only Indian group remaining in the west. The northeastern section of the area, which includes the Bajío and the Basin of Aguascalientes, was inhabited by the nomadic Chichimec, who left no cultural heritage.

The mixing of Indian and Spanish cultures that was so characteristic of other parts of Central Mexico therefore occurred in the west only on a modest scale. Today, it is a land of predominantly Hispanic culture. The rural houses are of Andalusian and Extremaduran origin; the ox draws the wooden plow in the fields; and Indian slash-burn cultivation of wooded slopes is unimportant. Although the aboriginal crop complex of maize-beans-squash predominates in subsistence agriculture, the cultivation of wheat, barley, and the European horse bean (*haba*) is not insignificant.

Another distinctive feature of the west is its colonial land-tenure system. Until the Revolution, there were many large haciendas, chiefly for raising livestock, and the small rancho, of 50 to 500 acres, is still a significant holding for both subsistence and commercial agriculture. The land is usually worked by a single family, either mestizo or of pure Spanish descent. The proud, Spanish-like peasantry is best exemplified by the tall, blue-eyed men of the Los Altos district of northeastern Jalisco, around the towns of Arandas, Tepatitlán, and San Juan de los Lagos. The people of this *patria chica* are deeply religious Roman Catholics and are among the most conservative of all Mexicans.

Not all of the *rancheros* of the west are farmers, however; many are small-scale stockmen of long tradition. From this group comes the famous *charro,* the distinctively costumed Mexican horseman who has been popularized in song and legend throughout the nation.

Although there are agricultural villages throughout the west, the dispersed ranchero dwellings are equally characteristic of the rural settlement pattern. Like the core area, the west contains a number of medium-sized cities overshadowed by a large urban area— in this case, Guadalajara (population, 734,-000). Although its sphere of political and commercial influence is less than it was in colonial times, Guadalajara remains the metropolis of western Mexico, and is of growing industrial importance. Like Mexico City, it is connected to a seaport (Manzanillo, on the Pacific coast) by railroad and highway via a steep escarpment route. The smaller cities of the western area, as well as many medium-sized towns, have grown from pueblos or villas founded by Spanish settlers in the sixteenth and seventeenth centuries and still retain much of their colonial Hispanic flavor in architecture and custom. Most of the towns function as market centers for restricted areas. The largest and most rapidly growing cities are those of the Bajío, where León (226,000), Irapuato (83,000), Celaya (59,-000), and Salamanca (30,000) form an urban cluster ripe for industrial expansion.

The Bajío is a special geographical entity within the western culture area. Though its role as the breadbasket of Mexico has diminished in recent years, it remains one of the most productive agricultural sections of the country (Figure 12.4). Despite the abun-

Figure 12.4
Harvesting Garlic Near Apaseo in the Eastern Part of the Bajío of Guanajuato. Various parts of the fertile Bajío specialize in growing certain crops. For example, Apaseo is known for its garlic, Irapuato for its strawberries, and Salvatierra for its peanuts.

dance of *ejidos* created from expropriated haciendas within the basin, the Bajío is still a stronghold of the western *rancheros,* whose holdings, now reduced to small farms through divisions by inheritance, date from the colonial period.

The Gulf Coast Area

In terms of physical environment and economy, the coastal zones of Veracruz and Tabasco stand apart from the adjacent highlands. Yet these lowlands show many historicultural attachments to the core area. Before the Spanish Conquest, the central Gulf coast formed an integral part of the Aztec tribute state, supplying tropical and marine products to highland markets and the Valley of Mexico nobility—a function continued through the colonial period and retained still today. Many Indian language groups flourished before the Conquest, and Nahuatl was widely spoken in many lowland villages and was the trade language throughout the coastal zones. From the time of the Conquest, the port of Veracruz and the escarpment roads have closely bound the central Gulf coast to the core area.

The outstanding physical characteristics of the central Gulf lowlands include the tropical, practically frost-free climate (*tierra caliente*) and the fertile alluvial soils that border the numerous streams that flow from the highlands to the Gulf (see Chapter 2). Most of the area is hilly, and in some places low elevations are interrupted by mountains, such as the volcanic Sierra de Tuxtlas in southern Veracruz. Extensive plains occur only in Tabasco.

Like the core area, the Gulf coast is today mainly mestizo in race and culture. Only a few purely Indian groups remain. The lowland Huastec (about 25,000 native-language speakers) and the lowland Totonac (50,000) live in scattered pueblos and rancherias in northern Veracruz; small groups of Nahuatl-speaking folk are found on the lower escarpments; and the few remaining Popoluca oc-

cupy the eastern portion of the Sierra de Tuxtlas. Nevertheless, the mestizos (many of pure Indian blood) of Veracruz and Tabasco retain a large number of aboriginal traits in their largely Hispanic culture. One which is immediately expressed on the landscape is slash-burn cultivation, especially on hillsides or, as in Tabasco, in level forested areas. Indian houses typical of the *tierra caliente* (mainly of wattle construction) predominate throughout the lowlands.

The rural mestizos of lowland Veracruz are known as *Jarochos.* This folk name implies a number of culture traits peculiar to the Veracruzanos, including a distinct Spanish dialect and regional foods, dress, music, and attitudes. In northern Veracruz live the *Jarochos del Norte,* who are cattle herders and slash-burn cultivators, some with private holdings, others with individual *ejidos.* The *Jarochos del Interior* are farmers who cultivate the fertile stream alluvium and hillsides of the lower escarpment, west and southwest of Veracruz; and the people of the Sotavento, descendants of the colonial herders, are chiefly cattlemen who still run sizable herds on the savannas and coastal marshes between Veracruz City and the Tuxtla Sierra. Another subculture area corresponds to the Tuxtlas volcanic highlands, still largely an Indian enclave, which was opened to commercial agriculture (tobacco) in the last century and is now important for the cultivation of the famous small black beans of Veracruz. Steeped in the colonial tradition of cattle raising and commercial cacao production, the people of Tabasco have developed a kind of *patria chica* within the coastal lowlands; the local area called "the Chontalpa," the alluvial deltaic plain of the Mezcalapa River in the western part of the state, has a long history of cacao cultivation and subsistence farming on natural levees along the abandoned distributaries of the river.

Long neglected because of tropical diseases, the Gulf coast area has, within the last half-century, become one of Mexico's most rapidly developing economic regions. Various new developments in land use in Veracruz and Tabasco, mentioned earlier (Chapter 11) include: (1) the new growth of stock raising in northern Veracruz made possible by planting nutritious grasses for pasture and improving cattle breeds; (2) the increase in tropical commercial farming with cultivation of sugar cane, citrus fruit, and cacao on river flood plains and terraces; (3) the development of government-sponsored agricultural and industrial projects for colonizing and resettling the coastal areas, such as the Papaloapan Valley Authority in southern Veracruz and the Grijalva Commission in Tabasco; and (4) possibly the most significant, the growth of the petroleum industry, including the recent beginnings of petro-chemical manufactures based on local oil, natural gas, salt, sulphur, and abundant supplies of water. Perhaps no other large region of Mexico has undergone such rapid and fundamental changes in the past three decades and holds greater promise for the future than the Gulf coast area.

The Balsas Lowland

Sandwiched between the Mesa Central and the southern highlands of Mexico, the Balsas lowland forms a distinct natural region characterized by a peculiar cultural pattern. This structural depression, 350 miles long, has the dubious distinction of being the hottest part of Mexico the year round. The highland Tarascan Indians still call it *jurío* ("the infernal region"). Deprived of moist air from both the Pacific and the Gulf, it is also quite dry, some rain falling only in the summer months. Consequently, low, tropical scrub covers most of the depression, including the lower slopes of the adjacent escarpments. Although it is low in elevation (500–1,500 feet), most of the surface is hilly, level land occurring as spots of alluvium along the Balsas River and its tributaries and as alluvial piedmont plains north of the Río Tepalcatepec.

In most of the lowland, a sparse mestizo population ekes out a precarious living on scattered ranchos and *ejidos* by herding cattle, farming, gathering a few wild plant products, and trading. Since the Spanish Conquest, cattle raising has been the most widespread activity of the Balsas. There the herder is completely clothed in tough leather, and even his horse wears an apron of rawhide as protection against the thorny bush.

Besides hides and dried meat, one of the most typical products of the smaller Balsas cattle ranchos is a soft, salty, white cheese (*queso blanco*), traded widely in the adjacent highlands. Subsistence farmers, using slash-burn techniques, plant maize, beans, and squash on hillside plots or till the fertile spots of alluvium along the rivers with the plow or the ancient *coa*. Since 1870, some of the best alluvial stretches along the rivers have been planted to sesame, which yields abundantly in this hot land; today these lowlands yield more than 80 per cent of Mexico's sesame seed, from which a fine industrial oil is extracted. Mention has already been made of the irrigation developments in the Tapalcatepec piedmont plain, where cotton, rice, coconuts, and limes comprise the main commercial crops.

A sizable number of Balsas lowland people make a living by gathering wild plants, such as the fronds of low palm which are used in the plateau villages to the north for making hats. A more important product is the pod of the cascalote, a low leguminous tree, which yields tannin for the leather industry.

Since aboriginal times, there has been active trading between the hot lands of the Balsas and the cool Mesa Central to the north. During the colonial period, the mule driver (*arriero*) became important in the Balsas and escarpment areas. Long mule trains carried tropical products, hides, and cheese to the highland markets and returned with wheat flour and clothing for the Balsas rancheros. Lowland towns such as Apatzingán and Churumuco originated as trading stations. Today, with the advent of auto roads, many of the old Balsas trails have fallen into disuse, and the *arriero* is rapidly disappearing here, as in all parts of Mexico.

The Southern Highlands

The rugged Sierra Madre del Sur of southern Michoacán and Guerrero states and the equally mountainous Mesa del Sur of Oaxaca comprise a culture area that is here called "the southern highlands." As defined, it includes not only the cool uplands, but also the steep, scrub-covered Pacific escarpment, the hot coastal fringe, and the semiarid plains and hills on the southern side of the Isthmus of Tehuantepec. Moreover, the northern edge laps over into the dry upper Balsas drainage, and the eastern border includes portions of the humid escarpment that overlooks the Gulf lowlands of southern Veracruz. The difficult terrain of this jumbled highland mass, as well as its relatively poor, overworked and eroded soils, help make it one of the most backward and poverty-stricken parts of Mexico.

The Valley of Oaxaca, in the center of the Mesa del Sur, is the only extensive level section in the uplands. Intensively cultivated for over 2,000 years, the once fertile soils of the valley are now badly depleted. In terms of arable land, most of the southern highlands are overpopulated despite a low over-all population density. The uneven distribution of people and lack of good communications are reflections of the highly complex terrain. The recent irrigation developments in the Tehuantepec Isthmus and the spectacular growth of tourism along the Guerrero coast are the only bright spots in the picture.

The rugged surface of the southern highlands has made it an ideal refuge for remnant Indian groups, and it is consequently one of the most aboriginal parts of the country. Its cultural core is the state of Oaxaca, where approximately 600,000 individuals, 35 per cent of the state's population, speak Indian languages and retain a good part of their aboriginal culture. Of a total of 14 different

major Indian languages spoken in Oaxaca before the Conquest, 12 are still extant, and possibly 35 to 40 dialects and subdialects of these languages are still spoken. The two most important Indian language groups are the Zapotec (200,000 individuals) in the eastern part of the state, and the Mixtec (185,000) in the western half. Other large aboriginal groups include the Mazatec (75,000) in northern Oaxaca; the Mije (45,000) who inhabit the high, isolated mountains of east-central Oaxaca; and the Chinantec (30,000), who dwell on warm, humid eastern slopes of the Oaxaca plateau.

Culturally, the western part of the highlands (the Sierra Madre del Sur of Guerrero state and southern Michoacán) is peripheral to the Oaxacan core. Only in eastern Guerrero are Indian languages still spoken (Nahuatl, Tlapanec, and Amusgo), and only by a few thousand people. Nevertheless, certain aspects of aboriginal life, such as primitive slash-burn cultivation, wattle-daub and thatch house construction, Indian foods, and a fatalistic outlook characterize the mixbloods of the Sierra Madre del Sur.

Subsistence farming is the chief economy of the southern highlands. Except for the use of the plow on level-to-rolling terrain, cultivation techniques are essentially aboriginal (Figure 12.5). However, some Old World farming practices, in particular, wheat cultivation and sheep rearing, have been adopted by the mountain Indians of Oaxaca. On mountain slopes above 8,000 feet, many Indians plant small patches of wheat as a cash crop; in all parts of the highlands, but especially around the Mixtec villages in western Oaxaca, the annual wool clip from small herds of sheep furnishes supplemental income. In addition, there are the usual cottage industries common in most Indian areas.

The few spots of modern commercial agriculture within the southern highlands occupy tropical or subtropical zones on the Pacific escarpment and coast; these include the Pochutla coffee zone along the southern escarpment, the irrigated plains of Tehuante-

Figure 12.5
Cultivating Maize with Oxen-Drawn Wooden Plows (Ards) in a Small Valley in Oaxaca.
Such scenes are typical in rural sections of Mexico.

pec, and the long stretch of coconut plantations along the beach ridges of the Guerrero
coast.

In the Oaxaca and Guerrero highlands,
the landholding village is the basic unit of
settlement among the Indians and many
mestizos. As in ancient times, the village lands
are often worked communally, though many
villagers now have legal title to individual
plots. Usually a number of villages and their
satellite rancherias (small groups of scattered
dwellings on the mountainside) surround the
larger market towns inhabited by mestizos and
some whites; there the Indians hold the
colorful weekly, or even daily, markets that
are the delight of foreign visitors. There are
few cities in the southern highlands. Oaxaca
City (68,000 inhabitants) and Chilpancingo
(17,000) are both state capitals and the
largest urban centers in the mountainous
interior. Modern Acapulco (60,000), on the
Guerrero coast, is an aberrant development
and foreign to the native culture of southern
Mexico.

Prior to the Agrarian Revolution of 1910,
large haciendas controlled the best agricultural lands in the southern highlands, especially those in the Valley of Oaxaca. Similarly,
the stock-raising districts in the Pacific lowlands of Oaxaca and Guerrero, as well as
the pastures of Tehuantepec, were in large
holdings. In the Mesa del Sur, however, the
hacienda was never the important institution
that it was in central Mexico. Today the
federal government has expropriated most of
the large estates within the Valley of Oaxaca,
granting some lands to the surrounding
Indian villages and creating *ejidos* with the
remainder. Elsewhere in the uplands, the
ejidos derived from expropriated haciendas
are overshadowed in importance by communal Indian village lands.

A large number of *patrias chicas*, or small
culture units, characterize the southern highlands. Most of these are based primarily on
geographical area and aboriginal language;
secondarily, on economy, dress, and social
organization. All such culture units have
particular names known to all the inhabitants
of neighboring *patrias*. One of the best known
is the Mixteca Alta, which covers the high
mountains of west-central Oaxaca—the present stronghold of the Mixtec-speaking Indians
and the center of ancient Mixtec culture.
Immediately southward is the Mixteca Baja,
which comprises the rugged surfaces with

warm valleys of low elevation where sub-tropical crops are grown. The highland Zapotec in eastern Oaxaca has formed several small cultural units, all distinct in landscape and culture from the lowland Zapotec of Tehuantepec, where the women are famed for their beauty and their colorful native dress.

Chiapas

Most of the state of Chiapas is culturally more closely associated with Guatemala than with Mexico. Except for the Soconusco Coast along the Pacific, pre-Conquest Chiapas formed part of the ancient highland Maya culture area. During the colonial period it was a province attached to the Captaincy of Guatemala, and it did not become a Mexican state until 1824.

Today, Chiapas is composed of two cultural units. One is the predominately mestizo southern half which includes the Valley of Chiapas (drained by the upper Río Grijalva), the Sierra Madre de Chiapas, and the narrow Pacific coastal plain. The other is the predominately Indian plateau (the Meseta Central de Chiapas) and adjacent limestone ranges in the northern part of the state. The major cultural aspects of both areas stem from the colonial period; except for some agricultural developments in the Sierra Madre and the Pacific coastal plain, the cultural landscape of Chiapas has changed little since the end of the eighteenth century.

Attracted by spots of savanna grasslands scattered through the tropical scrub, Spanish stockmen occupied the valley of Chiapas early in the sixteenth century; Spanish encomenderos also quickly assumed control of the native cacao groves along the Soconusco coast. In these lowland areas, the Indian population gradually dwindled; by the end of the colonial period, the people of southern Chiapas had become largely mestizo in blood and culture. The only remaining significant Indian area is at the eastern end of the Sierra Madre, where a Mam-speaking group extends across the Guatemalan border into Mexican territory.

Stock raising remains a major occupation in the valley of Chiapas; but with the redistribution of many hacienda lands to *ejidos,* the area devoted to subsistence agriculture has increased. This has been especially true on the gentle northern slope of the Sierra de Chiapas, where the *llanos,* the wide grassy valleys which were formerly pasture, are now fields of maize and beans. The present coffee zone along the steep Pacific escarpment of the sierra and the rapidly expanding commercial growing of bananas and sugar cane on the Pacific coastal plain around Tapachula are extensions of similar economic activities in neighboring Guatemala.

High and cold (6,500–9,000 feet elevation), and forested with pine and oak, the Meseta Central of Chiapas (sometimes called the "Sierra de San Cristóbal") attracted few Spaniards during the colonial period. The administrative and religious centers of Ciudad Real (now San Cristóbal) and Comitán were the only important Spanish settlements on the plateau. Today, the northern Chiapas highlands are the refuge of numerous Indian groups, most of which speak languages related to Maya. Approximately 200,000 Indians, comprising about half the highland population, live in agglomerated villages and semidispersed rancherias scattered over the rough plateau surface. The Tzotzil and Tzeltal (about 125,000 people) are the most important aboriginal groups.

The international boundary between Mexico and Guatemala, which runs directly through Indian country, has little meaning for the related families on either side of the border. Long isolated from outside influences, the Chiapas Indians are perhaps the least Hispanicized in southern Mexico. The highly publicized Lacandon people who inhabit the rain forest of northeastern Chiapas now live more primitively than did their Mayan ancestors. Cultivation is of the slash-burn dibble variety, land is held by the village, houses are pre-Conquest types, and dress, particu-

Figure 12.6

The Chiapas Highlands Near San Cristóbal de las Casas, Showing Pine-Clad Slopes and a Mountain Meadow, Where Indian Women and Children Tend Flocks of Sheep.

larly of the women, is typically Indian. Among the few elements of Old World culture that the Indians of Chiapas (like other highland aborigines) have integrated into their present way of life are sheep raising and the use of wool for making homespun cloth (Figure 12.6).

San Cristóbal de las Casas (15,000 population) is the only large town in the Chiapas highlands. It is the administrative and commercial center of the entire area, and its daily market draws Indian traders from most parts of the plateau. Located on the paved Inter-American highway, San Cristóbal is now sharing in Mexico's rich tourist industry.

Yucatan

Although physically a peninsula of the mainland, Yucatan is culturally an island. It is probably the least Mexican portion of the country; even today, many inhabitants of the peninsula consider themselves Yucatecos, not

Mexicans. This provincial attitude is the ultimate expression of the *patria chica* concept that has created so many Mexicos.

The limestone lowlands of Yucatan contrast with the mountainous character of most of Mexico. As we mentioned earlier (Chapter 2), the porous character of the limestone in the northern third of the peninsula has led to the development of underground, rather than surface drainage. *Cenotes,* or steep-sided sinkholes, are the major landform, and important sources of drinking water. Soils are red, thin, and not very fertile. The tropical scrub forest that covers most of northern Yucatan results from paucity of soil moisture and centuries of slash-burn farming.

The hilly southern part of the peninsula, including the Petén of northern Guatemala, receives more rainfall than the northern plains and is covered by heavy rain forest. Once the center of classical Mayan culture, and famed for its numerous elaborate stone temples and palaces, this area was practically depopulated long before the Conquest. Since colonial times, the rain forest of this *despoblado* has served as a barrier to human movement, isolating densely populated northern Yucatan from direct contact with both Mexico and Guatemala.

An equally important isolating factor was the conservative and hostile attitude of the Maya Indians toward the Spaniards. Initially difficult to subdue, the Mayas of northern Yucatan rebelled many times against the Spanish encomenderos and *hacendados* who had usurped a large part of the best Indian lands during the colonial period. The last serious native rebellion occurred in 1847, when Mexican estate owners came close to losing the entire peninsula to the Indians.

Like most of the other culture areas of southeastern Mexico, Yucatan contains a large Indian population. About 300,000 Maya-speaking people, mainly poverty-stricken subsistence farmers, comprise nearly half the population of the northern part of the peninsula, including the state of Yucatan and parts of Campeche and Quintana Roo.

These Indians retain a large number of aboriginal traits. Slash-burn dibble farming and the ancient maize-bean-squash crop complex form the basic subsistence economy. The Indians reject almost completely the Old World ox-drawn plow, both from conservatism and from the impracticability of the tool in the small, rocky milpa patches. Although the native apsidal, straw-thatched house is typical, the prevailing agglomerated village with a gridlike street plan stems from the Spanish resettlement program of the sixteenth and seventeenth centuries.

During the colonial era, Spaniards established large cattle haciendas in the northern part of the peninsula. By the end of the nineteenth century, most Indian villages had lost their anciently held lands to the encroaching haciendas, but the villagers were permitted to till parts of the estate for subsistence crops. As we explained earlier (Chapter 11), henequen cultivation and processing began on a large scale in northern Yucatan during the last quarter of the nineteenth century, the biggest plantations taking over the best agricultural lands in the vicinity of Mérida, the capital city of Yucatan state. This enterprise gave rise to a class of wealthy Yucatecos, mestizo and white, whose palatial houses in Mérida are now but a reminder of the days just prior to the outbreak of the Agrarian Revolution in 1910. Today, most of the large henequen plantations have been broken up into *ejidos*, and estate lands that rightfully belonged to Indian villages have been returned. Although henequen cultivation still forms an important part of the economy of northern Yucatan, the Maya Indians utilize most of the peninsula for subsistence farming, practicing ancient slash-burn cultivation on the thin soils, just as their ancestors did a thousand years ago.

Except for the immediate coasts, where commercial coconut farming has developed in recent years, most of the southern part of the peninsula is a sparsely inhabited wilderness. Some lumbering of tropical timbers goes on, but the most widespread activity in the rain forest for the past half-century has been the collecting of *chicle,* the latex of the chicosapote tree (Achras sapota), which is used for chewing gum. Hundreds of Mayan *chicleros* wander through the unsettled forest, tapping trees for the latex which they bring to collecting stations for shipment to processing plants in Campeche and Chetumal. Most of the chicle is sent to the United States, where chewing gum has been used since the 1890's.

THE EUROPEAN-MESTIZO NORTH

More so than in the Indian-mestizo south, the landscape of northern Mexico reflects, in settlement forms, house types, and economic activities, the impact of Hispanic culture. Although the population is predominantly mestizo, the north contains a large number of whites, mainly members of proud families descendent of Spanish colonists. Only in northwestern Mexico are there some Indian groups, the remnants of a once sizable aboriginal farming population. Elsewhere in the north, the bands of primitive nomads that formerly scourged Spanish settlements have long since disappeared, leaving few traces of their culture.

Northern Mexico, which comprises 60 per cent of the national territory, contains but a quarter of the country's people. In this arid to semiarid land, spots of dense rural population occur chiefly along river oases and in irrigated zones. Large desert areas in Baja California, northwestern Sonora, and on the Mesa del Norte are totally uninhabited, forming true *despoblados*.

Since the sixteenth century, northern Mexico has been an area of frontier expansion. The Spaniards, attracted by silver deposits and grasslands, spread northward from central Mexico, carrying with them their Hispanic culture (see Chapter 9). Today, as new irrigation districts are opened or expanded and as industry grows in the cities, Mexicans continue to migrate northward from the overpopulated central part of the country.

The European-mestizo north is here divided into four smaller culture areas: (1) the north-central area, corresponding generally to the Mesa del Norte; (2) the northeast, including the states of Tamaulipas, most of Nuevo León, and the northeastern part of Coahuila; (3) the northwest, principally the states of Sonora and Sinaloa; and (4) the peninsula of Baja California (Figure 12.1).

The North-Central Area

This highland desert-steppe area forms both a physical and cultural entity. Throughout the area, the Spanish economic complex of mining and stock raising, firmly established in colonial times, still prevails.

In this section, the large estates devoted to stock raising have been little affected by the Agrarian Revolution. The most favored area for the establishment of the ranch-mine complex was the wide belt of grassland that occupies the semiarid foothills and basins on the eastern side of the Sierra Madre Occidental. In this Silver Belt, the present cities of Zacatecas, Durango, Parral, and Chihuahua grew out of the administrative centers of colonial mining and stock-raising settlements. Eastward, Spanish miners and stockmen also colonized the less favorable areas of desert basins and ranges, founding centers such as Matehuala, Mazapil, and Saltillo.

Irrigated farming, begun on a modest scale in colonial times, has boomed in the Mesa del Norte during the present century. The productive Laguna area of central Coahuila and the Las Delicias district on the Conchos River in Chihuahua are now among the most productive mechanized farming areas of Mexico. In other desert oases that were settled during colonial days are found practices of Mediterranean origin, such as wheat and barley cultivation, vineyards and wine making; the widespread use of the ox-drawn wooden plow and the two-wheeled cart. Such practices, plus the ubiquitous flat-roofed adobe rural house of Moorish origin, give the north-central area a definite Hispanic cast (Figure 12.7).

In contrast to the predominant Spanish cultural heritage in the Mesa del Norte, an

Figure 12.7

A Small Hacienda Center Near Saltillo, Coahuila State. Flat-roofed adobe structures and a small church contrast with the pretentious hacienda buildings of Central Mexico. In the background irrigated fields of maize, wheat, and grapevines occupy the central portion of the basin oasis.

economy that may derive from the nomadic Indian still prevails in the desert. Here the wild desert plants are gathered for processing into useful products, an occupation which provides a livelihood for an estimated 40,000 families that live in small hamlets scattered throughout the desert basins and mountain slopes (Figure 12.8). One of the most important products is *ixtle,* a fiber obtained from the short, fleshy leaves of a small agave (lechuguilla) and from the spiny leaves of a yucca (palma). Both these plants are widespread in the eastern portion of the central desert south of Saltillo (Figure 12.9). Rope, twine, sacks, and huaraches, or native sandals, are made from *ixtle* fiber and, since the 1930's, foreign demand for twine and rope has greatly increased Mexican *ixtle* production. Other desert plants gathered in north-central Mexico include *candelilla,* a small euphorb that produces a wax used in industry; *guayule,* which yields a rubber-producing latex; and *tuna,* the fruit of the pricklypear cactus, once an important Indian food, now processed to make nutritious confections such as *queso de tuna* ("tuna cheese"). The ex-

ploitation of these plants has been so intensive in the last few decades that some have disappeared from the scant vegetation of large sections of north-central Mexico. As a result, many desert gatherers have been forced to migrate to the cities to find other occupations.

Since the end of the last century, some religious groups have migrated to north-central Mexico. In 1885, Mormons from the United States formed several agricultural villages in the vicinity of Casas Grandes, northwestern Chihuahua. By 1912, the colonies contained 4,000 people, but the rigors of the Revolutionary period forced most of the colonists to disband and only a handful remain. In 1922, the Mexican government permitted the entry of several hundred Mennonites (of German-Russian descent) from Canada. They founded agricultural colonies at Cuauhtemoc, west of Chihuahua City; at Patos, north of Durango City; and near Saltillo, in Coahuila. Today over 12,000 German-speaking Mennonites live in 65 villages on the Cuauhtemoc colony alone, with lesser numbers in Durango and

Figure 12.8
A Typical Desert House in a Small Community of *Ixtleros,* or Lechuguilla Collectors, Northern San Luis Potosí State, Mesa del Norte.

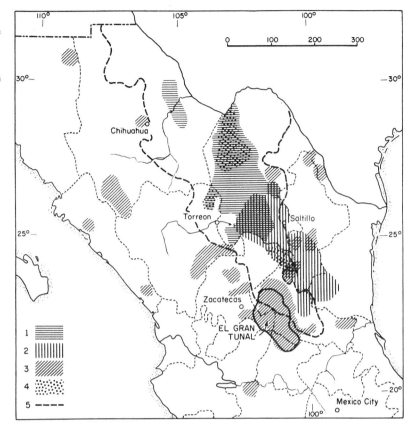

Figure 12.9

Gathering of Wild Desert Plants:
Main Areas of Production.
1. Candelilla (wax)
2. Lechuguilla (agave fiber)
   and palma (yucca-leaf fiber)
3. Tuna cactus fruit
4. Guayule latex
5. Interior desert of northern
   Mexico

Coahuila. So populous have these settlements become that many Mennonites are migrating to British Honduras to form new cells. The Mennonite settlements in Mexico are characterized by elongated, European-type street villages; by names such as Kleefeld, Blumengart, and Schanzenfeld; by north-German houses and barns; and by dairy farming which emphasizes the production of cheese and butter.

The Northeast

This region covers the subhumid coastal lowlands and the adjacent hill areas between the Pánuco River and the Rio Grande. An isolated, poverty-stricken land a century ago, it is today one of the most progressive sections of Mexico. The state of Nuevo León and its capital and industrial city, Monterrey, form the regional hub, overshadowing the adjacent state of Tamaulipas and its administrative center, Ciudad Victoria.

Although Spanish stockmen settled the central part of Nuevo León in the late sixteenth century, the Crown did not effectively occupy most of the northeast until the mid-eighteenth century, when Spanish farmers entered after the defeat of the Indian nomads. Thus, the cultural landscape of the northeast (like the north-central desert area) is chiefly Hispanic in origin and character and, excepting for the recently arrived mestizos from central Mexico, both the rural and urban families are predominantly of Caucasian stock. One of the most interesting cultural features of the northeast is its distinctive rural house, with white stone or plastered walls, neatly thatched or tiled roofs, and quaint outside chimney (the latter possibly an introduction from Anglo-America) (Figure 12.10).

Figure 12.10
Typical Rural House of Northeastern Mexico.

Within the last 50 years, the northeast has become a leading industrial and agricultural section of Mexico. The exploitation of the Sabinas coal deposits, the lower Rio Grande gas fields, and the oil reserves north of the Río Pánuco have been significant factors in the rise of Monterrey and towns adjacent to it as the leading industrial center of the north. Iron and steel are two of the main products of this area. The recent development of mechanized cotton farming on irrigated lands in the Rio Grande delta, and the opening of new agricultural areas on the rich calcareous soils in southern Tamaulipas, have also furthered the economic development of the northeast.

A particular feature of this area is its close economic and cultural ties with the United States. Three paved highways and two railways lead directly from Monterrey to the United States border. Another main highway leads from Brownsville to Ciudad Victoria and from Piedras Negras to Monclova, Saltillo, and Monterrey. Four large border towns, each with its United States counterpart, are within the northeast. It is not surprising that Monterrey has many characteristics of a North American city, in contrast to the definite Hispanic cast of most other north Mexican urban centers.

The Northwest

Physically and culturally, the northwest is the most complex region of northern Mexico. As defined here, it includes all of Sonora, most of Sinaloa, the extreme western parts of Chihuahua and Durango, and the northeast corner of Baja California. The northwest comprises three major physical zones: (1) the dry coastal lowlands, which include fertile river flood plains and deltas; (2) the subhumid basins and ranges of eastern Sonora and Sinaloa; and (3) the moist, rugged, pine- and oak-covered Sierra Madre Occidental.

Despite its physical complexity, the area retains some cultural unity through its aboriginal heritage, now greatly modified by Hispanic peoples and traits. The northwest today is the most Indian area of northern Mexico. Before the Conquest, it was the only significant part of the north that was inhabited by large groups of sedentary farmers. Today, the most numerous of these are the Mayo (28,000), who live in the flood plains and deltas of southern Sonora and northern Sinaloa, and the Tarahumar (23,000), primitive mountain farmers and hunters of the northern Sierra Madre Occidental in Chihuahua. Others, now reduced to small remnants, include the Yaqui (4,000) of southern Sonora and a few Pima in northwestern Sonora, both flood-plain dwellers; a small number of Opata in the basins of central Sonora; and a handful of primitive Seri, who now fish off the desert coast of Tiburón Island in the Gulf of California. Except the Tarahumar and Seri, most Indian groups have been fairly well integrated into modern Mexican rural life. Indian culture, however, has left its mark on the landscape—the maize-beans-squash crop complex still dominates subsistence farming and the aboriginal wattle and daub rural houses are the prevailing type.

More important in the northwest, however, is the mark of the colonial Spaniard. As in the Mesa del Norte, the mining of silver and the raising of livestock became the prevailing colonial economy, lasting, especially in Sonora, until the present time. Mission settlements among the Indians, and presidios or garrisons placed at strategic points to protect settlement and trade from frequent Apache raids, were also features of Hispanic settlement in the northwest. Spanish control centered in the high grassy basins within the Ópata Indian area of northeastern Sonora (towns of Ures, Arispe, Nacozari) and in the flood plain of the Río Culiacán in northern Sinaloa.

The last half-century has brought great changes to the northwest—mechanized farming, new highway and rail transport, and port facilities. Perhaps the most significant of these has been the rise of commercial agriculture in the coastal river flood plains and deltas (see Chapter 11, pp. 329–30).

Through government construction of dams and reservoirs for irrigation water, the arid coast from the Colorado delta (Mexicali area) to central Sinaloa has become Mexico's foremost producer of cotton, wheat, and winter vegetables (Figure 12.11). This has resulted in drastic changes in the landscape of those coastal areas where water is available for irrigation. The scrub-covered range lands of the cattle haciendas were converted to large irrigated fields which now belong to *ejidos* or to small private holders who cultivate by modern, mechanized methods.

The development of modern port facilities is another important change in the northwest. Guaymas and Mazatlán, formerly small fishing villages, now export agricultural products and mineral concentrates and import machinery and Mexican petroleum for the mechanized farms. The growing fishing industry in the Gulf of California, encouraged

Figure 12.11
Irrigated Lands of the Deltaic Plain of the Fuerte River, Northwestern Mexico. These contrast with the dry, cactus-covered slopes of the surrounding hills. Tomato packing plants are seen in the middle background.

by the new port facilities and processing plants, has enhanced the importance of the northwest in modern Mexican economy.

As we have already indicated, much of the impetus and the technical knowledge for the recent agricultural developments in the northwest derives from the United States. Similarly, the renascence of mining in Sonora came with the opening of the Cananea and Nacazori copper deposits by United States investors and engineers at the beginning of this century. Moreover, the proximity of the northwest to the stock-raising areas of southern Arizona, as well as to the landholdings of American stockmen in Sonora, facilitated the introduction of the improved cattle breeds which are now replacing the rangy *criollo* stock in northern Mexico.

Baja California

Far from central Mexico, effectively isolated from the mainland by the Gulf of California, and poor in economic resources, the long, arid peninsula of Baja California has always stood apart from the rest of the country. Only since World War II, with the increase of rapid air travel across the Gulf and the construction of a paved highway and railroad around the north side of the Gulf, has the peninsula become easily accessible to the Mexican heartland. Like Yucatan, Baja California, though physically a peninsula, was long a cultural island.

Aridity is the basic characteristic of most of Baja California. Only the northwestern Pacific coastal plain and the adjacent interior mountains, which receive winter cyclonic rains, and the cape region at the peninsula's southern tip, which is moistened by late summer tropical storms, fall outside the area of desert climate. The central part of the peninsula, which receives less than four inches of rain annually, is probably the most arid section of Middle America. There are no sizable rivers like those of Sinaloa and Sonora to serve as a physical base for agriculture in Baja California. The scant settle-

ment in the desert clusters around springs that issue from old lava flows.

During the colonial era, the Spaniards found little to attract them to the peninsula. The Catholic orders from the mainland, founding mission settlements among the scant, nomadic, hunting and gathering Indians were the actual colonizers. The missions in the desert between the cape area and the moist northwestern sector were founded at spring oasis sites. After the near extermination of the Indian population in the early nineteenth century by European diseases, the mission settlements reverted to small stock-raising centers and producers of irrigated Old World fruits such as dates, figs, and citrus. Oasis towns such as Mulugé, Comondú, San Ignacio, and San José de Gracia, with their date and citrus orchards, resemble places in southeastern Spain or in the Sahara of North Africa. Most of the village farmers and stockmen are of Spanish or mestizo origin.

Mining has been relatively unimportant in Baja California. Only one mining center is of any significance—that of Santa Rosalía on the desolate Gulf coast, where copper ore has been extracted and smelted on a large scale since 1885. The demand for local agricultural products in the mining town is the sole economic basis for the continued existence of the oasis farming settlements in the desert interior.

The cape region of Baja California, having climatic and cultural affinities with the adjacent mainland coast, is geographically distinct from the rest of the peninsula. Although moistened by summer tropical rains (10–25 inches yearly), the area is semiarid. Cattle and goats browse over most of the scrub-covered hill lands; but tropical products such as sugar cane, plantains, and citrus, as well as truck crops, are cultivated by irrigation in the alluvial valleys and coastal lowlands. The largest urban center is La Paz (24,000), the capital of Baja California Sur territory and the center of a growing tourist industry based on deep-sea fishing off the coast.

Geographically, northwestern Baja California is more akin to southern California of the United States than to the rest of the peninsula. Winter rains and chaparral vegetation extend southward, beyond the United States border, as far as San Quintín on the coast. Moreover, California-type farming, of Spanish origin, including the cultivation of wheat, citrus fruits, and the vine, are characteristic of northwestern Baja. Since the 1930's, wine production has become a major industry in this part of Mexico, and the vineyards around Ensenada and Tecate vie

with those of Parras and Coahuila in north-central Mexico, both in output and in the quality of the wine and brandies. Northern Baja California, together with the Mexicali irrigated cotton area (here considered part of the northwest culture area), is the most populous and economically important section of the peninsula. The border city Tijuana (150,000) and Ensenada (45,000) attract thousands of United States tourists yearly and also boast a growing industry, based mainly on tuna fishing off the coast.

SELECTED REFERENCES

Beltrán, E., *El Hombre y su Ambiente: Ensayo sobre el Valle de México*. Mexico, D.F.: Fondo de Cultura Económica, 1958.

Dicken, S. N., "The Basin Settlements of the Middle Sierra Madre Oriental, Mexico," *Annals of the Association of American Geographers*, XXVI, No. 3 (1936), 157–78.

Gierloff-Emden, H. G., "Die Halbinsel Baja California: Ein Entwicklungsgebiet Mexikos," *Mitteilungen der Geographischen Gesellschaft in Hamburg*, LV (1964), 1–160.

Helbig, K. M., "Das Stromgebiet des obern Río Grijalva: Eine Landschaftsstudie aus Chiapas, Süd-Mexiko," *Mitteilungen der Geographischen Gesellschaft in Hamburg*, LIV (1961), 5–274.

Megee, M. C., *Monterrey, Mexico: Internal Patterns and External Relations,* University of Chicago, Department of Geography, Research Paper No. 59. Chicago: University of Chicago Press, 1958.

Pfeifer, G., "Sinaloa und Sonora: Beiträge zur Landeskunde und Kulturgeographie des nordwestlichen Mexico," *Mitteilungen der Geographischen Gesellschaft in Hamburg*, XLVI (1939), 289–460.

Redfield, R., *The Folk Culture of Yucatan.* Chicago: University of Chicago Press, 1941.

Schmiedehaus, W., "A Beleaguered People: The Mennonites of Mexico," *Landscape,* IV, No. 1 (1954), 13–21.

Schmieder, O., "The Settlements of the Tzapotec and Mije Indians, State of Oaxaca, Mexico," *University of California Publications in Geography,* IV (1930), 1–184.

Soustelle, G., *Tequila: Un village nahuatl du Mexique oriental,* University of Paris, Institut d'Ethnologie, Travaux et Mémoires No. 62. Paris, 1958.

Stanislawski, D., *The Anatomy of Eleven Towns in Michoacán,* Latin-American Studies, No. 10. Austin, Tex.: University of Texas Press, 1950.

Taylor, P. S., *A Spanish-Mexican Peasant Community: Arandas in Jalisco, Mexico,* Ibero-Americana, No. 4. Berkeley, Calif.: University of California Press, 1933.

Termer, F., "Die Halbinsel Yucatán," *Petermanns Mitteilungen,* Ergänzungsheft No. 253, 1954.

Wagner, P., "Parras: A Case History in the Depletion of Natural Resources," *Landscape,* V, No. 1 (1955), 19–28.

Waibel, L., "Die Sierra Madre de Chiapas," *Mitteilungen der Geographischen Gesellschaft in Hamburg,* XLIII (1933), 12–154.

West, R. C., *Cultural Geography of the Modern Tarascan Area,* Institute of Social Anthropology Publication No. 7. Washington, D.C.: The Smithsonian Institution, 1948.

13

Present-Day Central America : Part One

Much of the present landscape of Central America, like that of Mexico, has its roots in the aboriginal and colonial past. But whereas some sections of the isthmian area have remained little changed since the eighteenth century, various political, social, and economic forces have greatly modified other sections. In this chapter and the one following, we shall trace the landscape changes that have occurred in each of the Central American countries since the early nineteenth century.

After it became independent of Spain in 1821, most of the colonial Captaincy General of Guatemala devolved into five small independent states, while Yucatan and Chiapas became part of Mexico. Much later, in 1903, Panama, a former province of Colombia, was made a separate country.

The nineteenth century also saw the introduction of new commercial export crops, such as coffee and bananas. These revolutionized the economy, introduced new forms of land tenure, and caused significant changes in settlement in many parts of Central America; they also helped to tie the Central American countries more closely to the United States in terms of trade and political and cultural influences. Banana culture, in particular, with its associated tropical plantation system and imported Antillean Negro labor, opened new agricultural areas and intensified the West Indian or Rimland character of the Caribbean littoral of Central America.

Again, it was during the nineteenth and early twentieth centuries that the transisthmian routes across Central America be-

came highways for international trade and travel, culminating in the completion of the Panama Canal in 1914. And, since World War II, Central America has experienced an even greater population explosion than Mexico, leading to the crowding of capital cities with rural refugees. But only in Costa Rica has the rapid population increase led to vigorous colonization of empty lands.

Although impressive advances have been made in some of its countries in recent years, Central America cannot boast of large-scale advancement of industry and transportation such as has occurred in Mexico during the last 30 years.

POLITICAL FRAGMENTATION

The division of Central America into a number of tiny nations is indeed striking. What are the reasons for this political fragmentation of a contiguous land area whose major way of life is Hispanic?

In colonial times (see Chapter 9), the area that now comprises five Central American countries formed provinces within the Captaincy General of Guatemala, whereas Panama came under the political jurisdiction of New Granada (Colombia). It appears that the present political separatism has its roots in these colonial provinces, for in each there developed around the provincial capital a single population cluster, usually separated from that of the neighboring province by sparsely peopled areas difficult of access. Examples of such clusters include the small

Meseta Central of highland Costa Rica, the lowland lake country of western Nicaragua, and the silver-mining area of the Honduran highlands. Largely neglected by a disinterested home government, the isolated Central American provinces were left much to their own devices. Moreover, the difficulties of travel between the provinces hindered cultural interchange. Thus, each population core tended to develop local loyalties and often distinctive culture patterns, to an even larger degree than in the *patrias chicas* of Mexico (see Chapter 12, p. 356).

Mainly for these reasons, the Spanish colonial provinces broke up into separate states despite attempts at political unification. Today, most Central American countries are still dominated by a single population core which contains the national capital. In some, however (e.g., Honduras), secondary centers which have been developing since the late nineteenth century now threaten to eclipse the traditional centers in economic and political importance.

Efforts to hold together the five Central American provinces after independence have included the abortive union with Mexico (1821–1822) and the longer-lasting but ineffective United Provinces of Central America, a federation which lasted from 1823 until 1839. By 1960 there had been no less than 25 separate attempts to revive political unity among the Central American republics, and all have failed.

CENTRAL AMERICAN POPULATION

Today over 13 million people live in Central America. Most are concentrated on the Pacific side of the isthmus, where they occupy both tropical lowland and highland environments. In contrast, the rainy, forested Caribbean versant is, with some exceptions, sparsely populated. This general distribution pattern has persisted in Central America since aboriginal times.

Population densities vary greatly even in the well-settled Pacific area, because of the traditional clustering of the populations. Rural densities of over 1,000 persons per square mile occur in the Meseta Central of Costa Rica, and the over-all density of little El Salvador, in the Pacific lowlands, is now approaching 350 people per square mile. On the other hand, certain rugged and mountainous sections of the Pacific slope may have population densities of 5 to 15 per square mile, as low as those in most parts of the Caribbean sector.

The population of Central America, almost stagnant during much of the colonial period, is now increasing more rapidly than that of any other major region in the world. Yearly rates of increase vary from 3 per cent in Honduras to more than 4 per cent in Costa Rica. The rapid increase in numbers, added to the high rural densities that already obtain in the overcrowded Pacific clusters has led to: (1) the sudden growth of urban centers, mainly the capitals, as people migrate to them from the country; and (2) the beginnings of colonization of the empty forests on the Caribbean slope.

The new colonization, which has progressed slowly in most of Central America, has gained momentum since World War II. Figure 13.1 shows the present frontiers. Pioneer colonization began first in Costa Rica (in the early nineteenth century) and has progressed farthest there. In Panama, peasants from the Pacific lowlands penetrated northward into the forest-covered mountainous interior, but the movement has stagnated at the continental divide. In Nicaragua, farmers from the densely settled lake lowlands and central highlands, encouraged by the government, are slowly moving into long unoccupied portions of the Caribbean versant. Similar movements have occurred in Honduras and are beginning in Guatemala, where the government has recently established agricultural colonies within the southern Petén in the northern part of the country. In overcrowded El Salvador, which has no Caribbean frontage, there has been movement toward the national frontier only to emigrate. With that exception, Central America still has abundant land (albeit much is of questionable farming quality) for its expanding population. However, a major problem is the reluctance of conservative rural folk, deeply attached to their crowded places of birth and to their local customs, to move to unfamiliar environments.

Racially, the Central Americans are highly varied. Half of Guatemala's population is Indian, but only remnants of aboriginal groups are found in the rest of the isthmus. The Costa Ricans are unique for their high percentage of Caucasian blood, most of the highlanders being almost wholly white. Elsewhere in the well-settled Pacific versant, Central Americans are largely mixed Indian-

white with occasional traces of Negro blood.

Much of the Caribbean coast is noted for its high percentage of Negroid population (Figure 13.2). Negro slaves were brought to the Caribbean shores by English woodcutters and smugglers as early as the seventeenth century, but most of the present-day Negroes descend from English-speaking West Indian islanders who came to work on the banana plantations and the Panama Canal at the beginning of this century. These Negroes and their offspring live in well-defined areas on the Caribbean side of Panama, Costa Rica, and Nicaragua. The Black Caribs, descendent of mixed Negro-Indians from the Leeward Islands whom the British forcibly marooned in the Bay Islands of Honduras at the end of the eighteenth cen-

Figure 13.1
Status of Settlement in Central America: Mid-Twentieth Century. (*After G. Sandner*)

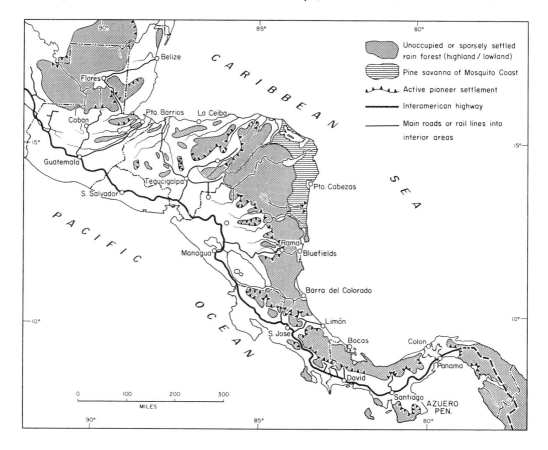

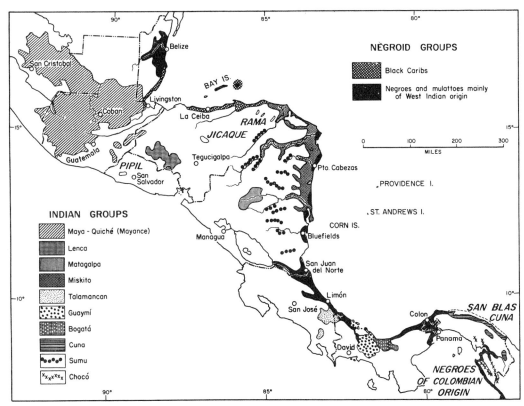

Figure 13.2
Distribution of Indian and Negroid Groups in Central America : c. 1960.

tury, form still another Negroid group. Nearly 30,000 of these curious people, who speak an Arawakan dialect, are subsistence farmers and fishers along the Caribbean shores of Honduras, Guatemala, and British Honduras.

THE ISTHMIAN FUNCTION OF CENTRAL AMERICA

Because of its form and geographic position, the long, narrow land of Central America has played two important roles in the cultural history of the Americas. Central America served, first, as a land bridge connecting North and South America. In prehistoric times, it was a roadway over which plants and animals moved between the two continents. Later, American Indians used it

for migrations and cultural interchange. After the Spanish Conquest, when the narrow land mass became a barrier to seafaring Europeans who wished to cross from one ocean to the next, the isthmus assumed a second role. The constrictions—the narrowest and lowest portions—of the mountainous isthmus became key points for the Spaniards; the same constrictions are still important crossing points.

As we saw in Chapter 10, the earliest and most significant crossing was Panama, the narrowest portion of the Central American isthmus. Other colonial crossings included the Nicaragua Rift, the Comayagua Depression in Honduras, and, occasionally, the Isthmus of Tehuantepec in southern Mexico. Owing to economic depression and political turmoil, however, transport over the isthmian crossings lagged in the eighteenth and early nineteenth centuries.

Traffic was suddenly revived after the discovery of gold in California in 1848. Rather than endure the long, dangerous trip overland across the United States, thousands of Europeans and eastern North American gold seekers took sea passage to California via the Central American crossings, particularly the route between Puerto Bello and Panama City. In 1855, to facilitate this growing traffic, North American interests completed the Panama Railway. The crossing via the Nicaragua Rift—up the San Juan River from Greytown and across Lake Nicaragua to San Juan del Sur on the Pacific—became another important route to the California gold fields. And, although less important, the Tehuantepec crossing was sufficiently used to instigate the construction of a transisthmian railway from the Pacific coast to Coatzacoalcos on the Gulf of Mexico, not completed until 1902.

Since colonial times, men had envisioned the construction of sea-level canals across the Central American isthmus, but it was only with the increase in oceanic traffic following the opening of the American west and the rise of the United States as a two-ocean

sea power that serious consideration was given to such a gigantic undertaking. Between 1850 and 1900, United States and European engineers surveyed more than 30 transisthmian canal routes from the Isthmus of Tehuantepec to the Atrato River and its lower tributaries in northwestern Colombia. Of these, the old Panamanian route was favored, mainly because of its short 50-mile distance between the two oceans.

French interests first began excavations of a canal across this route in 1882, but yellow fever and inadequate machinery forced them to abandon the project. After political maneuvering and outright military intervention that resulted in the independence of Panama from Colombia, the United States, in 1903, obtained from the newly organized nation the right to build the canal. Completed in 1914, the Panama Canal, together with the Canal Zone, came under virtual United States sovereignty. In recent years the Canal has become inadequate and a new waterway, to be constructed through one of the many possible transisthmian routes, is under consideration (Figure 13.3).

Central America's old isthmian role of land bridge between the two continents may soon be revived with the completion of the

Figure 13.3
Transisthmian Routes of Central America.

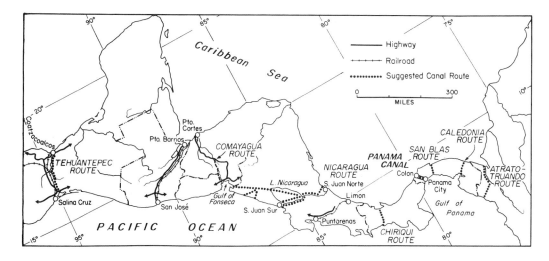

Inter-American Highway. However, a 400-mile stretch through sparsely populated rain forest in eastern Panama and northwestern Colombia remains to be constructed before the highway can actually resume that function. Although short sections of the Inter-American Highway were completed for local use in the 1930's, it was not until World War II that military necessity forced a unified construction program, financed mainly by the United States. In 1964, it finally became possible to drive with comparative ease from the United States to Panama City over this highway.

THE CENTRAL AMERICAN ECONOMY

Agriculture

Today, Central America's economy revolves around agriculture, much as it did in colonial days. At present, for example, more than two-thirds of the area's 13 million people gain their living by farming; agriculture contributes 37 per cent of the area's gross product; agricultural products account for 90 per cent of the value of Central American exports—this despite the fact that less than 10 per cent of the land is under cultivation.

In Central America, food crops and techniques for subsistence cultivation have not changed appreciably since colonial, or even pre-Conquest, times. Primitive slash-burn or dibble farming is even more widespread here than in Mexico, and more common among subsistence farmers than is the ox-drawn wooden plow. Maize, beans, and squash still form the major crop complex of subsistence farmers of Mesoamerican Indian heritage living in Guatemala, El Salvador, much of Honduras, and western Nicaragua; whereas in eastern Nicaragua, Costa Rica, and Panama, tubers of South American Indian origin are as important as maize in the rural diet and Old World rice is now becoming more common than any of the aboriginal foods.

That part of the Central American economy that has undergone the greatest change during the last 100 years is commercial agriculture. In Chapter 10 we saw that stock raising and the cultivation of indigo and cacao formed the economic cornerstone of most of the Central American provinces during the colonial period. This pattern continued until the mid-nineteenth century. Thereafter, the growing of coffee in the tropical highlands revolutionized commercial farming and changed the rural landscape of many Central American states. A second revolution in commercial farming came near the end of the nineteenth cntury, when North American fruit companies established large banana plantations in the Caribbean lowlands. Still a third change, the growth of mechanized cotton farming on large estates in the hot Pacific lowlands, occurred after World War II.

Today, coffee, bananas, and cotton are Central America's most remunerative products; together they constitute nearly 80 per cent of the value of its exports. These three crops occupy the best agricultural lands, yet they supply no food for the area. Much of the foreign exchange that the Central American countries gain through the sale or taxing of these products must be used to import staple foods such as wheat and wheat flour, maize, and rice to feed their expanding urban populations.

Coffee. The central highlands of Costa Rica are the heartland of coffee cultivation in Central America. Although the plant was introduced there as a curiosity from Cuba in 1796, it was not until 1832 that the first coffee beans were exported. By 1850, the coffee farm *(finca)* was an established institution in the Meseta Central, and it still dominates Costa Rica's economy. From Costa Rica, coffee cultivation spread to El Salvador in 1840, to Nicaragua in the 1850's, and became established on the Pacific slope of

Guatemala in the 1860's. In all four countries today this crop is the major export, and in all four the *fincas* occupy fertile lands along the volcanic axis of Central America. Honduras and Panama were the last of the Central American nations to enter the world coffee market. The crop was grown on a small scale in the Honduran highlands in the nineteenth century, but sizable amounts have been exported only since the 1940's. In Panama, coffee was first cultivated in the western highlands at the turn of this century, but significant exporting did not begin until 1957.

Today the economies of Guatemala, El Salvador, and Costa Rica are so closely tied to coffee that any considerable drop in the world price creates economic difficulties, just as a substantial rise in price brings prosperity. Traditionally, both the United States and western Europe (chiefly Germany) have been the main buyers of Central American coffee. The beans are of high quality and delicate flavor, and are often blended with cheaper grade Brazilian coffee.

Bananas. The story of the commercial banana industry in Central America is one of the most dramatic episodes in the cultural history of this area. The development of large-scale production of this delicate tropical fruit in Central America at the end of the last century was based chiefly on three factors: (1) the availability of large tracts of unoccupied fertile land in the hot, rainy Caribbean lowlands; (2) the establishment by North American interests of large tropical plantations, on which efficient and standardized production was achieved by scientific agricultural methods and modern transportation techniques; and (3) the presence of a large nearby market in the heavily populated, industrialized eastern United States.

The many river flood plains of Caribbean Central America afforded almost ideal conditions for banana production. Highly fertile, friable, and well-drained, the alluvial clay-loam soils of the natural levees bordering the large rivers lacked only sufficient quantities of nitrogen for the exacting banana plant. Throughout most of the lowlands, continuously high temperatures and an average annual rainfall of 80 to 120 inches with only a month-long dry season, insured year-round harvests.

Numerous individuals had experimented with commercial banana production as early as the 1860's, near Puerto Bello, in Panama, and in the Ulúa-Chamelecón basin of northern Honduras. In the 1870's, small quantities were shipped out of the lowlands around Limón, in Costa Rica, in order to supply freight for a railroad under construction. Substantial exports, however, did not develop until the 1880's, after small North American and local companies had established plantations in the Matina valley of Costa Rica, the Bocas del Toro district of northwestern Panama, and along the Escondido River back of Bluefields, Nicaragua. Figure 13.4 shows the major banana plantation areas of Central America and southern Mexico.

The vast tropical plantation usually associated with banana production in Central America did not fully develop until after the establishment of the United Fruit Company in 1899. Much later, in 1924, several small fruit companies merged to form the second big banana corporation, the Standard Fruit and Steamship Company. Clearing of large forested tracts and construction of drainage canals, railway networks, company labor and administrative towns, and shipping ports, as well as the maintenance of fleets of refrigerated fruit ships—was all undertaken by these United States companies and their predecessors. During this time, too, large numbers of West Indian Negroes, chiefly Jamaicans, were imported to work on the Caribbean plantations. United Fruit established plantations in the Limón district of Costa Rica; Bocas del Toro, Panama; Ulúa-Chamelecón, Honduras; and the lower Motagua valley, Guatemala. Standard Fruit's holdings were mainly along the north coast of Honduras. Only El Salvador, whose coast is completely on the Pacific, failed to experience the big Central

American banana boom of 1900–1930. As is indicated in Figure 13.5, banana exports, mainly to the United States, grew steadily after 1900, reaching a peak of 48 million stems in 1930. More than half these exports came from the Caribbean coast of Honduras, which at that time produced one-third of the world's bananas.

By the 1930's, the Caribbean plantations were so ridden with Panama disease, a banana plague, that production suffered a serious decline. This disease, which affects root systems, was detected in Panama as early as 1880. By 1900, thousands of acres of banana lands had been abandoned throughout the Caribbean lowlands. In 1938, banana leaf blight, Sigatoka, entered the area, causing further damage. Sigatoka can be controlled

with copper sulphate spray, but no effective remedy has yet been found for Panama disease.

The most significant consequence of Panama disease was the shift of the Central American banana industry from the Caribbean to the Pacific coastal lowlands, where the plague had not penetrated. This movement began in 1927, when United Fruit transferred its Panamanian operations from Bocas del Toro, on the Caribbean, to the Puerto Armuelles district on the Pacific coast. By the late 1930's, the company had established plantations on the Pacific side of both Costa Rica and Guatemala, until recently the main banana-producing areas of those countries (Figure 13.4). In the Pacific lowlands, owing to the need for irrigation arising

Figure 13.4

Major Banana-Producing Areas in Central America. Banana ports:

1. Frontera	6. Puerto Castilla	10. Puerto Limón	14. La Palma
2. Puerto Barrios	7. Puerto Cabesas	11. Sixaola	15. Puerto Armuelles
3. Puerto Cortés	8. Río Grande	12. Almirante	16. Golfito
4. Tela	9. Bluefields	13. Colón	17. Quepos
5. La Ceiba			

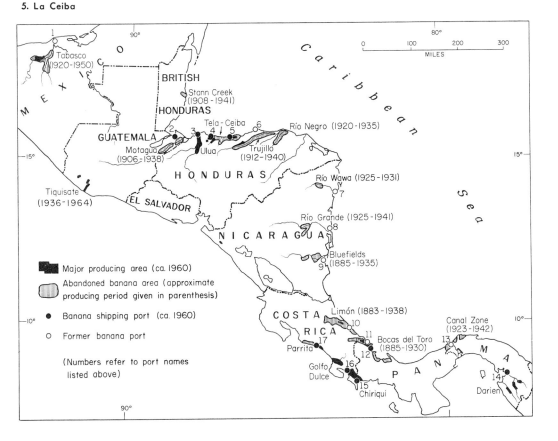

from the long dry season and to the frequent destructive winds, production costs have proved to be higher than on the Caribbean. Furthermore, both Panama disease and Sigatoka have invaded the Pacific lowlands, and caused abandonment of banana lands there. For example, in 1964, United Fruit closed out its banana properties at Tiquisate on the Pacific coast of Guatemala.

Considerable banana production, however, has been retained on the Caribbean side. Plantations in the Ulúa district of Honduras have been maintaind through flood fallowing, which has helped to control Panama disease. And since 1960, many Caribbean plantations have turned to the cultivation of disease-resistant varieties of bananas, which are rapidly supplanting the better-known Gros Michel. In consequence, banana exports, from both the Pacific and Caribbean sides of Central America, have reached all-time highs since World War II, as is indicated in Figure 13.5. Moreover, production systems are rapidly changing in the banana industry. The big plantation is still significant, but an increasing part of production comes from the small fruit grower, who sells to the large companies which control overseas transport.

Despite the spectacular rise of the banana industry in Central America, in only two of the republics—Honduras and Panama—have bananas been the most valuable export for any appreciable length of time. In most of Central America, the term "banana republic" and all that it implies, including control of the national economy and politics by foreign fruit companies, is but a myth. It would be more appropriate to call the Central American nations "coffee republics."

Cotton. The sudden rise of cotton production has been even more spectacular than that of bananas. After World War II, the great demand for cotton fiber and the consequent high prices prompted many large landowners on the dry Pacific side of Central America to invest in large-scale mechanized cotton cultivation. In three countries—Nicaragua, El Salvador, and Guatemala—cotton has become second only to coffee as the most remunerative commercial product. Exports go mainly to Japan and western Europe.

Other Segments of the Economy

In Central America, some of the traditional occupations, such as stock raising and forest exploitation, are still significant. Commercial fishing, however, has developed only since 1950. Shrimping off the Pacific coasts of Guatemala, El Salvador, and Panama, and the export of frozen shrimp to the United States, constitute the main portion of this activity.

Like most of the world's developing countries, the Central American nations are deeply interested in expanding their manufacturing. It is true that such development helps

Figure 13.5
Banana Exports from Central America : 1900–1960.

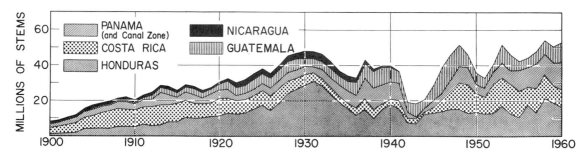

to strengthen economies whose commercial survival depends on one or two agricultural products, yet industrialization is too often regarded as a panacea for all national ills.

Unfortunately, industrialization has not progressed far in Central America. Unlike Mexico, the area lacks the basic raw materials: no profitably exploitable deposits of hydrocarbon fuels have been discovered and there are few large reserves of industrial mineral ores. However, there is a sizable hydroelectric potential for power to run light industry.

The Central American Common Market

Within the last few years the Central American countries have been working toward economic unity, having been encouraged by the success of the western European common market bloc. In 1960, five countries, all except Panama, agreed in principle to a Central American Common Market, which would endeavor to: (1) abolish all tariffs on goods traded among them; and (2) fix common tariffs on all goods entering Central America. It was further agreed to establish a Central American Bank to issue loans to each of the nations for industrialization. Foreign investments were to be attracted to Central America by still another agency. By 1963, all five countries had signed the agreement. The Central American Common Market has already increased threefold the intraregional trade among the signatories and has decreased their dependence on foreign trade. Moreover, in order to lessen industrial duplication and competition, each country is to obtain monopolistic control over certain manufactures and produce them for all of Central America. Under this arrangement, Guatemala, for example, now produces automobile tires for the five.

The breaking down of trade barriers, aided by increasing transportation and communications facilities in Central America, such as the recent completion of the Inter-American Highway and improvement of air travel, may be the first step to the effective political union that has evaded these small Central American countries for a century.

Guatemala

Of the six small republics that comprise the isthmus of Central America, Guatemala is physically and culturally perhaps the most distinctive. Guatemala is smaller than the state of Louisiana, yet the physical landscape is almost as diverse as Mexico's. Culturally, Guatemala is the most Indian country in all Middle America; of its four million people, more than half are aborigines who live much as their pre-Columbian ancestors did. Like most Latin American nations, Guatemala has been much beset by political strife since independence from Spain early in the nineteenth century. The lack of political stability, the cultural conservatism of both the Indians and the landed aristocracy of Spanish descent, and a comparatively poor endowment of natural resources have slowed the country's economic development. Much more than Mexico, Guatemala still lives in its aboriginal and colonial past.

THE PHYSICAL LANDSCAPE

The gross physical characteristics of the Central American countries have already been described (see Chapter 2). The following summary of the salient features of the land configuration, climate, and vegetation of Guatemala provides a review and reemphasis.

Mountainous highlands make up the southern half of Guatemala. These consist of two high ranges, geologically related to the Old Antillean tectonic belt that runs west-east through northern Central America. Between the ranges lies the deep, dry, scrub-covered Motagua River depression. The northern range, composed chiefly of lime-stone, extends eastward from southern Mexico into Guatemala as the Alto Cuchumatanes plateau (9,000–11,000 feet elevation) and the lower folded ranges of Alta Verapaz (Figure 13.6.). South of the Motagua depression rises the high southern range, topped by a series of magnificent volcanoes interspersed with lava plateaus and ash-filled basins, forming the northwestern end of the Central American volcanic axis. The largest volcanoes (10,000–14,000 feet elevation) and the highest basins (6,000–8,000 feet) lie in the western portion of the southern range, aptly called "Los Altos." The uplands above 5,000 feet enjoy a cool, bracing tropical highland climate with well-marked dry (November–April) and wet (May–October) seasons. Remnants of a once-extensive pine and oak forest cover most of these highlands.

Facing southward toward the Pacific Ocean, the escarpment of the volcanic range descends abruptly to the coastal plain. Often called the "Boca Costa," or the "Piedmont," the lower half of the escarpment today forms Guatemala's most productive agricultural area. The upper portion of the Boca Costa (1,500–5,000 feet elevation) lies within the *tierra templada* altitudinal zone of the Middle American tropics. Rain-drenched and once covered with a dense tropical rain forest, the upper Boca Costa has, since the mid-nineteenth century, become Guatemala's major coffee belt. The lower Boca Costa (300–1,500 feet elevation), entirely within the *tierra caliente,* comprises the lower portions of the great alluvial fans that have been formed at the base of the escarpment by rivers flowing from the volcanic axis. Beyond the rolling landscape of the lower Boca Costa, the Pacific plain (locally called "La Costa") stretches seaward as a low, hot, flattish, grass-and-forest-covered surface to the coastal lagoons.

A much larger tropical lowland, the Petén, forms the northern third of Guatemala. The

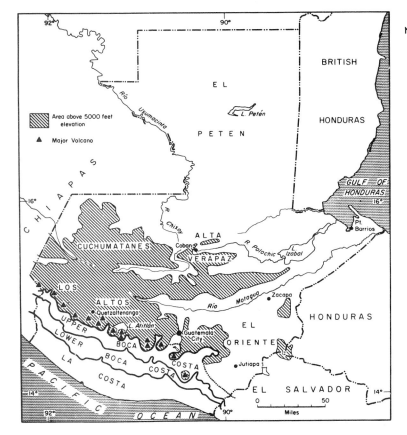

Figure 13.6
Natural-Cultural Areas of Guatemala.

flattish-to-rolling surface of this limestone area is a southern continuation of the Yucatan Platform. Covered by a dense rain forest and scattered savannas, it represents one of the great sparsely populated regions (*despoblados*) of Middle America.

THE GUATEMALAN PEOPLE

Numbers and Densities

With nearly four million inhabitants, Guatemala is the most populous of the Central American countries. As in most of Middle America, the population increase has been extraordinarily rapid since 1940 (Figure 13.7) and, between 1958 and 1962, it has been estimated at 3.2 per cent yearly. This rapid growth stems entirely from natural population increase, for immigration has been negligible since the colonial period.

Since pre-Columbian times, most of the people have lived in the southern highlands, the cultural core of the country. Although the over-all population density of Guatemala averages 90 persons per square mile, the volcanic basins of the southwestern highlands, or Los Altos, often have rural populations of over 300 persons per square mile. Indeed, nearly one-third of Guatemala's entire population is concentrated in the highland basins and on the lower mountain slopes of Los Altos.

Since the introduction of coffee as a cash crop in the last century, population densities have greatly increased in the upper Boca Costa zone of the volcanic escarpment. In addition, portions of the Pacific coastal plain (La Costa), sparsely peopled during the colonial period, are today being cleared and settled. The lowest population densities occur in the northern third of the country. The vast, forest-covered lowlands of the Petén contain only one person per square mile, a relative emptiness that dates from the abandonment of the area by the highly cultured Maya Indians more than a thousand years ago. The forested mountains and low-

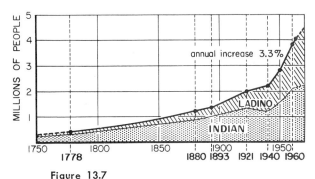

Figure 13.7

Population Growth in Guatemala : 1750–1960.

lands around Lake Izabal and within the lower Motagua valley near the Caribbean coast are also sparsely populated, but the area has higher densities (10 to 20 persons per square mile) than the Petén.

Racial and Cultural Dichotomy

Guatemalans, like Mexicans, are of two main racial groups: pure Indian stock and mixed Indian-Caucasian ancestry. In Guatemala, however, the pure-blooded Indian makes up an estimated 55 per cent of the total population, whereas he is in a minority in the other mainland countries of Middle America. Only an insignificant proportion of Guatemalans are Caucasian (chiefly in urban centers) or Negroid (mainly along the Caribbean coast).

The term "Indian" has a cultural rather than a racial meaning in Guatemala, as it does in most of Central America. Thus, Guatemalans comprise two main culture groups: (1) the Indian, who has usually retained his language and a large number of indigenous customs; and (2) the non-Indian, or *Ladino*,[1]

---

[1] The term "Ladino," used chiefly in Guatemala, El Salvador, and Honduras, has an even greater cultural connotation than "mestizo," which is employed in Mexico, Nicaragua, and Panama. Caucasians, as well as mixbloods and Indians, may be called "Ladinos," whereas pure whites are usually not referred to as "mestizos."

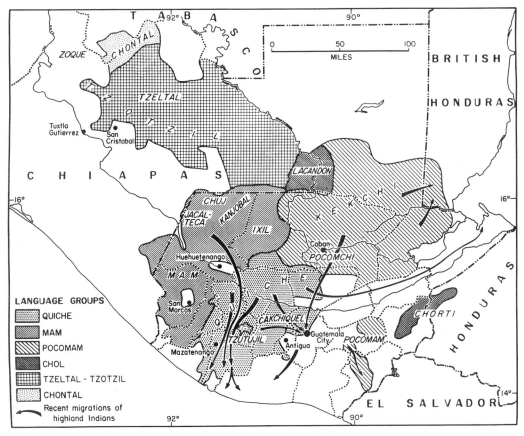

Figure 13.8

Present-day Indian Language Groups in Guatemala and Chiapas. Shaded areas are those in which 40 per cent or more of the total population speaks Indian languages.

who speaks only Spanish and whose customs are largely of Spanish origin. To be sure, most Ladinos are either mixbloods or Caucasians, but full-blooded Indians may become Ladinos on losing their Indian ways and adopting European modes of living. Figure 13.7 indicates that the Ladinos have increased from approximately 25 per cent of the Guatemalan population, in 1893, to 45 per cent in 1960. The Ladino element will probably continue to gain at the expense of Indian culture.

The Indian. The Guatemalan Indians are concentrated in the highlands, chiefly in Los Altos, west of Guatemala City, and in the isolated Alto Cuchumatanes Plateau and

mountains of Alta Verapaz, where in many sections they comprise over 90 per cent of the rural population. These areas, together with the northern highlands of adjacent Chiapas in southern Mexico, form the largest and most populous continuous aboriginal area of Middle America (Figure 13.8). The Indian languages spoken throughout the area belong to the large Mayance, or Maya-Quiché, family. Thus, the Guatemala-Chiapas Indian area in the south and the Maya-speaking section of Yucatan in Mexico form the two large aboriginal remnants of the pre-Conquest Maya culture area.

According to the 1950 Guatemalan census, 15 different Mayance languages are spoken by more than one million people, about 40 per cent of the country's total population.[2] The largest groups are the Quiché (340,000), Cakchiquel (170,000), and Mam (178,000), who inhabit the highland basins of Los Altos, the most densely peopled area of Guatemala. The Kekchi (134,000), who occupy the isolated limestone ridges and valleys of Alta Verapaz and southern Petén, are among the least acculturated Indians of the country.

Most of the Guatemalan Indians are both subsistence and commercial farmers, cultivating maize, beans, and squash (the crop trilogy of Mesoamerica) much as their ancestors did in pre-Conquest times. Slash-burn farming is often practiced on steep slopes but, in the fertile volcanic basins and adjacent slopes of Los Altos, a series of wide ridges and furrows are laboriously constructed on permanent fields with a heavy metal hoe (*azadón*). Borrowed from the Spaniard, this instrument probably replaced the aboriginal wooden *coa*. Throughout most of the Indian area of Guatemala, as in Chiapas and Yucatan, the farmers have rejected the Spanish ox-drawn plow.

Hoe cultivation, however, often yields surplus crops that can be sold for cash. At high elevations, wheat is now a cash crop, although Guatemala still imports wheat and flour for her bread-eating urban folk. As in most highland Indian areas of Latin America, sheep raising is now an important subsidiary occupation, especially on the high alpine grasslands of the southwestern highlands. In the past 50 years, some Indian communities in Los Altos, such as those surrounding Lake Atitlán, have specialized in the cultivation of vegetables as cash crops, employing elaborate gardening techniques introduced by Europeans. Among most of the indigenous groups, individual farms are small—two to ten acres —and are either privately owned or are communal village lands, as in pre-Conquest times. In many instances, the plot of an Indian family is too small to produce enough food for the household. As was indicated in Chapter 9, the colonial Spaniards established few large estates among the dense Indian population in the cold, pine-covered southwestern highlands of Guatemala. Today, in this area, aboriginal land tenure systems prevail, along with newer, small private holdings (Figure 13.9).

[2] The discrepancy between the estimated percentages of Indians (55) and aboriginal-language speakers (40) arises from the fact that approximately 13 per cent of Guatemalans are considered "Transitional Indians," who no longer speak the aboriginal tongues but retain other Indian ways of life.

Figure 13.9

A Portion of the Pine- and Oak-Clad Volcanic Plateau of Los Altos, Southwestern Guatemala. In the background at right are the twin volcanoes of Tolimán (10,400 feet elevation) and Atitlán (11,600 feet) ; to the left is that of San Lucas (7,300 feet) ; all form part of the volcanic axis.

As in most Latin American areas of high pre-Conquest culture, the Indians of the Guatemalan highland supplement their farming activities with cottage industries. The pre-Conquest custom of community specialization persists throughout the Indian area, and pottery, baskets, reed mats, blankets, together with surplus farm produce, are carried on human backs to colorful weekly village markets. Often the artisans take their own handicrafts to market, but usually they are purchased by merchants who travel from village to village, buying the wares for resale. Surplus crops are usually carried to market and sold by women, who squat before their wares in long, colorful rows. Such market towns are centers of Indian economic, social, and religious activity, just as they were in the pre-Columbian period. Thus, the present Guatemalan Indian economy, though strongly aboriginal, is in many ways a market economy based on specialized production and on money as a medium of exchange (Figure 13.10).

Although the Indians of Guatemala retain a common culture, there is little social or political unity among the various language groups. In fact, the individual Indian community, which corresponds to the small political unit called the *municipio* ("municipality"), usually constitutes a distinct cultural grouping based on blood relation, local customs and, sometimes, dialect. The women of a given *municipio* all wear the same kind of native dress, distinct in color and design from that of neighboring communities. Such customs contribute to the kaleidoscopic cultural scene that so enchants the foreign visitor. The cultural distinctiveness of the Indian communities is also enhanced by physical

Figure 13.10
Guatemalan Indian Women Weaving *Rebozos* (Shawls) on the Traditional Belt Loom. *(Delta Air Lines)*

isolation. This is especially true among the Kekchi in the rugged mountains of Alta Verapaz and in the southwestern highlands (Los Altos), where streams have eroded deep canyons in the soft volcanic ash, effectively discouraging communication between *municipios*.

A distinctive settlement pattern, partially derived from pre-Columbian times, characterizes most Indian *municipios* in Guatemala: There is one main settlement that functions as the administrative center and the market, and most of the rural population lives on farmsteads dispersed throughout the political unit. Some centers may be relatively large, nucleated towns containing 1,000 to 5,000 rural and urban inhabitants. Others may consist of only a market place and a few small public buildings, with the rural dwellers dispersed for miles around; they are usually vacant except on market days or religious holidays, and so they are sometimes called "concourse centers." These have been likened to the small pre-Conquest ceremonial centers, the ruins of which dot the Guatemalan highlands. In addition, small cities that serve as political capitals of departments (states) and as regional economic centers lie within the Indian areas. Administrative towns in colonial times, these cities, such as Quetzaltenango and Cobán, now contain large numbers of Ladinos, who compose the commercial and professional urban classes.

Since the Spanish Conquest in Guatemala, Indians have served as the main source of labor for commercial agriculture on large Ladino estates and for public works. As in Mexico, abuses of Indian labor continued after independence in the form of debt peonage, and even the colonial work levy (*repartimiento*) was not stopped until the end of the nineteenth century. Actually, all kinds of forced Indian labor, including debt peonage, continued to some extent in Guatemala until the enactment of the Constitution of 1945.

A gradual extension of Indian settlement, from the highlands into the western portion of the Pacific piedmont and coastal plain, has occurred within the past hundred years. Since the mid-nineteenth century, the most frequent use of Indian labor in Guatemala has been in coffee cultivation and harvest, chiefly in the upper Boca Costa of the Pacific piedmont. More recently, the developing sugar and banana plantations on the Pacific coastal plain have also relied heavily on Indian labor from the adjacent highlands. Although the demand for workers during the coffee harvest is largely seasonal, many Indian families have settled in the coffee area. Moreover, the need for a permanent labor force on the banana and sugar plantations in the lower Boca Costa has steadily grown since World War II.

Figure 13.8 shows that the major language groups involved in the expansion of settlement from highland to lowland include chiefly the Quiché of the Los Altos district and the Mam of the Alto Cuchumatanes. Both groups have settled mainly in the coffee zone above Mazatenango and in the coastal plain, toward the Tiquisate banana area. Another migratory trend has been the movement of Indians from the rural areas to the national capital, Guatemala City, where they are attracted by the dubious amenities of city life and the expectation of well-paying jobs.

The problem of bringing the large Indian population into the stream of Guatemalan national life is much greater than it is in Mexico. The Indian's principal social and political allegiance is to his *municipio*—to his *patria chica*—not to the nation. On the other hand, although many are illiterate and speak little Spanish, most Guatemalan Indians are successful farmers, craftsmen, or tradesmen within their own communities. They may be considered as an aboriginal peasantry, proud of their Indian heritage, rather than an abject and underdeveloped ethnic minority.

The Ladinos and Their Culture. In contrast to the Indians' occupance of the high, cool areas of the country, the Ladinos, or non-Indians, have generally settled in the lower, warmer, and drier regions. The relatively low (3,000–5,000 feet) eastern highlands and, immediately northward, the hot, dry Motagua depression have formed the core of Ladino or Spanish settlement in Guatemala since the colonial period. Today only small islands of remnant Indian culture remain in these eastern areas, locally termed "El Oriente." Other predominantly Ladino sections include the eastern part of the Pacific piedmont (Boca Costa) and the Pacific coastal plain. Moreover, the highland basins that contain the colonial and present political and administrative centers of Guatemala— Antigua and Guatemala City—are also predominantly Ladino. These cities hold strategic positions between the Indian and Spanish sections of the country. In addition, a few enclaves of Ladino culture, such as those around Huehuetenango and San Marcos, surround some of the departmental capital towns in the predominantly Indian western highlands.

The present concentration of Guatemala's Ladino population in the eastern part of the country stems mainly from early Spanish settlement in the low, dry areas which afforded abundant grass and scrub for raising livestock. Colonial cattle ranches centered in the hot, arid plains around Zacapa in the Motagua depression and in the higher grassy basins of Jutiapa and Chiquimula, in the eastern highlands, where stock raising is still a major occupation. The non-Mayan Indians who inhabited most of the eastern area seem to have disappeared soon after the Conquest, leaving only small groups of Mayan-affiliated Chorti and Pocomam to resist Spanish settlement. Within the past 50 years, the Ladino population has expanded into the entire Pacific lowland belt and into the lower part of the Motagua depression near the Caribbean, following the development of stock raising and plantation agriculture.

Today, the Ladinos of eastern Guatemala retain a Spanish colonial way of life that has been influenced by many Indian traits.

Though most of the people are mixbloods, many families of pure Spanish ancestry live in small urban centers. Settlement follows the traditional southern European pattern of compact town and hamlet, in contrast to the dispersed dwellings of the highland Indians. The hamlets (*aldeas*) may be semi-dispersed, with houses scattered over a sizable area. As in colonial times, most of the people rely upon subsistence farming and stock raising for a livelihood. Although some large cattle haciendas remain around Jutiapa, most of the land is in medium-sized holdings of 50 to 100 acres. Many landless farmers of the *aldeas* work as day laborers, sharecroppers, or cowherds on the larger farms, forming a socioeconomic system found in much of non-Indian Central America. Ladino farmers have adopted the aboriginal maize-beans-squash crop complex and, as among the Indians, the maize tortilla is the staff of rural life. On the other hand, although the dibble is often used as a planting stick, the main farming tools are the European, ox-drawn, wooden plow; the hoe; and a hooked-shape machete. A patch of sugar cane is often planted near the farmhouse, and a small mill (*trapiche*) for making sugar, or panela, forms a common element of the house assemblage. Finally, the ox-drawn, two-wheeled cart (*carreta*) for hauling farm produce, and the small Spanish style adobe, tiled-roofed farmhouse completes the rural landscape of eastern Guatemala.

Cottage industries and the market complex, so important to the Indian way of life, are quite secondary in most Ladino communities. Individuals within an *aldea* or pueblo manufacture baskets, furniture, and other necessities for local use and sale, but the great specialization in particular handicrafts found in the villages of western Guatemala is lacking in the Ladino east.

The national capital and its immediate surroundings form a special Ladino area. Guatemala City, founded in 1773 after a severe earthquake had destroyed the old colonial capital (Antigua), had a population of over 400,000 in 1963, making it the largest urban center in Central America. The Indians who continue to flock into the city from rural areas soon lose their aboriginal ways and many young folk intermarry with mixbloods. In this sense Guatemala City is a racial and cultural melting pot, but it is also the home of the conservative landed aristocracy of Spanish descent, who still control the country.

THE GUATEMALAN COMMERCIAL ECONOMY

Like most Central American nations, Guatemala is a land of farmers. Nearly 85 per cent of its people live by the soil. The Indian and Ladino farmers described above form two distinct groups of rural peasantry that have given rise to two contrasting cultural landscapes in Guatemala since the colonial period. Economically, both cultures are basically subsistent in character, and their local commercial farming and small-scale home industries are subordinate in the national economy.

Large-scale commercial agriculture is far more significant to the Guatemalan economy. In terms of value, 95 per cent of the country's exports are coffee, bananas, and cotton. These crops are raised chiefly on large holdings owned and operated by: (1) a Ladino aristocracy of European descent; (2) foreign fruit companies; and (3) the national government, in some instances since World War II. Commercial agriculture, much of it on tropical plantations, forms a third kind of cultural landscape in Guatemala.

Since colonial times, the main areas of commercial agriculture in Guatemala have been the Pacific piedmont, or Boca Costa, and the Pacific coastal plain (Figure 13.11). Favored by fertile, well-drained soils derived from volcanic ash and alluvium and by a humid tropical climate, these areas today form Guatemala's richest source of wealth. Another significant region of tropical commercial agriculture is the humid, lower Motagua Corridor, where the fertile alluvium of the wide river flood plain was first cleared of rain forests in 1906 for banana plantations.

Coffee

Guatemala's most important commercial crop is coffee, which alone accounts for three-fourths of the country's export revenue. Since the mid-nineteenth century, the upper

Figure 13.11

Vertical Cross Section of the Pacific Slope of Guatemala.

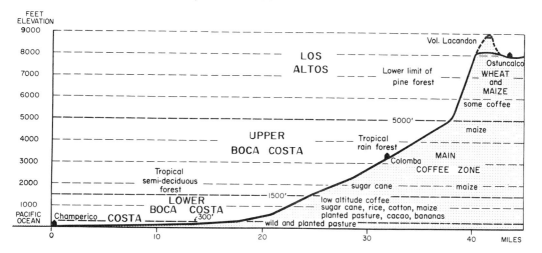

Boca Costa of the Pacific escarpment has been the main coffee area; it now produces nearly 80 per cent of the total crop. The isolated Cobán district within rugged Alta Verapaz is the second, but much less significant, coffee zone.

Local estate owners, following the lead of planters in other Central American countries, began coffee cultivation on the escarpment south of Guatemala City around 1860. It was a small group of foreign planters, however, aided by outside capital and agricultural acumen, who gave impetus to the Guatemalan coffee industry. Most successful were German planters who in 1869 established the first *fincas,* or coffee estates, in the Cobán area of Alta Verapaz, using the local Kekchi Indians as laborers, and the extraordinarily cheap Indian labor has probably been the main factor in the persistence of coffee cultivation in Alta Verapaz. In this limestone area, good soils occur only in small swales and valleys; moreover, the isolation of this rugged land and the lack of good transportation mean high transport costs.

The upper Boca Costa coffee zone began to boom in the 1870's. German planters moved chiefly into the westernmost sector of San Marcos department, while local Guatemalans and a few Englishmen and North Americans opened *fincas* in the central and eastern parts of the escarpment. Rich volcanic soils, correct air temperatures at elevations between 1,600 and 5,000 feet, and plentiful moisture with a five-month dry season (December–April) for harvest and processing were almost ideal for coffee cultivation (Figure 13.12). And there was an abundance of long-unoccupied, forest-covered land, easily convertible to a tree crop. Moreover, transport along the lower piedmont to Pacific ports, and even to the Caribbean via the Motagua Corridor, was not difficult. Most important, however, was the abundant supply of cheap Indian labor close by in the adjacent highlands of Los Altos. By the end of the nineteenth century,

the coffee industry of the upper Boca Costa was well established and, by World War I, the German planters had acquired approximately 30 per cent of the producing *fincas.*

In both Alta Verapaz and the upper Boca Costa coffee areas, semipermanent laborers are usually contracted for a period of four years. Formerly, workers could be held on the *finca* for a much longer time through the pernicious system of debt peonage. The contract laborers (*colonos*) are given use rights to small plots of land on the *fincas,* and on these they cultivate their maize. During the harvest period, when large numbers of coffee pickers are needed, the *finca* owners contract for seasonal workers (*cuadrilleros*)[3] who return to their own villages in time to plant maize at the onset of the rainy season. Even today in the Boca Costa, during the last days of March, one can observe long lines of Indian families slowly trudging up the steep escarpment slope from the *fincas* toward their highland villages. This spectacle, however, is rapidly disappearing, for many highland Indians have migrated permanently into or below the coffee zone, and there is now bus service over the new roads that connect the Pacific piedmont with Los Altos.

The coffee *fincas,* which range in size from approximately 25 to 4,500 acres, form the main landscape element in the upper Boca Costa. From afar, the *finca* appears as a forested slope, for the coffee shrub is cultivated under the shade of large trees in Guatemala and other Middle American countries. This technique, as well as careful harvesting of the beans, is said to be responsible for the high quality coffee for which Guatemala is famous. Each *finca* has a household center (*casco*) of the owner or overseer, near which may be the huts (*ranchos*) of the Indian workers. A large *finca* may also operate a coffee processing plant (*beneficio de café*). During World War II, the Guatemalan government expro-

---

3 From *cuadrilla* ("labor gang").

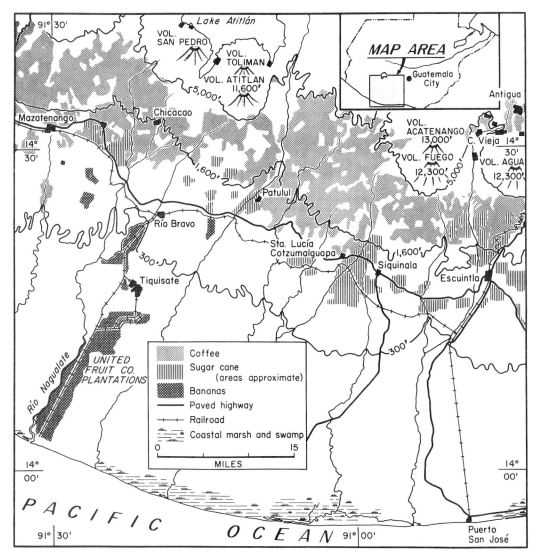

Figure 13.12

Commercial Agriculture Within a Portion of the Guatemalan Pacific Piedmont and Coastal Plain: 1960. The blank areas within the coastal plain are chiefly in pasture, forest, and newly formed cotton farms.

priated all coffee and other holdings of German nationals, and the government still controls a large number of these "national farms," which produce around 25 per cent of the country's coffee crop.

With the growth of coffee cultivation in the upper Boca Costa, a series of market towns developed along the major transport route that follows the great alluvial fans of the lower piedmont. The more important coffee market centers include Coatepeque,

Retalhuleu, Mazatenango, and Escuintla, cities of 30,000 to 40,000. The pack trains of mules that once carried sacks of green coffee from the market centers to Guatemala City and Puerto Barrios have long since been replaced by rail or truck transport.

Other Commercial Crops

Whereas coffee has been the mainstay of Guatemala's economy for the last century, the cultivation of other commercial tropical crops has had a chequered history. Since colonial times, sugar cane has been grown in the hot valleys of El Oriente and in the lower Boca Costa on the Pacific slope, but largely for local consumption. In the 1880's, Chiquimula, in eastern Guatemala, was the leading sugar area of the country, the cane being raised by irrigation on large estates. Today, the main commercial sugar-growing areas occupy the alluvial fans of the lower Boca Costa, where cacao and indigo were the chief crops 100 years ago. The largest plantations, some over a thousand acres, are concentrated on the large fans around Escuintla just below the coffee zone (Figure 13.12).

Bananas. The interesting history of the banana plantations in Central America is summarized earlier in this chapter. Despite the ravages of plant diseases in Guatemala, there are two principal areas which produce most of the commercial crop and which account for about 16 per cent of the country's export revenue. One is in the lower Motagua valley around Bananera. During the period 1906–1940 this area was one of the most productive banana sections in Central America, but thereafter it was abandoned for many years, mainly because of plant diseases. Since 1962, however, the United Fruit Company has re-established many plantations near Bananera by introducing disease-resistant banana varieties, such as the Valery, which must be boxed for shipment. The second area of commercial banana production, Tiquisate, lies within the Pacific coastal plain along the flood plain of the Nagualate River.

The opening of the Tiquisate plantations in 1936 by United Fruit was one of the important shifts of commercial banana cultivation from the Caribbean to the Pacific side of Central America, leading the development of commercial tropical agriculture on Guatemala's extensive and fertile coastal plain. The Pacific area, however, has certain disadvantages, as we observed earlier, notably: a long dry season which necessitates irrigation; frequent and destructive windstorms; the necessity of hauling the fruit 300 miles to Puerto Barrios on the Caribbean side, the main banana port and the one nearest to the major market in the eastern United States; and the fact that the banana diseases have spread to the Pacific area and have proved just as damaging there. Owing to these problems, the United Fruit Company in 1964 closed out its banana operations at Tiquisate. Nonetheless, smaller independent Guatemalan banana producers in the Tiquisate and Retalhuleu areas, who are using agricultural practices introduced by the North American fruit companies, still main-

Figure 13.13
Overhead Irrigation in Banana Plantation, Tiquisate, Pacific Coastal Plain of Guatemala. *(United Fruit Company)*

tain some commercial production in the Pacific coastal plain. The banana operations have drawn thousands of Ladino and Indian highlanders into the hot coastal area, where they work on the plantations or settle on the abandoned banana lands (Figure 13.13).

Cotton. Since 1950, cotton production on large holdings in the lower Boca Costa and the coastal plain has increased steadily, so that today this crop holds third place after coffee and bananas in Guatemala's agricultural exports. The recent rise of cotton cultivation in Guatemala parallels a similar development in Mexico and in other Central American countries. In the coastal plain, the large estate owners are clearing alluvial forest land for cotton and obtaining some of the world's highest yields per acre.

Rice. Rice is another crop that is spreading into the coastal plain, especially in the extreme southeastern part of the country, near El Salvador. Unlike cotton, rice is cultivated on small holdings, as it is over most of the southeastern highlands where it has been grown since colonial times. As rice is a prestige food of growing importance among urban folk in Guatemala, large amounts must still be imported from El Salvador, Mexico, and the United States.

Commercial Stock Raising

The greater part of La Costa, the hot Pacific coastal plain, is devoted to the raising of livestock on large haciendas, most of which are owned by wealthy Ladinos living in Guatemala City. In colonial times, La Costa's lush grasslands were fattening pastures for range cattle bred in the eastern highlands of Guatemala, in western and central Honduras, and even in Nicaragua. Still today, large herds of Honduran cattle are driven annually into Guatemala and fattened on the coastal haciendas, within

easy rail distance of Escuintla's large meat processing plant and the large market in the national capital. Although artificial pastures of Guinea grass have been planted in recent years, most coastal haciendas still retain the natural savanna bunch grasses, which are burned annually to control brush and ticks. The recent crossbreeding of the rangy *criollo* cattle with Brahma bulls is gradually decreasing the importation of feeder stock from Honduras.

Figure 13.12 shows the great extent of the remaining savanna grassland and forest of the Pacific coastal plain, even though commercial agriculture is rapidly developing. The colonial landscape of vast pastures, herds of grazing cattle, isolated hacienda centers with makeshift corrals, and smoke from burning grass still pervades the greater part of La Costa. Further improvement of pastures and livestock, plus disease and tick control, could make Guatemala's coastal plain a leading tropical livestock area of Central America.

Agrarian Reform and Colonization

Guatemala's agrarian problems are as acute as those in most of Latin America. The Indians' tiny, intensively cultivated plots in the western highlands contrast with the immense and often unused estates of the lower Boca Costa and the Pacific coastal plain; only in the eastern highlands, with its predominantly Spanish peasant culture, do medium-sized farms prevail. According to the Guatemalan 1950 census, one-half the farmland is owned by only 0.3 per cent of the farmers; nearly one-half the farmers work plots of less than 3.5 acres. The inequality of the land distribution underlies many of Guatemala's economic and social problems.

The first real attempt at agrarian reform in Guatemala did not occur until 1952–1954, when a scheme roughly similar to the Mexican *ejido* system was hurriedly started by the leftist-oriented Arbenz regime. Fearing communist domination, the landed aristocracy, with outside help, succeeded in overthrowing Arbenz and ending the radical reforms. Today's approaches to the agrarian problem are more conservative, emphasizing orderly colonization of unused lands and the resettlement of farmers from the densely peopled highlands. As part of the Rural Development Program of 1956, several apparently successful colonies have been established on unused tracts expropriated from North American fruit companies and from German nationals in the fertile Pacific coastal plain. Within a given colony, each resettled family is given legal title to a farm up to 50 acres in size. With wise planning, adequate sanitation (chiefly malaria control), and construction of a network of farm-to-market roads, the new rural colonization program within the Pacific *tierra caliente* may prove to be a partial solution to Guatemala's land problem.

Forest Products of the Petén

The vast rain forests of northern Guatemala—the Petén and much of the adjacent Caribbean lowlands of Izabal department—to date have contributed little to the Guatemalan economy, except insofar as the forest products have been exploited. The banana plantations of the lower Motagua valley and the small coffee *fincas* overlooking the Polochic River and Lake Izabal are the only commercial agriculture practiced in this sparsely peopled area. The only settlements of any significance in the Petén—the town of Flores (the departmental capital) and a few villages of Mayan and Ladino subsistence farmers which date from the seventeenth century—cluster around Lake Petén.

The gathering of chicle latex from the wild chicosapote tree is the most important economic activity in the Petén, just as it is northward in adjacent Mexican territory (Campeche and Quintana Roo). This industry began on a large scale during the first decades of this century, and practically all of the latex gathered in Guatemalan territory is exported to the United States and used in the manufacture of chewing gum. With the recent development of synthetics for chewing gum, chicle gathering has declined drastically, but during its heyday (1920–1950) American companies (mainly Wrigley) constructed numerous airplane landing strips within the Petén rain forest to carry out the chicle latex to Puerto Barrios. The chicle gatherers, Ladinos and Indians,

Figure 13.14
Temporary Camp of a *Chiclero*, or Chicle Gatherer, in the Petén. This camp consists of a crude lean-to of palm fronds, under which a hammock is slung. (*Zeb Smith*)

establish temporary camps, from which they wander into the wilderness seeking out and tapping the chicosapote tree (Figure 13.14). It is said that most of the known Mayan ruins of the Petén, and northward into Campeche, were discovered by the *chicleros*; the chicosapote tree, although scattered, tends to grow in groves in once-disturbed areas, as around old Mayan sites.

Mahogany and tropical cedar also abound in the Petén rain forest. Since the last century, these have been exploited chiefly by North American lumber companies but few roads exist in the Petén and the extraction of timber is costly. The few rivers sufficiently large for rafting flow either into Mexico or British Honduras; thus, much timber formerly was floated down the Usumacinta River to the Mexican Gulf port of Frontera, and today mahogany rafts are often smuggled into British Honduras via the Belize and Hondo rivers.

The possibilities for agricultural colonization of the Petén appear to be slim indeed. The heavy annual rainfall (80–150 inches), the short dry season, and the relatively poor limestone soils are not attractive, and the lack of roads and the long distances from markets are further deterrents. Isolated, poor in resources and population, the Petén still lies outside the national life of Guatemala, despite recent attempts at government-sponsored colonization.

Industrial Development

Like other Central American countries, but quite unlike neighboring Mexico, Guatemala has little industry and has to import most modern manufactured products. The country is poor in mineral resources. The few lead and zinc mines are of little consequence; hydrocarbon fuels are either lacking or are insufficient for exploitation. During the 1950's, North American companies searched intensively but in vain for large deposits of oil and gas in the folded geological structures of southern Petén and northern Alta

Verapaz; thus, almost all the needed petroleum must be imported. A hydroelectric power potential, however, exists on small streams as they drop down the Pacific escarpment from the volcanic highlands. Several small plants now furnish electrical power to the urban centers and larger ones may be constructed in the future.

Aside from the native cottage industries, most of Guatemala's industrial effort has been put into food processing—instant coffee manufacture, sugar refining, meat packing, flour milling, brewing, and the like. Since 1958, however, with the inauguration of the Central American Common Market program, a spate of new industrial activity has begun: a large tire plant is under way in Guatemala City; a small oil refinery has been completed in the new port of Matías de Gálvez near Puerto Barrios and another is under construction at Escuintla, south of Guatemala City; a new paper mill is in operation in Escuintla, and many more industrial enterprises are planned.

Thus, since 1960, a few small industrial centers have been emerging in Guatemala. One is Escuintla, the piedmont town on the main line of communication between the Pacific coast and the national capital; the other is Guatemala City, with its large reservoir of cheap labor and its growing urban market.

Transport and Trade

The pattern of Guatemala's main land routes for travel and commerce have varied little since colonial times. Three lines dominate the pattern: (1) a transisthmian route determined chiefly by the Motagua Corridor; (2) a highland route, mainly along the volcanic axis from Mexico to El Salvador; and (3) a Pacific piedmont route that follows the alluvial fans at the base of the volcanic axis from Mexico into El Salvador (Figure 13.15).

The transisthmian route, connecting the Pacific lowlands with the Caribbean ports

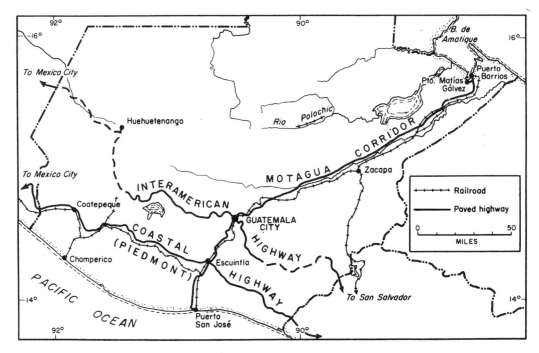

Figure 13.15
Gross Transport Pattern in Guatemala.

via the national capital, contains Guatemala's most heavily traveled railroad and paved highways. It is the principal communication axis of the country. Leaving the Motagua depression in its middle sector, the road crosses the volcanic highlands through a gentle pass, the Valle de las Vacas, which is the site of Guatemala City (5,000 feet elevation). Thence it continues down the Pacific piedmont via the long, gently sloping alluvial fan of Escuintla to the coastal plain. Both the old colonial capital, Antigua, and Guatemala City were strategically located in relation to the Motagua Corridor and the Escuintla fan.

Railroad construction began in the late nineteenth century to transport coffee to the ports. Between 1880 and 1890, North American contractors completed the Pacific coastal rail system connecting the ports of San José and Champerico with the coffee areas and with Guatemala City. Within the next two

decades, the line was extended down the Motagua Corridor to the new banana-shipping port of Puerto Barrios. In 1912, the entire Guatemalan railroad system was made part of the present American-owned and operated International Railways of Central America (IRCA), which connect with El Salvador. Coffee and bananas destined for the Caribbean port of Puerto Barrios are the chief cargo on the transisthmian portion of the railroad.

All-weather roads date from the 1930's, when most of the highland route of the old Pan-American Highway was completed from Guatemala City. Between 1955 and 1963, the Coastal Highway and the Interoceanic Highway through the Motagua Corridor were completely paved. Although passable, parts of the new Inter-American Highway through the highlands are still under construction.

As we mentioned in the first section of

this chapter, Guatemala, like most of the Central American countries, looks toward the Caribbean for its main contact with foreign commerce, a trade orientation which has obtained since the colonial period despite the location of population centers close to the Pacific side of the isthmus. Guatemala's principal markets (the eastern United States and northwestern Europe) are on the Atlantic shore; equally important, her best harbors are on the Caribbean. Since the sixteenth century, the sheltered Bay of Amatique and Golfo Dulce on the Caribbean have been the chief outlets for overseas trade, and the hazardous roadstead harbors on the straight, open Pacific coast have been less important.

After 1912, the IRCA constructed modern port facilities at Puerto Barrios to export bananas and coffee and to handle much of Guatemala's import trade. In terms of export tonnage, Puerto Barrios is one of the leading ports of Central America, for its hinterland includes not only Guatemala but also El Salvador, which ships much of its coffee over the IRCA railway to the Caribbean terminus. Having incomplete control over the company-managed facilities, the Guatemalan government in 1952 began the construction of a new port, called Puerto Matías de Gálvez, at the site of the old colonial docks of Santo Tomás a few miles south of Puerto Barrios. The new port is designed to be the country's main port of entry, leaving only the banana trade to Puerto Barrios. On the Pacific coast, San José serves as a major import port, through which move bulk goods such as wheat and petroleum products. This small roadstead consists of a single long pier for unloading lighters that transfer freight from ships anchored off coast.

British Honduras

The small English colony of British Honduras, or Belize, represents the only successful North European foothold on the Middle American mainland. Once a part of the pre-Columbian Maya culture area, the colony adjoins Guatemala on its northeastern border, and Guatemala has continued to claim for more than a century this Caribbean territory. However, as we saw in Chapter 9 (p. 305), the early cultural history of British Honduras was quite distinct from that of Guatemala. The coastal sector of the colony is today chiefly English-speaking, Negro or mulatto in racial composition, and Caribbean in general cultural attitudes. Like much of the eastern coast of Central America, British Honduras is a mainland extension of the Caribbean Island, or Rimland, cultural realm of Middle America.

MAJOR PHYSICAL CHARACTERISTICS

Physically, much of British Honduras is a continuation of the Guatemalan Petén— rolling limestone hills covered by a heavy tropical rain forest. The Maya Mountains, an igneous mass with maximum elevations of 3,000 to 4,000 feet, extend from the Petén into the west-central portion of the colony. Several rivers, flowing northeastward from the Petén across British Honduras, form narrow flood plains through the limestone hills. Near the coast, ancient beach ridges of sand and shell support stands of pine (Pinus caribea) and are consequently called "pine ridges." Thousands of coral and limestone reefs and islands fringe the swampy, mangrove-ridden coast. These coastal conditions make navigation hazardous, but favor an abundant tropical sea life. The heavy rainfall, dense forests, and leached, infertile soils of British Honduras have not been conducive to settlement and economic development; moreover, the colony lies athwart the Caribbean hurricane belt and its coastal towns and forests are ravaged by frequent storms. Hurricane Hattie, in November, 1961, almost completely destroyed Belize, the capital city, and seriously damaged northern settlements.

THE PEOPLE

Less than 100,000 people inhabit British Honduras, giving it an average density of only 10 persons per square mile. The population is unevenly distributed, however, one-third being concentrated in Belize alone. The rest live in towns and villages along the coast and on subsistence farms inland along the river banks, with the greatest densities in the northern districts.

Figure 13.16
Selected Economies and Settlement in British Honduras.

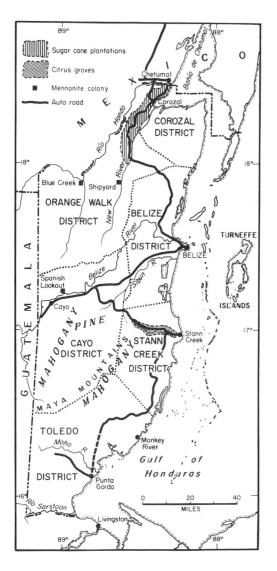

This small population has a highly varied racial and cultural makeup. English-speaking Negroes and mulattoes, descendants of slaves brought in by British woodcutters in the eighteenth and nineteenth centuries, comprise approximately 60 per cent of the population; they live mainly in the central coastal area, particularly in Belize District, which forms the cultural core of the colony (Figure 13.16). A quite distinct Negroid group, the Black Caribs, inhabits the coast south of Stann Creek and continues into Guatemala to the town of Livingston. These people, who stem from mixed Carib Indian-Negro exiles from the Lesser Antilles, have spread along the Caribbean coast from Nicaragua to British Honduras since the close of the eighteenth century. Among themselves, the Black Caribs use a curious language that is basically Arawak, but many are trilingual, speaking broken English and Spanish as well. In their almost wholly subsistence economy, the women do most of the farming, still cultivating the Antillean bitter manioc as the staple foodstuff, while the men engage in fishing off coast.

A third culture group consists of Spanish-speaking whites and mixbloods, who make up 25 per cent of the British Honduran population and occupy the northern district of Corozal and the sparsely populated interior near the Guatemalan and Mexican frontiers. Those in the north are mainly descendants of Mexican refugees who fled Yucatan during the Indian wars of the last century. Those on the western frontier are Guatemalan immigrants from the Petén, now engaged in cattle ranching. Within the Spanish area of British Honduras, a fourth ethnic group consists of Indians—Maya-speakers in the northwest and Kekchi, recent migrants from Guatemala, in the extreme southwest.

The most recently settled rural group consists of German-speaking Mennonite farmers from northern Mexico. The first of their closed communities was founded in 1958, on the upper Hondo River, where the elders had purchased a large tract of cut-over forest across from the Mexican border. Later, the Mennonites established two other communities, one on New River in the north, the other on the upper Belize. Unaccustomed to the climate, soils, and diseases of the humid tropics, the Mennonites nearly foundered in the initial settlement, but they appear to have made a successful adjustment, and some 2,500 are now engaged in subsistence farming and some commercial agriculture.

The racial and cultural complexity of the colony reaches its maximum in Belize. Here are found representatives of all the groups mentioned above, plus English civil servants, North American businessmen, and East Indian, Syrian, and Chinese merchants.

THE ECONOMY

Forest Products

Since the entry of the Baymen, or English pirates and logwood-cutters, in the seven-teenth century, the commercial economy of British Honduras has revolved around the exploitation of its forests. It is still a land of woodcutters; so little surplus is produced on the scattered subsistence farms that most of the food for the coastal towns must be imported.

At present, between 50 and 75 per cent of the colony's export revenue comes from lumber, naval stores, and chicle. During the nineteenth and early twentieth centuries, mahogany and tropical cedar were the main exports; in recent years, the extensive pine forests have been cut to export building material to the Caribbean Islands. Labor for the logging crews and sawmills comes from the Negroid group of the central coast, among whom the wielding of axe and saw has been a tradition for more than 200 years. The logs, formerly rafted downriver to the coastal sawmills, are now trucked out from the new mills in the interior over auto roads constructed since 1940.

Intensive long-term exploitation has de-

Figure 13.17
A Sawmill in the Sibun River Valley, Northern Flank of the Maya Mountains, British Honduras. Mahogany logs in the foreground have been salvaged from the surrounding rain forest ravaged by Hurricane Hattie in 1961.

pleted the tropical forests of British Honduras more than most lumbering areas in Middle America. The dyewoods near the coast were long ago cut out; most of the prime mahogany has disappeared during the last hundred years; and now the once-abundant stands of pine are seriously depleted. The isolated Maya Mountains contain one of the last remaining virgin forests in the colony (Figure 13.17). In 1940, the colonial government made plans for forest conservation and regeneration through large-scale planting of mahogany and pine in cut-over areas, but few positive results have been attained.

Commercial Agriculture

Although commercial agriculture has never been notable in British Honduras, there are a few areas of specialized farming. One is the sugar cane area in the northern district of Corozal, where Spanish-speaking landowners have established small plantations. One large sugar mill and numerous smaller *trapiches* manufacture refined sugar and panela for local consumption and some for export.

Between Belize and the Guatemalan frontier is the famous Stann Creek valley, a long, narrow trench cut into the northeastern flank of the Maya Mountains. This valley has enjoyed a number of agricultural booms. Between 1900 and 1910, it was the center of a profitable banana area in the southern part of the colony, but Panama disease caused its abandonment. Citrus orchards gradually replaced the banana groves in Stann Creek and, since World War II, the valley and adjacent slopes have been completely covered with groves of orange and grapefruit. High-quality canned juice and frozen concentrate, the chief exports of the valley, bring premium prices on the British market.

Another instance of specialized commercial agriculture occurs in the Sibun River valley, immediately southwest of Belize, where thriving cacao farms have been established since 1950. Finally, in the far south of the colony, inland from the town of Punta Gorda (Toledo District), lies a fertile section that has recently become significant for its rice production under government supervision.

Aside from these few examples of commercial agriculture, most farming in British Honduras involves only rudimentary subsistence cultivation of small patches of maize and plantains along river banks.

Figure 13.18
Part of the British Honduran Fishing Fleet Tied Up in Haulover Creek in Belize City.

Fishing

The rich fish resource in the offshore tropical waters is little developed commercially. A profitable sponge-gathering industry used to exist on the Turneffe Islands off Belize, but disease soon wiped out the beds. Today the local fishermen make profitable hauls of red snapper, and the take of the spiny lobster, processed at a freezing plant in Belize and shipped to Florida for the New York market, affords considerable income. The British Honduran fisherman, however, lacks the equipment to take advantage of the rich shrimp beds at the mouth of the Sarstoon River, which are occasionally, but illegally, exploited by United States trawlers (Figure 13.18).

Future Development

Despite its small population, British Honduras cannot feed itself. Agricultural development has been neglected in an economy built on traditional exploitive enterprises. The fate of this small territory after it becomes an independent nation a few years hence hangs in doubt.

El Salvador

El Salvador is the smallest mainland country of Latin America. It is also the most heavily populated, having in 1960 a density of 320 persons per square mile. Within all of Middle America, only some of the Caribbean islands have similar over-all population densities.

El Salvador is the only Central American country without a Caribbean coast; it thus lacks a port facing eastward toward its United States and European markets. It also lacks unsettled land for its expanding population, unlike the other isthmian countries. Confined, overcrowded, and plagued by the evils of *latifundia,* El Salvador suffers some of the most acute social and economic problems in Middle America. Twenty-seven per cent of its total territory is under cultivation —the highest ratio in Latin America. Its natural cover of vegetation has been almost completely destroyed or highly altered and its originally fertile soils are greatly eroded in many sectors. As in most Latin American countries, the best lands are owned by a few rich families, who raise commercial crops (chiefly coffee) for export, not food for the nation. Today, although the economy appears to prosper in many respects, El Salvador has one of the most poorly fed populations in Middle America; the per capita daily average food intake is only 1,975 calories, whereas 2,500 to 3,000 are considered necessary for a healthy diet. In Middle America only the people of the Dominican Republic and Haiti consume fewer calories daily (1,950 and 1,780 per capita, respectively).

In contrast to neighboring Guatemala, El Salvador lacks great variety of landscapes and cultures. Yet it possesses an individuality that has been derived largely from its colonial past. During the colonial period, most of the present national territory formed the province of San Salvador within the Captaincy General of Guatemala (see Figure 9.3). Like the eastern section of the Guatemalan Pacific piedmont, this province was settled by Spanish stockmen and growers of cacao and indigo, and lands were concentrated in the hands of a few Spanish families. Indians, whites, and some Negro slaves gradually intermixed to form, by 1800, a predominately mestizo proletariat, landless and poverty-stricken, with a mixed Indian and southern European culture. This colonial socioeconomic pattern still prevails in rural El Salvador.

THE NATURAL LANDSCAPE

El Salvador is a land of volcanoes. Its entire territory lies within the Central American volcanic axis. Southeastward from Guatemala, the volcanic range decreases in

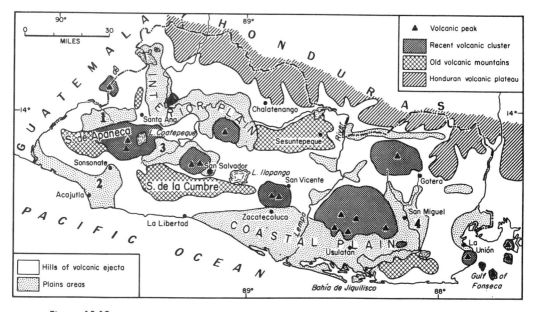

Figure 13.19

Surface Configuration of El Salvador. Numbers refer to names of plains :
   1. Chalchuapa
   2. Sonsonate
   3. Zapotitlán basin
   4. San Miguel basin

elevation, so that in El Salvador individual peaks do not rise above 7,800 feet. Figure 13.19 depicts two rows of recent volcanoes that extend east-west through the country. The southern one contains the largest cones, which have spewed out vast quantities of ash and lava for miles around. Several eruptions have occurred in El Salvador within historic times. Izalco, first formed in 1770, is still active; in 1917, Volcán Boquerón, near the capital city San Salvador, ejected a large flow of lava that destroyed many coffee plantations on its northern flank.

Between the large composite cones are low, flattish, alluvial basins and rolling hills eroded from ash deposits, which have formed sites favored for human settlement since pre-Columbian times. As in Guatemala, highly fertile soils have weathered from the recent volcanic ejecta. Other volcanic phenomena include fumerole and geyser fields, which are so abundant that plans for converting hot underground steam into electrical energy have often been suggested. The northern frontier of El Salvador lies along the edge of the high, rugged volcanic plateau of southern Honduras, an area that is physiographically distinct from the lower Salvadorean territory.

Recent vulcanism has so disrupted normal drainage that El Salvador can boast of only one large river, the Río Lempa, which today is the source of hydroelectric power for local industry. The upper course of the river flows through a dry interior basin, but its lower course and other short streams have built up an alluvial coastal plain, 15 to 20 miles wide, in the southeastern part of the country. This plain, formerly the exclusive domain of cattle ranchers, is now one of the prime areas of commercial agriculture (chiefly cotton) which lie along the Pacific coast of Central America.

With most of its surface below 3,000 feet elevation, El Salvador lies almost entirely in *tierra caliente*. The higher slopes of the large volcanoes reach into the *tierra templada,* where coffee is the main crop. Like most of the Pacific side of Central America, El Salvador experiences a long dry season (December–April), to which most agricultural activity is closely adjusted.

POPULATION CHARACTERISTICS

El Salvador's population is approaching three million and is increasing at the rate of 3.5 per cent annually. If this rapid growth is maintained, by 1970 the country's population density will have grown from the present 320 to over 400 persons per square mile. Although the people are fairly evenly distributed throughout the country, there are heavy concentrations of both urban and rural dwellers in the central basins and adjacent volcanic slopes where the soil is most fertile. The coastal plains have fewer inhabitants, chiefly because of the large cattle haciendas. The areas near the Honduras border, characterized by rugged terrain and poor soils, are the most sparsely settled.

The bulk of the Salvadoreans are a racial mixture of Indian and white, with some traces of Negro blood. It is estimated that perhaps 20 per cent of the population may be of pure Indian blood, but fewer than 3 per cent retain even a modified aboriginal way of life. These—the sole remnant of the populous Pipil-speaking Indians of Mexican origin who once covered western El Salvador to the Lempa River—occupy a few villages on the southern slopes of the Sierra de Apaneca, north of Sonsonate in the southwestern part of the country. Culturally, most other Salvadoreans are Ladinos who speak only Spanish but who practice many Indian as well as European customs. At the apex of the cultural system stand the few affluent, land-rich families, most of which trace their lineage from the colonial era.

The rapid increase of people, especially since 1940, has caused a number of significant migrations. One has been the gradual

filling of the country east of the Lempa River by landless farmers from the central area, who rent land for subsistence or work as day laborers on the new cotton plantations. Similar, but smaller, migrations have taken place within the Sonsonate coastal plain in the southwest. Another movement has been from the overcrowded rural areas into the cities, especially into San Salvador, the national capital, whose population grew from 105,000 in 1940, to 230,000 in 1960. Finally, with few rural areas within the country left unoccupied, Salvadoreans have begun to migrate into Honduras. Thousands now rent small farms or illegally squat on hillside plots in the southern and central highlands of Honduras, often causing international ill feeling. Many also migrate temporarily to the north coast of Honduras to work on the large banana plantations; others have settled permanently in Guatemala, Nicaragua, and elsewhere in central America.

A LAND OF FARMERS

The economy of El Salvador varies little from that of its Central American neighbors. Agriculture and stock raising are basic; well over half (62 per cent) of the Salvadorean people are farmers. Industrialization, a possible partial solution to the nagging problem of overpopulation, is still in its infancy. The hydrocarbon fuels are lacking and the mining of metals has never been outstanding.

The agricultural system is dualistic. On the one hand, commercial farming, which is done on the best lands, held in large tracts by the elite, produces chiefly for export (coffee, cotton) and gives the country its monetary wealth. On the other hand, subsistence cultivation of small hillside plots occupies the great majority of Salvadorean farmers, who produce the bulk of the food crops. Under such a system, the country has not been able to feed itself and, since the nineteenth century, El Salvador has imported basic foods—maize, wheat, and rice —from Honduras or from overseas.

The poverty of the small subsistence farmer in El Salvador is indicated by the size of his holdings. Forty per cent of the farms are smaller than 2.5 acres, but they comprise only 2 per cent of the total farmland. Many of the small farmers hold legal title to such plots *(terrenos),* but most are tenants, paying rent in kind or cash to the landowner. Such small farms are found in all parts of the country, but the smallest plots are concentrated in the central and northern sections on generally poor soils. The steep slopes have been badly eroded by the complete stripping of the original vegetation and overcropping; and the fertility of much of the land used for subsistence farms was greatly depleted by large-scale cultivation of indigo during the eighteenth and nineteenth centuries. Subsistence farming is also practiced on the large coffee and cotton estates, where owners customarily permit the permanent laborers *(colonos)* to till small plots.

In El Salvador, as in most of mainland Middle America, subsistence farming revolves around the cultivation of maize; the aboriginal maize tortilla and tamale are the staff of life. Other basic food crops include beans, rice, sugar cane, and sorghum. Within the last century grain sorghum *(maicillo,* of African origin) has become as important as maize in El Salvador; its cultivation now extends from eastern Guatemala to northern Nicaragua (Figure 13.20). It does well in dry areas and on poor soils, and is often interplanted with maize as insurance against drought. Probably because of its use by Negro slaves on the indigo plantations and in the mines during the colonial era, sorghum is regarded by most Central Americans as a poor man's food which carries a certain social stigma; even a Salvadorean sharecropper will rarely admit that tortillas of sorghum are served in his house. Nevertheless, in overcrowded El Salvador, as much sorghum as maize is harvested.

Depending on the terrain, the Salvadorean

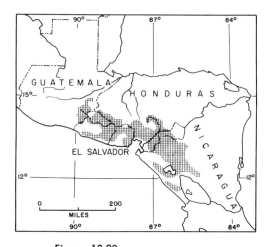

Figure 13.20
Area of Grain Sorghum Cultivation in Central America.

subsistence farmer practices either Indian-derived dibble tillage or southern European plow cultivation. The former is used on steep slopes, the latter on level-to-rolling land. The dibble, or planting stick, is normally associated with slash-burn, shifting cultivation; in El Salvador, however, land is at such a premium that steep slopes are often tilled with the hoe and planting stick year after year, with the result that the soil becomes eroded and its fertility suffers. In plow cultivation, the ox-drawn wooden ard is still used in the traditional fashion, but fields are rarely fallowed or fertilizers applied. Although two or more consecutive maize crops per year are climatically possible in the *tierra caliente,* most Salvadoreans raise but one, during the wet season from May to September; at the onset of the dry period in December, large numbers of farmers leave their tiny plots and flock to the coffee or cotton estates to bring in the harvest, in this way supplementing their family income.

The majority of Salvadorean subsistence farmers live in small hamlets *(aldeas)* or in farmsteads dispersed throughout the countryside. A century ago, however, most farmers in El Salvador lived in compact villages or towns in the old Spanish tradition, and the fields were located in the surrounding area. Apparently the present semidispersed rural settlement pattern is a result of the pressure of population. The rural houses, essentially Indian in form and building materials, contrast sharply with the whitewashed-adobe walled and red-tile roofed town houses. Square or rectangular huts with wattle-daub walls, thatched roofs, and dirt floors predominate (Figure 13.21). The two-wheeled *carreta* is a far more common means of transportation in El Salvador than in Guatemala. The rural scene in the subsistence areas of El Salvador exemplifies the amalgam of aboriginal and south European traits that is so common in Latin America.

Cottage industries have maintained their importance in many rural sections of El Salvador. While the highly developed village specialization of a century ago has largely broken down under the influence of improved transportation and of modern urban manufactures, in northeastern San Salvador many villages still specialize in the manufacture of fiber goods, for which they are renowned throughout Central America. Such products include rope, twine, saddlebags, and hammocks of agave fiber; wicker baskets for the coffee harvest; hats of palm leaves; and sleeping mats of tule reeds. Crafts and surplus agricultural products are sold in the traditional village markets, in most sections of the country (Figure 13.22). Notwithstanding its predominantly Ladino culture, El Salvador, lying within the ancient Mesoamerican area, retains a considerable pre-Columbian tradition.

Figure 13.22

Market Day in Chalatenango, Northern El Salvador. Ladino merchants spread their wares beneath the corridors of buildings and in cloth-shaded stalls along the cobbled streets.

Commercial Farming

Agricultural exports have been the mainstay of Salvadorean economy since the colonial period. Then, it was cacao and indigo that gave the country its economic wealth. Today it is coffee and cotton.

Independence from Spain (1821) opened Central America to world trade and foreign investments, and the Salvadorean indigo industry reached its peak in the mid-nineteenth century, most of the dyestuff being exported to Germany. The plantations were concentrated in the low, hot lands around San Salvador in the central part of the country, and in the plain of San Miguel and the lower Río Lempa in the east, where the ruins of the processing plants *(obrajes)* can still be seen. The perfection of synthetic aniline dyes in the 1860's caused the indigo industry to decline.

Coffee. Fortunately for El Salvador, coffee was introduced in 1840. Within a decade, it had become a significant export, eventually replacing indigo as the main commercial crop. Thereafter, for a hundred years

Figure 13.21

Typical Rural House Assemblage in El Salvador. The kitchen is the separate structure to the right of the main house.

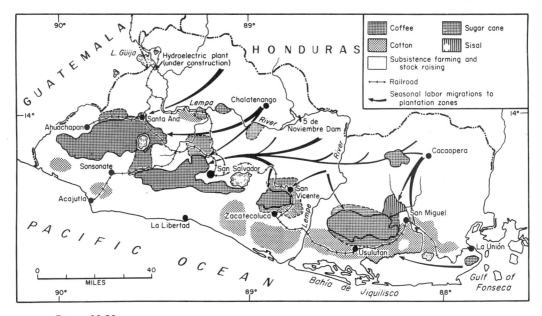

Figure 13.23

Areas of Commercial Agriculture in El Salvador.

Figure 13.24

Lower Slopes of Volcano San Vicente in El Salvador. The slopes are covered with fields of sugar cane and pasture, above which are coffee *fincas* that appear as wooded areas. Near the left peak farmers using slash-burn cultivation are destroying remnants of the original forest.

(1860–1960), El Salvador's national economy depended on this one crop. Between 1880 and 1950, coffee furnished from 80 to 90 per cent of the country's export revenue. With the recent rise of cotton, however, that percentage has now fallen to approximately 50.

The best coffee lands in El Salvador are areas above 2,000 feet elevation within the southern row of recent volcanoes (Figure 13.23). One-third of the entire crop comes from the highland west and south of Santa Ana; other areas include the highlands westward from San Salvador and, in the eastern part of the country, the slopes of the volcanoes San Vicente and San Miguel. As in Guatemala, the coffee *fincas* vary greatly in size, but the larger and more productive ones are immense estates of 3,000 to 4,000 acres. Eighty per cent of the land in coffee belongs to 15 leading Salvadorean families, who usually control the country's politics as well (Figure 13.24).

The coffee landscape of El Salvador is quite similar to that of Guatemala. The *colonos* live in hamlets on the *fincas* and grow their own food on small plots. With the beginning of the coffee harvest in December, an estimated 250,000 seasonal workers, chiefly men, women and children from the subsistence farming areas, migrate to the *fincas* as pickers *(cortadores)*. The provenience of the seasonal workers is shown in Figure 13.23.

Cotton. Cotton, presently the second most important commercial crop in El Salvador, was a minor plantation crop in the last century. But, as in other Central American countries, the present cotton boom did not get under way until after World War II. The plantations are largely in the east, for example, in the San Miguel basin and the southeastern coastal plain, where the towns of Zacatecoluca and Usulután are the main market and supply centers. Unlike coffee cultivation, cotton farming is becoming mechanized, although some plantations still employ ox-drawn plows. Cooperatives have even been formed for dusting the cotton fields from airplanes. Thousands of peasants are seasonal workers at harvest time and since 1940, the lowland of southeastern El Salvador has developed from a sparsely settled cattle range to an intensely cultivated farming area containing many new hamlets and towns for the permanent laborers.

Sisal and Sugar. Sisal and sugar cane are also grown commercially in El Salvador, but neither is a significant export. The cultivation of sisal is closely connected with the local coffee industry, for, since 1900, several large plantations north of San Miguel have supplied fiber for coffee sacks.

Large sugar plantations and modern sugar mills *(centrales)* were not organized in El Salvador until the turn of the century. These occupy fertile basins near the national capital and supply most of the country's refined sugar. Smaller, oxen-powered mills *(trapiches)*, found throughout the country, make brown *panela,* the poor man's sugar, from locally grown cane, as in colonial times.

STOCK RAISING

Despite its dense human population, El Salvador still maintains a large livestock industry, a heritage of the colonial period. About 35 per cent of the total area is in permanent pasture. Cattle, which comprise 85 per cent of the livestock, are raised in all parts of the country, for even the subsistence tenant farmer may own a few head. Commercial stock raising, however, is concentrated on the large haciendas in the coastal lowlands and in some of the dry interior basins, for example, the upper Lempa River plain.

Nearly half the pastures in the coastal areas grow nutritious grasses imported from Brazil and Africa. Some are even irrigated to provide green forage through the long dry season. Most of the interior grasslands, however, are so-called natural pastures. These include original savannas; grasslands culturally induced by cutting and burning the original forest; and abandoned farmlands, now grass-covered. Such pastures are kept free of invading bush by annual burning during the dry season. Near the coast are natural marshes, inundated during the rains, but dry and lush in the dry season. Probably since colonial times these grassy marshes have formed the basis for a kind of transhumance practiced in El Salvador and adjacent Central American areas. During the dry season (December–April) when the interior pastures wither, herds are driven to the coastal marshes to graze, returning to the interior at the onset of the rains. Livestock are also moved from the lowland pastures, during the dry season, to highland cloud-forest meadows near or across the Honduran border. Since all land in El Salvador is now in private holdings, such movements are more difficult today than formerly, but stockmen often own both summer and winter pastures, or pay other landowners for grazing rights.

FISHERIES

Though still minor in the total economy, commercial fishing has been slowly developing along the Pacific coast of Central America since the 1950's. Shrimp, which command a high price in the North American market, are the most important sea resource. The large lagoon called Bahía de Jiquilisco was El Salvador's initial shrimping ground, but local fishermen now trawl most of the catch from the clayey sea bottom off coast. Quick-frozen at small mainland plants, the shrimp are exported to the United States. The steady and uncontrolled growth of shrimping in Central American waters, however, will probably deplete the beds, as it did in the Gulf of California.

The further development of offshore fin-fisheries for home consumption would be highly desirable, in view of El Salvador's dense, underfed population. However, high prices, as well as local prejudice, have kept this protein-rich food out of reach of the masses.

INDUSTRIAL ACTIVITY

El Salvador is usually considered the most industrialized country of Central America, yet, aside from cottage crafts, manufacturing accounts for only a small percentage of the nation's employment and income. Nevertheless, El Salvador's industrial growth, chiefly because of population pressure, has been longer and faster than elsewhere in Central America. Production, aided by the government and the Central American Common Market, increased 30 per cent between 1959 and 1963.

The country's most important industry is cotton textiles. Most of the cloth is for national consumption, but much is exported to neighboring countries under the common market arrangement. The textile mills, as well as other light industry including food processing, are concentrated around the national capital and in the large towns of San Miguel and Santa Ana, where abundant labor and local markets are close at hand. A small center of heavy manufacturing has recently been established in the new port of Acajutla. There, a small oil refinery (using crude imported from Venezuela), a cement establishment, and a chemical fertilizer plant may foreshadow an important new industrial center.

Lacking coal and petroleum deposits, El Salvador could not have developed its industry without hydroelectric energy. In 1954, the large dam and hydroelectric plant, *5 de Noviembre,* was inaugurated on the middle course of the Lempa River, and a second plant is under construction on Lake Güija in the northwestern corner of the country.

TRANSPORT FACILITIES

Its small area, comparatively easy terrain, and intensive land utilization help explain El Salvador's highly developed transportation system. The rail network, a part of the International Railways of Central America, was completed early in this century, chiefly to bring out coffee.[4] Two trunk highways traverse the country: one, part of the Inter-American Highway system, keeps to the southern line of volcanoes and passes through the coffee belt and the main population centers; the other, completed in 1962, forms the eastern extension of the Coastal Highway that runs from Mexico to the Gulf of Fonseca. From these two arteries, paved feeder roads interconnect the important areas of commercial agriculture, giv-

---

[4] The only railway in the country that is outside the IRCA system is the nationalized line (formerly British-owned) which connects San Salvador with the port of Acajutla.

ing El Salvador the best road system in Central America. The poverty-stricken northern sections toward the Honduran border, however, still lack good roads. Direct trade across the northern border is today almost as difficult as in the last century.

As we mentioned previously, much of El Salvador's coffee goes by rail to the Guatemalan port of Puerto Barrios in the Caribbean. Three Pacific ports, however, handle the bulk of Salvadorean overseas trade. Two of these are roadsteads: La Libertad and Acajutla. Acajutla is connected with its hinterland by both rail and highway. The completely new deep-water harbor protected by large sea walls, opened there in 1961, may eventually make it the country's leading port, as well as an industrial center. The third port, and the current leader in tonnage, is Cutuco, near the town of La Unión on the well-protected Gulf of Fonseca. A deep-water dock permits the direct loading of cargo, mainly coffee, onto large freighters.

SELECTED REFERENCES

Adams, R. N., *Cultural Surveys of Panama, Nicaragua, Guatemala, El Salvador, Honduras.* Washington, D.C.: Pan American Sanitary Bureau, 1957.

Bergmann, J. F., "Cacao and its Production in Central America," *Tijdschrift voor economische en sociale Geografie,* XLVIII, No. 2 (1957), 43–9.

Dege, W., "Die Karibische Küste Guatemalas und ihre Häfen," *Geographische Rundschau,* X, Heft 7 (1958), 252–60.

Dozier, C. L., *Indigenous Tropical Agriculture in Central America: Land Use, Systems, and Problems,* National Research Council Publication No. 594. Washington, D.C., 1958.

Gigax, W. R., "The Central American Common Market," *Inter-American Economic Affairs,* XVI, No. 2 (1962), 59–77.

Helbig, K., "Zentralamerika; natürliche Grundlagen, ihre gegenwärtige und Künftig mögliche Auswertung," *Petermanns Mitteilungen,* CVIII,

Heft 3 (1964), 161–81; Heft 4 (1964), 241–60.

Higbee, E., "The Agricultural Regions of Guatemala," *Geographical Review,* XXXVII, No. 2 (1947), 177–201.

McBride, G. M., and M. A. McBride, "Highland Guatemala and its Maya Communities," *Geographical Review,* XXXII, No. 2 (1942), 252–68.

McBryde, F. W., *Cultural and Historical Geography of Southwest Guatemala,* Institute of Social Anthropology Publication No. 4. Washington, D.C.: The Smithsonian Institution, 1947.

Sandner, G., "Die Erschließung der karibischen Waldregion im südlichen Zentralamerika," *Die Erde,* XCV, Heft 2 (1964), 111–30.

Smith, R. S., "Population and Economic Growth in Central America," *Economic Development and Cultural Change,* X, No. 2, Part 1 (1962), 134–49.

Tax, S., *Penny Capitalism: A Guatemalan*

Indian Economy, Institute of Social Anthropology Publication No. 16. Washington, D.C.: The Smithsonian Institution, 1953.

Termer, F., "Zur Geographie der Republik Guatemala, II Teil, Beiträge zur Kultur- und Wirtschaftsgeographie von Mittel- und Süd-Guatemala," *Mitteilungen der Geographischen Gesellschaft in Hamburg,* XLVII (1941), 1–262.

Waddell, D. A. G., *British Honduras: A Historical and Contemporary Survey.* London: Oxford University Press, 1961.

Whetten, N. L., *Guatemala: The Land and the People.* New Haven, Conn.: Yale University Press, 1961.

14

Present-Day Central America: Part Two

Honduras

Honduras occupies a distinctive geographical and economic segment of Central America. Most of its surface is covered with the oldest and most highly mineralized rocks of the isthmus. Its land is mountainous and difficult to traverse. Its soils, except on the Caribbean coast, are generally infertile. Thus, from colonial times to the early twentieth century, Honduras was a land of mines and livestock, of little agriculture, of a scant and isolated population, and of indifferent colonial and unstable republican governments.

Among its sister republics, this rather unfortunate country has been regarded as the most backward economically and culturally of the Central American states. Much of the country still lives under almost colonial conditions. Honduras is also considered the prototype of the "banana republics," with commercial economies based on a single export crop under the complete control of large North American companies. This is, however, not correct, for the Honduran economy includes much more than the banana industry, although only since World War II has the country seen substantial economic diversification and growth of transportation and settlement.

THE PHYSICAL BASE

As we saw in Chapter 2, Honduras lies completely within the land mass of geologic Old Antillia, characterized by its east-west-trending mountain ranges of ancient crystalline rock often capped by limestone or sandstone. In southwestern Honduras, the ancient rock is covered by thick layers of old lava and other volcanics that have been highly eroded to form a rugged surface, parts of which rise above 9,000 feet. The volcanic axis of Central America skirts the southern edge of Honduras, leaving but a few volcanoes as islets within the Gulf of Fonseca. Honduras thus lacks the covering of recent volcanic ash that has created the fertile soils of Central America's Pacific versant. In the central and northern parts of the country, northeast-southwest-trending crystalline ranges rise to maximum elevations of 9,000 feet, with deep valleys between.

In terms of human settlement, the most significant physiographic features of the interior highlands are numerous flat-floored basins of 1,000 to 3,000 feet elevation, called *valles,* the more important of which are shown in Figure 14.1. One of the largest is that of Comayagua, some 5 by 25 miles in extent. This *valle* occupies part of a north-south structural depression which was a transisthmian land route from colonial days through the nineteenth century. Dry and hot, grass and shrub-covered, the *valles* have been centers for stock raising since the sixteenth century and some have recently become important for commercial agriculture.

Much of the mountainous interior of Honduras supports an oak and pine forest, one of the most extensive in Middle America. Elevations above 7,000 feet, however,

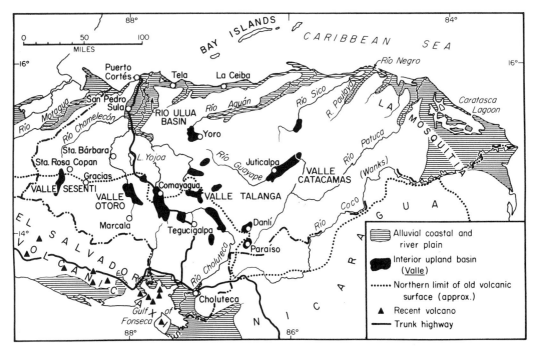

Figure 14.1
Selected Landscape Features of Honduras and Adjacent Areas.

carry remnants of dense cloud forest, called "montañas." The southern and central highlands receive 30 to 60 inches of rain between May and December, the rest of the year being quite dry. The Pacific slope, somewhat wetter, carries a semideciduous tropical forest and patches of savanna. On the Caribbean side, heavy rains (70 to 100 inches a year) and a short dry season give rise to a tropical rain forest, now greatly altered by man, that once covered mountain slopes and valley floors.

The Caribbean lowlands, which the Hondurans call "La Costa," form a distinct physiographic unit. Narrow river flood plains extend like fingers far inland, following depressions between mountain ranges. The fertile alluvium of the valleys and adjacent coastal plains, cultivated since pre-Columbian times, now contain large banana plantations. Of these productive lowlands, the Ulúa River basin is the most intensively developed.

In the far northeast lies the most extensive Caribbean lowland, the Mosquitia, which continues southward into eastern Nicaragua. This sparsely peopled Honduran lowland and the adjacent mountain ranges comprise one of the least known sections of all Middle America.

Honduras reaches the Pacific only along the northern side of the Gulf of Fonseca. Back of the mangrove-fringed shore lie narrow coastal and river plains, the most extensive of which is that of Choluteca, famed for its savanna pastures and its livestock industry since the sixteenth century.

THE HONDURANS

One of the sharpest demographic contrasts in Central America is that between relatively underpopulated Honduras (45 persons per square mile) and overcrowded El Salvador (320). About two million *Hon-*

dureños—just two-thirds the number of Salvadoreans—live in an area five times larger than its tiny neighbor to the south. Most of the Honduran people are concentrated in the central and southern uplands, but even in the highland departments population densities do not exceed 100 persons per square mile. This contrast in population density has existed since aboriginal times, and is reflected in the present overflow of Salvadorean migrants into Honduras and in Honduras's traditional role of exporter of surplus food to El Salvador.

The Honduran people, like their neighbors, are increasing at the high rate of 3 per cent annually. Partly because of the poor soil and the mountainous terrain, many rural sections of the interior are already relatively overpopulated. Thus, within the last 50 years there has been considerable migration of peasant farmers to the empty northern highlands and to the developing Caribbean lowlands.

Hondurans are distributed unevenly over their mountainous land, and more than two-thirds live in the western and southern highlands. Since the development of the banana plantations along the Caribbean during this century, the population of the lowland floodplains and the coast has grown remarkably; this area now contains a fourth of the total number of Hondurans. Thus, in terms of both population distribution and cultural pattern, there are now two Hondurases: (1) the mountainous interior of colonial tradition, centered on the national capital, Tegucigalpa (160,000 population) ; and (2) the newly developed Caribbean lowlands, or La Costa, centered on the banana plantations and the market city of San Pedro Sula (95,-000 population) in the Ulúa River basin. The northeastern lowlands of La Mosquitia, comparatively empty, still remain outside the course of national development.

Racially, 90 per cent of the Hondurans are mixed Indian and white, with some Negro blood as well. Only 7 per cent are considered full-blooded Indians, 2 per cent Negro, and 1 per cent white. Culturally, the great bulk of the population is Ladino, having a mixed Spanish and aboriginal tradition.

Excepting its western portion, Honduran territory lay outside the area of aboriginal Mesoamerican culture. The pre-Conquest Indian population was never dense, and during the colonial period most of it was destroyed or greatly modified. At present, the so-called traditional Indians, who have been little influenced by western culture, consist of a handful of Sumu and Paya riverine forest people in the far northeast. In the same area, several hundred Miskito Indians, now mixed with Negro, live along the Río Cocos. In southwestern Honduras, some 65,000 Indians, whose culture is now greatly modified, form a remnant of the once-extensive Lenca language group. Although they have lost their native language, the Lencas maintain many aboriginal customs and are considered to be Indians by their Ladino neighbors. In addition, several thousand Chorti-speaking Indians of Mayan affinity live on the Honduras-Guatemala border, and a few Jicaque are found within the cloud forests on isolated mountain peaks in the north-central highlands.

The small Negroid element in Honduras lives mainly along the Caribbean coast. One group consists of English-speaking descendants of Jamaican contract laborers who were imported from the West Indies early in the century to work on banana plantations. These people now make up a sizable element in the port towns and add to the West Indian cultural flavor that characterizes much of the Caribbean coast of Central America. The second Negroid group consists of several thousand Black Caribs, locally called *morenos,* who live in small villages and carry on a subsistence livelihood much as they do in British Honduras and Guatemala.

Off the northern coast of Honduras, the English-speaking white, mulatto, and Negro population of the Bay Islands adds to the cultural complexity of the Caribbean coastal scene. The Bay Islanders (some 10,000 in 1960) are descendants of English whites and

Negroes who migrated from British Honduras and the Cayman Islands in the 1830's. Although they have been under Honduran rule since 1859, these interesting people have maintained their Caribbean culture almost intact. Most fish or grow coconuts for copra exports.

THE ECONOMY OF HONDURAS

In the preceding paragraphs we have noted that one of the fundamental features of present-day Honduras is its twofold physical and cultural division into the mountainous interior and the Caribbean lowlands. This dichotomy exists not only in population and settlement characteristics, but also in types of economy. In the mountainous interior are found the traditional colonial occupations of stock raising, mining, and subsistence farming; in the recently developed Caribbean lowlands, the tropical plantation system based on large-scale production of bananas and other commercial crops is domi-

nant. The Caribbean lowlands have now surpassed the interior in economic wealth, rate of population growth, and rapidity of landscape change.

The Mountainous Interior

Mining. To understand better the present economic pattern of the interior, the Honduran mining industry should first be considered briefly. Although today of little consequence, the production of gold and silver was the mainstay of Honduran economy throughout the colonial period and the nineteenth century. As late as 1915, silver bullion led all other exports in terms of value.

After Honduras won its independence from Spain, mining companies owned by North American, British, and French interests began to take over the abandoned colonial silver mines in the interior and, by 1860, those around Tegucigalpa and Yuscarán were in full operation. Because of its increasing economic importance, Tegucigalpa was made the national capital in 1880, gain-

Figure 14.2

Old Mining Town of Cedros, Central Highlands of Honduras. The town retains much of its colonial and nineteenth-century architectural charm.

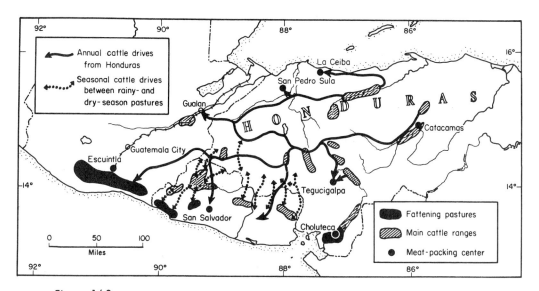

Figure 14.3
Cattle Industry of Northern Central America.

ing political ascendancy over its rival, Coma-yagua, the old colonial administrative center. Exploitation of the gold placers along the Guayape River, of colonial fame, was also revived at mid-century. After reaching a peak of production in the 1890's, the mining industry gradually declined, owing to depletion and to political instability. In 1954, the most productive silver mine of Honduras, El Rosario, at San Juancito a few miles northeast of Tegucigalpa, closed down, leaving the United States-operated Morochito mine west of Lake Yojoa as the only large silver producer in the country. In the 1890's, silver and gold accounted for 75 per cent of Honduran exports by value; by 1963, this had declined to 4 per cent.

Many small mines still operate and, in the old silver centers, folk miners *(güirises)* grub for rich ores in abandoned shafts. Some also pan gold along the Río Guayape. But the picturesque mining towns such as Yuscarán, San Antonio and Cedros in the central highlands, are, like those in Mexico, mere reminders of a more prosperous past (Figure 14.2).

Stock Raising. As in northern Mexico, the mining industry in Honduras encouraged

stock raising, for mining centers consumed quantities of animal products. Thus, from colonial times the raising of cattle and mules has been a leading activity in the mountainous interior as well as in the Pacific lowlands. Since the sixteenth century, cattle haciendas have occupied the best lands—the grassy floors of the upland basins *(valles)*, such as those of Comayagua, Catacamas, and Yoro. In the Pacific lowlands, the savannas of the lower Choluteca plain are still renowned for the production of mules and cattle. When colonial mining declined in the eighteenth century, Honduran stockmen began to drive cattle to Salvadorean and Guatemalan markets. By mid-nineteenth century, cattle from the savannas of the upper Aguán River valley, destined for export to the West Indies, were being driven to Caribbean ports. To this day, Honduran stockmen export animals and animal products; some 40,000 to 50,000 steers are driven annually into Guatemala and El Salvador alone (Figure 14.3).

Until recently, little was done to improve either the quality of the *criollo* cattle or of the native pastures in the upland *valles*. The pastures of the large haciendas have a low carrying capacity, and grasslands must be

Figure 14.4
Corral on Cattle Ranch, Northern Honduras. *(United Fruit Company)*

burned annually to prevent invasion of thorny scrub. Today some stockmen are attempting, with government help, to upgrade herds by introducing Brahma and Santa Gertrudis breeding stock from the United States. The improved herds maintained on United Fruit Company holdings also have set examples for upland stockmen (Figure 14.4).

Since 1960, several large meat-packing and freezing plants have been established in various parts of the country. The largest is at Choluteca, whence frozen beef is flown to the United States. Livestock and animal products now account for nearly 12 per cent of the total Honduran export revenue.

Subsistence Agriculture. A third, and the most widespread, human activity in the mountainous interior of Honduras is the

cultivation of foodstuffs by peasant farmers. It, too, reflects the long influence of the colonial mining era. Because the cattle haciendas occupy most of the grass-covered basin floors, subsistence farming is ordinarily relegated to small plots on mountain slopes where the soil is least fertile. Probably this agricultural pattern goes back even to aboriginal times, for, possessing only the stone axe, the dibble, and fire, the Indians could hardly have worked the tough grassy sod of the more fertile basins. The introduction of the plow did not have the effect of making farmland of the *valles,* however, for the colonial cattle barons forbade the cultivation of their haciendas. Hillside farming is still prevalent in many parts of Latin America, and it is one of the factors militating against increased food production.

Today over 80 per cent of the working

population of Honduras are farmers, and most cultivate hillside plots of 15 to 25 acres. Many holdings are privately owned, and worked by the owner and his family; others are sharecropped. However, in the Indian-dominant southwestern highlands, especially, most properties are *ejidal* lands and belong to the municipality; plots are assigned only to community members for use. Finally, national lands, found on high mountain ridges and in the sparsely peopled northeastern lowlands, are available to any farmer. In contrast to El Salvador, un-occupied lands, particularly on high mountain slopes, are abundant in much of central and northern Honduras; the more serious agrarian problems occur in the heavily populated southern and western sections.

Following the aboriginal crop pattern of most Central American countries, the Honduran mountain *campesino* cultivates chiefly maize and beans. At altitudes below 5,000 feet, sweet manioc (*yuca*) is an important staple, as are the African grain sorghum and cooking banana (plantain), rice, and sugar cane (for homemade panela). Wheat was formerly cultivated as a cash crop at elevations above 6,000 feet, but production has greatly declined in recent years.

In colonial times, the hillside Indian and Ladino farmers supplied food for nearby mining communities, and since the nineteenth century, Honduras has exported large amounts of maize and beans to overpopulated El Salvador. A surplus crop is normal in many parts of the Honduran highlands.

The dibble, hoe, and machete are the highlander's main agricultural tools, although southern Honduran subsistence farmers use wooden plows and oxen on gentle slopes and valley flats. Modified primitive slash-burn cultivation, with only two to three years of fallow after an equal period of continuous cropping, is typical practice on the mountain slopes. As in El Salvador, this has caused serious soil erosion; in some places, the complete removal of the topsoil has turned sizable areas into reddish-colored wasteland, fit

only for scrub pine. The best lands that remain to the highland farmer are the montañas, cloud forests on high mountain ridges of deep, rich soils. Unfortunately, the cloud-forest remnants are rapidly being destroyed by slash-burn cultivation. Erosion soon removes the topsoil, and the abandoned fields are colonized by pine rather than by the original broad-leaved evergreen forest.

The rural settlement pattern of highland Honduras resembles that of eastern Guatemala. Most of the subsistence farmers live in small semidispersed hamlets (*aldeas* or *caseríos*), with individual dwellings scattered about the mountainous terrain—a pattern well-suited to hillside cultivation. Larger compact villages and towns, often located within or on the edge of valleys and basins, serve as market and municipal administrative centers. In the old mining sector of the central highlands, the compact Spanish-type village, often precariously perched on steep slopes near worked out mineral deposits, is dominant. Both the wattle and daub, thatched-roof hut and the more substantial adobe, tiled-roof structure are common. The Lenca Indian settlements of southwestern Honduras paralled those of the aboriginal parts of Guatemala: dispersed farm houses, concourse centers for markets and religious functions, and Ladino towns as commercial and administrative centers. Craft specialization also characterizes the Lenca community, as it does many Ladino towns in the southern uplands near the Salvadorean border.

The poverty of Honduras is reflected in these upland rural people who comprise well over half the nation's population. Their primitive farming technology, small land holdings, low crop yields on poor soils, and physical isolation from ready markets create serious economic problems.

Commercial Agriculture. Since colonial times, parts of the Honduran highlands have specialized in the production of certain crops. One of the oldest is the tobacco area of Santa Rosa de Copán near the Guatemalan border, already famed in the eighteenth century for its high quality cigar leaf. Since 1950 cultivation has expanded, most of the product being shipped to San Pedro Sula for cigarettes.

Parts of the large cattle haciendas in a few of the upland basins (*valles*) have lately been converted to farms producing cotton, maize, and beans. For example, sizable cotton plantations are now cultivated with mechanized equipment in the Comayagua Valley and, in the well-watered valleys of Danlí and Paraíso near the Nicaraguan border, small farms specialize in the commercial production of potatoes and beans.

The most significant cash crop of the highlands, however, is coffee. It has been important only since World War II, since Honduras was one of the last Central American countries to enter the world coffee market. The coffee *fincas* are concentrated in the high mountain slopes near the lower edge of the cloud forests, where soil and moisture are favorable. North of the Salvadorean border around Marcala, the high regions to the west and east of Lake Yojoa, and the mountains near Danlí and Choluteca in the far southwest are the major producing areas. Unlike those of Guatemala and El Salvador, the *fincas* are small—25 to 50 acres—and many were started by Salvadorean immigrants, who introduced the industry into Honduras. Since 1950, the export value of coffee (15 per cent of the total exports) has been second only to bananas, and its economic importance is increasing yearly.

The Caribbean Coastal Lowlands

The rapid rise of the western part of the Honduran Caribbean coast during this century is a remarkable example of modern economic and social development in the humid lowland tropics. Whereas in the mid-nineteenth century the Caribbean area was sparsely inhabited, forested, and disease-ridden, its western sector now contains over a quarter of the country's total population,

accounts for half its export revenue, possesses its entire railway network, and is rapidly becoming its most industrialized region. Partly because of these developments, a sharp political rivalry has evolved between the rich, progressive north coast and the poor, backward, mountainous interior.

Bananas. The modern development of the north coast began with the rise of the banana industry in long, fertile river valleys that extend inland from the sea. Of these, the largest and most intensively utilized is the Ulúa-Chamelecón river basin, in the northwestern corner of the country. Filled by rich, deep alluvium deposited by the rivers, this basin, 20 by 60 miles in extent, forms the northern end of the Comayagua transisthmian depression mentioned previously. San Pedro Sula, the second largest city of Honduras and rapidly growing, functions as an administrative and market center for the whole western lowland region. Farther east, the narrow river valleys of León, Aguán, and Negro, formerly all large producers of bananas, are now secondary to the Ulúa-Chamelecón basin.

As early as 1860, a few Honduran planters on the Caribbean coast were cultivating bananas on a small scale and selling them to freighters that stopped at the old ports of Omoa and Trujillo. By 1896, bananas accounted for nearly a quarter of the value of Honduran exports.

The big banana plantation system was introduced into Honduras after the turn of this century by North American fruit companies, aided by government concessions of extensive lands in the coastal lowland. The United Fruit Company concentrated its efforts in the Ulúa-Chamelecón basin, the León River valley and adjacent coastal plain near Tela, and in the Río Negro valley and coastal area east of Trujillo. The Standard Fruit and Steamship Company developed plantations mainly in the long Aguán River valley and on the coastal plain near La Ceiba. Peak banana production was reached in Honduras in 1929 to 1931, when nearly 30 million bunches, about one-third of the world's exports, were shipped annually to the United States. To handle this enormous export, the fruit companies constructed port facilities at Puerto Cortés, Tela, La Ceiba, and Puerto Castilla (immediately north of Trujillo), and laid nearly 1,000 miles of standard and narrow-gauge rail throughout the lowland areas.

By 1945, however, disease had wiped out most of the eastern plantings in the Negro and Aguán valleys, and production had declined drastically in the Ulúa basin. By 1960, Honduran banana exports had fallen to 10 million bunches. But, despite adverse natural conditions (floods, hurricanes, and plant disease), the Ulúa-Chamelecón basin continues to be the major banana region of the Central American Caribbean coast (Figure 14.5). Disease is now controlled, with moderate success, by flood-fallowing, a system whereby large tracts are diked and flooded for several months to kill the damaging parasites and, more recently, disease-resistant Giant Cavendish, Valery, and Lacatan bananas have been replacing the Gros Michel variety. In the early 1930's, bananas constituted from 70 to 80 per cent of Honduran exports by value and, through export taxes, virtually financed

the Honduran government. Today this ratio has dropped to about 50 per cent, not only because of the decrease in production, but also because of the growth of highland exports, such as coffee.

People flowed from the interior of Honduras into the Caribbean lowlands to work on the banana plantations and, despite the decline of banana production, this influx continues, especially into the Ulúa-Chamelecón basin. There, the banana boom gave impetus to the commercial production of foodstuffs, sugar cane, and livestock; to the growth of market towns and transportation centers, such as San Pedro Sula, El Progreso, and Puerto Cortés; and to the beginnings of light industry, especially food processing. The United Fruit Company donated large tracts of abandoned banana lands to subsistence and commercial farmers; it also introduced new plantation crops, such as African oil palm. Between 1930 and 1962, the population of the Ulúa area increased sevenfold (approximately from 35,000 to 250,000), and San Pedro Sula increased sixfold (from 15,000 to 95,000 people). The population density of the area, around 130 per square mile, is one of the highest in Honduras. The cultural scene of this formerly forested tropi-

Figure 14.5
Banana Plantation, Ulúa-Chamelecón Lowland in Northern Honduras. The living quarters in the foreground are part of a "farm," one of the large blocks of land into which a plantation is divided. *(United Fruit Company)*

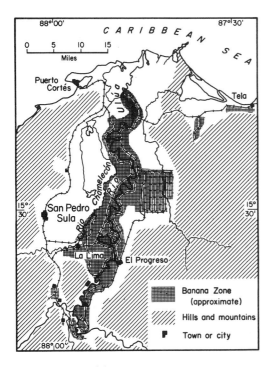

Figure 14.6
The Ulúa-Chamelecón River Basin, Northern Honduras.

cal lowland is today one of intensive land use, a dense network of railways, and large numbers of agricultural hamlets and towns (Figure 14.6). The recent expansion of banana plantings in the León River valley and the transfer of United Fruit headquarters from La Lima in the Ulúa basin to the port of Tela may result in another highly developed area on the Caribbean coast.

Forest Exploitation

Had they been wisely exploited, the extensive forests that once covered much of Honduras might have been that country's greatest resource today. Unfortunately, perhaps more senseless destruction of the forest cover has occurred here than in any other Central American area.

For nearly two centuries (1750–1930) Honduras was renowned for the fine mahogany of its Caribbean rain forest. Today,

with practically no virgin trees left, the mahogany trade is insignificant. On the other hand, the pine forests of the mountainous interior and the northeastern lowlands, although somewhat depleted, are still an important part of Honduran natural wealth.

The greater part of the interior pine forests was altered or destroyed by slash-burn farming and by the burning of undergrowth and grass to improve pasturage for livestock. Today, however, scores of sawmills, large and small, are seen everywhere in the remaining pine stands, cutting timber for local use and for export. The most extensive stands left are in isolated mountains of Olancho department in the north central part of the country. Since the 1950's, pine from Olancho and from other interior forests has become the third-ranking export of Honduras. Most of the sawed lumber now goes to the timber-poor West Indian islands and to El Salvador, but wood pulp and paper manufacture may soon develop as part of the Central American common market program (Figure 14.7).

Figure 14.7
Typical Cut-Over Pine Forest in the Central Highlands of Honduras Near Tegucigalpa.

Manufacturing and Transport

The relative poverty of Honduras is reflected in its position as one of the least industrialized Central American countries. Only since 1950 has manufacturing employed 6 per cent of the working population. Food processing plants (e.g., meat products, beverages, vegetable oils), a few textile mills and clothing factories, tobacco products plants, and the like are concentrated either in Tegucigalpa or San Pedro Sula. San Pedro Sula, situated within one of the most rapidly growing sections of the country, appears to have the greater potential for further industrial expansion. The Lake Yojoa hydroelectric project, near completion, will supply power to both cities.

Still another index of Honduras's economic backwardness is its rudimentary transport system. The only railways coincide with the banana areas on the Caribbean coast. In 1860, British interests contracted to build a transisthmian railroad across Honduras through the Comayagua depression, but only some 60 miles of the line were completed, from Puerto Cortés southward to the edge of the Ulúa basin.

Since the 1940's, the Honduran government has constructed a number of all-weather, but extremely rough, truck roads in many parts of the rugged interior highlands. However, the short portion of the Inter-American Highway that traverses southern Honduras, the Southern Highway from the Gulf of Fonseca to Tegucigalpa, and one highway in the Ulúa basin are, to date, the only sizable stretches of paved roads in the country. It is estimated that half the population must still travel to markets on foot or horseback.

The main ports are also in the banana areas. Puerto Cortés (formerly Puerto Caballos), the chief port since colonial times, still handles about half the country's foreign trade. One meager Pacific port, Amapala, which occupies a volcanic island in the Gulf of Fonseca, handles only a small part of Honduran imports and exports.

Nicaragua

Like Honduras, Nicaragua has had an unfortunate history. It was neglected by Spain in colonial times, was fraught with internal strife after independence, and has been embroiled in wars and disputes with its sister republics, and its economy has developed slowly. On the other hand, two outstanding geographic features have given Nicaragua a much greater economic potential than Honduras: (1) the natural passway across the isthmus through the Nicaraguan Rift; and (2) the highly fertile volcanic soils on the Pacific side of the country. Nonetheless, the colonial past is still deeply entrenched in Nicaragua's social and economic patterns, which are reflected strongly in the present cultural landscape.

Perhaps more than any other Central American country, Panama excepted, Nicaragua has felt the direct influence of the United States in its politics and economy. American interests utilized the Nicaraguan Rift as a transisthmian route in the mid-nineteenth century; during the same period activities of the American filibuster, William Walker, in Nicaragua engendered a lasting resentment of a large segment of the Central American people against the United States. Between 1911 and 1932, actual military intervention in Nicaragua by United States forces was effected to protect American lives and investments, to manage the custom houses, and to supervise elections within the country. During this period Nicaragua was a virtual protectorate of the United States. Although needed health measures were introduced and North American investments and trade in Nicaragua sharply increased during the occupation, Latin Americans often point to this period of intervention as an example of United States "imperialism." The Nicaraguan Rift and its strategic value as a canal route has been one of the significant geographical factors that has maintained the interest of the United States in this Central American country for the last 100 years.

PHYSICAL PATTERNS

Nicaragua is the largest country of Central America and as varied physically as any. The most salient physiographic feature is the great graben, the structural rift or depression that passes through the southern and western sections of the country, athwart the Central American isthmus. This lowland contains lakes Managua and Nicaragua, the two largest natural bodies of fresh water in Middle America. Both drain to the Caribbean via the San Juan River (Figure 14.8). Narrow plains surround the lakes, but the largest area of flattish lowland within the depression lies northwest of Lake Managua. From the Gulf of Fonseca to the southern shore of Lake Nicaragua, the depression is intruded by a single range of volcanoes— a part of the Central American volcanic axis. This range contains some of the most active volcanoes in Middle America. Among them are a line of low cones within the plain northwest of Lake Managua, including the beauti-

fully symmetrical Momotombo; the famous caldera of Masaya, near Granada, which between 1946 and 1956 emitted sulfurous fumes which were destructive to agriculture for miles around; and various volcanic peaks that form islands within the lakes, such as Isla de Ometepe with its cones of Madera and Concepción. Concepción erupted violently in 1958, and the ashes caused widespread agricultural damage.

On the western side of the Nicaraguan Depression, a narrow up-faulted block of earth forms a series of uplands (Sierra de Managua, Carazo Plateau) which we shall call the Diriamba highlands. These, together with the low Rivas Isthmus to the south, separate the lakes from the Pacific Ocean. The Diriamba highlands, of 700 to 3,000 feet elevation, are thickly mantled with ash spewed from the adjacent volcanoes and blown westward by the prevailing trade winds.

Although the frequent eruptions and accompanying earthquakes have often been de-

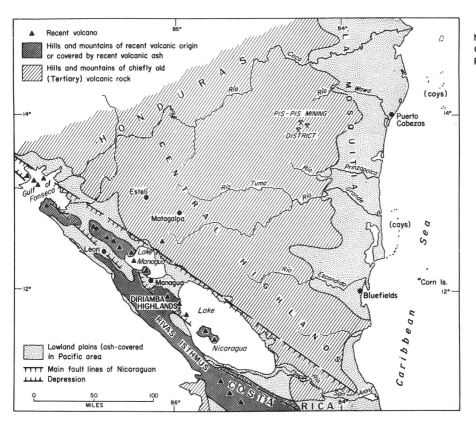

Figure 14.8

Nicaragua: Surface Configuration and Related Geology.

structive, the volcanic ash that falls on the surrounding lowland plains and flanking uplands of the Nicaraguan Depression weathers into highly fertile soil. This, and plentiful rain (40 to 60 inches) from May to October, have attracted people to the northwestern portion of the depression and its adjacent uplands. For perhaps 2,000 years, the area has supported a dense population. In pre-Columbian times it was the locale of high Chorotegan Indian culture, the southernmost extent of Mesoamerican civilization; today, it forms the core of Nicaragua in terms of people, agricultural production, and natural wealth.

Eastward from the lake and volcano-studded depression lie the central highlands. Old volcanic lava and ash, which have buried most of the underlying granitic rocks of Old Antillia, comprise this rugged mountain mass —a southern continuation of the Honduran uplands. The higher mountain ridges reach 3,000 to 6,500 feet, and between them are deep valleys that drain eastward to the Caribbean Sea. Drenched by heavy rains (70 to 100 inches yearly), most of the crests and eastern slopes of the central highlands are covered by a dense rain forest; but in the north, near the Honduran border, extensive pine forests form the southernmost limit of the North American upland conifers. A semideciduous tropical forest once covered the drier western versant of the highlands, located in the lee of the prevailing trades. Since colonial times, settlers have pushed slowly eastward into the central highlands from the densely occupied Nicaraguan Depression. The drier western and northern portions of the highlands are now well settled, but the wet, forest-covered, eastern flanks are still pioneer country.

The extensive, sparsely settled Caribbean lowlands, sometimes called "La Mosquitia," comprise the eastern third of Nicaragua. This hot, humid area includes the coastal plains of leached, infertile, gravelly soils; the lower eastern spurs of the central highlands; and the San Juan River basin. Receiving between 100 and 250 inches of rain yearly, with a

short dry period in February and March, the lowland is the wettest section of Middle America. The pine and palm savannas that begin in easternmost Honduras extend southward along the coast to Pearl Lagoon, whereas the rest of the lowland is clothed in rain forest. Numerous rivers that drain the central highlands cross the Mosquitia as they flow to the Caribbean Sea. The area's only fertile soils are in the narrow floodplains of these streams, along which are concentrated the few lowland farming settlements. This great empty area contrasts sharply with the crowded western part of the country.

THE NICARAGUAN PEOPLE

Population Distribution

Three-fourths of Nicaragua's 1.6 million people live on the Pacific side of the country, mainly within the fertile plains of the lake lowlands and the adjacent Diriamba highlands and Rivas Isthmus. In these areas, population averages more than 150 per square mile; in some sections (as around Masaya near Lake Nicaragua), rural densities reach beyond 400 (Figure 14.9).

Figure 14.9
Population Density in Nicaragua, by Departments.

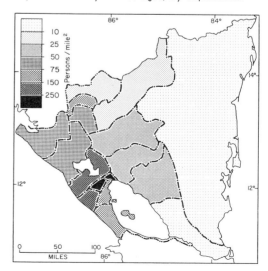

The Nicaraguan Depression likewise contains most of the cities. The capital, Managua, has 230,000 inhabitants, nearly 15 per cent of the country's population. One of Latin America's youngest national capitals, Managua was chosen in 1858 as a compromise site midway between the two rival colonial cities of León (now 50,000 population) and Granada (28,000) (Figure 14.10). A secondary population center lies in the northern part of the central highlands. Only lightly settled by Spaniards in colonial times, this area began to receive an influx of settlers drawn by coffee cultivation during the mid-nineteenth century and has steadily grown since. The main settlements cluster around the towns of Estelí, Matagalpa, and Somoto, where densities range from 50 to 80 persons per square mile. In sharp contrast, the Caribbean lowlands average only 4 persons per square mile, and most of the interfluves are uninhabited.

The population distribution of Nicaragua has changed little since pre-Conquest times. As we have seen, at Spanish contact the lake lowlands and adjacent uplands supported a dense Indian population; a smaller number of less advanced aboriginal farmers lived in the central highlands; and the Caribbean lowlands contained a few small tropical forest tribes scattered along the river courses. Perhaps better than any other Central American country, Nicaragua illustrates the persistence of ancient patterns of population distribution.

Like the people of other Middle American

Figure 14.10
Aerial View of Managua City and Vicinity, Southwestern Shore of Lake Managua. In the foreground is Lake Tiscapa (165 feet deep), which occupies the crater of a large cinder cone. The presidential palace is perched on the far rim of the crater. In the distance one sees the symmetrical slopes of Momotombo Volcano. *(Compañía Mexicana Aerofoto)*

nations, Nicaraguans are increasing more than 3 per cent annually. In order to relieve population pressure in the overcrowded Pacific area, the Nicaraguan government has encouraged colonization within the central highlands and the Caribbean lowlands. Since World War II, Nicaraguan farmers have been settling in the north portion of the central highlands, but colonists from the Pacific area have made little headway into the Caribbean tropical forests.

Racial Composition

Nicaragua is a land of mixbloods. Seventy-five per cent of the people are mestizo, or mixed Indian-white, most of whom live in the populous Pacific area and the northern portion of the central highlands. At mid-nineteenth century, a third of the population of these areas was still Indian, but practically all the purely aboriginal racial element has since disappeared from the lake lowlands, and only a small remnant of culturally modified Matagalpa Indians persist in the central highlands. In the Caribbean lowlands, however, a sizable number (about 20,000) of Miskito Indians (about half of whom are sambos, or mixed Indian-Negro) live as subsistence farmers and fishers along the Cocos and other rivers (see Figure 13.2, p. 381). In addition, small groups of Sumu Indians occupy isolated stretches of streams on the eastern flank of the central highlands. The Caribbean lowland is also the home of most of Nicaragua's Negro population (10 per cent of the total), most of whom entered the country as laborers on banana plantations early in this century. Ten per cent of the Nicaraguan people are classed as Caucasian; these are mainly descendants of colonial families who live in urban centers and form the upper landholding class.

ECONOMY AND CULTURE AREAS

Like its Central American neighbors, Nicaragua is a nation of farmers. Nearly 70 per cent of its economically active population is engaged in agriculture and 80 per cent of its exports by value are farm products: this despite the fact that only 5 per cent of the country is farmed. Most of the people are either landless laborers on large estates or subsistence farmers working hillside plots, and a smaller number own and cultivate medium-sized farms (*fincas*). The large hacienda owners possess most, and the best, of the arable lands and pastures. A heritage of the colonial past, this threefold rural class structure and land tenure system permeates Nicaraguan life.

Nicaragua's agricultural economy tends to coincide with the country's three distinct culture areas, which in turn reflect basic physical conditions. These areas are: (1) the Pacific area, including the lake lowlands and adjacent uplands; (2) the northern part of the central highlands; and (3) the Caribbean lowlands.

THE PACIFIC AREA

Since early colonial times, the densely peopled Pacific area has been Nicaragua's main center of subsistence and commercial agriculture. Most of the land is in large estates, or haciendas, on which the bulk of the rural people are employed as farm hands (*mozos*). Most of the *mozos* and their families live in nucleated hamlets and villages on or near hacienda lands in much the same way their Indian ancestors did in the colonial period. Most of their houses, Indianlike, have wattled walls and grass-thatched roofs. On rented subsistence plots near their settlements, many hacienda workers raise the native maize, beans, and squash, and the introduced rice and sorghum. Among the most typical foods are the aboriginal maize-chocolate gruel (*tiste*) and the Mesoamerican tortilla, tamale, and *atole*. The ox-drawn wooden plow and the two-wheeled cart are widespread. Thus, the rural cultural pattern of the Pacific area is a composite of Hispanic and Indian traits little changed, except for the growing of certain commercial crops, from the colonial period.

Stock Raising

Since colonial times, most of Nicaragua's wealth has come from large haciendas. Livestock and indigo continued to be the country's main exports until the mid-nineteenth century. Today, indigo has disappeared, but cattle raising is still significant and the main pastures are still centered in the hilly savannas of Chontales and Boaco on the eastern side of Lake Nicaragua. Only recently have the cattle barons begun to improve the traditional hide-and-tallow producing herds by crossing them with Brahma and other beef-yielding breeds. Today chilled beef, shipped by air mainly to the United States, is the country's third most valuable export.

Commercial Agriculture

The commercial crops produced on large estates in the Pacific area include coffee, cotton, bananas, sugar cane, and sesame seed. Coffee and cotton are by far the most important.

Coffee. In the 1850's, Nicaragua's commercial agriculture was revolutionized by the introduction of coffee. First grown in the volcanic hills west of Managua, by 1860 coffee had spread into the fertile ash-covered Diriamba uplands between the lake plains and the Pacific. It is grown on estates of 100 to 4,000 acres, particularly in a small area of 1,000 to 3,000 feet elevation called "Los Pueblos," where the towns of Diriamba, San Marcos, and Jinotepe serve as market centers for the crop (Figure 14.11). In the

Figure 14.11
Commercial Agriculture in Western Nicaragua.

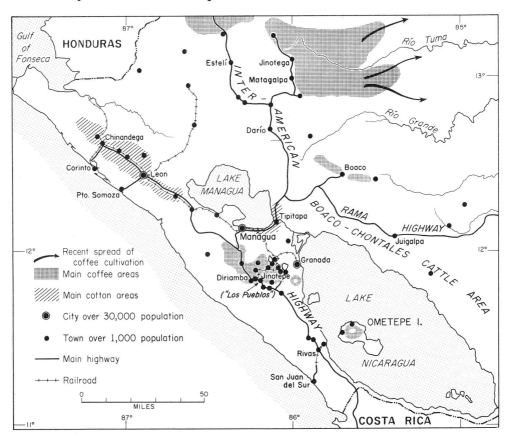

Figure 14.12

Wide Floodplain of the Río Sebaco, Western Side of the Central Highlands of Nicaragua. The view shows large-scale mechanized farming of maize, cotton, and rice on hacienda lands.

1920's, the Diriamba upland produced 90 per cent of Nicaragua's coffee; today it produces less than half the total, owing to the expansion of cultivation in the north central highlands. For more than a century, coffee has been Nicaragua's foremost export and one of the main sources of wealth for the estate owners.

Cotton. Cotton has become very significant since 1950, and it now vies with coffee as Nicaragua's most valuable export. Production is centered in the northwestern lowland plains between Lake Managua and the Gulf of Fonseca. There, the deep, black soil, weathered from volcanic ash, is among the best in Central America. The most productive section lies around the booming market town of Chinandega, where cattle haciendas have been transformed into large cotton plantations (Figure 14.12). A secondary cotton-growing area lies along the southern side of Lake Managua between the capital and Tipitapa. Although large holdings and a flattish terrain have facilitated extensive mechanization, a large labor force is still needed to harvest the crop, and new *mozo* settlements have mushroomed throughout the

cotton zone. Practically all the crop is exported to Japan and western Europe through the new deepwater port of Corinto, constructed in 1958 near the old colonial harbor of Realejo.

Bananas. The most recent estate crop in Nicaragua's fertile Pacific zone is bananas. In 1962, large-scale plantings were made along the coastal plain inland from Corinto. If successful, this venture by large landholders may revive the long-dormant banana industry that once flourished in Nicaragua's Caribbean lowlands.

THE CENTRAL HIGHLANDS

During the colonial period, the central highlands underwent a cultural and economic development quite distinct from that of the Pacific area. Only the Nueva Segovia gold and silver deposits and the pastures for stock raising in the northern part of the highlands attracted Spaniards in any numbers, and the threat of pirate and Miskito Indian raids from the Caribbean caused frequent abandonment of these settlements. Moreover, the rugged terrain, and the poor soils, as well as the scant and hostile Indian population combined to discourage agricultural developments similar to those of the Pacific lowlands. Thus, subsistence farming, small landholdings, and dispersed settlement characterized the rural scene of the central highlands well into the nineteenth century.

Coffee. The first significant change came in the 1890's, when German, North America, and English colonists introduced coffee cultivation into the hardwood forests of the Matagalpa and Jinotega areas. The success of these *fincas* attracted large numbers of peasant farmhands from the lake lowlands. Many of these, as well as the native Matagalpa Indians, established small coffee farms and slash-burn subsistence plots, pushing the settlement frontier eastward. Although interrupted by civil strife between 1911 and 1934, this eastward expansion now continues apace and has now reached well into the densely forested Caribbean versant of the central highlands.

Today, the Matagalpa and Jinotega area produces nearly half Nicaragua's coffee crop. In contrast to the large, crowded estates in the Diriamba district, the coffee *fincas* are small-to-medium holdings (25 to 75 acres), dispersed over wide areas.

The Cultural Landscape. In addition to growing coffee, many small independent farmers (*finqueros*) run cattle and plant subsistence crops of maize and sorghum in slash-burn hillside plots with the dibble and hoe. The plow and ox-cart, so common in the Pacific area, are rarely seen in the rugged central highlands; rather, away from the recently constructed truck roads, mule transport is the rule. The cultural landscape of the north-central highlands is that of a recently settled and expanding pioneer zone, a characteristic that sets it apart from the long and densely settled Pacific belt of feudal Indian-Hispanic heritage.

The South-Central Highlands

The southern part of the central highlands remains sparsely occupied. Since World War II, some cattle ranchers from the Chontales savannas have spread into the mountains, felling the forest to plant grass for artificial pastures, and coffee cultivation has been started in the mountains back of Boaco. Like the vast, forested Caribbean lowland, this part of the central highland is an area for future colonization.

THE CARIBBEAN LOWLANDS

As we noted in the first part of this chapter, the Caribbean lowlands of Nicaragua constitute a part of the eastern versant of Central America that falls outside the area of mainland Hispanic life. This is a territory whose littoral is a part of the Middle American Rimland (Caribbean Negroid culture) and whose interior still belongs largely to primitive forest Indian groups. As such, the eastern third of Nicaragua is, culturally and physically, a world apart from the rest of the country—a forested, sparsely peopled area that still lies outside the effective national territory.

The vast contrast between the Nicaraguan Pacific core and the Caribbean versant was equally pronounced in aboriginal times, for the civilized Chorotegans of the lake lowlands had little contact with the primitive fishers and farmers of the Caribbean tropical forests. During the colonial period, the Spaniards normally shunned the Caribbean forests; they traversed the lowlands only occasionally, via the San Juan River, to transport merchandise between the Caribbean port of San Juan del Norte and Granada on Lake Nicaragua. In Chapter 10, we told how English pirates and smugglers used the unoccupied Caribbean coast for bases during the seventeenth and eighteenth centuries and how they organized the Miskito Indians into kind of a kingdom that lasted until the mid-nineteenth century. During this time, the English established the ports of Bluefields and Greytown (the site of San Juan del Norte) along the Caribbean coast to encourage trade and white colonization and to control their Indian protectorate. Although the Kingdom of Mosquitia was abolished by treaty in 1850, Nicaragua did not take formal military possession of the Caribbean coast until 1893.

Since the mid-nineteenth century, the economy of the Caribbean lowlands has revolved mainly around three activities, all of which have been largely in the hands of foreign interests: (1) exploitation of wild forest products; (2) gold mining; and (3) plantation agriculture. All three have been characterized by boom periods followed by decline and abandonment. Moreover, save for port towns, little permanent settlement has resulted from these activities.

Exploitation of the Forests

Between 1860 and World War I, the gathering of latex from wild rubber trees (*Castilla elastica; balata*) became a significant industry in the Caribbean rain forest. Thousands of mestizos from the Pacific belt, as well as local Matagalpa and Miskito Indians, ranged the forests in search of rubber, especially on the eastern slopes of the central highlands in the San Juan basin. By 1900, Nicaragua had become the leading producer of rubber north of the Amazon basin. With the rise of the rubber plantations in southeast Asia after 1915, the gathering industry collapsed in both Nicaragua and Brazil, reviving briefly during World War II.

Lumbering has been more permanent, particularly the cutting of mahogany and Spanish cedar, which are scattered through the tropical rain forest, and of slash pine (*Pinus caribea*), which grows in solid stands in the Mosquito Coast savannas. Early in the nineteenth century, English woodcutters were floating out mahogany logs along the many lowland rivers to the coast, and during World War I this tropical cabinet wood became Nicaragua's second most important export. In 1924, a company from New Orleans began lumbering slash pine in the Mosquito savanna and built a new port at Puerto Cabezas to handle exports to the United States and to the Caribbean islands. Intensive logging still continues, but most of the better stands of pine are depleted and, in 1963, operations ceased in the Puerto Cabezas area.

Gold Mining

Since the sixteenth century, gold has been a significant Nicaraguan export. Until the latter half of the nineteenth century most of the mines were located in the central highlands. But, in the 1890's, the rich deposits of Pis-Pis were discovered in an isolated, low, forested mountain spur inland from Puerto Cabezas (Figure 14.8). Worked off and on by North American companies, it became Nicaragua's leading gold district in the 1940's. Between 1938 and 1949, gold surpassed coffee as the country's leading export, with more than half the production coming from Pis-Pis. By 1963, however, the ores were greatly depleted and the mining centers of Siuna and Bonanza in the Pis-Pis district were closed down.

Plantation Agriculture

One of the most promising attempts to open the Caribbean lowlands to permanent settlement was the establishment of banana plantations along the river flood plains during the late nineteenth and early twentieth centuries. As we mentioned in Chapter 13, commercial banana production in Nicaragua first began on the middle course of the Escondido River in 1883, inland from Bluefields (see Figure 13.4, p. 385). Until 1920, this rich alluvial area remained the chief banana area in Nicaragua, production being in the hands of a large number of independent growers. Thereafter cultivation spread to other rivers, especially the Río Grande and Río Wawa farther north, and the large fruit companies acquired control of most of the production. 1929 was the peak banana year in Nicaragua (four million stems), but the harvest was far below that of other Central American countries. Panama disease and Sigatoka adversely affected the industry after 1938, and the banana lands in the Nicaraguan lowlands were completely abandoned by the end of World War II. During the height of production, English-speaking Jamaican Negroes were brought in as plantation laborers. Many of their descendants now live in the major port towns such as Puerto Cabezas, Río Grande, and Bluefields, where they have entered various trades; few have become farmers.

Despite varied economic activity in the Caribbean lowlands during the last hundred years, the land is relatively unpopulated. Since the close of World War II, the Nicaraguan government has encouraged mestizos from the Pacific to colonize the lowlands, but only one significant penetration has been made—along the new highway constructed from Managua through the central highlands to the town of Rama, center of the former banana plantations on the middle Escondido River. Along the alluvial flood plain, colonists have established small subsistence and commercial farms. Although the all-weather highway to the population centers on the Pacific facilitates movement of produce to markets, the success of the colony is still uncertain.

TRANSPORT

Nicaragua's rail and highway network is another index of the concentration of economic wealth in the Pacific lowlands. The 216-mile rail system, now a government utility, was constructed piecemeal between 1878 and 1903, mainly to haul coffee from the Diriamba highlands to the port of Corinto. Until the completion of the Panama Canal in 1914, the San Juan River also was a cheap, but hazardous, export route for the coffee crop via the Caribbean coast.

Few auto roads existed in Nicaragua before World War II, but, in 1958 and 1960, paved highways were completed between Managua and the port of San Juan del Sur and between the capital and the port of Corinto. The postwar period also saw the completion of the Inter-American Highway and of many feeder truck roads through the north-central highlands, linking the Matagalpa coffee area with the Pacific lowlands. The Rama road, connecting the Pacific with the Caribbean lowlands, was started in 1942 as a military measure, but was not completed until 20 years later.

INDUSTRY

Like Honduras, Nicaragua is one of the least industrialized of the Central American countries. The few plants constructed since World War II are in the four major towns of the Pacific lowlands: Managua, León, Granada, and Chinandega; some minor industries are established also in Matagalpa, in the north-central highlands. Possessing the bulk of surplus urban labor and 90 per cent of the country's electrical power, Managua is the largest industrial center. Food and lumber processing, textiles, steel tubing manufacture, and an oil refinery are among the industries of the capital city. With the completion of a hydroelectric development on the Tuma River, on the eastern slope of the central highlands, the power base for industrialization and rural electrification in Nicaragua will be greatly increased.

Costa Rica

This delightful country is unique among Latin American nations. About 80 per cent of the Costa Ricans claim to be unmixed white descendants of Spanish colonists, and most of these are small farmers in a confined highland area—the Meseta Central. The people also claim the highest literacy rate, the most democratic government, and the most comfortable living standard in Latin America. In striking contrast to its Central American neighbors, Costa Rica has suffered only one serious political upheaval (1948) during a long, peaceful period lasting from 1886 to the present. Unusual, also, has been the spontaneous colonization of the virgin forest lands from the surrounding, densely populated Meseta Central during the last 125 years, a vigorous and continuing pioneer movement.

Except for its northwestern province (Guanacaste), Costa Rica, in pre-Spanish times, lay outside the cultural influence of aboriginal Mesoamerica. Thus, the strong Indian heritage that Mesoamerican culture has given to Guatemala, El Salvador, and western Nicaragua is absent in most of Costa Rica. The Indians of South American (Chibchan) cultural affinity who lived in the Costa Rican highlands disappeared rapidly after the Conquest, leaving that area open to the Spanish colonists. Without a large number of Indians to work for them, the Spaniards in the highlands failed to develop

the large landed estate and accompanying serfdom that is usually associated with Hispanic occupation. Rather, there arose, as the prevailing cultural pattern, a Spanish peasantry occupied with subsistence farming, a pattern that still dominates the rural scene of much of highland Costa Rica.

PHYSICAL CHARACTERISTICS

Although of extreme local complexity, the physical structure of Costa Rica is roughly the threefold Central American division of: (1) cool central highlands; (2) warm Pacific lowland and leeward mountain slopes with well-defined wet and dry seasons; (3) Caribbean lowlands and eastward-facing escarpments, rain-drenched and forest-covered. Together with the Panamanian isthmus, the narrow Costa Rican land mass forms a bridge that connects Old Antillia with South America.

The Central Highlands

Figure 14.13 indicates that the Costa Rican highlands consist of a northern volcanic range (Cordillera Volcánica) and a

Figure 14.13

Costa Rica and Panama: Surface Configuration and Associated Geology.

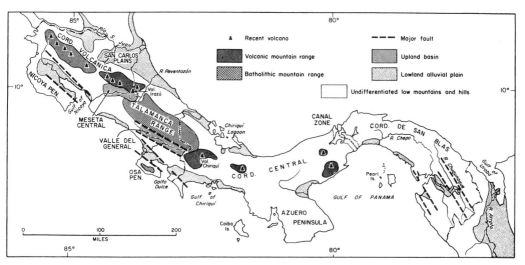

southern mountain mass formed by the intrusion of a gigantic batholith of granitic rock (Talamanca Range). Between these two distinctly different mountain ranges lies a small upland area known as the Meseta Central, the most significant physiographic unit of Costa Rica in terms of its cultural development.

The northern range, a part of the Central American volcanic axis, consists of a series of cones perched atop an elevated mass of lava and ash. The highest and most active volcanoes are toward the southeast, where Irazú (11,500 feet elevation) suddenly erupted in 1963, causing extensive damage by ash throughout central Costa Rica.

Immediately south of the highest volcanoes lies the Meseta Central, itself a product of vulcanism. Two small basins comprise this upland. The higher, eastern one is Cartago (5,000 feet elevation), drained by the headwaters of the Reventazón River which flows to the Caribbean. To the west lies the lower and larger basin, San José (3,000 to 4,000 feet elevation), site of the present capital city and drained toward the Pacific by the headwaters of the Río Grande de Tárcoles.

Between the two basins a low range of volcanic hills forms the continental divide. Ashfalls, avalanches of glowing cinders, and mudflows from the adjacent volcanoes have filled the basins to their present elevations. On this volcanic floor, eroding streams have formed the rolling surface and numerous terraces that characterize the basins today. As elsewhere along the volcanic axis, the ash and cinder deposits have weathered into highly fertile soil. Situated in the *tierra templada* altitudinal zone, the Meseta Central enjoys one of the most equable climates in Middle America. Frost-free and sufficiently moist, the Meseta can produce a wide range of tropical and midlatitude crops and, since pre-Columbian times, it has supported a dense population (Figure 14.14).

Another upland basin, the Valle del General, lies between the Talamanca Range and the coastal mountains in southwestern Costa Rica. This isolated structural depression, composed of river flood plains, terraces, and rolling hills 1,000 to 3,500 feet above the sea, has been occupied only recently by farmers migrating out of the overcrowded Meseta Central.

Figure 14.14
Basin of Cartago, Which Forms the Eastern Portion of the Meseta Central. Small fields of maize and pasture cover the surrounding slopes.

The Pacific Lowlands

Unlike the straight Pacific shoreline of northern Central America, that of Costa Rica is indented by a series of peninsulas and gulfs, mostly as a consequence of faulting (Figure 14.13). The down-faulted blocks (grabens) produce the gulfs of Nicoya and Dulce as well as adjacent alluvial lowlands; the up-faulted blocks (horsts) give rise to the mountainous peninsulas of Nicoya, Osa, and Burica with their steep, rocky shore lines. The alluvial plains afford fertile soils for tropical lowland farming and some, as the Golfo Dulce graben, contain large banana plantations. Despite a four-month dry season (January through April), the annual rainfall (80 to 120 inches) is sufficient to support a heavy rain forest. In the northwestern province of Guanacaste, where the interior plains receive less than 60 inches of rain, there are open deciduous forests, most of which man has transformed, by burning, into tropical grasslands.

The Caribbean Lowlands

The belt of heavy precipitation and tropical rain forest that characterizes the Caribbean lowlands of Nicaragua extends southward into Costa Rica, where the annual rainfall is 150 to 200 inches and there is a short or no dry season. Wetness and disease have discouraged modern settlement of these hot lands, despite the rich alluvial soils of many sections. Nevertheless, some parts, such as the Matina valley near Limón, have been occupied intermittently by Europeans since the colonial era and, between 1880 and 1940, other sections became centers of large-scale banana production.

Costa Rica's largest alluvial plain within the Caribbean lowland is the San Juan River basin, which borders on Nicaragua. This plain continues as the Llanos de Santa Clara southeastward along the coast, in a narrowing wedge to the vicinity of Limón. The vast accumulation of sediment that comprises both of these plains comes mainly from the numerous streams that drain the ash-covered northeastern slopes of the Cordillera Volcánica. Between the plain and the steep mountain escarpment, the same streams have created immense alluvial fans, and these have coalesced to form a continuous alluvial piedmont of fertile, well-drained soils, most of which are ideally suited for tropical agriculture. Farther south, along the Panamanian border, the Sixaola River forms a smaller alluvial plain, part of which extends into Costa Rican territory.

THE COSTA RICANS

Better than any other Middle American country, Costa Rica displays a single-cluster distribution of population. Well over half the country's 1.4 million people are concentrated in the Meseta Central, and the concentration used to be even greater. San José basin alone contains some of the most densely populated rural areas in Central America (300 to 1,500 per square mile); it also contains the country's largest towns and cities, including the national capital within whose metropolitan area live 275,000 people, 20 per cent of Costa Rica's population. Moreover, between 1958 and 1962 Costa Ricans increased at the rate of 4.3 per cent annually, one of the highest national growth rates in the world. Population growth, as well as the clustering within the Meseta Central, dates from the late colonial period. The small Meseta Central, only 15 by 40 miles, is truly the political, social, and economic core —and historically the cultural hearth—of Costa Rica.

The people who live outside the Meseta Central are scattered unevenly in various sections of the country which have been settled mainly since independence (1821). The Pacific versant and the Reventazón River valley from Cartago basin to Turrialba has received most of these settlers. In the Caribbean, only the former banana areas contain a sizable population; the rest of the forested lowlands and eastern escarpments are largely unoccupied. The greatest *despoblado* of Costa Rica, however, is the high, forested Talamanca Range.

Racial Composition

A characteristic in which the Costa Rican highlander takes special pride is his direct ancestry from colonial settlers who came chiefly from Extremadura and Andalusia in west-central and southern Spain. Within the Meseta Central and surrounding highlands, as we have noted, probably 90 per cent of the people consider themselves pure Caucasians. An estimated 17 per cent of the entire country's population is mestizo; most of these live in the northwestern province of Guanacaste and the Pacific coast. Only 2 per cent of all Costa Ricans are Negro; descendants of English-speaking Jamaicans, they are confined mainly to the former banana lands on the Caribbean coast. Isolated remnants of Indians who long ago fled into the remoteness of the Talamanca Range comprise today less than 1 per cent of the population.

The Spread of Settlement

The spread of settlement which has occurred in Costa Rica is unique in Middle America. This outward movement has taken place without a decrease of population within the Meseta Central, the core area. Moreover, the settlers have come almost solely from the natural increase of the Costa Rican population. The national government has not controlled this expansion; it has been a spontaneous, unplanned movement of surplus peasants who were seeking new lands for subsistence and commercial farming. Generally, the more important movements have followed new lines of communication. Some colonists, however, have filtered into isolated, rugged hills and mountains far from established roads.

Today, about three-fifths of Costa Rica

has been settled, whereas in 1860 less than one-fifth was occupied; and new settlement continues at an ever-growing pace. Large sections of the remaining frontier zones within the Caribbean lowlands and the high interior mountain areas may be occupied in the near future.

The exceedingly slow population growth and settlement of the Meseta Central during the colonial period was outlined briefly in Chapter 9. Figure 14.15 depicts the major lines of expansion during the nineteenth and twentieth centuries. With the spread of commercial coffee cultivation in the 1820's, the population of the Meseta Central began to increase markedly, doubling between 1824 and 1844. At that time, settlement spread westward from the Meseta, following a cart road constructed to haul coffee to Puntarenas on the Pacific coast. During the next 20 years, farmers continued to settle northwestward into the Pacific escarpment and on the Guanacaste savannas along the foot of the Cordillera Volcánica. With the completion of a railroad between the Meseta and the Caribbean port of Limón in 1892, settlement expanded eastward along this route down the Reventazón valley, near which the towns of Juan Viñas and Turrialba were founded.

By the close of the century, cattlemen and subsistence farmers had spilled northward across the volcanic range toward the San Carlos plain in the San Juan lowlands. Colonists had also pushed southward to settle the northern foothills of the Talamanca Range and thence westward into the rugged Turrubares hills; some penetrated as far south as the upper Valle del General, which later became a major route of expansion in southwestern Costa Rica. In the Caribbean lowlands, the rapid growth of the banana industry attracted many highland merchants and professionals to the port of Limón and to the market towns that arose along the rail lines within the plantation area. But few white peasant farmers from the Meseta Central ventured into the rainy, malarial *tierra caliente*, and Negroes imported to labor

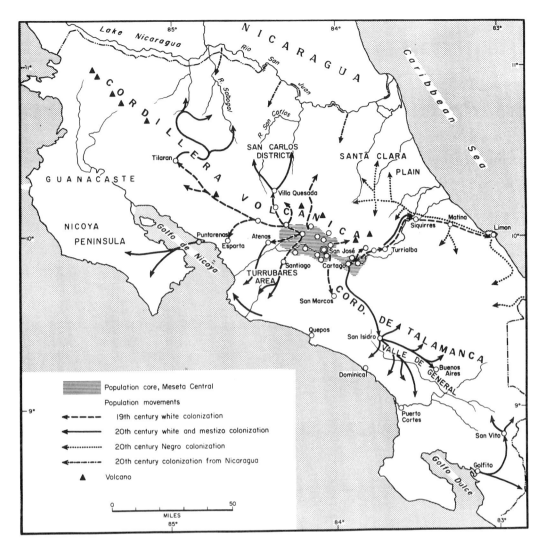

Figure 14.15
Rural Colonization in Costa Rica : Nineteenth and Twentieth Centuries.

on the plantations there became the dominant racial group. For many years, the town of Turrialba (1,600 feet elevation) remained the lower limit of white colonization on the eastern escarpment. Since the 1930's, however, large numbers of white highlanders have settled on the abandoned banana lands northwest of Limón and have become successful tropical lowland subsistence farmers.

The greatest expansion of settlement in the entire history of Costa Rica took place between 1930 and 1960. During this time, the United Fruit Company shifted its banana industry from the Caribbean to the Pacific coastal lowlands. This change involved the inducement of large labor forces—mainly mestizos from Guanacaste and Puntarenas—into the previously sparsely peopled lowlands around Parrita and Golfo Dulce. A more spectacular colonizing boom took place into the Valle del General, after the Inter-American Highway was completed through the northern end of the Talamanca Range. In 1927, the valley was almost a forested wilderness, containing only 4,800 people. In 1962, it contained more than 55,000 inhabitants, about 20,000 having immigrated from the Meseta Central between 1950 and 1960, to farm and to pasture livestock on its fertile river flood plains and alluvial terraces. The valley's market towns—San Isidro, Buenos Aires, and Volcán—reflect their recency in their makeshift wooden stores, their muddy streets, and the noisy truck traffic. In 1962, the Inter-American Highway was completed into Panama, providing a connection to the Golfo Dulce banana area and opening new areas for settlement. A branch highway taps the southern end of the Valle del General, where the thriving Italian agricultural colony of San Vito was established in 1952 near the Panamanian border.

Highland farmers continue to push northward into the forested lowlands of the San Juan basin. In 1957, a truck road was completed from the Meseta Central into the eastern portion of the northern lowlands. However, the comparatively few highland farmers who have entered this extremely humid area have done poorly; only a small number of large-scale cattle ranches and sugar plantations have been profitable. The less humid San Carlos plain, to the west, has been more successfully colonized by both small farmers and big cattle ranchers. Connected with the Meseta Central by auto road in 1945, the town of Ciudad Quesada has become the area's administrative and market center. On the higher plains near the mountains, small farmers intensively cultivate coffee, sugar cane, and foodstuffs; at lower elevations, ranchers have converted big tracts of rain forest to lush artificial pastures for large herds of cattle. The San Carlos plain appears to be the most promising section of Costa Rica's northern humid lowlands for future settlement.

PATTERNS OF LIVELIHOOD

Costa Rica is basically an agricultural country. More than half the working population is directly engaged in farming; 95 per cent of all exports, by value, are agricultural —chiefly coffee, bananas, and cacao; proceeds from crops and livestock make up nearly 40 per cent of the gross national product.

Patterns of agricultural land use in Costa Rica correspond closely with natural geographic regions and are usually synonymous with a given way of life.

Farming in the Meseta Central

The Meseta Central produces most of Costa Rica's coffee, sugar cane, commercial dairy products, and a substantial amount of the general food crops (Figure 14.16). Of these, coffee is outstanding; since the 1840's, it has been Costa Rica's main export, and its successful cultivation symbolizes wealth and prestige to the small, independent highland farmer.

The main coffee belt occupies the eastern portion of San José basin, including the valley floor and the surrounding mountain slopes up to about 4,200 feet elevation. Natural conditions are almost ideal for high quality coffee: deep, friable, volcanic soils rich in organic matter; mild, frost-free temperatures; and an average rainfall of 70 inches, with a dry season between January and April for harvesting and processing the coffee beans. An important feature of the area is that the coffee *fincas* are small or of medium size, averaging less than 25 acres. This system of *minifundia* also characterizes many of the newly colonized areas outside the area[1] (Figure 14.17).

Small holdings within the coffee belt formerly were more numerous than they are today. As the cost of cultivation and processing has risen, many contiguous holdings have been purchased by individuals and companies to form larger and more efficient *fincas,* and the former owners of the small *fincas* often continue to work on the enlarged holdings as hired hands (*peones*). Large coffee *fincas*

[1] According to the 1955 Census, 44 per cent of Costa Rica's farms are smaller than 17 acres, and another 36 per cent are between 17 and 85 acres. Slightly less than 17 per cent of the farms are between 85 and 425 acres. Only 3.5 per cent exceed 425 acres, but this group includes the large haciendas and accounts for more than half the total farm acreage.

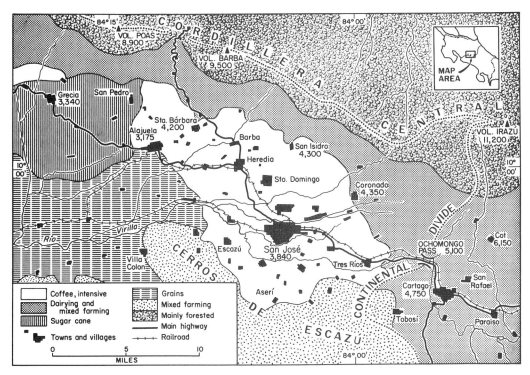

Figure 14.16
Land Utilization: Meseta Central of Costa Rica. Figures indicate feet above sea level.

Figure 14.17
Portion of a Small Coffee *Finca* Near Alajuela, Meseta Central. Throughout Central America coffee is grown under shade. In this scene the low coffee bushes form the understory, and are shaded by the tall leguminous trees. *(Instituto Costarricense de Turismo)*

are even more common in the Reventazón valley, where some are larger than 500 acres. The consolidation of coffee lands has gone so far in Costa Rica that, today, less than 2 per cent of the growers produce more than half the crop. Thus, the big agricultural estate in highlands Costa Rica is of relatively recent development, unlike the haciendas in most other Central American countries, which originated in the feudal land tenure system introduced by the Spanish colonist (Figure 14.18).

In recent years, production on both small and large Costa Rican coffee *fincas* has been substantially increased by more scientific methods—fertilizer, insecticides, and so forth. Between 1952 and 1962, for example, the coffee harvest was doubled with no increase

Figure 14.18

Coffee Pickers on a *Finca* Near San José, Costa Rica. *(Pan American Union)*

in acreage. Excepting in the war years, when transatlantic shipping was curtailed, Costa Rica's best coffee market has been western Europe, especially Germany, where the high quality beans bring special prices. Since 1955, approximately one-third of the harvest has been shipped to the United States, two-thirds to western Europe.

The coffee belt of the Meseta Central contains an unusually large rural population. Most of the roads within the San José basin are bordered almost continuously by dwellings which form line settlements. These wooden, tiled-roofed houses, often brightly painted, are the homes of small coffee growers or of *peones* who work on nearby *fincas*. Each *peon* usually owns or rents a subsistence plot, of one acre or less, near his house, and grows food for his large family. Formerly, each small coffee grower owned a *carreta*, a two-wheeled cart drawn by a yoke of oxen, to haul coffee and other products to the processing plant and market, but, since World War II, the motor truck has come into use and the famed, brightly painted Costa Rican *carreta* is now common only in the more remote rural areas (Figure 14.19). Auto roads now form a dense network throughout the Meseta Central. Although they are dangerously narrow, most are paved or graveled and lead to the principal markets and administrative centers such as San José, Heredia, and Alajuela.

In the dry, low, and hilly western part of the Meseta Central, the coffee *finca* gives way to small holdings on which maize, rice, and other cereal crops are produced. This cereal belt continues westward down the Pacific escarpment, following the Río Grande de Tárcoles valley, which has become the main rice-growing area of the country. West from Alajeula to the town of Grecia, that portion of the Meseta below 2,500 feet is planted chiefly in sugar cane. This area, and the terraces that border the Reventazón River east of Cartago, produce the bulk of Costa Rica's sugar (Figure 14.20).

On the high mountain slopes above the

Figure 14.19
Brightly Painted Costa Rican *Carreta*. The *carreta* is used for hauling many things. Here firewood is being hauled into San José. *(Pan American Union)*

Figure 14.20
Sugar Center of Juan Viñas, Upper Reventazón Valley. Fields of sugar cane cover the rolling volcanic surface in the background.

coffee belt is located one of the most distinctive economies of Costa Rica: a well-developed dairy industry based on native highland grasses and pastures planted at elevations between 4,500 and 7,000 feet. This belt now extends eastward to include the southern slopes of Irazú and Turrialba volcanoes, as well as the basin of Cartago which forms the eastern portion of the Meseta Central. Settlers from the San José coffee zone began to form small dairy farms on the cool, wet mountain slopes in the 1880's. Since that time, the individual farms have been consolidated, and few small holdings remain. The herds include some of the finest dairy stock in Latin America, derived from Holstein, Jersey, and Guernsey breeds imported from Europe. Quite unlike his Central American neighbors, the Costa Rican highlander, or "Tico," as he is often nicknamed, consumes large quantities of fresh pasteurized milk, butter, and cheese, mostly from the mountain dairy belt, which is connected with the larger towns in the Meseta by paved roads. A large cooperative does most of the processing in the area, including that of powdered milk and ice cream. Unfortunately, the fall of ash from the Irazú eruption of 1963–1964 has greatly curtailed milk production by destroying a large portion of the pastures, just as it has badly damaged the coffee *fincas* of San José basin.

Southwestern Uplands

This large area has a pioneer character. It consists chiefly of low, rugged coastal mountains, the northern and western slopes of the Talamanca Range, and the Valle del General. As we have seen, much of it was settled only in the past 50 years, and it is still being colonized. The white subsistence farmers who first came to these mountains as squatters used primitive slash-burn cultivation, destroying large sections of the original forest to make clearings for their small plots of maize, beans, upland rice, and yucca (sweet manioc). Subsequently, erosion stripped the rather infertile red clay soils from many hillsides, but most of the cleared sections were converted to pasture after a few years of cropping. On higher slopes, above 2,000 feet, some squatters grow small cash crops of coffee. However, produce is difficult to market, for few good roads exist in the mountainous zones and farmers live in isolated homesteads or in small hamlets dispersed on the steep slopes.

Pioneer farming conditions are better in the Valle del General, where level land, fairly fertile soils, and good roads prevail. Here, in addition to subsistence agriculture, large-scale commercial production of maize, as well as of tropical fruits such as pineapple, has recently been developed. Cattle ranches, using both natural savanna and artificial pas-

Figure 14.21

Landscape in the Upper Valle del General, Showing Cultivation on Stream Terraces and Hillslopes.

tures for grazing, are multiplying. Connected by paved highway to both the Meseta Central and the Golfo Dulce banana plantations, the once-isolated Valle del General now enjoys excellent truck transport for marketing agricultural products (Figure 14.21).

The prevalence of squatting by landless colonists on whatever unoccupied land is available has produced a serious tenure problem in many parts of Costa Rica, especially in the southwestern uplands. The chief motive of Costa Rica's agrarian reform program of 1961 was to legalize the holdings of the present squatters, or *parásitos* ("parasites"), for they number into the thousands. At the same time, steps are being taken to halt squatting (*parasitismo*) entirely and to preserve the remaining virgin forests from destruction by the squatter's ax and fires.

The Guanacaste

The northwestern corner of Costa Rica—the province of Guanacaste—until recently was a world apart from the central highlands. Throughout the colonial period, this province belonged to Nicaragua, from which it received its major cultural patterns. Not until 1824 was it incorporated into Costa Rica, and only in the past half-century have portions of the area been settled by sizable groups of Costa Rican highlanders.

The Guanacaste lies mainly within the *tierra caliente* and is composed of: (1) the mountainous, forest-covered Nicoya peninsula; and (2) the savanna plains of the adjacent structural lowland. Each of the two natural divisions presents a distinct cultural landscape.

Since the sixteenth century, the savanna lowland, locally called "Los Llanos," has been occupied by large cattle haciendas. The few Spanish ranchers that came from Nicaragua mixed readily with the native Chorotegan Indian women; in the eighteenth century many mixbloods (sambos and mulattoes) from Nicaragua entered the plains as cattle hands and subsistence farmers. From these racial elements is derived the present-day *nicoyano* or *paisano* population of the Guanacaste lowlands. Stock raising still dominates most of the savanna areas, but, on the plains bordering the western side of Nicoya Gulf, most of the large landholders have turned to mechanized cultivation of cotton, sesame, rice, and sorghum. Scattered throughout the plains are hamlets of subsistence farmers who cultivate maize, beans, and squash and prepare the traditional Mesoamerican tortillas and tamales as did their Chorotegan predecessors in pre-Columbian times.

Since 1890, large numbers of white highlanders, mainly landless peasants from Cartago basin, have migrated to the Guanacaste. Most of these people have settled in the forested peninsular hills and mountains south and west of the cattle country. Small, dispersed holdings on steep slopes, cultivation of beans and upland rice in slash-burn plots for subsistence together with small fields of coffee and sugar cane for cash crops, raising of hogs and milk cows, use of the highland *carreta*—such are the Costa Rican traits and landscape features introduced by the Cartagos into the Nicoya peninsula. The development of such a cultural dichotomy in Guanacaste province within the last 60 years illustrates the changes that are taking place in Costa Rica, as well as the great diversity of the landscape.

The Caribbean Lowlands

By reason of their peculiar physical character and settlement history, the Caribbean lowlands form a distinct economic region. Only 5 per cent of the country's people reside in this hot, rainy zone, giving it an average density of 20 persons per square mile. Some lowland areas, such as parts of the San Juan basin, are completely unpopulated; others, in which tropical agriculture has been well developed, have population densities of over 100 per square mile.

As we observed earlier, effective settlement of the Caribbean lowlands did not take place until the introduction of large-scale banana plantations in the 1880's. Banana planters considered the area nearly ideal, for: it has an annual rainfall of 100 inches or more with no dry season; there is abundant, fertile, well-drained alluvial soil close to the coast; and windstorms are infrequent.

The Matina River valley, famed for its cacao groves in colonial days, was the first large area planted to bananas by foreign interests. Plantations next spread westward to the lower Reventazón River in the vicinity of Siquirres. After its incorporation in 1899, the United Fruit Company acquired almost complete control of banana production in Costa Rica and extended cultivation northwestward from the Reventazón along the lower alluvial piedmont within the Santa Clara plains. Later, the company established plantations southward from Limón along the coastal plain to the Río Estrella and, in 1906, began the development of banana tracts on the Costa Rican side of the Sixaola River valley across from Panama. Between 1880 and World War I, Costa Rica led all Central American countries in banana production, the peak coming in 1913 with the export of 11 million stems. During this heyday, United Fruit extended rail lines throughout the producing areas to transport fruit to Limón, which was developed as a major Caribbean port. Along the railways, company towns were established to house the English-speaking Jamaican Negroes imported as laborers. Thus, by 1910, the whole complex of Caribbean plantation economy had been implanted in the Costa Rican lowlands.

Chiefly because of plant disease, production declined steadily after 1913. Panama disease was first noticed in the Matina valley in 1890, and by 1926 United Fruit was forced to abandon large tracts of land in the Santa Clara plain. In 1938, Sigatoka appeared and the company decided to shift its operations to the Pacific coast.

On their former banana lands in the Caribbean lowlands, United Fruit began large-scale cultivation of various commercial crops. Cacao replaced bananas in the coastal areas between Limón and the Reventazón River. Management of the groves was turned over to former Negro plantation workers, who continued to live in the company towns and along the railroads. Abacá, or Manila hemp, was introduced during World War II. Today, cacao is an important product of the Caribbean lowlands, and ranks third in Costa Rican exports, after coffee and bananas.

In 1957, the Standard Fruit Company revived commercial banana production near Limón on a 5,000-acre tract which had long before been abandoned by its rival, United Fruit. Growing the disease-resistant Giant Cavendish banana, the new Standard plantations and small independent holdings reached an annual production of nearly two million stems, one-fourth of Costa Rica's total banana output, by 1962. The new variety has made possible a substantial revival of the banana plantations in the Caribbean lowlands.

Since the 1930's, the subsistence farmer has become a significant part of the Caribbean lowland landscape. Many have settled on abandoned banana lands, especially in the upper Santa Clara alluvial piedmont northwest of the Reventazón River. In 1933, the government purchased most of United Fruit's holdings in this area and parceled them out in small plots to former Negro plantation workers and to newly arrived white families from the highlands. In addition, hundreds of landless Negroes, mulattoes, and white *parásitos* squatted there. Although some farmers cultivate cash crops such as cacao, most raise only maize, sweet manioc, and plantains. Negroes have also penetrated into the mountain slopes, where their primitive slash-burn fields, crops, and tools resemble those of their Jamaican homeland. Peasant settlement into the tropical lowlands is still continuing northeastward into the lower Santa Clara plain, where virgin forest lands are being opened to subsistence cultivation.

Plantation Zones of the Pacific Coast

The alluvial lowlands along Costa Rica's southwestern littoral have been the scene of one of the most recent developments of the tropical plantation in Central America. During 1938 and 1939, the United Fruit Company shifted its banana interests to two disease-free areas on the Pacific coast: (1) the Quepos-Parrita coastal plain and adjacent river valleys; and (2) the Golfo Dulce lowland, near the Panamanian border (see Figure 13.4, p. 385). Both areas are favored by fertile alluvial soils and over 100 inches of rainfall yearly, but a three-month dry season makes irrigation necessary in some sections. Moreover, the Pacific coast suffers from occasional, violent tropical storms.

Typical large-scale plantations, complete with a rail network, roads, and company labor towns, were laid out in both areas, and two new ports—Quepos in the northern section, Golfito in the Golfo Dulce—were completed by 1940 as banana shipping centers. The boom in the Parrita-Quepos area, however, was short-lived. After reaching peak production in 1948, most of the plantations became diseased and had to be abandoned. Subsequently, United Fruit planted much of

the banana land near Parrita to African oil palm and cacao; other holdings, near Quepos, were reduced to small properties and sold to independent cacao and banana farmers.

Although also affected by disease, the company plantations in the Golfo Dulce area produced nearly three-quarters of Costa Rica's banana crop in 1963. Harvests come chiefly from two small alluvial plains: the lower Río Grande de Térraba north of the gulf (the Palmar section) and the Río Coto drainage adjacent to the Panamanian border. When disease forces the abandonment of tracts, new forested land is cleared for planting. Banana exports leave the Golfo Dulce area through the ports of Golfito on the eastern gulf shore and Puerto Cortés on the Térraba River (Figure 14.22).

One of the most spectacular aspects of the banana boom in southwestern Costa Rica has been the rapid influx of people into the coastal zone. Between 1938 and 1963, the population of the banana areas increased from a few hundred subsistence farmers to

Figure 14.22
Portion of the Banana Port of Golfito, Southwestern Costa Rica. A United Fruit Company refrigerated ship lies alongside the pier, which is equipped with modern loading cranes. In the background are the local railway terminal and a part of the residential section. (*United Fruit Company*)

over 70,000 people. These migrants came mainly from the Guanacaste and the Meseta Central, but thousands also entered from Nicaragua and adjacent Chiriquí province in Panama. They came as day laborers on the plantations and small merchants in the new port and administrative towns. Thus, a medley of mulattoes, sambos, mestizos, and whites now compose the population along the southwestern coast. Many have taken to subsistence farming in the hills, where the small, scattered slash-burn plots and oddly shaped pastures within the tropical rain forest provide a contrast to the rectangular and well-regulated company plantations on the alluvial plains.

TRANSPORT PATTERNS

Since the close of the colonial period, Costa Rica's transport pattern has been dominated by two short routes that connect the Meseta Central with the Pacific and Caribbean coasts. Together these routes form an east-west transisthmian axis, significant not only for trade but also for channeling settlement into the escarpment and coastal areas.

The Pacific segment of the axis was first a mere cart road to carry coffee to the port of Puntarenas during most of the nineteenth century. However, expense of shipping from the Pacific coast to Europe and the eastern United States via the long route around Cape Horn spurred the construction of a railroad between the Meseta Central and Puerto Limón on the Caribbean. Started in 1871, this line was finally completed to San José in 1892. It not only captured the coffee trade but also stimulated the development of the banana industry on the Caribbean coast. Not until 1927 was a railroad constructed to Puntarenas on the Pacific side, thereby completing a transisthmian connection across the country. Today, a paved highway (part of the Inter-American route) also connects San José and Puntarenas, but a similar road to the Caribbean is yet to be constructed. Al-

though more tonnage is exported from the new banana docks of Golfito, Limón and Puntarenas remain the country's principal ports.

Since World War II, Costa Rica's transport pattern has been modified by the completion of the Inter-American Highway from western Nicaragua, via the Guanacaste, Meseta Central, and the Valle del General to Panama. In addition, there are many feeder auto roads that extend outward in all directions from the Meseta Central, all of which have helped to channel the new settlements, as have the rail lines constructed by the United Fruit Company in the Caribbean lowlands.

INDUSTRIAL DEVELOPMENT

Like other Central American countries, Costa Rica aspires to industrialize in an attempt to occupy the growing labor force of the urban areas and to raise the national standard of living. In 1960, manufacturing accounted for about 13 per cent of the gross national product, as compared to 20 per cent for Guatemala, 14 for Nicaragua, and 11 for Honduras. Predictably, industrial development is centered in the capital, San José, and in the neighboring towns of Alajuela, Heredia, and Cartago in the Meseta Central, where both the major labor supply and local markets are located. Here are concentrated food processing plants, textile mills, and many small shoe and clothing manufacturing shops. Power comes from a large number of small hydroelectric plants scattered throughout the central highland.

Costa Rica's first heavy industry, a nitrogen fertilizer plant at Puntarenas on the Pacific coast, began operating in 1963. At Limón, on the Caribbean coast, an oil refinery financed by French capital was nearing completion in 1965. As such developments increase, and plans for industrial expansion under the Central American Common Market arrangement are put into effect,

Costa Rica may be freed of its complete economic reliance on the two agricultural exports, coffee and bananas.

Panama

In many ways, this narrow country differs from the other isthmian nations. As we noted earlier, it was a province of Colombia until 1903 and, since colonial times, has been considered, culturally and politically, to be South American. Its neighbors still regard Panama as apart from the "five" Central American republics. As a Colombian province, it was never associated with the attempts at political union that occurred among the other isthmian countries during the last century, and even now Panama is not a full participant in the Central American Common Market.

Moreover, during the nineteenth century Panama's status as a Colombian province was at best tenuous. Separated from Colombia by the almost trackless rain forest of Darien, communication with federal authority was perforce by sea. Provincial Panama thus retained a feeling of political and cultural separateness that was engendered in colonial times, and which, after independence, was to develop into an intense nationalism.

Unlike Costa Rica, Panama has retained much of its South American Indian heritage. Aboriginal techniques of cultivation, subsistence crops, food habits, rural house types, and the like predominate in the countryside. In addition, several Indian groups inhabit the back country and perpetuate their languages, their tribal ceremonies, and their subsistence economies.

The most distinguishing feature of Panama is its historic role as the principal transisthmian transit zone of Central America. Since 1914, the Canal, the Canal Zone, and their associated functions have so dominated the country's economy and politics that few outsiders are aware even of the existence of other important regions of Panama.

THE PHYSICAL SETTING

The three main natural divisions (central highlands, wet Caribbean lowlands, and subhumid Pacific versant) that characterize most of Central America continue through Panama to the Canal Zone. The eastern third of the country, however, begins to exhibit land forms, climate, and vegetation characteristic of northwestern South America.

Interrupted by the granitic Talamanca Range in southeastern Costa Rica, the Central American volcanic axis resumes in westernmost Panama with the high cone of Chiriquí which rises over 12,000 feet above the sea. Other recent, but lower, cones continue eastward atop or adjacent to a mass of old volcanic material that forms the Cordillera Central, the backbone of western Panama (see Figure 14.13, p. 437). Like Costa Rica, Panama has an irregular Pacific coast. Many of the off-shore islands, as well as the large Azuero peninsula, appear to be remnants of an older land mass of granitic rock. Only narrow coastal plains line the Gulf of Chiriquí and the western part of the Gulf of Panama. But between the mountainous Azuero peninsula and the Cordillera Central lies a wide depression of savanna-covered plains and rolling hills, which the Panamanians call "El Interior." Since the pre-Conquest period, this lowland has been one of Panama's most densely populated areas and it is today the most important rural section of the country. The Pacific side of Panama, west of the Canal Zone, receives an average rainfall of 60 to 120 inches, but it also enjoys a three-month dry season from January through March.

In contrast, the Caribbean versant is drenched yearly by more than 120 inches of rain, with no definite dry period. It is covered by a heavy rain forest that extends inland beyond the crest of the Cordillera Central. Along most of the Caribbean shore between Costa Rica and the Canal Zone, the mountains reach the sea, forming a cliffed coast. The only large indentation is the island-studded Chiriquí lagoon, around which a few rivers have formed small alluvial pockets. Near the Costa Rican border, the Changuinola and Sixaola river systems have built the area's largest alluvial valleys, famed for their plantation agriculture since the late nineteenth century.

Geologically, most of the country that lies between the Canal Zone and the Colombian border is the northwesternmost extent of South America. Along the Caribbean coast runs the Serranía de San Blas (1,000 to 3,200 feet), an extension of a northern prong of the Andes. On the Pacific side, the Serranía de Baudó of northwestern Colombia extends into Panamanian territory and continues westward as low hills beyond the Gulf of San Miguel. Between these two low ranges lies a structural depression occupied by the Chepo and Chucunaque river systems. A yearly rainfall of 80 to 120 inches, with a dry period during February and March, is sufficient to support a heavy rain forest, similar to that of northwestern Colombia. Except for flurries of gold mining in Darien, Europeans and mixbloods alike have shunned the hot, humid, disease-ridden forests of eastern Panama since the Spanish Conquest, leaving the area to small groups of Negroes and Indians.

POPULATION

Most of Panama's 1.2 million people live in two well-defined regions. One-third are concentrated within the present transit area which includes the United States-administered Canal Zone and adjacent Panama City and Colón. Nearly 60 per cent of the total population (and three-quarters of the rural people) inhabit the Pacific lowland and adjacent mountain slopes west of the Canal. These two areas of population concentration underscore the duality of Panama's geographical personality. The transit zone is chiefly urban and its people are cosmopolitan, of many races and nationalities; the western Pacific lowland is rural and its people are truly Panamanian, of mixed blood. This fundamental geographical pattern dates from the late sixteenth century, after the rise of Peruvian trade with Spain and the establishment of the transit route across the Panamanian isthmus near the present canal.

Whereas the over-all population density of Panama is 40 per square mile, that of the western Pacific lowland averages between 50 and 60; the savanna of El Interior in Herrera province has rural densities exceeding 100 persons per square mile. Within the transit zone, the capital, Panama City, alone contained 250,000 people, nearly 24 per cent of the national total in 1960. The Caribbean slope of Panama and the province of Darien near Colombia are the least populated sections of the country. There, over-all densities range from 3 to 10 persons per square mile, and many forested areas are completely uninhabited. The Caribbean coast has been settled to some degree, chiefly around the Chiriquí lagoon and the Changuinola and Sixaola river valleys, the former locale of the Bocas del Toro banana plantations. Moreover, within the past 200 years, the San Blas Cuna Indians have effectively occupied the off-shore coral islets along the Caribbean coast east of the Canal Zone. Elsewhere, both the Caribbean versant and the eastern forests remain places for future colonization.

The racial composition of the Panamanians is highly varied. Most of the rural folk who live in the western Pacific lowlands are mixed Indian, white, and often Negro, a mixture which stems from colonial times when the few Spanish cattlemen and, often, their Negro slaves took Indian wives. More recently, the construction of the Panama Canal attracted English-speaking Negroes from Jamaica and Barbados as laborers. Today, a large part of the 40,000 people in the Canal Zone are descendants of these blacks, and many Negroes of Jamaican descent now live in Panama City and Colón. A second English-speaking Negro concentration is found in the plantation zone of Bocas del Toro on the western side of Chiriquí lagoon. Since the 1940's, many of these Negroes have migrated to the new banana plantations on the Pacific coast in the vicinity of Puerto Armuelles. Negro communities also occur in Darien province, eastern Panama, mainly along the lower courses of rivers that flow into the Gulf of San Miguel. These, however, are Spanish-speaking migrants from the Colombian Chocó, and differ from the aggressive Jamaicans in attitudes and customs. The 1940 census[2] classified almost 15 per cent of the population of Panama as Negro.

Although Indians are now only 6 per cent of the population, aboriginal groups occupy a large area of the country. Most have retained much of their individuality by retreating into the back country and refusing to blend their culture with the Hispanic (see Figure 13.2, p. 381). Mention has been made of the San Blas Cuna along the Caribbean coast of eastern Panama. Most of the 19,000 Cuna have isolated themselves on the offshore coral islands, where they cultivate maize and manioc for subsistence and coconuts for cash. Only a handful now occupy their original homeland along the rivers in the interior. The Guaymí, who have retreated into the forested slopes of the Cordillera Central in western Panama, are the largest Indian group in the country. Some 21,000 today form the remnant of a large pre-Conquest population that once occupied most of central Panama. A much smaller group, a few hundred Chocó, live on the upper river courses in Darien near the Colombian border; these forest people are the least acculturated Indians in Middle America.

Some 10 to 12 per cent of the Panamanians are classified as Caucasians. Most of these are descendants of old Spanish families who form the upper class and live principally in Panama City.

2 This was the last census taken in Panama that identified racial groups other than Indian.

THE PANAMANIAN ECONOMY

Panama's dual personality—the urban cosmopolitanism of the transit zone and the rural provincialism of the western Pacific lowlands—is reflected not only in population distribution, but even more so in the nation's economy. Well over half Panama's income derives directly from trade, transport, and related activities within the transit area. Only one-quarter of the country's wealth comes from agriculture and stock raising, mainly in the western Pacific lowlands and adjacent mountain slopes. Agriculturally, Panama is the least developed of the Central American countries. Less than 6 per cent of the national territory is cultivated, although about half of the economically active population is engaged in farming or stock raising. Until recently, the country had to import large quantities of rice and maize and the transit area, especially the Canal Zone, still imports much food from the United States. Until 1963, however, farm products (chiefly bananas from foreign-owned plantations) accounted for nearly two-thirds of Panama's total exports by value.

Agricultural Patterns

Since colonial times, the western Pacific lowland has been the country's most important farming and stock-raising area, supplying meat and some grains to the transit area. By the mid-sixteenth century, Spanish cattlemen occupied the rolling central savannas of El Interior. By the end of the eighteenth century, a mestizo population of white, Indian, and Negro mixtures had developed in this area. Many were employed as cowhands on the large haciendas; others owned small tracts on which they raised food and cattle, shipping their surplus to Panama City; but most had become small subsistence farmers practicing the ancient Indian system of slash-burn cultivation on forested hill slopes inland from the savannas. Out of these elements has evolved the present-day peasant (*campesino*) of El Interior. This area is the hearth of Panamanian rural life. Here are still found most of the old food habits, house types, and social customs typical of the peasant during the last century; from here, migrants settled other parts of the western Pacific lowlands in the early nineteenth century.

Subsistence Farming. Most of the *campesinos* of the western Pacific lowland, as elsewhere in Panama, are migratory slash-burn farmers who have inherited many Indian farming practices. They hold no property titles, but cultivate government land by usufruct or land rented from large owners. They live in scattered dwellings or small hamlets on forested hillslopes, raising rice, maize, beans, plantains, and a variety of root crops in small plots that are abandoned after two or three years of continuous cropping. Around their aboriginal-type dwellings (*bohios*) of thatch and wattle, small patches of sugar cane and clumps of peach palms (*pejibaye*) or coconuts add to the typical rural scene (Figure 14.23). The machete and the dibble are the main tools of the *campesino*. Ox-drawn wooden plows are rare.

Since the colonial period, rice, introduced by the Spaniards not later than 1600, has become the main food in both urban and rural Panama. Mixed beans and rice (*guacho*) is the national dish of the *campesino*. Of nearly equal importance are yuca (sweet manioc), arrowroot (*otó*), and the Old World plantain. Panamanian country folk eat much less maize than their Central American neighbors, chiefly in the form of the Mesoamerican tortilla and tamale and the South American maize cake (*arepa*) and mildly fermented corn beer (*chicha*).

The prevalence of primitive slash-burn farming (*roza*) in Panama is made evident by the fact that from the small hillside plots come 75 per cent of the country's rice crop and almost all its maize, beans, plantains, and starchy tubers. With the improvement of roads, an increasingly larger part of this produce is reaching urban markets.

Figure 14.23

The Typical *Bohio* of Rural Panama. Wattle-daub walls and thatched roof derive from Indian culture; the attached kitchen with tiled roof may be of Spanish origin.

A variant of the slash-burn farming in the western Pacific lowlands occurs in the more level parts of El Interior, where *campesinos* combine crop cultivation with small-scale stock raising. Their holdings, of 50 to 100 acres, are chiefly planted pastures that graze as many as 100 head of cattle. However, these farmers consider their small rice and maize fields to be their major source of food and cash. Such cattle-*roza* farms are characteristic of the dry eastern side of Azuero peninsula near the market towns of Chitré and Las Tablas. This area is also the center of Hispanic culture within El Interior, and here one finds a concentration of tile-roofed houses, ox-carts, and a large percentage of Caucasian blood. It is likewise the most densely populated rural section of Panama, whence many migrants are slowly penetrating northward to colonize the forest lands along the crest of the Cordillera Central.

Commercial Stock Raising. The large stock ranch is the oldest agricultural enterprise of Spanish origin in Panama. Many cattle haciendas in the Pacific lowlands were settled in colonial times on the savannas of the dry plains and hills in the eastern section of El Interior within Coclé and Herrera provinces. Since the mid-nineteenth century, many more prosperous ones have been established in cleared sections within the southern versant of the Cordillera Central and in the wet coastal plain of Chiriquí province near David. On both the old and new estates, cattlemen have improved their breeds with the Asiatic Brahma strain. They have also increased the carrying capacity of the land by planting nutritious African grasses, such as *faragua* and Pará. The principal market for the cattle haciendas is the transit area—the slaughterhouses and packing plants of Panama City, Colón, and the Canal Zone. Most of the animals destined for this market originate in the coastal pastures of Chiriquí (Figure 14.24).

Commercial Agriculture. Large-scale commercial farming began with the banana plantations of Panama's Caribbean coast during the 1880's. Plant disease caused this large enterprise to shift to the Pacific coastal plain in the late 1920's, and the western Pacific lowland has since become Panama's main producer of agricultural exports and the center of mechanized farming (Figure 14.25).

Mechanized farming is exemplified by large, irrigated rice plantations of the wet coastal plain of Chiriquí, near David, and along the Coclé coast in the vicinity of Antón

Figure 14.24
Artificial Pasture of Pará Grass Near Chitré, Central Savannas of Panama. (R.H. Fuson)

Figure 14.25
Commercial Economy of Panama. Only Selected Items Are Shown.

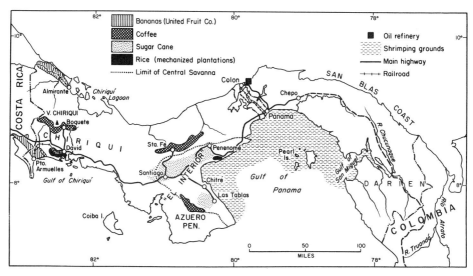

Figure 14.26
A Field of Irrigated Rice Near Divisa, Central Savannas of Panama. *(R.H. Fuson)*

(Figure 14.26). Their high yields furnish a quarter of the country's rice, and they have made Panama a self-sufficient producer of its major staple food since 1953. The few sugar cane plantations and associated mills in the eastern part of El Interior (Coclé province) illustrate another kind of commercial farming. Most of Panama's sugar crop, however, is harvested on small plots, and the energy-giving panela is sold throughout the rural areas.

Coffee has never been a major commercial crop in Panama. It was first planted in the rich soils of the Boquete valley on the southern slopes of Chiriquí volcano about 1900, and became a significant crop only after World War II. As late as 1957, coffee was still being imported but, with increased production in the Boquete area and the establishment of small coffee *fincas* on the Pacific slope of the Cordillera Central in Veraguas province, Panama finally entered the world coffee market in 1958.

The United Fruit Company's banana plantations in extreme southwestern Panama, in the vicinity of Puerto Armuelles, are the most highly developed form of commercial agriculture in the country. This small area is an eastward continuation of the company's Costa Rican banana holdings in the Coto River plain and possesses the same natural advantages—heavy rainfall (120 inches annually) and fertile alluvial soils (within the

Chiriquí River flood plain). As early as 1927, the United Fruit Company transferred some of its operations from the disease-ridden Bocas del Toro district to the Pacific side. By the early 1940's, the Puerto Armuelles plantations were in full production, only to be curtailed by the lack of shipping facilities during World War II. Production of nine million stems yearly had been resumed by 1948, and, until 1960, banana exports from the area were 40 to 60 per cent of Panama's total exports by value.

In the old banana lands in the Bocas del Toro district on the Caribbean, the United Fruit Company established large acreages of cacao and abacá, mainly in the Changuinola River valley. In 1950, however, the company began flood fallowing and, by 1962, over six million stems, one-third of Panama's banana production, were shipped from the refurbished port of Almirante in the Bocas del Toro area.

In Panama, bananas are produced for export not only by the highly organized company plantations, but also by small, semi-subsistence farmers. Today such production occurs chiefly in small river valleys: (1) along the Caribbean coast between the Canal Zone and Chiriquí lagoon; and (2) in the eastern province of Darien. Production is greatest in Darien, where, since 1924, Negroes and Chocó Indians have cultivated small groves along the rivers that flow into the Gulf of San Miguel. Launches collect the stems at the river mouths for transfer to the refrigerated banana boats anchored in the gulf. This production, which accounts for only a small part of Panama's banana exports, is being increasingly relied on by the large fruit companies, and the small farms may one day replace the large, complex tropical plantation.

Commercial Fishing

One of Panama's most spectacular economic developments since World War II is the rise of shrimping in the shallow, muddy coastal waters around the Gulf of Panama (Figure 14.25). By 1960, shrimping contributed one-fourth of the country's total export receipts. The catch is frozen in seven packing plants in Panama City, and most of it is shipped to the United States. A fleet of about 200 trawlers, chiefly of Panamanian registry, now operate in the gulf. Trash fish caught in shrimp nets, as well as commercial catches of anchovies and herring off the coast, are processed into fish meal fertilizer in plants near Panama City. As in Mexico

and El Salvador, the rapid rise of shrimping is a belated exploitation of the coastal fish resource of Middle America. It also illustrates the relation of resource development to a United States market which fluctuates according to public taste and affluence.

The Transit Zone

Even as a Colombian province, Panama lived mainly by the trade and transport conducted over its transisthmian road. This pattern continues today, for Panama has a special political and economic relationship with the United States and has become highly dependent on the Canal. Moreover, because of its strategic position in world oceanic shipping and its military vulnerability, the Panamanian transit zone is now one of the world's most politically sensitive areas.

The present transit area, as here defined, includes the United States-administered Canal Zone, the terminal cities of Panama and Colón, and the area adjacent to the transisthmian highway which passes through national territory a few miles east of the Zone (Figure 14.27). Within this area

Figure 14.27
The Transit Zone of Panama.

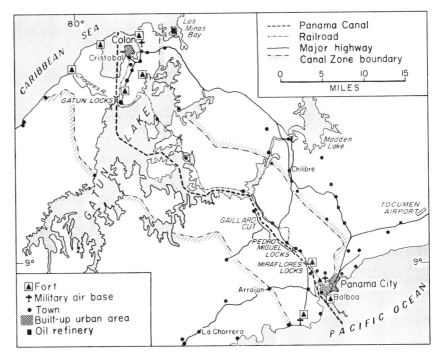

live 400,000 people, 95 per cent of whom are urban, and who comprise one-third of Panama's total population. Apart from the Canal itself, the Zone is a complex of cities, towns, military installations, highways, and railroads. The bustling economic activity within the area generates over half the national income, partly in the form of wages paid to nationals working in the Zone and partly through trade with United States citizens who are Zone residents, and with tourists and foreign transients. Panama's growing manufacturing industries are also concentrated in or near the transit area.

The Canal Zone. According to the United States-Panama treaty of 1903, the Zone comprises a strip of land extending five miles on either side of the Canal, including Gatun Lake. This area, however, excludes Panama City and the coastal plain eastward thereof, as well as the city of Colón on the Caribbean. The treaty gave the United States what has amounted to "perpetual sovereignty" over the Canal Zone, but the interpretation of such rights has caused much friction between the two nations in recent years. In return, the United States now pays Panama an annuity of nearly two million dollars.

Today Panamanians resent American occupation of what they consider to be the most important segment of their national territory. This resentment, an outgrowth of intense nationalism, has increased to the extent that most Panamanians now favor the demand that the United States relinquish control of the Canal and the Canal Zone to their country.

The Canal is a lock-and-lake type, with elaborate sets of locks that raise ships from ocean level to Gatun Lake, normally 85 feet above the sea. Gatun Lake, a reservoir created by damming the Chagres River, supplies water for the locks and serves as a waterway for half the 51-mile distance across the isthmus (Figure 14.28). Hydroelectric plants at Gatun Dam and Madden Dam (completed in 1935) furnish power for the

entire Canal Zone, including operation of the locks. The Canal crosses the continental divide through the famous eight-mile Gaillard Cut, a 200-foot-deep trench constructed by United States engineers and British West Indian Negro laborers at the expense of many lives and after seven years of toil (1907–1914).

In recent years, the constantly increasing traffic (12,000 ships in 1963) making the eight-hour trip through the Canal has led to serious congestion; moreover, the locks are too narrow (110 feet) to accommodate the largest ships. In addition, the locks are militarily vulnerable and Panama is seriously challenging the United States' complete control of the Zone. All of these factors have prompted serious planning for a new sea-level canal in some other part of the Central American isthmus.

As a United States owned reservation, the Canal Zone functions to operate, maintain, and protect the Canal and its installations. For this purpose about 40,000 people inhabit the Zone; of these, 40 per cent are Negroes, chiefly descendants of West Indian laborers, and the rest are United States white residents, or "Zonians," the administrators, engineers, and skilled laborers who operate and maintain the Canal installations. They live in cities and towns scattered through the Zone, the largest being Balboa, adjacent to Panama City, and Cristóbal, which borders Colón on the Caribbean. Balboa and Cristóbal, the terminal stations of the Canal, contain the main docks in the transit area for ocean-going ships. In addition, the Zone bristles with military installations—army camps, forts, airfields, naval yards, and communication centers—all of which house a sizable personnel.

Rapid transit lines connect the terminal points of the isthmus. The Panama Railroad, which parallels the Canal, was constructed as a convenience to transisthmian ship passengers and to facilitate maintenance of installations. As a military measure during World War II, the United States government

Figure 14.28
Miraflores Locks on the Pacific Side of the Panama Canal. In the background is Miraflores Lake and the Pedro Miguel Locks, through which ships are lifted to the level of Gaillard Cut and Gatun Lake. *(Panama Canal Company)*

built the Transisthmian Highway within Panamanian territory a few miles east of the Zone, cutting transit time from Panama City to Colón to less than two hours by auto.

Panama City and Colón. That part of the transit area under direct Panamanian jurisdiction is dominated by two cities, the capital and Colón. Panama City, with 250,000 people, 24 per cent of the nation's population, crammed into its confines, exemplifies the dominance of the primate city better than any other Middle American capital. The next largest urban center is Colón, with 50,000 inhabitants, and then the small provincial cities of David (23,000) and Puerto Armuelles (10,700). Highly mixed racially and nationally, both Panama City and Colón live by trade. A duty-free zone, opened in Colón in 1951, created an economic boom there; the dependence of Panama City on tourist and transient trade was underscored

by the local economic depression that followed the Canal Zone riots of 1964.

Since World War II, Panama City and Colón have been becoming industrialized. A substantial part of the nation's light industry is located in Panama City, which has food processing plants, wood products factories, and clothing manufacturing shops. Panama's first heavy industry (1958) was a small steel mill using local scrap; the latest, which is the most spectacular recent industrial development in all Central America, is the new petroleum refinery in Las Minas Bay, five miles east of Colón. This United States-owned refinery began operations in 1962 with a 55,000 barrel-per-day capacity. Using imported Venezuelan crude, the refinery now supplies Panama's needs and furnishes many Central American countries with several kinds of petroleum products. Within a single year after its opening, this plant changed the pattern of Panama's export trade; in 1963, petroleum products led all other items, accounting for more than one-third of the country's total export revenues.

Transportation

The main axis of Panamanian transport was covered in the preceding section on the transisthmian transit zone. A secondary axis trends east-west along the Pacific lowlands, where the Inter-American Highway has now been completed through the settled part of the country from Costa Rica to Panama City. Eastward, the road continues only 54 miles to the village of Chepo. Beyond lies the vast forest-covered wilderness of eastern Panama and the Chocó of northwestern Colombia, which forms today the only gap in the Inter-American Highway from Fairbanks, Alaska, to Buenos Aires.

SELECTED REFERENCES

Checchi, V., *et al.,* eds., *Honduras: A Problem in Economic Development.* New York: The Twentieth Century Fund, 1959.

Fox, D., "Prospects for the Panama Canal," *Tijdschrift voor economische en sociale geografie,* LV, No. 4 (1964), 86–101.

Fuson, R. H., "House Types of Central Panama," *Annals of the Association of American Geographers,* LIV, No. 2 (1964), 190–208.

Guzmán, L. E., *Farming and Farmlands in Panama,* University of Chicago, Department of Geography Research Paper No. 44. Chicago: University of Chicago Press, 1956.

Helbig, K. M., "Die Landschaften von Nordost-Honduras," *Petermanns Mitteilungen,* Ergänzungsheft No. 268 (1959), pp. 1–270.

León, Jorge, "Land Utilization in Costa Rica," *Geographical Review,* XXXVIII, No. 3 (1948), 444–56.

Nunley, R. E., *The Distribution of Population in Costa Rica,* National Research Council Publication No. 743. Washington, D.C., 1960.

Parsons, J. J., "Gold Mining in the Nicaragua Rain Forest," *Yearbook of the Association of Pacific Coast Geographers,* XVII (1955), 49–55.

Rubio, A., and L. Guzmán, "Regiones geográficas panameñas," *Revista Geográfica,* XXIV, No. 50 (1959), 53–66.

Sandner, G., *Agrar-kolonisation in Costa Rica: Siedlung, Wirtschaft und Sozialgefüge an der Pioniergrenze.* Schriften des Geographischen Instituts der Universität Kiel, XIX, Heft 3 (Kiel, 1961). [Spanish trans.: *La colonización agrícola de Costa Rica.* (San José: Instituto Geográfico de Costa Rica, 1962–1964)].

Squier, E. G., *Honduras: Descriptive, Historical and Statistical.* London: Trübner and Co., 1870.

————, *Nicaragua: Its People, Scenery, Monuments, and the Proposed Interoceanic Canal.* New York: Appleton-Century-Crofts, Inc., 1852.

Taylor, B. W., *Ecological Land Use Surveys in Nicaragua.* Managua: Instituto de Fomento Nacional, 1959–1961.

Wagner, P. L., "Nicoya, a Cultural Geography," *University of California Publications in Geography,* XII, No. 3 (1958), 195–250.

15

Middle America: Summary and Outlook

It is difficult to generalize about the lands and peoples of Middle America. The effect of a varied history on an equally varied physical environment has been to create a vast array of landscapes, cultures, and ways of life. No one economic model can portray the numerous ways in which the land is exploited; no single cultural description can embrace the ethnic, linguistic, and religious heterogeneity of the people; and no chart of organization can outline the many forms of government. The area's diversity is rooted in pre-Columbian times and the Conquest (see Chapter 1); it has persisted and it has even been increased by poor communications, special economic interests, and political disunity.

Nor is it easy to classify or pattern the area's landscape and folkways. Except in a few cases, such as Hispaniola, international boundaries are seldom a meaningful guide to cultural differentiation. Ways of life frequently vary more within the same country than between countries. Many of the ways of the southern Mexicans, for example, are more like the Guatemalans than the northern Mexicans' (see Chapters 7, 8, and 9). Similarly, the patterns which create uniformity in the Rimland as contrasted to the Mainland (see Chapter 1) have evolved with little regard to state boundaries.

Frequently, the most obvious common denominators in Middle America are its problems. Thus, the localism born of diversity has made it difficult to establish stable government almost everywhere. The same localism is also partially responsible for the fragmentation of the area into a multiplicity of states, most of which are too limited in size and resources to be economically viable. Note, for example, the failure of the West Indies Federation and the many obstacles which impede the progress of the Central American Common Market.

Cultural diversity and localism have also militated against the crystallization of a strong sense of nation in many territories. To what extent do the Indians of Guatemala or the Jamaican Negroes of Costa Rica participate in national life? Is it realistic to consider the Creoles and East Indians of Trinidad as the same nation? The strong bond of nation which unites the people of the United States, or of Japan, or of most European states requires a degree of cultural uniformity, a sharing of common goals, a knowledge of history, and a communication of ideas which are largely lacking to the indigenous and peasant populations of most Middle American countries.

The most important problems which the peoples of Middle America share are economic. Chief among these are a history of exploitation by outsiders; a narrow commerce which is subject to the whims of foreign markets; a distribution of wealth so unequal as to create extreme poverty and great affluence; and, above all, an increase in population which is dangerously out of proportion to the countries' economic growth.

Population

Growth Trends. One measure of the growing pressure of population in Middle America
is the high rate of natural increase in recent
years. Mexico's death rate, for instance, decreased by 40 per cent from 1940 to 1960,
while her birth rate continued to be twice
that of the United States. Comparable and
even higher increases of population are taking place in most of Central America and
the West Indies, with the result that Middle
America's total population jumped from 50
million in 1950 to roughly 60 million in 1960.
Only in a few spots, such as Puerto Rico and
Barbados, does the growth rate seem to be
leveling off.

People-to-land ratios are highest in the
Antilles but, because of the irregular distribution of population, the pressure of population
is almost as high in the settled sectors of the
Mainland. In Mexico, the bulk of the inhabitants are still concentrated in the old
Mesoamerican highland centers; the Mesa
Central, only 16 per cent of the country's
area, contains over 55 per cent of its population. Over 90 per cent of the inhabitants of
Central America live on the Pacific side of
the isthmus, the highest densities being in the
western highlands and in the foothills bordering the coastal lowlands.

Immigration and Emigration. From the days
of the Discovery until roughly 1875, Middle
America was an area which received immigrants. Since then, emigration has been
more important, although the nature, the
extent, and the impact of immigration and
emigration have varied. Movements within
the area have also been of great importance.

The most important immigrants to Middle
America were the Spaniards, the northern
Europeans, and the Africans. After the influx
of Europeans from the sixteenth to the eighteenth centuries, immigration came to a virtual standstill except for the vital ebb and
flow of the African slave trade, which affected chiefly the Rimland.

It was not until the abolition of slavery
and the development of plantations in Cuba
and Puerto Rico in the nineteenth century
that new waves of non-African immigrants
reached Middle America. Hundreds of thousands of Europeans arrived in the 1800's and
the first decades of the 1900's, primarily from
Spain. In an effort to fill the labor gap
created by the emancipation of slavery, the
British and, to a lesser extent, the French and
Dutch imported indentured workers from the
Orient. The indentured immigrants, who arrived at various times during the latter nineteenth and early twentieth centuries, included
small numbers of Chinese and Indonesians
and moderately large numbers of East Indians from what was then British India. Virtually every colony of the North European
nations received a few Oriental immigrants,
but they left a major mark only in Trinidad.
In the past century, small numbers of Syrians,
Portuguese, Corsicans, Anglo-Americans, and
others have arrived.

In contrast, emigration from Middle
America has never been large. The poverty
and ignorance of most of the people, the
restrictions of slavery and peonage, and more
recently, the barriers against non-white immigration of the United States and other
countries have discouraged emigration. Before the twentieth century, there was no
emigration to speak of except for the handful
of white colonials who returned to Europe
at various times, the slaves sold in West Indian marts to United States planters, the
small number of Mexicans who went to
Texas and the American Southwest before
1845, and the smaller number of Cubans who
fled to Florida. Emigration in the twentieth
century has been more pronounced. Mexican
braceros and Puerto Ricans have moved to
the United States; French West Indians, to
cities in France; British West Indians, to
northern South America, Harlem, and lately,
Britain; and smaller movements, such as the
continued flow of Cubans to Florida and of
selected Panamanian and other Latin American immigrants to North American cities.

Inter-Regional Movements. Data on the inter-regional migrations in Middle America are fragmentary, particularly for the period preceding the mid-nineteenth century. We can assume that there were post-Columbian moves associated with early European settlement and that slave labor was shifted from one territory to another. Negro uprisings in Hispaniola at the end of the eighteenth century caused many French and Spanish families to move to other islands, including Cuba, Puerto Rico, and Trinidad.

The later inter-regional movements have, by and large, been from populous territories, such as Haiti, Jamaica, Barbados, the Windwards, or from some of the more crowded Mainland centers, to the less densely populated zones, such as Cuba, the Dominican Republic, and the Caribbean lowlands of Central America. The most important movements have been from Haiti to the Dominican Republic and to eastern Cuba; from Barbados, the Windwards, and Leewards to the less crowded British territories, especially Trinidad; and from Jamaica, Barbados, and other West Indies to the Panama Canal Zone and to the plantation and lumber centers of the Caribbean coast of Central America.

The movements from the Mainland centers have been less publicized. Many migrants have come from densely populated El Salvador to Honduras, Guatemala, and other Central American countries. Similarly, there is an important flow of Nicaraguans to northwestern Costa Rica. One of the more recent movements—from the Central American uplands to the lowlands of both the Pacific and Caribbean coasts—may soon involve large numbers of people. Currently, the areas most chosen for settlement are the Pacific lowlands of Costa Rica and Guatemala and the Caribbean lowlands of Costa Rica.

Middle America is also being affected by a strong movement from country to town. Everywhere apparent, this trend is perhaps most conspicuous in the West Indies. In a few instances, it is created by expanding economic opportunities, such as the industrialization of the San Juan area of Puerto Rico. More often, however, the flow to the town is simply an escape from the poverty and hopelessness of the countryside. This artificial urbanization is increasing unemployment, slums, and crime in the cities, while the rural districts are suffering from a shortage of labor.

Settlement

In the whole of Middle America, settlement is characterized by nucleation, a sharp contrast between the city and the countryside, and the differences in the types of settlement on the Mainland and on the Antilles.

Nucleation. Nucleation, initially begun by the selective occupance of the colonial Spanish, persists particularly on the Mainland, although it is also found on the larger islands of the West Indies. There are clearcut concentrations of population, each forming the tributary area of a major city and separated by empty or lightly occupied areas across which transportation is often very difficult. Overlapping of tributary areas of the major urban centers, so common in Anglo-America and Western Europe where cities tend to develop specialized functions, is rare in Middle America.

In most political entities of Middle America, there is a single concentrated area of settlement, spreading out from the territory's chief city and capital. This is so everywhere in the West Indies except in Hispaniola, and it is so in most of Central America, except in Panama where the Canal has necessitated more than one nucleus, and in Honduras, which has a highland population clustered around Tegucigalpa and a Caribbean nucleus around San Pedro Sula, Tela, and La Ceiba. In Haiti and the Dominican Republic, there are two concentrated settlements—one in the north, around Cap-Haïtien and Santiago, and one in the south, around Port-au-Prince and Santo Domingo. In Mexico there are several concentrated settlements, each with its urban center, but most of these are on the Mesa Central and are less clear-cut. Where more than one concentrated settlement exists, the area which contains the territory's capital city is generally larger, has a greater population, and is more economically developed.

Urban-Rural Contrasts. An enormous socio-economic gulf separates the urban centers from their rural tributaries. In the city, the streets are often crowded with automobiles, the stores are modern and well-stocked, beautiful buildings and monuments are much in evidence, and professional services compare favorably with those of Anglo-American centers. If one can overlook their beggars and the odoriferous shanties on their fringes, the cities of Middle America—like the cities everywhere in Latin America—create the impression of wealth and conspicuous consumption. But often, only a few miles outside the city, the conditions are those of another world and another era. Gone are the automobiles— not only because the country people cannot afford them but because the roads are inadequate. The well-stocked store is replaced by the little *kiosko* or *tienda,* which sells codfish or beans, work clothes, and cheap native liquor; the city's beautiful buildings give way to one-room *bohios* or adobe huts and the only monuments are the scars of erosion on the misused land.

That the cities of Middle America consume the wealth produced by their hinterlands is in keeping with the feudal tradition established by the early Spaniards and, to a lesser degree, by the northern European planters and merchants. From the first, their cities drew the landowners, the clerical and lay officials, and the other elements which were to become aristocracy, and they brought their colored and mestizo servants and their artisans. The early locus of wealth and activity, the city has had a magnetic attraction for the poverty-stricken people of the countryside ever since. As a result, the cities are too big, and the line of rural settlements too thin. The proportion of people who live in

cities is surprisingly high. Not every city is equally magnetic, however. In each country there is one city, usually the capital, which is several times larger than its runner-up.

The Middle American city is the collecting and distributing center, the administrative center, the educational center, and the religious center of the area around it. The city provides all the services available to its hinterland. Since urban areas rarely overlap and since the economy is based largely on agriculture, grazing, and mining, a city with specialized functions (such as Monterrey, in Mexico) is a great exception. In the Rimland, most of the chief cities are also ports. On the Mainland, where the chief urban center is almost invariably in the upland interior, twin cities, one a port, have evolved. Mexico City and Veracruz are such twin cities.

Although the urban population everywhere in Middle America is increasing more rapidly than the population as a whole, the great majority of Middle Americans, on the Mainland and the Rimland, still live in rural settlements. The economy would not permit otherwise. The percentage of rural population varies, however. On some of the West Indian islands, for example, the rural population may be as high as 85 per cent of the total. In the crowded territories, such as Barbados and Haiti, it is often difficult to differentiate between urban and rural settlement—not only because of the high density of rural population but also because of the women, especially, who walk daily to the markets in the towns. In Middle America as a whole, rural populations are from 65 to 75 per cent of the total.

There are also wide differences in the type of rural settlement. The dominant rural settlement on the Mainland is an agglomerated one. Less than 1 per cent of the Mexican people, for example, live in dispersed, isolated farmsteads; roughly 10 per cent live in hamlets whose populations are under 100; more than half live in villages whose populations are 101 to 2,500; and the remainder live in even larger settlements. In the Rimland, the plantation manor houses were the core of agglomerated hamlets. Many of these remain, but dispersed settlement is more widespread than on the Mainland, for several reasons. In many of the West Indian islands, the terrain is mountainous. This confined the plantations to the coastal plains and valley bottoms, leaving the highlands to small holders and squatters. In Puerto Rico, for example, and in Cuba, to a lesser degree, a white peasantry invaded the less desirable mountain lands at an early date and developed a semisubsistence agriculture which included the growing of tobacco and, sometimes, coffee, for sale. Virtually everywhere in the West Indies, the emancipation of the slaves increased the dispersion of rural settlement. Wherever sufficient land was available, the emancipated Negroes abandoned the estates in large numbers and established themselves as subsistence farmers. Generally, the land which was not already pre-empted was in the uplands, but, even in the lowlands, the subdivision and sale of some bankrupt estates provided the Negroes with dispersed plots.

In most of Middle America, the trend seems to be toward agglomerated settlements. This may be partly due to the tempo of urbanization and partly to improved transportation and other factors. As roads penetrate into previously inaccessible areas, hamlets often string out along the artery. There are some exceptions to the general rule of increasing agglomeration, however, especially in El Salvador, Honduras, Costa Rica, and other Central American territories.

Economic Aspects

From the very beginnings of colonization, Middle America was regarded as a source of quick wealth either for the ruling metropolis or the small group of local aristocrats. Inevitably, the colonial economy developed in lopsided fashion. Only the exploitation of immediately profitable products and resources was undertaken long-range; systematic development of the territories and the welfare of the masses were disregarded by the privileged. More than four centuries after Columbus, a large part of the area's economy is still essentially colonial.

Agriculture. Nothing illustrates the imbalance and the colonialism of Middle America's economy more dramatically than agriculture, the area's chief occupation. In most territories, the economic structure is like an inverted pyramid resting on a few export crops, and it is so precariously balanced that any threat to the exports threatens the entire economic structure.

Equally serious problems stem from land use and tenure, from primitive agricultural techniques and practices, from plant disease, from erosion, from poor soils, and from other factors. The soil, for example, is not generally abundant or exceptionally fertile. Some soils, as in northern Mexico, receive too little rain and cannot be cultivated without costly irrigation; others, particularly the leached clays of the humid tropical lowland, cannot be permanently cultivated without heavy applications of fertilizer or frequent fallowing. Still others are on mountains too steep to cultivate.

As a result, agriculture in Middle America is spotty. Production is concentrated, for the most part, on narrow strips of coastal plains, on irrigated oases, on river valleys, or on suitable mountain basins. The volcanic soils of the upland areas and the riverine alluvial deposits are generally the most productive. Elsewhere the yield is low, because of natural infertility, long use and misuse, erosion, and inefficient farming. The percentage of land under cultivation varies widely, but it is generally much higher in the more densely populated West Indies than on the Mainland. In Mexico and Central America, the land in crops amounts to less than one-tenth of the total, though in a few crowded spots, such as El Salvador, it is as high as one-quarter.

Perhaps even more than the modest or

poor soils, the traditional systems of land tenure account for the deficient state of agriculture in Middle America. These systems normally include: (1) large landholdings (*latifundia*), i.e., haciendas, plantations, or estates, which may be family or corporate-owned and which are devoted to commercial production; and (2) small holdings (*minifundia*), i.e., peasant-owned parcels, tenant worker plots on estates, communal lands, leased-lands, and share-cropped lands.

The best lands are owned by the large holders, a practice which has roots in both the Hispanic and northern European traditions in Middle America. On these large tracts are produced the commercial crops which may benefit a few and contribute little to the well-being of the area. True, some workers are employed and otherwise benefited, but the lion's share of the profits goes to the owners. The small farmer, the bulk of Middle America's population, is forced to cultivate the marginal lands. *Latifundia* also fosters the prestige of ownership. Land is bought for this reason or for possibly expanded operations, or simply in the hope that its value will rise. Much of this reserve land is put to little or no use.

On the *latifundia* are produced sugar, coffee, cacao, cotton, sisal, animal products, and food crops such as wheat. These products may be sold overseas, as is most of the Rimland produce and the coffee, cotton, and sisal produced on the Mainland, or they may be sold locally. In either case, they stimulate monoculture and retard, if not prevent, the emergence of a well-rounded agricultural economy. When the market is overseas, there is a slavish dependence on the vagaries of foreign demand and price. A drop of a few cents in the price of coffee on the New York Commodities Exchange creates widespread distress in the coffee regions of Central America.

The small holders grow food, primarily for their families but also for the local market. In Middle America as a whole, these small growers are the bulk of the agricultural labor force; yet food has to be imported into many areas and most of the people are poorly nourished. The major food crops on most of the Mainland, particularly on the old Indian centers, are corn, beans, squash, and a variety of peppers. Crops may vary, especially in the different climatic zones of the highlands. In the Rimland, corn is less important. Starchy vegetable tubers, such as yams and manioc, and tree crops, such as breadfruit, plantains, and bananas, are grown. Rice is a staple in much of Middle America and is raised in many territories, but much is also imported from the Far East and the United States. Wheat is also widely grown and often imported.

Yields of the small holdings are low, partly because they are marginal lands and partly because they are not worked well. Most subsistence farmers are still using primitive techniques which originated with the Mainland Indians and on the Rimland with African slaves. Simple iron tools, such as the machete and the hoe are probably the most widespread technological innovations. The ox and the plow are not extensively used for food crops even on some of the haciendas.

Outside the grazing areas, farm animals are few, and here are often scavengers such as pigs, poultry, and goats. This scarcity of animals precludes the use of barnyard manure as fertilizer, and commercial fertilizer is beyond the means of the small holder. Crop rotation is known, but fertile land is so scarce that it is often under the same basic crops. The marginal land cultivated by small holders is often on hillslopes, and erosion is a major problem virtually everywhere.

Forests and Fisheries. The exploitation of the forests is locally important in a few areas, such as Hispaniola and parts of Central America and Mexico, but its contribution to the over-all economy of Middle America is negligible. The more accessible forests have been virtually destroyed by the expansion of agriculture and the lack of conservation. This is particularly true of the once-extensive

Caribbean lowland pine forests of Cuba. Even now, there is heavy and destructive cutting of Central American lowland pine, from British Honduras to Nicaragua. The mountain pine forests, which are less accessible, have been less exploited, but now highland pine forests, such as those of the Dominican Republic and Mexico, are being subjected to heavy cutting. Once valuable areas of cabinet woods such as tropical cedar and mahogany, in the West Indies and Central America, have been logged dry.

Tropical forest industries, such as the gathering of drugs, resins, gums, and other items, have lost their markets to synthetic products. Despite the decreasing commercial importance of forestry in Middle America, however, the native subsistence economy relies heavily on the trees for buildings, fences, and charcoal fuel.

The history of the fisheries has been even more tragic. In pre-Columbian days, many of the circum-Caribbean tribes, such as the Caribs, relied heavily on the sea harvest to supplement the food produced by farming. Fish from the rivers, mollusks from the coast, and sea turtles and manatees were once important to the Europeans in the Rimland also. But overexploitation has erased this abundance, and, except possibly in Mexico, only a handful of part-time workers fish in each territory. In fact, much of the fish, such as the dried salt cod which is consumed in many areas, is imported from Canada, the United States, and Europe.

Minerals and Energy Fuels. The list of minerals in Middle America is a long one, but only a few are plentiful enough to warrant exploitation, and these are irregularly distributed. Mexico is easily the leading repository of mineral wealth. In Central America, except for the limited production of precious metals, especially in Honduras and Nicaragua, mining is negligible. Minerals are of only token importance in Cuba and the Dominican Republic, but important to the economies of Trinidad and Jamaica. Petro-leum, the fond hope of the Rimland, is produced in significant quantities only in Mexico and Trinidad. Other mineral resources of some importance are copper, lead, zinc, silver, and iron, in Mexico; bauxite, in Jamaica; and nickel and manganese, in Cuba. Water power is an important potential source of energy, but only about 1 per cent has been actually developed. A deficiency of minerals and fuels is the rule in Middle America.

Manufacturing. The census data for most Middle American territories generally include a large number of factories. Most of these, however, are household enterprises or small establishments, which employ less than a dozen workers. They produce bricks, bread, and other items for their own localities. The larger establishments are often sugar *centrales* and other processing plants. In most of the large cities, where manufacturing is concentrated, the list of products includes beverages, matches, building materials, pharmaceutical products, and the like. Mexico's Monterrey and Monclova are the sole examples of industrial specialization.

No country in Middle America is industrialized in the modern sense, but industrialization is spreading. Virtually every territory is attempting to attract industry from abroad with offers of tax exemption, cheap labor, and other inducements. A few, such as Puerto Rico, are achieving surprising success, but industrial development is beset by too many obstacles to offer any immediate promise.

In addition, the resources, as we have observed, are inadequate for industry. Industrial development would have to overcome the same obstacles which have impeded agriculture: (1) the small populations, with limited purchasing power, spread over great distances, and with poor means of communication; (2) the lack of capital, of skills, and of facilities for generating power; (3) the prestige of landholding and the lack of prestige of manual labor; (4) the investor's preference for land, real estate, jewels, and precious metals; (5) an unwillingness to risk capital in untried enterprises and an expectation of large and rapid returns from investments; (6) and a strong and pervasive traditionalism especially among the upper classes, who tend to view innovation as a threat to their status.

Tourism. Virtually every part of Middle America has enjoyed a marked rise in tourism since the end of World War II. In a few territories, such as the Bahamas and the American Virgin Islands, tourism is now the primary industry; in others, such as Mexico, Puerto Rico, and Jamaica, it is one of the two or three main sources of income; and in the remaining territories, it is a hope.

The continued prosperity of the United States plus improved transportation facilities were perhaps the principal causes of the growth of the tourist trade in Middle America. In the Bahamas and the West Indies, the airplane has largely replaced the cruise ship. The expansion of air travel has also helped to increase the flow of tourists to the Mainland countries. Many drive to Mexico and, to a lesser extent, to Central America, however.

Transportation. Commercially and culturally, Middle America has faced the sea since the earliest colonial period. The sea orientation of the Rimland was inescapable, and the Rimland's destiny was repeatedly shaped by the particular power which controlled the sea lanes of the Gulf-Caribbean complex. Even in the interior Mainland settlements, an effort was made from the beginning to link the chief city and other centers with a coastal outlet. The sea, which was the major avenue for commerce and contact with the rest of the world, often became the principal means of contact with immediate neighbors as well. On the islands this was a matter of necessity, but on the Mainland it was chosen because of the difficulty of moving over land.

Land transportation is poorly developed even now. Dispersed settlements, the difficult

terrain, the climate, and, above all, the lack of economic incentive are largely responsible for retarding transportation to the point where it is a major obstacle to economic development. Railroads, often financed by foreign capital, have made only the barest impression on most of Middle America. Mexico has about the best developed railroad system in Middle America, but the only zone which has a dense rail network is the core area of the Mexican plateau. Mexico is connected with the United States system at several points along the border, and her railroads also join the Guatemalan line.

In Central America, short lines connect the upland populations with their coastal outlets. Some territories, such as Guatemala, El Salvador, and Costa Rica, have more miles of rails than, say, Honduras and Nicaragua, but nowhere do the railways serve the entire country. In the West Indies, Trinidad and all the Greater Antilles have railroads, many of which were built to transport sugar cane and other plantation crops to the *centrales* and to the ports. Cuba, which has the largest area and the strongest sugar economy, has the most extensive railways. The advent of highways and truck transportation, however, has rendered obsolete many of the West Indian railways on the smaller islands such as Puerto Rico and the Dominican Republic.

Middle America is now building more highways than railroads. On the Mainland, the interest in highways has been stimulated by the much-discussed Inter-American Highway; in the West Indies, highways have proved superior to rails. Again, however, development is spotty and, compared with the United States or western Europe, poor. Some of the islands, particularly Puerto Rico, Cuba, and the Dominican Republic, are developing excellent all-weather, paved systems. Considering its size and other difficulties, Mexico is also achieving a measure of success in road building. Americans may now motor into Mexico on at least three modern highways, one of which is the Inter-American Highway. In Central America, however, outside the major cities, the roads are nonexistent or rough, even if one includes the unpaved, fair-weather arteries and the extension of the Inter-American Highway.

With land transportation so poorly developed and costly, Middle America hailed the advent of air transport with great hope in the late 1930's. And the airplane was an immediate and outstanding success as a passenger vehicle. The movement of freight by airplane is costly, but land transport is so poor that many items, such as machinery and other valuable finished goods, are being flown in and out in increasing quantities. There are several international and national airlines, and many small operators offer common carrier services over short distances, linking even the most remote regions of the Mainland with its major centers. There are often more airports and landing strips than railroad stations, especially where land transport is poorest.

Commerce. The outstanding characteristics of Middle American commerce are: (1) its dependence on the exportation of a limited list of raw materials for the foreign exchange with which to buy finished products, fuel, and food; (2) the negligible importance of inter-regional trade as compared with extraregional trade; (3) the dominance of the United States as the source of imports and the market for the exports of the entire area, except in a few territories which retain an association with European powers.

In varying degree, commerce spells economic life or death virtually everywhere, except in those local areas whose populations are almost totally subsistent. This dependence on commerce is more pronounced in the Rimland than in the Mainland and, in the Mainland, it is more pronounced in Central America than in Mexico. In Mexico the development of a more balanced economy during recent decades is making the country less vulnerable to the vagaries of international trade.

The cultural and physical diversity of the component units of Middle America has not created a basis for economic exchange within the area. Trade is still oriented outward, as it has been since the colonial period. Too often, the basic exports of the various territories are the same—sugar, coffee, bananas, or cotton. But even when they are not, they are raw materials from farm and mine, destined for use by more industrialized areas. The postwar industrial growth of Puerto Rico has increased that island's trade with other territories of Middle America, however.

The dominant position of the United States in Middle America's trade is not surprising. Its geographic proximity, the differences in its climate which create corresponding differences in its agricultural products, its industrial production which requires raw materials, its heavy capital investment in many commercial enterprises of Middle America—all these conditions, and others, make the United States the logical area with which to exchange. It is perhaps less logical, although understandable, for Middle Americans to blame the United States for their economic ills.

The remaining European possessions in Middle America are integrated commercially with the mother countries because of political and economic expediency. Again, there are exceptions, chiefly the Dutch oil-refining islands, the Bahamas, and the British Virgin Islands.

THE OUTLOOK

Middle America is in ferment, and its transition is disquieting. Like much of the underdeveloped world, it is struggling against the inhibiting legacy of the past and toward modernization. This is not a new struggle. In Mexico, it has been continuously pressed since the Revolution of 1910. In the area as a whole, however, the fight to overcome the inertia of centuries has become intense only recently.

The tempo of modernization varies from place to place, but no major segment of Middle America is untouched by it. The threat, if not the impact, of change is being felt economically, technologically, politically and socially. Traditional patterns of settlement are being altered; there is a disturbing flow of population from country to town; new techniques of exploiting resources are being introduced; and new industries and other expressions of material culture are appearing on the landscape. An acute awareness of the need for change permeates every level of administration, from the national government to the village and community councils.

But the break with the past is neither complete nor painless. Modernization is hampered by the problems we have already mentioned, including the opposition of the upper classes. And the effort has become enmeshed in the conflict between the Communist countries and the West.

The ferment in Middle America requires reform or revolution. In the face of this dilemma, Cuba and, at an earlier date, Mexico chose revolution. Puerto Rico, with American aid, is taking the more peaceful path of reform. How will the others choose? The answer to this question may be as vital to the United States, and ultimately to the world, as it is to the peoples of Middle America.

Middle America's importance to the United States stems not only from economic and strategic considerations (see Chapter 1) but also from the challenge which it poses for American policy and leadership vis-à-vis the emerging nations. Because of its geographic proximity, its largely non-white population, and its lack of development, the area is a proving ground for America. Failure of American policy so close to home would not enhance its image elsewhere in Latin America, or in Asia, or in Africa. To date, however, our record in Middle America is less than brilliant. The United States' lack of sympathy for the goals of the Mexican Revolution during its early, critical stage added little to America's reputation as a champion of *Los de abajo*.[1] Cuba is a more recent illustration of failure, and the dispatching of American troops to the Dominican Republic in 1965 was not a signal of success.

Sophisticated explanations of American failures is beyond the scope of this volume or the ken of its authors. We can only hope that the complex mosaic of lands, peoples, and cultures which we have tried to reveal will provide one or two clues. Middle America's unrest is too deeply rooted in its geography and its history to be approached only by contemporary economic and political engineering. To grasp the meaning of Middle America's struggle for modernization, it is essential to know the particulars—what was, what is, and where. Such a perspective reveals that the social unrest is primarily a mass revolt against the inequities of the past, particularly against the institutions which have perpetuated the exploitation of land and labor. To the privileged groups of Middle America and some Washington policy makers, the revolt looks like a radical conspiracy, but this view may be both naïve and dangerous. "Revolution is a mettlesome horse. One must either ride it or be trampled to death by it."[2]

[1] *Los de abajo* (*The Underdogs*) is the title of Mariano Azuela's classic novel of The Mexican Revolution.
[2] Arnold Toynbee, *The Economy of the Western Hemisphere* (London, Oxford University Press, 1963).

SELECTED REFERENCES

Ericksen, E. G., *The West Indies Population Problem*. Lawrence, Kansas: The University of Kansas Libraries, 1962.

Hansen, A. T., "The Ecology of a Latin American City," in E. B. Reuter, ed., *Race and Culture Contacts*. New York: McGraw-Hill Book Company, 1934.

Powelson, J. P., *Latin America: Today's Economic and Social Revolution*. New York: McGraw-Hill Book Company, 1964.

Proudfoot, M. J., *Population Movements in the Caribbean*. Port of Spain, Trinidad: Caribbean Commission, Central Secretariat, 1950.

Reubens, E. P., *Migration and Development in the West Indies*. Mona, Jamaica: University College of the West Indies, 1961.

Index

471

70582

DATE DUE
